Third Edition

Religion in America

Third Edition

RELIGION IN AMERICA

Winthrop S. Hudson

*An historical account of the development
of American religious life*

CHARLES SCRIBNER'S SONS
New York

Copyright © 1981, 1973, 1965, Charles Scribner's Sons

Library of Congress Cataloging in Publication Data

Hudson, Winthrop Still, 1911–
   Religion in America.

   Bibliography: p.
   Includes index.
   1. United States—
Religion.   I. Title.
BL2530.U6H8   1981   291'.0973   81–2152
ISBN 0–684–17010–8   AACR2
ISBN 0–684–17002–7 (pbk.)

5 7 9 11 13 15 17 19 K/P 20 18 16 14 12 10 8 6
1 3 5 7 9 11 13 15 17 19 H/C 20 18 16 14 12 10 8 6 4 2

Printed in the United States of America

To
CHARLES M. NIELSEN
friend and colleague

Preface to the Third Edition

While religion in the United States can be analyzed from the perspective of various scholarly disciplines, there is no substitute at the outset for a straightforward historical account to provide structure and context for one who wishes to explore restricted aspects of the American religious scene. It is such an introduction, which may be supplemented by other readings, that this volume is designed to supply.

Several features of the book should be called to the attention of readers that they may be forewarned of what to expect and thus forearmed against misunderstanding.

First, my concern has not been to chronicle the life of individual religious groups. Although the history of the various denominations has not been ignored, the central purpose has been to depict the religious life of the American people as a whole in interaction with other dimensions of their experience.

Second, I have sought to show the unity exhibited in American religious life as well as its particularities. For the European population of the thirteen colonies and the new nation, there was only a limited pluralism. Early American society was largely homogeneous, sharing common assumptions and common patterns of behavior. The diversity was primarily ecclesiastical, a variety of forms within the context of a common religious faith.

Third, ethnic and religious diversity steadily increased during the nineteenth century as immigration mounted and transformed small minorities into major population segments. At the same time a previous

Protestant homogeneity was progressively fragmented along lines of social and cultural division—North and South, black and white, liberal and conservative—and at other points of disaffection.

Fourth, in spite of the seemingly rampant pluralism which developed under conditions of religious freedom, at a deeper level of the American experience there remained an underlying unity. Quite apart from the churches, there was a national faith—a belief in providence and the mission of America—which was shared by Catholics and Jews as well as by Protestants. It was a faith which even former slaves did not reject out-of-hand, but sought rather to have it more perfectly exemplified so that they too could become inheritors of its promises. Though sorely tested, often perverted, and increasingly diluted, this national faith retained sufficient health, prior to the spreading disenchantment of the late 1960's, for Martin Luther King to be able to touch the conscience of much of the nation by reminding Americans of their common national faith.

Fifth, an attempt has been made to maintain balance in the attention devoted to the several epochs in the story of religion in America. A corollary of this concern for balance has been to present each epoch in terms of its own dominant motifs. This mode of organizing the narrative becomes clear in the treatment accorded "late-blooming" religious groups. Judaism, for example, had a long history, but it did not emerge as a major community in America until the twentieth century.[1] Rather than scattering snippets of information throughout the book, most references to groups of this sort have been postponed so that a unified account could be given at the time when they began to loom large on the American scene. In similar fashion, some groups that were prominent in the colonial period receive little attention thereafter, while the Mormons who were so conspicuous in the 1830's and 1840's are not mentioned again until, bursting out of their intra-mountain empire after World War II, they began to out-pace in growth most other religious bodies.

Sixth, the attentive reader also will note references in every period to transatlantic contacts and influences which indicate that religion in America can be understood only within the context of the larger European society. The same would be true of English-speaking Canada, and to a slightly lesser degree of French-speaking Canada.

[1] The full influence of most immigrant groups, including east European Jews, was delayed until they escaped from language imposed isolation.

Seventh, there were and are regional differences in the United States, just as in England, France, Germany, and other nations. But in each of these lands these differences were being subordinated and, with a few striking exceptions, tended to be less important than the continuities which made them nations. Evidence of continuity in the United States can most easily be seen in surviving architecture. Indeed, the moving population tended to recreate, not only the architectural fabric, but the layout and design of the villages from whence they had come. Place names provided equally eloquent testimony of continuity. Evidence of continuity stretched from the Atlantic to the Pacific. It was no accident that Berkeley was chosen as the name for the site of the University of California.

A high priority has been to keep *Religion in America* to a reasonable length to permit the use of supplementary readings. For things omitted the only apology is an acknowledgment that choices had to be made. Others would have chosen differently. Few would contend, however, that a more encyclopedic coverage would have been preferable had it been effected by including scattered cryptic references which served only to oversimplify and distort. For those who wish to pursue specific subjects in greater detail, bibliographical references have been placed in notes adjacent to the text where it is believed that they will be most useful as well as in an appended list of Suggestions for Further Reading (see pp. 463ff).[2]

The task of preparing a third edition of *Religion in America*— revising, correcting, clarifying, and rewriting nearly half the pages of the book to incorporate recent scholarship, fresh insights, and new material —has been a pleasure as well as a responsibility. It calls to mind the

[2] For further guidance, two excellent bibliographies are available: Ernest R. Sandeen, *American Religion and Philosophy: Guide to Information and Sources* (Detroit, 1978), and Nelson R. Burr, *Religion in American Life: Goldentree Bibliography* (N.Y., 1971). The latter is a condensation and supplement to Burr's two-volume *A Critical Bibliography of Religion in America*, published as part of *Religion in American Life* (Princeton, 1961). For quick reference, see the bibliographies appended to S. F. Ahlstrom, *A Religious History of the American People* (New Haven, 1972), and R. T. Handy, *A History of the Churches in the United States and Canada* (N.Y., 1976).

Other useful reference volumes are: H. W. Bowden, *Dictionary of American Religious Biography* (Westport, Conn., 1977), and E. S. Gaustad, *Historical Atlas of Religion in America*, 2nd. ed. (N.Y., 1976). For individual religious groups and movements, A. C. Piepkorn's projected seven volume, *Profiles in Belief: The Religious Bodies of North America* (N.Y., 1977–   ), is unsurpassed. These volumes as they appear replace those of Piepkorn's former colleague, F. E. Mayer, *The Religious Bodies of America*, 2nd. ed. (St. Louis, 1956) which also are unusually perceptive and well-informed.

names of many friends from whom I have learned much and to whom I am deeply indebted. It is a list which grows longer with each passing year as comments, suggestions, and criticisms are received from colleagues who are using the book as a text.

For this third edition, I am most deeply indebted to Professor Grant Wacker, by whom *Religion in America* has been classroom-tested in a detailed and systematic fashion with undergraduates at the University of North Carolina and with theological students at Duke Divinity School. The response of students was positive and appreciative. But, as a result of Professor Wacker's close attention to detail with the students, words whose meaning was not readily apparent have been replaced, allusions made more pointed, confused syntax simplified, and issues that passed unnoticed by students restated. Professor Wacker has made a further contribution by aiding me in my understanding of the various strands of the "new conservatism," including a rough draft of some materials to be included in the final chapter which brings the story of religion in America up-to-date. The new conservatism is an area in which his interest has given him unusual scholarly competence.

Attempts to make sense of past and present complexities of American religious life have necessitated interpretive judgments. It is my hope that these have been judicious and that they will stimulate constructive reflection.

WINTHROP S. HUDSON

University of North Carolina
Chapel Hill, North Carolina

Contents

Third Edition

Religion in America

PART I

THE FORMATIVE YEARS

1607–1789

I

The American Context

After a long period in which historians have emphasized the uniqueness of almost everything American, it is becoming increasingly clear that the United States can properly be understood only as an integral part of a larger European society.[1]

Our roots as a nation go back to the remarkable burst of colonizing activity which transformed the Atlantic Ocean into the *Mare Nostrum* of western Europe. There is little that we, as Americans, can claim as exclusively our own. Our language is not our own, nor are our tables of weights and measures. Our most characteristic proverbs and our most familiar nursery rhymes have been inherited from others. Our concept of trial by jury came to us from abroad. Indeed, the whole structure of our legal system, with its guarantees of liberty and provisions for constitutional government, is the product of a longer history than ours. Even after

[1] See C. J. H. Hayes, "The American Frontier—Frontier of What?" *American Historical Review*, II (1946), 199–216; and W. S. Hudson, "How American Is Religion in America?" in J. C. Brauer, ed., *Reinterpretation in American Church History* (Chicago, 1968), 153–67.

our declaration of political independence, we remained part of this larger society—reading the works of European poets, studying the writings of European philosophers, listening to the music of European composers, utilizing the discoveries of European scientists, reaping the benefits of European capital invested in our railroads and mines, recruiting European "hands" for our mills and factories. In almost every respect, we have been and are part of Europe; and this is as true in religion as it is in literature, law, philosophy, art, or science.

The religious heritage which links us to Europe is immediately apparent to any visitor to the British Isles. When an American walks down the street of an English city, he will be reminded of home as he passes Anglican (Protestant Episcopal), Presbyterian, Congregational, Baptist, Methodist, and Roman Catholic churches. He may be handed a Plymouth Brethren tract, encounter a Salvation Army lassie, or find a Quaker meetinghouse or Jewish synagogue half hidden in a side street. Traveling north of the Tweed, he will discover that many of the Presbyterian divisions at home had their origin in divisions which took place in Scotland.

But it is not from the British Isles only that our churches have come, for there are German, Swedish, Danish, Norwegian, and Finnish Lutheran churches; German, Dutch, and Hungarian Reformed churches; Mennonite, Moravian, Dunker, and Schwenkfelder communities. And more recent immigration from central and eastern Europe has swelled the Roman Catholic and Jewish population in the United States and has introduced the numerous national churches of Eastern Orthodoxy into the American scene.

With only a few exceptions, the varied religious groups of America have their rootage abroad; and throughout the years their relationship to the lands from which their fathers came has been intimate and continuous. The continuing European religious influence is no more than barely suggested by the names of Kant, Schleiermacher, and Ritschl; Pascal, Kierkegaard, and Von Hügel; Newman, Maurice, and Temple; Barth, Buber, and Bultmann. In religion, as in other areas of our common life, we have been and we have continued to be part of a larger European society.

The recognition that the United States, in all the fundamental features of its life save geographic location, is a part of Europe must not obscure the parallel fact that we are Americans as well as Europeans. European society has never been a monolithic whole. Within the common culture, there have always been diverse local and national traditions; and this is as true in America as it is in England and France and Germany. America has drawn most heavily, as the mere fact of language so eloquently testifies, from the English-speaking segment of European society. But it is far from an exact transcript, even of this segment, that has been reproduced on American soil. There have been modifications and adaptations of the European inheritance from the very beginning.

In part the changes that have occurred in America have been due to the differing circumstances of life in a new land; in part they have been the product of the intermingling in varying proportion of several European traditions; in part they have been the consequence of the constitutional arrangements which were effected to bring thirteen newly independent and somewhat recalcitrant colonies together under one government; and in part they have been the result of the growing and evolving life that is characteristic of any intimately related segment of a larger community. Thus while we have been and continue to be debtors to Europe, we have also developed within the larger context a distinctive life of our own and we have made contributions of our own to the European society of which we are a part.

Although it is the European heritage that has given American religious life its basic shape and substance, the purpose of this initial chapter is to focus attention upon the distinctive ethos and character of religion in America.

England as the "Bridge" from the Old World to the New

As early as 1622 John Donne was asserting with remarkable prescience that England, which hitherto as an island had been "but as the suburbs" of Europe, was destined to occupy a much more central position in the future as the "bridge" between the Old World and the New.[2] His words were prophetic so far as the Atlantic coast of North America was concerned, and the most obvious conditioning factor in American religious life has been its English beginnings. The thirteen colonies were English colonies, the vast proportion of the population was of English stock, and

[2] Louis B. Wright, *Religion and Empire* (Chapel Hill, N.C., 1943), 111.

5

the American Revolution was fought—so the colonists asserted—to defend and preserve their rights as Englishmen.

PROTESTANT PREDOMINANCE. The fact that the American colonies were English colonies meant, first of all, that the colonists in background if not always in active affiliation would be predominantly Protestant. Even the non-English minorities—the Scots, the Scotch-Irish, the Germans, the Dutch, the French, and the Swedes—were almost wholly Protestant in background. Only in Maryland was there a significant number of Roman Catholics and even in Maryland they were a minority. Judaism was limited to a handful of tiny congregations. Thus, to the extent that the mind of colonial America was shaped by a religious faith, it was shaped perforce by Protestantism.

This overwhelmingly Protestant religious orientation was equally true of the new nation as its borders pushed westward. In the Northwest Territory, the French trading posts on the Great Lakes were not deeply enough rooted as permanent settlements to become centers of a continuing cultural or religious tradition. Nor did the Louisiana Purchase of 1803 change the picture to any marked degree. The permanent non-Protestant area of settlement was confined to a relatively small enclave at the southern tip of the vast area embraced in the Purchase. It was not until the nineteenth century was well advanced, when their numbers began to be augmented by large-scale immigration, that Roman Catholics became sufficiently numerous to constitute a significant minority in American life; and it was not until the end of the nineteenth century that major Jewish and Eastern Orthodox communities came into existence.

As a consequence of Protestant predominance, even non-Protestant groups tended to take on a somewhat Protestant coloration in the American environment. The earnest "moralism" of American Roman Catholicism has often been attributed to the influence of a Protestant culture; and on occasion American Roman Catholics have had to defend themselves against charges of undue "Americanism," a term which usually implied the adoption of Protestant presuppositions. A more complete adjustment was represented by Reform Judaism which initially adopted even the forms of Protestant Sunday worship. Nor has Eastern Orthodoxy remained unaffected. A spokesman for the Greek church, after staunchly defending at an ecumenical gathering the unchanging integrity of the Orthodox witness, commented privately that the Orthodox in America scarcely dare admit even to themselves the extent to which their life has been modified by an encounter with Protestantism.

After World War I, to be sure, the older Protestant predominance had been so greatly reduced by the shifting tide of immigration that influences which once moved only in one direction tended to become reciprocal. Not the least of the influences, for example, reshaping the Protestant understanding of the pastoral office and Protestant liturgical practice has been the influence exerted by Roman Catholicism.

THE PURITAN HERITAGE. While the United States by virtue of its English antecedents and character was predominantly Protestant throughout its early history, it was an English Protestantism with a difference. At home the great majority of the people were Anglicans, members of the Church of England; and the "Dissenting" interest composed of Presbyterians, Congregationalists, Baptists, and Quakers was relatively small. In the colonies this situation was reversed. By the end of the colonial period the Congregationalists and the Presbyterians were the two largest American denominations. The Baptists and the Anglicans were roughly equal in size, and the Quakers—widely dispersed throughout all the colonies—ranked fifth in number of adherents. It was this difference in the religious make-up of the population that Edmund Burke had in mind when he noted in his speech *On Conciliation with the American Colonies* (1775) that "the people [of the colonies] are Protestants, and of that kind which is the most adverse to all implicit subjection of mind and opinion."

What was the character of this early American Protestantism? While diverse in outward ecclesiastical form, its diversity found expression mostly within the limits of the common faith of English Puritanism.[3] The tendency in popular mythology to stress the priority of Plymouth at the expense of Jamestown is not historically accurate, but in a deeper sense it is a true recognition that the American people over a considerable portion of their history have had their fundamental rootage in a Puritanism which they have found most easy to identify in terms of New England.

André Siegfried, a French observer of twentieth-century America,

[3] See David Hall, "Understanding the Puritans," in J. M. Mulder and J. F. Wilson, eds., *Religion in American History* (Englewood Cliffs, N.J., 1978), 1–16; Alan Simpson, *Puritanism in Old and New England* (Chicago, 1962) ; and the readings collected by Michael McGiffert in *Puritanism and the American Revolution* (Reading, Mass., 1969).

confirmed the estimate that is implicit in the prominence given to the story of the landing of the Pilgrims when he asserted: "If we wish to understand the real sources of American inspiration we must go back to the English Puritanism of the seventeenth century." James Bryce also emphasized this feature of American life in 1888 as he sought to describe the American commonwealth to his fellow countrymen at home. "There is a hearty Puritanism in the view of human nature which pervades the instrument of 1787," he wrote. "It is the work of men who believed in original sin, and were resolved to leave open for transgressors no door which they could possibly shut. Compare this spirit with the enthusiastic optimism of the Frenchmen of 1789. It is not merely a difference of race and temperaments; it is a difference of fundamental ideas." [4]

The same verdict had been expressed by Philip Schaff (1819–93) in 1844 when, shortly after his arrival from Germany, he sought to analyze the main features of American religious life. "Puritan Protestantism forms properly the main trunk of our North American church," he declared in his inaugural address as professor of church history in the Mercersburg Theological Seminary. "Viewed as a whole," the American church "owes her general characteristic features, her distinctive image, neither to the German or Continental Reformed, nor to the English Episcopal communion," but to the Puritans of New England. "To this New England influence must be added indeed the no less important weight of Presbyterianism, as derived subsequently from Scotland and Ireland. But this may be regarded as in all essential respects the same life. The reigning theology of the country . . . is the theology of the Westminster Confession." A few years later he asserted that "the six northeastern states included under the name of New England . . . are . . . in regard to culture and Christianity, the garden of America"; and from this seedbed has come "the leading religious influence in the Union," exerting "a powerful influence upon the religious, social, and political life of the whole nation." [5]

Philip Schaff's only error was to identify this Puritanism so exclusively with New England. Puritanism was far from monolithic. In England it was a many-faceted movement that embraced Presbyterians, Congrega-

[4] André Siegfried, *America Comes of Age* (N.Y., 1927), 33. James Bryce, *The American Commonwealth* (N.Y., 1910), I, 306.
[5] Philip Schaff, *The Principle of Protestantism as Related to the Present State of the Church* (Chambersburg, 1845), 114; quoted by J. H. Nichols, *Romanticism in American Theology* (Chicago, 1961), 2. Philip Schaff, *America: A Sketch of Its Political, Social, and Religious Character*, ed. Perry Miller (Cambridge, Mass., 1961), 54, 89, 107; see also 116–17.

tionalists, Baptists, large numbers of Episcopalians, and even the Quakers. It is a mistake, therefore, to limit Puritan influence in America to New England Congregationalism, for in other forms of English dissent it was strongly represented in all the colonies. As Philip Schaff noted, the Presbyterians—including those from Scotland and Ireland—stood shoulder-to-shoulder with the Congregationalists at every important point. This was equally true of the Baptists who also had adopted a modified form of the 1647 Westminster Confession [6] as their statement of faith. Nor was colonial Anglicanism for the most part "the high-flying Anglicanism" of the Restoration divines; it was "the Calvinistic Low Church Anglicanism of the period before Laud." [7] Whether in Virginia or in New England, the same books of religious edification were read, the same doctrines were taught from the pulpits, and the same laws were passed to enforce religious duties. When the Quakers, who represented the left-wing of the Puritan movement, are brought into the picture, it is evident that the Puritan influence in early America was overwhelmingly dominant. So pervasive was its influence that, as Schaff reports, even many of the Lutheran churches were remade in the Puritan image.[8]

One further word of caution that needs to be spoken is an acknowledgment that what was labeled as Puritan by Schaff, Bryce, and Siegfried was not a static theological point of view. As the Calvinism of the early Puritans was not precisely the same as the Calvinism of Geneva, so the Puritanism of nineteenth-century America was not that of seventeenth-century England and it might more properly be described as Evangelicalism. There was constant modification and change and development. But there were also large elements of continuity; and even when theological foundations were altered or eroded, habitual ways of thinking and feeling

[6] The Westminster Confession of Faith, with the modifications made by the Congregationalists, is reproduced in Williston Walker, *The Creeds and Platforms of Congregationalism* (N.Y., 1893). The Baptist recension is in W. L. Lumpkin, *Baptist Confessions of Faith* (Philadelphia, 1959). John Witherspoon, president of Princeton, noted the basic unity of the denominations in this tradition when he described the religious situation in New Jersey at the close of the Revolution. "The Baptists," he said, "are Presbyterians in all other respects, only differing in the point of infant baptism; their political weight goes the same way as the Presbyterians." *Essays on Important Subjects* (Edinburgh, 1805), IV, 203.

[7] The comment is William Haller's in *The Constitution Reconsidered*, ed. Conyers Read (N.Y., 1938), 136. This "Calvinism" owed more perhaps to Zurich than Geneva, the term being used as shorthand for the whole Reformed tradition.

[8] Schaff, *America*, 93, 150–54. For further elaboration of Americans' New England self-image, see W. S. Hudson, *Nationalism and Religion in America* (N.Y., 1970), 2–6. The writing of American history was monopolized by sons of Harvard almost to the end of the nineteenth century.

persisted and continued to give form and structure to the common life.

RELIGIOUS DIVERSITY. The fact that the American colonies were English colonies also explains in large measure the multiplicity of religious bodies which was so prominent a feature of the English colonial scene in contrast to the religious uniformity which prevailed in the French and Spanish domains, for a deliberate policy of religious toleration was adopted by the English colonial authorities.

At the outset, to be sure, it was assumed that there would be and should be uniformity of religion in the new settlements; but in keeping with the whole system—or lack of system—of English colonial administration, the instructions at this point were not always observed. The Separatists who landed at Plymouth in 1620, for example, had set sail with the permission of the Virginia Company to establish a settlement within its territory, even though the second Virginia charter stated that no one, such as the Separatists, who refused to take the Oath of Supremacy should be allowed to embark for Virginia. In colonies other than Virginia, English administrative laxity was transformed into an explicit policy of toleration, and in no colony other than Virginia did the English authorities even attempt to impose a pattern of religious uniformity. When such attempts were made in the colonies, as in Massachusetts Bay, it was by the colonists themselves, and it was in spite of rather than because of English policy.

One important factor determining the tolerant attitude of the English government was the economic advantage to be gained by a policy of toleration. From the point of view of the English government, the colonies were commercial ventures designed to contribute to the wealth and prosperity of the mother country. The great need if they were to be profitable was to attract settlers who would provide the manpower to exploit the untapped resources of field and forest. Jails were emptied to provide colonists, the impoverished were sent out, adventurers were enlisted. But it soon became obvious that those who suffered from disabilities at home because of their religious profession would be prime recruits if they could be induced to leave the homeland by the prospect of greater freedom abroad.

The Dutch had early discovered the economic folly of adopting rigorous measures to suppress religious dissent, and Peter Stuyvesant was rebuked for attempting to institute such a policy in New Amsterdam. The Dutch authorities informed him that his "vigorous proceedings" should be discontinued lest he "check and destroy" the population. The secret of the prosperity of old Amsterdam, he was reminded, was the moderation displayed by the magistrates in dealing with religious minorities, with the result that "people have flocked" from every land "to this asylum." He was informed that a similar policy should be pursued in New Amsterdam. "It is our opinion that some connivance would be useful; that the consciences of men, at least, ought ever to remain free and unshackled." [9]

English policy was of a piece with the Dutch. This is self-evident in the grants that were made to Lord Baltimore and William Penn, but the clearest statement of the motivation which lay behind the policy is to be found in a communication from the Lords of Trade in London to the Council of Virginia: "A free exercise of religion . . . is essential to enriching and improving a trading nation; it should be ever held sacred in His Majesty's colonies. We must, therefore, recommend it to your care that nothing be done which can in the least affect that great point." [10] Non-English settlers were welcomed and some were even recruited with the promise of freedom to establish their own religious institutions. Most of these non-English groups arrived relatively late in the colonial period [11] and constituted, proportionately, a small segment of the total population, but they did serve to give added variety to the religious spectrum.

Economic advantage alone, however, does not explain the relative equanimity with which dissent was viewed by both the Dutch and the English. A major contributing factor was the fact that the "maxims of moderation" were already being practiced at home. The English were more halting in their progress in this direction, but throughout the colonial period England was moving steadily toward an ever broadening toleration of religious dissent. At times the toleration at home was within narrow limits. At other times, as during the two decades following the meeting of the Long Parliament in 1640, it was very broad. For brief periods under Charles I and Charles II there were efforts to impose a rigid conformity, but these efforts were never wholly successful and were not long pursued. With the adoption of the Act of Toleration in 1689, the acceptance of

[9] The text of the letter is printed in W. W. Sweet, *Religion in Colonial America* (N.Y., 1942), 151–52.

[10] *Historical Collections Relating to the American Colonial Church*, ed. William S. Perry (Hartford, 1871–78), I, 379–81.

[11] The great influx of the Germans and Scotch-Irish, the major non-English elements in the population, occurred during the last third of the colonial period.

religious diversity within the limits of trinitarian Protestantism became the settled domestic policy of the English government. Thus its religious policy in the colonies was in many ways merely a reflection of a policy that was being developed at home, and in the end England did little more than export her own religious diversity.

A new beginning in a new land

While the English inheritance was the most important single influence determining the form and substance of religious life in the colonies, both the necessities and the opportunities of life in the New World introduced changes of emphasis and modifications of practice. Faced with the task of beginning anew, the leaders of the churches found themselves far more dependent upon the laity than had hitherto been true, and they were forced to concede to the laity far greater powers than the laity had previously enjoyed. Furthermore, the long sea journey had removed many of the inhibitions and restraints to which most of the churches had been subject, leaving them free to experiment in reshaping their life to conform more closely to long-cherished convictions than had been possible at home. Finally, given the view of history that prevailed, the mere fact that a new beginning could be made cultivated an eager expectancy that this was "the Lord's doing" and was but a foretaste of the near-approaching time when all things would be made new.

THE IMPORTANCE OF THE LAITY. The Protestant Reformation with its emphasis upon the priesthood of believers and its appeal to the plain testimony of Scripture had tended to elevate the laity in the life of the church. This tendency was arrested, however, by the establishment of national churches, sanctioned and maintained by the state. The clergy, being appointed by and responsible to the state, took charge and left to the people a purely passive role. Thus, within the limits of state control, the church tended to become a clerically dominated institution. In England, to be sure, the post-Reformation struggle for dominance between contending parties within the church necessitated appeals for lay support and thus gave added influence to the laity,[12] but this influence was always limited by ordered structures of church life. In the colonies, on the other hand, the

[12] See James F. Maclear, "The Making of the Lay Tradition," *Journal of Religion,* XXXIII (1953), 113–36.

restraint provided by an established church order was reduced to a minimum.

One of the facts of life in the New World was that a new beginning had to be made, and for most of the churches this new beginning had to be made by individual clergymen recruiting their own congregations out of a population that was largely unchurched. The ready-made congregations of early New England and the parishes created by legislative fiat in Virginia were not typical. Elsewhere there were neither closely knit bodies of believers already in existence nor parishes established by law. Nor was there any ecclesiastical body close at hand to supervise and regulate the life of the churches. Furthermore, because of the diversity that prevailed, the clergy often had to compete for the allegiance of the people. Far removed from the status-giving context of an ordered church life and dependent upon what support they could enlist among the laity both for the formation and the maintenance of the congregations they served, the only real authority the clergy possessed was the authority they could command by their powers of persuasion and the force of their example. Given these circumstances, it is scarcely surprising that the laity soon began to exercise a decisive voice in church affairs, with "everything," as Henry M. Muhlenberg (1711–87) was to explain, dependent "on the vote of the majority." [13]

Even in New England, where churches had been constituted at the outset with ministers as a "speaking aristocracy" and congregations reduced to a "silent democracy," this state of affairs did not long persist. Men who had gained independent status as property holders by clearing their own land with flintlocks close at hand were not the type to be unduly submissive, and their self-assertiveness soon stripped the New England clergy of much of their independence. The same process was at work in Virginia where lay vestries gained effective control by neglecting to present the clergy to the governor for permanent induction into office, thus retaining, as the Archbishop of Canterbury complained, the right to hire and fire them like "domestic servants." [14]

[13] *The Journals of Henry Melchior Muhlenberg* (Philadelphia, 1942), I, 67. For a perceptive discussion of this point, see Sidney E. Mead, "The Rise of the Evangelical Conception of the Ministry," in *The Ministry in Historical Perspectives*, ed. H. Richard Niebuhr and D. D. Williams (N.Y., 1956), 212–18.
[14] Elizabeth Davidson, *The Establishment of the English Church in Continental American Colonies* (Durham, N.C., 1936), 19.

A further consequence of this lay predominance in the affairs of the churches was the strong support that was given to what was later described as "local autonomy." With single congregations beginning of necessity as independent self-governing units, resistance developed when attempts were made to regularize their status by subordinating them to larger units of ecclesiastical control. The laity were fearful of losing the prerogatives they possessed in the local church. Thus in Virginia and other southern colonies, where the Anglican laity had gained decisive powers in local "vestries," there was vigorous opposition to the attempt to establish an episcopate in America. A similar apprehension among the Congregational laity in Massachusetts thwarted the proposal to complete the Congregational structure there with a yearly consultative synod, while the Presbyterians in 1758 were forced to come to terms with this sentiment by conceding extensive powers to local presbyteries at the expense of synodical authority.

Thus, whatever the denomination and whatever the polity that was ostensibly professed, all the colonial churches tended to be characterized by a strong emphasis upon local autonomy and lay control. This emphasis persisted and it was only partially curtailed in the nineteenth and twentieth centuries through strenuous efforts of Presbyterian, Methodist, and Roman Catholic clergy alike to have all church property transferred to and vested in presbytery, conference, or bishop. The objective was to place a limitation upon local lay power by gaining control of the church property.

THE BREAKDOWN OF THE PARISH SYSTEM. A further consequence of the conditions that prevailed in the New World was the shattering of the parish system of ecclesiastical organization and the transformation of all the churches into what are usually described as "gathered" churches.

For almost a thousand years in western Europe, it had been generally assumed that every member of society was automatically a member of the church. Richard Hooker (1554?–1600), speaking of the situation in England, had voiced this common assumption in these words: "There is not any member of the Church of England but the same man is also a member of the commonwealth; nor any member of the commonwealth which is not also [a member] of the Church of England." [15] For purposes of worship, instruction, and discipline, people were divided geographically

[15] *Hooker's Ecclesiastical Polity: Book VIII*, ed. R. A. Houk (N.Y., 1931), 156.

into parishes. This was the basic unit of church life, established and maintained by the state. It was in marked contrast to a self-supporting congregation whose membership was defined by voluntary affiliation.

Only in Virginia and in New England did a parish system, designed to embrace a total community, function with any real degree of success, and in Virginia the success was limited. The pattern of settlement in Virginia was the major problem. With the population thinly distributed on large plantations bordering the navigable rivers, a single parish could be from thirty to one hundred miles in length. In such a situation, it was difficult for the parish incumbent even to keep in touch with his parishioners, to say nothing of maintaining regular services of worship and a systematic program of instruction for them. In New England the pattern of settlement on small landholdings gathered about a village center was more conducive to an effective parish system and it was maintained largely unimpaired until the inroads of dissent destroyed the religious homogeneity of the population.

Elsewhere in the colonies, the religious diversity which was present from the beginning compromised any attempt to establish a system which presupposed that the whole community would belong to a single church. A thin façade of parish structure was maintained by legislative action in Maryland, the Carolinas, Georgia, and the environs of New York City, but none of these parish churches could claim more than a minority of the population. South of Virginia most parishes existed only on paper, never having been supplied with clergymen. The only thing that made possible even the pretense of maintaining a parish system was governmental authority, and the moment it was withdrawn the whole flimsy structure toppled. By this time the Anglicans had become a minority even in Virginia, and the adoption of Thomas Jefferson's "Bill for Establishing Religious Freedom" (1786) was equally effective in exposing as fiction the notion that the Anglican parishes there were anything more than "gathered" churches composed of voluntary adherents.

The New England story was somewhat more complex, for in New England the attempt was made to preserve "gathered" churches within a parish structure. This posed no great problem during the early years when the total population was largely a "sifted" people. But when the children of believers were unable to exhibit the minimum qualifications for church membership, the problem became acute. In an effort to preserve the parish concept, a form of "birthright" membership was adopted and by this means the collapse of the parish system in New England was deferred until the increase of dissent made its defense a hopeless cause. A full century before disestablishment stripped away the lingering traces of the parish structure in New England, Jonathan Edwards (1703–58) had recognized that its days were numbered and had called upon his fellow Congregationalists to return to their initial emphasis upon the church as a covenanted community of convinced believers. While certain privileges were retained until the first decades of the nineteenth century, the defenders of the attenuated "establishment" that survived during these final years found it necessary to adopt all the techniques of the "gathered" churches in order to carry on a rear guard defense of its few remaining prerogatives.

The "techniques of the 'gathered' churches" is a key phrase, for it calls attention to the necessity that was laid upon the churches to win support and gain recruits by voluntary means. No longer could they depend upon people being automatically members of the church and subject to its discipline. The churches had to utilize all their powers of persuasion if they were to maintain and perpetuate themselves. The techniques they devised to this end were many and varied: the fostering of revivals, the organization of mission societies, the establishment of Sunday schools, the development of programs of visitation, the publication of tracts, and more recently the utilization of advertisements in periodicals. This vigorous evangelistic and instructional activity, imposed upon the churches by their status as "gathered" groups of convinced believers, was to become one of the most distinctive features of American church life. And in the end, in order to maintain themselves on this basis, some of the churches—most notably the Roman Catholic Church—felt compelled to embark on the even more ambitious venture of establishing weekday schools for the complete education of their children.

THE POSSIBILITY OF THOROUGHGOING REFORM. The prominence of religious radicals and left-wing groups in America has frequently been noted, and it is not surprising that they should have come to the New World in disproportionate numbers. Members of the established churches in Europe could only view the situation in America with some dismay, for the necessity to make a new beginning forced them to improvise and served to shatter many of their previously cherished patterns of ecclesiastical life. In New Amsterdam, for example, Jonas Michaelius (b. 1584) was acutely conscious of the coercions imposed by the conditions of life in a new land, and he felt compelled to explain the irregularities which attended the formation of his church. "One cannot," he wrote to the authorities at home, "observe strictly all the usual formalities in making a beginning under such circumstances." [16] The nonestablished churches of Europe, however, were in a reverse situation. They welcomed the opportunity to make a new beginning free from the restraints to which they were subjected at home. This was the great attraction which enticed the Mennonites and the Moravians to risk the hazards of beginning life anew in the American wilderness. It was this prospect also which exerted so strong an appeal to that hardy band of Pilgrims who settled at Plymouth in 1620 and encouraged the founders of Massachusetts Bay Colony in 1629 to undertake their "great migration."

The necessity to make a new beginning was seen by these minority groups as something more than a mere negative release. It was an opportunity to undertake a positive work of construction. William Penn (1644–1718) could never have launched his "holy experiment" in England where the existing patterns and institutions of a settled community would have dictated compromises from the start. He needed an opportunity to begin anew where there would be "room," as he put it, for "such an experiment," and it was this opportunity that was given him in America.

The significance of the opportunity to make a new beginning can be seen most clearly through the eyes of those who sailed with the Winthrop fleet to Massachusetts Bay. Michaelius had to "make do" in New Amsterdam, but the early New Englanders had had to "make do" at home. In England they had been compelled to adjust to the irregularities imposed upon them by the requirements of the established church, and the shift to the New World was viewed by them as a release from this bondage. "It is one thing," explained John Cotton (1564–1652), "for . . . members of the church loyally to submit unto any form of [church] government when it is above their calling to reform it"; it is quite another matter for them to "choose a form of government and governors discrepant from the rule." The Great Migration had been organized with the specific purpose of providing them with this freedom to "choose," and John Winthrop

[16] His letter is printed in *American Christianity: An Historical Interpretation with Representative Documents*, ed. H. Shelton Smith, Robert T. Handy, and Lefferts A. Loetscher (N.Y., 1960–63), I, 56–59.

(1588–1649) standing on the deck of the *Arbella* made explicit the duty that was thus laid upon them. It was to "bring into familiar and constant practice" that which they previously had been able to "maintain as truth in profession only." Their purpose was clear. "We go," said Francis Higginson (1586–1630), "to practice the positive part of church reformation." [17]

America was for them, as it was to become for others, a land of opportunity, a land where a "wide door" of "liberty" had been set open before them. No longer were they to be compelled to resort to devious expedients, as they had been at home, in order to avoid "corruptions." This necessity had been lifted. But more important was the freedom they possessed to undertake a radical reconstruction of church life to conform to what they regarded as the plain prescriptions of God's "most holy Word." The goal was a full and complete restoration of the primitive church in all its pristine glory. This was their opportunity, and they were determined to take advantage of it. Looking back in 1677 to the early days of settlement, Increase Mather (1639–1723) declared: "There never was a generation that did so perfectly shake off the dust of Babylon . . . as the first generation of Christians that came to this land for the Gospel's sake." [18]

The early New Englanders were seeking freedom for themselves alone, but others found in America an equal freedom to "shake off the dust of Babylon." There was and there continued to be space enough for everyone.[19] It was this sense of being freed from the necessity to give heed to compromising restraints in making a new beginning that was to give a perfectionist cast to much of American religious life and to foster the uninhibited experimentation by smaller fringe groups that was to be the dismay of European churchmen.

THE SENSE OF EXPECTANCY. A new beginning is always a heady experience that breeds an eager expectancy among those who participate in it. Hopes are kindled and, as imagination takes over, the future becomes

[17] See Perry Miller, *Orthodoxy in Massachusetts* (Cambridge, Mass., 1933), 137, 146. Winthrop's address, "A Model of Christian Charity," is printed in *The Puritans*, ed. Perry Miller and T. H. Johnson (N.Y., 1963), I, 195–99, and in Smith, Handy, Loetscher, *American Christianity*, I, 97–102.

[18] Quoted by W. W. Sweet, *Religion in Colonial America* (N.Y., 1950), 2.

[19] For a discussion of the significance of geographic space, see S. E. Mead, "The American People: Their Space, Time, and Religion," *Journal of Religion*, XXXIV (1954), 244–55; reprinted in S. E. Mead, *The Lively Experiment* (N.Y., 1963).

pregnant with possibility. This was doubly true of the new beginning that was made in America, for European peoples had always lived with the hope—sometimes faint but never absent—that the Lord's promise in Isaiah and Revelation to "make all things new" would some day be fulfilled. And the very term "New World," which was used to describe the setting in which they were making their new beginning, was calculated to remind them of the Lord's promise.

Since every Englishman had been taught from childhood to view the course of history as predetermined by God's overruling providence, no one could regard the colonizing activity in America as an ordinary venture. As early as 1613, William Strachey was insisting that God had kept America hidden for a purpose and that those who had established the small settlement in Virginia were but pursuing a course of action which God had foreseen and willed and was now carrying to its foreordained completion.[20] This purpose of necessity was related to God's final act of redemption, for this was the end toward which all history was directed.

The specific understanding of the past which illumined God's activity in the present was that which had been made the common possession of all Englishmen by John Foxe's "Book of Martyrs"—a volume that in 1571 had been placed by official decree in every cathedral church for all to read and was later to have a place of honor beside the Bible in every Protestant home.[21] Through the eyes of Foxe the shifting course of past events was seen to be a movement within a set pattern which God had adopted as a means of instructing mankind in the ways of righteousness. Throughout the centuries there had been alternating periods of impiety and faithfulness, corruption and reform, decline and renewal. After a long period of decline in which darkness had been demonstrated to be the only result of the folly of unrighteousness, Foxe pointed out that by 1300 God had begun to summon his servants to a renewed witness to him and thus to serve as

[20] Perry Miller, *Errand into the Wilderness* (Cambridge, Mass., 1956), 111, 117.

[21] The first edition of 1554 was a small octavo volume which recounted the martyrdoms of the precursors of the Protestant Reformation, and to these the accounts of martyrdoms under Mary Tudor were soon added. By the time it reached its final form in 1583, it was a folio of almost 2,500 pages and its full title had become *Acts and Monuments of Matters Most Special and Memorable, Happening in the Church, with an Universal History of the Same.* See William Haller, "John Foxe and the Puritan Revolution," in *The Seventeenth Century: Studies in the History of English Thought and Literature from Bacon to Pope,* by Richard F. Jones and others (Palo Alto, Calif., 1951); and also Haller's *The Elect Nation* (N.Y., 1963).

harbingers of the new dispensation which was to be inaugurated with the Protestant Reformation.

When a full century had passed after the posting of the "Ninety-five Theses" by Martin Luther, it had become clear to scattered groups in England that Foxe had been overoptimistic in his estimate of the immediate outcome of the Reformation. The godly forces in Europe had proved to be unequal to the task to which God had summoned them. Why this should be so, they could only speculate; it was evident that God intended to pursue a new tactic to effect the final thrust into the new age.

The early New Englanders shared this sense of disappointment and as they reflected upon the significance of their venture in the New World they felt certain that it was to implement God's over-all design that they had been sent, as Samuel Danforth (1626–74) put it, on an "errand into the wilderness." When old England "began to decline in religion," declared Edward Johnson (1598–1672), Christ raised "an army out of our English nation, for freeing his people from their long servitude" and created "a new England to muster up the first of his forces in." This new England, he continued, "is the place where the Lord will create a new heaven and a new earth in, new churches and a new commonwealth together." [22]

God had "sifted a whole nation" in order to plant his "choice grain" in the American wilderness, but his purpose was more far-ranging than merely to enable them to escape the inhibitions they had suffered at home. They were not fleeing from persecution; they were executing a flank attack upon the forces of unrighteousness everywhere. Their role, John Winthrop had reminded them, was to be "a city set on a hill" to demonstrate before "the eyes of the world" what the result would be when a whole people was brought into open covenant with God. As part of God's program of instruction, they were to provide the nations with a working model of a godly society and by the contagion of their example were to be God's instruments in effecting the release from bondage of all mankind. [23]

The New Englanders, however, were not alone in the conviction that America had a decisive role to play in God's plan of redemption. William

[22] *Johnson's Wonder-working Providence, 1628–1651,* ed. J. F. Jameson (N.Y., 1910), 23, 25. A portion of Johnson's narrative is in *The Puritans,* ed. Perry Miller and T. H. Johnson (N.Y., 1938), I, 143–62.

[23] Smith, Handy, and Loetscher, *American Christianity,* I, 102; *The Puritans,* ed. Miller and Johnson, I, 199. Perry Miller discusses this "errand" in *Errand into the Wilderness,* 11 f.

Penn was equally convinced that God intended his "holy experiment" to be "an example . . . to the nations" and a means of forwarding the remodeling of life everywhere. And Samuel Purchas' history of Virginia, written in 1625, began its account of that colony's varied experiences with Adam and Eve in order to "show how God had so managed the past that English colonization in the present was the fulfillment of his plan." [24] Even Roger Williams (1604?-84), "the New England firebrand" who dissented at several crucial points from his neighbors in the Bay Colony, lived in daily expectation of a new dispensation.

This understanding of the decisive role that America was to have in the divine economy was appropriated and popularized in the eighteenth century by leaders of the Great Awakening. (For the Great Awakening, see Chap. III.) Jonathan Edwards, reflecting upon the outbreak of the revival, was convinced that "this work of God's Spirit, so extraordinary and wonderful, is the dawning or at least a prelude of that glorious work of God so often foretold in Scripture, which in the progress and issue of it shall renew the world of mankind." He saw the Awakening as the vindication, after so many successive disappointments, of the earlier expectation that the final act of God's work of redemption would begin in America. And if "in any part of America," he continued, "I think if we consider the circumstances of the settlement of New England, it must needs appear the most likely of all American colonies to be the place whence this work shall principally take its rise." [25] Whatever other leaders of the revival may have thought of Edwards' speculation as to the precise point at which the new age would first manifest itself, they shared his belief that God's Spirit was making itself felt in an unusual way and that God had a special destiny in store for America.

This mood of eager expectancy was to continue to be characteristic of American religious life. Having escaped in so many ways the limitations of a bounded existence, men and women were easily persuaded of the reality of unlimited possibilities. The hope of all things being made new, in the course of time, was often subtly secularized and frequently restated in political terms. But the conviction remained that somehow this was God's country with a mission to perform. For the churches this sense of mission was the source of much of their restless energy as they sought to keep

[24] Miller, *Errand into the Wilderness*, 115. See also Wright, *Religion and Empire*, 115–33.

[25] *The Works of Jonathan Edwards*, Vol. IV, *The Great Awakening*, ed. C. C. Goen (New Haven, 1972), 353, 358.

abreast of the western tide of migration and to make sure that the United States would fulfill its calling as a godly nation.

THE OUTSIDERS. One should keep in mind, as a continuing feature of the American context, two segments of the population which were unable to share the eager expectation of the dominant majority. The native Americans quickly became strangers in the land with no heady vision of the future to sustain them. To evangelize the Indians and make them joint-heirs of the promise had been one of the motives of colonization, and there was intermittent missionary activity. For the most part, however, Indians were treated as an alien presence to be pushed back beyond the forward-moving edge of "civilization." In similar fashion captives brought from Africa as slaves were outsiders who had little reason to view the future as pregnant with the possibility of all things being made new.

Mostly only at times of sporadic revolt did the outsiders achieve momentary visibility as persons. It is true that some Indian missions were successful, with converts being accepted and assimilated to new modes of life, but this was not the typical outcome of the encounter between the colonists and the first Americans. A few blacks also gained visibility in churches of their own in the years surrounding the American Revolution. The dating is shadowy but two black Baptist preachers, David George and George Liele, gathered a congregation in 1775 at Silver Bluff, South Carolina. Three years later there was a black congregation down river in Savannah. With the British evacuation David George was carried to Nova Scotia where he gathered a church in 1784, while Liele escaped to Jamaica to carry on Baptist activity there. The first permanent African Baptist church in Savannah was established in 1788 by Andrew Bryan.[26] Meanwhile, in 1776, a black church was founded at Williamsburg, and in 1780 another black Baptist church was formed in Petersburg, Virginia, followed a decade later by one organized in Lexington, Kentucky. By the 1790's there were also black Methodist churches in Philadelphia and New York City. Despite these beginnings it was to be a century and a half before either native Americans or blacks were to achieve sufficient visibility to become major participants in the shaping of a common destiny for all Americans.

26 See Albert J. Raboteau, *Slave Religion* (N.Y., 1978).

II

Transplanted Churches

Where to begin an account of the various religious groups in colonial America is a puzzling question. There was no single dominant group to provide a logical point of departure and to serve as a foil for the discussion of the others. The Congregationalists were the largest of the denominations but they were a regional group. The Anglicans were the first to establish themselves on the American scene but they were to be neither the largest nor the most influential of the colonial religious bodies. The Presbyterians and the Baptists were to be both numerous and widely dispersed by the end of the colonial period but their growth was relatively late and presupposed in part the founding of Pennsylvania by the Quakers. A purely chronological approach would be awkward and confusing, for it would introduce the Dutch Reformed and the Swedish Lutherans much too early in a story whose dominant motif was almost wholly English. Even the attempt to deal with the various groups on a regional basis would involve distortion, for few of them were confined to a single area. The most satisfactory solution would seem to be to provide a brief review of the founding and the religious complexion of each of the colonies, and then to deal with each of the English-speaking denominations in roughly chronological order before giving attention to the highly significant but much less numerous groups of Continental origin.

Religious characteristics of the different colonies

The thirteen colonies came into being as a result of two great waves of English colonizing activity separated by the twenty distracting years (1640–60) of the English civil wars and the regime of Oliver Cromwell. Virginia, Maryland, the several New England colonies, and the island possessions (Bermuda, Barbados, St. Kitts, Nevis, and Antigua) were products of the early years. Following the restoration of the Stuarts to the English throne in 1660, the gap between Maryland and New England on the Atlantic coast was closed by the capture of New Netherlands from the Dutch in 1664 and by the founding of New Jersey in 1674 and of Pennsylvania and Delaware in 1681 and 1682. The southern frontier was extended by the settlement of Charleston in 1670 in accordance with a proprietary patent to the territory which was later divided into the royal colonies of South and North Carolina. Georgia, the last of the thirteen colonies, was founded in 1733.

THE SOUTHERN COLONIES. Virginia, the earliest of the colonies, was unique in several other respects. In Virginia alone did the Anglicans command a clear majority of the religious population; in Virginia alone was Anglicanism the established religion from the beginning; and in Virginia alone of all the colonies was provision made to enforce conformity to the Church of England. The instructions of James I in the first charter of Virginia were explicit. "The true word and service of God" was to be "preached, planted, and used" in the new colony "according to the doctrine, rights [rites?], and religion now professed and established within our realm of England." [1] To this end, chaplains were appointed by the Company, and repeated legislation required everyone to attend the services of the church. It is true that these laws were seldom rigorously enforced, but the intention was that there should be no toleration of dissent.

[1] Peter G. Mode, Source Book . . . for American Church History (Menasha, Wisc., 1920), 10.

The first major break in the pattern of religious uniformity in Virginia came after 1660 when Quaker missionaries were successful in establishing scattered communities of adherents, but it was not until the later decades of the colonial period that the Anglican predominance was to be sharply reduced and then surpassed as new population flowed into the area which lay beyond the tidewater region. The surge of non-Anglican strength was partially the result of Anglican neglect to form parishes and to provide a ministry for the new arrivals, but it was more largely due to other factors. Many of the new settlers who spread out in the territory adjacent to the Shenandoah were Scots from northern Ireland, some were Germans, others were from New England. The potential Presbyterian strength represented by the Scotch-Irish was marshaled with great effectiveness by Samuel Davies (1723–61) who had been sent to Virginia by the Synod of New York in 1748 and who continued to spearhead the Presbyterian advance until 1759 when he became president of the College of New Jersey (now Princeton). The moderate growth of the Baptists was transformed into a phenomenal expansion by the exciting preaching of a transplanted New Englander, Shubal Stearns (1706–71), who began his activity in Virginia in 1754. The success of these dissenting groups was facilitated by the tension that existed between the older and newer areas of settlement. Anglicanism suffered because of its identification with the early planters of the tidewater region, whose descendants had become a ruling aristocracy which controlled the Assembly, denied full representation to the upcountry districts, and refused to heed their grievances. Furthermore, the attempts to suppress dissent by this time could be countered by an appeal to rights guaranteed by the English Act of Toleration of 1689.

From the standpoint of religion, North Carolina, South Carolina, and Georgia had little in common with Virginia beyond a nominal establishment of Anglicanism as the official faith of the three colonies. Religious toleration was granted at the outset and the population had little homogeneity. The settlement of North Carolina was haphazard, and it resembled Pennsylvania in its religious diversity. The early inhabitants were runaway servants from Virginia. For many years Quakers were the largest religious group. Later the Scotch-Irish sweeping up the Shenandoah valley gave Presbyterians major strength in the southern colonies, and the Baptists were active and growing rapidly at the close of the colonial period. Strong German communities—mostly Lutherans and Moravians—were found in both North Carolina and Georgia. Only in South Carolina was there any significant Anglican strength south of Virginia. In 1704 "by dint of political trickery" an act was passed by the South Carolina Assembly providing for an Anglican establishment, and after some modifications it was put into effect in 1706. Its provisions, however, were never fully carried out because of lack of clergymen, and at best it was a highly precarious establishment depending upon shifting majorities in an Assembly controlled at intervals by the dissenting groups. A similar establishment was secured in North Carolina in 1715 and in Georgia in 1758, but in neither colony did the establishment become operative in more than a handful of parishes.

Maryland, founded in 1634 by the second Lord Baltimore, had many affinities with the middle colonies, both geographic and otherwise. Its proprietor was Roman Catholic; and like the Quaker William Penn, he was as interested in providing a place where his co-religionists could settle as he was in making his colony a profitable financial investment. And for both these reasons, like Penn, he pursued a forthright policy of religious toleration from the beginning. In actuality, of course, for the first decade or two, Roman Catholics were the only persons in Maryland who received any benefit from this toleration, for there were no other dissenting groups. The non-Catholic Christians there were Anglicans, and one can scarcely speak of tolerating in English territory a church whose "supreme governor" was the English monarch himself. Indeed, the charter presupposed that churches would be "dedicated and consecrated according to the ecclesiastical laws of our kingdom of England."

The Roman Catholics who participated in the colonization of Maryland were a minority of even the first contingent that sailed for the new colony; and in order not to jeopardize the charter they were instructed by the proprietor that "no scandal nor offense" was "to be given any of the Protestants." On shipboard they were "to cause all acts of the Roman Catholic religion to be done as privately as may be" and were "to be silent upon all occasion of discourse concerning matters of religion."[2]

The wise precautions by which the proprietor sought to secure the toleration of his co-religionists were not entirely successful, for Roman

[2] "The Calvert Papers," No. 1, *Maryland Historical Society Proceedings*, XXVIII (Baltimore, 1889), 132.

Catholics were disfranchised for a brief period in the 1650's after their leaders had proclaimed allegiance to Charles II in opposition to the authority of the English Parliament. And after the expulsion of James II from the English throne because of his efforts to subvert the Protestant faith, Roman Catholics in Maryland were again subjected to various disabilities. Nevertheless, they remained one of the most important and influential segments of Maryland society.

By 1677 both Roman Catholics and Anglicans had been reduced to the status of minority groups if credence is to be given Lord Baltimore's report to the Privy Council concerning the shifts that had occurred in the religious affiliations of the Maryland populace. "The greatest part of the inhabitants of that province (three of four at least) do consist of Presbyterians, Independents, Anabaptists, and Quakers; those of the Church of England, as well as those of the Romish, being the fewest." [3] In spite of this numerical inferiority, the overthrow of James II in 1688 marked the beginning of a vigorous campaign to secure an Anglican establishment in Maryland, an objective which was achieved in 1702 when the Board of Trade and Plantations in London was finally satisfied that the rights of other minorities would be adequately safeguarded. By this time Presbyterians, Baptists, and Quakers were becoming more numerous, and German Protestants were soon to spill over the border from Pennsylvania.

THE NEW ENGLAND COLONIES. Plymouth, the first of the New England colonies, was almost immediately overshadowed by and in 1691 was absorbed into Massachusetts Bay Colony, and its religious history differed in no significant way from its larger neighbor. Both colonies were established by Congregationalists: Plymouth by Separatist Congregationalists; Massachusetts Bay by Nonseparatist Congregationalists (see pp. 36–37), but in the New World this difference was not of great moment.

A degree of intrigue and perhaps deception lay behind the establishment of Massachusetts Bay. In 1629, when the repressive ecclesiastical measures of William Laud, bishop of London (later archbishop of Canterbury) and chief advisor to the king, had begun to make life in England difficult for them, a group of Nonseparatist Congregationalists obtained from Charles I a royal charter for the Massachusetts Bay Company. For some reason the usual clause which required the headquarters of such a

[3] L. J. Trinterud, *The Forming of an American Tradition* (Philadelphia, 1949), 26.

company to be in England and thus subject to the immediate control of the crown was omitted from the charter. This could scarcely have been an oversight, for when the great Winthrop fleet sailed in the summer of 1630 it carried with it all the officers and stockholders of the company together with the charter itself. With charter and company in America, the colony was in effect an independent republic. The stockholders were called "freemen" and they became the electorate; the directors or "deputies" became legislators; and the governor of the company became the chief executive of the colony. When it became inconvenient for the whole body of freemen to attend the annual meeting or "general court" of the company, a representative system was devised whereby their "assistants" became a second house of the legislative assembly. When the English authorities finally discovered what had occurred, efforts were made to have the charter returned and the status of the colony regularized. Tactics of delay, however, were adopted; the turmoil of the two decades from 1640 to 1660 intervened; and it was not until 1684 that the charter was finally revoked and a royal governor appointed.

With freedom to pursue an independent course, the early settlers of Massachusetts Bay were in no mood to permit dissent from the "due form" of ecclesiastical government which they established. Having forsaken their homes to found a new Zion in the American wilderness, they saw no reason why their endeavor should be compromised by dissidence. Others, they contended, had full liberty to stay away; and they noted that there was ample room elsewhere in America for them to establish settlements of their own. As early as 1635 the first of a long succession of heresy trials imposing banishment as the most common penalty was held.[4]

The attempt to suppress dissent in Massachusetts Bay was never wholly successful for several reasons. The mere fact of space, even in Massachusetts itself, made policing difficult. And the policy of banishment created centers just across its borders from which the contagion of dissent filtered back to the older settlements. Furthermore, their fellow Congregationalists in England were embarrassed by their proceedings and exerted constant pressure upon them to adopt a more liberal policy. But the major reason was the fact that within the heart of New England Puritanism there was a steady and persistent acknowledgment that "the Lord hath more

---

[4] Among those banished were Roger Williams, Samuel Gorton, William Coddington, John Wheelwright, and Anne Hutchinson.

light yet to break forth out of his Holy Word" and that therefore they must ever be ready "to receive whatever truth shall be made known . . . from the written Word of God." [5] These were the words of John Robinson (1576?–1625), pastor of those who came to Plymouth in 1620 when they were exiles at Leyden, but they represent the basic assumption upon which the whole Congregationalist enterprise was founded. In the light of this fundamental principle, it is not surprising that Congregationalism was forever spawning its own dissidents—men and even women who defended themselves by appealing to the truth that had been made known to them from "the written Word of God."

While these three factors reduced the effectiveness of the attempt by the Massachusetts Bay authorities to enforce conformity, they persisted in their endeavor until 1684 when the loss of the charter made it impossible for them to proceed independently of English authority. Three years later the end of the Congregational monopoly in the colony was dramatically signalized in Boston when the governor forced the Congregationalists to permit the Old South meetinghouse to be utilized for Anglican worship.

New Hampshire, in its basic pattern of church life, was little more than an extension of Massachusetts Bay. This was also largely true of Connecticut, founded by Thomas Hooker (1586?–1647) in 1635 and later incorporating the smaller colony of New Haven. Connecticut in several respects was more conservative than Massachusetts, and the *Saybrook Platform* of 1708 provided a more centralized control over the churches.

Rhode Island was a different story. The territory around Narragansett Bay had become the refuge for many of those expelled for reasons of religious dissent from Massachusetts Bay. Roger Williams, who was to be briefly a Baptist and then a Seeker, made his way there in 1636.[6] Anne Hutchinson (1591–1643), the "antinomian" prophetess whose trial shook the whole ruling hierarchy of the Bay colony, arrived with a number of her adherents in 1637. John Coggeshall and William Aspinwall came in 1638,

---

[5] Cotton Mather, *Magnalia Christi Americana* (Hartford, 1855), I, 64.

[6] For Williams, see Perry Miller, *Roger Williams: His Contribution to the American Tradition* (Indianapolis, 1953), W. C. Gilpin, *The Millenarian Piety of Roger Williams* (Chicago, 1979), and Mauro Calamandrei, "Neglected Aspects of Roger Williams' Thought," *Church History*, XXI (1952), 239–58. For a brief account of his characteristic emphases, see Introduction to his *Experiments of Spiritual Life and Health*, ed. W. S. Hudson (Philadelphia, 1951).

and a little later were joined by John Clarke (1609–76) and William Coddington. Samuel Gorton (1592?–1677), a contentious mystic who was always as ready to stir up a fight over politics and property rights as over religion, arrived in 1640. Williams, fearful lest the leading of God's Spirit and one's faithfulness to Christ be impaired by the sinful corruption of men, was a firm advocate of complete religious freedom. On this basis he succeeded in bringing together the disparate religious elements represented in the communities at Providence, Portsmouth, Newport, and Warwick to form the colony of Rhode Island and Providence Plantations, traveling to England in 1643 to secure the necessary patent from the English Parliament. Although the Baptists initially were the largest group in Rhode Island, they were soon rivaled and then surpassed by the Quakers who utilized the freedom the colony afforded as a base from which to attempt the evangelization of other parts of New England.

THE MIDDLE COLONIES. When the English took over control of New Netherlands in 1664, the new colony was the most religiously heterogeneous area in America. The Dutch Reformed church quite understandably was the largest single religious group, and throughout the seventeenth century it was to continue to have more adherents than all other groups combined. But, as Governor Dongan (a Roman Catholic) reported in 1687, there were also French Calvinists, German Lutherans, Congregationalists from New England, several varieties of Quakers, Mennonites, Baptists, some Roman Catholics, and a few Jews. "In short," he explained, "of all sorts of opinion there are some, and of the most part none at all."

The terms of capitulation to England provided that the Dutch should have freedom of conscience, worship, and church discipline. This was interpreted to mean that the Dutch Reformed church retained a measure of its established character, and the early English governors considered that the Dutch Reformed ministers were entitled to support from public funds. The Duke of York, to whom the colony had been granted by royal patent, also issued instructions that no one who professed the Christian faith was to be in any way disturbed for differing judgment in religious matters. Thus the policy of religious toleration which hitherto had prevailed was continued, with only the status of the Jews left in doubt.

After the Glorious Revolution of 1688 which brought William and Mary to the English throne, the governor of New York was instructed to secure an Anglican establishment in the colony. After repeated rebuffs, the

Assembly was finally induced in 1693 to adopt a measure which stipulated only that a "sufficient Protestant minister" should be supported by an annual tax in each of six parishes to be set up in New York City and three adjoining counties. Although the governor protested the vagueness of the wording and sought without success to have the act amended, he interpreted it (contrary to the intention of the Assembly) as a legal establishment of the Church of England. It was a small victory, for there were too few Anglicans in the colony to give it much substance. As the chaplain of the English garrison reported two years later, there were only ninety Anglican families in the entire colony in contrast to the 1,754 Dutch Reformed families and the 1,355 families of various types of English dissent.

The colony of New Jersey had a checkered development. Initially it was part of the grant to the Duke of York in 1664, but almost immediately he gave it to two friends. A few hundred Dutch and New England emigrés were already there and in order to attract more settlers laws were promulgated which provided for freedom of conscience and an Assembly. In 1674 West New Jersey was sold to two Quakers who let William Penn become one of the proprietors, and it was not until 1702, when New Jersey became a royal colony, that the two sections were reunited. Delaware was purchased by Penn from the Duke of York in 1682 and was administered jointly with Pennsylvania until it was given a separate Assembly in 1704.

William Penn founded Pennsylvania in 1681. Son of an admiral, Penn was converted to Quakerism in 1667 at the age of 23, after having made a grand tour of the Continent and spending a period of time at the lively court in Dublin. Penn was eager to secure a colony where, free from the pressure of bad example and worldly corruption, he could carry out a "holy experiment" in establishing a society fashioned in accordance with Quaker ideals. His share of West (New) Jersey did not satisfy his ambitions and a tactful reminder to the Duke of York of a debt to his father that had not been repaid led to his becoming the proprietor of the vast slice of territory which was given the name Pennsylvania.

The settlement of the new colony began without delay. A few Swedes, Finns, and Dutch were already there, and large-scale Quaker immigration set in at once. Other English-speaking inhabitants were enticed by the easy terms for the purchase of land described in Penn's promotional brochure,

Some Account of the Province of Pennsylvania (1681). The prospect of religious freedom attracted several German minority religious groups (see below pp. 51–58), while the lure of economic advantage drew many other Germans from the economically depressed Palatinate. The population was also swelled by large numbers of Scotch-Irish Presbyterians driven from home by the economic consequences of the Woolens Act of 1699 and by religious disabilities imposed in 1704. Quakers, however, continued to set the tone of the colony and, due to unbalanced representation in the Assembly, long maintained political dominance.

The English-speaking denominations

The Church of England was drastically reformed at the time of the Protestant Reformation. Ties with Rome were severed, monastaries suppressed, prayers for the dead abolished, tables replaced altars, the liturgy reshaped and rewritten, worship conducted in English, and the monarch acknowledged as "supreme governor" of the church. Although the English church was indebted to the major Reformed theologians—Bucer, Bullinger, and Calvin—for its theology, the impact of the varient form of Calvinism known as Arminianism [7] began to be felt soon after the first colonies were settled. During the reigns of Elizabeth (1558–1603) and James I (1603–25), a strong Puritan movement developed within the church which sought to remove a few remaining popish "ornaments," to promote godly preaching throughout the land, and to secure greater self-government for the church. A policy which gave Puritan consciences considerable latitude avoided, except for a few small separatist groups, any open break until after Charles I came to the throne. In the 1630's, however, Archbishop Laud's attempt to enforce rigid conformity by means of extra-legal royal prerogative courts helped fuel the flames which resulted in civil war between king and parliament in the 1640's. When the Long Parliament met in 1640 almost everyone was opposed to the "prelacy" represented by Laud. Beyond that there was no agreement. Some favored a reformed episcopacy, some favored a presbyterian system of church government after the Scottish model, some became

---

[7] Jacob Arminius (1560–1609) was a Dutch Calvinist who opposed the hyper-Calvinism of the late sixteenth century. Later the term "Arminian" was used in England to designate a "Romish" tendency to stress the human role in redemption. A century later John Wesley used the term with a still different connotation, see the portion of his "What Is an Arminian?" printed in H. E. Fosdick, *Great Voices of the Reformation* (N.Y., 1952), 514–17.

independents (congregationalists) who stressed the rights of local congregations. Some of the latter advocated believers' baptism. In the confusion following the defeat and execution of the king, still other groups appeared, the Quakers being the most prominent. When the Stuart line was restored in 1660, a new attempt was made to enforce a rigid conformity, a policy which ended with the Glorious Revolution of 1688 when James II was expelled and the Act of Toleration of 1689 was adopted. Henceforth the Church of England was to be in fact and in law the church of only part of the English people. A further anomaly for an "established" or "state church" was the fact that the monarch when in Scotland ceased to be an Anglican and became a Presbyterian.

THE ANGLICANS. In colonial America, Virginia was the great center of Anglican strength.[8] The first ministers were chaplains sent out by the Virginia Company, but between 1619 and 1622 a rudimentary parish system was set up with assessments levied and land set aside for parochial support. Lay vestries with responsibility for ordering parish life probably were introduced at this time. They were given statutory authority in 1643 when the Assembly ordered that vestrymen should be chosen by the voters of each parish. Later the vestries became self-perpetuating bodies, the preserves of the socially and economically privileged.

There was a perennial shortage of ministers throughout the colonial years. This was partly due to the fact that the establishment of a college to train a native ministry, though earnestly sought, was long delayed. Although Harvard College was founded as early as 1636, it was not until 1693 that Virginia was able to secure a similar institution for training its clergy. Even after William and Mary opened its doors, the problem was not wholly solved. Since a bishop alone could ordain, young Anglicans who wished to enter the ministry were compelled to undertake the long and hazardous journey to England to secure ordination.

Among expedients used to entice ministers to Virginia was the payment of a bounty of twenty pounds to anyone who would transport a "sufficient minister" to the colony. Later the bounty was paid directly to the minister. Clergymen secured by such means were of uneven quality. While several were of unusual ability, many were not. But even the competent and faithful had a difficult time. Parishes were large, population

[8] For an account of Anglicanism in colonial Virginia, see G. MacLaren Brydon, *Virginia's Mother Church*, 2 vols. (Richmond, 1947–52).

was scattered, and a legal technicality frequently deprived them of security and authority. A 1629 act directed the governor to "induct" a minister "into any parish that shall make presentation of him." Vestries discovered that by neglecting to present their ministers for induction, the parish remained technically vacant and the minister could be made subservient by hiring him on a yearly basis. If the faithful and competent had a difficult time by being subjected to the whims of the vestry, clergy of less zeal and devotion found the absence of episcopal supervision a distinct advantage. Charges of indolence, drunkenness, and immorality were not uncommon. While abuses were not as widespread as some suggested, there were few means by which they could be corrected.

The Anglican clergy in the colonies were nominally under the supervision of the bishop of London, but, apart from certain formalities, his jurisdiction was not given any practical implementation until after the Revolution of 1688 when Bishop Compton began to delegate his disciplinary authority to resident "Commissaries," the most notable of whom were James Blair (1655–1743) in Virginia and Thomas Bray (1656–1730) in Maryland.[9] Although they did much to improve the condition of both church and clergy, they lacked the full episcopal powers which were indispensable to a fully developed church life. Bray was one of the first men to make an earnest plea for an American episcopate, but despite continuing agitation this was to remain an unrealized hope throughout the whole colonial period. Much of the opposition to the appointment of a bishop came from the laity who felt that he would jeopardize their own prerogatives in the church. William White (1748–1836), who became one of the first bishops of the newly formed Protestant Episcopal Church after the American Revolution, declared in 1782 that "there cannot be produced an instance of laymen in America, unless in the very infancy of the settlements, soliciting the introduction of a bishop." Even the clergy in the southern parishes were opposed to the establishment of an American episcopate, Samuel Auchmuty reported, since without a bishop they were "their own pastors." [10]

The missionaries sent out by the Society for the Propagation of the Gospel (S.P.G.) presented a brighter picture than did the general run of

9 For Bray, see Henry P. Thompson, *Thomas Bray* (London, 1954).
10 William White, *The Case of the Episcopal Churches in the United States Considered*, ed. R. G. Salomon (Philadelphia, 1954), 29. Carl Bridenbaugh, *Mitre and Sceptre* (N.Y., 1962), 249.

the parish clergy. The primary objective of the Society, which was organized in 1701 at the insistence of Thomas Bray and with the full support of the Archbishop of Canterbury, was to provide for "the administration of God's Word and the sacraments" in those areas where there were no settled Anglican clergy. From the time of its inception until 1783 when it officially ceased operations in the newly independent colonies, eighty-four of its missionaries labored in New England, fifty-eight in New York, fifty-four in South Carolina, forty-seven in Pennsylvania, forty-four in New Jersey, thirty-three in North Carolina, thirteen in Georgia, five in Maryland, and only two in Virginia. In all, three hundred and nine missionaries were recruited to serve in these colonies and well over one million dollars (£227,454) was raised in England for their support.[11]

The S.P.G. missionaries constituted a superior caste among the Anglican clergy. A measure of idealism and devotion was required of those whose only prospect of financial remuneration was the relatively small stipend provided by the Society. A life of ease and modest comfort might be envisioned by those who sought appointment to established parishes but this was never the lot of the missionaries. Furthermore, the absence of episcopal authority and discipline was in a measure remedied by the Society. The Society, to be sure, could not unfrock an erring minister, but it could and did dismiss the indolent, the disobedient, and the immoral from its service. Everywhere, even in New England and Pennsylvania, the missionaries had the advantage of varying degrees of official support, an advantage which they were not slow to exploit. The advantage, of course, became a liability with the coming of the American Revolution. The missionaries almost to a man identified themselves completely with the English cause and in the end few of them remained to carry on the ministry of the Protestant Episcopal Church in the United States.

Since the S.P.G. missionaries were to disappear with the coming of independence, a development of greater long-range significance was the emergence of an indigenous Anglicanism in New England. The break came on the day after commencement in September, 1722, when Timothy Cutler (1684–1765), president of Yale College, announced to the astonished trustees that he and one of the tutors and three neighboring ministers had been persuaded that their Congregational ordinations were invalid.

[11] C. S. Pascoe, *An Historical Account of the Society for the Propagation of the Gospel* (London, 1901), 86–87.

This change of view went back in part to a gift of books to the library, some of which detailed the Anglican claim to be the lineal descendant of the apostolic church. A more decisive factor perhaps was the influence exerted by an S.P.G. missionary stationed at Stratford, for Cutler and his friends did not reveal their new sentiments until they had been assured of support by the Society. Four of the converts went abroad to seek episcopal ordination. One of them died there of the smallpox but the others returned to serve as missionaries of the Society—Cutler becoming the first rector of Christ Church in Boston, James Whetmore serving the mission station at Rye, and Samuel Johnson (1696–1772) ultimately becoming the first president of King's College (Columbia University) in New York.

The apostasy of the president of Yale was a traumatic shock to New England Congregationalism, and as a result of his influence and example there were to be continuing conversions among the students at New Haven. These conversions gave the Church of England in the colonies a nucleus of native-born and native-trained ministers who were "convinced" rather than "birthright" Anglicans, and they brought to their pastoral endeavors all the zeal and ardor that is commonly found among converts.

THE CONGREGATIONALISTS. The "congregationalism" of the early New Englanders was the product of the peculiar history of the English Reformation which in several respects was an "arrested" reformation. Some of the early advocates of a more thoroughgoing reform, especially liturgical reform, broke from the parish churches and established independent churches of their own. These were the Separatists.[12] They restricted church membership to convinced believers and insisted that, since all members were equally priests, all should share in the determination of church affairs. Others who were dissatisfied with the slow pace of official reform found a considerable measure of freedom to carry out their desired reforms within the established parishes. So long as they engaged in no concerted organizational activity, both Elizabeth and James I were content for the most part to leave them to their own devices. When pressure was applied they found patrons to aid them, and they became adept at defending their rights in the common-law courts. They did not reject the Church of England as a false church, although they acknowledged that in many ways it was deformed and tainted with corruptions. This point of

[12] Robert Browne (1550?–1633?), author of *Reformation without Tarrying for Any[one]* (1582), was the early leader.

view was made explicit in the words Francis Higginson is reported to have said on shipboard as the shores of England faded from view:

> We will not say as the Separatists are wont to say at their leaving England, "Farewell Babylon, Farewell Rome"; but we will say, "Farewell dear England, Farewell the Church of God in England and all the Christian friends there." We do not go to New England as Separatists from the Church of England, though we cannot but separate from the corruptions in it.[13]

Prior to Higginson's departure in 1629, these Nonseparatist Congregationalists had elaborated the theory that in the hidden essence of its constitution the Church of England was basically congregational in structure. They differed from the Presbyterians at two points. Since they had had unworthy and unwanted ministers thrust upon them in their parish churches, they were unwilling to concede the power of ordination even to a presbytery, reserving it to the local congregation alone. Furthermore, since they had been pressured on occasion by the threat of excommunication wielded by a bishop, they were insistent that this power also must be reserved to the local congregation so that an individual might be tried by those who knew him best and not by any higher judicatory.

The Separatists provided the nucleus of the settlement at Plymouth, while those who came to Massachusetts Bay were Congregationalists of the Nonseparatist variety. The difference between the two groups was not great, and two factors served to obliterate it. First, shortly before their departure from their refuge in the Netherlands, the leader of this particular group of Separatists, John Robinson, had been persuaded of the validity of most of the Nonseparatist contentions. Second, in the New World the old issue that had divided them, whether or not the parish churches of England could in some way be viewed as true churches, was not of great significance, for they had to establish new churches of their own. Thus they became joint representatives of what was to be a single denomination. There were a few isolated individuals like Roger Williams, of course, who insisted that they should repudiate the Church of England in profession as well as in practice, but this counsel was rejected as politically inexpedient.

---

[13] Cotton Mather, *Magnalia*, I, 362. For an elaboration of the Separatist-Nonseparatist distinction, see Perry Miller, *Orthodoxy in Massachusetts*, 53–101.

Unlike other religious groups the Congregationalists in America were well supplied with ministers from the beginning, with no less than one hundred and thirty graduates of Cambridge and Oxford having come out to serve the churches prior to 1647. "Such a concentration of educated men in a new settlement in proportion to the population," it has been stated, "has never occurred before or since," and one of the first concerns of the early settlers was to make provision for the future supply of educated ministers. *New England's First Fruits* (1643) emphasized this point in its account of the founding of Harvard in 1636.

> After God had carried us safe to New England and we had builded our houses, provided necessaries for our livelihood, reared convenient places for God's worship, and settled the civil government; one of the next things we longed for and looked after was to advance learning and perpetuate it to posterity, dreading to leave an illiterate ministry to the churches when our present ministers shall lie in the dust.[14]

So successful were they in this endeavor that of the 1,586 ministers who served the Congregational churches of New England during the colonial period, only 79 were not college graduates.

Elementary education was of equal concern, it being "one chief project of that old deluder Satan to keep men from the knowledge of the Scriptures."[15] To counter this "project," a grammar school was established in every town. The consequence of this systematic effort, as Andrew Eliot informed Thomas Hollis in 1761, was that "scarce any are to be found among us, even in the obscurest parts, who are not able to read and write with tolerable propriety."

"The convenient places for God's worship" that were erected were called "meetinghouses" so that people would not be confused and make the mistake of thinking that the church was a building. These houses in which the church met were plain structures, often beautiful in their simplicity, with the people gathered about the table which stood at the center and with a high pulpit on one side for the reading and preaching of God's Word. The worship was equally plain, with the singing of psalms, a

---

[14] A portion of *New England's First Fruits* is printed in Smith, Handy, Loetscher, *American Christianity*, I, 123–26; and in *The Puritans*, ed. Miller and Johnson, II, 701–7.

[15] S. E. Morison, *The Puritan Pronaos: Studies in the Intellectual Life of New England in the Seventeenth Century* (N.Y., 1936), 65.

long prayer, the reading of Scripture, and a sermon being the principal features. The government of these churches was given its classic definition in the *Cambridge Platform* of 1648,[16] a document drafted and adopted in response to a "Remonstrance" which challenged the Congregational way of proceeding and threatened an appeal to the English Parliament if the restrictions upon church membership and voting were not liberalized. The same synod which framed the *Platform* also adopted as a statement of the Congregationalist doctrinal position the Confession of Faith which had just been issued in England by the Westminster Assembly of Divines, thus emphasizing their doctrinal solidarity with both the English and Scottish Presbyterians.

The *Cambridge Platform* had sidestepped one issue with regard to church membership which had begun to trouble the churches, and it proved to be an issue which could not long be ignored. According to Congregational theory both the believing adult and his infant child belonged to the church, the latter being "federally holy" and entitled to receive baptism. On reaching the age of discretion, however, the child was required to give an account of his own repentance and faith in order to qualify for full communicant standing, including the right to partake of the Lord's Supper and to vote at church meetings. It was understood that true faith, even among the weakest Christians, would be confirmed by some specific experience of God's redeeming grace, and that in the absence of such an experience a person was not to be admitted to full membership. This practice posed no problem until grandchildren began to be born whose parents were but "half-way" embraced within the covenant community and the question was raised as to whether their children were "federally" related to the church and qualified to receive baptism.

The controversy that ensued was heated, for whatever the decision, one of two equally cherished "goods" would be sacrificed. If baptism were denied to children of unregenerate parents, the integrity of the churches as gathered communities of convinced believers would be preserved but an increasing proportion of the population would be removed from the discipline of the church, and the endeavor to fashion a holy commonwealth in the American wilderness would be brought to naught. If baptism were granted, the churches would be in danger of becoming "mixed multitudes"

[16] A portion is reprinted in Smith, Handy, Loetscher, *American Christianity*, I, 128–40. The full text is in Walker, *Creeds and Platforms of Congregationalism*.

of the regenerate and unregenerate. Seventeen ministers from Massachusetts and Connecticut met in Boston in 1657 and announced that they were persuaded that the children of half-way convenanters should be baptized. Their action served only to inflame the opposition which was led by Charles Chauncy (1589–1672), president of Harvard. Finally the General Court of Massachusetts Bay intervened in 1662 and sought to end the controversy by summoning a synod of the churches to reach an authoritative decision. When the vote was taken after long debate, the earlier judgment of the seventeen ministers was sustained.

The decision of the synod opened the door to further laxity. Within little more than a decade, the restriction which kept unregenerate church members from partaking of the Lord's Supper began to break down. Solomon Stoddard (1643–1729), pastor of the church at Northampton, became the chief advocate of lowering the bar at this point. He insisted that the germ of grace is latent in all the children of the covenant and that it should be nourished by partaking of the Lord's Supper as soon as possible. To him it seemed contradictory that those who were in need of grace should be denied this means of grace because of their weakness in grace. His arguments were persuasive to many and his practice was widely adopted.

A further breach was effected in Boston toward the close of the century. The instigators were two Harvard tutors, William Brattle (1662–1717) and William Leverett (1662–1724), who insisted that all distinctions among church members should be discarded and that even those who could not testify to an experience of grace should be allowed to participate in the government of the church, including the right to vote in the selection of the minister. Without the consent of the other churches, they proceeded to organize a new church upon this basis.

The formation of the Brattle Street Church in 1699, which was followed by Increase Mather's ejection from the presidency of Harvard in 1701, stirred the conservatives to action. Their plan, embodied in the *Massachusetts Proposals* of 1705, was to bring the churches under a form of synodical control so that further innovation could be held in check. This proposal of the ministers received no support from the governor and council appointed under the new charter of 1691, for they had no intent to diminish their power by setting up an instrument for independent action by the clergy. The *Proposals* received equally short shrift from many church members whose fear that their rights and privileges might thereby be lost was articulated by John Wise (1652–1725) of Ipswich in two tracts which later became part of the ideological arsenal of the American Revolution.[17]

Though defeated in Massachusetts, the conservative party was more successful in Connecticut where Yale College had been founded in 1701 with the aid of the Mathers as a counter to the lax influences emanating from Harvard. The *Saybrook Platform* of 1708 embodied all the essential features of the *Massachusetts Proposals*. It provided that the churches of each county were to be formed into a Consociation which was to have disciplinary oversight over them and from whose decision there was to be no appeal. These churches were further bound together by a General Association made up of delegates from each of the local Associations. The approval of the colonial authorities was secured by including the proviso that no church should be compelled to join the "united churches" or hindered, if allowed by the general laws of Connecticut, from exercising discipline in its own way.

As a result of the stabilizing influence exerted by Yale and the achievement of a measure of disciplinary oversight of the churches, Connecticut became the citadel of Congregational orthodoxy. Over the course of time, many of the Connecticut Congregationalists came to feel a greater sense of kinship with the Presbyterians than they did with their fellow Congregationalists of Massachusetts, who had been unable to complete their system with any connectional body, and thus pursued a more independent development.

THE PRESBYTERIANS. The classic form of Presbyterianism, with its presbyteries, synods, and general assembly, took shape in Scotland where the Reformation had been carried forward under the leadership of John Knox, after his return from John Calvin's Geneva, and it did not differ greatly from the structures devised by the other Reformed churches on the Continent. Incipient presbyterian tendencies had long been present in English Puritanism, and they came to the fore when the Long Parliament met in 1640. One reason for the strength of the Presbyterian party that emerged at that time was the influence of the Scottish Commissioners. The

---

[17] *The Churches Quarrel Espoused* (1713) and *A Vindication of the Government of New England Churches* (1717). An excerpt from the latter tract is printed in Smith, Handy, Loetscher, *American Christianity*, I, 384–92; and in *The Puritans*, ed. Miller and Johnson, I, 257–69.

meeting of Parliament had been precipitated by a Scottish invasion which in turn had been occasioned by an attempt to impose "Laud's liturgy" upon the Scottish churches. The Scots supported Parliament in its controversy with the King but they insisted, as a condition of their support, that the Church of England be brought into conformity with the Church of Scotland so that the occasion for future strife might be avoided.

Presbyterian sentiment was constantly cropping out in early New England and gained strength from the course of events at home. Hingham and Newbury were two notable centers, and several Presbyterian churches were established by migrating New Englanders, first on Long Island, and then in New Jersey, Pennsylvania, Maryland, and South Carolina. Several of these churches were brought together to form the Presbytery of Philadelphia in 1706. Ten years later three additional presbyteries were organized and the Synod of Philadelphia was established with representatives from each of the four subsidiary presbyteries. Although there were scattered groups of Scotch-Irish in the colonies as early as the 1680's, the great influx of population from northern Ireland which contributed so greatly to Presbyterian strength did not begin until 1720. Those who settled in the backcountry of New England tended to be absorbed into the Congregational churches, but the major flow of Scotch-Irish was into the middle colonies and up the Shenandoah valley into the Piedmont region of the South, and these areas became the great centers of Presbyterian strength and influence.

Francis Makemie (1658?–1708), a Scotch-Irishman with strong ties to both England and New England, was the key figure in the early growth of American Presbyterianism. He was in effect a missionary-at-large, itinerating widely to gather churches and to supervise their work. He had been sent to the colonies in 1683 by the Presbytery of Laggan in Ireland, but after 1691 he served as the agent of the newly formed United Brethren (Congregationalists and Presbyterians) in London, receiving support from their General Fund. Although he was the leading spirit in the formation of the Presbytery of Philadelphia in 1706, he did not think in terms of denominational aggrandizement and he insisted that it was the height of folly to magnify the small differences that existed among Protestants.

In 1707 Makemie became one of the heroes of the struggle for religious freedom. He had been arrested by the governor of New York for unlicensed preaching, and he responded that "to give bond not to preach" was one thing he did not dare do. He appealed to the Boston ministers for help; they enlisted the aid of the United Brethren in London, and the case became a *cause célèbre*.[18] Makemie was acquitted after a brilliant defense but the governor forced him to pay the costs of his own prosecution, the rather considerable sum of £83/7s/6d. This injustice so incensed the colonial legislature that an act was passed prohibiting the assessment of such costs in the future. Charges were also brought against the governor, which led to his being recalled to London in disgrace.

Makemie died in 1708 and the subsequent history of the Presbyterians in colonial America was to be inextricably entangled in the story of the Great Awakening. This was true even of the Adopting Act of 1729 [19] by which the Synod of Philadelphia established the Westminster Confession of Faith as the doctrinal standard of American Presbyterianism, since freedom was given the presbyteries to distinguish between the essential and nonessential doctrines contained therein.

THE BAPTISTS. The English Baptists were another offshoot of the Puritan movement. The Baptists were Congregationalists who had become convinced that if churches were to be composed of believers only, then baptism should be restricted to those who were able to give some account of their own faith. Prior to 1640 the Baptists in England were few in number. It was during the decade that followed that they became a significant and influential group, with their most notable strength being gained among the officers and men of Cromwell's army. Some of the Baptists—the General Baptists—were Arminian in theology, deriving their name from their adherence to the doctrine of a general atonement. What was destined to be the major Baptist body, however, was firmly rooted in the Calvinistic tradition which found its classic expression in the Westminster Confession of Faith.[20]

Baptist beginnings in America closely paralleled those of the Presbyterians. It was not the intention of the founders of New England to foster

18 An account of Makemie's apprehension and examination is printed in *The Presbyterian Enterprise: Sources of American Presbyterian History*, ed. M. W. Armstrong, L. A. Loetscher and C. A. Anderson (Philadelphia, 1956), 13–18. For an account of colonial Presbyterianism, see L. J. Trinterud, *The Forming of an American Tradition.*

19 Printed in *The Presbyterian Enterprise*, 30–32. See also Jonathan Dickinson's *Remarks* in Smith, Handy, Loetscher, *American Christianity*, I, 262–68.

20 The several strands of Baptist life are discussed in *Baptist Concepts of the Church*, ed. W. S. Hudson (Philadelphia, 1959), 11–29.

dissent, but dissent there was from the start, and the considerations which had led some of the English Congregationalists to become Baptists were equally persuasive to some New Englanders. Henry Dunster (1609–59?), for example, rejected infant baptism in 1654 and was forced to resign as president of Harvard. The key figure initially, however, was Roger Williams who was instrumental in forming a Baptist church at Providence in 1639, three years after establishing a settlement there. Williams soon abdicated his Baptist leadership, for he became convinced that all existing churches, including the newly established Providence church, lacked a proper foundation, a defect which could be remedied only by a new apostolic dispensation in which new apostles, authoritatively commissioned and divinely authenticated, would appear to re-establish the true church. A more important person in early Baptist history was John Clarke who had gathered a church at Newport, Rhode Island, in 1641. It was Clarke's *Ill News from New England* (1652) which gave notoriety to the case of Obadiah Holmes who was publicly whipped by the Massachusetts authorities for conducting unauthorized worship in Lynn.

While Rhode Island remained a center of Baptist activity and a Baptist church was organized in Boston as early as 1665, the major Baptist growth prior to the Great Awakening stemmed from the formation of the Philadelphia Baptist Association in 1707. This Association was founded almost simultaneously with the Presbytery of Philadelphia and was similar in character to the presbytery although it lacked the latter's "authoritative" judicial power. Initially the Association was composed of churches in New Jersey, Pennsylvania, and Delaware; later it also included churches in Connecticut, New York, Maryland, and Virginia; ultimately subsidiary Associations were formed in Massachusetts and Virginia, and a relationship was established with the Charleston Association in the Carolinas. The Association carried on vigorous missionary activity from Nova Scotia to Georgia, and established the College of Rhode Island (Brown University) as a training center for its ministers. The Philadelphia Confession of Faith of these American Baptists was a slightly emended version of the Westminster Confession of Faith, following the changes introduced by the Savoy Declaration (1658) of the English Congregationalists with an additional modification at the point of baptism.[21]

[21] The "Platform of Government" which the English Congregationalists had appended to the Savoy Declaration was incorporated in the body of the Confession by the Baptists.

While the growth of the Baptists was substantial during the first half of the eighteenth century, the large-scale accessions which made them one of the major religious groups in America occurred just prior to and during the American Revolution.

THE QUAKERS. The Society of Friends, as the Quakers are more properly termed, emerged in England around 1650 out of the turmoil and confusion of the religious controversies which had accompanied the English civil wars.[22] During these years many people had pursued what was in effect a spiritual pilgrimage from one group to another. In the end there were many who became completely disenchanted by the welter of competing claims and, like Roger Williams, became Seekers waiting for a new apostolic dispensation when the true Church would be restored. Others, whom Oliver Cromwell was to describe as "happy finders," believed that the new dispensation, in the form of a new age of the Spirit, had already arrived. It was from among these "happy finders" that George Fox gathered the people known as Quakers. They were a plain people—plain in dress, plain in speech, and plain in behavior. They gathered in silence for worship until one of their number was led by the Spirit to speak. Many of them became itinerant "publishers of truth," moving from place to place to declare that Christ had already returned to reign, that he was rising up as the "Christ within" in innumerable sons and daughters, and that the terrible day of the Lord was at hand when the whole creation would be purged of dross and corruption.

Few groups have exhibited the intense missionary zeal that characterized the early Quakers. In many ways they were a most attractive people of simple honesty and integrity, but in terms of their missionary activity they were frequently the most troublesome of people. It became customary for them to invade churches and to interrupt the sermon with denunciations of false worship and the folly of seeking God through empty forms and human inventions. A few felt themselves called by the Spirit to even more bizarre behavior, such as going naked through the streets of a town as a "sign." By 1700, however, the early excesses had disappeared and

[22] For the Puritan antecedents, see G. F. Nuttall, *The Holy Spirit in Puritan Faith and Experience* (Oxford, Eng., 1946). Two standard accounts of the Quakers are Howard Brinton, *Friends for 300 Years: The History and Beliefs of the Society of Friends* (N.Y., 1952), and Rufus M. Jones, *The Quakers in the American Colonies* (London, 1911). See also S. V. James, *A People among Peoples: Quaker Benevolence in Eighteenth Century America* (Cambridge, Mass., 1963), and F. B. Tolles, *Quakers and the Atlantic Culture* (N.Y., 1960).

Quakerism entered a period of "quietism." Henceforth they were to be the most restrained of people in their behavior and were to become increasingly esteemed for their humanitarian sympathies and concerns. John Woolman (1720–72) is the most famous representative of this latter tendency and the journal in which he tells of his itinerant ministry in bearing testimony against the slave trade is a moving testament of devotion.[23]

The first Quaker missionaries to reach the New World were two women, Mary Fisher and Ann Austin, who arrived in Boston in 1656 and were followed a few weeks later by eight additional publishers of truth. The following year Quaker missionaries made their appearance in New Amsterdam and Virginia. Everywhere, except in Rhode Island, they were harried with fines, imprisonment, and deportation. The most savage persecution occurred in Massachusetts where a law was enacted subjecting Quaker missionaries who returned to the colony, after once having been banished, to the death penalty. Four suffered martyrdom before Charles II intervened in 1661 and put an end to the executions.

Rhode Island and Long Island, where the followers of Anne Hutchinson had been embryonic Quakers for twenty years, quickly became centers of Quaker strength. By the time George Fox and his twelve companions arrived for a missionary tour in 1672 persecution had practically ceased and Quaker "meetings" were to be found in every colony from New Hampshire to South Carolina. Two years later, when West (New) Jersey came under the control of Quaker proprietors, the flow of Quaker settlers to the New World set in, and the number of Quaker immigrants swelled to a great tide after Pennsylvania was established as a Quaker domain in 1681. As a result of the earlier missionary activity and the later migration, the Quakers ranked fifth numerically among the various religious bodies at the close of the colonial period and were one of the most widely dispersed of all the denominations.

As the number of Quakers increased, zeal tended to diminish. The passage of time and growing prosperity took their inevitable toll. In 1764 an aged Quaker minister summarized the decline that had taken place over the past sixty years. He well remembered, he declared, that in the early days

---

[23] *The Journal of John Woolman* (Chicago, 1950).

Friends were a plain lowly minded people and that there was much tenderness and contrition in their meetings; and that at the end of twenty years from that time, the Society increasing in wealth and in some degree conforming to the fashions of the world, true humility decreased and their meetings in general were not so lively and edifying; that at the end of forty years many of the Society were grown rich, that wearing of fine costly garments and with fashionable furniture, silver watches became customary with many and with their sons and daughters, and as these things prevailed in the Society and appeared in our meetings of ministers and elders so the powerful overshadowings of the Holy Spirit were less manifested amongst us . . . and that the weakness amongst us in not living up to our principles and supporting the testimony of truth in faithfulness was matter of much sorrow.[24]

With the passing of the first generation, there were many who were Quakers by birth rather than conviction. This tendency was both accelerated and sanctioned by the action of the London Yearly Meeting in 1737 which permitted "the wife and children to be deemed members of the Monthly Meeting of which the husband or father is a member, not only during his life but after his decease." Thus the Quakers with their "birthright membership" were pursuing much the same path as the New England Congregationalists with their progressive lowering of the bars to church membership after the adoption of the Half-way Covenant.

THE ROMAN CATHOLICS. Of all the churches which took definitive shape at the time of the Reformation, the Roman Catholic Church was by far the largest. As certain elements in the pre-Reformation church had been made normative for Lutherans by the Augsburg Confession and the Formula of Concord, so other elements were made normative for Roman Catholics by the decrees of the Council of Trent (1545–63). In spite of their predominance in many parts of Europe, the Roman Catholics were a small minority in England. Although their faith was proscribed by law, few Roman Catholics found the hard conditions of life in America an attractive prospect. In England they were mostly landed gentry and they had friends at Court to offer them protection. Consequently, enjoying at least modest comfort and relative security, these English Roman Catholics did not bulk large in the colonizing activity of their compatriots. Since there was to be

[24] F. B. Tolles, *Meeting House and Counting House* (Chapel Hill, N.C., 1948), 123–24.

no significant Roman Catholic immigration from the Continent until after the American Revolution, the Roman Catholic population in the colonies was largely limited to Maryland where the proprietor had granted large manors to his Catholic friends. There were a few Roman Catholics in New York and a larger number in Pennsylvania, but elsewhere only isolated individuals were to be found.[25]

When the *Ark* sailed from England late in 1633 with the first contingent of settlers for Maryland, it stopped briefly at the Isle of Wight to pick up two Jesuit priests, Fathers Andrew White (1579–1656) and John Altham (1589–1640), who were to distinguish themselves in the new colony by their earnest pastoral care and by their missionary activity among the Indians. Later they became involved in controversy with the proprietor because of their zeal in attempting to proselyte among non-Catholics and because of their purchase of land directly from the Indians. In different ways both of these proceedings appeared to threaten Lord Baltimore's authority, and when he carried the issue to Rome they were ordered to yield to his demands. The resolution of the controversy was hastened by the arrival of two secular priests in 1642 to replace the dissident Jesuits. In 1669 the proprietor complained that only two priests remained in the colony, and as a result two Franciscans were sent out in 1673 and were joined four years later by three additional Franciscans and three more Jesuits. Within a few years Catholic families were moving northward into Pennsylvania, and in 1706 the Jesuits opened a mission near the border of Pennsylvania and for a brief period conducted a school there. This school was apparently the only Catholic educational venture until the founding of Georgetown Academy in 1791.

Denominations of Continental origin

With the exception of African slaves and native Americans who had little opportunity to develop independent religious institutions, there were only three nationality groups of measurable size at the end of the colonial period that were of non-British stock. These were the Germans with roughly 9 per cent of the white population; the Dutch 3 per cent; and the French, 1.7 per cent.[26] Of these, the Dutch and the French were the earliest arrivals, with most of the latter initially being French-speaking

[25] For a brief account of Roman Catholicism in colonial America, see John Tracy Ellis, *American Catholicism* (Chicago, 1969), 1–39.
[26] W. L. Sperry, *Religion in America* (N.Y., 1946), 266–70.

Walloons. Practically all these people, whether Dutch, French, or German, were of Protestant background.

THE DUTCH AND FRENCH REFORMED. Reformed Protestantism had no single outstanding early leader. It had its origin as a distinct movement within the pre-Reformation church in the reforming activity of such men as Huldreich Zwingli, Henry Bullinger, Martin Bucer, and William Farel. Later John Calvin emerged as the most influential of the Reformed theologians, and his *Institutes of the Christian Religion* became the most representative statement of the Reformed understanding of the Christian faith. Almost everywhere the Reformed churches had to struggle for existence, and in the face of unrelenting persecution they stressed the sovereignty of God and man's duty to glorify him by full and unyielding obedience.

The efforts to suppress the Reformed church in France led to a series of inconclusive Wars of Religion between 1562 and 1593. A resolution of the conflict was effected when Henry of Navarre, the Protestant, or Huguenot, leader, succeeded to the throne, declared himself a Catholic, and in 1598 issued the Edict of Nantes guaranteeing freedom of worship to the Protestants. During the same period, the Dutch were struggling to free themselves from the rule of Spain, a struggle that was intensified by the religious issue as a result of the Spanish attempt to stamp out Dutch Protestantism. The armed revolt which broke out in 1566 culminated in a declaration of independence by the five northern provinces at Utrecht in 1581, and by 1609 the Dutch had made good their claim to independence.

With the energies released by their struggle for independence, the Dutch became the great trading power of Europe with the largest and most efficient merchant marine in the world. Dutch traders were everywhere, reaching Java as early as 1595. Within the next few decades they had driven the Portuguese out of most of their trading posts in the Far East, had conquered Brazil, and had occupied several islands in the West Indies. Their attention had been called to the possibilities of the fur trade in North America by the pioneering voyages of Henry Hudson, and in the same year that they gained control of Brazil they established a trading-post at the present site of Albany on the Hudson River. Two years later, in 1626, another trading-post—New Amsterdam—was established on the tip of Manhattan Island.

Peter Minuit, the first Director of New Netherlands, had been a ruling elder of the French Reformed church at Wesel, and he brought with him in 1626 two "comforters of the sick" to minister to the religious needs of the infant settlement. In 1628 the first minister, Jonas Michaelius, arrived and immediately organized a church. Michaelius reported that there were "fifty communicants, Walloons and Dutch," at the first administration of the Lord's Supper, it being observed with "great joy and comfort to many." Since few of the Walloons and others from French-speaking areas could not understand Dutch, Michaelius thought it unnecessary to have weekly services for them in their own tongue. Every four months, however, he did administer the Lord's Supper "in the French language and according to the French mode." On these occasions he read his sermon because, as he explained, he was not sufficiently fluent in French to speak extemporaneously. When Michaelius returned to Holland in 1632 he brought charges of incompetence and irregularity against the Director with the result that both men were replaced.

New Amsterdam was a typical sailors' town. Many of the inhabitants were rough and boisterous, and the lot of the early ministers was far from easy. It was not until Peter Stuyvesant became the Director of the colony in 1647 that they received any real support from the governing authority. Stuyvesant, the son and son-in-law of Dutch Reformed ministers, was a zealous churchman and a strict disciplinarian. He restricted the sale of liquor, ordered strict observance of the Sabbath, decreed that there should be preaching in the afternoon as well as in the morning on the Sabbath, and required all persons to attend the services of the church. Stuyvesant's zeal included an attempt to impose a rigid religious uniformity upon the colony, but his treatment of Lutherans, Quakers, and Jews earned him a stern rebuke and he was ordered to leave any dissenter "unmolested as long as he is modest, moderate, [and] his political conduct irreproachable."

By the time the colony was surrendered to the English in 1664, there were eleven Dutch Reformed churches in the colony which included settlements in what was to be New Jersey. Although the shift to English control involved problems of readjustment, the Dutch Reformed churches continued to grow with the natural increase in the Dutch population; and it has been estimated that there were one hundred and twenty Dutch Reformed congregations at the time of the Declaration of Independence.

For at least two decades prior to the revocation of the Edict of Nantes in 1685, the increasing pressures which were brought to bear upon them led many Huguenots to leave France and seek refuge in other European countries. Some of them made their way to America, with the largest number settling in New York and South Carolina. Several of the Dutch Reformed ministers had made it a practice to preach in French, and the French Reformed in New York had generally become members of the Dutch churches. In 1683, however, the French Reformed in New York secured a pastor of their own, and congregations also were formed at New Rochelle and New Paltz. By the end of the century there were five or six French Reformed churches in the vicinity of New York City. Another church had been formed in Boston, at least one in Virginia, and several in South Carolina. The tendency everywhere was for the Huguenots to disperse and to become denationalized, due partly perhaps to an eagerness to forget the language and customs of the native land that had subjected them to such relentless persecution. In the South they tended to become Anglicans. In New York they were absorbed by the Dutch Reformed; the "French church" at New Paltz, for example, kept its records in Dutch after the first fifty years of its existence.

MENNONITES, DUNKERS, AND MORAVIANS. Pennsylvania was the great center of German immigration to the colonies, for William Penn's efforts to recruit settlers found an eager response among the inhabitants of the Palatinate (an area between the upper Rhine and France) which had been repeatedly ravaged and devastated by the armies of Louis XIV. This eager response was movingly expressed in a letter, dated February 6, 1681, from a father in Heilbron to his son who had been among the first to arrive in the new colony.

> Dear Son:—Your letter from far away America . . . gave us great joy. . . . America, according to your writing, must be a beautiful land. . . .
> Dear Henry, since you have been away from us conditions in South Germany have become very much worse. The French have wrought much devastation . . . , and besides we now suffer from the plague of high taxes. Thousands would gladly leave the Fatherland if they had the means to do so.
> A merchant from Frankfort was with us last week and informed us how along the Rhine a number of families have banded together to

accept the invitation of an Englishman named William Penn, who had recently visited that community, to settle in that beautiful land and there establish new homes.

After I had received this information I went at once to our minister, whose parents live at Worms on the Rhine, and begged him earnestly to learn what truth there was in these reports and to find out, if possible, if there would be any opportunity for us to join them. . . . He then informed me that these reports were all true. . . .

It is the good providence of God that has shown these burdened people so glorious a land. We . . . are only waiting for a good opportunity when the dear Lord will bring us to you. Your brother Peter is learning shoemaking and will soon be free. America is the only dream of Elizabeth. Catharine, only six years old, asks us daily, "Will we soon be going to our brother in America?" [27]

While a half dozen different religious groups were to be represented in the German migration to Pennsylvania, the family at Heilbron were Mennonites, an Anabaptist group which took its name from Menno Simons (1492–1559).[28]

Of all the Reformation groups none had been subjected to more bitter persecution than the Anabaptists. They were earnest people, deeply devout, who rejected infant baptism and sought to practice full obedience to the commands of Christ, refusing among other things to take oaths, hold public office, or bear arms. They had managed to survive in small scattered communities throughout the Rhineland from Rotterdam to the valleys of Switzerland. The earliest Mennonite group to arrive in Pennsylvania came from Krefeld in 1683. Most of this initial contingent had been won to Quaker views prior to their departure, and separate Mennonite worship was not established until 1690. The Swiss Mennonites who began arriving around 1710 settled in what is now Lancaster County and this became the principal Mennonite center. Each Mennonite congregation conducted its own affairs, frequently choosing its officers—a bishop, elders, and deacons—by lot. Consequently they were seldom troubled by lack of ministerial leadership and they never needed to await the arrival of a minister in order to organize their church life

The Dunkers (Church of the Brethren) in many ways were not

---

[27] Smith, Handy, Loetscher, *American Christianity*, I, 183.
[28] See C. Henry Smith, *The Mennonites of America*, 4th ed., rev. by Cornelius Krahn (Newton, Kan., 1957); George H. Williams, *The Radical Reformation* (Philadelphia, 1962); and Franklin H. Littell, *The Anabaptist View of the Church* (Boston, 1958).

unlike the Mennonites. They also were a "plain" people who sought to live in strict obedience to New Testament precepts. Their founder was Alexander Mack, a man of some means who had come under Pietistic influences after reacting against the spiritual lethargy of the German Reformed church in which he had been reared. At Schwarzenau in Hesse-Kassel in 1708 he formed into a church the little group he had gathered for Bible study, and other congregations were soon formed in neighboring provinces. Unlike the Mennonites, many of whose practices they adopted, the Dunkers baptized by a threefold immersion rather than by pouring. It was this practice that gave them their popular name. Their worship centered in the Lord's Supper, which was preceded by a "love feast" and the washing of feet, and was concluded with the "holy kiss of charity" and the "right hand of fellowship." The Dunker migration to America was initiated in 1719 by the congregation at Krefeld, and four years later their first church in America was formed at Germantown.

The Schwenkfelders were a much smaller group than either the Mennonites or the Dunkers, and they differed from the larger groups in that they looked to the Holy Spirit rather than to the "letter" of Scripture for guidance. They stemmed from one of Martin Luther's fellow reformers, Caspar Schwenkfeld, who anticipated George Fox's emphasis upon the authority of the "Christ within." Condemned as a heretic, Schwenkfeld managed to gather a small following and for almost a century these hunted people were able to maintain a precarious existence in southern Germany. When the Emperor Charles VI undertook their final extermination in 1720, some of them found refuge on the estates of a Saxon nobleman, Nicholas Ludwig, Count von Zinzendorf (1700–60). From there they made their way in 1734 to Pennsylvania.

Zinzendorf was the key figure in the story of the Moravians. He was a Lutheran who early in life had come under the influence of Pietism, a movement which, in reaction to the seeming lifelessness of Lutheran and Reformed orthodoxy, stressed the importance of religious experience and the practical aspects of the devotional life.[29] Its most characteristic feature

[29] Pietism stemmed from the activities of Philipp J. Spener (1635–1705) and August H. Francke (1663–1727). The former gathered small groups for Bible study, prayer, and discussion of the Sunday sermon in his home at Frankfort. The latter developed a similar ministry among students at the University of Leipzig. The founding of the University of Halle in 1691 by the Elector of Brandenburg provided them with a center for the dissemination of their views.

was the gathering of earnest Christians in small groups to study the Bible, sing hymns, and engage in prayer. The Pietists were not hostile to the churches and they were far from heterodox, but they found theological discussion distasteful and regarded it as a source of division and strife among Christians. Christianity was a life, they insisted, not a creed. Thus the Pietists tended to sit rather loosely to their confessional traditions, to emphasize the common experience of Christ which bound all Christians together, and to be characterized by a strong missionary fervor. It was this spirit that Zinzendorf imbibed and it led him to welcome to his estates any refugees among whom he espied any signs of true piety.

The Moravians, or the Unitas Fratrum, had their origin in the evangelical movement which sprang from the preaching of John Hus of Prague in the fifteenth century.[30] They had been buffeted by persecution for more than two centuries when Zinzendorf offered them asylum in 1722. Zinzendorf, together with other Lutheran Pietists whom he had gathered about him, soon became deeply involved in the activities of the Moravian community. He gradually emerged as their leader and was consecrated Bishop in 1737. Under his leadership the Moravians launched a far-flung missionary campaign which had several objectives—the conversion of the heathen, the renewal of spiritual life among nominal Christians, and the reuniting of all Christian groups in a single spiritual communion. An early project had been the establishment of a Moravian settlement in Georgia in 1735 where some missionary work was carried on among the Indians and Negroes. Their refusal to bear arms, however, aroused the opposition of the colonial authorities and in 1740 the Moravians moved to Pennsylvania where they established the towns of Nazareth and Bethlehem. Later Salem, North Carolina, became a major Moravian center.

In the meantime Zinzendorf, having been charged with harboring religious fanatics and promoting views contrary to accepted Lutheran standards, had been banished in 1738 from his estates. He utilized his banishment as an opportunity to embark on a missionary tour which brought him to Pennsylvania in 1741. His immediate objective was to draw together the various German Protestant denominations in Pennsylvania to form what he called "the Church of God in the Spirit." His intention was to create spiritual ties among them by an acknowledgment of

[30] See Edward Langton, *History of the Moravian Church* (London, 1956), and J. R. Weinlick, *Count Zinzendorf* (N.Y., 1956).

agreement in "essentials," but this intention was misunderstood and the project interpreted as a scheme to subordinate all the churches to Moravian control and direction. As a result the seven consultations which were held with representatives of the different denominations ended in failure. During the remaining months of his stay, Zinzendorf busied himself in establishing contact with the Indians and in organizing churches and schools at scattered points in Pennsylvania and New York. For a brief time he served as pastor of the Lutheran congregation in Philadelphia. Before his departure in 1743 he made arrangements for the orderly supervision of both the itinerant preachers and the rapidly expanding missionary activity among the Indians. In 1753 a tract of land was secured in North Carolina and this became another major Moravian center.

THE GERMAN LUTHERANS AND THE GERMAN REFORMED. The economic havoc wrought by Louis XIV's repeated spoliation of the Palatinate which had spurred the emigration of the small religious minorities was equally effective in prompting other inhabitants of the region to respond to William Penn's promotional efforts to recruit settlers for his new colony. There had been Germans of Reformed background in New Netherlands and a Dutch Lutheran congregation had been formed there. There were also Swedish Lutherans who remained in America after the short-lived Swedish colony on the Delaware was taken over by the Dutch. The Lutherans and the German Reformed, however, derived their major strength from the flow of Palatine Germans into Pennsylvania.

Organized church life among the German Lutherans and German Reformed was not effected immediately for several reasons. For one thing, they migrated as individuals and not as religious communities. They generally had no financial resources of their own and they had no group to help provide the expense of travel. Many of them came as "redemptioners," given free passage by shipowners who recouped themselves financially by selling their passengers for a term of service as indentured servants. Others were assisted by the English government which recognized the need for settlers but had placed restrictions upon the emigration of English subjects lest the homeland should be impoverished. Most of these Germans had no strong religious interest, and neither the Reformed nor the Lutherans had a tradition of lay initiative in church affairs. Consequently their adherents tended to be dependent upon outside help for leadership in the formation of churches.

Although a Swedish Lutheran church had been formed in 1639 and the Dutch Lutheran church in New Amsterdam had secured a minister as early as 1658, the first German Lutheran church was not organized until 1703. This was the church at New Hanover, Pennsylvania, and it was established under the leadership of Daniel Falckner (1666–1741?). In the same year his brother, Justus Falckner (1672–1723), became pastor of the Dutch Lutheran church in New York where the growing German population became the primary concern of his pastoral labors. These were small beginnings and further work among the Germans who were swarming into Pennsylvania was long delayed. Another minister, Anthony Jacob Henke, arrived in 1717 and John Casper Stover and his son in 1728. The latter worked mostly as an itinerant missionary following the German population into Maryland and Virginia. There were a few other early ministers but a decisive change did not occur until the arrival of Henry Melchior Muhlenberg in 1742.

Muhlenberg was sent to America by the Pietists at Halle in response to a plea for help which had been made much earlier by the Lutherans of Philadelphia. The failure to respond immediately had been occasioned by the unwillingness of the American congregations to commit themselves to a definite salary, but when news of Zinzendorf's activities reached Halle the debate as to salary ceased and Muhlenberg set out without further delay. When he arrived he found the people badly divided. Some had been drawn away by Zinzendorf, while others had come under the influence of a minister of dubious character, Johann Valentin Kraft. Within six weeks Muhlenberg had mastered the situation and was installed as pastor of the Philadelphia Lutherans. He soon took additional churches under his care, and ultimately seven churches looked to him for pastoral leadership. Whenever possible he responded to calls for help from more distant places and frequently was asked to arbitrate church quarrels. The regular reports which he sent to Halle stimulated further interest in his work and brought reinforcements in both men and money. Muhlenberg's most important achievement was the forming of the Ministerium of Pennsylvania in 1748. This was the first permanent Lutheran Synod in America, and its influence became decisive in the developing life of the churches.

While most of the Lutheran population in the colonies stemmed from the influx of Germans into Pennsylvania, being largely a dispersion from this center, the Salzburg Lutherans in Georgia were the product of an independent odyssey. They had been driven from their homes in Austria in

1731 by the Roman Catholic archbishop of Salzburg. Fourteen thousan of them in the dead of winter made the long trek to Prussia where they had been promised refuge. Accounts of their sufferings aroused interest in England and provision was made to send some of them to Georgia, where they arrived in four contingents between 1734 and 1741. The first group was accompanied by two ministers who had been trained at Halle, and they had a vigorous church life from the beginning.

The plight of the German Reformed in America was much the same as that of the Lutherans. They also came without pastors and with meager economic resources. The first churches to be formed among them were an exception to the general rule of waiting until a minister appeared on the scene. John Philip Boehm (1683–1749) had settled in Pennsylvania in 1720 as a farmer. He was the son of a Reformed minister at Frankfort-on-the-Main and he had taught school for a period of twelve years. Almost immediately after his arrival his neighbors persuaded him to conduct religious services for them. Five years later the three informal congregations he had gathered pressed him to assume the pastoral office. With some reluctance he agreed to do so, although he was not ordained. When a German Reformed minister, George Michael Weiss, arrived two years later, he was scandalized by Boehm's action, challenged his right to assume ministerial prerogatives, and attempted to take over his congregations. The people rallied to Boehm's support, appealed to the Dutch Reformed ministers in New York for advice, and were referred by them to the Classis of Amsterdam for a decision. In due time an answer was received which approved Boehm's emergency assumption of pastoral duties but advised him to seek ordination. As a result he was ordained by the Dutch Reformed ministers of New York on November 23, 1729. Weiss was present at the ordination and afterward the two worked together in complete harmony.

Although several German Reformed ministers came to America in the next two decades, most of the people of German Reformed background were without either ministers or churches. Their numbers were rapidly increasing, being augmented by an influx of settlers from Switzerland, and they were becoming widely dispersed in the backcountry of most of the colonies. The appeal to the Classis of Amsterdam had enlisted the interest of the Synods of Holland in the plight of the German immigrants, and a committee of the Synods was appointed to send aid—money, Bibles, and medicines—to the German Reformed congregations in America. In 1746

Michael Schlatter (1716–90), a Swiss who had been educated and ordained in the Netherlands, was sent to Pennsylvania as the representative of the Dutch Synods with instructions to visit the existing congregations, to form new ones where needed, and to bring them together as soon as possible in a presbytery, or "coetus," subject to the Synods of Holland. He immediately made a tour of the churches and discovered that in Pennsylvania there were four ordained men to care for an estimated German Reformed population of fifteen thousand. Within a year he had organized the "coetus," and in 1751 he returned to Europe to plead the cause of the German Reformed churches. When he returned the following year, he brought with him six young ministers, seven hundred Bibles, and the promise of an annual subsidy of two thousand gulden from the states of Holland and West Friesland.

THE JEWS. With the exception of such transient groups as the Sandemanians, Rogerenes, and the Ephrata community, the Jews were the smallest of the religious minorities in colonial America.[31] Twenty-three Jews, fleeing from Brazil when the Portuguese regained control from the Dutch, arrived in New Amsterdam in 1654. Most of them failed to remain but those who did were not permitted to maintain public worship until after the end of Dutch control. Their number gradually increased and by 1695 they were worshiping in a rented room. Thirty-five years later, in 1730, a synagogue was built and dedicated. There were isolated Jews in New England as early as 1649 and a community was gathered in Newport, Rhode Island, about 1658. This early congregation had disappeared by 1690 and was not revived until about 1750. The beautiful synagogue which still survives in Newport was erected in 1763. Apart from these two centers, the only other congregations in America prior to the American Revolution were at Savannah (1733), Philadelphia (1747), and Charleston, South Carolina (1749).

This account of denominational beginnings in America can be misleading. While there was a profusion of religious groups, most of the people belonged to no church at all. It was not until the Great Awakening, when America experienced its "national conversion,"[32] that this situation began to change.

[31] See Jacob R. Marcus, *Early American Jewry*, 2 vols (Philadelphia, 1951–53).
[32] The term is supplied and explicated by H. Richard Niebuhr, *The Kingdom of God in America* (N.Y., 1959), 126.

III

The Great Awakening

The Great Awakening, which was to exert a decisive and far-reaching influence upon the development of American religious life, was but one manifestation of a general spiritual quickening during the eighteenth century. There were scattered "awakenings" of new religious life in England, Scotland, and Wales, as well as in America, and the Pietist movement on the Continent was a parallel phenomenon. These several awakenings quickly reinforced each other and initiated the great tide of evangelical religion which swept through the English-speaking world, reaching a crest of influence in the latter half of the nineteenth century before it began to ebb away. Churches of all denominations were caught up in the surge of religious fervor and were profoundly affected by its impact. A new type of preaching dominated the pulpits, the structure of public worship was altered, and the "revival" became the most widely accepted means of introducing people to the Christian life.

Although the immediate effect of the Awakening was to arouse opposition, split congregations, set minister against minister, and divide

most of the denominations, the opposition in the end was almost everywhere overwhelmed and the ultimate consequence was to mold the various
denominations to a common pattern, to subordinate differences, and to
make possible wide-ranging cooperative endeavors. Above all, this surging
tide of evangelical religion supplied the dynamic which emboldened the
Protestant churches of America to undertake the enormous task of
Christianizing a continent, nerved those of the British Isles to assume a
similar responsibility for an expanding population at home and overseas,
and led both the British and the American churches to join forces in a vast
mission to the entire non-Christian world.

Why the spark provided by any one of the local quickenings should
suddenly have ignited a general conflagration is something of a mystery.
The earlier drive and enthusiasm of the Puritan movement, which sprang
from a transforming experience of God's grace and a consequent dedication to warfare against sin, had long since lost much of its force.[1] For some
the consciousness of entering the Christian life through a "new birth" had
been replaced by an insistence upon mere assent to orthodox beliefs as the
foundation of the Christian life. Others stressed the reasonable character
of the "grand essentials" of all religion and emphasized moral behavior as
the distinguishing mark of the Christian. At best the successors of the
Puritans tended to appeal to the head without captivating the heart; at
worst they promoted a spirit of rationalism (an attempt to validate the
Christian faith by human reason) that frequently ended in indifference.
There were, of course, exceptions to this general characterization. When
Jonathan Edwards spoke of "the time of extraordinary dullness in religion" which preceded the outbreak of the revival in Northampton,
Massachusetts, he was but echoing the lament that had been voiced by
many of the New England clergy for the better part of a century. And from
time to time there had been local awakenings—even in Northampton
under the preaching of Solomon Stoddard—when consciences would be
touched, faith awakened, and people brought into the churches in unusual
numbers. But no general revival had occurred.

Nor is the suggestion that the revivals were the product of the
unsettled conditions of frontier life an adequate explanation of a phenomenon that was equally widespread in both Britain and America. Further-

For the definition of Puritanism as a "revival" and its relationship to Evangelicalism, see Alan Simpson, *Puritanism in Old and New England*, 103–10.

more, the communities along the Connecticut River and between New York and Philadelphia, where the revivals first appeared, were centers of an established agrarian economy rather than frontier settlements. Even after revivalism became an accepted feature of American religious life, revivals seldom occurred in an area until the frontier period was over; and they manifested themselves with equal power in many of the oldest communities.[2]

It is true that the revivals were initially welcomed and later eagerly promoted as an answer to the problem posed by the fact that a large part of the population, in both England and America, stood outside the churches altogether. In England the parish system, which through custom and tradition provided the possibility of long-term nurture and instruction in the Christian faith, had broken down.[3] And in America, with the possible exception of New England, the parish system had never been successfully established. Even in New England the loss of the charter in Massachusetts had made it clear that little confidence could be placed in external guarantees that were designed to ensure that at least the outward formalities of religion would continue to be observed. Thus the churches were confronted by a clear-cut summons to missionary endeavor. Given the circumstances that prevailed, the time was ripe for a type of preaching that would prick the conscience, convict men of sin, and lead them through the agony of repentance into a personally apprehended experience of the new life that was to be found in Christ. The mystery nonetheless remains, for such preaching had never completely disappeared. The novelty of the Awakening was the widespread response it suddenly elicited, a response so unexpected that it surprised even those who sought it.

The first stirrings of revival

The Great Awakening in America had its antecedents in local revivals which developed among the Dutch Reformed churches of northern New Jersey under the leadership of Theodore J. Frelinghuysen (1691–1748?); among the Presbyterian churches of the same general

[2] The appearance of revivals in postfrontier areas is documented in the illuminating study of Whitney R. Cross, *The Burned-over District: the Social and Intellectual History of Enthusiastic Religion in Western New York, 1800–1850* (Ithaca, N.Y., 1950), 75–76.
[3] For the significance of unaltered parish boundaries in relationship to England's shifting population, see Winthrop S. Hudson, *The Great Tradition of the American Churches* (N.Y., 1963), 99–100.

area under the leadership of the Tennents, father and sons; and in Northampton and other communities of the Connecticut valley under the leadership of Jonathan Edwards. Although these local revivals were not to be consolidated into one great movement until George Whitefield (1714–70) arrived on the scene, they provided a foretaste of what was to come and did much to shape the subsequent outburst of religious fervor and activity.

THEODORE J. FRELINGHUYSEN. The "beginner of the great work" [4] in America was a German born near the Dutch border, educated under Dutch auspices, ordained to the ministry of the Dutch Reformed church, and sent to America in 1719 to become the pastor of four Dutch Reformed churches in the Raritan valley of New Jersey. Although he has sometimes been described as a German Pietist, his real affinities and affiliation were with a group of Dutch Calvinists who had been deeply influenced by the experiential piety of the English Puritans.[5]

When Frelinghuysen assumed his new responsibilities, he discovered, much to his dismay, that most of his parishioners were content with a perfunctory orthodoxy which had become for them more a symbol of their Dutch nationality than an expression of any deep-seated Christian conviction. He immediately embarked on a program of reform, seeking to rouse them from their lethargy by a strict enforcement of the provisions of the Reformed discipline with regard to admission to the Lord's Supper, by personal conferences in their homes, and above all by pointed evangelistic preaching which sought to induce the members of his congregations to take seriously the understanding of the Christian faith they ostensibly professed.[6] Perhaps the emotional response he evoked was partially due to the vigor of the opposition he aroused. Many were scandalized by his bluntness, and his congregations were disrupted and thrown into turmoil. The cause of the disaffected was championed by the Dutch ministers of New York, one of whom visited them in their homes to encourage their opposition. Frelinghuysen, however, refused to be daunted and conversions became so frequent in the heated atmosphere that opposition within

[4] The phrase is Whitefield's; quoted by L. J. Trinterud, *The Forming of an American Tradition*, 34.

[5] The absence of any trace of Pietist influence is discussed by Trinterud, *op. cit.* 54–57.

[6] His program of reform is illustrated in a sermon, a portion of which is printed in Smith, Handy, Loetscher, *American Christianity*, I, 316–21.

his own congregations was silenced. By 1726 the revival was at its height, had begun to spread to other Dutch communities, and within the next few years Frelinghuysen was to gain the support of the majority of the Dutch ministers. Nevertheless the rift between the two parties persisted and was not healed for several decades.

THE TENNENTS. William Tennent (1673–1746) and his sons were the key figures in the outbreak of the revival among the Presbyterians. A graduate of the University of Edinburgh and an unusually able teacher and scholar, the father followed Irish precedent in giving his sons their theological training in his own home while he was a pastor at Bedford, New York, from 1720 to 1727. Gilbert Tennent (1703–64), his eldest son, received a Master's degree from Yale in 1725, perhaps in partial compensation for his father's disappointment in not being named to succeed Timothy Cutler as president of that institution. Two years later, the father moved to Neshaminy, Pennsylvania, where he established an embryo college of his own. Deeply indebted to the Puritan devotional classics for his own understanding of the Christian faith, the elder Tennent succeeded in transmitting his earnest concern for a vital inward faith both to his sons and to the graduates of his "log college" at Neshaminy.

The chronology of the awakening among the Presbyterians is somewhat obscure, for Gilbert Tennent reports that his brother John had the first actual revival.[7] This must have been sometime in 1727 or 1728 when he was serving as a licentiate in the Presbytery of New Castle. Later, when John Tennent was pastor at Freehold, New Jersey (1730–32), another revival occurred which was carried forward after John's death by his brother William, Jr. Gilbert Tennent, however, was the most important of the brothers. He was the outstanding preacher and the natural leader of the men his father had trained.

In 1726 Gilbert Tennent had been called to the Presbyterian church at New Brunswick, New Jersey, where the revival among the Dutch Reformed was at its height. He and Frelinghuysen immediately recognized each other as kindred spirits, for the views of both men had been shaped by the characteristic emphases of evangelical Puritanism. Tennent's ministry, by his own account, was not conspicuously successful at first, but Frelinghuysen encouraged him and Frelinghuysen's success served both as

---

[7] Trinterud, *op. cit.*, 58–59. This account of the Tennents is largely based on the careful and thorough research of Trinterud.

a rebuke and as an inspiration. After a period of sickness, during which he was "exceedingly grieved" that he had "done so little for God" and had vowed to "promote his kingdom" with all his might if God would be pleased to spare him for this purpose, Tennent began to secure the response his father had taught him to seek.

The nub of the problem, as Tennent defined it, was what he called the "presumptuous security" of those who professed to be Christians. They had been baptized, catechized, and inducted into full membership in the church. They affirmed orthodox doctrines and were fully persuaded that one is saved by faith and not by works. But faith was interpreted as merely assent to orthodox ideas and was quite unrelated to most of the Christian graces. There was little of the inwardness and transforming power of the Christian faith to be found among them. To counter this smugness and complacency Tennent adopted the old Puritan technique of preaching for "conviction"—an acknowledgment or conviction of one's own sinful estate. He insisted that no one ever became a Christian without first being subjected to the terrifying realization that he is not a Christian. He must first know himself as a sinful creature, estranged from God, and rightfully subject to condemnation, before he can apprehend and receive God's forgiveness and acceptance.

Tennent's preaching had the desired effect and by 1729 scattered Presbyterian congregations from New Brunswick to Staten Island had begun to throb with new life under his leadership. Other products of his father's tuition, notably Samuel Blair (1712–51), were equally active. The participation of Presbyterian ministers of New England background, such as Jonathan Dickinson (1688–1747) at Elizabeth and Aaron Burr (1716–57) at Newark, was also enlisted. By the end of the 1730's there had been eight or ten local revivals of some degree of intensity. In the meantime Gilbert Tennent was gaining a wider hearing through the publication in 1735 of three of his sermons in New York and one in Boston. Earlier in the same year two sermons by John Tennent with an account of the revival at Freehold had also been published in Boston.

JONATHAN EDWARDS. The third manifestation of religious excitement occurred in the Connecticut valley with Jonathan Edwards playing the central role. Edwards, one of the most brilliant and original minds America has produced, scarcely conforms to the popular image of the revivalist. His interests seem to have been wholly academic, and he spent long hours each day in his study. His sermons were tightly knit and closely reasoned expositions of theological doctrine which he read rather than speaking extemporaneously. But, however one may explain it, a revival of extraordinary power did spring from his preaching.

Edwards had been educated at Yale, graduating in 1720 at the age of seventeen. For some years he served there as a tutor, leaving in 1727 to assist his grandfather, Solomon Stoddard, who was pastor of the church at Northampton, Massachusetts, and succeeding him two years later when he died. Edwards was greatly distressed by the "licentiousness" which so generally prevailed among the youth of the town.

> Many of them [were] very much addicted to night walking, and frequenting the tavern, and lewd practices. . . . It was their manner very frequently to get together in conventions of both sexes for mirth and jollity, which they called frollics, and they would often spend the greater part of the night in them.

Furthermore, many of them were "indecent in their carriage at meeting." Edwards began to meet with the young people in their homes; they in turn responded to his pastoral concern; reformation in behavior set in; and by 1733 Edwards was able to report that they had grown "observably more decent in their attendance on public worship." [8]

In the meantime he had been becoming increasingly alarmed by the complacency that was being engendered by the spread of "Arminian" principles. The doctrine of human ability, he was convinced, destroyed the very foundation of the Christian faith. To counter this threat, he preached a series of five sermons in 1734 on justification by faith alone. This, Edwards reported, proved to be "a word spoken in season" and was attended by "a very remarkable blessing of heaven to the souls of the people in this town." A young woman of questionable morals was converted, other young people were stirred by her example, the tempo of religious interest increased, and conversions multiplied.

> This work of God . . . made a glorious alteration in the town, so that in the spring and summer following (anno 1735) the town seemed to be full of the presence of God. It never was so full of love, nor so full of joy, and yet so full of distress, as it was then. There

[8] *A Faithful Narrative of the Surprising Work of God in the Conversion of Many Hundred Souls in Northampton and Neighboring Towns* (London, 1737), reprinted in *The Works of Jonathan Edwards*, Vol. IV, *The Great Awakening*, ed. C. C. Goen (New Haven, 1972), 146–47.

were remarkable tokens of God's presence in almost every house. It was a time of joy in families on the account of salvation being brought unto them; parents rejoicing over their children as new born, and husbands over their wives, and wives over their husbands.

There had been other revivals from time to time in the valley, most notably those which occurred under the ministry of Edwards' grandfather, Solomon Stoddard. None of them, however, had proved to be contagious. With the quickening of 1734 it was otherwise. News was carried to other communities, visitors came to Northampton, Edwards was invited to preach in neighboring churches, and by 1736 the revival had spread throughout the Connecticut valley. But by 1737 the revival in Northampton had come to a halt, ceasing almost as abruptly as it had begun. Even this, Edwards interpreted as further evidence of God's mercy, for by withdrawing his Spirit to other places he was but demonstrating "how entirely and immediately the great work lately wrought was his" and "how little we can do and how little effect great things have without him." [9]

Edwards' fame as a revivalist was the product in part of his *Faithful Narrative of the Surprising Work of God in the Conversion of Many Hundred Souls in Northampton* which was published in London in 1737 and reprinted in Boston in 1738. John Wesley read it as he walked from London to Oxford, George Whitefield read it during his first brief visit to Georgia in 1738, and it had a decisive effect upon both men. Much more important than the stimulation and inspiration the book provided was the way in which it shaped subsequent revival efforts by the precise and detailed account it gave of how the revival at Northampton actually developed. The duplication of this pattern, of course, became a major objective of those who followed him. Even the conversion process itself tended to become stereotyped. Less influential but of greater inherent significance was the series of writings—*The Distinguishing Marks of a Work of the Spirit of God* (1741), *Some Thoughts concerning the Present Revival of Religion* (1742), and *A Treatise concerning Religious Affections* (1746)—in which he analyzed with amazing psychological insight and scientific detachment the twin phenomena of conversion and revival.[10]

[9] Quoted by Edwin S. Gaustad, *The Great Awakening in New England* (N.Y., 1957), 22.
[10] For Edwards' life, see Ola E. Winslow, *Jonathan Edwards, 1703–1758* (N.Y., 1940). For his thought, see Perry Miller, *Jonathan Edwards* (N.Y., 1949); and C. H. Faust and T. H. Johnson, *Jonathan Edwards: Representative Selections* (N.Y., 1935).

The Great Awakening

It was not until 1740 that the local manifestations of intense religious interest and concern were transformed into a Great Awakening which was to spread throughout every colony from Nova Scotia to Georgia and to touch every area—urban and rural, tidewater and backcountry—and every class—rich and poor, educated and uneducated—before its power was finally dissipated. There had been interconnections, to be sure, between the revival movements led by Frelinghuysen, the Tennents, and Edwards. Frelinghuysen and Gilbert Tennent actively supported one another. Edwards was at Yale when William Tennent was sufficiently well known there to think of himself as a possible choice for the presidency and when Gilbert Tennent received a degree. In his *Faithful Narrative* Edwards mentions an earlier revival "under the ministry of a very pious young gentleman, a Dutch minister, whose name as I remember was Frelinghuysen." But these were mostly tenuous connections and the revivals remained local in character until they were consolidated into a single movement by the itinerant activity of George Whitefield.

"THE GRAND ITINERANT." A recent graduate of Oxford University, where he had been an intimate friend of the Wesleys and a member of the "Holy Club," Whitefield had spent a few months in Georgia in 1738. Upon his return to England he had adopted, much to the dismay of John Wesley, the expedient of preaching in the open air. Since both men had come to look upon "all the world" as their "parish" to the extent that they were convinced that wherever they chanced to be it was their "bounden duty to declare unto all that are willing to hear the glad tidings of salvation," Whitefield's expedient had the distinct advantage of making it unnecessary to secure an invitation from a local church in order to have an opportunity to preach. Moreover Whitefield's preaching in the open air met with such success that by the time he returned to America late in 1739 he had persuaded Wesley to "become more vile" and to preach in his stead to the great throngs he had assembled in the vicinity of Bristol.

Whitefield arrived in Philadelphia on November 2, 1739. He was a "slim slender youth," twenty-four years of age, with a strong but mellow voice, perfect enunciation, a keen sense of the dramatic, and an ability by subtle inflection to clothe almost any word with emotion. Later it was said that by merely pronouncing the word "Mesopotamia" he could bring tears to the eyes of his listeners. Although his intention had been to proceed immediately to Georgia to look after the affairs of his projected orphanage, Whitefield was prevailed upon to preach first in the Anglican church, then in other churches, and finally he spoke to great crowds each evening from the steps of the courthouse. The response was astonishing. Even Benjamin Franklin was impressed, both with the young man himself and with the good moral effect of his preaching. William Tennent visited him and persuaded him to make a rapid evangelistic tour of the area between Philadelphia and New York, which had already been stirred by revivals. Conscious of the new opportunity that had opened before him, Whitefield determined to preach his way to Georgia, traveling by land instead of going by ship. After a brief period in Savannah, he was back in the Philadelphia area from the middle of April to the middle of May to collect funds for the building of his orphanage, announcing his intention to visit New England in the autumn on a similar mission.

Whitefield arrived at Newport, Rhode Island, on September 14, 1740, having sailed from Charleston three weeks before. His arrival had been well publicized, and the Boston newspapers carried advertisements of numerous books and tracts by and about Whitefield and even called attention to other writings which he approved. During the next seventy-three days he was to travel eight hundred miles and to preach one hundred and thirty sermons. He was met everywhere by great throngs. The ministers of Boston were enthusiastic in the welcome they extended (Charles Chauncy may have had some reservations), Harvard and Yale threw open their doors, the visit to Jonathan Edwards at Northampton was a triumphant pilgrimage, and by the time Whitefield had made his way through New York and New Jersey to Philadelphia he was convinced that America was to be his "chief scene of action." [11] While this was not to be true, he did make three other tours of the colonies and had just embarked upon a fourth when he died at Newburyport, Massachusetts, on September 30, 1770.

If America was not the chief scene of his labors, Whitefield nonetheless did as much to shape the future of American religious life as anyone else. Previous to his coming the "quickening" sermons had been preached in churches and at stated hours of public worship. And when sermons were delivered to congregations other than one's own it was at the invitation of

[11] Joseph Tracy, *The Great Awakening* (Boston, 1842), 112. For Whitefield's life, see Stuart C. Henry, *George Whitefield: Wayfaring Witness* (N.Y., 1957).

the pastor. But Whitefield knew no such restrictions. He preached whenever and wherever he could find anyone to listen, and in this, as well as in his extemporaneous preaching, he had many imitators. Through him also, with his incessant traveling and a catholicity of spirit that welcomed an opportunity to preach from any pulpit that was opened to him, the revival impulse permeated every denomination. America in turn did much to shape Whitefield. He was early indebted to Edwards, and Gilbert Tennent helped win him to a type of Calvinism that later cost him the friendship of the Wesleys.[12] Henceforth he was to be firmly convinced that the doctrine of election was the only sure guard against the notion that one is saved by one's own choice and decision.

THE MOUNTING OPPOSITION. Although the early revivals among the Dutch Reformed and Presbyterians had provoked discord and strife and although Whitefield had encountered vigorous opposition among his fellow Anglican ministers, the Edwardsean revival and the subsequent visit of Whitefield to New England had been viewed with remarkable equanimity and approval. In 1741, however, the storm broke.

Among the Presbyterians the occasion for the violent rupture was Gilbert Tennent's sermon on *The Danger of an Unconverted Ministry*, delivered at Nottingham, Pennsylvania, on March 8, 1740, and published at Philadelphia before the end of the year. It was an intemperate discourse. Even though he had been goaded into a denunciation of "phariseeteachers" by the persistent efforts of men who gave little evidence of any serious Christian concern to sabotage his father's "log college," Gilbert Tennent's response only served further to inflame them. "Is a blind man," he asked,

> fit to be a guide in a very dangerous way? Is a dead man fit to bring others to life? . . . Is an ignorant rustic that has never been at sea in his life fit to be a pilot? . . . Isn't an unconverted minister like a man who would learn others to swim before he has learned it himself, and so is drowned in the act and dies like a fool?

And the sermon ended with an open invitation for people to forsake the ministry of "natural" men and to seek out instead a congregation where they would receive profitable instruction.[13]

[12] Trinterud, *Forming of an American Tradition*, 88.

[13] A major portion of the sermon is reprinted in Smith, Handy, and Loetscher, *American Christianity*, I, 321–28; and a smaller portion in Armstrong, Loetscher, Anderson, *The Presbyterian Enterprise*, 40–44.

The result could have been predicted. The opposition was both consolidated and angered. At the meeting of the Synod of Philadelphia in 1741 the revivalist group was expelled, and later formed the rival Synod of New York.[14] At the time of the expulsion the antirevivalist group was slightly stronger with twenty-seven ministers as against the twenty-two members of the Tennent party. Seventeen years later, in 1758, when the schism was finally healed with the formation of the Synod of New York and Philadelphia, the antirevivalist ministers in the old Synod of Philadelphia had dwindled in number to twenty-three while the ministers of the newer Synod of New York had more than tripled in number to seventy-three. The initial defeat was turned into an ultimate triumph by the withering of the antirevivalist party and by the subsequent conciliatory spirit displayed by Gilbert Tennent.

When Whitefield left New England on his way to Philadelphia he had met Gilbert Tennent and had insisted that Tennent must go to New England in order to carry forward the work Whitefield had begun. Tennent's tour, from December 13, 1740, to March 3, 1741, was marked by the same large crowds that had greeted Whitefield, and at New Haven many of the students were converted. There was, however, an undercurrent of opposition among some of the clergy. Charles Chauncy (1705–87) in particular had had second thoughts which caused him to regard Tennent's preaching as unlearned, confused, ill-prepared, and ill-delivered. Rumors had begun to circulate concerning Tennent's Nottingham sermon which, if the rumors were true, was clearly calculated to undermine and foster disrespect for ministerial authority.

After Tennent's departure a sizable portion of the New England clergy exploded in indignation. Not only were the rumors concerning Tennent's sermon confirmed, but printed copies of Whitefield's journal of his New England tour were found to contain disparaging comments concerning the caliber of many of the New England ministers. Whitefield, to be sure, had paid tribute to the general level of religious life in New England which he regarded as exceeding that of any other part of the world, but many of those who preached, he felt, did not "experimentally know Christ."

---

[14] Technically the revivalists withdrew, but it was under duress. Furthermore, it is clear that the powers reserved to the presbyteries by the Adopting Act of 1729 had been usurped by the Synod.

The ministers' preaching almost universally by note is a certain mark they have in a great measure lost the old spirit of preaching. . . . It is a sad symptom of decay of vital religion when reading sermons becomes fashionable where extempore preaching did once almost universally prevail.

Whitefield even echoed Tennent's denunciation of unconverted ministers. The reason that congregations have been dead, he wrote, is that "dead men preach to them," and "how can dead men beget living children?" God may, if he chooses, "convert people by the Devil," and he may also "by unconverted ministers," but "he seldom or never makes use of either of them for this purpose." Nor could one look to the New England colleges, Harvard and Yale, to supply ministers of different caliber, said Whitefield, for "their light is become darkness, darkness that may be felt and is complained of by the most godly ministers." [15]

Opposition was further aroused by the fanatical spirit and emotional extravagance of James Davenport (1716–57) who projected himself on the scene at this particular juncture. The revival preaching, to be sure, was highly emotional and on occasion people were known to cry out, to weep and sob, and even to faint and swoon. But the leaders of the revival were careful to restrain such public displays and to cast doubt upon them as evidence of conversion. Thomas Prince (1687–1758) reported that he did not "remember any crying out or falling down or fainting, either under Mr. Whitefield's or Mr. Tennent's ministry all the while they were here [in Boston]." [16] It was otherwise with James Davenport who did so much to bring the revival into disrepute by encouraging all manner of excess.

The grandson of the founder of New Haven and a graduate of Yale, Davenport had been called to a pastorate on Long Island in 1738. Stirred by the revival excitement, he crossed to Connecticut in the summer of 1741 to follow the itinerant path blazed by Whitefield and Tennent. His sermons were marked by invective, incoherent ejaculations, and indiscriminate denunciations of ministers. He sang as he made his way through the streets to the place of worship. He claimed to be able to distinguish infallibly the elect from the damned, publicly greeting the former as "brethren" and the latter as "neighbors." He was obviously unbalanced mentally, and the

[15] Gaustad, The Great Awakening in New England, 30; C. C. Goen, Revivalism and Separatism in New England, 1740–1800 (New Haven, 1962), 49.
[16] Goen, Revivalism and Separatism in New England, 18.

leaders of the revival immediately sought to dissociate themselves from him. But the damage was done, and the revival cause was brought into further disrepute when Davenport invaded Massachusetts the following summer. He had been arrested in Connecticut and transported under guard out of the colony. In Massachusetts he was jailed, again adjudged insane, and sent back to Long Island. In the end his sanity seems to have been restored, and through the friendly counsel of Eleazar Wheelock and Solomon Williams he came to see the error of his ways. In 1744 he published his *Confessions and Retractions,* expressing the hope that this would remove the prejudices which his extravagant behavior had evoked. It was a vain hope, for those who had been affronted by Whitefield's ill-considered observations were only too happy to utilize Davenport's excesses as a weapon to discredit the revivalists as a whole.

Charles Chauncy led the attack and blasted the revival from the pulpit of the First Church of Boston in a sermon entitled *Enthusiasm Described and Cautioned Against.* This was followed in 1743 by a more extended denunciation, *Seasonable Thoughts on the State of Religion in New England.* The Harvard faculty was also incensed. When Whitefield had first visited Boston he had been entertained and commended by the president of the college, and the Overseers had set aside a day of thanksgiving for the beneficent effects of his labors. When he returned in 1744 the doors of the college were closed to him and the faculty issued a statement, later endorsed by the Yale faculty, blistering his message, his methods, and his character.

The situation was quite confused and the ministers were badly divided. The "Old Lights," under the leadership of Chauncy, embraced perhaps a third of the ministers of New England. They tended to move in the direction of "rationalism" in theology and constituted the group out of which Unitarianism was later to emerge. As many as another third were "New Lights" who favored the revival and participated wholeheartedly in it, while deploring the unfortunate excesses which the "Old Lights" so vigorously denounced. Only a handful were ready to insist upon emotional manifestations as evidence of conversion and to defend itinerancy and lay preaching. The others were uncommitted. This basic division among the Congregational ministers of New England between "Old Lights" and "New Lights," with certain subsequent refinements and shifts in alignments, was to persist until it was finally obliterated in the first quarter of the nineteenth century by the coming of the "Second Great Awakening" and by the withdrawal of the Unitarians from the Congregationalist fold (see below, pp. 160–63).

In the meantime a further split began to develop within the revivalist camp. Some of those who had been persuaded of the necessity of a work of grace as the indispensable door to the Christian life became disturbed by the continued reception and retention of unconverted members by the churches. For all its emphasis upon conversion, the revival had not led to the abrogation of the lax membership practices which had been introduced by the adoption of the Half-way Covenant. Even when ministers wished to tighten disciplinary procedures, few congregations were willing to accept the rigorous standards implicit in the preaching of their pastors. The most shocking evidence of this fact was the callous ejection of Jonathan Edwards from his Northampton church in 1750 when he insisted upon some evidence of a personal religious experience as a prerequisite to church membership. The unhappiness of the more "experienced" Christians with this lax state of affairs led a considerable number of them to withdraw and to form separate churches of their own.

While the movement was fairly general throughout New England, the real stronghold of the "Separate" or "Strict" Congregationalists was in eastern Connecticut. It has been suggested that this was a lower-class revolt but a careful examination of the Separate churches has revealed that they were composed of a representative cross-section of the population and included prominent and even wealthy members of their respective communities.[17] The constant factor was the earnestness of their religious concern. In all, no fewer than ninety-eight Separate churches were formed, and there were at least thirty-two temporary separations. But this scarcely indicates their full strength, for the strong and ultimately overwhelming tendency was for the Separates to become Baptists. The doctrine of believer's baptism, of course, was a fitting expression of the Separates' conception of the church as a community of "experienced" Christians. At least nineteen of the Separate Congregational churches became Baptist, but a better indication of the Separates' strength is the additional one hundred and thirty Baptist churches that were formed by disaffected Congregationalists. Although not participating directly in the earliest New

[17] This is the conclusion reached by C. C. Goen as a result of his thorough and careful research, *Revivalism and Separatism*, 188–91.

England revivals, the Baptists reaped the largest harvest, siphoning off the strength of the remaining Separate churches to such an extent that they tended to dwindle and die.

THE SOUTHERN PHASE OF THE AWAKENING. In the South the Awakening developed more slowly. Although Whitefield preached to large numbers in the South, the way had not been prepared for him by earlier revivals and there was little leadership to conserve the results he obtained. The old established areas of Virginia were Anglican territory and the Anglican clergy were unsympathetic and even hostile. The other areas were more recently settled and, without a modicum of leisure and existing centers of church life, there had been scant opportunity for revivals to develop. Thus throughout the South it was Whitefield who blazed the way for the spread of the Awakening instead of consolidating existing interest into a single movement as he had done elsewhere.

The earliest indication of a spiritual quickening in Virginia occurred east of the mountains in Hanover county. As a result of Whitefield's influence as he made his way overland to Georgia in December, 1739, a few lay people had begun to meet in private homes to read some of Whitefield's sermons and other devotional literature. A spontaneous revival broke out. As religious concern spread, the homes of the leaders became too small to hold the gatherings and "reading houses" were erected. This was the situation when William Robinson (d. 1746), a graduate of William Tennent's "log college," was sent by the New Brunswick Presbytery on a missionary tour of Virginia during the winter of 1742–43. Those who had erected the "reading houses" invited him to preach and were persuaded by him to become Presbyterians. Robinson was followed by a succession of revivalist itinerants sent out by the Synod of New York and its subsidiary presbyteries, the most important of whom was to be Samuel Davies who succeeded Robinson at Hanover in 1747.[18] Under his leadership the revival spread rapidly, numerous churches were organized, which were brought together in 1755 to form a new presbytery. After Davies' departure in 1759 to become president of Princeton, the Presbyterian activity became less pronounced.

In the meantime the revival had broken out in another quarter. Two brothers-in-law, Shubal Stearns and Daniel Marshall (1706–84), had come to Virginia from New England in 1754. They had been converted by

[18] See George H. Bost, *Samuel Davies* (Chicago, 1944).

Whitefield, had become Separate Congregationalist itinerants, and then had been ordained as Baptist preachers. Within a year of their arrival in Virginia they were told of a large tract across the border in North Carolina where there was no preaching of any kind and the people "so eager to hear that they would come forty miles each way when they could have opportunity to hear a sermon." Here at Sandy Creek a church was gathered. In three years two additional churches had been formed, and in seventeen years there were forty-two churches. Daniel Marshall went on to Georgia where he labored with almost equal success, and throughout the whole Piedmont region, but especially in Virginia, Separate Baptist churches multiplied at an astonishing rate. At first considerable tension existed between the hyperenthusiastic Separates and the old "regular" Baptist churches which had been formed or reorganized by itinerant evangelists of the Philadelphia Baptist Association. By 1787, however, this breach was beginning to be healed, first in Virginia, then later in North Carolina, Kentucky, and elsewhere.

As Hanover was the center of Presbyterian expansion, and Sandy Creek the center from which radiated Baptist evangelistic activity, so Dinwiddie County was to be the center of the revival impulse among the Anglicans. It was a delayed response, for no leader appeared until Devereux Jarratt (1733–1801) was installed in 1763 as rector at Bath. He had been influenced in his early years by Whitefield, and when he went to England for ordination he had come into contact with both Whitefield and John Wesley. Under Jarratt's zealous preaching his three churches became so crowded that he was compelled to hold services in adjacent groves, and he followed the precedent of Whitefield and Wesley in meeting with the more earnest Christians in small groups.

As early as 1765 two of John Wesley's lay preachers had come to America as immigrants—Robert Strawbridge (d. 1781) to Maryland and Philip Embury (1728–73) to New York. They were followed by two others who arrived in 1769, and in the same year Wesley commissioned the first two of eight officially appointed lay missionaries to serve in America. In 1772 Robert Williams, one of Wesley's lay preachers, appeared in Dinwiddie County and enlisted Jarratt's participation in a more widespread endeavor. Jarratt began to itinerate beyond the bounds of his own parish and the great assemblies gathered in the open air to hear him preach were impressive. Jesse Lee, one of his young converts, reported:

I have been at meetings where the whole congregation would be bathed in tears, and sometimes their cries would be so loud that the preacher's voice could not be heard. Some would be seized with trembling and in a few moments drop on the floor as if they were dead, while others were embracing each other with streaming eyes and all were lost in wonder, love, and praise. [19]

With the assistance of several lay preachers, Jarratt was busily forming converts into "methodist" societies, and as a result of his activity the great strength of the revival movement among the Anglicans was to be found in Virginia and the adjoining counties of North Carolina. By 1777 there were 4,379 members of the societies in this area, while the total for all the colonies was only 6,968. After the Revolution when the societies broke with Anglicanism and formed the Methodist Episcopal Church in 1784, Jarratt expressed resentment at the separation. He felt that he had been deceived by the assurances of loyalty that he had received from the lay preachers. Within a few years his bitterness was gone, but he remained within the Anglican fold where his influence contributed greatly to the strength of the evangelical movement within the newly formed Protestant Episcopal Church.

The impact of the Awakening

The Awakening was much more than the activity of a few conspicuous leaders. It was "Great" because it was general. People everywhere were caught up in the movement, and its influence was spread by innumerable local pastors, passing itinerants, and lay exhorters. No one could escape the excitement or avoid the necessity to declare himself as friend or foe.

And because the Awakening was general, it played an important role in forming a national consciousness among people of different colonies whose primary ties were with Europe rather than with one another. As a spontaneous movement which swept across all colonial boundaries, generated a common interest and a common loyalty, bound people together in a common cause, and reinforced the conviction that God had a special destiny in store for America, the Awakening contributed greatly to the development of a sense of cohesiveness among the American people. It was

[19] W. W. Sweet, *Methodism in American History* (N.Y., 1954), 76.

more influential in this respect than all the colonial wars the colonists were called upon to fight, more influential in fact than many of the political squabbles they had had with the mother country since the latter as often served to separate as to unite them. Whitefield, Tennent, and Edwards were rallying names for Americans a full three decades before Washington, Jefferson, Franklin, and Samuel Adams became familiar household names. Perhaps it is significant that the Awakening did not reach Nova Scotia until 1776, too late to create the intangible ties which bound the other colonies together.

INSTITUTIONAL CONSEQUENCES. No exact estimate can be made of members added to the churches by the Awakening, but the number in all denominations was large. Interest in Indian missions was revived. A wide variety of charitable projects, including schools for Indians, Negroes, and the children of indentured servants, were initiated. The role of the laity in the churches was enhanced. The setting of minister against minister undermined ministerial authority at a time when a stress upon a self-authenticating religious experience was freeing the individual from dependence upon clerical opinion. On the other hand, quite paradoxically, the ministerial office was also given added luster by the fame of the revivalists, and the number of young men drawn into the ranks of the ministry rapidly mounted.

Apart from the multiplication of churches, the major institutional survivals of the Awakening came from the impulse that was given to higher education by the necessity to provide educational opportunities for the swelling number of ministerial recruits. The Presbyterians were especially active in this endeavor and many of their ministers established classical academies, similar in character to William Tennent's "Log College" and patterned after the small private Presbyterian academies of Ireland and the Dissenting academies of England which at this time enjoyed an educational reputation that was greater than that of the ancient universities. Several colleges—Washington and Lee, Washington and Jefferson, and Dickinson—trace their ancestry back to these early academies. In 1746 the Synod of New York secured a charter for the College of New Jersey (Princeton) which was designed as the capstone of the Presbyterian educational structure, and in 1776 the Hanover Presbytery in Virginia established Hampden-Sydney College. The Baptists also organized several academies and in 1764 founded the College of Rhode Island (Brown University) as their major center for the training of the ministry. In 1766 the prorevivalists among the Dutch Reformed obtained a charter for Queen's College (Rutgers University). Dartmouth, an outgrowth of an Indian charity school, was incorporated in 1769. Columbia University (originally King's College), of course, had no connection with the Awakening, nor did the University of Pennsylvania which became a degree-granting college in 1755. The latter, it is true, had its origin in the tabernacle which had been constructed in 1740 for George Whitefield to use when inclement weather made it impossible for him to speak in the open air.

Although the clergy of the English settlements along the seaboard did not have the opportunity to duplicate the work of the priests who accompanied the French traders and trappers on their far-ranging travels through the interior of the continent, the evangelization of those tribes with whom the English came into contact did not suffer neglect.[20] The effect of the Awakening was to pour new enthusiasm into this task. Eleazar Wheelock, Samuel Kirkland, David Brainerd, and for a time Jonathan Edwards were among those who devoted themselves to Indian missions. The diary of David Brainerd, edited by Jonathan Edwards, is a moving testament of devotion which tells the story of his experiences among the Indians, and it inspired many others to give themselves to mission work.

THE THEOLOGICAL TEMPER GENERATED BY THE AWAKENING. Evangelicalism, to use the term by which the new surge of spiritual life is usually described, has often been interpreted as a revolt against Calvinism. While this may have been its ultimate consequence, it was far from that in the beginning. The understanding of the Christian faith as set forth in the great Reformed Confessions was taken for granted. John Wesley was an important exception but, in many respects, even Wesley stood firmly within the Genevan tradition. Evangelicalism, however, was much more a mood and an emphasis than a theological system. Its stress was upon the importance of personal religious experience. If it was a revolt against anything, it was a revolt against the notion that the Christian life involved little more than observing the outward formalities of religion.

Only in New England was significant theological discussion pro-

---

[20] Anglicans lost heart for Indian missions for many years after the 1622 massacre of 300 colonists, but others did not. For Indian missions, see R. P. Beaver, *Pioneers in Mission* (Grand Rapids, 1966) and *Church, State, and the American Indians* (St. Louis, 1966); and F. P. Purcha, *Americanizing the American Indians* (Cambridge, 1973) and *American Indian Policy in Crisis* (Norman, Okla., 1973).

voked by the Awakening and only in New England did clearly defined theological alignments appear. From a theological standpoint the "Consistent Calvinists" or Edwardseans made the most impressive contribution to the debate. This "New England Theology" was fashioned by Jonathan Edwards and his two most influential disciples, Joseph Bellamy (1719–90) and Samuel Hopkins (1721–1803), in an effort to buttress the revival by a bold and intellectually rigorous restatement of those doctrines which they were convinced had been verified by the revival.[21] The truth that man's redemption was effected by God's sovereign grace alone was to be defended at whatever cost to human pride, and all attempts to substitute man's moral attainments for the righteousness that comes only as a gift were to be resolutely opposed. Arrayed against them, especially in the vicinity of Boston, were those charged with being "Arminians"—ministers who regarded Edwardsean doctrines as unduly harsh as well as being an affront to common sense in that they tended to undermine all morality. The doctrine of original sin, pictured in terms of innocent infants burning in hell, was denounced as inhuman, unreasonable, and indefensible; while the doctrine of predestination was condemned as destructive of all moral effort. Between the embattled extremes was a varied group of middle-of-the-roaders who for some unaccountable reason became known as "Old Calvinists." Whether more traditionally oriented or more liberally inclined, members of this group were dismayed and distressed by theological wrangling, viewing it as the consequence of an overly fussy concern for "theological niceties" and advocating instead a "large measure of charity." Ezra Stiles (1727–95) was typical of their point of view when he announced that the reigning theological debate was only a verbal dispute.

> Interrogating so-called Arminians, he found they believed in the redemptive grace of Christ; inquiring of so-called Calvinists, he learned that they did not deny the importance of good works. On the whole, "I cannot perceive any very essential real difference in their opinions respecting the fundamental principles of religion." [22]

[21] See Joseph Haroutunian, *Piety Versus Moralism, the Passing of the New England Theology* (N.Y., 1932), and Conrad Wright, *The Liberal Christians* (Boston, 1970).

[22] Gaustad, *The Great Awakening*, 130. Stiles was a representative figure through whom many of the tendencies of the age are to be seen. A graduate of Yale, he was pastor at Newport, R.I., and Portsmouth, N.H., before returning to Yale in 1778 as president of the college. See Edmund S. Morgan, *The Gentle Puritan: A Life of Ezra Stiles, 1727–1795* (New Haven, 1962).

In this lack of concern for careful theological distinctions and in the emphasis upon "the fundamental principles of religion," the moderates were more closely akin to the general spirit of Evangelicalism than were the Edwardseans. Evangelicalism as a whole tended to prize a "warm heart" and to be impatient with theological controversy. What distinguished the Edwardseans from other Evangelicals was their firm conviction that a warm heart was not enough. In keeping with the earlier Puritan heritage they insisted that both heart and head—faith and reason—must be brought together in the service of God. Thus the Edwardseans were to provide the major portion of whatever intellectual content Evangelicalism was to have. Without the influence of this theological structure which Evangelicalism took largely for granted, Evangelicalism would have had small staying power. Reduced to little more than sentiment, its thrust would quickly have evaporated.

Although the Awakening was productive of controversy and strife, it was, paradoxically, at the same time a great unifying force which gave to "four-fifths" of the Christians in America "a common understanding of the Christian life and the Christian faith." [23] Since the revival had penetrated many denominations quite indiscriminately, this common understanding tended to minimize the importance of denominational distinctions and to provide a basis for mutual respect, appreciation, and cooperation. Typical of the new spirit was John Wesley's emphatic declaration that he renounced and detested all distinctions among Christians, and refused to be distinguished from other men by anything but "the common principles of Christianity." From "real Christians" he had no desire to be distinguished at all. "Dost thou love and fear God? It is enough! I give thee the right hand of fellowship." [24] This catholicity of spirit was even more conspicuously exhibited in George Whitefield. Whitefield spoke with equal readiness from Anglican, Presbyterian, Congregational, Baptist, and Dutch Reformed pulpits, and he counted men of all denominations among his converts. Preaching from the courthouse balcony in Philadelphia, he raised his eyes to the heavens and cried out:

> Father Abraham, whom have you in heaven? Any Episcopalians? No! Any Presbyterians? No! Any Independents or Methodists? No, no,

---

[23] Trinterud, *Forming of an American Tradition*, 197.
[24] From *The Character of a Methodist*, reprinted in *The Works of John Wesley*, 4th ed. (London, 1841), VIII, 332–33.

no! Whom have you there? We don't know those names here. All who are here are Christians. . . . Oh, is this the case? Then God help us to forget party names and to become Christians in deed and truth.

His attitude was echoed by Samuel Davies in Virginia.

My brethren, I would now warn you against this wretched, mischievous spirit of party. . . . A Christian! a Christian! Let that be your highest distinction; let that be the name which you labor to deserve. God forbid that my ministry should be the occasion of diverting your attention to anything else. . . . It has . . . been the great object of my zeal to inculcate upon you the grand essentials of our holy religion, and make you sincere practical Christians. Alas! . . . unless I succeed in this, I labor to very little purpose though I should presbyterianize the whole colony.[25]

In addition to a common theological outlook, a specific understanding of the nature of the Church underlay this broad-minded spirit.

THE DENOMINATIONAL CONCEPT. What has been called the "denominational" concept of the Church had been elaborated a century earlier by the Dissenting Brethren of the Westminster Assembly of Divines.[26] This concept was to be of decisive future importance in the shaping of American religious life. Denominationalism, as these men used the term, was the opposite of sectarianism. A "sect" regards itself alone as the true Church. By definition a "sect" is exclusive. "Denomination," on the other hand, was adopted as a neutral and inclusive term. It implied that the group referred to is but one member, called or denominated by a particular name, of a larger group—the Church—to which other denominations belong. Gilbert Tennent stated the concept with clarity and incisiveness when he declared: "All societies who profess Christianity and retain the foundational principles thereof, notwithstanding their different denominations and diversity of sentiments in

[25] A. L. Drummond, *The Story of American Protestantism* (Boston, 1950), 115. Samuel Davies, *Sermons on Important Subjects* (N.Y., 1842), I, 217-18.

[26] The Assembly was summoned in 1643 by the Long Parliament to advise the Parliament in its task of effecting a religious settlement for the nation. Presbyterian sentiment was predominant among the assembled clergy. The Congregational minority became known as the Dissenting Brethren. The case for "denominationalism," as developed by these dissenters, is discussed in Russell E. Richey, ed., *Denominationalism* (Nashville, 1977), 19-42; and also in Winthrop S. Hudson, *American Protestantism* (Chicago, 1961), 33-48. Jacob Neusner provides an unusually incisive discussion of the same concept in *Understanding American Judaism* (N.Y., 1971), II, 259-77.

smaller things, are in reality but one Church of Christ, but several branches (more or less pure in minuter points) of one visible kingdom of the Messiah."[27]

On the basis of this understanding of the Church which acknowledged the unity that existed within the diversity of outward ecclesiastical forms, the Protestant churches were able to develop a functional catholicity which was to find expression in the creation of a whole system of voluntary societies for the promotion of a host of worthy causes. There were societies devoted to missions, Bible and tract distribution, education, charitable enterprises, and to a wide-ranging spectrum of moral and social reforms. These societies were to be the instruments into which much of the evangelical fervor released by the Awakening was subsequently to be channeled when the Protestant churches jointly addressed themselves to the task of spreading churches and schools across a continent while devoting themselves, at the same time, to reforming the nation. From a modern perspective, two of the more important causes forwarded by these societies were the abolition of slavery and the emancipation of women. In many ways the full promise for slaves and for women was to remain unfulfilled, but, if much remained to be accomplished, significant progress was made. From the perspective of the early nineteenth century, however, in contrast to that of a later time, the missionary task in its various ramifications was regarded as fundamental to the achievement of all other objectives.

All this, however, was in the future. The immediate problem at hand was the relationship of the colonies to England.

[27] Trinterud, *Forming of an American Tradition*, 132.

IV

The Birth of the Republic

When Edmund Burke in 1775 sought to help his fellow members of Parliament understand the "love of freedom" and "fierce spirit of liberty" which had occasioned the uproar in the colonies over sugar and stamps and tea and taxes, he reminded them that "the people of the colonies are descendants of Englishmen." And then he added:

> England, Sir, is a nation which still I hope respects, and formerly adored, her freedom. The colonists emigrated from you when this part of your character was most predominant; and they took this bias and direction the moment they parted from your hands. They are therefore not only devoted to liberty, but to liberty according to English ideals, and on English principles.

Representative institutions in harmony with English practice had indeed developed very early in all the colonies. Some of the colonial charters were explicit in guaranteeing that the settlers would have "the rights of Englishmen," and the colonists had become accustomed through long practice to the idea that they could not be taxed except by their own consent as expressed in the colonial assemblies.

Religion and politics

While the "love of freedom" had deep and ancient roots in English society, it had been nurtured and transformed into a "fierce spirit of liberty" during the first half of the seventeenth century when the religious issue had come to the fore and had become inextricably intermingled with the liberties of Englishmen. During the course of the constitutional struggle in England it became evident to the participants that certain theological convictions had definite political implications, and these implications were rather fully explored and explicated by both royalists and parliamentarians before the nation finally regained its equilibrium. It was the emotion and spirit generated in the struggle between King and Parliament that Burke had in mind when he noted that the colonists were not only Englishmen but "Protestants, and of that kind which is the most adverse to all implicit subjection of mind and opinion."

THE PURITAN POLITICAL HERITAGE. These Protestants whom Burke described as "the most adverse to all subjection of mind and opinion" had their rootage in Reformed or Calvinist Christianity. It has been said of the early Calvinists that they feared God so much that they could not fear any man, be he king or emperor. And they had much to fear from men, for almost everywhere the Reformed churches were "churches under the cross"—suffering persecution and struggling to survive. But they remained undaunted, sustained in part by a firm confidence in God's overruling providence and impelled by a strong conviction that the chief end of man is to glorify God and insisting that God is glorified by full and complete obedience. When John Knox informed Queen Mary that "right religion takes neither origin nor authority from worldly princes but from the eternal God alone" and then told her that subjects therefore must not "frame their religion according to the appetite of their princes," he was speaking in an accent that was familiar to all sons of Geneva.[1]

[1] See John T. McNeill, "The Democratic Element in Calvin's Thought," *Church History* (1949), 153–71, and W. S. Hudson, "Theological Convictions and Democratic Government," *Theology Today*, X (1953), 230–39. There is no satisfactory treatment of the whole Calvinist political tradition, but G. P. Gooch, *English Democratic Ideas in the Seventeenth Century* (Cambridge, Eng., 1927) and A. S. P. Woodhouse, *Puritanism and Liberty* (London, 1938) are useful.

The Reformed churches were prodded into political theorizing. While they remembered the apostle Paul's admonition that Christians must be subject to "the powers that be," they were not of a temper patiently to endure bloody repression if a plausible excuse for active resistance could be found. Goaded by the burnings in England under Mary Tudor, the persecution in Scotland under Mary Stuart, the wars of religion in France, and the massacre of the Dutch by the Spanish troops of the Duke of Alva, the Reformed leaders explored every possible concept that could be utilized to justify resistance and rebellion. Rights derived from natural law and from the origin of government in a compact between the ruler and the ruled were explicated, and the role of lesser magistrates as guardians of the liberties of the people was carefully defined. Even tyrannicide, in exceptional circumstances, was defended.[2]

Doctrines of resistance and rebellion were purely negative features of Reformed political thought. From a positive point of view, a distinct preference was exhibited for the checks and balances of a "mixed state." Noting with characteristic irony that "it very rarely happens that kings regulate themselves so that their will is never at variance with justice and rectitude," Calvin himself had suggested the importance of broadening the franchise so that the self-interest of the one may be checked by the self-interest of the many. "It is safer and more tolerable for the government to be in the hands of the many that they may afford each other mutual assistance and admonition, and that if any one arrogate to himself more than is right, the many may act as censors and masters to restrain his ambition." "No kind of government is more happy than this, . . . and I consider those most happy people who are permitted to enjoy such a condition" in which they have the right and the duty to "exert their strenuous and constant efforts" to preserve their liberties.[3]

This was the seedbed of the Puritan political thought which reshaped the English constitution through the ordeal of civil war and became so deeply rooted in the consciousness of Englishmen that the ejection of

[2] See, e.g., *A Defense of Liberty against Tyrants: A Translation of the Vindiciae contra Tyrannos*, ed. H. J. Laski (London, 1924) and John Ponet, *A Shorte Treatise of Politike Power*, facsimile reproduction in W. S. Hudson, *John Ponet: Advocate of Limited Monarchy* (Chicago, 1942).

[3] John Calvin, *Institutes of the Christian Religion*, IV, xx, 8; and *Commentary on Micah*, 5:5. For a later explication of the necessity for checks and balances, see the preface to John Cotton's *The Keys of the Kingdom of Heaven* (1644) by Thomas Goodwin and Philip Nye; reprinted in A. S. P. Woodhouse, *Puritanism and Liberty*, 293-98.

James II from the throne in 1688 was effected by a "bloodless" revolution. Defenders of the royal prerogative had few doubts as to the source of the rebellious and seditious notions of the time. Richard Bancroft, chaplain to Elizabeth's Archbishop of Canterbury and soon to be archbishop himself pointed an accusing finger at Geneva in his book *Dangerous Positions and Proceedings* (1593). James I echoed the accusation at the Hampton Court Conference in 1604. And in 1663 Robert South repeated it, saying: "In our account of the sons of Geneva, we will begin with the father of the faithful (faithful, I mean, to their old antimonarchical doctrines and assertions), this is, the great mufti of Geneva" —John Calvin.

The fact that this "fierce spirit of liberty" was part of the intellectual baggage carried to the New World by the Puritans has been obscured by two much-quoted statements of John Winthrop and John Cotton. "A democracy," said Winthrop, "is among most civil nations accounted the meanest and worst of all forms of government." "Democracy?" Cotton asked rhetorically. "I do not conceive that ever God did ordain it as a fit government either for church or commonwealth." [4] Winthrop and Cotton, of course, used the word in its classical meaning which had no connotation of indirect representation. The democracy they repudiated was not the "mixed" government which the nineteenth century became accustomed to calling democracy. Cotton's inclusion of "church" in his rejection of democracy should make it clear that definition of terms is required, for Cotton was a major architect of the "congregational" form of church government.[4a] Even Thomas Jefferson did not believe that democracy "would be practicable beyond the extent of a New England township." [5] What Winthrop and Cotton were advocating, and what the Founding Fathers sought to establish, was a "mixed government" with a separation of powers that would provide "guards for their future security."

No one was more aware than John Cotton that all men and especially men in power are prone to corruption. "Let all the world," he declared, "learn to give mortal man no greater power than they are content they

---

[4] R. C. Winthrop, *Life and Letters of John Winthrop* (Boston, 1869), II, 430; and Cotton's "Letter to Lord Say and Seal" in *The Puritans*, ed. Miller and Johnson, I, 209.

[4a] It has often been noted that experience gained in self-governing New England Congregational churches contributed to the political views of the colonists. Less seldom recognized was the "fierce spirit of liberty" generated by the Anglican "vestry system" in the southern colonies and also the familiarity with representative government in Presbyterian and other churches.

[5] *The Constitution Reconsidered*, ed. Conyers Read (N.Y., 1938), 106.

shall use, for use it they will. . . . It is necessary that all power that is on earth be limited. . . . It is counted a matter of danger to the state to limit prerogatives, but it is a further danger not to have them limited." John Winthrop told the men of Hingham that in signing the covenant they had agreed to submit to the rulers which were thus set over them for their own good, but this admonition had the important qualification—unless they could prove that their rulers were violating the good they had been appointed to serve.[6] This was the common conviction. Thus, while minority rights were not cherished with equal ardor by all Protestant churches in America, most of them through tradition, conviction, and experience had developed an ingrained antipathy to arbitrary rule and had been taught that upon just occasion people had the right and even the duty to rebel.

FEARS GENERATED BY ANGLICAN AGGRESSIVENESS. In the colonies the Puritan political heritage had not been allowed to fade into the past as mere ancient history, nor had the memory of distant events which surrounded that heritage with deep emotion been permitted to grow dim. Provoked by an Anglican aggressiveness which aroused old fears of ecclesiastical tyranny, both pulpit and press rehearsed past history to counter what was considered a present threat. And because the royal power and the episcopal pretensions were so closely linked, the controversy generated a widespread spirit of disaffection which in the course of time was transformed into a deeply rooted rebellious temper. Since the most prominent of the immediate grievances which led to the American Declaration of Independence were economic and political, the importance of the ecclesiastical issue as a major factor in precipitating the American Revolution has been frequently neglected.[7]

The Glorious Revolution of 1688 which brought William and Mary to the English and Scottish thrones had a marked effect upon Anglican fortunes in the New World. Under James II the Church of England had

---

[6] John Cotton, *An Exposition of the Thirteenth Chapter of Revelation* (London, 1656), 72, as reprinted in *The Puritans*, ed. Miller and Johnson, I, 213. For Winthrop, see Perry Miller, "From the Covenant to the Revival," in *The Shaping of American Religion*, ed. J. W. Smith and A. L. Jamison (Princeton, 1961), 334–35. It is made clear by Edmund Morgan, *The Puritan Dilemma: the Story of John Winthrop* (Boston, 1958), that Winthrop's (and also Cotton's) emphasis was usually upon the duty of obedience.

[7] Carl Bridenbaugh, *Mitre and Sceptre: Transatlantic Faiths, Ideas, and Politics, 1689–1775* (N.Y., 1962), explored in detail this aspect of the Revolutionary background. For another aspect, see Norman C. Hatch, *The Sacred Cause of Liberty: Republican Thought and the Millennium in the American Revolution* (New Haven, 1977).

been given scant support in the colonies, had numbered few adherents, and had been officially established only in Virginia. This situation was altered by the Revolution. Dissenting "dissidence" at home was temporarily quieted by the Act of Toleration, while the Anglican bishops were freed from their almost complete preoccupation with the domestic problems created by a Roman Catholic king. Thus the way was cleared for a more aggressive Anglican policy in the colonies. With the support of a sympathetic Court it now became possible to marshal sufficient pressure to secure Anglican establishments in Maryland, South Carolina, and the city of New York, with North Carolina and Georgia later being brought into line.

The Society for the Propagation of the Gospel was designed to spearhead and implement the new Anglican thrust. It had been organized in 1701, with royal and archiepiscopal blessing, to send "orthodox clergymen" to the colonies to instruct such as lacked "the administration of God's Word and Sacraments" in the "principles of true religion." If the clause in the charter which defined the purpose of the Society had been interpreted to mean providing a ministry for the numerous communities in the middle and southern colonies that lacked any ministry whatsoever, the Society would have aroused little opposition. The Society, however, was determined that Anglicanism should shed its regional character and this meant expansion into the older settled areas north of Maryland. Consequently the charter was interpreted as a directive to proselyte members of other communions. In 1750, for example, one-third of the S.P.G. missionaries were stationed in New England where already there was at least one "orthodox minister" in every town and where the converts to Anglicanism were drawn almost exclusively from the ranks of professing Christians. Elsewhere in the colonies S.P.G. activity was similarly restricted to a very great degree to older communities which already had a settled ministry, and the zeal of its missionaries was primarily engaged in making Anglicans out of Quakers, Presbyterians, Baptists, Lutherans, and Reformed.

Under such circumstances it is scarcely surprising that friction developed—a friction that was augmented, as Jonathan Edwards and the "Associated Ministers of Hampshire" explained, by the "uncharitable and unchristian spirit" of the missionaries in "intimating that our ministry is no ministry, not having had episcopal ordination," and thereby inferring with self-evident satisfaction that all other "churches are no churches of Christ, and that our people are to be looked upon as strangers to the commonwealth of Israel—a tenet or principle which came from Rome and which in years past has been disclaimed in England and is still by all the other reformed churches in Europe." The "grand business" of the missionaries, a correspondent of the *Boston Evening Post* declared, "seems to be not to convert men from paganism to Christianity but to proselyte Protestant Dissenters to the Church of England, as if they imagine there can be no salvation out of that church." [8]

Other irritations and grievances, some of them profoundly disturbing, stemmed from what William Smith, Jr. (1728–93), of New York called the Anglican "lust for dominion." Anglican clergy in the middle and northern colonies sought to impress the local populace by convening their conventions in the presence of the governor and by having them preceded by a public procession of the clergy in gowns and cassocks. This ostentation was a minor annoyance but it was not calculated to reduce friction. More serious were deliberate harassments, such as the arrest of Francis Makemie for preaching in the city; the ejection of a Presbyterian minister at Jamaica, New York, with an S.P.G. missionary installed in his place; the repeated intervention of the S.P.G. to prevent non-Anglican churches in New York from being incorporated so that title to their property might be made secure; the order of the Board of Trade that no schoolmasters from England were to be permitted to teach in New Hampshire without a license from the Bishop of London; the attempt of the missionaries to thwart the founding of the College of New Jersey by the Presbyterians, their efforts to subvert the interdenominational character of King's College and the College of Philadelphia, their constant scheming to gain control of Harvard and Yale, their effective role in frustrating the establishment of a Presbyterian college in North Carolina; and the successful intimidation of printers so that for a time there was no freedom of the press for non-Anglicans in New York. Even the granting of a charter to enable Congregationalists to carry on mission work among the Indians was denied. Ill-feeling was further intensified when news was received that the plight of the Dissenters in England had worsened after Queen Anne had come to the throne, with the disabilities imposed by the Occasional Conformity Act and the Schism Act being added to those of the Test and

[8] Bridenbaugh, *Mitre and Sceptre*, 79–80, 90.

Corporation Acts.[9] Nor were reports of the burning of Dissenting meeting-houses by English mobs reassuring.

It was, however, the persistent efforts of S.P.G. missionaries to persuade the British government to establish an Anglican episcopate in America that did more than anything else to awaken old fears and to spread a spirit of disaffection. The proposal to send bishops to regularize the status of colonial Anglicanism seems innocuous enough if one fails to take into account the close link that existed between Anglican ecclesiastical authority and British political authority. To many of the colonists, bishops were a symbol of incipient tyranny; and Anglican activity in America had done little to disabuse them of the notion that powers, once granted to bishops, would be extended and abused. Jonathan Mayhew (1720–66) put the point succinctly when he stated: "People have no security against being unmercifully priest-ridden but by keeping all imperious bishops and other clergymen who love to lord it over God's heritage from getting their feet into the stirrup at all." [10] Even so, the traditional fear of bishops might not have evoked such a concerted and long-sustained campaign of opposition had the proposal not been promoted from time to time as part and parcel of a plan to secure a tax-supported Anglican establishment in all the colonies and had it not, in order to facilitate this goal, involved a scheme for regrouping the colonies in more efficient administrative units which would necessitate the withdrawal of the existing colonial charters. The struggle against bishops thus came to be regarded by many as a struggle to defend both the civil and the religious liberties of the colonists.

A further alienation occurred when the S.P.G. missionaries sought to advance their cause by suggesting that an American episcopate would bind the colonists more closely to England. No argument could have been better calculated to antagonize the other churches, for its plain implication was that their members were an alien and disloyal people. Nor did the missionaries hesitate to spell out this implication. In seeking to counter the antibishop attack, they accused "dissenting" churchmen of being "avowed

[9] The Test and Corporation Acts excluded non-Anglicans from governmental positions. The Occasional Conformity Act tightened this restriction and the Schism Act required all teachers to be licensed by a bishop and to teach nothing but the Anglican catechism. Had the latter act been enforced, it would have suppressed all schools run by Dissenters and would have taken from Dissenters the education of their children.

[10] A. L. Cross, *Anglican Episcopate*, 145.

republicans," "enemies to monarchy," and constituting a "restless and turbulent faction"; whereas if the Church of England were properly established the populace would quickly be reduced to "passive obedience" since the Anglican clergy "inculcate the great principles of loyalty and submission to government." An article in the *Boston News-Letter* in 1750 reached back to the Hampton Court Conference of 1604 to find the proper slogan to state the case for episcopacy as the indispensable support of monarchy: "The good old saying, 'No Bishop, no King,' however grating it may be to some people, ought to be the standing maxim of the English government." [11]

Although the tactical skill and political connections of the Dissenting Deputies [12] in London thwarted the successive schemes to secure an American episcopate, the fears and apprehensions that were aroused created a smouldering fire of discontent and provided repeated occasion for preachers to utilize their sermons for purposes of political instruction. The campaign for bishops had been launched by the first S.P.G. missionaries and had been pushed with intermittent vigor in succeeding decades, but in the 1760's the agitation was stepped up and a mounting militancy of political activity reached its peak in 1770. This coincided with the new economic and political policies of the government which were to result in a general conflagration. Within this context, according to the *St. James's Chronicle*, "stamping and episcopizing" were commonly regarded as "only different branches of the same plan of power"; and Ezra Stiles indicated that much of the opposition to the Stamp Act was based on a recognition that if "a Parliamentary revenue had been established independent of the [colonial] Assemblies," the door would have been opened to the appropriation of funds "for half a dozen bishops on this continent." John Adams put it more bluntly: "If Parliament could tax us, they could establish the Church of England with all its creeds, articles, tests, ceremonies, and tithes; and prohibit all other churches as conventicles and schism shops." [13]

In the seventeenth century the Church of England had reaped a

---

[11] Bridenbaugh, *Mitre and Sceptre*, 102, 181, 262.

[12] A committee of lay representatives of "the Three Denominations" (Congregationalists, Presbyterians, and Baptists) which was formed in 1732 to direct the political agitation of English Dissenters in their struggle to secure the repeal of restrictive legislation. See B. L. Manning, *The Protestant Dissenting Deputies* (N.Y., 1952).

[13] Bridenbaugh, *Mitre and Sceptre*, 239, 259. Anson Phelps Stokes, *Church and State in the United States* (N.Y., 1950), I, 234.

whirlwind of disaster when Archbishop Laud identified it so completely with the ill-considered economic and political policies of Charles I that the church became an equal victim with the crown in the Revolution that followed. In the eighteenth century the role was reversed. The colonial structure came tumbling down at least partly because the Church of England identified the crown so intimately with its own "lust for dominion" in the New World that it became an albatross about the neck of the government. The precise weight to be given ecclesiastical grievances as a contributing cause of the American Revolution is impossible to determine, but John Adams, the most reflective and perceptive participant in the events which led to war, always insisted that "the apprehensions of episcopacy contributed . . . as much as any other cause to arouse the attention not only of the inquiring mind but the common people and urge them to close thinking on the constitutional authority of parliament over the colonies." [14]

DEISM. While a pervasive Puritanism as recast by Evangelicalism was the dominant religious emphasis in colonial America, a minimal faith known as Deism had become fashionable in some upper-class circles during the decades immediately preceding the American Revolution. Several of the most conspicuous leaders of the struggle for independence (George Washington, Thomas Jefferson, Benjamin Franklin, and Thomas Paine were notable examples) were Deists.

Deism had a double rootage. First of all, it may be traced back to seventeenth-century men of "latitude" in England who sought to overcome the divisions among Christians by suggesting that only those affirmations on which all Christians agree are essential articles of faith. Rejecting any dependence upon biblical revelation and appealing only to unaided natural reason, Deists pushed this reductionist tendency a step farther. They reduced the "essentials" of religion to a simple fivefold affirmation that God exists, that he is to be worshipped, that the practice of virtue is the true worship of God, that people must repent of wrongdoing, and that there are future rewards and punishments. To these five points, American Deists at least added a belief in God as a governing and over-ruling Providence who guides and determines the destinies of nations.

If Deism was partly the product of latitudinarian sentiment, it

[14] *The Works of John Adams*, ed. C. F. Adams (Boston, 1850–56), X, 185.

was also related to the rationalism which was associated with "the Age of Reason" or the era of the "Enlightenment." The period from the Peace of Westphalia (1648) to the French Revolution (1789) was a time of rapid scientific advance, an advance that is best epitomized in the work of Sir Isaac Newton (1642–1727). To many contemporaries Newton seemed to have solved all the chief problems of astronomy, optics, physics, and mathematics. Alexander Pope voiced this estimate when he wrote:

> Nature and Nature's Law lay hid in night.
> God said 'Let Newton be!' and all was light.

As a result of his studies, Newton was thought to have discovered "a universal law of nature" which banished mystery from the world." [15] The universe was simply a vast mechanism—intelligible, harmonious, and thoroughly rational—the product of God the Great Mathematician. It was within this context that two chief publicists of Deism, John Toland in *Christianity Not Mysterious* (1696) and Matthew Tindal in *Christianity as Old as Creation* (1730), affirmed that the "essentials" of religion are those truths which can be known by human reason alone without the aid of any special revelation.

The alliance of Christians with Deists in carrying forward the Revolution was not as strange as it may seem to be, for Deists did little more than appropriate Puritan political ideas. English Puritans as early as the 1640's had made a distinction between the realm of nature and the realm of grace, between natural revelation and special revelation. By the end of the seventeenth century this distinction had become integral to the thinking of representative figures ranging from Increase Mather through Jonathan Edwards and his heirs to Jonathan Dickinson, Samuel Davies, and John Witherspoon.[16] So long as Deists made no direct attack upon "revealed" religion (see below, pp. 131–32), Christians had no difficulty uniting with Deists for common political ends on the basis of the shared assumptions of "natural" religion.

William Penn (1644–1718), Algernon Sidney (1622–83), and John Locke (1632–1704) served as transmitters of Puritan political

---

[15] Newton had no such idea for he spent much of his time doing "biblical arithmetic" in an attempt to date the millennium.

[16] See Conrad Wright, *The Liberal Christians* (Boston, 1970), 17–20.

ideas to the Revolutionary generation. Locke was perhaps the most important. His *Essay concerning Human Understanding* (1690) and his *Reasonableness of Christianity* (1695) exalted the powers of human reason without rejecting biblical revelation or denying the messiahship of Jesus. But in 1776 his decisive influence was exerted by his *Treatises on Government* (1690) and his *Letter concerning Toleration* (1689), both of which were written in connection with the Revolution of 1688. In the former he asserted that all peaceful governments were established by the consent of the governed in order to protect their natural rights to life, liberty, and property, and that whenever this trust is betrayed the people have the right to resist.

Locke's political views were little more than a distillation of concepts that had long been current coin in Calvinist political theory—a fact which John Adams acknowledged [17]—and had become fundamental postulates of a large portion of the English people in earlier conflicts between King and Parliament. Although Thomas Jefferson wrote the Declaration of Independence, the key paragraph which justified the resort to arms could quite easily have been written by a Puritan divine. When it came to writing a constitution for the new nation, the happier view of human nature implicit in John Adams' assertion that unaided reason is "a revelation from its maker which can never be disputed or doubted" gave way to a more pessimistic estimate.[18] Even those who thought people were good enough to win heaven by their own efforts were skeptical about statesmen making the grade and insisted that the exercise of power must be checked by adequate safeguards.

The winning of independence

During the years prior to the Revolution "rational religion" exerted little influence in America except among some of the "intellectuals" of the coastal ports and among some of the plantation owners of the South. Few

[17] *Works*, VI, 4. For an explication of this point, see W. S. Hudson, "John Locke: Heir of Puritan Political Theorists," in G. L. Hunt, *Calvinism and the Political Order* (Philadelphia, 1965). For Penn, see W. S. Hudson, "William Penn's *English Liberties:* Tract for Several Times," *William and Mary Quarterly*, XXVI (1969), 578–85.

[18] For an analysis of the basic Puritan-Calvinist assumptions reflected in the United States Constitution, see H. Richard Niebuhr, *The Kingdom of God in America*, 45–87. See also Henry F. May, *The Enlightenment in America* (N.Y., 1976), 48–65, 88–99, 155–64. The application of theological assumptions in the drafting of the Constitution is discussed by W. S. Hudson, "Theological Convictions and Democratic Government," *Theology Today*, X (1953), 230–39.

of those who regarded themselves as emancipated from traditional Christian doctrine had any desire to promote their views among the populace at large. Believing as they did that orthodox religion served to inculcate the necessary principles of private and public morality among the common people, the rationalists tended to maintain at least a nominal connection with the existing churches and to contribute to their support. Thus to the extent that religious concerns played a decisive part in enlisting mass support for the colonial cause, this support of necessity was marshaled by the orthodox churches.

THE ATTITUDE OF THE VARIOUS DENOMINATIONS. Not all the churches, of course, supported the war with Great Britain, nor did any single denomination present an unbroken front. There were both Tories and Patriots in every religious group, as well as many who were apathetic. Nevertheless the general attitude which was to characterize each of them would not have been difficult to predict.

The Church of England had a long tradition of intimate identification with the English government and in the colonies this governmental relationship constituted its major source of strength. It is not surprising therefore that the Anglican clergy, with a few notable exceptions, were zealous Tories who condemned the conflict as an unjustified rebellion against constituted authority. The Anglican laity in the South, on the other hand, gave strong support to the struggle for independence. The pacifist groups—Quakers, Mennonites, Moravians, and Dunkers—held themselves aloof as a matter of principle. The Dutch and German Reformed and the Lutheran churches had no real stake in the perpetuation of British rule. While many sought to avoid taking sides in the conflict, the majority ranged themselves on the side of the colonists. This was also true of Roman Catholics and Jews, with Charles Carroll among the former contributing notable service to the colonial cause. These latter groups, however, were relatively small. The more significant support came from the Congregational, Presbyterian, and Baptist churches.

The Congregationalists had early nurtured a tradition of independence in the colonies which they had founded, and later British rule came to be associated in their minds both with Anglican proselyting activity and with pressure to give increased recognition to the status of the Church of England as the official church of the governing authority. But above all, Congregationalists had been fed a steady diet of "election sermons" which emphasized concepts of fundamental law, constitutional rights, limited government, and the duty to resist abuses of power—all of which were notions calculated to create a climate of opinion opposed to any infringement of the people's liberties.

These latter concepts which were so important in generating a revolutionary temper were not, of course, the exclusive possession of the Congregationalists. Having been formulated by early Calvinist political theorists and further refined by English Puritan and Scottish Presbyterian divines, they were shared in America by Presbyterians, Baptists, and others who stood within the Reformed tradition. Indeed, as we have seen, they had been popularized in the "political Calvinism" of John Locke, and in this form they had been appropriated by many who regarded themselves as otherwise quite emancipated from key doctrines of the Reformed understanding of the Christian faith.

The Presbyterians and the Baptists embraced these ideas the more zealously because of the disabilities to which they had been subjected in several of the colonies. Even in New England where Congregationalists often made life difficult for Baptists, the Baptists responded by accusing the Congregationalists of being disloyal to their own tradition and by asserting that the Baptists were the true heirs of the founders of New England.[19] In Virginia both Presbyterians and Baptists were thrown into a perpetual state of disaffection by irritations arising from Anglican tactics of oppression. The attitude of the Scotch-Irish among the Presbyterians was further colored by bitter memories of the ill-treatment their fathers had received at the hands of the English in northern Ireland.

THE ROLE OF THE CLERGY. In 1781 when arch-Tory Peter Oliver (1713–91) reviewed the course of the Revolution in his *Origin and Progress of the American Rebellion*, he suggested that if one wished to understand the inflamed public opinion which swept the colonies into war one must look to "Mr. Otis's black regiment, the dissenting clergy."[20] They certainly were key figures, for their influence penetrated remote communities that were seldom reached by newspapers and books. And if it is true, as a British official reported of the people of rural Connecticut, that "they are all politicians and Scripture learnt," this was the result of the

[19] This was the whole thrust of the argument of Isaac Backus in his *History of New England, with Particular Reference to . . . the Baptists* (Boston, 1777–96).

[20] James Otis (1725–83), a Boston lawyer, was one of the most conspicuous and effective leaders in arousing anti-British sentiment.

work of the preachers. Practical politics may have been learned at the town meeting but the undergirding political theory was picked up from the Sunday sermon and the weekly lecture as well as from the annual election sermon. So well rehearsed were these common folk in political thought that they knew all the arguments, delighted in the subtleties of debate, and were familiar with the facts of past crises which pointed up the present moral. Ezra Stiles could refer to "half a dozen bishops on this continent and a long string of &c. &c. &c.," in perfect confidence that the reader would recognize the allusion to be to the "Et cetera Oath" which had troubled the consciences of Englishmen more than a century before. Thus a few cliché-studded sentences were often sufficient to evoke a broad context of meaning. Perhaps the general run of the populace was best informed in New England, but elsewhere less widespread literacy and less ample access to the press made people even more dependent upon the preachers for information concerning issues of the day.[21]

The role of the clergy was not restricted to fostering and perpetuating notions of fundamental and "inalienable" rights. What Peter Oliver had in mind when he spoke of the importance of "Mr. Otis's black regiment" was the indispensable aid they provided in enlisting active support by "preaching up" the Revolution in innumerable "fast day" and recruiting sermons. This they did in a curiously roundabout fashion. While American rights were defended, there was little stress upon American righteousness and few direct and forthright attempts to enlist divine aid against the British. Their understanding of God's relationship to his people in terms of a covenant that involved more responsibilities than privileges left scant room for such unabashed presumption, and they knew that a simple invocation of the powers of heaven was no way to secure the assistance of a Supreme Governor whose favor was far from capricious.[22]

The preachers and those who had been taught by them knew that under the providential government of God the occasion for troubles and disasters must be sought within rather than without. Thus they viewed the present affliction that had been visited upon the colonies as less the result of the iniquity of the British than the consequence of the infidelity of the Americans. The remedy therefore was to confess their sins and to mend

[21] Bridenbaugh, *Mitre and Sceptre,* 189, 259.
[22] For an analysis of this type of approach, see Perry Miller, "From the Covenant to Revival," in *The Shaping of American Religion,* ed. J. W. Smith and A. L. Jamison, 322–68.

their ways. Only then could they reasonably expect that God would impart the necessary wisdom, energy, and will to push the war to a successful completion.

The successive "recommendations" of the Continental Congress that days of "public humiliation, fasting, and prayer" be observed played upon this theme as a repetitive refrain, expressing the hope that "we may with united hearts and voices unfeignedly confess and deplore our many sins, and offer up our joint supplications to the all-wise, omnipotent, and merciful Disposer of all events; humbly beseeching him to forgive our iniquities, to remove our present calamities, to avert those desolating judgments with which we are threatened" (1775); summoning the colonists to "implore the mercy and forgiveness of God, and beseech him that vice, prophaneness, and extortion, and every evil may be done away and that we may be a reformed and happy people" (1777); lamenting the fact that "too few have been sufficiently awakened to a sense of their guilt, or warmed with gratitude, or taught to amend their lives and turn from their sins, so he might turn from his wrath" (1779); and asking God's gracious intervention "to make us sincerely penitent for our transgressions; to prepare us for deliverance, and to remove the evil with which he hath been pleased to visit us; to banish vice and irreligion among us, and to establish virtue and piety by his divine grace" (1780).

This call to repentance, revival, and reform was a familiar theme to all who had been nurtured in the piety of the early Puritans and their revivalist successors. And it had always elicited not a failure of nerve but a vigorous response, for a program of action in terms of obedience to the ordinances of God was always implicit in their summons to repentance. It may seem strange to a later generation that this theme of abnegation would have been coupled with another theme from their past which demanded immediate and concerted action against any magistrate who violated the fundamental rights of the people. But to the great mass of the religiously oriented in the Revolutionary generation there was no contradiction. These rights, if variously derived, were divinely ordained, and to defend them—even when their abrogation was viewed as punishment for their sins—was part of their Christian obedience. The outcome was always in the hands of God, but since he uses men as instruments to serve the purposes of his providential government, the call to repentance and humiliation was at the same time a summons to battle.

RELIGIOUS FREEDOM. The securing of religious freedom in America is sometimes viewed as a sequel to the winning of independence, but this is a mistake. Philip Schaff was right when he asserted that the whole question of religious freedom had been settled prior to the formation of the national government by the previous history of the American colonies.[23] Of the original thirteen colonies, four—Rhode Island, New Jersey, Pennsylvania, and Delaware—had long been fully committed to a policy of religious liberty, and the Anglican establishments in five of the remaining colonies—in New York, Maryland, North Carolina, South Carolina, and Georgia—quickly toppled after the outbreak of hostilities when the supporting prop of English authority was withdrawn. The speedy action of New York in repealing all laws or acts which "may be construed to establish or maintain any particular denomination of Christians" was typical. Indeed, the North Carolina Assembly anticipated the repudiation of British authority when it refused in 1773 to renew the Vestry Act, an action which had the practical effect of bringing the establishment there to an end. Only in Virginia, and in Massachusetts, Connecticut, and New Hampshire, was there any delay; and even in these four areas the struggle for religious liberty was carried on during the war years as part of the revolutionary struggle itself. In Virginia, as early as June 12, 1776, an effort was made to forestall the popular tide and to preserve some remnant of the establishment by adopting a "Declaration of Rights" which asserted that "all men are equally entitled to the free exercise of religion."[24]

Obviously the urgent necessity which the war imposed to find a basis of unity among people who were religiously diverse was a compelling consideration in this rapid shift of many of the former colonies to a policy of full religious freedom. But the story is much more complex than simple necessity would suggest. For one thing, the shift was facilitated by a growing spirit of harmony and good will among many of the denominations. The Great Awakening had done much to promote this irenic ecclesiastical temper, bridging religious barriers in much the same way as

[23] Schaff, *Church and State in the United States* (N.Y., 1888), 23. The literature dealing with the church-state issue in America is voluminous. Much of the relevant source material has been assembled in Stokes, *Church and State in the United States*. Sidney E. Mead, *The Lively Experiment* (N.Y., 1963) is a perceptive and discerning commentary on the consequences that have flowed from the policy of religious freedom.

[24] The motion for its adoption was made by a conservative, Edmund Pendleton, who viewed the *Declaration* as a means of relieving the pressure for the more radical action of disestablishment. Stokes, *Church and State in the United States*, I, 380.

it had tended to dissolve colonial boundaries by the sweeping tide of new religious life and activity. At the same time the major non-Anglican religious groups also were being drawn together to resist Anglican encroachments, and both a catholic spirit and a developing national consciousness were fostered by the interdenominational and intercolonial committees of correspondence that were set up to coordinate this resistance. But an even more important factor in the movement toward full and complete religious freedom was a developing awareness among the colonists of the meaning of the American experience.

While all non-Anglican churchmen cherished the security and safety they had found in the vast expanse of the New World, the classic interpretation of their common experience which gave meaning to the American adventure was fashioned by the New Englanders. As clear a statement as any of this meaning was supplied by Cotton Mather (1663–1728) in an election sermon before the General Court of Massachusetts early in the 1690's. "What went ye into the wilderness to see?" the forefathers were asked rhetorically.

> And the answer to it is not only too excellent but also too notorious to be dissembled. Let all mankind know that we came into the wilderness because we would worship God without that Episcopacy, that Common Prayer, and those unwarranted ceremonies with which the "land of our forefathers' sepulchures" had been defiled. We came hither because we would have our posterity settled under pure and full dispensation of the gospel, defended by rulers that should be ourselves.

It is true that these early settlers were seeking freedom for themselves and not for others, but they were being constantly needled by their fellow Congregationalists in England to adopt a more liberal policy than that of reminding those who differed from them that they had equal freedom to establish settlements of their own in the American wilderness. By the early decades of the eighteenth century this more liberal policy had been forced upon them by the concessions they had been compelled to grant Anglicans, Baptists, and Quakers. Thus the tables were turned when the Anglicans launched their drive for ecclesiastical power in New England. Formerly the Congregationalists had squirmed under charges of intolerance, but now they could pin the label of bigotry upon the Anglicans and could remind them that the New England Congregationalists conceded more freedom to Anglicans than the Anglicans in England were willing to concede to Congregationalists.

Under this Anglican pressure, the New Englanders turned increasingly in their sermons, lectures, and writings to recasting the story of their past to bring it into accord with the necessities of the present. The Founding Fathers were pictured as apostles of liberty, and the need to maintain intact the liberties that had been bequeathed to them was constantly reiterated. Typical was the pointed application that was given by Thomas Prince in the dedication of his *Chronological History of New England* (1736) in which he spoke of

> the worthy Fathers of these plantations, whom yourselves and posterity cannot but have in everlasting honor, not only for their eminent self-denial and piety wherein they set examples for future ages to admire and imitate, but also for their great concern that the same vital and pure Christianity and LIBERTY, both *civil and ecclesiastical,* might be continued to their successors, for which they left their own and their fathers' houses in the most pleasant places then on earth with many of their dearest relatives, and came over the ocean into this then hideous wilderness.

By 1760 Ezra Stiles was declaring:

> The right of conscience and private judgment is unalienable; and it is truly the interest of all mankind to unite themselves into one body for the liberty, free exercise, and unmolested enjoyment of this right. . . . And being possessed of the precious jewel of religious liberty, a jewel of inestimable worth, let us prize it highly and esteem it too dear to be parted with on any terms lest we be again entangled with that yoke of bondage which our fathers could not, would not, and God grant that we may never, submit to bear. . . . Let the grand errand into America never be forgotten.[25]

And five years later, in an essay on canon law, John Adams rehearsed once again the history of New England and issued a peremptory summons: "Let the pulpit resound with the doctrines and sentiments of religious liberty," for there is "a direct and formal design on foot to enslave America."

So effective a propaganda device was not neglected in the other

[25] Bridenbaugh, *Mitre and Sceptre,* 3.

colonies. In New York, William Livingston (1723–90) shrewdly included the Dutch forefathers with the English when he reminded the governor in 1755 that

> the greatest number of our inhabitants are descended from those who with a brave and invincible spirit repelled the Spanish tyranny in the *Netherlands,* or from those who for their ever-memorable opposition to the arbitrary measures of King Charles I were constrained to seek a refuge from the relentless sword of persecution in the then inhospitable wilds of AMERICA. From such ancestors we inherit the highest relish for civil and religious LIBERTY.

The following year the Anglican William Smith (1727–1803) of Philadelphia sent word to London that "the impartial Presbyterian historian," William Smith, Jr., of New York, had explained the prevailing discontent of the people as the product of their desire "for an equal universal toleration of Protestants" and their aversion to "any kind of an ecclesiastical establishment." Twelve years later Livingston asserted that all good and loyal Protestants affirm "the natural right of every man to choose his own religion." Everywhere the religious issue was inextricably entangled with the revolutionary struggle. From South Carolina the Anglican Commissary, Charles Martyn, reported to the Bishop of London that the principles of most of the colonists "are independent in matters of religion as well as republican in those of government" and that "it would be as unsafe for an American bishop . . . to come hither as it is at present for a distributor of stamps." The watchword which united them all was "liberty, both civil and religious." Little wonder then that, with the cry of religious liberty having been constantly upon their lips, the Assemblies in those areas where Anglicanism had been established took immediate steps at the outbreak of war to give substance to one of the major slogans under which the colonists were being called upon to do battle.[26]

All the details of what was involved in a policy of religious freedom, to be sure, had not been worked out. In most of the newly independent colonies, for example, voting was restricted to Christians, Trinitarian Christians, or Protestants. In Massachusetts, Connecticut, and New Hampshire, those in control were confident that a policy of religious liberty had long since been put into practice. To be sure, their policy had differed

[26] *Ibid.,* 167, 176, 249, 304.

from colonies where no faith enjoyed any privileges. As Ezra Stiles explained it, "the happy policy of establishing one sect without infringing on the essential rights of others is peculiar to the three New England provinces where Congregationalism is the establishment." Basic to this "happy" situation was the dominant Congregational polity. This polity, he contended, provided a guarantee against ecclesiastical despotism, since each congregation enjoys sole power in the regulation of its own affairs. Moreover, other religious groups are permitted to exist, and while all inhabitants are taxed for the support of religion, they are allowed to assign their taxes to a church of their choice. This latitude, Stiles concluded, made possible "the friendly cohabitation of all." [27] Obviously this was an idealized portrait. Isaac Backus thought it a fraud. In a shrewd propaganda move, he turned the tables and insisted that Baptists, with their uncompromising defense of full religious liberty, were the true heirs of the Founding Fathers of New England. While Backus was unrelenting in his attack upon the remaining ecclesiastical privileges of the New England establishment, the crucial struggle for religious liberty was to be fought in Virginia.

Although the penalties imposed on religious dissent in Virginia were progressively eliminated during the war years as a result of Baptist and Presbyterian pressure, the Anglicans who dominated the "unreapportioned" Assembly had continued to fight a rear-guard action in defense of the establishment. Their last endeavor was the attempt in 1784, after the coercion imposed by the necessity to maintain united support for the war effort had been removed, to regain some measure of tax support for the Anglican church by levying a "general assessment" to be distributed impartially among all Christian churches. It was this "general assessment," again as a result of Baptist and Presbyterian pressure, that was defeated as inconsistent with the principles of liberty. Since the proposed benefits would be restricted to Christian churches, the point was made that the state would be required to determine what constitutes Christianity and thus would be compelled to set up its own standard of orthodoxy. Furthermore, "the same authority which can establish Christianity in exclusion of all other religions may establish with the same ease any particular sect of Christians in exclusion of all other sects" and "the same authority which can force a citizen to contribute threepence only of his

[27] *A Discourse on the Christian Union* (Boston, 1761), 37, 43, 97–99.

property for the support of any one establishment may force him to conform to any other establishment." [28] In January, 1786, the issue was settled with the adoption of the "Bill for Establishing Religious Freedom" which rejected the whole idea of any multiple establishment as well as any religious test for public office.

When the delegates assembled to draft the United States Constitution, the controversy in Virginia had been brought to an end and for most Americans the issue of religious liberty was no longer a subject for debate. If the Constitution in its primary form failed to deal with the issue beyond providing that "no religious test shall ever be required as a qualification to any office or public trust under the United States," it was not because there was any question at this point but because the instrument of 1787 gave the federal government no powers to deal with religious matters and it was assumed that no other guarantee was needed. As soon as it became apparent that an affirmative statement was necessary to win ratification by reluctant states, the necessary affirmation was promptly made by amendment—an amendment carefully devised to establish religious freedom, defined in terms worked out in Virginia, as binding national policy. The restrictions of the federal Bill of Rights did not apply to acts of the individual states, but only Massachusetts, Connecticut, and New Hampshire, with their emasculated Congregational establishments, remained out of step with the rest of the country. And long before the courts by invoking the Fourteenth Amendment (1868) imposed federal policy at this point upon the states, Connecticut (1818), New Hampshire (1819), and Massachusetts (1833) had fallen into line with guarantees in their own constitutions which gave to all religious groups a purely voluntary status.

Partisans of differing camps have quarreled as to who should receive primary credit or blame for the government surrendering all control over the religious life of its citizens. In many respects this is a fruitless debate. Beyond the decisive necessity imposed by the simple fact of religious diversity, claims and counterclaims can easily be made. The Virginia Bill for Establishing Religious Freedom was drafted by Thomas Jefferson, and Jefferson was both a "rationalist" and an ardent advocate of full and

[28] The arguments were presented in the "Memorial and Remonstrance" of 1784 drafted by James Madison. See Stokes, *Church and State*, I, 341–42, 344. The "Bill for Establishing Religious Freedom" is reprinted in Smith, Handy, Loetscher, *American Christianity*, I, 445–48.

complete religious liberty. But other "rationalists" were not as clear as was Jefferson at this point. Washington favored the "general assessment" in Virginia; Franklin had favored an American episcopate and was not unduly disturbed by the Congregational establishment in New England; and John Adams was vigorous in his defense of the New England pattern. The low-pressure religion of the pre-Revolutionary "rationalists," on the whole, did not lend itself to a crusading spirit, and an establishment that did not interfere with private reflection was frequently viewed as a good thing for the masses.

Few of the more orthodox religious groups, on the other hand, presented an entirely unbroken front in support of full and complete religious freedom. The Congregationalists developed an intricate defense of their own distinctive solution to the problem. At least a majority of the Presbyterian clergy in Virginia were ready to settle for a "general assessment" in contrast to the lay elders who were adamant in rejecting it. Even some Baptist churches in New Hampshire accepted the status and legal privileges of establishment in their respective towns. What seems clear is this. In several of the crucial struggles, leadership was supplied by "rationalists" while the ardor and indispensable political pressures were supplied by troops in the field who represented more conventional religious ideas. The latter created the problem, popularized the orthodox Protestant conviction expressed by Jefferson that all "legislators and rulers, civil as well as ecclesiastical," are "but fallible and uninspired men" (a conviction which struck at the heart of any rationalization of enforced conformity), and committed the war effort to the slogan of "liberty, both civil and ecclesiastical."

For good or ill—whether as a result of mere necessity, the influence of "rational" religion, or the principles of liberty that had been resounding from orthodox pulpits for more than a generation—the revolutionary struggle committed the new nation at its birth to a policy of complete voluntaryism in religion. Freed from threats of governmental interference, the churches were also denied the possibility of governmental support.

SEPARATION OF CHURCH AND STATE.   A curious misunderstanding was to develop concerning the First Amendment: "Congress shall make no law respecting an establishment of religion nor prohibiting the free exercise thereof." A *New York Times* editorial of April 23, 1960, began with the words: "We start with the premise, shared by every American who believes in the constitutional principles on which our country is founded, that religion has no proper place in American politics." This was a curious statement because when the First Amendment was adopted no one thought that the provision for the "separation of church and state," to use the terminology of the Supreme Court, implied any separation of religion and politics. The colonial clergy, according to their differing convictions, both "preached up" and "preached down" the American Revolution. They debated, for example, the issue of God-given rights. Since then political issues have never been absent from American pulpits. In similar fashion political leaders cast their thought within religious categories and used religious rhetoric to express political convictions.

The separation of church and state is a separation of institutions—a separation of "church" and "state." Ecclesiastical institutions have no connection with the state. They shall not be "established," i.e., they shall receive no state support, patronage, or privilege. Nor shall religious institutions be subject to any state control. Any interference with the "free exercise of religion" is strictly forbidden. No individual shall be penalized for belief or unbelief. Churches shall be wholly voluntary, dependent upon purely persuasive powers to marshal support to maintain themselves and to make their influence felt.

This seems very clear, plain, and simple, but the terms should be plural rather than singular. Americans have neither a monolithic church nor a monolithic state. What we do have are churches and a multiplicity of governmental units which come into contact at many different points and in many different ways. The principle of separation is clear but the line of separation follows a meandering course that must be repeatedly defined, adjudicated, and applied under a variety of circumstances in specific cases. What must be kept in mind is that the principle of institutional separation and its strict application has been of great utility both to the nation and the churches. It has contributed to public peace and tranquility by avoiding the religious antagonisms which have lacerated public life in Europe. At the same time, under conditions imposed by the American constitution, religious institutions of all traditions have flourished and exerted influence in the shaping of American society.

❧ PART II

THE NEW NATION

1789–1860

V

The Religion of the Republic and the State of the Churches

The winning of independence presented to the American people a prospect that was at first exhilarating and then sobering. The initial exuberant optimism was voiced by Ezra Stiles in the Connecticut election sermon of 1783, entitled *The United States Elevated to Glory and Honor.*

> This will be a great, a very great nation, nearly equal to half Europe. . . . Before the millennium the English settlements in America may become more numerous millions than that greatest domain on earth, the Chinese Empire. Should this prove to be a future fact, how applicable would be . . . [our] text [Deut. 26:19] when the Lord shall have made his American Israel high above all nations which he has made—in numbers, and in praise, and in name, and in honor.
>
> I am sensible some will consider these as visionary utopian ideas; and so they would have judged had they been told . . . at the battle of Lexington that in less than eight years the independence and sovereignty of the United States should be acknowledged by four European sovereignties, one of which should be Britain herself. How wonderful the revolutions, the events, of Providence! We live in an age of

wonders; we have lived an age in a few years; we have seen more wonders accomplished in eight years than are usually unfolded in a century.

Nor was the prospect dismaying to Stiles that the churches were to be
dependent solely upon their powers of persuasion, for he was confident
that in a free market truth would prevail. "Here Deism will have its full
chance; nor need libertines [any] more to complain of being overcome
by any weapons but the gentle, the powerful ones of argument and truth.
Revelation will be found to stand the test to the ten thousandth examination." [1]

But when the exhilaration of the moment was past, there were second
thoughts. The war had left the former colonies exhausted, impoverished,
and disorganized. Soon the government of the Confederation was mired in
confusion, and the very grounds of promise—vast expanse of territory,
multiplying population, and diversity of interest—came to be seen as
dangers which threatened the nation. Hopefulness gave way to anxiety,
and several decades were to elapse before it became evident that the
multiple experiment in independence, republicanism, federal union, and
religious liberty would be crowned with success. In the interim, Americans
were sustained by the conviction that had nerved them in the struggle for
independence—the belief that God had a special vocation in store for
America.

The mission of America

It is somewhat misleading to speak of the religious pluralism of the
United States. From the beginning there was a pluralism of religious
bodies, denominations, churches. But most of these had a common understanding of the Christian faith, an understanding which under the impact
of the Awakening came to be known as "evangelical" or "spiritual" religion (see above, pp. 7–9, 78–82). In addition to the common faith of the
churches, there was also a "general" religion which was not pluralistic,
a "civic" religion which was the religion of most people, a "religion
of the republic" with its own beliefs, myths, and symbols; its own ceremonies and rituals; its own days of remembrance and thanksgiving. The

[1] The sermon is reprinted in John W. Thornton, *The Pulpit of the American Revolution* (Boston, 1860). See pp. 440–441, 471.

religion of the churches and the religion of the republic existed side by side. Since they were regarded as mutually supportive, the distinction between them was often blurred. Still the operating assumption was that the nation had its own independent religious vocation.[2]

THE RELIGION OF THE REPUBLIC. The theoretical basis for distinguishing between the vocation of the nation and the vocation of churches had been developed in the 1640's by English Puritans who were dismayed that religious differences should result in civil war. They posited a distinction between the realm of nature and the realm of grace. The realm of nature was God's "great kingdom, the world." The realm of grace was "his special or peculiar kingdom, the kingdom of grace." In the first, God rules "every natural man" by "the light of nature to a civil outward good and end." In the second, God rules the Christian by his special revelation in Christ to an inward and spiritual end. Whereas spiritual religion is available only to the "saints" through the gift of faith, natural religion is available to all men through "natural reason," i.e., through the lessons of history, including the history of the Hebrew people, which make plain the manner of God's providential dealings with civil communities. "General religion," William Penn called it; beliefs and principles, including the Ten Commandments (the epitome of natural law) common to Christian and Jew alike. By the end of the seventeenth century, this distinction had received its most influential expression in John Locke's famous *Letter concerning Toleration* (1689).[3]

Throughout the colonial period many Americans had viewed themselves as sharing in some decisive way the role in history which they believed God had reserved for England. The Revolution brought about a shift in thinking at this point, making it clear to the citizens of the new republic that a headstrong and heedless England had forfeited her place in God's plan for the nations. Even prior to the war some Americans were audacious enough to believe that the colonists alone were God's new Israel. After the war this became the general conviction. Through his providential

[2] See R. N. Bellah, "Civil Religion in America," *Daedalus*, XCVI (1967), 1–19; reprinted in W. S. Hudson, *Nationalism and Religion in Amerca* (N.Y., 1970). See also Elwyn A. Smith, *The Religion of the Republic* (Phila., 1971); Conrad Cherry, *God's New Israel* (Englewood Cliffs, N.J., 1971); and S. E. Mead, "The Nation with the Soul of a Church," *Church History*, XXXVI (1967), 262–83.

[3] For this distinction, see A. S. P. Woodhouse, *Puritanism and Liberty* (London, 1938), Introduction, 38–43. For Locke, see George L. Hunt, *Calvinism and the Public Order* (Phila., 1965), 115–16, 118–24.

control of events, God had fashioned the United States as a new instrument to effect his purposes for mankind. Thomas Jefferson, Benjamin Franklin, John Adams, and other members of the Constitutional Convention were as vigorous as any clergyman in asserting that the United States had come into being as a grand design of Providence for "the illumination of the ignorant and the emancipation of the slavish part of mankind over all the earth." [4]

This faith of the new republic was neither sectarian nor parochial. Its roots were Hebraic. Its explication was cast in Hebraic metaphors— chosen people, covenanted nation, Egyptian bondage, promised land. Its eager millennial expectation was expressed in the vivid imagery of the Hebrew prophets. Its potentially unbridled exuberance was kept in partial check by an Hebraic awareness that divine displeasure could quickly bring divine judgment upon the nation.[5] Nor was the faith of the republic parochial. Members of the Revolutionary and post-Revolutionary generation frequently referred to themselves as "citizens of the world." The blessings they had won were blessings which of right belonged to all people. And the cautionary reminder that "the eyes of the world are upon you" remained a standard item in the rhetoric of the nation.

There were two versions of the mission of America. The initial version stressed the role of the United States as "a light to the nations," forwarding the emancipation of mankind by the contagion of its example and the power of its attraction. The second version emphasized the American role as "the liberator of the oppressed."

The firm belief in the contagious influence of American example was never more eloquently expressed than by Lyman Beecher in an address at Plymouth in 1827.

> To accomplish . . . changes in the civil and religious condition of the world, revolutions and convulsions are doubtless indispensable. . . . To the perfection of this work a great example is required of which the world may take knowledge, and which shall inspire hope and rouse and concentrate the energies of man. But where could such a nation be found? It must be created for it had no existence upon the earth. Look now at the history of our fathers and behold what God hath

[4] *Works of John Adams*, ed. C. F. Adams (Boston, 1850–56), I, 66.
[5] See W. S. Hudson, "Fast Days and Civil Religion," *Theology in Sixteenth and Seventeenth Century England: Papers read at a Clark Library Seminar, February 6, 1971* (Los Angeles, 1971).

wrought . . . , a powerful nation in full enjoyment of civil and religious liberty, where all the energies of men . . . find scope and excitement on purpose to show the world by experiment of what man is capable. . . .

When the light of such a hemisphere shall go up to the heavens it will throw its beams beyond the waves; . . . it will awaken desire and hope and effort and produce revolutions and overturnings until the world is free.

From our revolutionary struggle proceeded the revolution in France and all of which followed in Naples, Portugal, Spain, and Greece. And though the bolt of every chain has been again driven, they can no more hold the heaving mass than the chains of Xerxes could hold the Hellespont vexed with storms. Floods have been poured on the rising flame, but they can no more extinguish it than they can extinguish the fires of Etna. Still it burns, and still the mountain heaves and murmurs. And soon it will explode with voices and thunderings and great earthquakes. Then will the trumpet of Jubilee sound, and earth's debased millions will leap from the dust, and shake off their chains, and cry, "Hosanna to the Son of David." [6]

In the interim preceding that glorious day, the United States would continue as an "asylum for the oppressed," drawing to herself the tired, the poor, the huddled masses yearning to be free. Likewise, by the simple power of attraction, the new nation would bring the blessings of liberty to all North America as settlers in more distant parts of the continent petitioned to be received into the Union.

The second version of the mission of America was no less idealistic. Unlike the "example to the nations" theme, the second version stressed a more active role. This was the servant image of a nation called to help liberate the captive and the oppressed. It was foreshadowed in Thomas Jefferson's purchase of Louisiana, and it found expression in Andrew Jackson's determination to "extend the area of freedom," in subsequent military adventures, and in the sacrificial foreign mission activity of the churches. The latter enterprise, among other objectives, sought to banish ignorance, superstition, poverty, and disease in far corners of the earth as a prelude to Beecher's day of Jubilee when the oppressed everywhere would shake off their chains and the whole world would be free.

[6] For Beecher's address, see W. S. Hudson, *Nationalism and Religion in America*, 99–105.

Unfortunately a servant image is easily·transmuted into a master image, with the master image being justified (through benefits conferred) as no more than an extension of the servant roll. Still a tension remained between those who wished simply to liberate and those, often equally idealistic, who viewed themselves as tutors to mankind. Albert J. Beveridge, who insisted that God had made Americans stewards of civilization and their brothers' keepers, was to be a conspicuous exemplar of the muscular Americanism which sought to impose American ways, institutions, and commercial enterprise on peoples who were less than willing to receive them. The significant point is that this robust self-righteous vision of America's mission always encountered resistance. The resistance was not always successful, but it had sufficient rootage in tradition to maintain a degree of ambivalence in the public mind as to America's role in world affairs, whether it was to be that of an example, a servant, or a benevolent master.

The major counter to an uninhibited imperialist thrust was an acknowledgment, deeply grounded in American consciousness, that America's election was conditional. "Covenant mercies" presuppose "covenant duties" was the way John Higginson phrased it in his preface to Cotton Mather's *Magnalia*. The sense of divine vocation was paralleled by a sense of divine judgment, by an awareness that the judgment of God is harshest on those who are most favored. Again and again Americans were cautioned that desolation and destruction is the fate of a wayward people, that the United States has no unqualified promise from God that it will endure, and that God is prepared to raise up another people unto himself if those entrusted with his mission should fail him.

SPIRITUAL RELIGION. The distinction between "civic religion" and "spiritual religion" has often been understood as a distinction between a religion of the head ("natural religion") and a religion of the heart ("evangelical religion"). Although drawing the distinction in this way involves some distortion and much oversimplification, it is still useful in pointing to a major distinction in role. "Civic religion," the "religion of the republic," was *public* religion, a religion available to all through natural reason. "Spiritual religion" was *private* religion, an "experienced" religion that was intensely personal. The one was preoccupied with the nation and its mission; the other was preoccupied with individuals and their redemption. The one provided a bond which united the nation and gave it a reassuring sense of a God-given vocation; the other rescued individuals from sin and, in reconciling them to God, established them in the paths of virtue.

While civic religion and spiritual religion could be viewed as somewhat autonomous, still they were not unrelated. Both fell within the scope of God's ultimate purpose for mankind, and their respective millennial visions ("political emancipation" and "spiritual emancipation") often tended to become intermingled. Moreover, both were generally regarded as mutually supportive. Spiritual religion, free and unconstrained, depended upon the devotion to liberty which stood at the heart of the national faith. On the other hand, it was clear to most proponents of "reasonable" religion (including Benjamin Franklin, for example) that for the rank and file of the populace a more personal "experienced" religion was indispensable in a society based largely on voluntary obedience.

A SOCIETY OF VOLUNTARY OBEDIENCE. In his later years Jefferson expressed confidence that everyone would one day be able to act rationally in serving the common good on the basis of natural reason alone, but even Jefferson in the early days of the republic exhibited a pragmatic concern for church or private religion, being convinced of its utility in inculcating morality and virtuous behavior among the people. Others less pragmatic and more devout were equally convinced that the heart must be touched to secure the voluntary obedience required in a society designed to maximize liberty and minimize coercion. In a self-governing society which presupposed the common consent and voluntary obedience of most citizens, few could regard the future with equanimity in the absence of a prevailing sense of moral obligation. Hence the dual emphasis, an emphasis on "the religion of the republic" common to all, and an emphasis on "spiritual religion," a more personal faith which was not of the republic but which was regarded by many as indispensable to the well-being of the republic. It was for this reason that when Lyman Beecher voiced his concern for the republic, he stressed the need for "revivals."

Colonial experience had taught leaders of the churches that "spiritual" or "evangelical" religion was most readily fostered in and through revivals. Many of the churches, however, were ill-prepared to undertake aggressive action to promote a resurgence of spiritual religion. Church life had been disrupted by the war. Pastors had marched off with the troops, congregations had been scattered, meeting-houses had been requisitioned as barracks, colleges established for training ministerial recruits had been forced to close, synods and associations had been unable to meet. When President Witherspoon of Princeton and President Stiles of Yale acknowledged that God had blessed the American people beyond all expectation in the winning of independence, they both knew that before the churches could give themselves wholeheartedly to renewing the "spiritual" life of the nation, the churches had many institutional problems of their own to put in order.

The reordering of denominational life

While no denomination escaped the disruption and dislocation of the war years, they survived the conflict with varying fortunes. Anglicans, Quakers, Mennonites, and Moravians suffered most. Congregationalists and Presbyterians were less affected. Baptists and the as yet unorganized Methodists actually prospered, multiplying in number. The Revolution was a time of troubles for the peace churches. Often their members were subjected to fines, abuse, and public opprobrium. Conflicting loyalties led to defections which reduced their membership. Moravians, Mennonites, and Dunkers withdrew into greater isolation as small enclaves within the larger society. This was less true of Quakers who lacked the defensive rampart of another language. Quakers on occasion were to move into the world to exercise an influence far greater than their numbers warranted, but the war helped introduce the internal divisions which ushered in what Howard Brinton called their period of "conflict and decline." Never again were Quakers to be one of the major religious denominations in America.

ANGLICANS. The Church of England was the greatest casualty of the American Revolution, being stripped almost overnight of its privileges, prestige, and support. As the church of the royal officials it was disliked and distrusted, and its unpopularity was augmented by the ardent Toryism of many of its clergy, most of whom "to the utmost of their power opposed the spirit of disaffection and rebellion." Its ranks were also depleted by the Methodist defection in the South and by the emigration to Canada of "United Empire Loyalists" in the North. In the end only a remnant survived the war, and this remnant continued to diminish.

The surviving Anglicans faced a triple coercion. First, to be indigenous to America, an explicit break with a church that acknowledged the King of England as its "supreme governor" was required. Second, since the supervision of the Bishop of London's Commissaries had ended, a new governing structure had to be devised. Most urgent of all was the problem posed by a desperate shortage of clergymen, most of whom had fled. At this point Anglicans were plagued by dependence upon England. Not only was it impossible to secure ordination in America, English ordination required an oath of allegiance to the British crown.

An American bishop was the basic requirement. Samuel Seabury (1729–96), at the urging of ten Connecticut clergymen, secured episcopal consecration from the nonjuring bishops of Scotland, but this independent action was resented. The major role in organizing an American church was played by William White (1748–1836) and William Smith (1727–1803). White was rector of Christ Church in Philadelphia and chaplain to the Continental Congress. Smith's long association was with the College of Philadelphia but at the time he was in Maryland as rector at Chestertown. White was the one who rallied support, while Smith did the committee work. As a result of their efforts a General Convention met in 1785 to frame a constitution for the Protestant Episcopal Church, to revise the liturgy, and to arrange for consecration of bishops. White and Samuel Provoost (1742–1815) of New York were sent abroad to be consecrated, a reconciliation with Seabury was effected, and a fully equipped church met for the first time in the General Convention of 1789.[7]

Still the new church looked forward to no very hopeful future. Bishop Provoost relinquished his episcopal duties in 1801, convinced that the church would "die out with the old families." Others also believed that no more than a languishing life of brief duration could be expected.[7a] It was not until a new generation of men, most notably Bishops Griswold, Moore, Chase, and Hobart, infused new vigor into its leadership that the Protestant Episcopal Church began to make a significant recovery.

CONGREGATIONALISTS, PRESBYTERIANS, AND BAPTISTS. At the time of the formation of the new nation, the "three old denominations" of English Dissent, linked to one another by common adherence to the doctrines of the Westminster Confession, were the largest American denominations. In contrast to the Anglicans, they had survived the war with

[7] F. V. Mills, *Bishops by Ballot: An Eighteenth-Century Ecclesiastical Revolution* (London, 1978).
[7a] See L. W. Bacon, *A History of American Christianity* (N.Y., 1907), 213, 232.

increased prestige, each having been strongly identified with the colonial cause. At the beginning of the conflict Congregationalists had the largest number of churches and members, with Presbyterians ranking second. Baptists lagged considerably behind in a virtual standoff with the Anglicans. But while Anglican strength disintegrated during the war years, Baptist strength multiplied with astonishing rapidity. So marked was Baptist growth that by 1800 Baptists, as the popular wing of the Puritan-Reformed phalanx, had become the largest of the American denominations.

Outwardly the Congregationalists of New England were well prepared for independence. They had the largest number of churches as well as wealth, prestige, education, and able leaders. In 1760 Ezra Stiles had calculated that a century hence Congregationalists would have a "population" of seven million, and in 1783 he still was confident that Congregationalists and Presbyterians would far outdistance all other denominations in number of adherents. The promise was there but, in the event, his calculations proved hopelessly wrong. Despite outward signs of strength, Congregationalists were troubled by internal weaknesses, and energy was diverted to waging a rearguard defense of the special privileges they possessed in New England.

Presbyterians were equally well equipped for independence. They too had numbers, wealth, learning, and able leaders. They also enjoyed the prestige of being strongly identified with the winning side of a war which some had labeled a Presbyterian rebellion. "When the war is over," an agent of Lord Dartmouth had declared, it will become apparent that "Presbyterianism is really at the bottom of the whole conspiracy." [8] Furthermore, Presbyterians had the advantage of numerical strength on what was to be the growing edge of the country—a fact which led Theodore Roosevelt to call the Scotch-Irish Presbyterians America's first frontiersmen. Moreover, with the breach between the Old and New Side factions healed in 1758, Presbyterians were able to move quickly to fashion an effective structure to meet the needs of an expanding nation—local presbyteries being drawn into four regional synods and these in turn linked to a national General Assembly which met for the first time in 1789. Finally, as population moved westward Presbyterians were to inherit considerable Congregational strength.

[8] Trinterud, *Forming of an American Tradition*, 250. "Presbyterianism," of course, was used in the broad sense which included Congregationalists.

Of real significance was the fact that by the end of the colonial period most Presbyterians and Congregationalists had come to think of themselves as a single denomination. Ministers moved freely between the pulpits of the two groups, and the first three presidents of the Presbyterian college at Princeton were New England Congregationalists. In the years immediately preceding the Revolution, these intimate fraternal relationships produced a variety of joint committees, and this bond was formalized by an exchange of official delegates between their respective church judicatories. The common identification was further reinforced by the tendency of Congregationalists, especially in Connecticut and Rhode Island, to refer to themselves as Presbyterians.

Following the Revolution, Presbyterians and Congregationalists renewed and strengthened the ties which united them. The practice of exchanging delegates—with full right "to vote in all questions"—was revived. This "union" was further implemented when westward migration brought about an intermingling of Presbyterians and Congregationalists in the new settlements. Instead of dividing "the sparse population holding the same faith," as John Blair Smith (1756–99) put it, into "two distinct ecclesiastical organizations" and thus preventing "each from achieving those means of grace which both might sooner enjoy but for such division," it was proposed that Presbyterians and Congregationalists be encouraged to form union churches in frontier areas.[9] In 1801 this "Plan of Union" was put into effect, and seven years later it was strengthened by an "Accommodation Plan" which provided for more complete unity between the two denominations in a "uniform system of church government." For the next three decades Presbyterians and Congregationalists were to all intents and purposes a single denomination in New York, Ohio, Indiana, Illinois, Michigan, and Wisconsin.

In New England two factors forced Congregationalists to be content with the church structure they had been able to forge prior to the war. For one thing, their status as state churches in Massachusetts, Connecticut, and New Hampshire inhibited them from fashioning any official structure that would have provided a link across state lines. Moreover, a strong emphasis upon local autonomy had developed which fostered vigorous resistance to the surrender of local prerogatives. The jealous defense of local rights was most pronounced among those who were not church mem-

---

[9] The Plan of Union is printed in Smith, Handy, Loetscher, *American Christianity*, I, 545–47.

bers but who, as inhabitants of the towns, controlled many of the outward affairs of the state-established churches.

Lack of central organization was not necessarily a liability, as Baptists and later Disciples were to demonstrate. Nor was it an insuperable obstacle to cooperative endeavors, for Congregationalists appropriated the English technique of using voluntary societies of individuals to forward their corporate concerns—a technique permitting quick response to immediate needs and flexibility in marshalling support. It also facilitated joint efforts of Congregationalists and Presbyterians without raising too many ecclesiastical complications.

The major weakness of Congregationalism was division within its own ranks. The Great Awakening had created a split between revivalists and antirevivalists. This had led to schisms with large numbers of the revival faction being siphoned off into "Separate Congregational" and Baptist churches. As early as 1760 Ezra Stiles reported that there were already 22,000 Baptists in New England in comparison to 60,000 to 70,000 Congregational church members. During the next fifty years the gap steadily narrowed. In Connecticut there had been an upper-class defection to Anglicanism, and by 1800 Methodists were making significant inroads.

Congregationalism was also torn by doctrinal dissension. The differences were initially matters of emphasis, temperament, and cultural outlook. The "liberal" faction, centered in and about Harvard, represented a gradual softening of the characteristic tenets of Calvinism. Thoroughly alarmed by these "Arminian" tendencies, Jonathan Edwards and his heirs had occupied themselves with fashioning a tightly argued defence of a consistent Calvinism. The ensuing warfare was intense. Revivalism as a line of demarcation was inexact. Between the two extremes was a large body of moderate traditionalists who at the outset had made common cause with the antirevivalism of the "liberals," while later they came to acknowledge the utility of revivals. Party lines became increasingly polarized even in eastern Massachusetts. In 1808 Andover Theological Seminary was founded as a bulwark of orthodoxy, and after the explosion of 1815 (see p. 161), Congregational ranks were further depleted as the liberal wing found its spiritual home in an independent Unitarianism.

The growing ecclesiastical diversity in New England was accompanied by unrelenting attack upon the remnants of the Congregational establishments, and Congregationalists became preoccupied with defending what remained of the "Standing Order." At best this was a delaying action, for acts of disestablishment were passed in Connecticut in 1818, in New Hampshire in 1819, and in Massachusetts in 1833. It was only then that Congregationalists found "in their new insecurity and nakedness a kind of self-respect and self-reliance that made for good health."[10] A degree of doctrinal unity also had been restored by the conversion of the moderate conservatives to a revivalist point of view and by the defection of the Unitarians. By this time, however, the opportunity which had been theirs had been lost. Although New England exported vast segments of its population to the West, much of the Congregational blood in the newer regions was flowing through Presbyterian veins as a result of the agreement between the two denominations which did not fall apart until after 1837.

By 1800 Baptists had become the largest of the "three old denominations" of English Dissent, with twice as many adherents as any other religious group. In spite of striking gains they were to make in the West, Baptists were far from a frontier phenomenon. The greatest gains were made in the East. Throughout the nineteenth century most centers of Baptist strength were along the seaboard—in Maine, New Hampshire, Massachusetts, New York, Pennsylvania, the Carolinas, and Georgia.

Noah Worcester, a Congregational minister, was puzzled by the surge of Baptist growth, and in 1794 he sought to account for it in his *Impartial Inquiries concerning the Progress of the Baptist Denomination.* As reasons for their success, he mentioned the "coldness" of ministers and members of other denominations, the sympathy and respect gained from persecution, the advantage they had been able to take of revivals, the confident use they made of "irrelevant" Scripture, and finally "the want of qualifications in some Baptist teachers." Baptists did profit from revivals, for a stress upon the necessity for a "conversion" experience gave added weight to the doctrine of believers' baptism, and the appeal to Scripture was persuasive to those who had been taught to accept Scripture as their final authority. But Worcester's explanation of the influence exerted by "some Baptist teachers" who lacked "qualifications" (i.e. education) probably missed the point. "Many people," he said, "are so ignorant as to be [more] charmed with sound than sense."

> To them the want of knowledge in a teacher . . . may easily be

[10] E. S. Gaustad, *Historical Atlas of Religion in America* (N.Y., 1962), 42.

made up and overbalanced by great zeal, and affecting tone of voice, and a perpetual motion of the tongue. If a speaker can keep his tongue running . . . and can quote memoriter a large number of texts from . . . the Bible, it matters not to many of his hearers whether he speaks sense or nonsense.

Except in the back country of the South, not many of the Baptist preachers were unusually emotional in their preaching, nor did they prize an unlearned ministry. As Baptists multiplied in the closing decades of the eighteenth century, they were busy with projects for establishing academies and a college, and after the turn of the century they became increasingly active in promoting ministerial education. But, overwhelmed by the rapidity of their growth, Baptists had little opportunity to enforce educational standards. Mature men who exhibited gifts of leadership were called into service, and this readiness to utilize what leadership was available was one of the secrets of their growth. As was to be true of the Methodists, the Baptists helped to fill the vacuum left by the shortage of ministers among those denominations which adhered more rigidly to formal educational requirements.

METHODISTS AND "CHRISTIANS." Prior to 1784 Methodists were not a church but only a "religious society" nominally related to the Church of England.[11] Local Methodist societies had been formed in America during the decade prior to independence, mostly in the Chesapeake Bay region and southward through Virginia to North Carolina. One would suppose that the Revolution would have had the same disastrous effect upon Methodists as it had upon other Anglicans, for John Wesley was equally vocal in his opposition to American independence. Furthermore, all but one of the lay preachers Wesley had sent out to the colonies returned to England after the outbreak of hostilities. Francis Asbury (1745–1816) was the significant exception. When Barrett's chapel was being built in Delaware during the war years an observer voiced the common estimate of Methodist prospects: "It's no use putting up so large a dwelling for Methodists, for after the war a corncrib will hold them all." [12] This may have been the popular opinion, but it was wrong. The eager and contagious enthusiasm of the Methodist societies thrust forward native lay preachers to replace the departed English itinerants, and Asbury spent

11 John Wesley's tracts, *A Plain Account of the People Called Methodists* and *The Character of a Methodist*, are reprinted in Harry Emerson Fosdick, ed., *Great Voices of the Reformation* (N.Y., 1952), 499–513.

12 J. M. Buckley, *A History of Methodists in the United States* (N.Y., 1896), 186.

much of his time in the saddle supervising them. As a result, membership of the societies roughly doubled during the Revolution. Perhaps Methodists benefited from the suspicion with which they were viewed by the Tory Anglican clergy, but their great growth was basically little more than additional documentation of the truism that for the next three-quarters of a century the future in America—numerically speaking—belonged to those groups which could provide an ample supply of ministerial leadership, even if much of that leadership was restricted to lay preachers.

American Methodists seized upon the winning of independence as an opportunity to form themselves into a separate church. With so many of the Anglican clergy gone, John Wesley was prevailed upon in 1784 to ordain ministers for his American brethren so that they would not be denied the consolation of the sacraments. Although he was violating the laws of the Church of England, Wesley was convinced that ordination by presbyters was valid when dictated by necessity, and he found justification for it in the practice of the ancient church at Alexandria where presbyters had even ordained bishops. Thomas Vasey (1742–1826) and Richard Whatcoat (1736–1806) were the two men ordained, and when they sailed for America they were accompanied by the Rev. Thomas Coke (1747–1814) whom Wesley appointed to be "joint superintendent" with Asbury "over our brethren in North America." After their arrival, the "Christmas Conference" of 1784 was convened at Baltimore, Asbury was ordained, and the new Methodist Episcopal Church was constituted.

"The Revolutionary War now being closed and a general peace established," wrote Jesse Lee (1758–1816), the first official historian of Methodism, "we could go into all parts of the country without fear; and we soon began to enlarge our borders and to preach in many places where we had not been before." [13] The borders were enlarged and numbers also. In 1784 at the time of the Christmas Conference, Methodists had numbered almost 15,000. Six years later, in 1790, there were 57,631 members. By 1820 they had overtaken the Baptists and had become the largest American denomination. A major reason for the astonishingly rapid spread and growth of Methodism was the adoption of the "circuit system" which Wesley had devised for his English societies. Thus the new church was equipped with a highly mobile ministry of traveling preachers who covered a vast territory instead of being tied to a single locality. The more intimate nurture of the flocks they gathered was provided by local lay

[13] *Short History of the Methodists* (Baltimore, 1810), 84.

preachers and class leaders. No system could have been more admirably designed for moving quickly into new territory, whether that territory was in older settled regions of the seaboard or over the mountains into the new communities of the frontier. In both areas Methodists met with equal success. Had they not put down deep roots in the East, they would not have been able to move so boldly into the West with the initial tide of migration.

John Wesley was partly responsible for a second denomination which took shape in the early years of the new republic. It sprang from an effort to achieve unity among Christians by avoiding party names and "human" creeds and by adhering strictly to New Testament precedents in worship and government. Although his societies were nominally related to the Church of England, Wesley taught his followers to be impatient with theological points which served to divide "experienced" Christians from one another. To those seeking admission to his societies, Wesley wrote:

> Methodists do not impose in order to their admission any opinions whatever. Let them hold particular or general redemption, absolute or conditional decrees; let them be churchmen or dissenters, Presbyterians or Independents, it is no obstacle. . . . [Methodists] think and let think. One condition, and only one, is required—a real desire to save the soul. Where this is, it is enough; they desire no more; they lay stress upon nothing else; they only ask: "Is thy heart herein as my heart? If it be, give me thy hand." [14]

Leaders of the Great Awakening in America had exhibited a similar spirit and urged their converts to "forget party names," laboring instead to deserve the name "Christian" as their "highest distinction." These men were thinking primarily of the unity of spirit which bound together members of different denominations, permitted them to acknowledge one another as Christians, and impelled them to work together in common tasks without seeking partisan advantage. But there were to be others who thought that this type of thinking which affirmed the unity of all "experienced" Christians should lead to the abandonment of all denominational divisions. Believing that a return to the practices of the early church would provide a basis upon which all Christians could unite, their program of action was expressed in Thomas Campbell's slogan: "Where the Scriptures speak, we speak; where the Scriptures are silent, we are silent."

This sentiment first appeared in 1784 among a group of Virginia

[14] Quoted by W. W. Sweet, *The American Churches* (N.Y., 1948), 46–47.

Methodists led by James O'Kelly (1735?–1826). Impressed by the revivalist emphasis upon the name "Christian" as the bond which unites, they resolved to be known by no other name. In 1801 a similar movement was initiated in New England when Abner Jones (1772–1841), a Vermont Baptist, became convinced that "sectarian names and human creeds should be abandoned and that true piety alone . . . should be made the test of Christian fellowship and communion." Three years later in Kentucky the happy relationship with Methodists in the great camp meeting revivals persuaded several Presbyterian ministers, including Barton W. Stone (1772–1844), that Christians could and should live together in love, and they resolved to be known by no other name. A fourth point of origin was in western Pennsylvania where Thomas Campbell (1763–1854) had settled after his arrival from Ireland in 1807. As a student at Glasgow he had been deeply influenced by Scottish Evangelicalism, and he was dismayed that in America he was not permitted to invite all Christians to participate in the communion service. In 1809 he organized the "Christian Association of Washington County, Pa.," and issued a *Declaration and Address* to summon Christians of every denomination to abandon unscriptural doctrines and usages and to restore the original unity and purity of New Testament Christianity. A month later he was joined by his son Alexander (1788–1866), who was destined to become the best-known leader of the western "Christians," or "Disciples of Christ."

There was little communication between the eastern and western "Christians." In the East the "Christians" were gradually brought together in the General Convention of the Christian Church, a body which united with the Congregationalists in 1931. In the West the Campbellites and the Stoneites coalesced to form the larger "Christian" group (the Campbellites tended to prefer the name "Disciples of Christ"). While the Christian movement failed in its objective to unite all Christians, it did succeed in becoming one of the larger Protestant denominations.

In addition to the formation of Methodist or Christian churches, there were other indications of the spreading influence of Wesleyan theology and precept. From a small beginning in New Hampshire, Free-will Baptists penetrated much of the New England hinterland and upstate New York. Nor was the German-speaking population of the mid-Atlantic states immune to Wesleyan influence. Jacob Albright (1759–1808) became a Methodist in 1790, began to preach among the Germans of the mid-Atlantic area in 1796, and after forming his converts into what came to be called the Evangelical Association, was elected its bishop in 1807. Philip William Otterbein (1726–1813), a German Reformed minister in Baltimore, also appropriated Methodist theology and techniques, forming the United Brethren in Christ Church in 1800.[15] The spirit represented by the "Christian movement" also came to the fore among the Germans. Having been censured for revivalist preaching, John Winebrenner (1797–1860) withdrew from the German Reformed Church in 1825 and formed the General Eldership of the Church of God in 1830, announcing his opposition to nonbiblical names, creeds, and forms, and calling for a restoration of primitive purity as the only cure for sectarianism.

ROMAN CATHOLICS. Unlike Judaism whose adherents were not to be greatly augmented numerically until after the Civil War, Roman Catholicism began to experience a steady growth after the Revolution. Prior to independence Roman Catholics were a small minority, many of them landed gentry, concentrated almost exclusively in Maryland and Pennsylvania. The Quebec Act of 1774 had placed the territory between the Ohio and Mississippi rivers within the province of Quebec; this aroused ill-feeling among some ardent patriots who interpreted it as evidence that the British government was ready to surrender this vast inland empire to Roman Catholicism, and it was used as a religious issue to whip up anti-British feeling. By the end of the war, however, apprehensions thus generated had been largely forgotten. Charles Carroll (1737–1832) had rallied his coreligionists in Maryland to the colonial cause, and Irish Catholics in Pennsylvania had demonstrated their unwillingness to dishonor the memory of their fathers by any hesitancy to fight the English. This display of loyalty plus French military support allayed former suspicions, and the birth of the republic ushered in an era of general good feeling.

The Roman Catholic Church in the colonies had been under the jurisdiction of the Vicar Apostolic in London but independence made this arrangement inappropriate. In 1784 John Carroll (1735–1815), a cousin of Charles Carroll, was appointed "superior of the missions" with full responsibility to direct the affairs of the church in the United States, and six years later he was elevated to episcopal rank. In 1808 the diocese of Baltimore was given metropolitan status with Carroll as archbishop.

15 In 1946 the Evangelical Association and the United Brethren combined to form the Evangelical United Brethren Church. In 1968 the merged group united with the Methodist Church.

In the new republic the Roman Catholic Church experienced many growing pains. The number of adherents mounted rapidly, partly as the result of the acquisition of older settlements along the Mississippi but more largely a consequence of new immigration from Ireland and southern Germany. Tension between the older population and more recent arrivals was often acute, and this complicated the task of maintaining an orderly development of church life. The installation of refugee priests from France as pastors of Irish congregations also aroused much resentment.

"Lay trustees" posed one of the more serious problems. All churches in America had been vexed by the self-assertiveness of the laity and the Roman Catholic Church was no exception. In the immediate postwar years, Americans in general were especially conscious of their "rights" and "liberties" and were determined not to be pushed around. The effect of this pervasive spirit upon Roman Catholics was explained by Archbishop Ambrose Maréchal of Baltimore in 1818.

> The American people pursue with a most ardent love the civil liberty which they enjoy. For the principle of civil liberty is paramount with them, so that absolutely all the magistrates from the highest to the lowest are elected by popular vote. . . . Likewise all the Protestant sects . . . are governed by these same principles, and as a result they elect and dismiss their pastors at will. Catholics in turn, living in their midst, are . . . exposed to the danger of admitting the same principles of ecclesiastical government.[16]

They were not only exposed to the danger; many succumbed to it. As early as 1786 the trustees of St. Peter's Church in New York City asserted their right to choose and dismiss their pastor, and three years later the congregation of Holy Trinity Church in Philadelphia followed the example of St. Peter's in choosing their own pastor. Similar acts of disobedience occurred elsewhere. A congregation at Norfolk went so far as to assert that the bishop, according to the "civil rights and religious liberties" guaranteed by the laws of Virginia, had no authority to interfere in the affairs of any congregation or in "any of their religious matters whatever." Even where overt defiance was absent, chronic friction was fre-

---

[16] *Documents of American Catholic History*, ed. J. T. Ellis (Milwaukee, 1955), 219. For a discerning account of the tensions, see James Hennesey, "Square Peg in a Round Hole," *Records of the American Catholic Historical Society of Philadelphia*, LXXXIV (1973), 167–195.

quent. It was not until the custody of property was transferred to the bishops that the situation was finally regularized.

The flood of Roman Catholic immigrants constituted the greatest problem of the church during these years. No fewer than one million immigrants of Roman Catholic background arrived in the United States between 1790 and 1850. Had it not been for extensive assistance from abroad in the form of both funds and personnel, the task of ministering to these new Americans would have been completely impossible. As early as 1791 the French Sulpicians founded St. Mary's Seminary in Baltimore to provide training for a native priesthood but throughout the nineteenth century major reliance had to be placed upon men sent from Europe. The religious orders rendered notable service, especially in the field of education. Colleges, academies, and parochial schools were established. By 1840 there were at least two hundred parochial schools, staffed in part by American sisterhoods which had been growing in number since 1800. The controversy over tax support for parochial schools which was to agitate the life of the nation for more than a century was initiated in 1840 when Bishop John Hughes (1797–1864) of New York petitioned for Roman Catholics to be given a proportionate share of New York City public education funds for their parochial schools.

By 1852, when the First Plenary Council of American bishops was held, the Roman Catholic Church had become the largest single ecclesiastical body in the nation, and a number of noteworthy converts testified to its growing indigenous character. Among these converts were Elizabeth Bayley Seton (1774–1821) who founded the Sisters of Charity; Orestes A. Brownson (1803–1876) whose pilgrimage led him from Presbyterianism into the Universalist and then the Unitarian ministry before he became a Roman Catholic in 1844; and Isaac Thomas Hecker (1819–90), a colleague of Brownson at Brook Farm (see below, pp. 188–89), who became the founder of the Paulist Fathers. Compared with total membership, however, converts did not bulk large, and throughout the rest of the century Roman Catholicism continued to gain its great strength from immigration.

Estimating the influence of the churches

While Roman Catholicism made notable numerical gains during the first half of the nineteenth century, Protestantism in its varied ecclesiastical forms remained overwhelmingly predominant. Religious pluralism as a significant feature of American life was a post-Civil War development which reached its culmination in the twentieth century. By then non-Protestant groups had burgeoned as a result of new patterns of immigration, and Protestantism itself had become fragmented into separate camps by geographical, racial, and theological lines of demarcation which had little to do with the earlier denominational divisions. Unlike the earlier denominationalism, the new lines of Protestant division progressively eroded the earlier Protestant consensus.

During its early years, as we have seen, the United States was a two religion country, with neither faith being pluralistic in any fundamental sense. The one religion was of the republic, while the other was generally regarded as indispensable to the well-being of the republic. "This country," declared Samuel Worcester, "which . . . we may call *our own,* is still *not our own.* God owns it all." [17] God had his design for the nation as well as for the churches. Thus the American Revolution as well as the Great Awakening could be viewed as a prelude to God's perfecting of earthly existence. And while the two faiths were not necessarily related, still they were complementary and not antithetical, each having its own role to perform.

Subsequent chapters will detail the response of the churches to the larger problems bequeathed to them and to the nation by independence. The goal of the churches was a godly nation. Although there may be room for debate as to the adequacy of their understanding of what this implied and as to the propriety of the means they employed in forwarding the goal, one should not be misled in estimating the influence of the churches by interpreting early nineteenth-century statistics of church membership as if they are comparable to twentieth-century membership figures. Church statistics are always uncertain and ambiguous but it is probable that the estimated increase in church membership from one out of every fifteen persons in the total population in 1800 to one out of every eight in 1835 is reasonably accurate. The doubling of membership is significant at a time when requirements for membership had not been notably relaxed. The point at which misunderstanding occurs is when early nineteenth-century church membership is compared to post-Civil War and twentieth-century church membership, for they are not comparable. The American people were not as "unchurched" in 1800 as the statistics would seem to

[17] *Our Country and Our Work* (Salem, 1843), 7.

imply, nor was there as much expansion of the church-related portion of the population after 1835 as swelling membership statistics would seem to indicate. In fact it remained relatively stable throughout the remainder of the century. The confusion has been introduced by a progressive relaxation of membership requirements. The number of people attending Sunday morning worship in the 1830's was usually three times the membership of a church. Furthermore, churches customarily computed their "constituency" (those nominally related but not members) as approximately twice the number of attendants.[18] In terms of twentieth-century definitions of church membership (when what was once "constituency" had become "membership"), the increase of church members from 1800 to 1835 would have been from approximately 40 per cent to about 75 per cent of the population. The estimate of church "constituency" may have been overoptimistic, but the translation of the statistics into twentieth-century terms is sufficiently arresting to confirm reports of contemporaries that by 1835 the churches had won a conspicuous place in the life of the new nation.

But this is to anticipate the story. The initial outlook for the churches was far from auspicious. Most had little reason to expect that by the 1830's, when Alexis de Tocqueville visited the United States, he would report that "there is no country in the world in which the Christian religion retains a greater influence over the souls of men than in America." [19]

[18] Seymour Lipset noted the unanimity with which foreign observers commented on the "exceptional religiosity" of American society from 1830 to World War I and observed that there had been no drastic change in religious adherence during this extended period. *The First New Nation* (N.Y., 1963), 141–50. Allen Wiley, a pioneer presiding elder, provides specific evidence of the early definition of membership when he reported the membership of the Crawfordsville (Indiana) Methodist District for the 1837–38 conference year as roughly 3,000 while those present at services numbered 12,000. Allen Wiley, "Methodism in Southeastern Indiana," *Indiana Magazine of History* (1927). An English Congregationalist visiting Lexington, Kentucky, in 1835, reported that two Presbyterian churches had 300 members and 1,200 at services; two Baptist churches had 200 members and about 1,000 attendants; two Methodist societies had 400 members and 1,100 attendants. Andrew Reed and James Matheson, *A Narrative of the Visit to the American Churches* (N.Y., 1835), I, 132. See also E. S. Gaustad, *Historical Atlas of Religion in America*, 158; *Minutes of the Philadelphia Baptist Association, 1707–1807*, ed. A. D. Gillette (Phila., 1851), 458–59; and Robert Baird, *Religion in America* (N.Y., 1856), 378.

[19] *Democracy in America*, ed. Phillips Bradley (N.Y., 1945), I, 303.

VI

Protestant Expansion
and Consolidation

It took most Protestant churches until about 1800 to regroup and reorder their forces. The initial gloom, shared by Congregationalists and Episcopalians, was voiced by the Presbyterian General Assembly in 1798 when it bewailed the "general dereliction of religious principle and practice among our fellow citizens." Hidden behind such a lamentation of prevailing impiety was a demoralizing recognition these hitherto predominant denominations were rapidly being outpaced in number of adherents by Baptists and Methodists. Still there was sufficient conventional irreligion to disturb those who believed that the health of society depended upon moral principles and virtuous habits inculcated by true religion. More alarming was the aggressive Deism of Thomas Paine (1737–1809), Ethan Allen (1738–89), and Elihu Palmer (1764–1806), for they launched a frontal attack upon the whole concept of revealed religion.[1]

Deist sentiment was not new in America, but hitherto it had been confined to an aristocratic elite who frowned upon widespread dissemi-

[1] See G. A. Koch, *Republican Religion* (N.Y., 1933).

nation of their views because they believed that the "superstitions" of revealed religion did little harm and actually had the beneficial effect of promoting morality among the common people thereby helping preserve good order in society. In the first flush of enthusiasm evoked by the French Revolution, however, Deism was transformed into a popular movement. Pamphleteers began to attack the churches as enemies of progress. Although Robert Baird (1798–1863) later spoke of the French Revolution as that "volcano" which for a time "threatened to sweep the United States into its fiery stream," the danger was more apparent than real.[2] It is true that "deistical societies" were formed and college students took delight in shocking their elders by calling each other Voltaire and Rousseau, but in retrospect it is clear that this "radicalism" had no deep rootage. At the time, however, the danger posed by French "infidelity" seemed real and threatening. The depraved "state of nature" which engulfed France in the years following 1793 dismayed Americans generally and was utilized to discredit the Deist movement. For a decade or two it provided churchmen with an effective hortatory device to rouse the churches from their lethargy and summon them to action.

By 1800 the churches had become aware of another problem that was of continuing concern—the problem presented by the flow of population into the fertile valleys beyond the mountains. Even prior to Independence small pockets of settlement were to be found south of the Ohio River. After 1790 this westward migration became a stampede. Population spread quickly to the Mississippi River. Kentucky was admitted as a state in 1792, Tennessee in 1796, Ohio in 1803, Louisiana in 1812, Indiana in 1816, Alabama in 1817, Illinois in 1818, Mississippi in 1819. By 1821 the Mississippi River was sufficiently breached for Missouri to become a state. Then, without waiting for the intervening territory to be fully occupied, the rush to the Pacific began.

As early as 1760 Ezra Stiles had called attention to the importance of the West, and a sense of alarm was created when it became apparent that within a short time the balance of political power in the new nation would be in the hands of those who were migrating in such numbers to the newer settlements. The great fear was that the people of the West,

2 *Religion in America* (N.Y., 1844), 102. Baird's work is one of the classic accounts of the American religious scene. Philip Schaff drew heavily upon its insights when he wrote *America: A Sketch of Its Political, Social, and Religious Character.*

being far removed from the civilizing and Christianizing influence of the settled communities of the East, would revert to "barbarism" and thus subvert the moral order of society. Throughout the first half of the nineteenth century, an insistence upon the urgent necessity to find means of countering the lapse of the West into barbarism was a repetitive refrain on the lips of earnest churchmen.[3] John England (1786–1842), Roman Catholic bishop of Charleston, South Carolina, recognized the crucial importance of what was to become the heartland of the nation when he declared: "Give us the West, and we shall take care of the East."[4]

Establishing churches and providing a ministry in the newer settlements was to be a task of overwhelming magnitude, but it would be a mistake to draw too sharp a distinction between the East and the West, between conditions of life in the older settlements and on the frontier. The frontier rapidly receded and the new settlements quickly assumed the characteristics of the areas from which the settlers had come. Life in the Kentucky and Tennessee hills did not differ greatly from life in the backcountry regions of Virginia and the Carolinas. Plantations of the southern seaboard were duplicated in Alabama and Mississippi. Replicas of the mansions of Charleston dotted the banks of the Ohio. Farther north, along the trail of westward-migrating Yankees through western New York, Ohio, Michigan, Illinois, and Iowa, farmhouses and villages were almost indistinguishable from those of New England.

Nor did the manner of life differ greatly after the first years. It was a rural society both East and West, and in both East and West there was relative isolation for those who desired it. A European traveler in the East was apt to be as impressed with unbroken stretches of woodland as with vast expanses of open fields. In 1790 there were only six communities with as many as eight thousand inhabitants—New York, Philadelphia, Boston, Charleston, Baltimore, and Salem—and these as seaports were far from typical. And the West almost immediately began to produce port cities of its own. By 1820 Cincinnati and New Orleans were cities of consequence. By 1830 Pittsburgh, Rochester, Buffalo,

---

[3] The most eloquent statement of the threat was Horace Bushnell's *Barbarism, the First Danger* (N.Y., 1847). See also Lyman Beecher's *A Plea for the West* (Cincinnati, 1835), reprinted in part in M. W. Armstrong *et al, The Presbyterian Enterprise*, 140–43. John Mason Peck was also a key figure in publicizing the danger.

[4] Schaff, *America*, 187.

Louisville, and St. Louis were thriving centers with a population that ranked them among the top cities of the country. A decade later Cleveland, Detroit, Chicago, and Milwaukee had become boomtowns of importance.

There were differences, to be sure. The population in the West was younger and more uninhibited. Migration was a selective process. As a rule only the more adventurous and sturdy-spirited were willing to undertake the long trek to unsettled areas. But, basically, the population mirrored its own background. Where there were many who tended to be crude, turbulent, and illiterate, as was true along the tributaries of the lower Ohio, they did not differ greatly in these respects from the inhabitants of the regions from whence they had come. In religion, the strands linking the West to the East were equally evident. Methodists tended to be exuberant wherever they were. Kentucky revivalists were mostly products of Virginia and North Carolina. The revivalists who preceded and followed Charles G. Finney (see pp. 140–43) in western New York made repeated tours of New England. Lyman Beecher on one occasion, it is true, said that if Finney ever came to New England, he would meet him at the border and fight him all the way to Boston. But later it was Beecher who invited Finney to come to Boston. Edwin S. Gaustad has called attention to the fact that during the first half of the nineteenth century the churches were engaged not only in a "conquest of the West" but also in a "reconquest of the East," and both these conquests were closely interrelated and can be understood only as part of a single surge of new religious life and activity.[5]

The second awakening

As was to be expected in the light of past experience, an initial reaction of Protestant churches to the need for action was a renewed emphasis upon the tried and proved expedient of revivalistic preaching. This preaching, in turn, helped provoke the great wave of revivals, known as "the Second Great Awakening," which swept back and forth across the country for almost two generations.

The onset of the Second Awakening is difficult to chart,[6] for it

[5] *Historical Atlas of Religion in America*, 37, 42.
[6] See B. A. Weisberger, *They Gathered at the River* (Boston, 1958), and J. B. Boles, *The Great Revival, 1787–1805: Origins of the Southern Evangelical Mind* (Lexington, 1972).

appeared in many localities almost simultaneously. The earlier colonial Awakening had continued to some degree among both Baptists and Methodists. And during the 1790's scattered revivals had appeared among Congregationalists in more remote sections of New England. In Virginia the most significant event was a revival among students at Hampden-Sydney and Washington colleges in 1787, which sent thirty to forty men into the Presbyterian ministry. Joined by James Mc-Gready (1758?–1817), a graduate of the "log college" at Washington, Pennsylvania, these young men fanned out into the Carolinas, Kentucky, and Tennessee, and were responsible for the quickening religious interest which culminated in 1800 in a widely attended revival in Logan County, Kentucky. Excitement generated in Logan County spread rapidly throughout Kentucky and Tennessee; back into the Carolinas, Virginia, and western Pennsylvania; then northward into new settlements beyond the Ohio River. In central and western New York there were revivals of sufficient scope in 1800 for local annalists to refer to that year as the year of "the great revival." And in 1802 there was a revival at Yale where, as the result of a notable series of chapel sermons by Timothy Dwight (1752–1817), one-third of the students professed conversion. President Dwight stumbled into the revival inadvertently. Distressed by "freethinking" views among the students, he boldly launched an attack seeking to demonstrate that the only alternative to godliness was first anarchy and then despotism. The intensity of the response was surprising. It convinced Dwight that revivals could be exploited as an effective antidote to "infidelity," and this he proceeded to do.

The revival at Yale was significant for several reasons. Dwight commanded wide respect among conservatives and under his leadership the heirs of the moderate antirevivalist party in New England were brought into the revivalist camp. It was also significant in terms of the students it sent out to become leaders of the revival campaign, most notably Lyman Beecher (1775–1863) and Nathaniel W. Taylor (1786–1858). Beecher was to be the great organizer and promoter of the New England Awakening, while Taylor was the theologian who worked out the appeal and provided the intellectual defense.[7] Finally, through the contagion of Yale's example the revival spread to other

[7] See S. E. Mead, *Nathaniel W. Taylor* (Chicago, 1942).

colleges and soon became an established institution on most American campuses with the number of "hopeful converts" being regularly reported. In this way additional leadership was recruited to carry on the campaign.

The new revivalism was markedly different from the revivalism of the first Awakening under Jonathan Edwards when the outpouring of God's spirit was regarded as a by-product of the faithful preaching of God's Word. Christians "waited" for these earlier revivals, Calvin Colton remarked, "as men are wont to wait for showers of rain, without even imagining that any duty was incumbent upon them as instruments."[8] In the Second Awakening a change began to be introduced. More and more preachers sought to provoke a revival by utilizing "means" that were calculated to cause hearers to make a decision and to make it right. Thus the revival became a technique—a technique that had been taking shape earlier, but never had it been quite so instrumental in character. Heretofore the revival had always been in a sense an end in itself. Now it became an adjunct to other ends, and a discourse could be written on "The Necessity of Revivals of Religion to the Perpetuity of our Civil and Religious Institutions."[9]

The early revivals in the West were not greatly dissimilar in character to those in the East, but there was a more undisciplined emotionalism. The western revivalists in the early years were dealing with a moving, floating, migrating population, and they were operating in areas where opportunities for Christian nurture were few and often non-existent. Consequently they had to push for much quicker decisions than their eastern contemporaries. Subject to this coercion, revivalists in the West tended to turn on all the heat they could and appeal to the emotions more than to the intellect. This was especially true in Kentucky and Tennessee where much of the earlier population was unusually rough, turbulent, and unlettered. In the upland regions of the South, from whence they had come, opportunities for schooling had been scant, and uninhibited displays of religious emotion had been frequent. Many of them were like Augustus Longstreet's "honest Georgian" who "preferred his whiskey straight and his politics and religion red hot."

[8] *History and Character of American Revivals of Religion* (London, 1832), 2–6.
[9] It was published as an article in *The Spirit of the Pilgrims* of 1831. See *The Shaping of American Religion*, ed. J. W. Smith and A. L. Jamison, 362.

CAMP MEETINGS. A distinctive feature of frontier religious life was the camp meeting[10]—a technique developed by the fiery Presbyterian minister James McGready. McGready stormed into Kentucky in 1796 to become pastor of three small congregations in Logan county on the Tennessee border—a section Peter Cartwright (1785–1872) labeled "Rogue's Harbor." Of the area Cartwright said: "There was not a newspaper printed south of the Green River, no mill short of forty miles, and no schools worth the name. We killed our meat out of the woods, wild; and beat our meal. . . . As for coffee, I am not sure that I ever smelled it for ten years."[11] Among these backwoodsmen, McGready's impassioned preaching elicited a growing response. Many, he reported, were struck with "an awful sense of their lost estate." But it was not until 1800 that their pent-up emotions burst loose.

A four-day sacramental meeting was held at Red River in June. Two Presbyterian ministers, William Hodges and John Rankin, were there to assist McGready, and the two McGee brothers—William, a Presbyterian minister, and John, a Methodist minister—were also present. During the first three days McGready, Hodges, and Rankin spoke, and several times the audience was reduced to tears. On the final day, John McGee—the Methodist brother—could restrain himself no longer. He rose and began to exhort the people "to let the Lord Omnipotent reign in their hearts." When a woman "shouted" for mercy, he moved to her side.

> Several spoke to me: "You know these people. Presbyterians are much for order. They will not bear this confusion. Go back and be quiet." I turned to go back and was near falling, [but] the power of God was strong upon me. I turned again, and losing sight of fear of man, I went through the house shouting and exhorting with all possible ecstasy and energy.

Soon the floor was "covered by the slain" and "their screams for mercy pierced the heavens." According to McGready, the most notorious

[10] C. A. Johnson, *The Frontier Camp Meeting* (Dallas, 1955), and D. D. Bruce, *And They All Sang Hallelujah: Plain-folk Camp-meeting Religion* (Knoxville, 1974).
[11] Cartwright was a Methodist circuit-rider and his *Autobiography* is a vivid and fascinating account of frontier life. A voluminous collection of source materials is contained in W. W. Sweet's four volumes, *Religion on the American Frontier*.

"profane swearers and Sabbath-breakers" were "pricked to the heart" and many were "crying out 'what shall we do to be saved?' "[12]

News of the excitement at Red River spread rapidly, and it was duplicated at Gasper River in July where makeshift tents were erected to accommodate people coming from distances as great as 50 and 100 miles. Underbrush was cleared away so services could be held out-of-doors. Success at Gasper River led to the staging of other camp meetings which drew larger and larger crowds. The most famous of them all was at Cane Ridge in Bourbon county the following summer, when the number attending was variously estimated from ten to twenty-five thousand. Even ten thousand was a striking total at a time when Lexington, the largest settlement in the state, had only 1,795 inhabitants.

Whatever the actual numbers may have been at the camp meetings, there was abundant confusion. Preachers of every denomination attended and were encouraged to exhort the throng simultaneously from preaching stands erected at suitable distances. People would drift from one stand to another. They would gather in smaller groups to hear recent converts relate their experiences, then burst into hymns of praise. With "the traditionally slow cycle of guilt, despair, hope, and assurance" being compressed into a few days or even hours, the emotional stress was agonizingly intensified and it cut deep into normal restraint. Not only were there outbursts of weeping and shouts of joy; in the frenzied excitement of the moment individuals were suddenly swept into physical "exercises"—falling, running, jumping, jerking—which were attributed to the smiting power of the Holy Spirit. Accounts of these physical manifestations were undoubtedly exaggerated by both friendly and hostile witnesses but they were sufficiently numerous to arouse misgivings in the minds of many.

The camp meetings caused the faithful to rejoice. There is no way to prove that they elevated the moral tone of communities along the tributaries of the Ohio, but in 1801 George Baxter, president of Washington College in Virginia, had no doubts on this score.

> I found Kentucky . . . the most moral place I had ever been. A profane expression was hardly ever heard. A religious awe seemed to pervade the country. Upon the whole, I think the revival in Kentucky the most extraordinary that has ever visited the church of Christ; and

[12] Johnson, *The Frontier Camp Meeting*, 34–35. Weisberger, 24–25.

all things considered, it was peculiarly adapted to the circumstances of that country. . . . Something of an extraordinary nature seemed necessary to arrest the attention of a giddy people who were ready to conclude that Christianity was a fable and futurity a dream. This revival has done it. It has confounded infidelity, awed vice into silence, and brought numbers beyond calculation under serious impressions.[13]

More tangible evidence of the beneficent effect of camp meetings was the swelling membership of the churches. In Kentucky alone between 1800 and 1803 Baptists gained more than 10,000 members, and Methodists had an equal number of accessions. Presbyterian growth may have been as large but it was obscured and then reduced by a triple secession.

Many Presbyterians were disturbed by the camp-meeting extravagances they had helped foster. In 1805 the General Assembly expressed stern disapproval when it announced that "God is a God of order and not of confusion, and whatever tends to destroy the comely order of his worship is not from him." The disenchantment of the General Assembly had been hastened by the tendency of Presbyterian camp-meeting revivalists to accept "the doctrine of grace as held by the Methodists" and by their laxity in enforcing educational standards for ordination. Both issues led or were leading to schism. The first, centering on doctrine, was the "New Light" schism of 1803 which, under the leadership of Barton W. Stone, was quickly transmuted into the Kentucky wing of the "Christian movement." The second had its beginnings in 1805 when the Cumberland presbytery was dissolved by the Synod of Kentucky for ordaining "illiterate" exhorters. The problem of the presbytery had been to find ministers for mushrooming churches. When repeated appeals to the General Assembly proved unavailing, revivalist members of the presbytery formed what was to become the Cumberland Presbyterian Church. A third secession took place in 1805 when Shaker emissaries from New York won a considerable number of Presbyterians in Kentucky and southern Ohio, including three ministers, to the peculiar tenets of Ann Lee (see below, pp. 184–86).

If Presbyterians had trouble handling the energies generated by camp meetings, Methodists did not. They were accustomed to noise and excitement and were accustomed to "on-the-job" training for their

---

[13] Quoted from the *Methodist Magazine* (London), XXVI (1803), 93, by L. W. Bacon, *A History of American Christianity* (N.Y., 1907), 237.

preachers. Furthermore, the theology of the camp-meeting exhorters with its implicit rejection of predestination and its explicit emphasis upon salvation as potentially available to all, which proved so divisive among Presbyterians, posed no problem for Methodists. This was the gospel they had preached from the beginning. At Gasper River it was a Methodist preacher, John McGee, who set the theological tone for camp meetings by demonstrating that the hardest sinners would respond if it was made clear by a blunt approach that in winning one's way to heaven the help of the Holy Spirit would not be denied the truly penitent.

Within a few years camp meetings had become almost a Methodist preserve. By 1811 Methodists were holding their own camp meetings— at least four hundred of them scattered throughout the country. As camp meetings were domesticated by Methodists and adapted to conditions of life in other sections of the nation, much of the frenzied excitement of the first years disappeared. Grounds were policed, admittance restricted, crowds carefully controlled, and the meetings became much more sober, dignified, and orderly. By the 1830's, even among Methodists, camp meetings had become occasions when the faithful gathered to combine an annual outing with an opportunity to listen to inspirational addresses. Ultimately the camp grounds—at Chautauqua, New York; Ocean Grove, New Jersey; Junaluska, North Carolina; Oak Bluffs, Massachusetts; Bayview, Michigan; and elsewhere—became conference centers or summer resorts.

The camp meeting as such did not play a great part in the development of American religious life because it was the product of the scattered population and isolated life of frontier society. When this isolation was replaced by settled communities with a social life of their own, the death knell of the camp meeting as an effective evangelistic technique had been sounded. A new technique—the protracted meeting—was developed to marshal the group pressure that camp meetings had demonstrated to be so successful in inducing conversions.

NEW MEASURES. A distinctive thrust of the Second Awakening took shape in central and western New York under the aegis of Charles G. Finney (1792–1875).[14] Until Finney appeared, the northern phase

14 Whitney R. Cross, *The Burned-over District: The Social and Intellectual History of Enthusiastic Religion in Western New York*, a case-study of the westward transit of New England culture, details Finney's activities.

of the Awakening had been kept firmly in the hands of settled ministers and only ordinary "means of grace" had been used. Even when the "gifts" of a traveling evangelist such as Ashahel Nettleton (1783–1844) were utilized, the evangelist stayed with the local pastor, preached the Sunday sermons, delivered an extra lecture or two, participated in the prayer meeting, and visited the homes. Disorder and confusion were discouraged. If an audience began to show signs of undue emotion, the people were apt to be dismissed and the distraught counseled in private. Finney was too impatient to put up with such restraint. Before his conversion in 1821, Finney did not think Christians were really sincere. How could they believe that people "were on the verge of hell and yet be so indifferent in regard to this terrific fact"? If he were ever converted, he said, he would be a Christian in earnest and "pull men out of the fire."

At twenty-nine Finney, a lawyer in Adams, New York, was by his own confession a sinful, worldly man. He attended the Presbyterian church, led the choir, and debated theological points with the pastor. But the dazzling insight which led to his conversion was the product of his own reflection. While walking to his office one morning, it dawned upon him that salvation was much simpler than he had supposed. All that was needed to receive it was "my own consent to give up my sins and accept Christ." As he remembered it, he stopped in the middle of the street and said to himself: "I will accept it today or I will die in the attempt." He recalled the Scripture: "Then shall ye go and pray unto me, and I will hearken unto you" (Jer. 29:12). To Finney this was a contract and that night his prayers were answered with a "mighty baptism" that overwhelmed him. "The Holy Spirit descended upon me in a manner that seemed to go through me body and soul. . . . I wept aloud with joy and love; and I do not know but I should say, I literally bellowed out the unutterable gushings of my heart." The next morning when a deacon of the church reminded him of a case in court that was set for ten o'clock, Finney's response was immediate and decisive: "Deacon B———, I have a retainer from the Lord Jesus Christ to plead his cause, and I cannot plead yours."[15]

Finney pursued his theological studies under George W. Gale (1789–1861), the Presbyterian pastor at Adams, and began to make

[15] Finney's account of his conversion is printed in Smith, Handy, and Loetscher, *American Christianity*, II, 19–24.

preaching expeditions to nearby communities. In 1824 a Female Missionary Society sent him on a missionary tour of Jefferson County. He began at Evans Mills and Antwerp where he converted "the great mass of the population." He had equal success in other communities. Six feet two inches in height, with great piercing eyes that had an uncanny hypnotic effect, he was a commanding figure in the pulpit. He had few mannerisms. He spoke the simple language of everyday life. He said that he merely talked about things the preachers preached about, but he did it with a bluntness few could evade. In 1825 he moved into the Mohawk valley. The village of Western was the first to catch fire. Then Rome exploded, and Utica, Boonville, and Verona were swept by the conflagration. By this time Finney was attracting national attention. He was wanted everywhere at once. In 1817 he went to Wilmington, Delaware, spent the winter in Philadelphia, and in 1828 made a brief foray into New York City.

Finney is said to have arrived in New York City with "his backwoods invasion of civilization" at about the time Andrew Jackson entered the White House. The comment is misleading for neither Finney nor Jackson were backcountry rustics. Finney was trained as a lawyer, had mastered the points of theology with sufficient thoroughness to write a highly regarded book on systematic theology, and ended his career as a professor and then president of Oberlin. His great talent was to make complicated doctrines as clear and sensible as the multiplication table. He noted that his success was greatest with business and professional classes. Rochester, scene of his greatest triumph, was typical in this respect. "The exceptional feature," Whitney Cross observed, "was the phenomenal dignity of this awakening. No agonizing souls fell in the aisles, no raptured ones shouted hallelujahs. . . . The great evangelist, 'in an unclerical suit of gray,' acted 'like a lawyer arguing . . . before a court and jury,' talking precisely, logically, with wit, verve, and informality. Lawyers, real-estate magnates, millers, manufacturers, and commercial tycoons led the parade of the regenerated."[16]

The controversial feature of Finney's revivals were his "new measures."[17] As a lawyer, he refused to be inhibited from winning his case by being restricted to conventional means. His were the tactics of a trial lawyer. He said "you" instead of "they" when speaking of the wicked,

16 *The Burned-over District*, 155. For a detailed analysis, see P. E. Johnson, *A Shopkeeper's Millennium* (N.Y., 1978).

17 See his *Lectures on Revivals*, ed. W. G. McLoughlin (Cambridge, 1960).

and on occasion did not hesitate to mention a notorious sinner by name. The "convicted" were brought forward to the "anxious bench"— a front pew roughly analogous to the witness stand—where attention was centered upon them and where they dramatized the struggle for heaven in the soul of everyone. Women, to the scandal of many, were encouraged to testify and pray in public. The greatest "innovation" was Finney's adaptation of the revival to an urban environment. The entire community was mobilized by bands of workers visiting the homes. Prayer meetings were held at "unseasonable hours"—unseasonable, that is, for farmers. And the conventional routine of stated services—Sunday sermons and a weekday lecture—was displaced by special services held each night and prolonged for hours in inquiry sessions. This was the "protracted meeting"—a community-wide revival campaign of several weeks duration—which was designed to marshal the group pressure in settled areas that the camp meeting had been so effective in fostering on the frontier. In a real sense, the protracted meeting was the camp meeting brought to town.

While the urban phase of the Second Awakening can be seen most clearly in the person and activity of Finney, it must not be supposed that it was the work of a single man.[18] There were others who were already proceeding along the path he was to take, and Finney gathered about him many zestful young graduates of the revival-infected colleges, and he established training institutes for other young converts. In more remote areas his methods were widely copied—among Lutherans and Dutch Reformed as well as among Presbyterians, Congregationalists, Baptists, and Methodists. Even Quakers under the leadership of a visiting Englishman, Joseph John Gurney (1788–1847), conformed to the general pattern.[19] In 1832 Albert Barnes of Philadelphia reported that there was scarcely "a city or town or peaceful hamlet" in the country that had not been "hallowed" by a revival. A decade later Robert Baird noted that revivals has become "a constituent part of the religious system" to such an extent that "he who should oppose himself to revivals, as such, would be regarded by most of our evangelical Christians as, *ipso facto*, an enemy to spiritual religion itself."[20]

[18] Daniel Nash, Jedediah Burchard, James Boyle, Luther Myrick, Jabez Swan, and Jacob Knapp were a few of the better-known men who actively promoted the revival.
[19] See D. E. Swift, *Joseph John Gurney* (Middletown, Conn., 1962).
[20] Quoted by S. E. Mead in *The Ministry in Historical Perspectives*, ed. H. R. Niebuhr and D. D. Williams, 226, 227.

ROLE OF WOMEN. A striking feature of the revivals was the predominance of women among the converts. Women may or may not have been more religious than men, but for women a conversion experience could provide some release from the constraints of male domination. It could be something of a declaration of independence for it was a renunciation of the past and involved a resolute determination to pursue a new independent pattern of life. "The new birth," Donald G. Mathews has said, "was just what it was represented to be, a new entry into a new kind of life," often to the consternation of those upon whom a woman had been psychologically dependent.[21]

The ritual following conversion and preceding church membership also contributed to a woman's sense of self-confidence. She was expected to stand before the congregation and publicly profess her faith by relating her conversion experience. In many circles women, like children, were expected to be seen and not heard. For a woman to become the center of attention by engaging in an act of public speaking to an attentive audience conferred upon her a claim to respect and honor. "She had stood up in meeting on her own," says Mathews, and expressed "some of her most private thoughts which were accepted by the community as significant and praiseworthy." She also had learned to cite Biblical texts and opinions expressed by the preacher to counter pronouncements of other males, thus finding room for additional maneuver.

More important than these primary aspects of evangelical religion in creating psychological and social space for women was the way in which such evangelists as Finney used females in the organizational work of the revivals. In similar fashion female auxiliaries to the voluntary societies (see below pp. 146–47, 150–53) provided opportunities for women to participate in affairs outside the home, assume responsibility, and perfect leadership skills. Initially the auxiliaries were local groups, primarily responsible for accumulating funds for charitable and missionary projects, but in the end they served as channels to participation in affairs on the national scene. Moreover, on occasion, women in a more direct fashion would burst the bonds of male authority to function in a mixed society. This occurred when a woman's

[21] See *Religion in the Old South* (Chicago, 1977), 103–109.

account of her conversion was so profoundly moving that she would be asked to repeat her testimony and thus became in effect a traveling evangelist. This phenomenon was most common among Wesleyan groups (i.e., groups with a Wesleyan theology—Methodists, Free Will Baptists, Christians or Disciples), although it had long been commonplace among Quakers. It was to lead some women to become "prophetesses" with groups of their own.

Finally, imbued with the sense of mission generated by evangelicalism, the enthusiasm of women readily spilled over into their own specific concerns, the most prominent of which were female education and woman's suffrage (see below, pp. 155–56, 200, 204–05).

Missionary and educational activity

While revivals swelled membership rolls and generated enthusiasm and energy, Protestant expansion was primarily the product of missionary activity. This was especially true in Maine, Vermont, western New York, western Pennsylvania, and the vast area surrounding the Great Lakes; and it continued to be the principal means employed as the frontier marched westward to the Pacific. It was also true even in the camp meeting territory bounded by the watershed of the Ohio. Here the groundwork had been laid by men sent out to gather congregations and establish churches. Even among Methodists who utilized camp meetings most widely, the meetings did no more than supplement the regular work of churches carried on from day to day by circuit-riders and class leaders.

Prior to the Second Awakening, the typical form of missionary activity was for presbyteries, associations, and synods to secure the release of settled pastors for brief periods so that they could go on missionary tours of newer settlements. On these tours the pastors would seek out professing Christians, attempt to win new converts, and where possible establish churches. The major burden was carried by those bodies located nearest the frontier, since other synods and associations were less advantageously located to participate in this informal type of missionary endeavor.

By 1800 it was apparent that a more systematic approach to missionary activity was needed. With the stampede to the West that began in 1790, distances became too great and new settlements too numerous to be left to the haphazard and intermittent efforts of pastors on leave as short-term missionaries. For a task so large the full resources of the churches had to be marshaled. Recognition of this need coincided with the onset of the Second Awakening which quickened missionary interest and concern. The consequence was that the energies released by the revivals were channeled into a new missionary thrust.

EARLY MISSIONARY SOCIETIES. It has often been noted that whenever the English are confronted by an urgent need, the instinctive reaction is to form a committee or "voluntary society" of like-minded friends to do what needs to be done. In England this had been the technique of securing quick and concerted action throughout the seventeenth century, and at the beginning of the eighteenth century societies had been formed for a variety of ends, including the reformation of manners, the promotion of Christian knowledge, and the propagation of the gospel. With the rise of new evangelical zeal at the end of the century, this folk-pattern of response found expression in the formation of foreign mission, Bible, and tract societies. Nor had the colonists been oblivious to the advantages of the voluntary society technique. They used it to promote mission activity among the Indians, to forestall an American episcopate, to mobilize resistance to the Stamp Act, and—through committees of public safety—to initiate the Revolutionary struggle.

With this heritage, it was inevitable that voluntary societies would be formed to enable the churches to match the increasing pace of settlement with a more systematic and widely supported missionary endeavor.[22] The beginning of the new era in mission activity is usually dated from the founding of the New York Missionary Society in 1796 by Presbyterians, Baptists, and Dutch Reformed. The primary object of this society, however, was to promote Indian missions. The Missionary Society of Connecticut, organized by Congregationalists in 1798, was the first society to undertake the establishment of churches in frontier areas. Similar societies were formed in Massachusetts and New Hampshire. Baptists followed suit with the Massachusetts Baptist Domestic Missionary Society in 1802, a society in Pennsylvania in 1803, in Maine

[22] The two standard accounts of this development are O. W. Elsbree, *The Rise of the Missionary Spirit in America, 1780–1815* (Williamsport, Pa., 1928), and C. B. Goodykoontz, *Home Missions on the American Frontier* (Caldwell, Idaho, 1939).

in 1804, and in New York in 1806. Presbyterians were more ambivalent. For more than a generation they were unable to make up their minds whether to channel their efforts through voluntary societies or the General Assembly. Actually they did both. They formed the Western Missionary Society in 1800, participated in several New York societies, and at the same time the General Assembly in 1802 appointed a Standing Committee on Missions. Episcopalians, preoccupied with internal problems, gave little thought to the frontier. Not until 1821 was their Domestic and Foreign Missionary Society organized. Methodists were also tardy in forming their first missionary society (1819), but they had little need of this type of organization since every conference was in effect a missionary society and every itinerant a missionary. As soon as a traveling elder could be recruited, a circuit would be laid out that would take him to the newest settlements no matter how remote. A Presbyterian missionary in Kentucky paid tribute to the effectiveness of the Methodist system when he reported that wherever he went a circuit-rider had preceded him.

> I at length became ambitious to find a family whose cabin had not been entered by a Methodist preacher. . . . . I traveled from settlement to settlement . . . , but into every hovel I entered I learned that the Methodist missionary had been there before me.[23]

Nothing daunted the circuit-riders. This was made clear by the common remark, when people wished to describe the severity of a blizzard or cloudburst, that "nobody was out but crows and Methodist preachers."

The touring missionaries, whether Presbyterian, Congregational, or Baptist, functioned in much the same way as the circuit-riders.[24] They preached wherever they could gain a hearing, and had an ample supply of books and pamphlets to distribute. Instead of forming "classes," they formed any small cluster of hopeful Christians into a "conference." The goal of the missionaries was to transform one of the conferences as soon as possible into a church and to win sufficient support to become settled pastors. This allowed the sending society to utilize its funds to send out additional missionaries. For his part, the

[23] A. H. Redford, *History of Methodism in Kentucky* (Nashville, 1868–76), 530.
[24] See M. W. Armstrong, *et al.*, *The Presbyterian Enterprise*, 106–08, for an extract from the journal of a Presbyterian "circuit-rider."

former traveling missionary would provide what supervision he could to neighboring conferences, seeking to nurture them into full-fledged churches.

The transition from conference to church was not always easy to effect, for this implied assuming responsibility for paying the preacher, and money was scarce. But if money was scarce, land was not. Life was simple and one could readily become self-supporting. Ministers often supplemented their meager stipend by tilling a few acres. Sometimes they supported themselves until a church was strong enough to maintain them. The latter practice was most common among Baptists, particularly on the southern frontier. Typical in this respect was Joab Powell (1799–1873) of Tennessee who experienced a call to preach as a Baptist minister. Not waiting for a missionary society to send him, he went to Missouri where he spent twenty years farming and preaching, before moving on to Oregon where he gained fame as an itinerant revivalist. As early as 1757 the Synod of Philadelphia noted that Presbyterians in the newer settlements "were highly pleased with the prevailing principle that gospel ministers should work for their living and preach for charity" with the result that many have "struggled and earned their bread in a great measure with the sweat of their brows."[25] Three-quarters of a century later in Illinois, a Baptist missionary encountered the same spirit. He had preached sixty-nine sermons and baptized twenty-two persons, and the people had said to him: "We love to hear you preach. Come as often as you can." But when he reminded them that "the laborer is worthy of his hire," they began to grumble about "missionary-beggars" and "money-hunters."[26]

A clash of cultures along the Ohio River aggravated the problem. Farther north eastern-educated missionaries were readily accepted. In western New York, Aaron Kinne reported in 1793 that "the principal part of the inhabitants are directly or indirectly from New England and retain the spirit and manners of their native states," being "exemplary in their reverence for the Sabbath, zeal for religious worship, and the decent manner in which they attend." There were exceptions, as at Tioga on the Pennsylvania border where people were "intemperate," "contentious," and pleased to be "without law, without order, without

25 M. W. Armstrong, et al., The Presbyterian Enterprise, 69.
26 Goodykoontz, Home Missions on the American Frontier, 205.

Sabbaths, and without God in the world."[27] On the southern frontier, preachers had learned to address themselves to analogues of those at Tioga, and ill-feeling flared when the two streams of migration met. People from south of the Ohio had become accustomed to a stronger brew than missionaries were prepared to provide. Missionaries reminded Peter Cartwright, a rough-hewn Methodist circuit-rider, of "pale lettuce growing under the shade of a peach tree." He told one of them that he should "quit reading his old manuscript sermons and learn to speak extemporaneously" or "the Methodists would set the whole western world on fire before he could light his match."[28] Glasgow-educated Alexander Campbell was equally contemptuous of the products of the "priest factories" who had not learned to speak the idiom of the people. Missionaries who came into the area with the northern stream of migration, on the other hand, often sent back disparaging reports of preachers who had been schooled by the necessities of the southern frontier. John Mason Peck (1789–1838), pioneer Baptist missionary in southern Illinois and Missouri, reflected this bias when he declared that one-third of the preachers in this region were "doing positive injury to religion" while another third were able to render no more than "minor service."[29] Given these conflicting views, it is understandable that antimission sentiment should have arisen. Still it was localized and, apart from enclaves among Baptists, did not long endure.

VOLUNTARY SOCIETIES AND A NATIONAL STRATEGY. The initial decades of the nineteenth century witnessed, first, the proliferation of voluntary societies and, then, their coordination in the interest of a unified strategy for the nation as a whole.[30]

The earliest societies were local and regional missionary societies devoted to establishing churches. Other societies serviced the mission enterprise—Bible and tract societies furnished necessary literature, Sunday school societies provided religious instruction for children, and education societies established colleges and seminaries to supply trained missionary personnel and pastors. A third group of societies promoted a

27 *Ibid.*, 113.
28 Sweet, *Religion on the American Frontier*, III, 257–58.
29 Goodykoontz, *Home Missions on the American Frontier*, 33.
30 For the unified strategy, see C. I. Foster, *An Errand of Mercy: The Evangelical United Front* (Chapel Hill, N.C., 1958), 160. It is placed in context by R. T. Handy, *A Christian America* (N.Y., 1971).

wide variety of humanitarian causes and projects for moral and social reform. Societies became so numerous and varied that Orestes Brownson complained that "matters have come to such a pass that a peaceable man can hardly venture to eat or drink, to go to bed or get up, to correct his children or kiss his wife" without the guidance and sanction of some society.[31]

The picture of confusion that one might gain from the multiplicity of societies would be misleading. There was purpose in the apparent disorder. To understand this one must appreciate what was regarded as the peculiar genius of the voluntary society. The voluntary society, first of all, was an instrument for quick and concerted action by concerned individuals with no need to wait until some official body could be persuaded to act. A few friends could take the initiative and then, through the society they created, proceed to enlist the broadest possible support for the attainment of a single objective. Members of a society might be divided on other issues but on this single issue they could unite. Furthermore, by limiting a society to a single objective, the possibility of its energies being diverted and diluted by other concerns would be avoided. "Concentrated action is powerful action" was the way the manifesto of the American Bible Society put it. Finally, the voluntary societies which united "the best hearts, the most willing hands, and the most vigorous and untiring enterprise" in common tasks were regarded as the heaven-sent means by which the divided denominations could pool their efforts to meet particular needs.[32]

Four factors converged to give the voluntary societies their distinctive character. First, Protestants had become increasingly conscious of the ties binding them together. S. S. Schmucker (1799–1873) of the Lutheran seminary at Gettysburg declared that while each evangelical (the qualification is important) "denomination must naturally prefer its own peculiarities," it is a "dangerous error" to regard "these peculiarities as equal in importance with the great fundamentals of our holy religion held in common by all." In similar vein Samuel Miller (1769–1850) at Princeton said "it would never occur to us to place the peculiarities of our creed among the fundamentals of our common

[31] Stow Persons, *American Minds* (N.Y., 1958), 160.
[32] Smith, Handy, and Loetscher, *American Christianity*, I, 555; and Lyman Beecher writing of national needs in *The National Preacher*, III (1829), 154.

Christianity." Albert Barnes was even more explicit, asserting that "the church of Christ is not under the Episcopal form, or the Baptist, the Methodist, the Presbyterian or the Congregational form exclusively; all are, to all intents and purposes, to be recognized as parts of the one holy catholic church."[33]

Second, the revival campaigns stressed a doctrine of "disinterested benevolence" that had been elaborated by Samuel Hopkins and Nathaniel W. Taylor.[34] Sin was defined as including "selfishness," and the effect of conversion was to shift "the controlling preference of the mind" from a "preference for self-interest" to a "preference for disinterested benevolence." If one's conversion was genuine, it was insisted, this shift in the preference of the mind would express itself in action. The conversion experience, therefore, was not the end of the Christian life but only its beginning. Working was as necessary as believing, and working meant participating fully in every good cause.

Third, as a corollary to their understanding of conversion as a transformed ethical life, the revivalists merged a stress on Christian perfection with older Puritan theological ways of thinking. Nathaniel W. Taylor and Lyman Beecher led the way in making the adjustment, but Asa Mahan and Charles G. Finney were responsible for giving widespread currency to perfectionist ideas among non-Wesleyan Protestants and for elaborating them in ways that were congenial to Methodist piety.[35]

Fourth, the concern of the churches was not simply to evangelize individuals but also to remake society. They were heirs of the millennial tradition voiced by Mark Hopkins (1802–87), president of Williams College, when he declared that the time was coming when "wars, and intemperance, and licentiousness, and fraud, and slavery, and all oppression" shall be brought to an end "through the transforming influence of Christianity.[36] While this was to be "the Lord's doing," Christians could help speed the coming of the perfect society by promoting revivals, establishing churches, and participating in the host

[33] Schmucker, Miller, and Barnes are quoted by S. E. Mead in *The Ministry in Historical Perspectives*, ed. H. Richard Niebuhr and D. D. Williams, 222–24.
[34] See selection from Hopkins illustrating his view in Smith, Handy, and Loetscher, *American Christianity*, I, 539–45. For Taylor, see *ibid.*, II, 28–36.
[35] See Timothy L. Smith, "The Doctrine of the Sanctifying Spirit," *Wesleyan Theological Journal*, XIII (1978), 93–94.
[36] Ralph Gabriel, *The Course of American Democratic Thought* (N.Y., 1940), 36.

of societies designed to counter the evils Hopkins had listed as well as others he had neglected to mention.

The societies had local beginnings but within a decade or two they were pulled together into national organizations to coordinate their work throughout the country. This was particularly true after 1818 when the fight to save the establishment in Connecticut was lost, thus permitting Lyman Beecher—the real architect of the voluntary system in America—to devote full attention to transforming the societies into "a gigantic religious power," thoroughly "systematized" and "compact" in organization.[37]

There was little difficulty in combining most local reform and service societies into national organizations on an interdenominational basis. The American Bible Society and the American Education Society were the earliest, being formed in 1816; the American Colonization Society was next in 1817; then the American Sunday School Union was formed in 1824, the American Tract Society in 1825, the American Temperance Society in 1826, the American Peace Society in 1828, and the American Antislavery Society in 1833. Unlike the reform societies, extra precautions had to be taken to preserve the interdenominational character of the Sunday school and tract societies. The publishing committee of the American Tract Society, for example, was composed of an equal number of Baptists, Congregationalists, Dutch Reformed, Episcopalians, and Presbyterians who were charged with protecting their denominational "peculiarities," it being believed that there was sufficient common ground to load each tract with an ample measure of "divine truth." The missionary and education societies were of a different character. Their task was to establish churches and train ministers. This necessitated organization on a denominational basis. The Presbyterian United Domestic Missionary Society was reorganized in 1826 as the American Home Missionary Society and it became the arm of the Presbyterian-Congregational coalition. Similar national societies were formed for the other denominations.

The whole cluster of national societies has sometimes been referred to as the "benevolent empire." It is true that their activities were closely coordinated through a series of "interlocking directorates." Most of the leadership at the national level was concentrated in a rela-

[37] Gilbert H. Barnes, *The Anti-Slavery Impulse, 1830–1844* (N.Y., 1933), 17.

tively small group; and the annual meetings, held in New York in May, were so scheduled that one could participate in most of them. They did not act alone, an auxiliary society assured its members in 1826. They moved together "harmoniously" and thus formed "so many parts of the grand whole" in seeking to fulfill "that last command of our ascended Lord, 'Go and spread the influence of the gospel over every creature.' "[38]

Attention will be given the reform impulse in a subsequent chapter. Here the focus is on the concern with the importance of the growing cities and with the West. Impelled by the conviction that the cities were citadels which must be captured at all costs, Lyman Beecher had gone to Boston in 1826, Albert Barnes accepted a call to Philadelphia in 1830, and Charles G. Finney was persuaded to become a pastor in New York City in 1832. The cities were strategic for two reasons. They were centers of an influence which radiated to the remotest hamlet, and they were repositories of concentrated wealth. While Bible, tract, Sunday school, and missionary societies devoted great attention to the religious life of the cities, the leaders of the national societies were equally concerned with mastering the wealth of the urban centers. "The purposes of Christianity," declared Barnes, "require that that wealth should be consecrated to the Redeemer," and consecrating it to the Redeemer meant, among other things, devoting it to the work of the benevolent societies.[39] So successful was this enlistment of wealth that by 1834 the total annual receipts of the societies were in excess of nine million dollars.

The West became of even more urgent concern than it had been hitherto when Andrew Jackson's election as president in 1828 dramatized the shift of political power that was taking place. "The strength of the nation," a report of the American Home Missionary Society in 1829 declared, "lies beyond the Alleghany. The center of dominion is fast moving in that direction. The ruler of this country is growing up in the Great Valley. Leave him without the gospel and he will be a ruffian giant."[40] With this in mind the whole voluntary society apparatus

---

[38] Foster, *Errand of Mercy*, 143, 154.

[39] Albert Barnes, *Sermons on Revivals* (N.Y., 1841), 96. See also 109–10.

[40] W. B. Posey, *The Presbyterian Church in the Old Southwest, 1778–1838* (Richmond, 1952), 111. For the valley campaign of 1829–31, see Foster, *Errand of Mercy*, 190–205, and Hudson, *American Protestantism*, 84–90.

RELIGION IN AMERICA

launched a great "saturation" campaign to save the Mississippi valley and thus save the nation. The goal was a Bible for every family, a Sunday school in every neighborhood, a pastor in every locality, and tracts in abundance. Each of the societies—Bible, tract, Sunday school, missionary—was assigned its allotted task, and a single agent frequently worked for several societies. The statistics tell an incredible story of Bibles shipped, tracts distributed, Sunday schools organized, and churches established. So successful was the operation that by 1833, the societies were beginning to turn their attention to those sections of the South where the population was scattered and ignorance seemed widespread.

CONTRIBUTIONS TO EDUCATION. For those who feared that "barbarism" would overtake the nation, the provision of adequate educational opportunities was a primary concern. Both the political order of America and the ecclesiastical order of Protestantism presupposed a literate laity and, with only minor dissent, an educated leadership. Along the seaboard, churches had long been active in fostering education at all levels, and in the West the Ordinance of 1785 had set aside land in every township for the maintenance of publicly supported elementary schools. Even so, some time usually elapsed in newly opened territory before these schools could be brought into operation, and during this period ministers often filled the breach by serving as schoolmasters.

It was in the area of secondary and higher education, however, that the churches made their greatest contribution. Presbyterians and Congregationalists were the most active in founding academies and colleges. Baptists followed their example, as did Methodists after a delayed beginning. Other denominations made contributions in proportion to their numbers. For the greater part of the nineteenth century, most secondary and collegiate education was carried on under denominational auspices. Of the 516 colleges and universities founded before the Civil War, only a few had no religious affiliation.[41] Academies were

41 Some typical colleges were Transylvania (1783), Middlebury (1800), Hamilton (1812), Colgate (1817), Colby (1818), Hobart (1822), Center (1823), Kenyon (1824), Furman, Mississippi College, Western Reserve, and Illinois College (1826), Randolph-Macon (1830), Denison (1832), Mercer (1833), Wake Forest and Albion (1834), DePauw and Knox (1837).

often the product of an individual minister's zeal for learning, whereas the dominant motive in founding colleges was to provide an educated ministry. The classical education offered served also as preparation for other professions. This permitted enlistment of community as well as denominational support. It is interesting that denominational rivalry played small part in the founding of colleges and academies. There was little competition and little territorial duplication. A location preempted by one denomination was respected by the others. Still the mortality rate was high. Some infant enterprises were left stranded by changing patterns of settlement, some were victims of mismanagement, many were inadequately staffed.

Founding of theological seminaries was another feature of Protestant educational activity. Prior to 1800 specifically theological education, as distinguished from the classical education given aspiring ministers in the colleges, was commonly acquired under the direction of older clergymen. Such supervised training combined advanced study with practical experience, but there was a growing conviction that more adequate preparation could be given in a graduate professional school. New Brunswick Theological Seminary, which traces its beginnings back to 1784 when instruction was initiated in New York City, antedated the general movement which is usually considered to have begun with the founding of Andover Theological Seminary in 1808. In the next few years the movement rapidly gained momentum in most denominations.[42]

Part of the energy generated by revivals was directed toward efforts to provide educational opportunities for females and blacks. Emma Willard's Troy Female Seminary (1821) and Mary Lyon's similar endeavor at Mt. Holyoke (1837) are the most frequently cited examples of the former concern, but many such institutions flourished during the decades before the Civil War in widely scattered areas of the country. Lincoln University in Pennsylvania, founded in 1854, and Wilberforce in Ohio, founded in 1856, are specific examples of the latter concern—provision of educational opportunities for those of African

[42] The divinity schools at Harvard (1816) and Yale (1822) were paralleled by such theological seminaries as Princeton (1812), Union at Hampden-Sydney, later Richmond (1812), Hartwick (1816), Colgate, General, and Pittsburgh (1817), Auburn (1821), Bexley Hall (1824), Mercersburg and Newton (1825).

antecedents who had gained their freedom. Earlier, New York Central College, established in 1843 at McGrawville, N.Y., by abolitionist Baptists, regarded the education of blacks, who constituted a significant portion of its student body, as central to its mission. But it was Oberlin College (1832) that put the whole thrust of evangelical religion together.

Oberlin was dedicated to "universal reform," being rescued financially in 1835 by the Tappan brothers, New York City merchants, who stipulated that Finney serve as professor of theology and that the student rebels expelled from Lane Theological Seminary because of antislavery activity be accepted as students. Both women and blacks were admitted to the course of instruction. Its name[43] and the words "learning and labor" on its seal indicated that, like many evangelical colleges of the time, Oberlin was founded as a manual labor school to put into practice the latest educational theory which stressed the blending of head, hand, and heart in the instructional process. While the central purpose of Oberlin, in keeping with its revivalist concerns, was to send out well-equipped ministers and missionaries, there was scarcely a reform proposal which did not find ready reception and nurture in the congenial "perfectionist" atmosphere of the college.

THE MOOD OF THE SOUTH.   Academies and colleges multiplied in the South as they did in other parts of the country, but there was less self-generated activity by the voluntary societies. Perhaps the climate, before the advent of air-conditioning, slowed the pace of life. More likely the absence of the highly-organized and systematic procedures of the bustling cities of the North was responsible. It could not have been because the mood in areas of the South where evangelical religion was strong was any less exuberant and optimistic than in the North. Baptists, Methodists, and Presbyterians may have had fewer resources in the South than elsewhere, but they had done their work well.

Andrew Johnson, the future president but at the time a youthful adherent of Andrew Jackson, reflected the eager optimistic spirit of the time. He was addressing his constituents in the First Congressional District of Tennessee. He told them that democracy and Christianity

are going along, not in divergents, not in parallels, but in converging

[43] A life of the Swiss Protestant, Johann Frederick Oberlin (1740–1826), which gave impetus to the manual labor movement, was published by the American Sunday School Union in 1830. A year later Lewis Tappan and others founded the Society for Promoting Manual Labor in Literary Institutions.

lines—the one purifying and elevating man religiously, the other politically. . . . At what period of time they will have finished the work
of progress and elevation is not now for me to determine, but when
finished these two lines will have approximated each other—man being
perfected both in a religious and a political point of view.

As he continued, Johnson became lyrical in his vision of the future,
noting that as the lines converge then can

proclamation be made that the millennial morning has dawned and
that the time has come when the lion and the lamb shall lie down
together, when the "voice of the turtle" shall be "heard in our land,"
when . . . the glad tidings shall be proclaimed . . . of man's political
and religious redemption, and that there is "on earth, peace, good
will toward men."[44]

OVERSEAS MISSIONS.   Thus far attention has been centered on the
new nation, but the religious enthusiasm of the Second Awakening
could not be contained within national boundaries. Not only the nation but the world was to be redeemed. News of the Orient had been
seeping back into New England during the early years of the Awakening. This was the era of the clipper ships and the Pacific trade, and
every ship that returned to Salem or Boston brought tales of distant
lands and strange people. Also exciting reports of William Carey's pioneering missionary venture in India were being published in the religious press, and funds were being collected in Philadelphia and
elsewhere for his support. In 1810 the "banding" of a number of
students at Andover Theological Seminary—not far from Salem—to offer
themselves for foreign-mission service led to the founding of the American Board of Commissioners for Foreign Missions.[45] Two years later,
five of the students—Samuel Newell, Adoniram Judson, Luther Rice,
Samuel Nott, Jr., and Gordon Hall—set sail for India. Judson became
persuaded of the validity of Baptist contentions while on shipboard,

---

[44] Dixon Wector, *The Saga of American Society* (N.Y., 1937), 100. *The Papers
of Andrew Johnson*, ed. L. P. Graf and R. W. Haskins (Knoxville, 1970), II, 176–77.
See also D. G. Mathews, *Religion in the Old South* (Chicago, 1977), Erskine Clark,
Wrestlin Jacob: A Portrait of Religion in the Old South (Atlanta, 1979), and M. C.
Sernett, *Black Religion and American Evangelicalism* (Metuchen, N.J., 1975).

[45] See W. E. Strong, *The Story of the American Board* (Boston, 1910). An
overseas mission had been anticipated by David George when he sailed for Sierra
Leone in 1792 after having established a black church in Nova Scotia. Jamaica, Haiti,
and Liberia also became scenes of missionary activity by blacks from America.

and when he arrived in India he discovered that Rice had come to share his views while sailing on board another ship. When Judson went on to Burma, Rice returned to America to enlist Baptist support for Judson's mission. By 1850 the foreign mission work of all denominations called for an annual expenditure of about $650,000.

Protestant expansion in America during the decades that followed the formation of the new nation was part of a much larger movement of Protestant resurgence whose achievements led Kenneth Scott Latourette to describe the nineteenth century as "the great century" in the history of Christianity.[46] In Britain and on the continent of Europe, as well as in America, a sweeping tide of evangelical religion brought new life to Protestant churches at a time when the Roman Catholic Church was waging a defensive struggle against the forces of nationalism and "liberalism" in Roman Catholic lands. It was not until the end of the century that the Roman Catholic Church, either in America or elsewhere, was to be able to abandon its defensive posture. In the meantime, the Protestant churches in America were not without pressing problems of their own.

[46] Latourette's primary focus was upon the achievements of the far-flung missionary enterprise. Only by a repetitive refrain of superlatives could he describe what had taken place. "Never before in a period of equal length had Christianity or any other religion penetrated for the first time as large an area as it had in the nineteenth century." "Never before had any religion been planted over so large a portion of the earth's surface." "Never before had Christianity, or any other religion, been introduced to so many different peoples and cultures." "Never before had so many hundreds of thousands contributed voluntarily of their means to assist the spread of Christianity or any other religion." "Never before . . . had Christians come so near the goal of reaching all men with their message." "Never had it exerted so wide an influence upon the human race." "Measured by geographic extent and the effect upon mankind as a whole, the nineteenth century was the greatest thus far in the history of Christianity." *A History of the Expansion of Christianity* (N.Y., 1937–45), IV, 1, 4; V, 469; VI, 442, 443, 450; VII, 450.

VII

Divergent Trends and Movements

The evangelical religion of the first third of the nineteenth century bred a spirit of unity which was expressed both in the revivals of the period and in the activities of the voluntary societies. The societies were explicitly designed to secure the broadest possible cooperation in common tasks. And indispensable to the success of a revival in any community was the participation of a major portion of the churches, for without this broad participation the necessary psychological climate and group pressure could not be created. "The spirit of sectarianism," therefore, was the great "hindrance" and "quencher" of revivals; and Finney constantly warned his helpers not "to dwell upon sectarian distinctions or to be sticklish about sectarian points." [1] With Christians working side by side in the revivals and in the societies, further impetus was given to the development of cordial relations among the major denominations.

There were discordant notes, however, in the midst of the harmony.

[1] Calvin Colton, *History and Character of American Revivals*, 116–17. Finney, *Lectures on Revivals of Religion* (2nd. ed., N.Y., 1835), 369.

The Great Awakening of the colonial period, with its "New Lights" and "Old Lights," and "New Sides" and "Old Sides," had demonstrated that revivals could divide as well as unify. And the Second Awakening was equally productive of controversy and division. The reactions surprisingly were quite diverse. The doctrinal harshness of revivalist preaching, on the one hand, contributed to the Unitarian and Universalist defections; while its doctrinal laxity, on the other hand, helped to produce a reaction which led to a revived confessionalism. Still others found the lax churchmanship of the evangelicals disturbing, and this led to J. W. Nevin's stress upon the importance of the priestly office and the sacramental life and to John Henry Hobart's zealous defense of what he considered to be the primitive church order. All the dissenters, whatever form their protest might take, reacted strongly against what Horace Bushnell called the "artificial fireworks" and the "jump and stir" of the revivals.

Unitarians and Universalists

While Unitarianism (i.e., antitrinitarianism) in Boston was the product of many influences, its roots went back to the "liberal" tendencies which developed in reaction to the first Great Awakening, and during the succeeding years there had been a steady but barely perceptible drift toward greater emphasis upon the human role in redemption.[2] By the time Ashbel Green (1762–1848), a young Presbyterian minister from Philadelphia who was later to be president of Princeton University, made a tour of New England in 1791, he found many of the Boston ministers to be unsound in the faith. Among them, he reported, were Arminians, Universalists, Arians, and one professed Socinian. Ten years later Archibald Alexander (1772–1851), then president of Hampden-Sydney College in Virginia, found the situation in Boston even more dismaying. Heretical notions of all types abounded, and the only agreement he could discover was a rejection of the doctrine of the Trinity.[3]

The reports of Green and Alexander are somewhat misleading, for heretical doctrines were not being openly proclaimed. The only overt

[2] See Conrad Wright, *The Beginnings of Unitarianism in America* (Boston, 1955), and E. M. Wilbur, *A History of Unitarianism . . . in America* (Cambridge, Mass., 1952). Fresh perspectives are provided by Wright in *The Liberal Christians* (Boston, 1970). Key documents are printed in W. E. Channing, *Unitarian Christianity and Other Essays* (Indianapolis, 1957).

[3] Wilbur, *History of Unitarianism*, 399.

break occasioned by the theological ferment had occurred not among the Congregationalists but at King's Chapel, the former church of the royal governor. In 1782 the Episcopalian proprietors of the Chapel, being unable to obtain a minister, had invited James Freeman (1759–1835), a recent graduate of Harvard, to serve as reader. In deference to his scruples, the liturgy was revised to eliminate certain trinitarian references, the Athanasian and Nicene Creeds were omitted, and in 1787 the congregation proceeded to ordain him as its pastor. The Congregational clergy were much more cautious. Without the problem posed by a set of liturgy, most of them were content to let "sleeping dogmas lie." Orthodox doctrines were not openly opposed and rejected; they were quietly ignored. A clearcut party alignment began to appear only when Henry Ware (1764–1845), a known liberal, was elected to the Hollis professorship of divinity at Harvard in 1805, one consequence being the founding of Andover Seminary in 1808.

It was not until after 1815, however, that a definite separation took place. The event which brought the uneasy truce to an end was the publication in Boston of a chapter from the *Memoirs* of Theophilus Lindsey (1723–1808), which reproduced letters that had been written to the English Unitarian leader by several of the New England "liberals." One of the letters noted that, while most of the Boston clergy were Unitarian in sentiment, "the controversy is seldom or never introduced into the pulpit." But now names had been named and sentiments had been exposed, and there was little hope of preventing an open breach. A pamphlet war ensued with Jedediah Morse (1761–1826) writing a tract entitled *Are You of the Christian or the Boston Religion?* and John Lowell (1769–1840) replying in kind with one entitled *Are You a Christian or a Calvinist?*

The classic exposition of Unitarian doctrine was William Ellery Channing's (1780–1842) Baltimore sermon on "Unitarian Christianity" which he delivered in 1819 at the ordination of Jared Sparks.[4] The foundation was the inspired Word of God made manifest in the Scriptures; but, being "written for men" and "in the language of men," the meaning of Scripture must be sought "in the same manner as that of other books." The special divine office of Christ as Savior was not questioned. Though

---

[4] The sermon has been reprinted many times. A portion of it is in Smith, Handy, Loetscher, *American Christianity*, I, 493–502.

Jesus was not God, he was sent by the Father to effect the "moral and spiritual deliverance of mankind; that is, to rescue men from sin and its consequences, and to bring them to a state of everlasting purity and happiness." It is evident from other writings that if the early Unitarians were allowed to define their terms, they could have affirmed the Trinity. The basic issue which set them apart was their optimistic view of human nature. There is an "essential sameness" between God and man, declared Channing, and "all virtue has its foundation in the moral nature of man." The great significance of Jesus is that he leads and entices men to divine perfection. Having been made for "union" with the Creator, the "infinite perfection" of the Creator is "the only sufficient object and true resting place for the insatiable desires and unlimited capacities of the human mind." Later the Unitarian position was to be summarized in James Freeman Clarke's (1810–88) Affirmation of Faith: "The fatherhood of God, the brotherhood of man, the leadership of Jesus, salvation by character, and the progress of mankind onward and upward forever."

The publication of the extract from Lindsey's *Memoirs* precipitated a struggle for the possession of church property. Often the Trinitarians constituted a majority of church members, but the courts ruled in 1820 that church property was vested in the "parish" which embraced both church members and nonmembers. In many instances, with all the eligible voters of the parish or town participating in the decision, even a minority Unitarian faction among the church members was able to gain possession of the property. Oliver Wendell Holmes's "One-Hoss Shay" was supposed to be a symbol of the sudden crumbling of "Calvinism," but it collapsed only in eastern Massachusetts; and even there only momentarily, for within a very brief time orthodox Congregational churches were re-established in almost every parish. When the American Unitarian Association was formed in 1825 it numbered one hundred and twenty-five churches, one hundred of them in Massachusetts and most of them within forty miles of Boston, a fact which led the irreverent to quip that the Unitarians believed in the fatherhood of God, the brotherhood of man, and the neighborhood of Boston.

Unitarianism, on the whole, was the faith of well-to-do, urban New Englanders who rejected the notion of human depravity. Universalism was its counterpart among less urbane rural folk who were repelled by the idea of eternal damnation and thus led to affirm the doctrine of universal salvation.[5] Their mood in part was reflected in the reaction of a seventeen-year-old New Hampshire girl to uninhibited revivalist preaching: "We went this evening to hear Lorenzo Dow, a famous Methodist preacher, his appearance was enough to frighten one and his preaching disgusted all—the meeting house was crowded full. Think we should have been as wise if we had staid home." [6]

Although Universalism had been brought to America by John Murray (1741–1850) in 1770, it did not gain much headway until after Elhanan Winchester (1751–97), a Baptist minister, was converted in 1781. Later under the leadership of Hosea Ballou (1771–1852), whose *Treatise on Atonement* was published in 1805, the Universalists adopted an antitrinitarian position and, except for social status, became indistinguishable from the Unitarians. As a lower-class denomination, the Universalists competed with the Methodists and Wesleyan-oriented Free-Will Baptists for the allegiance of the common people. While the Universalists were concentrated initially in New England, they moved into the newer settlements of the West with such success that by 1850 they had more than twice as many churches as the Unitarians.

The resurgence of Old School "confessionalism"

The protest against revivalism was not limited to the "liberal" wing of the churches. Orthodox Calvinists also were alarmed by what they considered to be the dangerous narrowing of the distinction between Calvinism and Arminianism that was being effected by Nathaniel W. Taylor and Lyman Beecher in the interest of getting results, and the "new measures" employed by Finney in New York state seemed to them to be a clear confirmation of the unhappy practical consequences. Nathaniel Emmons (1745–1840), one of the most distinguished heirs of Jonathan Edwards, grumbled in his old age about the "undue excitements" of "modern" awakenings; and Asahel Nettleton, who had been one of the earliest leaders of the Second Awakening, was worried about the harm that was being done by "the imprudence of a few zealous individuals." Others were complaining that the revivals were becoming the work of "revival-makers" rather than a work of God. Even at Andover, which had been a

[5] See Richard Eddy's "History of Universalism" in Joseph Allen and Richard Eddy, *A History of the Unitarians and Universalists in the United States* (N.Y., 1894).
[6] Alice Felt Tyler, *Freedom's Ferment* (Minneapolis, 1944), 29.

seedbed of revival preachers, anxiety was beginning to be expressed.

Although strict Calvinists among the New England Congregationalists had fretted and chafed over the concessions that were being made, their dissent was muted by the necessity to maintain a united front to fight disestablishment and then to counter the Unitarian threat. Open conflict did not break out until 1828 when one of Taylor's more disturbing sermons, *Concio ad Clerum* ("Advice to the Clergy"), was published. The sermon dealt with the crucial issue of man's natural depravity and insisted that sin "is man's own act, consisting in a free choice of some object rather than God as his chief good." The "circumstances" of man's nature makes it certain that he will sin, but he has "power to the contrary." [7] The sermon made it abundantly clear to the conservatives that the New Haven Theology (or the "New Divinity" of Yale) had departed from orthodox Calvinism at one of its most essential points. The Yale group, on the other hand, argued that they were only offering a more acceptable and convincing explanation of the doctrine. The conservatives, finding the explanation neither convincing nor acceptable, raised the cry: "Shall we sustain our Calvinism or see it run down to the standard of Methodists and laxer men?" [8]

The pattern of response had been set at Andover where Jedediah Morse had persuaded the founders of the seminary to "guard against the insidious encroachments of innovation" by shackling the institution to two creeds: the *Westminster Shorter Catechism* and the so-called Andover Creed, which was based upon Samuel Hopkins' restatement of the views of Jonathan Edwards. The center of the controversy was in Connecticut, where a Pastoral Union was formed in 1833 and steps were taken to found a new seminary to combat the influence of Yale. The following year the (Hartford) Seminary was established at East Windsor and Bennet Tyler (1783–1858) was summoned from Portland, Maine, to assume the presidency. The integrity of both the Pastoral Union and the seminary was carefully guarded by Articles of Agreement which defined Calvinism in terms that would exclude any New Haven sentiments. The rift which was to continue for many years amounted to an open schism among the loosely organized Congregational churches.

A similar alarm among Presbyterian conservatives had precipitated

---

[7] The sermon is reprinted in Sydney E. Ahlstrom, ed., *Theology in America* (Indianapolis, 1967), 213–49.

[8] S. E. Mead, *Nathaniel W. Taylor*, 221

the formation of what came to be known as the Old School party in opposition to the New School or New Divinity men. The Presbyterian conservatives worked in close alliance with the strict Calvinists of New England, and as early as 1827 the Presbyterian *Christian Advocate*, published in Philadelphia and edited by Ashbel Green, was accusing the professors at Yale of promulgating doctrines which subverted the principles of orthodoxy. The ensuing controversy was marked by a whole series of heresy trials, beginning in 1831 when charges were brought against Albert Barnes in Philadelphia and ending in 1835 with the arraignment of Lyman Beecher before the Presbytery of Cincinnati. In each instance, after appeal to higher judicatories, the charges were dismissed, but the trials contributed greatly to the inflamed climate of opinion which led in 1837 to the exclusion of four New School synods in New York and Ohio from the Presbyterian church.[9]

While the theological issue was the most obvious factor in the division of 1837, the division was partly the product of a geographically based power struggle within the Presbyterian denomination, and lurking in the background was the disruptive issue of slavery. From the beginning Pennsylvania had been the center of power and prestige within the Presbyterian fold, but by 1828 its position of dominance had been badly eroded. In that year Ashbel Green noted that, whereas there were one hundred and ninety-six licentiates and ministers in Pennsylvania, New York had four hundred and twenty-six. And the damaging aspect of this imbalance was the fact that the New York ministers were within the New England rather than the Pennsylvania orbit of influence. Beecher, who had gone west to become president of the newly established Lane Theological Seminary, was certain that his trial for heresy was triggered by men of the Philadelphia-Pittsburgh axis who were alarmed at the prospect of a New England man rising to leadership in Cincinnati.

Within the Old School party, theological and political concerns intermingled and reinforced each other. The growing strength of the New School party heightened the apprehensions that had been aroused by the shifting emphasis of the New England Theology. In order to strengthen its

---

[9] The Old School-New School controversy is illuminated by documents reproduced in Maurice W. Armstrong, et. al., *The Presbyterian Enterprise*, 146–71. There is no satisfactory history of the Presbyterians for the period from 1789 to the Civil War, but the gap has been narrowed by G. M. Marsden, *The Evangelical Mind and the New School Presbyterian Experience* (New Haven, 1970), and by E. T. Thompson's study of the southern church.

position, the Old School group began to raise the issue of church government. The "union" with the Congregationalists had been welcomed initially by all parties within the church. Ashbel Green, for example, had been one of the leading proponents of the Plan of Union. But now the whole arrangement was brought under attack. Since the rival political power and the New School strength were both chiefly concentrated in the churches, presbyteries, and synods which had been formed under the provisions of the articles of "accommodation," these bodies were now denounced as being faulty in their constitutional foundation. Furthermore, since the great instrument of the New York–New School advance had been the independently controlled American Home Missionary Society and American Education Society, the Old School men demanded that these societies be repudiated and that all denominational funds be channeled through denominational boards that would be fully committed to the church's confessional position.

With the exception of a single year, the Old School party had not been able to gain control of the General Assembly prior to 1837. The balance of power was represented by Princeton Theological Seminary, and the faculty there hesitated to commit its influence to any program that would divide the church. Princeton regarded itself as the theological center of Presbyterian life, and it had looked with misgiving upon the establishment of Auburn Seminary in 1818 and Lane in 1829. But it was the founding of Union Theological Seminary in New York by New School men in 1836 that threw Princeton, though not without some reservations, behind the political program of the Old School Party. The new seminary in New York City could only be regarded as a direct challenge to Princeton's central role in the life of the church.

During the months preceding the General Assembly of 1837 the Old School faction had organized carefully to obtain a maximum representation, and when the Assembly met it proceeded with dispatch to carry out the Old School program. The "union" with the Congregationalists was abrogated, the relationship with the American Home Missionary Society and the American Education Society was severed, and three synods in New York and one in Ohio were expelled from the church. The following year, after attempting unsuccessfully to gain readmittance, the New School Presbyterians organized as a separate body which, with the adherence of scattered presbyteries and churches in other parts of the country, was roughly equal in size to the Old School body.

Although he took no great part in the division of 1837, Charles Hodge (1797–1878) was destined to be the great theologian of Old School Presbyterianism. He had been appointed to a professorship at Princeton Seminary in 1822 and he remained there for fifty years, sharing in the training of over three thousand ministers and contributing more than any other single person to the shaping of American Presbyterianism. He had been deeply influenced by Swiss orthodoxy, and a strong confessionalism became the hallmark of his theology. Hodge was convinced that "no such thing exists on the face of the earth as Christianity in the abstract. . . . Every man you see is either an Episcopalian or a Methodist, a Presbyterian or an Independent, an Arminian or a Calvinist. No one is a Christian in general." [10] His theological system was based solidly on the Westminster Standards and other Reformed confessions which he sought faithfully to expound and defend. It was with this in mind that he boasted that "a new idea never originated" at Princeton Seminary while he was there. His great monument and the source of much of his later influence was his three-volume *Systematic Theology* which was explicitly designed as a defensive rampart against all doctrinal aberrations.[11] While Hodge attempted to keep Presbyterianism in a theological strait jacket, it has been justly pointed out that his learning, doctrinal rigor, respect for confessional tradition, and insistence upon intelligible discussion did much in succeeding years to prevent anti-intellectual tendencies, sentimentality, and emotional partisanship from overwhelming theological concern.

During the 1830's the Baptists also were torn by an Old School–New School division which was in part a reaction to the growing influence in their ranks of the New England Theology.[12] The Baptist Old School party, however, failed to capture the denominational machinery which, above the

[10] *Biblical Repertory and Theological Review,* VIII (1836), 430.

[11] It is necessary to speak of "later" influence, for Hodge's *Systematic Theology* (N.Y., 1872–75) was not published until the last years of his life. Prior to this time his influence was mediated primarily through the classroom and his articles in the *Biblical Repertory and Theological Review* (later known as the *Princeton Review*).

[12] The theological issue was clearly delineated by Thomas Smiley (1759–1832), who was to become an Old School leader, in a letter to John Davis, April 27, 1811, and in his manuscript "History of the Chemung Association," 88–102, both of which are in the Samuel Colgate Baptist Historical Collection. Smiley, a pastor on the New York–Pennsylvania border, was shocked and dismayed by "the high Hopkinsian or all but fully Arminian sentiments" of the "Eastern missionaries" sent out by the Baptist board in Boston. For the missionaries' account of their tours through the Chemung River area, see the *Massachusetts Baptist Missionary Magazine,* II (1808–10), 302–7; and the *American Baptist Magazine,* I (1817–18), 269–71.

associational level, existed solely in the form of voluntary societies. A defection thereupon occurred both in the East and the West, but the defensive posture that these "Primitive Baptists" adopted became so permeated by an anti-mission spirit that the defecting churches and associations were left to eke out no more than a dwindling existence.

A revived confessionalism among the Reformed and the Lutherans came from another quarter. Both groups had been heavily infiltrated, first by Wesleyan doctrines, then by the more moderate evangelicalism of early Princeton, and finally by Taylorism and its associated Finneyite "new measures." In 1822 five ministers withdrew on doctrinal grounds from the Dutch Reformed Church, but their adherents were able to maintain only a meager church life until 1857 when the Christian Reformed Church was established on a strong confessional base by Dutch immigrants in Michigan. Not only did the new church prosper; its influence had the effect of drawing the older Dutch church back to a more conservative position.

A theological shift among the German Lutherans followed much the same pattern. S. S. Schmucker, graduate of Princeton and president of the Lutheran seminary at Gettysburg, was the great symbol of the Lutheran adjustment to the American theological climate.[13] It was Schmucker who issued in 1838 a *Fraternal Appeal* summoning all branches of evangelical Protestantism in America to unite in a single Apostolic Protestant Church, and who with other "liberal" leaders exerted strong influence on behalf of "new-measures" revivalism. The defeat of the Americanizing Lutherans, however, was foreshadowed by the arrival in Missouri of a group of immigrant Germans from Saxony the following year. They had left Germany because they could "see no possibility of retaining in their present home" the "pure and undefiled" faith of the historic Lutheran confessions and thus had felt "duty bound to emigrate and to look for a country where this Lutheran faith is not endangered."[14]

With their numbers augmented by continuing immigration, the Missouri group at a meeting in Chicago formed the Evangelical Lutheran Synod of Missouri in 1847. Other equally conservative synods were formed by immigrants from other parts of Germany—the Buffalo Synod in 1845, the Wisconsin Synod in 1850, and the Iowa Synod in 1854. While

13 See J. A. Brown, *The New Theology* (Philadelphia, 1857); Vergilius Ferm, *The Crisis in American Lutheran Theology*; E. Clifford Nelson, ed., *The Lutherans in North America* (Philadelphia, 1975).
14 A. R. Wentz, *A Basic History of Lutheranism* (Philadelphia, 1955), 116.

these synods engaged in doctrinal controversy among themselves, the conspicuous leader who influenced them all and who played a large part in the reshaping of American Lutheranism as a whole was Carl F. W. Walther (1811–87). As his biographer reports, he was "easily the most commanding figure in the Lutheran church in America during the nineteenth century," and another scholar has noted that Walther "stood almost alone in the nineteenth century American theological scene as one fully aware of the crucial importance of the problems of Law and Gospel to the Christian faith." In this latter respect he anticipated "the emphasis of Karl Barth and the 'Luther renaissance' of the next century, but by the same fact he doomed himself to attack and misunderstanding in his own time." [15]

The great wave of German immigration did not leave Lutheranism in the eastern part of the United States unscathed. Not only was pressure exerted by the newer synods in the West, but immigration also altered the theological complexion of the older synods in the East. By the 1850's, even at Gettysburg, Schmucker had been displaced in influence by Charles Philip Krauth (1797–1867) who was urging the churches to maintain their fidelity to the traditional Lutheran standards. Later his son, Charles Porterfield Krauth (1823–83), was to devote his attention to inaugurating a liturgical and sacramental renaissance among American Lutherans, and at this point his interests closely paralleled those of John W. Nevin. As a third-generation American, Krauth was an especially effective advocate of a revived confessionalism in the English-speaking Lutheran churches. [16]

"High Church" sentiment: *John W. Nevin and John Henry Hobart*

While others were fighting defensive battles against New School doctrines and assuming a rigid stance behind their confessional ramparts, John W. Nevin (1803–86)—the chief spokesman for what came to be known as "the Mercersburg theology" or "evangelical catholicism"—was undertaking the more positive task of restoring the sacramental life of the churches which, in his view, had been wrecked by rampant revivalism. [17]

---

[15] D. H. Steffens, *Carl F. W. Walther* (Philadelphia, 1917), 10. Sydney E. Ahlstrom, "Theology in America," in *The Shaping of American Religion*, ed. J. W. Smith and A. Leland Jamison, 275.

[16] See Charles Porterfield Krauth, *The Conservative Reformation and Its Theology* (Philadelphia, 1871), and Adolph Spaeth, *Charles Porterfield Krauth* (N.Y., 1898).

[17] See James H. Nichols, *Romanticism in American Theology: Nevin and Schaff at Mercersburg* (Chicago, 1961).

Born of Scotch-Irish parents in 1803, Nevin attended Union College and Princeton Seminary, and in 1829 became a professor of the Western Theological Seminary, a Princeton outpost at Allegheny, Pennsylvania. There his antislavery views involved him in constant controversy and, although theologically he was fully in accord with Old School views, he was violently attacked because he regarded the expulsion of the New School synods in 1837 as an unconstitutional act. Convinced that his future usefulness at Western had been impaired, he accepted a call in 1840 to the struggling German Reformed theological seminary at Mercersburg, a move which was interpreted to him as merely a shift from the "Scotch Reformed" branch of the church to the "German Presbyterian" branch. In the isolation of Mercersburg, Nevin underwent the radical theological reorientation that caused him to break with Princeton orthodoxy at three crucial points: its lack of any sense of historical development, its individualistic view of the church, and its Zwinglian view of the sacraments.

Many influences, some of long standing, combined to produce Nevin's change of front. Not the least of these was the influence of Coleridge, but Nevin reported that it was the writings of J. A. W. Neander (1789–1850), the German church historian, which had actually awakened him from his "dogmatic slumber." Neander taught him that Christianity was a life, an experience, a communion with invisible realities, rather than a dogmatic system. This enabled him to appreciate diverse doctrinal conceptions and to find in all the diversities a movement toward a divinely ordained purpose. Finally, at Mercersburg, Nevin was introduced to a psychology, based upon Hegel, which he discovered had direct bearing on doctrines of the Incarnation, the mystical union of Christ and the believer, and the presence of Christ in the Eucharist.

Nevin's shift to a new theological position was signalized in 1843 by the publication of *The Anxious Bench*, a forthright attack upon the "new-measures" revivalism which had invaded the German Reformed churches and which Nevin regarded as "unfavorable to deep, thorough, and intelligent piety," "fatal to the true idea of devotion," and "injurious to the worship of God." [18] His major work, *The Mystical Presence: A Vindication of the Reformed or Calvinistic Doctrine of the Holy Eucharist,*[19] was

[18] *The Anxious Bench* (Chambersburg, Pa., 1843), 56.
[19] Extensive selections from *The Mystical Presence* are reprinted in Ahlstrom, *Theology in America*, 374–426.

published three years later, and it brought him into a head-on clash with Hodge—a clash that ended with Nevin demolishing Hodge's attempt to marshal support from the Reformed confessions.

In contrast to those who understood Christianity as a relationship of individuals to Christ who are only subsequently brought together to form the church, Nevin held that individuals do not constitute the church. The church is not something added to the gospel; it is an essential part of the gospel. It is the context within which men have access to Christ's saving presence, the means by which the living Christ gives himself to his people. It was constituted and continues to be constituted as a "whole" through communion with Christ rather than being simply the sum total of predestined individuals—past, present, and future. Central to Nevin's understanding of communion with Christ was his conception of the Eucharist. "The question of the Eucharist," he declared, "is one of the most important belonging to the history of religion. It may be regarded indeed as in some sense central to the whole Christian system. For Christianity is grounded in the living union of the believer with the person of Christ; and this great fact is emphatically concentrated in the mystery of the Lord's Supper." [20] Thus it is in the mystical participation of the faithful in the life of Christ through the sacrament of the Lord's Supper that the church is most truly the Church.

Liturgical reform, ecumenical concern, and questions of ministerial order were other subjects to which Nevin devoted his attention, and his thought was enriched and in some instances explicated by his colleague Philip Schaff who arrived in Mercersburg from Germany in 1844. Nevin's views aroused much opposition from defenders of New School doctrines and practices, and after the Civil War the German Reformed Church was bitterly divided between the Nevinists and the anti-Nevinists. Competing educational insitutions were established and the denomination barely escaped actual schism.

Of Nevin it was said: "He is always instructive, even when he is in error." [21] Unfortunately, few were instructed, for he moved in a restricted circle. He belonged to a small denomination and taught in a remote seminary. But the main reason for his failure to be heard was the fact that

---

[20] *The Mystical Presence* (Philadelphia, 1846), 51.
[21] J. H. Nichols, "John Williamson Nevin," in *Sons of the Prophets*, ed. H. T. Kerr (Princeton, 1963), 81.

he addressed himself to issues which were not to be keenly felt until the twentieth century.

In some respects John H. Hobart (1775–1830), Episcopal bishop of New York, was a kindred spirit to Nevin. His emphases were much the same as those of the Mercersburg theologian, but he really lived in another world. Hobart's interest was practical rather than theological. Unlike Nevin he was stirred by no ecumenical vision and he had little appreciation of historical development. Hobart was a strict "denominationalist," a "sectarian" in the eyes of Evangelicals.

Consecrated bishop in 1811, Hobart spent the remaining nineteen years of his life in an amazing burst of activity directed to reviving the flagging fortunes of the Protestant Episcopal Church in the State of New York. He was constantly on the move visiting the churches of his diocese and establishing missions. He wrote and compiled handbooks as practical aids to the laity: *Companion for the Altar, Companion for the Festivals and Fasts, The Pocket Almanac, The Church Catechism, The Christian's Manual on Faith and Devotion.* He rebuked those who participated in the interdenominational voluntary societies, and to counter the influence of those societies he organized the Protestant Episcopal Tract Society, the Protestant Episcopal Sunday School Society, and the New York Bible and Common Prayer Book Society. In a church that was predominantly "Low Church" or "Evangelical" in sentiment, Hobart was proud to acknowledge the name "High Churchman," and the explication of what it meant to be a High Churchman was the constant theme of his annual "charges" as well as of his other writings.

A "Low Churchman" to Hobart was one "who deprecates the distinguishing characteristics of the Church or who is lukewarm or indifferent in advancing them," whereas the "High Churchman" exhibits "an eminent degree of attachment to the essential characteristics of the Church and zeal for their advancement." The essential characteristics were "those of the first and purest ages of Christianity, of the age of the apostles, of martyrs and confessors," and Hobart dedicated himself to arresting "the progress of an indifference and laxity of opinion" which threatened the destruction of the Church as "it was constituted by its divine head." [22]

[22] E. C. Chorley, *Men and Movements in the American Episcopal Church* (N.Y., 1946), 143, 146.

Hobart rejected what he called the "invidious distinction" that so many made "between the doctrine and the institutions of the gospel." Both, he insisted, "have a divine origin" and "are inseparably connected." Indispensable to the being of the Church are the "essential elements of doctrine, ministry, sacraments, and worship." In developing this fourfold form of the Church, Hobart displayed little creative thought. His liturgical interest was limited to defending the existing Episcopal liturgy as embodying evangelical truth in the "purest" language of devotion. While he regarded the sacraments as central and indispensable and thought that "he hazarded his salvation if he refused or neglected to receive these means and pledges of divine favor," he considered the bread and wine to be no more than "symbols and memorials of the body and blood of Christ." His interest in doctrine was equally commonplace. The point of his central concern was the ministry, as he made clear when he declared that the true High Churchman adheres "in all essential points to the faith, ministry, and worship which distinguished the apostolic and primitive Church, and particularly to the constitution of the Christian ministry under its three orders of bishops, priests, and deacons." [23]

Lawful ministers, Hobart maintained, are "those who derive their authority from Christ himself by regular succession from the apostles." Consequently, there cannot be "a lawful bishop, priest, or deacon who hath not had episcopal consecration or ordination." Episcopacy is the essential point and it is "unchangeable because it is the originally constituted mode of conveying that commission without which there can be no visible ministry, no visible sacraments, no visible Church." Thus "we continue in the fellowship of the apostles when we adhere to the ministry of bishops, priests, and deacons who have been from the apostles' times." Nor did Hobart hesitate to draw the harsh conclusion which offended so many of his fellow Episcopalians: "I could not maintain the divine authority of the Episcopal ministry without denying the validity of a nonepiscopal ministry." [24]

Scholars have often speculated as to the source of Hobart's uncompromising churchmanship which ran so counter to the spirit of his age. One clue perhaps is to be found in his family tradition, for his grandfather was a displaced New Englander who had become an Episcopalian. Another

[23] Ibid., 143–44, 147.
[24] Ibid., 142, 184, 186–87.

influence may have been a feeling of defensiveness that developed during his college days in the Presbyterian atmosphere of Princeton. More decisive undoubtedly was the influence of his father-in-law, Thomas Bradbury Chandler, who had led the fight for a colonial episcopate and who had taken care to make sure that his daughter was "well instructed in the doctrines of primitive episcopacy." But whatever their source Hobart's views, which represented only a minority opinion in his own time, were destined to become, after having been enriched and deepened by insights derived from the Oxford Movement in England, one of the dominant currents in the life of the Protestant Episcopal Church in the twentieth century.[25]

By the mid-nineteenth century, views analogous to those of Hobart had also begun to develop within Baptist ranks. This "High Church" sentiment, which emphasized apostolic succession through an unbroken line of New Testament churches, was the distinctive characteristic of a group of Baptists who called themselves "Landmarkists." The name was derived from a tract *An Old Landmark Reset* (1854) by James M. Pendleton (1811–91),[26] but the basic tenets, which included a refusal to recognize other "societies" as true churches and a rejection of "alien immersion" and "pulpit affiliation" with non-Baptists, had been set forth by James R. Graves (1820–93) three years earlier at a meeting in Cotton Grove, Tennessee. While the major Baptist bodies repeatedly repudiated the Landmarkists, their "High Church" views had gained wide currency in the South by the end of the century.

Transcendentalism

Little more than a decade after the founding of the American Unitarian Association, the Boston churches were torn again by a new reformation led by rebellious young preachers, members of the "Transcen-

[25] The Oxford Movement was initiated in 1833 by John Keble (1792–1866) with a sermon on "National Apostasy," and was carried forward through a series of *Tracts for the Times*, the first of which was published by J. H. Newman (1801–90) in the same year. The aim of the movement was to win support within the Church of England for the "High Church" views that had been explicated by seventeenth-century divines. A dominant motif of the movement was its renewed interest in primitive and medieval Christianity.

[26] See selection reprinted in Smith, Handy, Loetscher, *American Christianity*, II, 108–12. See also R. G. Torbet, "Landmarkism," in *Baptist Concepts of the Church*, ed. W. S. Hudson (Philadelphia, 1959), and J. E. Steely, "The Landmark Movement in the Southern Baptist Convention," in *What Is the Church?* ed. D. K. McCall (Nashville, 1958).

dental Club" which first met in the home of George Ripley (1802–80).[27] Among the more prominent of the rebel clergymen, in addition to Ripley, were Ralph Waldo Emerson (1803–82), Theodore Parker (1810–60), James Freeman Clarke (1810–88), Frederic Henry Hedge (1805–90), William Henry Channing (1810–84), and Orestes Brownson (1803–76). And they were ably abetted by several influential lay recruits, such as Bronson Alcott (1799–1888), Henry David Thoreau (1817–62), Margaret Fuller (1810–50), and Elizabeth Peabody (1804–94). Repelled by what they regarded as the cold logic of their Unitarian elders and deeply influenced by Coleridge's *Aids to Reflection,* the Transcendentalists sought to reconcile the rationalism of their tradition with the romanticism of their age by introducing a strong note of mysticism into Unitarian formulations.

Since they were basically eclectic in their approach to truth, it is difficult to characterize the Transcendentalists. No two of them agreed at every point; and while some exhibited an intense individualism, others displayed a passionate zeal for communal life. James Freeman Clarke on one occasion suggested that their group might be called "the Club of the Like-Minded" because "no two of us thought alike." They were, nonetheless, bound together by what they called "the spiritual principle"—a principle which was articulated in three major agreements: an insistence upon divine immanence, a dependence upon intuitive perception of truth, and a rejection of all external authority. Every created thing had deep religious meaning, and they found "sermons not just in stones but in bean rows at Walden Pond and mud puddles on Boston Common." They were called Transcendentalists, said Ripley, because they believed "in an order of truths which transcends the sphere of the external senses." And since "the truth of religion does not depend on tradition, nor historical facts, but has an unerring witness in the soul," they refused to acknowledge any authority beyond themselves. The Transcendentalist, Emerson declared, "believes in miracles, in the perpetual openness of the human mind to the new influx of light and power; he believes in inspiration and ecstasy." The individual soul is linked to God and through the gift of intuition—instinct,

[27] See William R. Hutchison, *The Transcendentalist Ministers* (New Haven, 1959). For basic documents, see *The Transcendentalists: An Anthology,* ed. Perry Miller, (Cambridge, Mass., 1950). There are several paperbacks containing Emerson's "Divinity School Address" and Theodore Parker's sermon on "The Transient and Permanent in Christianity," both key Transcendentalist documents. These also are reprinted in part in Smith, Handy, Loetscher, *American Christianity,* II, 130–52.

imagination, insight—the soul can penetrate beyond the outer shell of life and consummate the union with God by participating in the life of the "oversoul."[28]

Andrews Norton (1786–1853) and other old-line Unitarians were horrified by this "latest form of infidelity" and were restrained from ejecting the Transcendentalists from the Unitarian fellowship only by an awareness of the scandal that a heresy trial among the Unitarians would create. Consequently the members of the Club were permitted to proceed in their churches with their program of reformation. Unlike Nevin who had been spurred by Coleridge to move in a more churchly direction, the Transcendentalists were led by their romantic vision to a quite contrary emphasis. They sought to turn their churches into free religious associations in which the distinction between clergy and laity would disappear and worship would be so ordered that leadership might be rotated. Furthermore, their goal was a comprehension which would embrace the best elements of all former religious systems and within which radical movements would not be looked upon as heresies but as "providential" clues to some need which God wished the churches to fulfill.

The mediating theology of Horace Bushnell

After several false vocational starts, which included teaching, journalism, and law, a quiet conversion experience in the solitude of his own room sent Horace Bushnell (1802–76) to Yale Divinity School and from there to the pastorate of the North Congregational Church in Hartford, Connecticut, where he was to spend the rest of his active pastoral life.[29] Bushnell was to be both "conservative" and "liberal" in his emphases, finding much of Christian truth in the older tradition of New England and yet appropriating and incorporating into his thinking insights derived from the Unitarian critique. He could speak of "free," "self-governed" individuals, and yet emphasize the way in which individuals are bound, either for good or for evil, by the organic character of the communities—family, church, neighborhood, and nation—in which they

---

[28] Hutchison, *Transcendentalist Ministers*, vii, 29. Tyler, *Freedom's Ferment*, 48. O. B. Frothingham, *George Ripley* (Boston, 1882), 84–85. Key selections from Ripley, Emerson, Parker, and William Henry Channing are reprinted in Smith, Handy, Loetscher, *American Christianity*, II, 130–52.

[29] See Barbara M. Cross, *Horace Bushnell* (Chicago, 1958).

exist. His endeavor was to be a mediator, seeking to reconcile the intimations of Christian truth that were to be found in diverse theological camps. While Bushnell's views won little acceptance prior to the Civil War, they later became of major importance in preparing the way for the New Theology of the 1870's and 1880's.

Bushnell, Nevin, and the Transcendentalists all acknowledged the decisive influence that had been exerted upon them by the "mysticism" of Coleridge and Schleiermacher, but each domesticated this dual influence in different ways. The Transcendentalists were led to reject the past and to reduce the church to a pragmatically justified religious association. Nevin, on the other hand, experienced no such compulsion, for he had been freed from any notion of static orthodoxy by a sense of historical development which he derived from reading Neander. Thus his appreciation both of the past and of the Church as an embodiment of Christ had been enhanced by the stress on mystic communion. Bushnell's escape from orthodoxy was not dissimilar to that of Nevin, but for Bushnell it was made possible by a theory of language. To him language was an imprecise instrument. Words are but "faded metaphors" which cannot be transferred from mind to mind with their meaning clear and transparent. Each word is organically related to its own history, to the history of the one who uses it and of the one who hears it, and to the situation in which it is used. With these variables, all creedal statements and even the words of Scripture must be understood in a "spirit of accommodation," for they are but linguistic and hence poetic attempts to speak the unspeakable. Christian truth was something which lay behind doctrinal propositions, but Bushnell did not sympathize with the Unitarian rejection of creeds. They were testimonies to that which lay beyond them and he was ready to accept them all, for "when they are subjected to the deepest chemistry of thought . . . they become so elastic and run so freely into each other that one seldom need have any difficulty in accepting as many as are offered him." [30]

Horace Bushnell is best remembered as the author of *Christian Nurture* (1847) which, while not his most important work, was one of the most influential books ever to be published in America. It was a criticism of revivalism and a plea for what in its broadest sense could be called

---

[30] "Preliminary Dissertation on Language," in *God in Christ* (Hartford, 1849), 81–83. See also selections reprinted in H. Shelton Smith, ed., *Horace Bushnell* (N.Y., 1965), 69–105.

Christian education. With his understanding of language as a social phenomenon, Bushnell was driven to recognize the formative influence of the community of faith. No person exists in isolation. He lives within a social context which shapes and determines his character. There is no reason to suppose that a child of believing parents cannot "grow up in the Lord." Take any scheme of human nature you please, Bushnell declared, and you will find nothing in it "to forbid the possibility that a child should be led, in his first moral act, to cleave unto what is good and right." Instead of assuming that "the child is to grow up in sin, to be converted after he comes to mature age," the "aim, effort, and expectation" should be that he may "grow up a Christian and never know himself as being otherwise." The great trouble with revivalism, as Bushnell saw it, is that as a result of its "jump and stir" the ordinary operations of God's grace tend to be "swallowed up and lost in the extraordinary" and people are led to believe that the only entrance into the Christian life is through a convulsive conversion experience in a revival meeting.[31]

Bushnell was not opposed to revivals. He believed that they rendered a great and necessary service to those who have been caught in the web of the kingdom of evil. Sin no less than virtue can be transmitted by the social context.

> Evil, once beginning to exist, inevitably becomes organic and constructs a kind of principate or kingdom opposite to God. . . . Pride organizes caste and dominates in the sphere of fashion. Corrupt opinions, false judgments, bad manners, and a general body of conventionalisms that represent the motherhood of sin, come into vogue and reign. And so, doubtless, everywhere and in all worlds, sin has in its nature to organize, mount into the ascendant above God and truth, and reign in a kingdom opposite God.[32]

With God's help and the Christian nurture provided by family and church, no one need sink into the slough of sin; but if he has, then a drastic rebirth to change his "reigning love" is necessary. As early as 1838 Bushnell had published an article in the *Quarterly Christian Spectator* "to establish a higher and more solid confidence in revivals," an article in which he insisted that "nothing was ever achieved in the way of great and radical

[31] *Christian Nurture* (N.Y., 1923), 4, 10; "Spiritual Economy of Revivals of Religion," *Quarterly Christian Spectator*, X (1838), 143–45.
[32] *Nature and the Supernatural* (N.Y., 1858), 135.

change in men without some degree of excitement; and if any one expects to carry on the cause of salvation by a steady rolling on the same dead level and fears continually lest the axles wax hot and kindle into a flame, he is too timorous to hold the reins of the Lord's chariot." While religion need not be for everyone "a fireball shot from the moon," [33] for some it must be.

As Bushnell reconciled revivalism to the ordered life of home and congregation, so he reconciled the major contentions of the Unitarians with an evangelical understanding of the Christian faith. He refashioned his conception of God, of man, of Christ, and of the Atonement to take the force from the Unitarian critique, and in the process reached back to Jonathan Edwards for some of the themes that helped him to make his case. He reaffirmed the Trinity by acknowledging that it applied only to God as revealed and not as ultimate being, as descriptive not of his person but of the modes of self-disclosure by which he makes himself known as Father, Son, and Spirit. In similar fashion, Bushnell bridged the gap between the natural and the supernatural without allowing them to become completely indistinguishable.

The fate which befalls most mediators was not withheld from Bushnell. He was appreciated at one point and criticized at another. No one seemed completely happy with his solutions. He was saved from being subjected to a heresy trial only by the withdrawal of his church from the local Congregational association which was dominated by Bennet Tyler, president of Hartford Seminary and leader of the Old School forces in Connecticut. But Leonard Bacon (1802–81), pastor of the Center Church in New Haven who had stood astride the Taylor-Tyler controversy, pronounced what was to be the growing conviction when he said that "brother Bushnell is essentially sound." [34] During the second half of the century, Bushnell's "progressive orthodoxy" was to sweep through many of the seminaries, and men who had been deeply influenced by him were to be among the most distinguished preachers in the land.

The triumph of Methodism

Whatever the future verdict was to be, the men discussed in this chapter represented lost causes in their own generation. They were

[33] *An Argument for "Discourses on Christian Nurture"* (Hartford, 1847), 16.
[34] Roland H. Bainton, *Yale and the Ministry* (N.Y., 1957), 124.

minority voices in a time of evangelistic urgency. The tide was running in another direction, and the decades immediately preceding the Civil War witnessed the triumph of the distinctive emphases of Methodism in practically all the denominations.[35]

Earlier defections to Methodist views and techniques had produced a cluster of new ecclesiastical bodies such as the United Brethren, the Evangelical Association, the Winebrennerians, the Free-Will Baptists, the Cumberland Presbyterians, and the Disciples of Christ or "Christians"— the latter combining a Presbyterian heritage with Methodist doctrines and Baptist polity and practice. But more significant than these defections was the fact that the Calvinism of the other denominations was becoming so diluted as to be unrecognizable. Taking their lead from Nathaniel W. Taylor, the revivalists had placed such stress upon the ability of the sinner to acquire conversion as in effect to transform Calvinism into an operational Arminianism. Finney illustrated the progression that was taking place. He was first a Presbyterian and then a Congregationalist, but his theology became more and more that of the Methodists until he finally embraced the Wesleyan doctrine of Christian perfection. By mid-century Robert Baird was testifying that it was necessary in all progressive churches "to preach to sinners as if they believed them to be possessed of all the powers of moral agency, capable of turning to God, and on this account, and no other, inexcusable for not doing so."[36]

Curiously enough, Baird's comment appeared in—of all places—the *Princeton Review*. Old School Presbyterians had been greatly distressed by the infiltration of Arminian views and Finneyite techniques into their denominational life, but after the break of 1837 they exhibited astonishing alacrity in climbing on the bandwagon and turning again to revivalism as "the only effective weapon in the church's arsenal for turning back the tide of uncouthness, materialism, and moral disintegration."[37] Ultimately Barnes, Beecher, and even Finney were defended in the pages of the *Princeton Review;* and James W. Alexander (1804–59) could refer with equal approval to the Calvinist and Arminian revivals of the past, saying: "Accidents may vary but the essence is the same,"[38] It was Charles Hodge

---

[35] See W. S. Hudson, *American Protestantism*, 71–74, 99–104.
[36] *Princeton Review*, XXII (1850), 204.
[37] Elwyn A. Smith, *The Presbyterian Ministry in American Culture* (Philadelphia, 1962), 214.
[38] *Ibid.*, 215.

himself who was the architect of the theory that permitted Old School Presbyterians to reverse their basic commitment. He did this by adopting Jonathan Edwards' distinction between natural ability and moral inability and then glossing over the distinction to such an extent that his position was not dissimilar to that of New School revivalists.[39] With even Old School Presbyterians no longer untainted, it is apparent that "the Methodist age" of American Protestantism had reached maturity.

The "prayer meeting" or "businessmen's" revival of 1857–59 serves as a symbol of how thoroughly the oversimplified piety of the revivalists had become domesticated in the American scene. This was a laymen's revival, growing out of noonday prayer meetings sponsored by the New York Y.M.C.A. and being carried forward by Y.M.C.A.'s in other major cities. The emphasis upon "holiness" and "the higher Christian life" which characterized the revival was a reflection of the influence of Finney's doctrine of Christian perfection, but the revival itself was in the hands of the laity and revealed little theological sophistication. Its major feature was its thorough respectability. Unlike earlier revivals, it seems to have evoked no opposition. A contemporary report noted that "there was remarkable unanimity of approval among religious and secular observers alike, with scarcely a critical voice heard anywhere." [40]

While there was much that was superficial in this "Methodist" or "evangelical" piety, its achievements were not inconsiderable. Philip Schaff, when reporting the American scene in 1854 to his former colleagues in Berlin, felt compelled to confess despite his reservations that "the United States are by far the most religious and Christian country in the world." "Table prayer," he noted, is "almost universal," "daily family worship" is the rule "in religious circles," and church attendance is "inseparable from moral and social respectability." In contrast to Berlin where there were only forty churches for a population of 450,000 with an attendance at public worship of no more than 30,000, New York with a population of 600,000 had "over 250 well-attended churches, some of them quite costly and splendid." In Brooklyn the proportion of churches to the population was even larger, and a similar state of affairs prevailed throughout the country.[41]

[39] For a discussion of the Old School "capitulation," see Elwyn A. Smith, *op. cit.*, 220–24.

[40] J. E. Orr, *The Second Evangelical Awakening* (London, 1949), 21.

[41] Schaff, *America*, 11, 35, 56, 78.

VIII

Utopianism, Millennialism, and Humanitarianism

The first half of the nineteenth century in the United States was a time of eager expectancy, unbridled enthusiasm, and restless ferment. A new nation and a new world were being born, and to many anything and everything seemed possible. It was a period when the comet's tail was said to have swept America and everyone went a little mad. "We are all a little wild here with numberless projects of social reform," Emerson wrote to Carlyle in the autumn of 1840. "Not a reading man but has a draft of a new community in his waistcoat pocket." The hyperbole is obvious.

Not everyone went mad and many were sufficiently prosaic to think that nothing more than a watch belonged in a waistcoat pocket. Still there were many who were not of the mind or spirit to keep their expectations under control. While European visitors were impressed by the popularity and vigor of conventional religion, they were also struck by the many new ways to heaven that were being fashioned in the American environment and by the strenuous efforts of others to give the heavenly existence earthly embodiment.

Two factors combined to produce the unusual religious ferment of these years. One was the social context. The other was the religious climate. In the American environment there was an absence of tradition and a sense of pregnant possibility which encouraged a spirit of experimentation. Nor was this experimentation inhibited by law. Unlimited freedom had been granted religious expression, no matter how eccentric it might be. And an abundance of cheap land and open space provided an unequaled opportunity to implement and institutionalize religious ideas. If the context was hospitable to innovation, the actual impetus that gave rise to most of the novel cults, sects, and movements was the climate of opinion generated by successive waves of revivalism.

Noah Worcester had pointed out in 1794 that the "sects" had profited from revivals, and this continued to be true. Successive harvests were to be reaped by the Shakers, the Mormons, the Oneida community, the Millerites, the Spiritualists, and a host of smaller and more transient groups. The revivals left many individuals distraught and torn by anxiety; and, having tried without success to gain a sense of assurance in their own churches, they were in a receptive mood to listen to new prophets who offered definite guarantees of spiritual security. While the emotional disturbance which revivalism left in its wake explains why even the most bizarre groups, once established, could garner adherents, it does not account for their origin. Here it was the spirit—ideas, attitudes, hopes—fostered by the revivals which played the creative role.

Three emphases stimulated by revivalistic preaching would seem to have been of decisive importance in creating the climate of enthusiasm out of which the new cults, sects, and communities emerged. For one thing, the revivalists demanded an immediate confrontation with God. This often took the form of an ecstatic vision or mystical illumination which could easily be interpreted as a new revelation. Second, the revivalists placed increasing stress upon the possibility of perfect sanctification, thus arousing a hunger for holiness and a life free from sin. Finally, they tended to dwell upon the ancient millennial expectation of a golden age to come, whether inaugurated by the personal return of Christ or established through the preaching of the gospel. All the groups which deviated from the norm of conventional religion during these years stemmed from at least one of these emphases, and most of them represented a blending of all three.[1]

[1] See A. L. Jamison, "Religions on the Christian Perimeter," in *The Shaping of American Religion*, ed. J. W. Smith and A. L. Jamison, 197–202.

The utopian vision

A prominent feature of the first half of the nineteenth century in America was the rise and decline of a variety of communal societies. All of them were impelled by a vision of an ideal or perfect life which they sought to actualize. These societies were never numerous, nor was the total number of adherents great. Most of them quickly appeared and as quickly disappeared. Only a few maintained themselves for any considerable period of time. Some were nonreligious in origin and orientation, and these exhibited the least staying power. Some were imported from abroad—the Rappites at "Harmony" in western Pennsylvania and later at "Harmony" in Indiana; the Separatists of "Zoar" in Ohio; the followers of William Keil at "Bethel" in Missouri and "Aurora" in Oregon; the Amana Society (The Community of True Inspiration) at "Ebenezer" near Buffalo and then in Iowa; the community of Swedish immigrants established by Eric Janson at Bishop Hill in Illinois. With the partial exception of William Keil's Rappite seceders, all these immigrant groups remained isolated from American life. But there were also indigenous communal societies. Of the indigenous communities where men and women sought sanctification in a perfect society, the Shaker settlements of Ann Lee and the Oneida community of John Humphrey Noyes were the most important. The Transcendentalist ventures at Fruitlands, Brook Farm, and Hopedale, on the other hand, were more typical in that they illustrated the pathos of shattered hopes which was the lot of most of the communal enterprises.

THE SHAKERS. The followers of Ann Lee (1736–84) provide an outstanding example of the blending of new revelation with perfectionist and millenarian ideas in the formation of a communal society.[2] Although "Mother Ann" had come to America with eight followers in 1774, the United Society of Believers in Christ's Second Appearing was not organized until 1787, three years after her death, when a former Free-Will Baptist preacher took charge and gave the Society its definitive shape.

Ann was the wife of a blacksmith in Manchester, England, and the mother of four children, all of whom died in infancy. She had become a member of a small group of Shaking Quakers who were crying out warnings of Christ's approaching second advent and predicting that

[2] See Edward D. Andrews, *The People Called Shakers: A Search for the Perfect Society* (N.Y., 1953), and Henri Desroache, *The American Shakers: From Neo-Christianity to Presocialism* (Amherst, Mass., 1971).

famine and pestilence were about to descend upon the wicked. The distinguishing feature of their worship, which gave them their name, was the frequency with which they would be "seized with a mighty trembling, with violent agitations of the body, running and walking on the floor, with singing, shouting, and leaping for joy." [3] In 1770 Ann became the vehicle of a revelation that the root and foundation of human depravity and the source of all evils afflicting mankind was the sex act. This was the original sin of Adam and Eve. This was the forbidden fruit. In the words of a later Shaker hymn:

> As lust conceived by the Fall
> Hath more or less infected all;
> So we believe 'tis only this
> That keepeth souls from perfect bliss.

The basic summons was to a celibate life, and it was about this emphasis that Ann gathered her first little company of disciples.

After leaving England and settling in Watervliet, New York, Ann gained no new adherents until 1779 when a revival at New Lebanon proved so disturbing that it brought Joseph Meacham (1742–96) and several members of his congregation into the fold. Other recruits were won as scattered revivals began to appear in western Massachusetts and Connecticut. During the final four years of her life, Ann was reported to have performed miracles which convinced her followers that she was Christ in his "second appearing," making manifest the female element in the Godhead and inaugurating the beginning of the millennium by gathering a faithful remnant out of the churches of Antichrist.

In 1787, three years after the death of Mother Ann, Joseph Meacham assumed leadership of the group, gathered the members into several "families" for communal living, drafted the constitution of the United Society, and elaborated and systematized Shaker doctrine. Everything was carefully regulated, and the violence of the earlier physical manifestations was subdued and reduced to a ritualistic dance in which worship was expressed by the body as well as by speech and song. In the new order that was at hand, all that had been "earthly, sensual, devilish" would become "spiritual, divine, and heavenly," and the whole endeavor of the Shakers

[3] See contemporary account in Smith, Handy, and Loetscher, *American Christianity*, I, 586–96. Also D. W. Patterson, *The Shaker Spiritual* (Princeton, 1980).

was to live a life of perfection as preparation for the perfect state promised to them. Since there would be no further need for the propagation of the human race in the new age, the inclusion of celibacy among the twelve virtues which must be pursued and practiced did not seem unreasonable.

Under Meacham's leadership the Society experienced a surge of growth with the onset of the Second Awakening. Within five years ten communities with more than two thousand members had been formed in Maine, New Hampshire, Massachusetts, Connecticut, and New York. A second period of growth began in 1805 when emissaries were sent West to reap a harvest in the wake of the great Kentucky revival, including two of the prominent leaders of the revival—Richard McNemar and John Dunlavy. By 1825 there were at least twenty communities scattered throughout Ohio, Indiana, and Kentucky, as well as in New England and New York, and within a few years the Society had about six thousand members.

Economically the Shakers prospered from the beginning. Farming was the basis of their economy but they quickly developed successful commercial and handicraft enterprises. For five or six years after 1837 the various communities were troubled by a wild burst of spirit-inspired communications which had the result of creating a deep fear of any further enthusiasm. After this loss of fervor and with the waning of rural revivalism, the Shakers attracted fewer and fewer new members. Although the communities remained prosperous, a steady decline in numbers had set in by 1850. A century later only a handful of elderly men and women remained.

THE ONEIDA COMMUNITY. While the Shakers were seeking perfection in celibacy, others were going to the opposite extreme, moving in an antinomian direction with their claims to holiness and even lapsing into sexual promiscuity. While opposed to the "spiritual wifery" which swept through certain perfectionist circles, John Humphrey Noyes (1811–86) was the most conspicuous perfectionist leader who placed a stamp of approval upon a departure from the accepted code of sexual relationships.[4]

Noyes was a product of the Finney revivals. A graduate of Dartmouth and the son of a successful Vermont business man who was prominent in state politics, Noyes had begun the study of law when Finney

[4] See Lawrence Foster, *Religion and Sexuality: Three American Communal Experiments* (N.Y., 1980), and M. L. Carden, *Oneida: Utopian Community to Modern Corporation* (N.Y., 1977).

captured him for the ministry and sent him off for a year at Andover Seminary and two years at Yale Divinity School. When he asserted that conversion brought complete release from sin, he was refused ordination. This, however, did not keep him from preaching wherever he could find groups of like-minded perfectionists and from giving further study to what he called "the Sin system, the Marriage system, the Work system, and the Death system." After much pondering, he concluded that it was necessary to create a society in which conditions would be favorable to the practice of perfection. He was later to declare that, as "the revivalists had for their great idea the regeneration of the soul," he had as his great idea "the regeneration of society, which is the soul's environment." [5]

The system which Noyes worked out was based on three fundamental doctrines. The first was total security from sin, but this security was so defined that it did not eliminate the need of discipline and improvement. The second was the conviction that the millennium had been introduced in A.D. 70, but had been obscured by spurious post-millennial growths of the second and third centuries. The third and most distinctive principle was the insistence that, since the saints were equally yoked in dedication to faith, the practice of primitive Christian communism—a communism which included the marriage relationship—was the only logical arrangement.

Noyes gathered a small group in Putney, Vermont, and in the early 1840's instituted a communism of property. When this communism was extended in 1846 by putting into operation his theory of "complex marriage," the local citizens were aroused and to avoid the possibility of being mobbed the community was re-established at Oneida, New York, two years later. A major stroke of luck was the conversion of Samuel Newhouse, the inventor of a highly effective small-animal trap. Trap manufacturing placed the community on a sound financial basis, until it was replaced as the chief industry by silver plate ("Community Plate") production. But economic considerations were incidental. The philosophy of the community was stated by Noyes in these words:

> Our warfare is an assertion of human rights; first the right
> of man to be governed by God and to live in the social state of heaven;
> second the right of woman to dispose of her sexual nature by at-

---

[5] J. H. Noyes, *History of American Socialism* (Philadelphia, 1870), 24. See also Tyler, *Freedom's Ferment*, 186.

traction instead of by law and routine and to bear children only when she chooses; third the right of all to diminish the labors and increase the advantages of life by association.

These principles, he insisted, must find expression in "one living organization before the Kingdom of Heaven can come." Thus personal sanctification and social regeneration went hand-in-hand.[6]

While Noyes fashioned a detailed and closely supervised pattern of life for the community, including procedures for "mutual criticism" and innovations in the education of children, it was the theory and practice of "complex marriage" which gained for the community its notoriety. This theory, which regarded each woman in the group as the wife of every man and every man as the husband of every woman, was instituted on religious grounds. Noyes's followers thought of themselves as saints purified by religious experience and disciplined to the practice of absolute fellowship among themselves by a total love of God. As a consequence, they believed that there was a basic incompatibility between absolute good will among the regenerate and the exclusive legal and physical bonds of conventional marriage. "Sexual communion," Noyes insisted, "differs only in its superior intensity and beauty from other acts of love" and it contributes to true mutality. But when sexual communion is restricted to acts of "special love" it becomes unsocial and dangerous to communal interests. The Oneida perfectionists resented the charge that they were practicing "free love," for sexual intercourse among them was "organized" rather than promiscuous, and they believed that it was inspired by true spirituality.

For thirty years the community remained true to its original ideals, but pressure from the outside world persuaded Noyes in 1879 to abandon the practice of "complex marriage." This in turn led to the abandonment of communal ownership of property the following year. A joint-stock company was formed, the shares were distributed among the former communitarians, and silver-plated tableware became the chief reminder of their former effort to institutionalize a sinless life and thus provide a foretaste of the kingdom of God.

TRANSCENDENTALISM'S "WILD OATS." When Emerson spoke of the draft of utopia to be found in almost every reading man's waistcoat pocket, he was thinking pre-eminently of some of his fellow Transcendentalists, for

[6] Cross, *The Burned-over District*, 335, 337.

188

in a curiously romantic way they also had appropriated the perfectionist and millenarian tendencies of the time. Emerson himself remained skeptical, but others were driven by an overpowering desire to anticipate the millennium by perfecting human institutions. Three small communal societies—Fruitlands, Brook Farm, and Hopedale—were the product of what in retrospect can be seen as their moment of aberration.[7]

Louisa May Alcott's *The Transcendental Wild Oats* is a fictionalized account of Bronson Alcott's venture in communal living at Fruitlands which began with high hopes in the spring of 1843 and collapsed before winter set in. Believing that "our freer, but yet far from freed, land is the asylum . . . for the hope of man," Bronson Alcott was convinced that only in America could "the second Eden . . . be planted in which the divine seed is to bruise the head of Evil and restore Man to his rightful communion with God in the Paradise of Good." This was his vision of Fruitlands. Unfortunately, what might have been at least a summer's idyl was spoiled by the domineering spirit of Charles Lane, a dour ascetic Englishman, who was determined that every natural human desire should be denied. One by one the members slipped away, the crops were left unharvested, and Lane finally departed to join the Shakers.

Brook Farm was a happier experiment. George Ripley, Unitarian minister and leading member of the "Transcendental Club," was its founder and director. In 1840, before resigning from the pulpit of his Purchase Street congregation in Boston, Ripley had told his parishioners that it was the business of Christianity to overthrow every social evil, and Brook Farm was designed to be, "if not the sunrise," at least "the morning star" of the new day in which the thinker and the manual laborer would be united in a noncompetitive society.

Most of the literary lights of the time participated at Brook Farm either as members, visitors, or supporters. The intellectual life at the Farm was exciting, and the social life, which included plays, dances, picnics, and boating parties, was gay. Since the members were better dreamers than farmers, the community was dependent upon outside support except for the income derived from its school, which was recommended by the Harvard faculty as an excellent place to send young boys who aspired to

[7] See Clara E. Sears, *Bronson Alcott's Fruitlands, with Transcendental Wild Oats by Louisa Alcott* (Boston, 1915) ; Zoltan Haraszti, *The Idyll of Brook Farm* (Boston, 1937) ; Adin Ballou, *History of the Hopedale Community* (Lowell, 1897) ; Mark Holloway, *Heavens on Earth: Utopian Communities in America* (N.Y., 1966).

become college students. In 1844, however, the members became entranced by the ideas of the French socialist, Charles Fourier (1772–1837), and decided to turn Brook Farm into a Fourierist phalanx. This necessitated conforming to a rigid theory of social organization and involved establishing industries and forming specialized labor groups. Money was borrowed, the school was neglected, and in 1846 a fire left the community insolvent. By this time many of the sponsors had lost interest, having been diverted by newer fads, and in 1847 the community wound up its affairs. Later Nathaniel Hawthorne looked back with nostalgia to "our beautiful scheme of a noble and unselfish life" at the Farm. "How fair in that first summer appeared the prospect that it might endure for generations, and be perfected as the ages rolled by into the system of a people and a world. Were my former associates now there—were there only three or four of those true-hearted men still laboring in the sun—I sometimes fancy that I should direct my world-weary footsteps thitherward and entreat them to receive me for old friendship's sake."

The community at Hopedale was a less dilettante effort. Established near Milford, Massachusetts, in 1841, it managed to maintain itself for fifteen years. Adin Ballou (1803–90), a Universalist minister, was the founder and guiding spirit. He was not a member of the "Club," but was a Transcendentalist nonetheless and a friend of Channing and Parker. Since "it was one of the declared objects of Christ's labors to inaugurate the kingdom of heaven on earth," Ballou was convinced that "the imperative duty" of Christ's disciples is "to pray and to work for that sublime end." Working meant "actualizing" New Testament teachings in order to initiate a world movement toward the perfect life. Some thirty persons responded to Ballou's summons to subject themselves to "all the moral obligations" of the religion of Jesus and to take the lead in banishing from the world "all things known to be sinful against God or human nature." Ten years later the community had grown to nearly two hundred members and was a moderate financial success. But when Ballou retired from active leadership, it was decided that the common fund would be more productive if diverted to private enterprise, and in 1856 the whole project was liquidated. The failure, Ballou remarked with sadness, was not financial but "moral and spiritual"—"a deficiency among its members of those graces and powers of character which are requisite to the realization of the Christian ideal of human society."

Other variant religious groups

Utopian communities which sought to reproduce the heavenly existence in earthly institutions were but one manifestation of the religious ferment of the first half of the nineteenth century. Other variant groups came to the fore in which the perfectionist motif was more subdued. Such groups as the Mormons, the Millerites, and the Spiritualists were no less symptomatic of the energies released by the prevailing religious climate, but they found their primary orientation in some other point of emphasis—in a new and supplementary revelation, in the reduction of the millennial expectation to a definite timetable of events, in the sudden bursting of the barriers to the spirit world.

THE MORMONS. The Church of Jesus Christ of Latter-day Saints which was to create for itself a great intramountain empire in the West had its origin in the remarkable story of Joseph Smith (1805–44), who in 1816 at the age of ten had come with his parents from Vermont to the vicinity of Palmyra, New York.[8] Here he absorbed much from the religious excitement of what came to be called "the burned-over district." Smith later reported that he was greatly disturbed by the religious controversies that swirled about him. "In the midst of this war of words and tumult of opinions, I often said to myself, what is to be done? Who of all these parties be right? Or are they all wrong together?" Troubled by these anxieties, he "retired to the woods" to seek wisdom of God. His prayer was answered by the appearance of two heavenly personages—the Father and the Son—who told him to hold himself apart from the contending denominations for a special task was to be given him. After a period of testing in which he received a series of further revelations, he was guided by the angel Moroni to discover long-buried golden plates which told the story of the Nephites and Lamanites, descendants of a lost tribe of Israel, who had inhabited the American continent centuries before. Among them Christ had appeared after his resurrection and had established the proper church order. The Lamanites, progenitors of the Indians, had apostatized and had defeated the faithful Nephites in a battle in which all the Nephites

---

[8] A recent account of Mormonism is L. J. Arrington, *The Mormon Experience* (N.Y., 1979). See also T. F. O'Dea, *The Mormons* (Chicago, 1957), and Fawn Brodie, *No Man Knows My Name: The Life of Joseph Smith* (N.Y., 1946).

except Mormon and his son Moroni were slain. The records of this ancient people were buried by Moroni in the hill Cumorah, and it was there that Smith discovered them together with the translating spectacles which enabled him to decipher what he later described as the Reformed Egyptian hieroglyphics of the text. In 1830 Smith's translation of the *Book of Mormon* was published at Palmyra.

This new scripture provided a basis for resolving the sectarian jangling which Smith had found so disturbing throughout his adolescent years, for it gave an authoritative judgment upon almost every issue that was in dispute. This fact was quickly recognized by Alexander Campbell who pointed out in his *Delusions: An Analysis of the Book of Mormon* (1832) that the golden plates had anticipated and given a definitive answer to "every error and almost every truth discussed in New York for the last ten years," including "infant baptism, ordination, the trinity, regeneration, repentance, justification, the fall of man, the atonement, transubstantiation, fasting, penance, church government, religious experience, the call to the ministry, the general resurrection, eternal punishment, who may baptize, and even the question of freemasonry, republican government, and the rights of man." And the *Book of Mormon* both buttressed its own judgments and provided for the future adjudication of controversy by insisting that anyone who denies "the revelations of God" and says "that they are done away, that there are no revelations, nor prophecies, nor gifts, nor speaking with tongues and interpretation of tongues" betrays his ignorance and denies "the gospel of Christ."

It is scarcely surprising that one of the first converts to embrace the new revelation should have been Sidney Rigdon (1793–1876), an ex-Disciple minister who had once contested Campbell's leadership, for the *Book of Mormon* stressed many of the basic themes of Campbellite preaching—free grace, free will, repentance, restoration, plainness of doctrine, democratic church government, opposition to "priestcraft," rejection of infant baptism, and even the distinctive Campbellite doctrine of baptism "unto the remission of sins." Nor in view of this heritage is it surprising that when young Joseph Smith on October 30, 1830, met with five friends in Fayette, New York, to restore "the Church of Christ in these last days," he should have chosen the typically Campbellite designation of "Church of Christ" for his reincarnation of the ancient order of church life. Four years later, at the instigation of Rigdon, the name was changed to the Church of the Latter-day Saints, and in 1838 it was given its present expanded form.

A further theme running throughout the *Book of Mormon*, which had wide appeal to people who were stirred by the romantic nationalism of the time, was the portrayal of America as the promised land—"a land which is choice above all other lands," a land to which none shall come "save they shall be brought by the hand of the Lord." Indeed, the whole biblical setting of the drama of salvation was transferred to an American setting. To the successive declarations of political, economic, diplomatic, and intellectual independence penned by Jefferson, Clay, Monroe, and Emerson was now added a declaration of religious independence. The Old World heritage was declared to be both obsolete and irrelevant, for the restoration of the true church was dependent upon the recovery of an independent American tradition which extended back to the time of the Babylonian Exile and had been validated by the postresurrection appearance of Christ on American shores.

Prior to the formation of the new church, Smith had had a revelation in which John the Baptist had appeared and had ordained him and Oliver Cowdery [9] to the "Priesthood of Aaron, which holds the keys of the ministering of angels, and of the gospel of repentance, and of baptism by immersion for the remission of sins." Thus equipped, he was directed to form the church by a revelation which designated "Joseph Smith, Jun., who was called of God and ordained an apostle of Jesus Christ, to be the first elder of this church," and "Oliver Cowdery, who was also called of God, an apostle of Jesus Christ, to be the second elder of this church." Then at the first meeting of the church, Smith's full office was made clear by a further revelation which stated that he should "be called a seer, a translator, a prophet, an apostle of Jesus Christ, an elder of the church through the will of God the Father and the grace of your Lord Jesus Christ," with the added admonition that the church should "give heed unto all his words and commandments . . . for his word shall ye receive as if from mine own mouth."

[9] Cowdery was Smith's clerical assistant. While in Vermont prior to moving to Palmyra, Cowdery had embraced some "extraordinary doctrines, apparently involving millennial expectations and direct revelation as well as some mysterious treasure hunting." Cross, *Burned-over District*, 38–39.

By 1830 the new scripture had been published, the new church formed, and the new prophet designated with powers of immediate revelation to deal with troublesome problems as they arose. In the course of time more distinctive doctrines were elaborated—a plurality of gods, for example, as well as of wives—which set the Mormons further and further apart from the generality of Christians. Adaptations of Masonic ritual were introduced, marriage for time and eternity was adopted, baptism for the dead was instituted, and the priesthood of Melchizedek was restored by the miraculous intervention of Peter, James, and John. Mormon millennialism, on the other hand, remained moderate and never became the focal point of enthusiasm. Its perfectionism was restrained, and the communitarianism introduced by Rigdon at Kirtland, Ohio, probably owed more to the Campbellite stress on the authoritative example of the New Testament Church (see Acts 2:44–45; 4:34–35) than to any perfectionist drive. The communal tendencies were not central, being a peripheral feature sustained by the exigencies of their hegira, and the United Order of Enoch—a form of co-operative economic activity—was never transformed into a full communism. Still it was abundantly clear that the Mormons were not a part of conventional society, and their separateness created antagonism. This hostility, in turn, increased their sense of separateness, and the sense of separateness encouraged further innovation.

The impact of Joseph Smith's new church in the area of its origin was scant, for it was removed almost immediately to Kirtland, Ohio, where Sidney Rigdon's congregation provided a larger nucleus of adherents. The growth of the church was astonishing, and new recruits were won in Missouri to which missionaries had been dispatched in a fruitless endeavor to convert the Indians. Trouble at Kirtland, stemming in part from the failure of Smith's "Anti-Banking Company" (so named to circumvent the legislature's refusal to grant a bank charter) in the Panic of 1837, led to shifting the base of operations to Independence and then Far West, Missouri. Pitched battles there brought about another removal, this time to Nauvoo, Illinois, where Smith attempted to establish a semi-independent domain. The tragic murder of Smith by an angry mob in 1844 while he was confined in the jail at Carthage precipitated one of the epic stories of American history—the heroic trek of the majority of the Mormons under the leadership of Brigham Young (1801–77) to a new "Zion in the

Wilderness." Sheltered by the mountains surrounding the basin of the Great Salt Lake, they at last found a measure of peace and security. By 1870 the number of Mormons in the intramountain region exceeded 140,000, many of them converts that had been won abroad.

THE MILLERITES. The movement which created the greatest flurry of excitement during the years of religious ferment had as its single point of emphasis a specific date for the literal fulfillment of the ancient expectation that Christ would return in glory to rule upon the earth. In various forms the millennial hope had been a consistent theme of revivalistic preaching, and the increasing number and magnitude of revivals heightened the interest of many in the Second Coming. By 1825 references to the belief that the return of Christ was approaching began to become more numerous, and the phenomenal awakening of 1831 convinced many that it must be quite near. This millennial expectation was in part a reflection of the overpowering optimism and perfectionist temper of the American people, but the Panic of 1837 gave it another turn. With their buoyant optimism having been dissipated by the distress and disaster attendant upon an economic depression, many found in millennialism a compensatory substitute for their shattered hopes. An immediate judgment day became the simplest solution to all earthly problems, the shortest possible cut to millennial perfection, a panacea which would set all things right at a single stroke.

William Miller (1782–1849), a farmer at Low Hampton, New York, was the key figure in the Adventist excitement of the late 1830's and early 1840's.[10] After his conversion in 1816, he had become a member of the Baptist church and began to study the Bible with particular attention to the last times. Interested in calculating the date of Christ's return, he probably found the clue which pointed to 1843 in the Boston edition of the British *Christian Observer* or a similar publication. By nimble arithmetic (years of 360 days—twelve 30-day months—instead of 365), he ultimately was able to prove to his satisfaction that "God in his wisdom has so interwoven the several prophecies that . . . they tell us the same things." In 1828 he felt a "call" to tell the world of his discovery that Christ would come "about 1843." "I tried to excuse myself," he later

---

[10] See Ernest Sandeen's chapter "The Millenarian Tradition in the United States, 1800–1845," in his *The Roots of Fundamentalism* (Chicago, 1970); also F. D. Nichol, *The Midnight Cry* (Washington, D.C., 1944).

explained. "I told the Lord that I was not used to speaking . . . that I was slow of speech and slow of tongue. But I could get no relief." By 1831 he had developed sufficient courage to begin to issue local warnings by sharing his discovery with neighbors and friends. Then he was asked to discuss his views in a nearby church, and he suddenly found that on this one subject at least he was eloquent. Invitations multiplied and he began to gain a measure of local notoriety. Although he was never ordained, Miller's ministerial status was somewhat regularized in 1833 with a license to preach.

While revivalism had bred a mentality which predisposed many to become ready converts to Miller's dating of the end of time, three events combined to give him a more than local reputation. The first was the publication in 1836 of his computations in book form under the title *Evidence from Scripture and History of the Second Coming of Christ, About the Year 1843*. The second was the Panic of 1837 which created for the book at the moment of its publication an unusually receptive audience. The third was the chance discovery of Miller by Joshua V. Himes (1805–95) at Exeter, New Hampshire, in 1839 while Miller was on a speaking tour of New England. Minister of a Christian Connection church in Boston and an indefatigable promoter, Himes had all the gifts that a century later would be associated with Madison Avenue. He immediately sensed the potency of the message of the plain-spoken farmer, and attached himself to Miller as his manager and publicity agent. He equipped Miller with a great chart displaying Miller's calculations in graphic form, purchased the biggest tent in the country for Miller's meetings, edited two journals—the *Midnight Cry* in New York and *Signs of the Times* in Boston—and helped to found others in Philadelphia, Cincinnati, Cleveland, Rochester, and Montreal. Other evangelists were recruited and sent on speaking tours; camp meetings were organized; children's books, catechisms, tracts, pamphlets, and even a hymnbook— *The Millennial Harp*—were published.

Despite vigorous condemnation of the movement by the majority of the ministers and ridicule by neighbors and friends, thousands were convinced by Miller's detailed calculations. Members of all denominations were enlisted, for the Adventist cause was nonsectarian and noncreedal, but Baptists, Free-Will Baptists, and "Christians" seem to have been the most susceptible. At the height of the Millerite fever there were probably more than 50,000 convinced believers and there may have been as many as a million others who were skeptically expectant.

Miller had been hesitant to be more specific than to say that Christ would return "about 1843," but in January, 1843, he announced that *this* year (from March 21, 1843, to March 21, 1844, taking into account the change in the calendar year) must see the end of time. The tension mounted as the year progressed, and was heightened by the appearance of a comet in the heavens. Meetings grew larger and converts more numerous, but March 21, 1844, came—and time still continued. On May 2, Miller confessed his error and acknowledged his disappointment, but one of his followers called attention to Habakkuk 2:3 and Leviticus 25:9 and announced that there obviously was to be a "tarrying time" of seven months and ten days. October 22, 1844, was to be the day of Christ's triumphant return and people were rallied once again with the slogan: "The Tenth Day of the Seventh Month." Miller was finally converted to the new date: "I see a glory in the seventh month which I never saw before. Thank the Lord, O my soul! . . . I am almost home. Glory! Glory! Glory! I see that the time is correct." The excitement revived, and the number living each moment as if it were their last exceeded that of the preceding summer.

With the second disappointment, most of those who had been caught up in the movement were completely disillusioned and the reaction of others was often bitter. Miller, for example, was excommunicated by the Baptist church at Low Hampton, and in 1849 he died, discredited and almost forgotten. A few became Shakers, giving that group its last important influx of new members. Some of those who remained steadfast in their hope, believing that only a minor error in calculation had been made, met in Albany in 1845 to form a conference which later splintered into three groups, the largest of which was the Advent Christian Church. Others were persuaded by Ellen Gould White (1827–1915) that Christ's failure to appear was due to a neglect of proper Sabbath observance and they formed the nucleus of what was to become the Seventh-day Adventist Church.

THE SPIRITUALISTS. Before the Millerites had fully recovered from their disenchantment, "the Rochester rappings" of the Fox sisters in 1848 created a new sensation which led to the development of modern Spiritualism.[11] The way had been prepared by the teachings of Emanuel Swedenborg (1688–1772) whose views had become something of a vogue among religious liberals and whose works had just been republished in a new English edition. Swedenborg claimed to have received communications from the spirit world by which knowledge of all things in the heavens and below the heavens had been given him. Interest in his teachings was reinforced by the spread of Mesmerism which utilized the strange power of "animal magnetism" to produce a hypnotic trance which was thought to point to the basic laws of the spirit world and to give promise of unlocking the mysteries of the life beyond. All that was needed to transform these embryonic ideas into Spiritualism was a mechanism for communicating with the dead, and it was such a device that was supplied unwittingly by two young girls, Maggie and Katie Fox.

The "rappings" began at Hydesville, New York, as a childish prank which some adults took seriously and was exploited by an older sister who lived in nearby Rochester. Soon the Fox sisters were holding public seances and notable converts were being won, including Horace Greeley, editor of the *New York Tribune*. By 1851 seven Spiritualist periodicals were being published, and six years later the number had increased to sixty-seven. The Universalists provided the most recruits, and their denomination never really recovered from its encounter with the spirit world. While interest had begun to subside prior to the Civil War, the movement found institutional expression in a number of Spiritualist "associations" which were to enjoy several flurries of renewed enthusiasm. In 1888 the Fox sisters acknowledged their hoax and demonstrated how they had produced the "rappings" by cracking their toe joints, but this exposure had little effect upon convinced believers.

The humanitarian impulse

Utopian communities and novel sectarian emphases were not the only expressions of religious ferment. Most of the enthusiasm generated by the Second Awakening was devoted to more conventional enterprises in which the concerns of the evangelically awakened often paralleled those of

[11] See J. A. Hill, *Spiritualism, Its History, Phenomena, and Doctrine* (Garden City, N.Y., 1919), and R. L. Moore, *In Search of White Crows: Spiritualism, Parapsychology, and American Culture* (N.Y., 1976).

the heirs of Channing. The revivalists were generally postmillennialists who assumed that an era of peace, justice, and goodness would precede the return of Christ. Consequently where there were revivals, there must be reform. Every aspect of society began to be subjected to eager scrutiny in order to scour and purify the earth in preparation for God's final act of redemption. Scarcely any phase of American life was left untouched. Temperance, Sabbath observance, world peace, profanity, vice, women's rights, slavery, the condition of penal institutions, educational innovations—all became objects of concern. The whole impulse was carefully articulated in a series of related societies and closely integrated with revivalistic efforts, as was made clear in 1835 by Theodore Dwight Weld (1803–95) in a letter to Lewis Tappan.

> God has called some prophets, some apostles, and some teachers. All the members of the body of Christ have not the same office. Let Delevan drive temperance, McDowell moral reform, Finney revivals, Tappan antislavery, etc. Each of these is bound to make his own peculiar department his main business, and to promote collaterally as much as he can the other objects. I have no doubt but Finney has erred in not giving as much collateral attention to antislavery as the present emergent crisis demands. And I am equally certain that I have not done as much collaterally to promote temperance and revivals while I have been lecturing on slavery as I ought.[12]

The revivals provided the impetus, summoning men and women to battle against sin; and the reform movements were the implementation of the thrust toward the coming kingdom of righteousness. The task of those who enlisted in the struggle was put succinctly by Finney: "Every member must work or quit. No honorary members."

THE EXPANDING CONCERN. While initially the reforms were mainly limited to rectifying individual vices—such as infidelity, drunkenness, Sabbath-breaking, dueling, gambling, and profanity—by methods of persuasion, the concern quickly expanded to include larger social issues. The masthead of the *New York Evangelist* illustrated the broadening of the reform impulse. In 1831, when it was insisting that "the emancipation of the world must engross the desires . . . and the enterprise of the world,"

---

[12] *Letters of Theodore Dwight Weld*, ed. G. H. Barnes and D. L. Dumond (N.Y., 1934), I, 243.

the masthead announced that the paper was "Devoted to Revivals, Doctrinal Discussion and Religious Intelligence." In 1835 it added "Practical Godliness," and in 1837 "Human Rights." World peace was an early preoccupation, and colonization in Africa was promoted to solve the problem of slavery. Later antislavery sentiment was channeled into a demand for "immediate emancipation." Prison reform captured the interest of some, and a noted group of women spearheaded interest in female education and woman's rights. The latter concerns culminated in the 1848 Seneca Falls Convention, held in the heart of Finneyite territory and convened by Elizabeth Cady Stanton who had been introduced to evangelical reform activity first by her cousin and then by her husband.

While Lyman Beecher in 1827 listed "monopoly of the soil" and the factory system as twin evils to be combatted, economic problems did not bulk large in the thinking of evangelical reformers. This was partly because they tended to think that individual conversions would remedy the ills of poverty, but primarily it was because an abundance of unsettled land in a largely agrarian society served as an escape valve for economic discontent. Antislavery agitation, of course, had deep economic implications, and some dabbled with peripheral urban and labor problems when they established havens for out-of-work sailors and formed societies to reclaim prostitutes from their shame. The Panic of 1837 brought further hesitant steps in the direction of a social gospel. In 1842 revivalist Edward N. Kirk (1802–74) stressed the need to ferret out the causes of poverty and to apply remedies. In 1851 an influential Presbyterian layman, Stephen Colwell (1800–71), published *New Themes for the Protestant Clergy* in which he advocated legislative enactments to better the condition of workingmen. Two or three years later the *Independent* began to urge programs of urban renewal which would have as their aim low rents, clean buildings, and healthy surroundings.

Although the reform activity in the beginning was a balanced thrust with each reform being seen as part of a larger strategy, there was a tendency among many to move in the direction of what was called "ultraism" or "one-ideaism." This was a passionate concentration upon one particular reforming cause as the panacea for all human ills. Temperance, for example, tended to be thought of by many as the remedy for poverty, vice, corruption, brawling, ill health, premature death, and marital discord. The benefits to be derived from securing the rights of women were sometimes viewed from a similar universal perspective. Reforms of diet, dress, and education also became the objectives of specific crusades. Ultimately, the growth of antislavery sentiment terminated the "ultraist" dispersal of the reform movement by the simple expedient of focusing attention on the sin of slavery and absorbing the reformist energies and personnel into this one great cause.

THE SLAVERY CONTROVERSY. Of all the reform crusades, the one that disrupted the churches and shook the nation to its foundations was the antislavery movement.[13] Other reform movements had taken an individualistic turn which enabled the existing denominations for the most part to contain them. They had developed within the context of revivalism and most of them were no more than urgent summons to individuals to free themselves from the entanglement of sin. The antislavery crusade, as conducted by the evangelicals, had begun with the same emphasis. Although the adoption of the British motto—"immediate emancipation" —seemed to imply a drastic abolitionism, it was interpreted to mean "immediate emancipation gradually accomplished" or "gradual emancipation immediately begun." The emphasis was upon persuasion and a personal renunciation of slavery as sin. The campaign of Theodore Dwight Weld and his band of rebels recruited at Lane Theological Seminary and later expanded to a biblical "Seventy" exhibited all the characteristics and methods of revival meetings. The immediatism they preached was an immediate repentance of the sin of any personal involvement in and support of the slave system. However gradual the emancipation was to be, there was a point at which persuasion would end and abolition would be required, and as antislavery sentiment was intensified it became increasingly difficult to keep the movement from going beyond the scope of revivalism to a demand that its moral standard be imposed and enforced by legislative action.

The disruptive effect of the antislavery agitation was accentuated because it appeared at a time when an equally aggressive proslavery movement was developing. During the first third of the century, there were

---

[13] See G. H. Barnes, *The Antislavery Impulse, 1830–1844* (N.Y., 1933); D. L. Dumond, *Antislavery: The Crusade for Freedom* (Ann Arbor, Mich., 1961); Bertram Wyatt-Brown, *Lewis Tappan and the Evangelical War Against Slavery* (N.Y., 1971). For documents illustrating both proslavery and antislavery views, see Smith, Handy, and Loetscher, *American Christianity*, II, 167–210.

many in the South who were quite as critical of slavery as anyone in the North, but by the 1830's this sentiment had declined and highly vocal champions of the South's "peculiar institution" were beginning to dominate southern opinion. The most influential factor in this shift was the increasing importance of cotton in the South's economy and the accompanying conviction that profitable cotton production was dependent upon slave labor. The bitter attacks of northern and western abolitionists also contributed to the consolidation of proslavery sentiment in the South, as did the anxiety aroused by the growing minority status of the slaveholding states in a rapidly expanding nation.

Thomas R. Dew (1802–46), professor of political economy at the College of William and Mary, laid down the basic lines of the slavery defense in 1832 when he argued that slavery not only had been from earliest times the chief means of advancing civilization but that it had been established by divine authority.[14] Southern clergymen picked up this final point and began to respond to the antislavery arguments by appealing to the sanction of Scripture and by depicting the abolitionists as anti-Christian atheists who reject the Word of God. "We defend the cause of God," Benjamin Morgan Palmer, minister of the First Presbyterian Church of New Orleans, was to declare.

THE DISRUPTION OF THE CHURCHES. The disruptive effect of the slavery issue upon the churches was foreshadowed by its role in the hidden agenda of the Presbyterian Old School–New School division in 1837, and it was more clearly evident in the formation of perfectionist "union" churches and in perfectionist defections among Methodists, Baptists, and Lutherans. Perfectionist tendencies, of course, always threatened to get out of hand. The revivals had multiplied conversions so rapidly that it became increasingly easy to overlook the great obstacle which man's sinful nature placed in the path to perfection and to believe that it was only an individual's willful perversity which caused him to temporize with sin. Thus many were moving into a perfectionist phase, which emphasized the abolition of sin almost to the exclusion of any preoccupation with creed, just at the moment that slavery was coming to be regarded by many as the one great sin. Since the established denominations tended to play down

[14] See *The Pro-Slavery Argument as Maintained by the Most Distinguished Writers of the Southern States* (Charleston, S.C., 1852), and W. S. Jenkins, *Pro-Slavery Thought in the Old South* (Chapel Hill, N.C., 1935).

slavery in the interest of maintaining denominational unity, they appeared increasingly to be condoning sin.

Although this perfectionist antislavery sentiment was to become widespread, its early focal point was in upper New York State. As early as 1835, the reorganized Central (formerly Oneida) Evangelical Association, with fifteen ministers, eight licentiates, and seven churches, was proposing that it be considered as the nucleus of a network of true churches free from all sin to which all right-minded congregations could repair as they found their old denominations entangled in unrighteousness. "Union of feeling and sentiment," ran the resolution, can never be obtained until the churches "abandon their exclusive creeds and incorporate nothing in their articles that will shut off their fellowship with any child of God." The one thing demanded by these "union" churches was an unequivocal stand against slavery, since "proslavery or apparently neutral churches are anti-Christian." By 1855 there were no fewer than eighty-three of these "union" churches in New York State alone and others were scattered through New England and the Middle West. In addition the entire Genesee Association was read out of the Congregational fold in 1844 for its perfectionist tendencies.[15]

New York State was also the center of antislavery agitation among the Methodists. In spite of the attempt of the national General Conference in 1836 to stifle discussion of the issue, hundreds of petitions demanding disciplinary rules against slavery continued to flood in from New York, especially from the Genesee conference. The bishops resorted to expulsions and discriminatory appointments in an endeavor to silence the antislavery forces, and at the 1840 General Conference they maintained their ironclad control in the face of petitions signed by ten thousand laymen and five hundred preachers. Between 1839 and 1842 isolated groups in New England, New York, and Ohio began to withdraw from the church, and finally in 1843 at a meeting in Utica the Wesleyan Methodist Church was formed on a typically perfectionist platform which included abolitionism as one of its tests for membership.

The Baptists suffered a similar defection which extended from Maine through New York to Michigan. It took shape in the formation of a competing Baptist Free Mission Society in 1843 and in the establishment of New York Central College at McGraw, New York. Among the Lutherans

[15] Cross, *Burned-over District*, 261, 278–81.

an antislavery faction of twenty-one perfectionist congregations in central New York in 1837 formed the Franckean Synod which denied membership to anyone who sanctioned the principle of slavery.

These were minor schisms, and their growth was nipped by a shift in the policy of the major bodies. Responding to the increasing pressure of antislavery sentiment, the Methodist General Conference of 1844 adopted a strengthened antislavery rule which preserved the unity of the northern section of the church at the expense of the southern portion which departed the following year to form the Methodist Episcopal Church, South. The Baptist foreign and home mission societies also were forced to take a firmer stand, which resulted in the formation of the Southern Baptist Convention in 1845. The Congregationalists, as a regional denomination, were able to move into the abolitionist camp without suffering disruption, while the Disciple or "Christian" churches were too loosely affiliated to suffer schism. The Old School and the New School Presbyterian churches, having divided in 1837, sought to muffle the controversy in order to avoid further division. The New School group succeeded in doing so for a time but it finally split in 1857, while the Old School churches forestalled any break until after the Civil War began. Lutherans were torn by controversy but the General Synod was able to steer a neutral course. The Episcopalians and the Roman Catholics tended to remain aloof from the controversy. Remaining aloof, of course, often meant that the proponents of a slave-based social order were free to speak while their opponents were urged to avoid creating dissension by remaining silent.

The division of the churches was prophetic of the political division that was to follow. By 1860 the crisis was at hand. As soon as the outcome of the presidential election was certain, the South Carolina legislature summoned a state convention which met on December 20, 1860, and unanimously declared "that the Union now subsisting between South Carolina and other states under the name of 'The United States of America' is hereby dissolved." Four months later Fort Sumter was shelled and the Civil War had begun.

During the agitation preceding the conflict women had emerged for the first time to play a significant political role. Some were important in enlisting financial support; some devoted themselves to organizational tasks; others took to the platform as eloquent advocates of abolition. The Grimké sisters from South Carolina, Sarah and Angeline, toured New England as agents of the Anti-Slavery Society. Harriet Beecher Stowe, one of Lyman Beecher's gifted daughters,[16] probed the conscience of the nation with her emotion-laden indictment of slavery in *Uncle Tom's Cabin* (1852). And when the war began, it was Julia Ward Howe who provided the stirring words of "The Battle Hymn of the Republic," with its closing line "as he died to make men holy, let us die to make men free," as the marching song of the northern armies.

In both North and South, preachers marched with the troops—some to bear arms, others to serve as chaplains. Prayer meetings were a familiar feature of life in the camps and in the field, the sound of hymn singing echoed across the lines, and in the Confederate armies especially, a continuing revivalistic fervor was often maintained. The concern of people at home for the troops was expressed through such agencies of churchmen as the United States Christian Commission (the Civil War equivalent of the World War II USO) whose agents distributed incidental necessities—including mittens, scarves, taffy, writing paper—and wrote letters to loved ones for the seriously wounded or illiterate. The Red Cross, under the inspiration of Clara Barton, won its spurs in assisting the personnel of the Sanitary Commission. But the most fateful feature of the war was its fratricidal character and its magnitude. It was a war that bruised almost every family in the land, changed the face of the nation, and created new problems both for the country and for the churches.

[16] Beecher's daughters were no less gifted than his sons—Henry Ward, Edward, Charles, and Thomas K. All the daughters were active abolitionists. Harriet continued to write and also to fight for numerous causes. Catharine's great contribution was in education, desiring to secure "professional advantages of education for my sex equal to those bestowed on men." She wrote, she agitated, she established female seminaries and colleges, and she organized societies to support her educational ventures. Isabella fought with equal zeal for the "great and holy work" of woman suffrage. See Marie Caskey, *Chariot of Fire: Religion and the Beecher Family* (New Haven, 1978).

PART III

YEARS OF MIDPASSAGE

1860–1914

IX

Post-Civil War America

The Civil War was a watershed between an old and a new America. The American people became much more heterogeneous in background. The advent of modern science drastically altered the intellectual climate. And the quickening pace of industrialization created new centers of power in national life.

The changing composition of the population was one of the conspicuous contrasts between the old and the new America. After 1840 a sharply increasing percentage of the population was of foreign birth. From 1850 to 1860 the number of foreign born had increased 84.4 per cent. From 1860 to 1870, in spite of the dislocation of war, there was a further increase of 34.5 per cent. The first great influx had come from Ireland and Germany, but before the end of the century many nations were contributing to the growing number of new Americans. In contrast to the overwhelming predominance of British elements in the population at the beginning of the century, only a small percentage of the new arrivals were from England, Scotland, and Wales. By 1900, out of a population of 75 million, one-third were either of foreign birth or children of foreign-born parents. Of these 25 million new Americans, 8 million were German in background; 5 million were Irish; 2½ million had come from Austria, Hungary, Poland, and Italy; another 2½ million had come from the Scandinavian countries; 850,000 were French Canadians; and 774,000 had come from Russia. In addition to these totals, there were several million grandchildren of the immigrants who had arrived in the 1840's, 1850's, and 1860's.

A second contrast between the old and the new America was the radical shift in the intellectual climate. Geology, in the person of Charles Lyell (1797–1875), had been busy rewriting the Genesis account of the origin and early history of the earth. But it was the new biology, as set forth by Charles Darwin (1809–82) in his *Origin of the Species* (1859), that was to become the chief symbol of the intellectual revolution. The idea of evolution, of course, was not new. It had been championed by Hegel (1770–1831) and Comte (1798–1857), and the writings of Herbert Spencer (1820–1903) were to be more important than those of Darwin in pointing up the full implications of evolutionary thinking. Spencer adopted the doctrine of evolution as a unifying philosophical principle and sought to apply it to all phenomena. *Progress, Its Law and Cause* (1857) set forth the basic thesis that was elaborated in his subsequent writings: *First Principles* (1862), *Principles of Biology* (1864–67), *Principles of Psychology* (rev. ed., 1870–72), *Principles of Sociology* (1876–96), and *Principles of Ethics* (1892–93). With this evolutionism penetrating every realm of thought, a new history began to be written which was based on the application of evolutionary theories to the understanding of the past. And this new historical understanding bolstered the developing "higher criticism" of the Bible—first in Germany and then in Britain and America—which many were to find so disturbing.

A third feature of post-Civil War America was a marked shift in the center of power. Before the war the agrarian democracy envisaged by Jefferson still reigned supreme, although the lure of the city had begun to replace the lure of the West among young men of spirit and ambition. The census statistics for the decade 1840 to 1850, which revealed that the population of the cities had increased 90 per cent while the population of the country as a whole had increased only 36 per cent, gave a foretaste of what was to come. Ten years later, in 1860, the capital invested in industry, railroads, commerce, and urban property was greater than the value of all the farms from the Atlantic to the Pacific. The Civil War had "the effect of a hothouse" on this industrial growth. Military needs and currency inflation caused the mills to roar louder and the blast furnaces to flame higher. By the time Ulysses S. Grant took the oath of office as President of the United States, there was no longer any doubt that the dominant influence in American life had shifted from the rural countryside to the burgeoning urban communities. The successive efforts of Grangers, Greenbackers, and Populists to dislodge the commercial and industrial interests from the centers of power simply confirmed the fact that they were fighting a lost cause, for they never were able to win more than regional victories.

Each of these facets of post-Civil War society was to pose critical problems for the churches, but their full significance did not become clear for a decade or two. In the meantime, there were pressing problems which demanded immediate attention.

Reconstituting the nation

When Abraham Lincoln stood on the windswept fields of Gettysburg and spoke of those who "four score and seven years" before had "brought forth on this continent a new nation, conceived in liberty, and dedicated to the proposition that all men are created equal," he was recalling the theme which had given meaning and significance to the sense of American nationhood. But now this venture had been brought into question. Although Lincoln looked forward to the time when "this nation, under God, shall have a new birth of freedom," there was no blinking the stark, stubborn, present fact that the American people were engaged "in a great civil war, testing whether that nation, or any nation so conceived and so dedicated, can long endure."

THE BOND OF RELIGION. From the beginning of national life, religion had served as a bond of unity which helped to overcome the divisive effects of competing local interests and regional concerns. The Great Awakening had done much to make the several colonies emotionally one by binding them together in a common cause, generating a common loyalty, fostering common sentiments, and thrusting forward a common leadership. But it was a theological interpretation of the American past, present, and future that had contributed most to making them one nation.

211

What had welded the diverse people of the colonies—Englishman, Scots, and Germans; Georgians, Virginians, and New Yorkers—together was the consciousness of being summoned to a God-given mission. God had "designed this continent . . . to be the asylum of liberty" and had selected America to be an example to the nations. There was scarcely anyone who had not believed with Lyman Beecher that the establishment of the United States "in the full enjoyment of civil and religious liberty" had been a "design of Heaven" to demonstrate to the world "by one great successful experiment of what man is capable" and thereby to awaken among peoples everywhere the "desire and hope and effort" that would produce "revolutions and overturnings" until the whole world was free.[1] It was this conviction that had given Americans whatever sense of a common nationality they had, and it was this conviction that gave such moving power to the few brief words spoken by Lincoln at Gettysburg.

As tension had mounted between the North and the South, there had been agonized efforts to preserve the unity of the nation by reminding people of their God-given vocation. But the slavery question proved so disruptive that not even the churches could be kept from separating, and their divisions were prophetic of the tragedy that was to follow. Few had believed that the war could come. The notion that the nation could descend to fratricidal strife was unthinkable to most Americans. "There must be no war," had been a repetitive refrain. But the war had come, and its effect was shattering. The great "experiment" had gone wrong. The protective hand of divine Providence seemingly had been removed. No longer could Americans picture themselves as an example to the nations. Nor could they ease their tortured spirits by placing the blame for the disaster upon extraneous circumstance. The responsibility could not be sought beyond the American people themselves. No outside nation was involved. No foreign influence played any part in precipitating the tragedy. The machinery of peace was at hand in the orderly procedures of national life, but it had not been utilized.

The traumatic effect of the war was doubly compounded when what had been the bond of union was twisted to serve the cause of division. It was both natural and appropriate for the churches, North and South, to provide chaplains for the combatants and to organize agencies to minister to the temporal as well as the spiritual needs of the soldiers. It was no less

[1] Quoted by Tyler, *Freedom's Ferment*, 1.

natural for them to seek God's blessing and to claim divine sanction for their opposing armies, but it was profoundly disconcerting and disturbing. Those on both sides of the Mason-Dixon line in theology and piety were brothers, yet they offered contradictory prayers. In both North and South, the God who had made them a nation was being reduced to the partisan of a section.[2] When the bond which had united them was being utilized by apologists in both camps to justify the resort to arms, it was clear that the war itself must somehow be brought within the scope of a larger design of God if the nation were to be reunited.

Although not many gave themselves to this latter task, Lincoln was struggling throughout the war years to find a larger meaning to the conflict than that suggested by any simple alliance of Providence with either the North or the South.[3] Displaying a deeper theological perception than many preachers, he wrote to John Hay in 1862 that "it is quite possible that God's purpose is something different from the purpose of either party; and yet the human instrumentalities, working just as they do, are of the best adaptation to effect his purpose. I am almost ready to say that this is probably true; that God wills this contest, and wills that it shall not end yet." Later in the same year he told a Congressional delegation that he believed that God "will compel us to do right in order that he may do these things, not so much because we desire them as that they accord with his plans for dealing with this nation." And then he continued: "Sometimes it seems necessary that we should be confronted with perils which threaten us with disaster in order that we may not get puffed up and forget him who has much work for us yet to do." In his Second Inaugural Address, he reverted once again to this theme.

> On the occasion corresponding to this four years ago, all thoughts were anxiously directed to an impending civil war. . . . Neither party expected for the war the magnitude or the duration

[2] Two Presbyterian theologians, J. H. Thornwell and R. L. Dabney, were the most effective apologists in linking the position of the South with the cause of God and religion. Thornwell declared that "the Scriptures not only fail to condemn slavery, they as distinctly sanction it as any other social condition of man." To call slavery sinful, therefore, is to reject the Bible. "Our policy," wrote Dabney, must be "to push the Bible argument continually" and force the enemies of slavery to reveal their true infidel colors. Presbyterians, of course, were not alone in this enterprise. Episcopalians, Baptists, and Methodists played their part. Even John England, Roman Catholic bishop of Charleston, wrote a sturdy defense of slavery on biblical grounds. For representative statements, see Smith, Handy, Loetscher, *American Christianity*, II, 177–78, 182–86, 201–10.

[3] See W. J. Wolf, *Lincoln's Religion* (Chicago, 1974), and J. H. Moorhead, *American Apocalypse: Yankee Protestants and the Civil War* (New Haven, 1978).

which it has already attained. . . . Each looked for an easier triumph, and a result less fundamental and astounding. Both read the same Bible, and pray to the same God; and each invokes his aid against the other. It may seem strange that any men should dare to ask a just God's assistance in wringing their bread from the sweat of other men's faces; but let us judge not, that we be not judged. The prayers of both could not be answered—that of neither has been answered fully.

The Almighty has his own purposes. . . . If we shall suppose that American slavery is one of those offenses which, in the providence of God, must needs come, but which, having continued through his appointed time, he now wills to remove, and that he gives to both North and South this terrible war, as the woe due to those by whom the offense came, shall we discern therein any departure from divine attributes which the believers in a living God always ascribe to him?

Fondly do we hope—fervently do we pray—that this mighty scourge of war may speedily pass away. Yet, if God wills that it continue until all the wealth piled by the bondman's two hundred and fifty years of unrequited toil shall be sunk, and until every drop of blood drawn with the lash shall be paid by another drawn with the sword, as was said three thousand years ago, so still it must be said, "The judgments of the Lord are true and righteous altogether."

Lincoln, of course, was not alone in exploring the theme of God's hand in the conflict. Of the theologians who picked it up and elaborated it, Horace Bushnell and Philip Schaff were most prominent.[4] Like Lincoln, they both saw the war as the product of the guilt of the whole nation, the humiliation of an arrogant and boastful people, a supreme hour of trial designed to aid the nation to fulfill rather than to forfeit its destiny. Slavery had been the Achilles' heel of a nation called to exemplify what it meant for all men to be created free and equal, but slavery was not the sin of the South alone. The evil was inherited by the whole nation. Nor was slavery the real cause of the war. The real issue was whether or not the American people were to be a true people—a true nation—and thus

4 See W. A. Clebsch, *Christian Interpretations of the Civil War* (Philadelphia, 1969). Also Moorhead, *American Apocalypse*, and T. J. Pressly, *Americans Interpret Their Civil War* (N.Y., 1962).

capable of fulfilling their destiny. Hitherto—"half-loyally and half-lawlessly"—Americans had claimed a self-made and thus a false nationality. Too many had thought of the nation as their own creation and they had never given themselves fully to it. The several states had "simply kenneled under the Constitution" and had not been merged and compacted into a true nation.

As the product of the collective guilt of the American people, the war was an act of divine judgment. But to Bushnell and Schaff it was more than that, for it presented the possibility of redemption and renewal. Believing as they did that without the shedding of blood there is no atonement, they viewed the war as a sacrificial and cleansing tragedy that contained within it the possibility not only of preserving but also of regenerating the nation. The "baptism of blood" was thus to be seen as an act of divine mercy through which the nation could be reborn, purged of its sin, and recalled to its proper vocation. Upon the anvil of suffering and under the hammer of a providential God, it was to be hoped that what had been only a federation made up by a temporary surrender of power would be forged into a true nationhood. It seemed clear to them that nothing less than a common tragedy was sufficient to effect the necessary reconciliation that would unify a heterogeneous population into the free and responsible society which from the beginning had been God's intention for the American people.

What Lincoln, Bushnell, and Schaff were seeking to do was to restore to the American people their former bond of union by helping them to understand that even in the war itself God's will was being worked out in the life of the nation. The verdict of the war could then be accepted with grace both by those who gained the triumph and by those who suffered defeat, for by this reappropriation and reinterpretation of the American experience the conflict could be transmuted into something more than an occasion for future bitter memories. It was with this thought in mind that Lincoln looked forward to the future task as he brought his Second Inaugural Address to a close with words that have never been forgotten: "With malice toward none; with charity for all; with firmness in the right, as God gives us to see the right, let us strive on to finish the work we are in; to bind up the nation's wounds; to care for him who shall have borne the battle and for his widow and orphan—to do all which may achieve and cherish a just and lasting peace among ourselves, and with all nations."

THE FAILURE OF RECONSTRUCTION. Having compressed into four years a bloody slaughter that was comparable in magnitude only to the losses inflicted over a decade and a half by the Napoleonic wars, it was to be expected that festering sores would be left which would complicate and long delay the task of binding up the nation's wounds. Still there were many factors that could be counted upon to facilitate the healing process, not the least of which was the general weariness of the people with the war. The generous spirit exhibited by Grant in victory and the dignified acceptance of defeat by Lee had the immediate effect of tending to minimize recrimination. Reconciliation was further eased by "mystic chords of memory" which stretched back beyond the strife to the common history that previously had been shared. And having been schooled in the providential view of history, there were many who were prepared to accept the outcome of the war as a clear manifestation of God's will for the nation. Reduced to its simplest form, the plain implication of the providential understanding of defeat was stated by a young South Carolinian: "I think it was in the decrees of Almighty God that slavery was to be abolished in this way, and I don't murmur." [5] Other Southerners found it possible to take the more positive view articulated by Bushnell and Schaff. Stephen Elliott (1806–66) of Georgia and Richard H. Wilmer (1816–1900) of Alabama were conspicuous examples of theologians who were able to find in the war grounds for gratitude to God for settling "the meaning of the Constitution," restoring to the American people "one undivided country," and making clear the true mission of the nation.[6] Within this perspective, both Lee and Lincoln had served as instruments in the hands of God to effect his purposes; and it was this understanding which made it possible for both men to be lifted from the status of partisan leaders to that of national heroes.

Unfortunately the universal esteem in which Lincoln and Lee came to be held was deceptive, for the reconciliation was destined to be incomplete and a unified national life was never fully re-established. However decisive the war had been, the peace proved to be inconclusive. In the absence of strong leadership, the national government could not agree on what to make of its victory. Efforts at reconstruction were delayed, confused,

[5] Quoted by S. E. Mead, *Lively Experiment*, 143.
[6] Clebsch, *Christian Interpretations of the Civil War*.

indecisive, and of short duration.[7] There was little evidence of that "firmness" to "strive on to finish the work we are in" of which Lincoln had spoken. Some, to be sure, sought to gain political advantage by "waving the bloody shirt," but this did not conceal the increasing disposition in the North to leave the South to its own devices and to get on with the business of tapping the national till and reaping the profits of a booming economy. Seldom in history has a nation been so heedless of the fruits of victory. The issues which had stood at the center of the conflict were subordinated to partisan politics and the task of restoring the Union by protecting the fundamental rights of all its people was neglected.

As soon as it became apparent that little support was to be given the law-abiding elements in the South, unrepentant extremists became convinced that their cause was not wholly lost. Bands of hoodlums—Jayhawkers, Red Shirts, Knights of the White Camellia, and Klansmen—were recruited to intimidate law-abiding citizens by night-riding forays of pillage and torture. With amazing rapidity unreconstructed malcontents gained control of the former seccessionist states, silenced the dissent of other white Southerners, and put the Negroes "in their place"—a place that sometimes afforded them less protection than their previous status as slaves. While Lee continued to be revered, it was General Nathan Bedford Forrest—Grand Wizard of the Ku Klux Klan—who was to become the romantic hero that young white Southerners of spirit were encouraged to admire and emulate.

Although the outward ties of national life had been restored by the war, the resulting unity was far removed from that true nationhood which some had dared hope would be the consequence of the baptism of blood through which the American people had passed. In 1880, to be sure, Atticus G. Haygood (1839–96), Methodist president of Emory University, preached a Thanksgiving sermon on "The New South"[8] in which he repeated the theme that had been articulated by Elliott and Wilmer. But many of his fellow Southerners did not heed his appeal to recognize that the abolition of slavery had been a blessing and that their duty now was to

[7] See J. H. Franklin, *Reconstruction after the Civil War* (Chicago, 1961) ; C. Vann Woodward, *Reunion and Reaction: The Compromise of 1877 and the End of Reconstruction* (Boston, 1951) ; and Lawanda and J. H. Cox, *Politics, Principle, and Prejudice, 1865–1866* (N.Y., 1963).

[8] Reprinted in Smith, Handy, Loetscher, *American Christianity*, II, 372–77.

rejoin the Union in spirit as well as in fact. As early as 1865 another Methodist preacher in Mississippi had exhorted the South: "If we cannot gain our *political*, then let us establish our *mental* independence." [9] Actually, in the vacuum created by the withdrawal of national leadership, a very large degree of political independence was achieved, and this fostered a growing mental independence. The successful defiance of the brief effort at Reconstruction along the lines of a national policy made it possible for many Southerners to ignore the verdict of the war and to cling to an understanding of the American Constitution that had few points of contact with either the realities of the past or the necessities of the future. This essentially romantic interpretation of the American experience left the South intellectually and emotionally isolated from the rest of the nation. There was no conversion to an understanding that the nation was anything more than a mere aggregation of sovereign states. What unity there was had been achieved by leaving the major issues—so far as the South was concerned—unresolved, and from these unresolved issues a later generation was destined to reap a bitter harvest.

THE SOUTHERN CHURCHES.   The independent regional course of development that the South was permitted to pursue following the Civil War fostered a growing sectional self-consciousness that was to manifest itself in the religious as well as in the political and intellectual life of the southern states. There were, of course, some ecclesiastical links with the rest of the nation. Those denominations which had not divided over the issue of slavery prior to the Civil War experienced no great difficulty in resuming their former unified denominational life. For them there was no prewar heritage of bitterness to overcome, and they had had scant time and opportunity to develop the vested interests of an independent institutional life.

The ease with which the latter denominations effected the reunion of their severed branches is illustrated by the Protestant Episcopal Church. Although a separate Episcopal church had been formed in the South following Secession, the fact that a schism had occurred was never recognized nor accepted by northern Episcopalians. At the General Convention of 1862, the roll call included the southern dioceses—an action which implied that the missing bishops and deputies were only temporarily

[9] K. K. Bailey, "Southern White Protestantism at the Turn of the Century," *American Historical Review*, LXVIII (1963), 618.

absent. The next convention was held in October, 1865, six months after Lee had surrendered. Prior to the convention, the Presiding Bishop wrote to all the southern bishops inviting them to attend and assuring them of a cordial welcome. The response to the invitation was varied. Those who attended, however, were received with such friendly warmth that a month later the General Council of the southern Episcopal church voted that, since the circumstances which had brought it into existence had ceased, the southern dioceses were free to renew their former affiliation.

The denominations which were able to reunite, however, represented only a minority of southern church members. The three major denominations were the Methodists, Baptists, and Presbyterians. The Methodists and Baptists had gone their separate ways since 1845. While there was much initial sentiment for reunion in both communions, the Methodist Episcopal Church, South, and the Southern Baptist Convention had become too firmly established to be quickly dismantled. Time was needed to untangle the existing institutional structures, but each year of delay made the prospect of success less promising as a result of the steadily increasing southern regional self-consciousness. By 1869 the Methodist *Richmond Christian Advocate* was declaring: "We consider reunion neither possible nor desirable." [10]

The Presbyterian division was more recent but it was complicated by an earlier schism. Since 1837 the Presbyterians had been divided into Old School and New School bodies. In 1857 the New School Presbyterians divided over the issue of slavery, and in 1861 the southern Old School Presbyterians formed a separate church. In 1864 the New School and Old School Presbyterians in the South united. Thus at the close of hostilities the major body of Presbyterians was confronted by a three-way split. The first task seemed to be the healing of the breach in the North as a preparatory step to ending the schism between North and South. This occasioned delay, for negotiations initiated in 1866 were not brought to a successful conclusion until 1870. By this time an intense sectional spirit had reasserted itself in the South, and Presbyterians were to be no more successful than Methodists or Baptists in bridging the institutional barriers that had been erected.

The three large southern denominations justified their separate existence by constantly reminding themselves that Southerners were "a

[10] Sweet, *Virginia Methodism* (Richmond, 1955), 285.

different people," [11] and over the years their ecclesiastical isolation helped to give substance to their assertion. Several factors combined to produce this result. The most obvious, of course, was the mere fact of institutional separation which left most of the southern churches out of touch with the developing religious life of the rest of the nation. Equally important in giving the religious and ecclesiastical ethos of the South its own distinctive cast was the nostalgia which caused Southerners to idealize the past and to look askance at any innovation in either thought or practice. And further heightening the insularity of the southern churches was their role as the only available vehicle for the institutional expression of sectional feeling. Politically the South was divided into several states. Economically the South was not homogeneous and its new commercial and industrial ventures were tied to northern financial centers. Thus the southern Methodist church, the southern Presbyterian church, and the Southern Baptist Convention were the only institutional links which bound the South together. While the regional character of these denominations contributed to the popular esteem in which they were held throughout the South, this culturally grounded popularity tended to insulate them further from the larger Christian community.

The folk-religion of the southern churches was further heightened by an adherence to the doctrine of "the spirituality of the church." This concept had been first formulated by a Presbyterian, John Holt Rice

[11] The *New Orleans Christian Advocate* was to declare in 1880 that the "civilization of the two sections, and the customs and character of the people are in many things diverse. . . . One broad distinction is that the Southerner, as a matter of honor and principle, minds his own business, while the inborn nature of the North is to meddle. The South is tolerant, courteous, and refined in its contact with people in the ordinary associations of life. The North has a prying, inquisitive disposition, and is bent on bringing every one to its way of thinking and doing."
There are also differences in religion. "There is a south side to churches and religion, not so much in regard to their creeds, articles of religion, and church polity, as in the type of piety that prevails. Methodists and Presbyterians in the South profess the same faith as Methodists and Presbyterians in the North, and yet they are not the same people. The political meddling of the Northern churches is, of course, one difference. . . . There is a secularity about them, and a style that brings them into near fellowship with worldly enterprises and organizations. They *run* things up there—churches as well as factories and railroads. The style of their preaching is in contrast with ours, and is largely of the politico-sensational order. The North has been over-run with professional evangelists, whose methods and teachings have in many instances done harm. People raised in these churches, and imbued with their spirit, if converted, are apt to be essentially defective in the higher traits of Christian character. With many excellent people and exemplary Christians among them, and with much that is good and worthy of imitation in their church work, there is a spirit and practice, and a type of religion, that we should regret to see in our southern churches." Quoted by H. D. Farris, *The Circuit Rider Dismounts* (Richmond, 1938), 148–49.

(1777–1831). When it became apparent in 1827 that the slavery issue was apt to disrupt church life, Rice suggested that the church should "confine itself to making good Christians" and not concern itself with matters beyond its competence, such as the civil arrangements of society. By this means a bifurcation was introduced which permitted the churches to condone slavery while condemning card-playing and dancing, and which was reflected in the subsequent attitude of southern Methodist bishops who rejoiced that their church held aloof from political questions and was "satisfied to perform her own legitimate duties." [12]

Basically, however, the southern churches preserved and perpetuated the popular evangelicalism of the immediate prewar period, stressing sentimental preaching, periodic revivals, and heartfelt religion. While outsiders could point to many defects, including a rigid biblicism which sometimes tended to become obscurantist, there were also manifestations of an impressive vitality that on occasion broke the bonds of established custom. This southern evangelicalism was not distinctive in itself. Parallel expressions were to be found in other sections of the country. What made it distinctive was its almost complete predominance throughout the South and its success in withstanding any fundamental change in either thought or practice over a long period of time.

The churches and the freedmen

When he assumed the Presidency in 1861, Abraham Lincoln had noted the obligation imposed upon him by the Constitution to see that "the laws of the Union be faithfully executed in all the States." A month later he issued a call for seventy-five thousand volunteers in order to fulfill this constitutional duty. Combinations "too powerful to be suppressed by the ordinary course of judicial proceedings" had arisen, and this left him with no alternative but to utilize the armed forces of the United States "to cause the laws to be duly executed." The integrity of the nation was at stake, and the fundamental issue of the conflict that followed was the preservation of the nation. The precipitating cause of the war, however, had been the issue of human bondage, and before the strife was over the system of human slavery had been brought to an end by executive proclamation. As a

[12] E. T. Thompson, *The Spirituality of the Church* (Richmond, 1961), 21. Sweet, *Virginia Methodism*, 298. S. S. Hill, *Southern Churches in Crisis* (Boston, 1968).

consequence of the presidential action and the later constitutional amendment, American Negroes—for the first time in any significant numbers—were given an opportunity to determine their own destiny. Legal and extralegal restrictions were to limit this freedom, and its exercise was to prove hazardous in many localities. Nonetheless the Emancipation Proclamation marked the beginning of a new era.

EDUCATIONAL WORK AMONG THE NEGROES. Almost immediately after the outbreak of the war, the need of the Negro "contrabands" who were soon to become freedmen was self-evident—a need for food, clothing, shelter, work, and protection. But perhaps the greatest need was education, for throughout much of the South it had been illegal to teach a slave to read. While some slaveowners found it to their advantage to evade the law, the great mass of the Negroes were illiterate. It was at this point that the northern churches felt that they could best help, and a whole cluster of agencies—Julius H. Parmalee listed seventy-nine [13]—were organized for this purpose. The early interdenominational Freedmen's Aid Commissions quickly gave way to more firmly established denominational societies and boards, and their work was strongly supplemented for a five-year period after 1865 by the Freedmen's Bureau of the federal government.

As early as September, 1861, a representative of the American Missionary Association reported that among the "contrabands" at Fortress Monroe in Virginia there were many, both parents and children, who were delighted by the prospect of learning to read, and before the end of the month classes had been organized to provide them with the necessary instruction.[14] Shortly thereafter a representative of the American Baptist Home Mission Society was at Fortress Monroe to investigate conditions among the Negro refugees, and later another representative gave a dismaying account of the plight of the 15,000 "contrabands" in Washington, D.C., and Alexandria, Virginia. "What are we to do for the freedmen which are being thrown in increasing numbers upon our hands?" he asked. "One thing is certain, they must not be neglected." The response of the Society was an appeal for funds to send missionaries "to engage in such instruction of the colored people as will enable them to read the Bible and to become self-supporting." [15]

[13] "Freedmen's Aid Societies," U.S. Department of Interior, Office of Education, *Bulletin No. 38* (1916), 268-95.
[14] A. F. Beard, *A Crusade of Brotherhood* (Boston, 1909), 121.
[15] *Baptist Home Missions in North America* (N.Y., 1883), 398-99.

At the end of the war there were 3,500,000 freedmen and most of the denominations participated in the attempt to rectify the consequences of two centuries of neglect. The most extensive work was that of the American Missionary Association, a society primarily Congregational in support and personnel. By the end of 1863 it had eighty-three teachers in the field, and by 1867 the number had increased to 528. Among the surviving institutions which the Association fathered are Fisk, Atlanta, and Tougaloo universities, Talladega College, and Hampton Institute. Northern Methodists and Baptists also carried on broadscale programs among the freedmen, while more modest contributions were made by northern Presbyterians, Disciples, Episcopalians, Quakers, and Roman Catholics. The southern white churches exhibited a brief flurry of interest in Negro education at the end of the war, but hostile sentiment in the South soon put an end to almost all official activity. Isolated individuals continued to provide help, and by 1880 there were signs of a renewed interest in Negro education among southern Methodists, Baptists, and Presbyterians. The editor of the *Alabama Christian Advocate*, however, still spoke for many southern Christians in 1883 when he sought to squelch the emerging concern for Negro education in his denomination by calling it a "form of negrophilism" which smacks of "Yankee fanaticism." [16]

The men who went South to aid the Negroes were frequently distinguished persons. The Baptist missionary-teachers were typical in this respect. J. G. Binney had been president of Columbian College (now George Washington University) and a missionary to Burma; Nathaniel Colver was professor of biblical theology at Morgan Park Theological Seminary (later the Divinity School of the University of Chicago); Marsena Stone was a professor at Denison University; Joseph T. Robert had taught modern languages at Iowa State University and was president of Burlington University when he accepted a call to go to Augusta, Georgia; J. W. Parker had gained distinction during a twenty-year pastorate in Cambridge, Massachusetts; and Henry M. Tupper and Charles H. Corey were recent graduates of Newton Theological Seminary, one having served as an army chaplain and the other as an agent of the United States Christian Commission during the war. The young women who volunteered for service in the South were equally able and devoted.

The beginnings were crude and meager. Most of the pupils could

[16] Farish, *The Circuit Rider Dismounts*, 196–97.

neither read nor write, and those who could had little further training. Housing was a major problem. Few whites dared sell or lease a building to the missionaries. In Richmond they had to make-do with an old slave pen known as "Lumpkin's Jail." In Raleigh two old log cabins and a delapidated cotton shed served to house the fledgling institution that was established. In Nashville an abandoned government building was purchased. And the missionaries were subjected to all manner of harassment by rougher elements among the whites. They were ostracized, threatened, and on occasion the school buildings were burned. Even the church press of the South invited the "white cravatted gentlemen from Andover" and the "pretty Yankee girls" to go home.[17]

The opposition to the missionary-teachers was based on a determination to keep the Negro "in his place." "He is and must continue to be," declared the *New Orleans Christian Advocate* in 1867, "the laboring man of the South, because he is not fitted . . . for anything higher."[18] Particular scorn was directed at the idea of providing the Negro with a classical education. The Rev. Samuel A. Steele of Mississippi declared: "*Hic, haec, hoc* will be the ruin of the African." Actually, of course, little classical education was provided. In addition to instruction in the most rudimentary subjects, most of the curriculum was pre-empted by industrial arts, agriculture, and homemaking, with due attention being given to Bible study. Prior to the twentieth century only a handful of institutions attained anything that even resembled a collegiate status. But the contribution that was made by those who gave themselves in sacrificial service to the education of the Negroes was great. Two-thirds of them were women, and an eloquent tribute was paid them by one who had been lifted from ignorance to enlightenment by their endeavors.

These noble women left homes, their friends, their social ties, and all that they held dear . . . to labor among the recently emancipated slaves. Their courage, their self-sacrificing devotion, sincerity of purpose, purity of motive, and their unshaken faith in God were their pass keys to the hearts of those for whom they came to labor. . . . Their monument is builded in the hopes of a race

[17] Franklin, *Reconstruction*, 52.
[18] R. M. Cameron, *Methodism and Society in Historical Perspective* (N.Y., 1961), 209.

struggling upward from ignorance. . . . As long as the human heart beats in grateful response to benefits received, these women shall not want a monument of living ebony and bronze.[19]

THE NEGRO DENOMINATIONS. Black Baptist churches were to be found in the South prior to 1790 but these were few and isolated.[20] Most blacks belonged to existing churches. This also was true in the North where a few served as pastors, but separate congregations began to be organized whenever a sizable Negro community developed. Among Methodists two independent denominations appeared at an early date. The African Methodist Episcopal Church, organized in 1816, grew out of a separation from other Methodists which occurred in Philadelphia in 1784; and the African Methodist Episcopal Zion Church, organized in 1820, stemmed from a similar separation in New York in 1796. Among Baptists local African congregations were formed in Boston in 1805, in New York in 1807, and in Philadelphia in 1809. There was a parallel movement in the West. In 1836 the Providence Baptist Association was formed of churches in Ohio, and in Pittsburgh, Detroit, and Buffalo. In 1838 the Wood River Association brought together churches in Illinois. Fifteen years later, in 1953 the Western Colored Baptist Convention was established. Although there was a Negro Congregational church in New Haven, Connecticut, in 1829, this was exceptional. Most independent African churches were either Baptist or Methodist.

In the South, Negro membership also was concentrated in Baptist and Methodist churches, and the Negro members of these churches sometimes far outnumbered the white members. In Richmond, Virginia, for example, there were 387 white members of the First Baptist Church in 1841 and 1,708 colored members. In 1846 the First Baptist Church of Charleston, South Carolina had 261 white members and 1,382 Negro members; at Georgetown, South Carolina, there were 33 and 798; at Natchez, Mississippi, there were 62 white and 380 colored. These figures were not exceptional and a similar situation prevailed among the Methodists. In isolated instances separate Negro churches were organized but few,

[19] Beard, Crusade of Brotherhood, 234.
[20] See E. F. Frazier and C. Eric Lincoln, The Negro Church in America and the Black Church Since Frazier (N.Y., 1974), and A. J. Raboteau, Slave Religion: The 'Invisible Institution' in the Antebellum South (N.Y., 1978), for interpretations of the development of the church among the black population.

if any, of them were permitted to be fully independent. The property was held by white trustees and the congregations were subject to the supervision of neighboring white-controlled churches. The single attempt of the African Methodist Episcopal Church to penetrate the South prior to the Civil War was quickly stamped out.

It is scarcely surprising that the defeat of the South should have been accompanied by the withdrawal of most Negroes from the churches of their former masters. For one thing, the mere act of leaving was a symbolic expression of their new freedom. Furthermore, few congregations were prepared to give the Negro any different status than he had had as a slave. He was still expected to sit in the back seats or the gallery, was given no voice in church affairs, and had little chance of attaining even the humblest office. Even had the churches pressed for some tangible integration, it is unlikely that the mass of Negroes would have gone along. As slaves they had had enough of white churches. Much of the preaching addressed specifically to them had not been particularly inspiring if Molly Finlay's report was at all typical. "He just say, 'Serve your masters; don't steal your master's turkey; don't steal your master's chicken; don't steal your master's hog; don't steal your master's meat; do whatsomever your master tell you to do." [21] Nor, even with the best of intentions, could white ministers have spoken pointedly and effectively to their needs, for the white ministers had not experienced what it meant to be a slave.

Negro Episcopalians and Presbyterians defected in large numbers. The Episcopalians made no effort to form them into a separate church, while the Presbyterians waited until 1898 to transfer its Negro remnant in a new Afro-American Presbyterian Church. The smaller Cumberland Presbyterians acted more expeditiously, organizing the Colored Cumberland Presbyterian Church as a separate body in 1874. Two other small withdrawals occurred when Negro members of Primitive (Old School) Baptist churches in the South established a separate organization in 1865 called the Colored Primitive Baptists in America, and when Negro members of the Methodist Protestant Church in 1866 formed the African Union Colored Methodist Protestant Church. The Roman Catholic Church also suffered defections, with the greatest number being lost in Louisiana, the center of Roman Catholic strength in the South.

The Methodist Episcopal Church, South, which had had a Negro

[21] Hodding Carter, *The Angry Scar: The Story of Reconstruction* (N.Y., 1959).

membership of 207,766 in 1860, had become an all-white body by 1870. A considerable number of the Negroes who had belonged to the southern Methodist church were formed into new congregations by missionaries of the northern Methodist church. But the greatest harvest of Negro Methodists in the South was reaped by the African Methodist Episcopal Church and the African Methodist Episcopal Zion Church. The former body grew from 20,000 members in 1864 to almost 400,000 twenty years later, while the latter group increased from 6,000 to approximately 300,000 during the same period. In 1866 the remaining 49,000 Negro members of the Methodist Episcopal Church, South, were placed in a separate conference, and four years later they were set adrift to pursue an independent existence as the Colored (Christian) Methodist Episcopal Church.

The largest number of Negroes were Baptists, and they rapidly outdistanced their only rival—the Methodists. This surge of growth was due perhaps to the ease with which Baptist congregations could be formed. Negro Baptist state conventions were organized in North Carolina in 1866, and in Virginia and Alabama in 1867. Within a few years every southern state had its own Negro Baptist convention. After several abortive attempts to establish a national organization, the majority of Negro Baptists were brought together in 1886 as constituent members of the National Baptist Convention.

The Negro churches made striking gains in membership which far surpassed the growth of other churches. Prior to the Civil War the percentage of Negroes who were church members was less than half that of the white population. By 1916 it was slightly larger, having increased from about 11 per cent to approximately 43 per cent. The popularity of the church among Negroes stemmed at least in part from the fact that it was one of the few institutions that was exclusively their own. Cut off from most areas of social and political life, the Negroes found in the church an opportunity for self-expression, recognition, and leadership. It was hardly a coincidence that until well into the twentieth century most of the outstanding Negro leaders had been ministers, for the ministry provided one of the few opportunities for leadership open to a Negro. Furthermore, the church was the primary agency of self-help in the Negro community, and it played an important role in maintaining group cohesion under difficult circumstances and in fostering the self-respect which is gained only through the exercise of independent responsibilities.

227

Renewal of home missionary concern

Apart from the South, where the white churches shared the impoverishment of their region, the post-Civil War years witnessed a marked resurgence of missionary activity. For more than two decades after 1840, the evangelistic thrust of the churches had been blunted by a variety of circumstances. The theological disputes spawned by Finneyite "new-measures" revivalism had proved to be divisive and distracting, and the available energy had been further sapped by the task of countering the disaffection created by the Mormons, Millerites, and Spiritualists. The attention of the churches was also diverted by the increasing demands of the slavery controversy, and finally the war itself had thrust to one side all other preoccupations. By the time the smoke had cleared from the battlefields, however, the earlier theological controversies had been forgotten and the churches in the North were ready to redirect to other pressing tasks the energy which had been devoted to ministering to the soldiers. Part of this energy was pre-empted by needs in the South, but the needs of the West and of the multiplying cities were not forgotten.

CHURCH EXTENSION IN THE WEST. The endeavor of the churches to match the pace of the westward migration was a continuation of their missionary activity on the earlier frontier, but "church extension" now became a more popular term than "home missions" to describe this activity. While a fairly substantial society had been established along the Pacific coast prior to the Civil War, the population was vastly augmented in the postwar years, and large numbers of people began to pour into the intervening territory. There was a steady succession of new states admitted to the Union, with four being added in 1889 alone.

The three enticements which drew people to the newer West were mining, cattle, and wheat. The initial discoveries of gold and silver in California, Nevada, and Colorado were followed by similar discoveries— including copper—in Arizona, Idaho, and Montana. Then the discovery that cattle could live on the prairie grass that stretched from the Missouri to the mountains and could survive the winter without shelter led to the creation of a great cattle empire. And when it became clear that it was feasible to raise winter wheat on the plains, there was a swelling influx of homesteaders. The whole development was spurred by the rapid extension of railroads throughout the area, with the first transcontinental track being completed in 1869.

Establishing churches in the new West was an unusually difficult enterprise, for the early population was scattered and transient. In the mining camps, the inhabitants—mostly men—had been stirred by a lust for gold and they had come not to establish homes but to make a "killing." Few men could have cared less than the miners about the desirability of establishing churches. When G. A. Reeder, a Methodist missionary at Yuma, attempted to hold meetings in the schoolhouse, he found himself preaching to empty seats. It was not until he took up a "position on the chief corner of the town, having the wholesale liquor establishment for my 'backing,' all the leading saloons near by, and a score of liquor dealers and drinkers within hearing," that he was able to make any impression on the community.[22] Effective missionary endeavor was equally difficult in the cow country, for it also had a floating population of men who were not greatly addicted to the practice of religion. And unlike the miners, the cowhands were not even gathered into temporary communities. The homesteaders provided a more stable population, but even among them a drought or a disastrous grasshopper infestation might provoke a further migration that would suddenly deplete the membership of a newly established church. With few exceptions, it was not until trading centers began to develop along the railroads that the churches were able to establish themselves on a permanent basis.

Methodists led the westward march of the churches, with Presbyterians, Congregationalists, and Baptists only a step behind.[23] The Methodist Church Extension Society was founded in 1864, and the Presbyterian and Baptist boards also allocated funds for the evangelization of the West. After the long period in which it had merged its interests with the Presbyterians, Congregationalism had developed a resurgent denominational consciousness and it was determined not to allow itself to be eclipsed on the new frontier. The Congregational General Council, which met in Boston in 1865, authorized the raising of a rather astonishingly large sum to be used in the West, and thereafter the Congregationalists engaged in a surge of church-building activity. By 1882 there was not a western state or territory in which Congregationalism was unrepresented. The Baptists

[22] W. C. Barclay, *History of Methodist Missions*, Vol. III, *Widening Horizons* (N.Y., 1957), 242.
[23] In addition to Barclay, see R. T. Handy, *A Christian America: Protestant Hopes and Historical Realities* (Oxford, 1971); C. M. Drury, *Presbyterian Panorama* (Phila., 1952); C. B. Goodykoontz, *Home Missions on the American Frontier* (Caldwell, Id, 1939); C. L. White, *Century of Faith* (Phila., 1932).

pioneered in the use of "chapel cars" which were shunted onto railroad sidings and used as places of worship until church buildings could be constructed. The Baptists also persuaded the Union Pacific and Central Pacific railroads to give them a site for a church and parsonage in every village along their rights-of-way. C. C. McCabe of the Methodist Church Extension Society rode up and down the western lines establishing churches, and boasted that the Methodists were building more than one Methodist church for every day in the year and proposed to make it two a day.

Other religious bodies were also represented in the West. The Disciples expanded into the new territory mostly through individual initiative until the church extension board was formed in 1884. The Episcopalians organized the whole area into missionary dioceses but they were hampered by the problem of recruiting a sufficient number of ministers to implement their ambitious plans. The Unitarians established a few churches, and the Lutherans exhibited real strength among German and Scandinavian immigrants who took up land in the West. Roman Catholics were to be found in increasing numbers in the mining centers, and their ranks were swelled by the acquisition of those territories in the Southwest which had a Spanish-speaking population. Furthermore, largely through the instrumentality of Bishop John Ireland (1838–1918) of St. Paul, Minnesota, colonies of Roman Catholics from Ireland were established in the northern tier of states.

URBAN REVIVALISM. While the churches were busy evangelizing the West, they continued to be concerned with the population flowing into the cities. The rural area of the nation was being enormously expanded as the frontier receded before the plows of the homesteaders, but even this expansion did not counterbalance the denuding of the older rural areas as young people left marginal farms to man the mills and the stores in the new communities that were springing up at every important railroad junction. And an even greater attraction was being exerted by the major metropolitan centers that were developing at key points throughout the country. In the 1830's Finney, Beecher, and Barnes had experimented with conducting revivals among urban people; and the "prayer meeting" revival of 1857–59 was an urban phenomenon. A fully systematized urban revivalism was to be the major contribution of Dwight L. Moody (1837–99) to American church life. Whereas Finney's great successes were won in communities where the population rarely exceeded ten thousand,[24] Moody was to achieve fame by galvanizing into action the religious forces of cities with a million or more inhabitants. Finney's triumphs in Western, Utica, Rome, and Rochester were duplicated by Moody in London, New York, Philadelphia, Boston, and Chicago.

If the new revivalism was shaped and systematized by Moody, it was fathered and promoted by the Y.M.C.A.[25] Contemporary observers noted that the move to the cities tended to relax the ties of habit, social pressure, and emotional association which had bound the new arrivals to the church in their former places of residence. The Young Men's Christian Association was a British import designed to counter this tendency among teenage boys who were striking out on their own for the first time. The Boston Y.M.C.A., organized on the British model in 1851, was quickly duplicated in other cities. Its prospectus expressed its hope of becoming "a social organization of those in whom the love of Christ has produced love to men; who shall meet the young stranger as he enters our city, take him to the church and Sabbath school, bring him to the Rooms of the Association, and in every way throw around him good influences, so that he may feel that he is not a stranger, but that noble and Christian spirits care for his soul."

Initially established as "a mission of the evangelical churches to young men," the eager members of the "Y" soon turned the tables and transformed the Y.M.C.A. into a mission to the whole community. They collected funds to aid the destitute and cared for the sick in hotels and lodging houses, but their principal activity was evangelistic—working in rescue missions, organizing groups for Bible study, distributing tracts, and going out to preach on street corners or wherever they could gather an audience. Soon they were to become the chief agency of the churches in promoting communitywide revival campaigns. It was through participation in such activities of the Chicago Y.M.C.A. that Dwight L. Moody was introduced to organized evangelistic work and induced to forsake his commercial pursuits in order to devote himself wholly to the business of conducting revivals.[26]

---

[24] Rochester, with a population of 14,404 in 1835, was the single exception.

[25] Out of a similar concern, women in 1858 began organizing Y.W.C.A.'s to surround young women in the cities with Christian influence. See C. H. Hopkins, *History of the Y.M.C.A. in North America* (N.Y., 1951).

[26] See J. F. Findlay, *Dwight L. Moody: American Evangelist* (Chicago, 1969).

The "business" of conducting revivals is the appropriate term for Moody. He not only was a businessman, he looked like a businessman, talked like a businessman, took things in hand like a businessman. By utilizing every technique of efficient business promotion—"planning, organization, publicity, vast sums of money, a host of workers, skillful executive direction"—Moody was able to demonstrate that citywide revivals could be produced almost at will, and in the process he became the first and foremost representative of a new breed of professional evangelists. Whitefield, Wesley, Nettleton, and Finney had made revivalism a full-time profession, but the "new breed" was distinguished by their strong emphasis upon the results to be gained by efficient business methods. Had Moody not been deflected from his business career, it is likely that with his ebullient energy and talent for organization he would have carved out a financial empire for himself analogous to those of such friends and supporters as Cyrus McCormick, Marshall Field, and John Wanamaker. As it was, he made a fortune in religious work, but gave it all away so that at his death his only estate was $500 which he did not know he had.

Moody had been born in Northfield, Massachusetts. He had gone to Boston at the age of seventeen to enter his uncle's shoe business, and two years later, in 1856, had shifted to Chicago in order to take advantage of the greater opportunities offered by that lustily growing city. "I can make more money here in a week than I could in Boston in a month," he wrote to his brother. Within five years he had an upper-bracket income and a comfortable nest egg in the bank. Having professed conversion in Boston, he displayed equal vigor in church work. In Chicago he participated in the activities of three different churches, organized a mission Sunday school, dragooned passers-by into the noonday prayer services of the Y.M.C.A., and served as chairman of its visitation committee. In 1861, finding Y.M.C.A. work—where every person was a potential customer—much more challenging than the shoe trade, he abandoned his business career in order to give full time to the "Y." The war years were spent commuting to army camps as an agent of the United States Christian Commission (the Civil War analogue of the United Service Organization of World War II), while at the same time continuing to look after his mission Sunday school. In the final year of the war, he organized the Illinois Street Church for those graduates of his mission who felt ill-at-ease in the other churches of the city.

After the war, Moody became something of a civic institution in Chicago. "Every man has his own gifts," he said. "Some start things; others can organize and carry them on. My gift is to get things in motion." Operating on the basis that "it is better to get ten men to work than to do ten men's work," he soon had a host of projects under way, most of them connected with the Y.M.C.A. of which he had now become "librarian and agent." By a clever scheme of financing he was instrumental in erecting a spacious building—including an auditorium that would seat three thousand persons—for the work of the association. At the dedication in 1867 he gave unabashed expression to his aggressive spirit: "When we stop trying to enlarge our work for the Lord and raise money for it, we shall become stale and stupid. . . . We must ask for money, *money*, MORE MONEY at every meeting; not for the support of the Association—as it now is—but to enlarge its operations." Shortly after its completion the building burned down, and before the embers were cool Moody is reported to have solicited sufficient new subscriptions to replace it.

In the meantime, through informal talks at meetings of one type and another and by shrewdly observing the successes and failures of the preachers who conducted services at his Illinois Street Church, Moody was gaining skill as an evangelist—a skill that he perfected in addresses at Y.M.C.A. and Sunday school conventions. It was a triumphal two-year tour of the British Isles from 1873 to 1875, however, which was to make him a public figure with a national reputation. A chance encounter with two philanthropic laymen on a visit to England in 1872 in connection with his Y.M.C.A. work had led to an invitation to come back the following year to conduct a series of evangelistic meetings. Taking Ira D. Sankey (1840–1908) with him as his song leader, the tour had begun inauspiciously at York. Minor triumphs in the north of England were followed by major victories at Edinburgh and Glasgow, and when London was invaded for a four-month period the total attendance at the meetings was more than two and one-half million.

With the unbroken series of successes of the British campaign having being reported in sensational terms by the press, Moody was greeted on his return to the United States by the query as to what he would do in America. If there was a question in the minds of others, there was no question in his. He had found his vocation. As a New England country boy, he knew that "water runs down hill," and he was convinced that in the life of the nation "the highest hills are the great cities." If we can stir the cities, he contended, "we shall stir the whole nation." In the next five years he duplicated his British triumphs in America. Beginning in Brooklyn, where a skating rink was remodeled to hold the crowds, he moved on to Philadelphia for the winter, with John Wanamaker purchasing a freight warehouse to serve as an auditorium. In New York, P. T. Barnum's Hippodrome was rented; and in Chicago and Boston, where no buildings of sufficient size could be found, tabernacles were constructed. From Boston, after a period spent in the smaller New England cities, he went on to Baltimore, St. Louis, Cleveland, and San Francisco.

An editorial in the *Nation* (March 9, 1876) commented that "the Moody and Sankey services are an old-fashioned revival with modern improvements." The improvements were mostly highly efficient methods of organization. Everything was carefully planned in advance. Nothing was left to chance. There were committees for finance, prayer, publicity, home visitation, Bible study, music, tickets, and ushering. An executive committee was appointed to make sure that all the other committees functioned properly. No advertising device was neglected, and considerable sums were spent on posters and newspaper notices. When someone complained that it was undignified to advertise religious services, Moody replied that he thought it more undignified to preach to empty pews. Cities were divided into districts, and squads of workers were trained and sent out to visit each home. Notables were recruited to grace the platform. Sankey's music was a great attraction, as was that of the massed choirs. And the singing of gospel songs by the congregation was a stirring experience. But it was Moody's warmhearted, slap-dash, no-nonsense, colloquial style of preaching that established complete rapport with those who attended and persuaded vast numbers to proceed to the inquiry rooms, where they were given "decision cards" to sign for the use of local pastors in following up the conversions that were professed.

Moody never pretended to be anything more than a layman. Such theology as he had was rudimentary at best. Finney had written a book of almost one thousand pages to explain the points at which he differed from orthodox Calvinist doctrine. Even had he had the necessary training, Moody would never have thought of embarking upon such an enterprise. Once when Moody was confronted by a woman who said that she did not believe in his theology, he answered: "My theology! I didn't know I had any." [27] He insisted that instead of troubling his hearers with the disconcerting intricacies of theology, he simply stuck to the "three R's" of the gospel: "Ruin by sin, Redemption by Christ, and Regeneration by the Holy Ghost." God loves everyone, and all that you need to do to be saved is to believe that Christ died for you. To the man who said, "I am so constituted I can't believe," Moody said, "Men can believe if they will. It is not because men cannot believe; it is because they will not believe." The central fact, so far as Moody was concerned, was that any man can obtain salvation. He called attention to Acts 17:30, God "commandeth all men to repent," and insisted that this left no room for questions of innate depravity, predestined election, and human inability. "When God commands anything, he gives you the power to obey," said Moody. "We are free agents. God allows us to choose." And it was a very simple choice, a "fair, square, practical" choice, that permitted no neutrality: "We are either for God or against him."

To those who criticized either his methods or his message, Moody had a stock reply: "It doesn't matter how you get a man to God provided you get him there." And to most of the churchmen of the time this was a persuasive answer. Endorsements of his campaigns cut across almost all denominational lines and embraced almost all shades of theological opinion, for he had developed what seemed to be a quick and easy system to reach the unchurched masses of the cities. After a few years, however, it became clear that Moody was not reaching "the masses." His audiences, as was repeatedly pointed out, were made up of "the better class of people." Nor was there much evidence, in spite of claims to the contrary, that the campaigns boosted the rate of growth of the churches.[28] Moody's greatest contribution was to lift the morale of the churchgoing segment of the population, to infuse it with new enthusiasm, and to stimulate giving to a wide variety of Christian enterprises.

Moody exerted his most lasting influence on the college campuses where the students were greatly impressed by his openhearted spirit of devotion. A surprising feature of his student conferences at Northfield was

[27] This disclaimer was a quip and not true; see S. N. Gundry, *Love Them In: The Proclamation Theology of D. L. Moody* (Chicago, 1976).
[28] W. G. McLoughlin made a careful statistical analysis which indicates that the Moody campaigns had little effect, either in Britain or America, in increasing church membership. *Modern Revivalism*, 202–06, 262–67.

their distinctly liberalizing effect. Moody found it helpful to invite as featured speakers some of the ablest theological scholars who were competent, as Moody was not, to deal with the acute threats to their faith that the students were experiencing as a result of the new scientific inquiries and the new biblical studies. In spite of feeling himself singularly ill-equipped to speak to students, Moody was successful in deeply influencing many of the "first minds" of the college campuses, including Henry Drummond, George Adam Smith, John R. Mott, Robert E. Speer, Sherwood Eddy, and Charles Foster Kent.

THE SUNDAY SCHOOL MOVEMENT. The other great evangelistic enterprise of the Protestant churches following the Civil War was the Sunday school movement.[29] Since early in the century missionaries of the American Sunday School Union had been busy establishing Sunday schools for the children of the nation, and they had been given powerful support when Horace Bushnell, in *Christian Nurture* (1847), argued the need to supplement revivals with "more natural" and "more constant means of grace." Though the Sunday School Union continued to exist, the dynamic new agency was to be the International Sunday School Association. This was a popular lay enterprise which carried forward the whole endeavor in a burst of new enthusiasm and devotion.

As was true of so many religious movements in the latter part of the nineteenth century, Dwight L. Moody was the chief instigator, having conceived the idea of breathing new life into Sunday school work and having recruited B. F. Jacobs (1834–1902), a Chicago wholesale grocer and real estate man, to forward the project. Described by his friends as "a steam engine of a man," Jacobs quickly became the key figure. He captured control of the informal conventions assembled at the time of the Sunday School Union meetings, and turned them into an independent organization which promoted city, county, state, and national conventions of Sunday school workers. The movement was frankly interdenominational, and its goal was to multiply through united effort the number of communities throughout the land where the influence of the Christian religion reigned supreme. This was to be done by enlisting, training, and inspiring a corps of dedicated teachers in every community to revitalize

---

[29] See E. M. Fergusson, *Historic Chapters in Christian Education in America* (N.Y., 1935); M. C. Brown, *Sunday School Movements in America* (N.Y., 1901); and *Encyclopedia of Sunday Schools and Religious Education*, ed., J. T. McFarland and B. S. Winchester, (N.Y., 1915).

the Sunday school and to supplement its traditional instructional purpose with a definite evangelistic objective. The heart of the project was a highly efficient county-convention system which utilized mass rallies to kindle ardor and zeal while at the same time introducing the workers to new methods and providing them with a modicum of training. So great was the enthusiasm awakened at the rallies that a convention often became the occasion for a revival in the city in which it was held.

One of the major innovations, which had been adopted at the insistence of Jacobs by the national convention of 1872, was the Uniform Lesson Plan. This was a plan proposed by John H. Vincent (1832–1920), a member of the Rock River Methodist Conference in Illinois who had become editor of Methodist Sunday school publications in 1868. The idea was to have each class within a Sunday school, and Sunday schools of all denominations, studying the same lesson each week. The plan had at least two distinct advantages. For one thing, "next Sunday's lesson" became a bond of union between members of different denominations and thus contributed to a growing sense of Protestant solidarity. But an equally great advantage was that it facilitated lesson preparation. Teachers of all age groups and of all Protestant denominations could be gathered on Saturday afternoon to study the lesson they were to teach the following day.

Vincent also was responsible for spearheading the development of teacher-training institutes. These institutes were designed primarily for prospective teachers and sought to equip them with tested methods of Bible teaching before they assumed any instructional responsibilities. The institute idea caught on quickly and swept across the country. In Chicago it ultimately found more elaborate institutional expression in the establishment of the Moody Bible Institute in 1886. At Chautauqua Lake in western New York, the summer training institute founded by Vincent in 1874 developed into the elaborate summer program of the Chautauqua Institution.

Within a very brief time, the Sunday school—benefiting from its surge of popularity—had begun to replace revivalism as the primary recruiting device of the churches. No longer was it merely a children's school. Adult classes were formed which frequently rivaled the stated services of the church in attendance. Slogans, such as "Each one win one," were adopted, and the whole program of instruction marched forward inexorably each year to "Decision Day." So great was the enthusiasm that by the end of the century annual Bible school parades had become a fixture in many communities, with the mayor and other civic notables ensconced in the reviewing stand. In 1910, when the Adult Bible Class Federation held its national convention in Washington, Congress adjourned to witness the parade. The following year at San Francisco the parade was headed by a platoon of mounted police, and there were ten thousand men in the line of march, each with a Bible, carrying banners, and singing hymns and official delegation songs. A more sober but scarcely less ecstatic expression of this enthusiasm was reflected in the 1888 Beecher lectures at Yale in which H. Clay Trumbull rehearsed the beneficent influence that was being exerted by the Sunday school. As a result of "God's blessing on the revival and expansion of the Bible school as his chosen agency for Christian evangelization and Christian training," Trumbull declared, "Bible study and Bible teaching have a prominence never before known in the world's history" and "vital godliness is shown and felt in unprecedented potency in the life and progress of mankind." [30]

The eager optimism of the Sunday school workers was not shared by everyone. The more thoughtful were aware of the serious problems being posed for the churches by the new intellectual climate and the new industrial growth. Furthermore, it was now becoming evident how drastically the shape of American religious life was being altered by immigration. Hitherto the population of the United States had been relatively homogeneous. After the Civil War, as immigration steadily mounted, it became much more heterogeneous. And this shift in the make-up of the population was immediately reflected in the proportionate strength of the various religious groups. By the end of the century the Lutherans had outdistanced the Presbyterians and were exceeded in number of adherents among Protestants only by the Methodists and the Baptists. Judaism had become a sizable community, Eastern Orthodoxy had been launched on its American career, and even Buddhism had made its appearance on the Pacific coast. But the most spectacular feature of the post-Civil War years was the growth of the Roman Catholic Church.

[30] *The Sunday School: The Lyman Beecher Lectures* (Philadelphia, 1888), 142. An unusually discerning overall account of the Sunday school movement has been provided by Robert W. Lynn and Elliott Wright, *The Big Little School: Sunday Child of American Protestantism* (N.Y., 1971). See also Theodore Morrison, *Chautauqua* (Chicago, 1974).

X

The New Americans

The influx of millions of Europeans into the United States during the fifty years from Appomattox to the assassination of Archduke Franz Ferdinand at Sarajevo was a phenomenon comparable in magnitude only to the migrations which overwhelmed the Roman Empire in the fifth and sixth centuries. The invasion was spurred by the spreading ganglia of the iron horse which had begun to bind the nation into a single economic unit on the eve of the Civil War. And even in the midst of the fighting, Congress had sped with lavish grants the advance of the railroads to the Pacific coast, thereby opening the whole continent to rapid settlement and creating a market, national in scope, that served as a powerful stimulus to commercial and industrial growth. With free farms awaiting the enterprising, employers bidding for cheap labor, and steamship companies drumming up passengers, the surge of immigrants broke all precedents. From 1865 to 1900 no fewer than 13½ million foreigners entered the United States. The pace at which they arrived was even greater after the turn of the century when almost 9 million immigrants passed through the ports of entry from 1900 through 1910. What this influx meant to the life of the nation can be fully understood only when it is remembered that the total population of the United States at the close of the Civil War was little more than 30 million.

The Irish and German invasions had begun prior to the war, with the incoming tide of Irish attaining major proportions during the "hungry forties" and the influx of Germans gaining momentum after the abortive Revolution of 1848. By the 1870's, when German immigration had reached floodtide and outstripped the Irish, the wave from Scandinavia had begun. Finally, from southern and eastern Europe came waves of Italians, Poles, Croats, Czechs, Slovaks, Hungarians, Greeks, Russians, and Romanians to work the mines, man the factories, and ply the needle in the garment trades.

Many of the Germans and most of the Scandinavians pushed on to the farmlands northwest of Chicago, but the other nationality groups tended to cluster in the cities. The ethnic composition of the cities changed in startling ways. Boston ceased to be the citadel of the Cabots and the Lodges and became the stronghold of the Kellys and the O'Briens. Other cities received a strong German, Polish, or Italian coloration. New York, as the chief port of entry, became a polyglot center of many nationalities. So rapid was the change that the number of foreign born in Chicago, for example, in 1890 nearly equaled the entire population of the city in 1880. The concentration of new Americans was even greater in some of the small industrial cities where almost all the inhabitants had been recruited abroad to staff the mills. Charles A. Beard, in describing the impact upon American society of the incoming tide of cheap labor, commented that "not since the patricians and capitalists of Rome scoured the known world for slaves—Celts, Iberians, Angles, Gauls, Saxons, Greeks, Jews, Egyptians, and Assyrians—to serve them," had the world witnessed such a drastic alteration in the composition of a social order as occurred in America during these years.[1]

The response of the older Americans

It is not surprising that so great a flood of immigrants should have created alarm among many of the older Americans. Peaceful coexistence

[1] *The Rise of American Civilization* (N.Y., 1927), II, 247.

seldom comes naturally. Tension usually develops whenever differing social groups first come into contact.

NATIVIST CONCERNS. The reasons for the sense of alarm that fostered a resurgence of nativist sentiment during the 1880's and 1890's were mixed. Apprehension built up at almost every level. There was a *cultural* concern at the introduction of differing folkways, customs, mores, and patterns of behavior. *Social* apprehensions were aroused by the poverty, illiteracy, and unsanitary habits of many of the immigrants. Whether the immigrants were herded into slums or created slums, there was widespread agreement that they constituted a social hazard. Even at best they had had a bad start. They were fleeing a life of poverty; and long, unsanitary voyages across the Atlantic meant that many of them went from the ship to the hospital to be cared for at public expense. Francis J. Lally has reported that a New York almshouse commissioner sadly exclaimed: "Many of them had far better been cast into the deep sea, than linger in the pangs of hunger, sickness, and pain, to draw their last agonizing breath in the streets of New York." [2] Not only did these new Americans tax the public dole, they committed crimes far out of proportion to their number. The *political* impact of the new arrivals was expressed in the saying that the immigrants "landed on Monday and voted on Tuesday," being met at the dock by the "bosses," quickly registered, and then shepherded to the polls. While this overstated the situation, the shifting of control in the cities from the native born to the foreign born was bound to produce unhappy reactions even without the suspicion that the immigrant vote was being manipulated. From an *economic* point of view, the new Americans also were not an unmixed blessing. They did provide cheap labor for an expanding America, but not too many of the native born appreciated this fact. Much more evident to them was the way in which the immigrants tended to depress wages and lower the standard of living by competing with the existing labor force.

All these factors were heightened by the sense of an alien intrusion into American life. The various nationality groups tended to cling together in "ghettos" of their own, separating themselves from the rest of the community. Many spoke no English. They were suspected of exalting foreign ties and cherishing foreign ideals. To many native Americans it

[2] *The Catholic Church in a Changing America* (Boston, 1962), 29–30.

seemed that the America they had known was doomed unless the immigrant invasion could somehow be checked.

In the post-Civil War period the labor leaders were the first to voice alarm at the threat posed by the incoming tide from Europe. At a later date even so uncompromising a "social liberal" as John A. Ryan (1869–1945) of Catholic University was to advocate restricting the flow of immigration. Only small victories, however, were won. The first general immigration law, adopted in 1882, excluded only convicts, lunatics, idiots, and those likely to become public charges. Nine years later polygamists and those suffering from dangerous diseases were banned. It was not until 1917 that a literacy test was imposed, and the highly restrictive "quota" system was not adopted until 1924.[3]

PROTESTANT-CATHOLIC TENSIONS. Nativist sentiment frequently had religious overtones, with Roman Catholicism being depicted as part of an international conspiracy to subvert the free institutions of America. This had been the theme of Samuel F. B. Morse (1791–1872), inventor of the telegraph, in a series of letters entitled "A Foreign Conspiracy against the Liberties of the United States" which he wrote to the *New York Observer* in 1834. During this early period, such prominent Protestant leaders as Lyman Beecher, Horace Bushnell, and Albert Barnes believed that there was a deliberate design by Roman Catholics to capture middle America, which was thus to be the great battlefield where the destinies of the world were to be decided. The Order of United Americans (the "Know-Nothing" party of the 1850's) both fed upon and generated this fear, but it subsided with the onset of the conflict between North and South. The conspiracy theme was revived, however, in 1887 with the formation of the American Protective Association (A.P.A.) at Clinton, Iowa, whose members were pledged to endeavor "to strike the shackles and chains of blind obedience to the Roman Catholic church from the hampered and bound consciences of a priest-ridden and church-oppressed people." The A.P.A. was a fringe group which flourished most in areas where Roman Catholics were least numerous, as in Iowa, Nebraska, and

[3] The renewed immigration after World War I coincided with a period of economic recession and brought renewed agitation for restrictive legislation. A temporary measure was adopted in 1921 limiting the number of immigrants annually to 3 per cent of the foreign born of each nationality resident in the United States in 1910. Three years later the Johnson-Reed Act restricted total annual immigration to 150,000 and assigned quotas to each nationality on the basis of its present representation in the population. A complete prohibition of Japanese immigration made the exclusion of Orientals almost complete.

Kansas. While the A.P.A. was an active political force which won local victories, it was bluntly rebuffed in its attempt to influence national politics, and it withered away within a few years. Anti-Catholic feeling, nevertheless, continued to persist among many segments of the American population.[4]

Although Joseph H. Fichter has suggested that anti-Catholicism in the United States was more largely rooted in ethnic than religious antagonisms,[5] the religious element should not be unduly minimized. It is true that much of the hostility to Roman Catholicism was generated by its "foreignness." And it is likely that native-born Catholics would have continued to be accepted, like other Americans, had Catholic immigrants not arrived in such overwhelming numbers. Moreover, nativist sentiment was not absent among Roman Catholics. Native-born Roman Catholics were often dismayed by the Irish immigrants, criticizing their lack of cleanliness, their boisterous conduct, their raucous laughter, their disgraceful fights. The Irish in turn frequently denounced the Germans with as much vigor as other nativists. In 1854 the Boston diocesan paper, the *Pilot*, welcomed a decline in immigration, urged the tightening of the naturalization laws, and was of the opinion that if the Know-Nothings succeeded in obstructing the Germans, posterity would overlook their crimes of bigotry. A few decades later, Archbishop John Ireland (1838–1918) alerted the Associated Press to the "general un-American character" of the American German Catholic Assembly. German Catholics exhibited similar hostility to still newer immigrant groups. And when Roman Catholics in the southern states were urged to welcome co-religionists from Ireland and Germany, they insisted that only those who would be friendly to southern interests be sent. "We must not," they declared, "warm vipers into life that may sting us when they grow warm." [6] While all this is true, religious concerns were present in the tension between Protestants and Roman Catholics.

[4] The excesses of the earlier anti-Catholic movement have been described in detail by R. A. Billington, *The Protestant Crusade, 1800–1860* (N.Y., 1938). For the later movement, see D. L. Kinzer, *An Episode in Anti-Catholicism: The American Protective Association* (Seattle, 1964).
[5] "The Americanization of Catholicism," in McAvoy, *Roman Catholicism and the American Way of Life*, 116–17.
[6] W. E. Wright, "The Native American Catholic, the Immigrant, and Immigration," in McAvoy, *Roman Catholicism and the American Way of Life*, 213–14, 216. See also C. J. Barry, "The German Catholic Immigrant," *ibid.*, 199. And Robert D. Cross, *The Emergence of Liberal Catholicism in America* (Cambridge, Mass., 1958), 92.

Protestants, of course, did not constitute a single homogeneous anti-Catholic bloc, a fact which Archbishop Ireland acknowledged and Robert D. Cross has documented.[7] Expressions of friendship and good will were not uncommon, and such organizations as the A.P.A. seldom reflected responsible Protestant opinion. There were nonetheless serious fears and apprehensions, stimulated in part by the harsh anti-Protestantism of some Roman Catholics. Michael Muller (1825–99), a Redemptorist Father, did little to foster good feeling when he published *The Catholic Dogma: Out of the Church There Is No Salvation* (1886). His purpose in writing the book, he said, was to refute "those soft, weak, timid, liberalizing Catholics, who labor to explain away all the points of Catholic faith offensive to non-Catholics, and to make it appear there is no question of life and death, of heaven and hell, involved in the difference between us and Protestants." There were other Catholics who felt no hesitancy in denouncing Protestants as infidels, and even the suggestion by a bishop in 1870 that non-Catholics could be persons of good faith and good character was sufficient to cause him to be called "a Luther or a Lucifer." Ten years later, Augustine Thébaud (1807–85), a Jesuit who had been in America since 1838, insisted that Protestants who "profess to be friendly to Catholics" are not sincere. And Archbishop John Hughes of New York denounced as "Protestant priests" those Catholic clergymen who enjoyed good relations with Protestants.[8]

Further antagonism was aroused by the generally negative attitude of some Catholics toward American life as a whole. The influential *Church Progress* of St. Louis was not particularly tactful when it made unfavorable comparisons between the United States and the Catholic nations of Europe, and the statement of Condé Pallen (1858–1929) that American culture "exhales an atmosphere filled with germs fatal to Catholic life" was hardly calculated to win friends. This negativism was most conspicuous among German-speaking Catholics. Anton Walburg, (1840–1910), a leading priest in Cincinnati, was emphatic in his criticism of the United States. In 1889 he depicted American culture as a "hotbed of fanaticism, intolerance, and radical ultra views on matters of politics and religion." Even the language, he insisted, was so permeated with Protestant ideas that an English-speaking Catholicism could never prosper. In contrast to

[7] Cross, *The Emergence of Liberal Catholicism in America*, 30, 32–37, 44, 48, 52, 65.
[8] *Ibid.*, 51–52, 56.

the United States, Father Walburg pointed to Germany as standing "foremost in the ranks of civilized nations," and he advised Americans to stop worrying about getting involved in European quarrels since the United States was too weak to defeat Ecuador, let alone a European power.[9]

While mutual animosities fostered mutual estrangement, Protestant uneasiness had its basic rootage in apprehensions concerning the changes that a continuing massive Roman Catholic immigration might introduce into American society. The existing social order, which embodied in so many ways the ideals and moralities of evangelical Protestantism, seemed to many thoughtful people to be in danger of being completely subverted. The most obvious, if perhaps the most superficial, threat was the challenge to two of the most conspicuous folk moralities of American Protestantism—Sabbath observance and temperance. The "Continental Sunday" of the immigrant groups both scandalized and spread consternation in the Protestant camp. And Protestants, long schooled in the evils of strong drink, noted with dismay that these new Americans were bringing "their grog shops like the frogs of Egypt upon us." [10]

Of more serious concern were the attacks leveled by Catholics against the public schools. Universal public education had been fostered as a counter to the project of that "old deluder Satan" to keep people from a knowledge of the Scriptures, and the "little red schoolhouse" was regarded, along with motherhood and the home, as one of the most cherished institutions of American life. While it was understandable that Catholics might wish schools of their own, nothing could have been better calculated to raise Protestant hackles than the attempt to drum up support for parochial education by attacking public education. The public schools were described as "godless," and those who defended them were charged with being "fanatics." Bishop Bernard McQuaid (1823–1909) called the public school system "a huge conspiracy against religion, individual liberty, and enterprise," while Michael Muller regarded it as a disease which would "break up and destroy the Christian family" and described the public schools as "hotbeds of immorality" where "courtesans have disguised themselves as school-girls in order the more surely to ply their foul vocation." Zachariah Montgomery was convinced that free love would

[9] *Ibid.*, 26, 28, 72, 90.
[10] Lally, *The Catholic Church in a Changing America*, 29.

be the ultimate consequence of free public education. "Free teaching draws after it free books, free clothes, free food, free time," he contended. "All this is going very far with the communists. . . . If we admit a right . . . to take the child out of the family, they will ask next for the wife." Other Catholics were convinced that not everyone should be taught to read, for this would serve to unfit them for the station in life into which they had been born. Still others argued that godly innocence was more often associated with childlike ignorance than with worldly knowledge. A few, appalled by the thought of a system that mixed innocents with the "crime-steeped progeny of the low and vile," went so far as to urge that all free (i.e., public) education be abandoned.[11]

Perhaps the greatest apprehension was aroused by the fear that Roman Catholicism might serve to undermine American democracy. While no more than a small minority of the American people may have shared the conviction of the radical nativist fringe that massive Catholic immigration was a deliberate plot to overthrow the free institutions of America, there were many who feared that the tenets and spirit of Roman Catholicism were antithetical to religious and political liberty. The memory of events in Europe after the defeat of Napoleon in 1814 and after the abortive revolutions of 1848–49 did little to reassure them, and they were equally disturbed by the condemnations contained in the *Syllabus of Errors* of 1864 and by the decrees of the Vatican Council in 1870. Moreover, in the encyclical letter *Immortale Dei* (The Christian Constitution of States) of 1885, Leo XIII had explicitly affirmed the right of the papacy to judge when the affairs of the civil order must yield to the superior authority of the Roman Church.[12] And somewhat later the Vatican newspaper *Osservatore Romano* pointed out that "as the Pope is the sovereign of the Church . . . , he is also the sovereign of every other society and of every other kingdom."[13] Some comments by American Catholics were no more reassuring. An article in the *American Catholic Quarterly Review* in 1877 dismissed the Declaration of Independence as a flock of vague clichés, and five years later a pastoral letter of the bishops of

[11] Cross, *The Emergence of Liberal Catholicism in America*, 95, 96, 98, 131–32, 135–36.

[12] For the *Syllabus of Errors*, see Smith, Handy, Loetscher, *American Christianity*, II, 112–15. The constitution promulgated at the Vatican Council in 1870 and the encyclical *Immortale Dei* are reprinted in W. S. Hudson, *Understanding Roman Catholicism* (Philadelphia, 1959), 37–45, 66–90.

[13] Cited in Cross, *Emergence of Liberal Catholicism*, 60.

the province of Cincinnati took a dim view of the notion that a people should rule themselves.[14]

Other Catholics, most notably Cardinal James Gibbons (1834–1921), Archbishop John Ireland, and Bishop John J. Keane (1839–1918), were as disturbed as most Protestants by the reactionary stance of the conservative wing of the Roman Catholic Church in America. They resented both the aspersions cast upon the public schools and the innuendoes which suggested that the American form of government was less desirable than the nondemocratic regimes of Europe. They repeatedly voiced their own approbation of American democratic principles, and were forthright in condemning the antidemocratic views of some of their fellow Catholics. In contrast to the conservative Catholics, the liberals were widely acclaimed and publicly honored by Protestants. Gibbons was invited to preach in Protestant pulpits, Keane gave the Dudleian lecture at Harvard, and a Baptist minister affectionately addressed Ireland as "my archbishop." The result of the Catholic ambivalence was a degree of ambivalence in the Protestant mind, with varying opinions being held as to the future course that the Roman Church would pursue in America.

PROTESTANT MINISTRIES TO THE IMMIGRANTS. The Protestant approach to the newcomers to the American scene was motivated by a varying mixture of religious concern, humanitarian sentiment, patriotic fervor, and anti-Catholic feeling. Not many after the turn of the century viewed the Catholic portion of the incoming tide as part and parcel of a carefully laid plot to capture the United States for the Pope. Many were convinced, however, that the "safety and welfare and Christian civilization of our country depends in no small degree upon transforming" the immigrant "into a true American," and that "nothing but Christianity, as incarnated in American Protestantism," can accomplish this end. The new arrivals, declared mission executive Charles A. Brooks (1871–1931), must be "born again of the American spirit." [15] In spite of attempts to enlist support for mission work among the immigrants by equating Protestantism with patriotism, the literature of the time makes it clear that much of the motivation was rooted in a truly humanitarian and religious solicitude for the friendless and poverty-stricken. Methodists, for example,

[14] *Ibid.*, 99.
[15] H. B. Grose, *Aliens or Americans?* (N.Y., 1906), 237, 255. C. A. Brooks, *Immigration: Its Extent, Its Effect on America, Its Call to the Churches* (N.Y., 1915), 8.

were as assiduous in their work among Lutherans from Sweden and Calvinists from Hungary as they were among Roman Catholics from any land.

Apart from informal "welfare" or "relief" programs, the major response of the Protestant churches to the presence of the new Americans in their midst was a strenuous effort to provide them with a religious ministry in their own language. Later, as a phase of their expanding humanitarian activity, the churches developed a systematized program of "Christian Americanization" or "Christian Friendliness" to assist the immigrant families in making a successful adjustment to American life. Women were enlisted to go into the homes to show mothers how to cook the food available in American stores, to teach them English, to help them prepare for naturalization examinations, and generally to befriend them.

Almost every Protestant denomination developed foreign-language ministries. Mission work was established among the Germans, Scandinavians, French Canadians, Italians, Poles, Hungarians, Czechs, Romanians, and Portuguese. Baptists, for example, maintained a ministry to twenty-one different nationality groups in as many different languages. The recruiting of a "native ministry" to labor among their fellow immigrants was haphazard at first, but as soon as any specific group began to arrive in significant numbers training institutes were organized to train converts for mission work. Within a relatively short time foreign-language "departments" were established in theological seminaries to provide more adequate ministerial training. The Baptists were typical in this respect, establishing a German department at Rochester Theological Seminary in 1858, a department for Swedish, Danish, and Norwegian students at the seminary in Chicago in 1871, a French-Canadian department at Newton in 1889, and an Italian department at Colgate Theological Seminary in 1907. "So ample were these facilities," Aaron I. Abell reported in his study of urban Protestantism, "that by 1900 a body of clergymen ready to meet all calls for independent or assistant pastorates had come into existence." As early as 1895 the problem of the Congregationalists had become one of sufficient financial support rather than of available personnel, for their home missionary society reported that the once "greatest desideratum —trained Congregational pastors—to supply these churches of foreign tongues, is now supplied in a degree almost beyond our power to use, through Oberlin and Chicago theological seminaries, whose well-equipped graduates stand ready to enlarge the field of our missionary service wherever the means are at the command of this society to employ them." [16]

While by no means negligible, the number of non-English-speaking immigrants added to the membership of churches of British background accounted for only a small fraction of the new Americans. As was to be expected, it was the churches of their homelands which experienced the great surge of growth.

Adjustments and tensions within Roman Catholicism

The most spectacular development in American religious life during the latter half of the nineteenth century was the growth of the Roman Catholic Church. In spite of repeated alarm that vast losses were being suffered among those who came to America, the Roman Catholic Church was remarkably successful in retaining the allegiance of Catholic immigrants.[17] Although the number of Roman Catholics had rapidly mounted during the pre-Civil War years, giant strides in membership took place in the decades that followed. The four million Catholics of 1870 increased to six million in 1880. Ten years later the total was nine million, and in 1900 it was twelve million. By 1920 every sixth person and every third church member was a Roman Catholic.[18]

INSTITUTIONAL DEVELOPMENT. The challenge presented to the Roman Catholic Church by the immigrant flood was prodigious. The immigrants were poor. They came from different countries, spoke different languages, and—within the limits of their common faith—had different

[16] A. I. Abell, *The Urban Impact upon American Protestantism* (Cambridge, Mass., 1943), 182, 183.

[17] The myth of vast losses was exploded by Gerald Shaughnessy, *Has the Immigrant Kept the Faith?* (N.Y., 1925). See also J. P. Dolan, *Catholic Revivalism* (Notre Dame, 1978).

[18] The older standard accounts of the Roman Catholic Church in America are John G. Shea, *History of the Catholic Church in the United States*, 4 vols. (N.Y., 1886–92), and Thomas O'Gorman, *A History of the Roman Catholic Church in the United States* (N.Y., 1895). These were supplemented by the popular and impressionistic account of Theodore Maynard, *The Story of American Catholicism* (N.Y., 1941), and the more scholarly study by J. T. Ellis, *American Catholicism* (Chicago, 1969). The most discerning brief account is James Hennesey, "Square Peg in a Round Hole," *Records of the American Catholic Historical Society of Philadelphia*, LXXXIV (1973), 167–95. Key documents of American Catholicism are printed in J. T. Ellis, *Documents of American Catholic History*, rev. ed. (Milwaukee, 1962).

traditions and customs and loyalties. Even had they not been poverty-stricken, they came in such numbers that the task of recruiting priests, erecting parishes, and building churches must have seemed almost insurmountable. Financial help did come from Europe. From France the Society for the Propagation of Faith had sent more than six million dollars by 1914. Additional help came from similar societies in Germany, Austria, and Switzerland. But the major financial burden was carried in America. In terms of personnel the assistance from abroad was much more important and substantial. Religious orders and congregations sent over priests, lay brothers, and nuns, with Ireland, Germany, France, and Belgium contributing the greatest number. Secular priests also were dispatched. Although the bishops constantly stressed the importance of encouraging vocations to the priesthood and founded seminaries to provide the necessary training, it was the recruits from abroad who made it possible for the ranks of the clergy to swell from slightly more than two thousand in 1860 to six thousand in 1880, to twelve thousand in 1900, and to seventeen thousand in 1910. Nor was it an easy task to maintain effective oversight of the multiplying parishes. New dioceses were constantly being formed. The seventeen dioceses in 1840 had increased to forty-four by 1860. From 1868 to 1900 forty more had been established, and by 1914 the total exceeded one hundred, grouped in fourteen provinces.

Prior to the period from 1846 to 1850 when five new provinces were constituted, there had been but a single province—that of Baltimore—in the United States. Beginning in 1829 the bishops had met approximately every three years in a provincial council to deal with their common problems. When other provinces were established, this procedure had to be altered. In place of the provincial gatherings, plenary councils of the whole American episcopate were summoned to coordinate the work of the church on a national basis with appropriate legislation. The first plenary council met in 1852, the second in 1866, and the third in 1884.[19] Thereafter such national councils were either suppressed or suspended, presumably to avoid the dangers implicit in the idea of a national church. A similar concern had dictated the refusal of Rome to accede to the petition of the bishops that the archbishop of Baltimore be granted the place of primacy among the bishops in the United States. In place of these alternatives, both

[19] For these councils, see Peter Guilday, *A History of the Councils of Baltimore, 1791–1884* (N.Y., 1932).

containing the potential hazard of undue independence, an Apostolic Delegate (papal representative) was appointed in 1893 to provide the necessary coordination and direction for the American church. With the structure of government having been completed in this fashion and with the arrangement functioning effectively, Pius X on June 29, 1908, removed the church in the United States from the jurisdiction of the Congregatio de Propaganda Fide. The effect was to place the Roman Catholic Church in America on a basis of full equality with the older branches of the church in Europe and to bring to an end its missionary status.

The resources of manpower, money, and ingenuity were further taxed by the policy of developing a whole system of Catholic education. The first provincial council of Baltimore in 1829 declared it to be "absolutely necessary that schools should be established in which the young may be taught the principles of faith and morality while being instructed in letters." In 1852 the first plenary council re-emphasized the need for parochial schools, and in 1884 the third plenary council decreed that schools should be established in every parish within the next two years unless the bishop permitted a postponement because of serious difficulties. Support for the program of parochial education, however, was not as uniform as these decrees suggest. German Catholics were among the most ardent proponents of parochial schools, viewing them as a means of preserving their German language and culture. Liberal prelates, such as Gibbons, Ireland, and Keane, preferred to work out an accommodation with public education as a means of integrating Catholics more fully into the main stream of American life. A hard-fought struggle ensued, with Irish conservatives, such as Archbishop Michael A. Corrigan (1839–1902) of New York City and Bishop McQuaid of Rochester, giving the Germans stanch support. Ultimately the issue was settled by papal intervention in favor of a complete system of parochial education, with deviations being tolerated if judged necessary by a bishop in the light of local conditions.

Progress in fulfilling the ideal of a school in every parish was slow. Had the Roman Catholic population not been concentrated in the major cities and in a few largely self-contained rural enclaves, the whole project would have been doomed from the start. And even with this concentration, parochial education was made possible only by the sacrificial devotion of

251

the members of numerous sisterhoods who were recruited to staff the schools. In spite of the fact that the council of 1884 had decreed that within two years every parish must have its own school, the parishes so equipped had increased only from 40 per cent to 44 per cent by 1892. Thereafter, with dissidence having been quelled, progress was somewhat more rapid. In 1914 the parochial schools enrolled over one million pupils, had over twenty thousand teachers, and were maintained at a cost of over $15,000,000 per year. But even an achievement of this magnitude was not enough, for a very large proportion of Catholic children were still being educated in the public schools.

Interest in secondary education lagged, with the total enrollment in 1915 being less than seventy-five thousand. Colleges and universities, on the other hand, were beginning to receive vigorous support after a long period of precarious existence.[20] Georgetown, St. Louis, Fordham, Notre Dame, and Holy Cross, among others, had become strong institutions, and in 1884 the third plenary council took the necessary decisive action to effect the establishment in 1889 of the Catholic University of America as a full-fledged graduate institution to serve as the capstone of the Catholic educational structure.

"AMERICANISM." In addition to their other problems, Roman Catholics had the difficult task of adjusting people of diverse nationality both to one another and to the American environment. To weld Irishmen, Germans, Italians, Czechs, French Canadians, and many others into a single church was a taxing effort. Tension often was acute. The earlier trustee controversy had been in part a rebellion of the Irish against the imported French priests who had been displaced from their homeland by the Revolution of 1789. After the Civil War the German-Irish tension came to the fore, and in the 1890's Polish dissatisfaction produced a schismatic movement which was to result in the formation of the Polish National Catholic Church.[21] In 1914 a parallel Lithuanian National Catholic Church was organized.

[20] Of thirty-eight colleges established between 1791 and 1850 only seven survived, and of fifty-five established between 1850 and 1865 only eighteen survived. Maynard, *The Story of American Catholicism*, 474.

[21] In 1916 the Polish group reported a membership of 28,245. Consecration of its bishops had been obtained from the Old Catholic Church in Europe, a small Dutch group which had refused to accept the decrees of the Council of Trent. Old Catholics in Germany and Switzerland had been alienated by the dogmatic pronouncements of the first Vatican Council in 1870.

The German-Irish issue, which had long smoldered and had been reflected in the school controversy, was brought to a head in 1891 when the St. Raphael Society of Switzerland, with Peter Paul Cahensly as its secretary, in a petition to Rome declared that in the United States the Roman Catholic Church had lost ten million souls through failure to make proper provision for them in their own language. As was true of other nationality groups, provision had been made for the establishment of German congregations under the leadership of German-speaking priests. And of the sixty-nine bishops in 1886, fifteen were of Germanic extraction. But this was not enough for the St. Raphael Society, which had been founded to aid German-speaking immigrants. In its petition to the papacy the Society proposed that each of the nationality groups in America be organized into separate dioceses. This attempt to fragment the church in America by institutionalizing Old World divisions was rejected by the papacy, but it serves to illustrate a difference in point of view as to the proper strategy to be pursued in the United States.

Most of the German leadership was convinced that the way to hold the immigrants was to keep them isolated from American life. German culture, customs, and language were defended with the slogan "Language Saves the Faith," and it was insisted that only priests proud of being German, and schools in which German was the language of instruction, could save German Catholics and their children from being de-Catholicized. To those who contended that "we are apostles to bring the people to Christ . . . , not to maintain or implant a nationality or to spread a language," the *Herald des Glaubens* responded that priests who voiced such sentiments "would rather see several million Germans go to hell than forego the opportunity to convert a few hundred Yankees." [22]

The Germans, of course, were not alone in believing that the only way to prevent defections was to insulate the faithful and to resist all accommodation to the American environment. Some of the most influential of the Irish bishops, while not concerned with the language problem, were equally uncompromising in their determination that no concessions should be made to American culture. There were others, however, who believed that resistance to Americanization not only created unnecessary antagonism and impeded the winning of converts, but actually was a policy

[22] *Roman Catholicism and the American Way of Life*, ed. McAvoy, 192–94; Cross, *Emergence of Liberal Catholicism*, 25–26, 91–92.

calculated to speed the defection of those who had been Catholics in their homelands. If being an American meant ceasing to be a Catholic, they had little doubt of the choice that many of them, especially their children, would make. While Isaac Hecker and the Paulist Fathers, the order of missionary priests which he had founded in 1859, were the most conspicuous advocates of this point of view, it found strong support among members of the hierarchy, most notably from the triumvirate of Gibbons, Ireland, and Keane.

Gibbons' *The Faith of Our Fathers* (1876) was one of the most successful Catholic apologetics ever written in English, and the response it elicited seemed a clear demonstration of the effectiveness of the Americanizing tactic. At the centenary in 1889 of Baltimore's establishment as a diocese, Gibbons re-emphasized the Americanist theme, saying that Carroll's aim had been "that the clergy and people—no matter from what country they sprung—should be thoroughly identified with the land in which their lot was cast; that they should study its laws and political constitution and be in harmony with its spirit; in a word, that they should become, as soon as possible, assimilated to the social body in all things pertaining to the common domain of civil life." And then, turning to the present, Gibbons called upon his contemporaries to emulate Carroll. Ireland was even more emphatic, believing that people unwilling to be assimilated did not deserve to be admitted to the country and that anyone who did not rejoice in the blessings of America "should in simple consistency betake his foreign soul to foreign shores, and crouch in misery and subjection beneath tyranny's sceptre."

> We should live in our age, know it, be in touch with it. . . . We should be in it and of it, if we would have its ear. . . . For the same reason, there is needed a thorough sympathy with the country. The Church of America must be, of course, as Catholic as even in Jerusalem or Rome; but as far as her garments assume color from the local atmosphere, she must be American. Let no one dare to paint her brow with a foreign taint or pin to her mantle foreign linings.[23]

But it was not simply a tactic that the liberal coterie had adopted. They were fully committed to American democracy, glorying in it,

[23] Roemer, *Catholic Church in the United States*, 303–04; Maynard, *Story of American Catholicism*, 511; Cross, *Emergence of Liberal Catholicism*, 89.

believing in it, and willing to defend it. "If I had the privilege of modifying the Constitution of the United States," declared Gibbons, "I would not expunge or alter a single paragraph, a single line, or a single word of that important instrument."

> The Constitution is admirably adapted to the growth and expansion of the Catholic religion, and the Catholic religion is admirably adapted to the genius of the Constitution. They fit together like two links of the same chain.

Furthermore, these Americanizers believed that America had a mission to the world. God intended America to be more than a "motherland," asserted Keane. "She was meant to be a teacher through whose lips and in whose life he was to solve the social problems of the Old World." [24]

The leaders of the liberal contingent also were certain that America could teach lessons in religion as well as in politics. The role of the laity was emphasized and lay congresses were organized. Close clerical supervision and direction were minimized by a stress upon the necessity for individual initiative in the apostolate of the church. The contemplative life exalted by most of the religious orders tended to be disparaged. "An honest ballot and social decorum," Ireland contended, "will do more for God's glory and the salvation of souls than midnight flagellations or Compestellan pilgrimages." Protestants were not to be regarded as implacable enemies but as "brothers to be brought back to the fold." Love and persuasion should replace harsh polemic. The technique of seeking to exert religious influence through the formation of a Catholic political party, a practice widely adopted in Europe, was likewise decried. Even the almost automatic identification of American Catholics with the Democratic party ("Have you heard the news? John Danaher has become a Republican!" "It can't be true. I saw him at mass just last Sunday.") was deplored on the ground that it deprived Catholics of influence because the Democrats took them for granted while the Republicans felt no obligation to them. [25]

The 1880's and 1890's were heady years for the liberals, but they were also years when the issue of "Americanism" was being sharply

---

[24] J. T. Ellis, *Perspectives in American Catholicism* (Baltimore, 1963), 124; Cross, *Emergence of Liberal Catholicism*, 184.

[25] Maynard, *Story of American Catholicism*, 514; Cross, *Emergence of Liberal Catholicism*, 187.

drawn.[26] The peak of the liberal ascendancy was reached in 1893 at the seventeen-day Parliament of Religions held in conjunction with the Chicago Columbian Exposition. The American archbishops, presumably influenced by Ireland, had decided that the Parliament presented a signal opportunity to present Catholic truth to those outside the fold. At the opening session, Archbishop Patrick A. Feehan (1829–1902) gave an address of welcome, and Cardinal Gibbons (he had received the red hat in 1886) led the assembly in the Protestant version of the Lord's Prayer. Bishop Keane presented two papers, read an address prepared by Gibbons, and presided on the day assigned for a specifically Catholic program. While those who participated felt that a real service had been rendered the Catholic Church, others were scandalized by the appearance given by Catholic participation of waiving the Roman claim to unique and final truth. By sharing the platform with every religious sect "from Mohammedanism and Buddhism down to the lowest form of evangelicalism and infidelity," the participating bishops were accused of having taken a dangerous first step toward "indifferentism." Even prior to this, in an article in the *American Catholic Quarterly Review,* the vicar general of Archbishop Corrigan had charged Ireland, Gibbons, and Keane of being guilty of the "liberalism" condemned by the *Syllabus of Errors.*[27]

Many issues, in addition to those strictly related to "Americanism," contributed to the coalescing of two parties in the church, each striving for ascendancy. There were differences of opinion over parochial schools and the language question, tensions between nationality groups, differing attitudes toward "temperance," and debates as to the position the church should take with regard to the Knights of Labor and the "single-tax" proposal of Henry George. The establishment of Catholic University in 1889 had been displeasing to many. Some feared it as a rival to their own institutions. Some were opposed to its location in Washington where students would be exposed to the corrupting influences of the nation's capital. Others were dismayed that an undergraduate college for women would be adjacent to a campus where priests and members of religious orders would be pursuing graduate studies. Still others were alienated by

[26] The two indispensable books dealing with the "Americanism" controversy are Cross, *Emergence of Liberal Catholicism,* and T. T. McAvoy, *The Great Crisis in American Catholic History, 1895–1900* (Chicago, 1957). The latter volume makes full use of archival material. It has been reprinted under a new title, *The Americanist Heresy in Roman Catholicism* (Notre Dame, Ind., 1963).

[27] McAvoy, *The Great Crisis in American Catholic History,* 76–77.

the "progressive" auspices under which the university had been established and by the pretension of its board of trustees to serve as a standing
council of the church. The latter pretension was related to a centralizing
tendency which also aroused antagonism. Gibbons was being encouraged
to assume the role of spokesman and unofficial primate of the church by
exploiting the precedence he derived from being the archbishop of
Baltimore and the only American cardinal, and the archbishops had
begun to function as a committee in a way that seemed to abridge
episcopal liberties. Perhaps as important as any of these issues in the
process of polarization was the personal rivalry of Archbishops Ireland
and Corrigan, each of whom aspired to be the next American to possess a
cardinal's hat. Thus ties of friendship, common convictions and ideals, and
mutual antipathies were involved in the struggle that was to take place.

When Archbishop Francesco Satolli was sent to represent the papacy
at the Chicago World's Fair in 1892, he was privately instructed to
adjudicate the controversies among American Catholics and to make
known at an appropriate time that Leo XIII wanted him to remain in
America as a resident apostolic delegate to ensure that the desired unity
would be maintained. For a variety of reasons, nearly all the bishops were
opposed to the appointment of any such permanent papal representative in
the United States. Ireland was the major exception to this opposition. He
had sensed the hopelessness of resistance and had decided to seek
advantage by being the first to welcome the establishment of an apostolic
delegation in Washington. He was confident that Satolli could be won to
the liberal cause. Ireland's confidence was buttressed by the favor he had
enjoyed at Rome during a visit of the preceding year, and by Leo XIII's
apparent sympathy with progressive views. Furthermore, Denis J. O'Connell (1849–1927), rector of the American College in Rome and a close
collaborator of the liberal triumvirate, had been assured that Satolli would
restore unity by driving Corrigan "to the wall." [28] Ireland therefore was far
from dismayed when Satolli announced on January 14, 1893, that he had
received a papal commission appointing him as apostolic delegate in the
United States.

For a time Ireland's hopes seemed to be confirmed. Satolli's early

---

[28] Cross, *Emergence of Liberal Catholicism*, 180. But McAvoy presents evidence
that Leo did not really favor either faction. See *Great Crisis in American Catholic History*,
89–90.

decisions were generally in harmony with the views of the liberals. The first indication that their fortunes were to suffer reverse came in 1895 when Leo XIII issued the encyclical letter *Longinqua Oceani* to the American church. After praising the notable accomplishments of American Catholics and noting the absence of any hostile legislation in the United States, Leo added the disturbing comment that it "would be very erroneous to draw the conclusion that in America is to be sought the type of the most desirable status of the Church." Indeed, the church in America "would bring forth more abundant fruits if, in addition to liberty, she enjoyed the favor of the laws and the patronage of the public authority." Ireland was so upset by this reprimand that he canceled a previous agreement to write an explanatory article on the anticipated encyclical for the *North American Review*. The encyclical was followed by a series of further blows. A papal warning later in 1895 against taking part in "promiscuous assemblies" was obviously directed against the liberals' enthusiasm for parliaments of religion. But the most shocking rebukes were the forced resignation in 1895 of Denis O'Connell as rector of the American College in Rome and the equally involuntary resignation in 1896 of Keane as rector of Catholic University. When news of Keane's dismissal reached Bishop McQuaid of Rochester, he wrote jubilantly to Corrigan:

> The failure of the University is known at last. . . . What collapses on every side! Gibbons, Ireland, and Keane!!! They were the cock of the walk for a while, and dictated to the country, and thought to run our dioceses for us.[29]

Several things had combined to change the attitude of Rome toward the liberal triumvirate. First, the appointment of Satolli had given the papal court its own independent source of information concerning American affairs, and his recommendations increasingly favored the conservatives. After initially relying on the advice of the liberal prelates, Satolli had been won to the views of their opponents through the influence of Joseph Schroeder, one of the few stanchly conservative professors at Catholic University. Second, Leo XIII himself had taken a conservative turn, having become disappointed by the failure of his liberal tactic to win support for the restoration of the temporal power of the papacy. Third, the

[29] Maynard, *Story of American Catholicism*, 518–19.

central issues of the dispute in America had been carried to Europe where they accentuated existing unrest and dissension. Ireland had toured France in 1892 calling upon the French to emulate the Americans, Keane had spoken in similar vein at Brussels in 1894, Gibbons had been equally eloquent at Rome some years earlier, and many of the speeches and writings of the Americanizers had been translated and circulated in Europe. The conservatives were no less active, with William Tappert reporting in Cologne that the American liberals had surrendered to rationalism, and Joseph Schroeder telling another German audience that they were attacking the universality of the church and undermining the authority of the papacy. The net result of this dual incursion was to win some support for the liberals but also to arouse an even more powerful opposition. Fourth, a papal rebuke of McQuaid for an intemperate attack upon Ireland had given McQuaid an opportunity to make a detailed reply and to state fully the conservative concern. He warned the Pope of a "false liberalism" in America "that, if not checked in time, will bring disaster on the Church," and it may have been this communication that tipped the scales against the progressive prelates.[30]

The liberal triumvirate refused to be daunted by its several defeats and immediately launched a counteroffensive. This in turn provoked a detailed indictment of their views in an article in the February, 1897, issue of the *American Ecclesiastical Review*. The liberals were accused of "an excessive 'flaunting' of American patriotism at the expense of Catholic loyalties; an undue reliance upon scholarship as a source of truth, coupled with a disregard for doctrinal uniformity; extreme libertarianism within the Church to the detriment of sound hierarchical principles; and a muting of Catholic truths in order to attract converts from Protestantism." [31] The article went on to declare that the church could be saved from this dangerous "American religious liberalism" only by the direct and forthright intervention of Rome. The sole liberal victory was Schroeder's forced departure from Catholic University at the beginning of 1898, but the price of this small triumph was to strengthen the demand for a formal condemnation of "Americanism." Meanwhile the "jingoism" of the American press in the months preceding the declaration of war against Spain heightened and consolidated European opposition. It gave substance to the

[30] McAvoy, *The Great Crisis in American Catholic History*, 124–25.
[31] Cross, *Emergence of Liberal Catholicism*, 198.

insistence of the Catholic conservatives that all forms of expansionism by the barbarous Americans were aimed at the destruction of the civilization of Christian Europe.

On January 22, 1899, Leo XIII issued a condemnation of what had become known as "Americanism" in the letter *"Testem Benevolentiae"* which he addressed to Cardinal Gibbons.[32] Although the purpose of the condemnation was "to put an end to certain contentions" which had "arisen lately" among American Catholics, the pretext for the letter was the controversy aroused by the publication in 1897 of an abridged French translation of Walter Elliott's *Life of Father Hecker* (1891).[33] Ireland was informed by Cardinal Rampolla, the papal secretary of state, that centering attention on the Hecker biography was designed to ease the embarrassment and humiliation of submitting to the papal directive. "The words of the letter," Ireland was told, would "allow us to say that the things condemned were never said or written in America" but "were set afloat in France" as a result of the translation and interpretation of the Hecker biography in a foreign language. He was further told that he should do his best "to spread this view." This was "small comfort," wrote Ireland, "but we must make the most of it." And then he added: "In my letter to the Pope, I accepted the letter, swore against all the opinions condemned in it, which I said had never been heard of in America, and declared it an insult to America to have covered such extravagances with the name of Americanism." [34]

Ireland was joined by Gibbons and Keane in coupling submission with a declaration that "Americanism" was a "phantom heresy" [35] which could only have flourished abroad. The conservatives, however, knew better. The bishops of the province of Milwaukee, incensed at the suggestion that the Pope had been "deceived by false reports" and "had beaten the air and chased after a shadow," affirmed that the condemned opinions

[32] The encyclical is reprinted in Smith, Handy, Loetscher, *American Christianity*, II, 336–40.

[33] Ireland had written a glowing introduction for the French translation, Keane had presented a copy to Leo XIII, O'Connell had rushed to the defense of Hecker in a speech at Fribourg during the summer of 1897, and Gibbons defended Hecker in a letter published in France, as "a providential agent for the spread of the Catholic faith" and rejoiced that through the biography Europeans had an opportunity to learn more about him. McAvoy, *The Great Crisis in American Catholic History*, 173–76, 180, 182–83, 200.

[34] For Ireland's letter from Rome, dated February 24, 1899, see *ibid.*, 281.

[35] The term was coined by Felix Klein, the leader of the Americanizing party in France. The fourth volume of his autobiography, *Americanism: A Phantom Heresy*, was published in an English translation in 1951.

had "most assuredly and evidently been proclaimed among us orally and in writing." McQuaid publicly denounced those who said the heresy did not exist, and Corrigan rejoiced that "the monster" had been "struck down dead" by the timely intervention of the Holy See.[36] It was obvious, of course, that Leo XIII had the United States in mind as the seat of the infection. He addressed the letter of condemnation to Gibbons and not to the primate of France, and directed that it be sent to other members of the American hierarchy. Furthermore, Keane was privately but specifically instructed, when appointed archbishop of Dubuque, to heed the warnings contained in the letter to Gibbons. And Ireland was placed under leash and died without his coveted cardinal's hat.

Roman Catholics in America, of necessity, had little time for creative theological reflection. Most of the priests and bishops were forced to be "brick and mortar" men rather than theologians. Their major preoccupation was building new churches and institutions to minister to the tremendous influx of Catholics from abroad. Thus the effect of the condemnation of "Americanism" was only to accentuate the generally conservative temper of American Catholicism. Whatever bold experimentation there had been now gave way to timidity. Discussion and debate within the church largely ceased, and any innovation tended to be viewed with suspicion. The papal condemnation of "Modernism"[37] in 1907 caused scarcely a ripple among American Catholics, although it did contribute further to the theological silence which was to characterize the Catholic Church in the United States for the next few decades.

Other immigrant faiths and accessions

While Roman Catholicism accounted for the largest number of the religiously affiliated among the new Americans, there were significant accessions to other churches and several additional faiths were introduced for the first time. Buddhism, for example, made its appearance among the Chinese and Japanese immigrants on the West coast, and a Young Men's Buddhist Association was founded in 1898. The annexation of Hawaii, also in 1898, gave added strength to the Buddhist community in the United States.

[36] McAvoy, *The Great Crisis in American Catholic History*, 293, 296, 329.
[37] Reprinted in Smith, Handy, Loetscher, *American Christianity*, II, 340–45.

LUTHERAN ACCESSIONS. Of the Protestant groups, the Lutherans benefited most from the growing immigrant tide. By 1910 the Lutherans had become the third largest Protestant denominational grouping, being exceeded in number only by the Methodists and the Baptists. From fewer than 500,000 confirmed members in 1870, they had increased to more than 2,225,000 communicants in 1910. During this period three million Germans had entered the country, with perhaps nearly two-thirds of them being of Protestant background; and during these same years one and three-quarters million Scandinavians had arrived, almost all of whom were Lutheran by heritage and tradition. While many of these new Americans were intensely anticlerical and served to swell the ranks of the unchurched, others among them were deeply pious and zealously orthodox.

So far as influence in the general religious life of the nation was concerned, the Lutheran segment of American church life remained something of a sleeping giant until after World War I. There were several obvious reasons for this. First, apart from some of the cities of the Middle West, the overwhelming proportion of Lutherans were located in largely self-contained and self-sufficient rural communities. Second, most of them were further isolated by language barriers. Third, their energies were almost wholly absorbed by the taxing demands of the attempt to keep abreast of the multiplying population from their homelands. Fourth, they had no organizational unity, being badly divided by national origin, place and time of settlement, and doctrinal differences. And throughout the period prior to World War I, they kept splintering apart, regrouping, and then splintering again. Among the German Lutherans, the major bodies were the General Synod, the General Council, the United Synod in the South, the Missouri Synod, and the Joint Synod of Ohio. The Scandinavians were represented by the Swedish Augustana Synod, the United Norwegian Lutheran Church, the Norwegian and Hauge synods, the Danish Lutheran Church, the United Danish Lutheran Church, and both Finnish and Icelandic churches. By 1900 there were twenty-four different Lutheran groups, with the family tree of most of them so complicated by constant reshuffling that it was difficult to chart even their individual histories.

OTHER PROTESTANT ACCESSIONS. The older German Reformed (Reformed Church in the United States) and Dutch Reformed (Reformed Church in America) churches both profited by the arrival of recruits from abroad. The Christian Reformed Church, though small, gained what strength it had from renewed Dutch immigration, and in 1904 Hungarian Reformed immigrants formed a church of their own. More significant statistically was the growth of the Evangelical Synod,[38] the American counterpart of the Prussian Union of 1817 (the Evangelical United Church of Prussia) which had brought both Lutherans and Reformed together in a single church. Although the Evangelical Synod had roots which antedated the Civil War, the scattered groups of "unionizing" Germans, whose major centers of strength were in the Midwest, were not fully organized as a united body until 1877. The number of Mennonites also multiplied as a result of successive infusions from Switzerland, Prussia, and Russia. But they remained small and divided, with a membership of 54,000 in 1910 distributed among eleven different Mennonite groups.

JUDAISM AND EASTERN ORTHODOX CHRISTIANITY. Immigration from eastern Europe, which peaked during the two decades that bridged the turn of the century, introduced the ancient churches of the East to the American scene and brought to Judaism the large-scale accessions which made it a major religious community in the United States.

Between 1880 and 1900 more than a half million Jews entered the country, fleeing the anti-Semitic pressures being directed against them in Russia, Poland, Austria-Hungary, and Romania. During the next decade and a half more than a million arrived. These were added to an estimated Jewish community of 250,000 in 1880. The figures, however, are somewhat deceptive, for only a small proportion initially became affiliated with a synagogue. And those who did become affiliated were sharply divided, some adhering to orthodox rabbis and others embracing the tenets of Reform Judaism.

The Eastern Orthodox Christians had a long history, antedating the gradual separation within the Roman Empire of the East from the West, the Greek from the Latin, the Byzantine from the Roman. The estrangement of eastern from western Christianity began in the sixth century, and the final breach occurred in 1054 when Rome and the ancient patriarchates of the East found it no longer possible to gloss over the divisive

---

[38] The Evangelical Synod should not be confused with the Methodist-oriented Evangelical Association which joined with the United Brethren in 1946 to become the Evangelical United Brethren Church and in 1968 became part of the United Methodist Church. The Evangelical Synod united with the Reformed Church in the U.S. in 1934 to form the Evangelical and Reformed Church, which united with the Congregational Christian Churches in 1957 to form the United Church of Christ.

issue of Roman primacy. Of the Eastern Christians, the Russian Orthodox have chronological priority in the United States by virtue of the purchase of Alaska in 1867. Apart from this former Russian territory, the Eastern Orthodox churches became statistically significant in America only in the twentieth century. By 1916 the Russian Orthodox and the Greek Orthodox churches each had a constituency of about 100,000 people. Although the Albanian, Bulgarian, Romanian, Serbian, Syrian, and Ukrainian Orthodox churches all had their beginnings in the United States prior to World War I, all of them were subordinated to the jurisdiction of the Russian church at that time.

Since Judaism and Eastern Orthodoxy both reached their full maturity in America after 1920 and since the course of their later development is intimately related to the problems raised and the issues faced in earlier years, a subsequent chapter provides a more meaningful context for a discussion of their initial growth (Chap. XIII).

Difficult as were the growing pains experienced by the churches of the new Americans, the churches of the older Americans had problems of their own during these years. The homogeneity of an evangelical Protestantism which transcended and minimized traditional denominational affiliations had been weakened and compromised by newer ecclesiastical separations into northern and southern, black and white churches. Now, in the last quarter of the century, as Arthur M. Schlesinger, Sr. pointed out, the path of these churches was to be beset with new "pitfalls and perils," being confronted simultaneously with "two great challenges"— the one to their "system of thought," the other to their "social program." [39] The first focuses attention on the new intellectual climate of the post-Civil War period, and the second on the new urban and industrial environment. The response to this dual challenge is the concern of the next two chapters.

[39] Schlesinger's essay, "A Critical Period in American Protestantism, 1875–1900," is printed in the *Massachusetts Historical Society Proceedings*, LXIV (1930–32), 523–48, and has been reprinted in John M. Mulder and John F. Wilson, eds. *Religion in American History* (Englewood Cliffs, N.J., 1978), 302–317. The best account of Protestantism's response to the twofold challenge is by Robert T. Handy, *A Christian America* (N.Y., 1971), 65–183.

XI

The New Intellectual Climate

During the post-Appomattox years when most of the Protestant churches were preoccupied with problems related to Reconstruction in the South and missionary expansion in the West and were devoting their energies to revival campaigns and Sunday school work, crucial theological issues were being raised by radical changes in the intellectual climate —issues that could not long be ignored.

Within a decade after the Civil War practically every important American scientist had been converted to Darwin's theory of biological evolution, and Herbert Spencer's "social Darwinism" was equally influential.[1] Indeed, as early as 1872, the *Atlantic Monthly* was able to report that within the scientific community "natural selection" had "quite won the day in Germany and England, and very nearly won it in America." This new intellectual current penetrated the public consciousness with astonishing rapidity. "Ten or fifteen years ago," Whitelaw Reid declared in an address at Dartmouth in 1873, "the staple subject here for reading

[1] See Richard Hofstadter, *Social Darwinism in American Thought* (N.Y., 1959).

and talk, outside study hours, was English poetry and fiction. Now it is English science. Herbert Spencer, John Stuart Mill, Huxley, Darwin, Tyndall, have usurped the places of Tennyson and Browning, and Matthew Arnold and Dickens." And the discussion was not limited to college students. Equally avid interest in the new scientific theories was displayed by the general public, if the amount of space devoted by the popular periodicals and newspapers to academic lectures and debates is an accurate index of what was being read and discussed.

The new biblical studies were another feature of the postwar intellectual climate. These studies, stemming mainly from the German universities but partly the work of British textual critics, utilized the techniques of "scientific history" to exhibit the Bible as a varied compilation of poetry, prophecy, history, and folklore that had been assembled over a period of a thousand years. The extent of the popular interest that was awakened by these studies is indicated by the reception that was given in 1881 to the English Revised Version of the New Testament which incorporated the results of scholarly analysis of the text. The *Chicago Times* and the *Chicago Tribune* both printed the entire text, while 200,000 copies of the revised New Testament were sold in New York within less than a week.

Furthermore, the study of comparative religion was coming to the fore as an academic discipline, and it soon became apparent that the non-Christian religions also were of fascinating interest to the reading public. James Freeman Clarke's sympathetic appraisal of *Ten Great Religions* went through twenty-one editions after it was published in 1871.[2] Toward the end of the century when a World's Parliament of Religions was held in connection with the Columbian Exposition of 1892–93 more than 150,000 people attended its sessions.

Finally, before the century was out the burgeoning "sciences" of psychology and sociology had made their appearance as forces to be reckoned with in the intellectual life of the nation. Almost immediately attention was centered on subjecting religious phenomena to psychological and sociological analysis. E. D. Starbuck (1866–1947) was one of the pioneers, and his *Psychology of Religion* (1899) was something of an overnight sensation. When William James (1842–1910) published his Gifford Lectures, *The Varieties of Religious Experience* (1902), the

[2] Clarke's views were initially expressed in an article published in 1857, a portion of which is reprinted in Smith, Handy, Loetscher, *American Christianity*, II, 160–64.

interest was so great that within a dozen years it had been reprinted twenty-one times. Ten years later J. H. Leuba (1868–1946) pointed up in provocative fashion the disturbing implications of the psychological approach in his *Psychological Study of Religion* (1912). In the meantime, William Graham Sumner (1840–1910) had published *Folkways* (1906), a sociological study of human behavior which stressed the socially conditioned character of religion and rejected any notion of absolute or eternal truth.

Each of these several currents of thought constituted a threat to accepted understandings of the Christian faith. The psychological and sociological studies tended to reduce religion to a social phenomenon. The accounts of other religions raised questions with regard to the uniqueness of the Christian faith. Both Darwinian biology and the new biblical studies seemed to undermine the authority of the Bible. How could one reconcile Darwinism with the Genesis accounts of creation? And how could one adjust the doctrine of biblical inspiration to take account of the errors and contradictions in the biblical text that were being noted by the scholars? What was one to make of a composite authorship of the books of Moses, with fragments of the text being assigned to different sources in widely separated times? What happened to the prophetic character of the book of Isaiah if parts of it were written by a later "second Isaiah" who was reporting events rather than predicting them? These were unsettling questions and their disturbing implications were made plain to the thousands who listened to Robert G. Ingersoll (1833–99), "the notorious infidel," as he ranged back and forth across the land questioning the basic tenets of Christian belief.[3] Other thousands read his lectures—*The Gods* (1872), *Some Mistakes of Moses* (1879), *Why I Am an Agnostic* (1896)—in printed form. On a less popular level, J. W. Draper sought to demonstrate the incompatibility of science and religion in his *History of the Conflict between Religion and Science* (1874), a task which was also undertaken by Andrew D. White in his *History of the Warfare of Science with Theology* (1896).

The pattern of response among Protestants, Roman Catholics, and Jews to the challenge of scientific modes of thought was remarkably

---

[3] Ingersoll, the son of a Congregational minister, was a great orator who had electrified the Republican convention of 1876 with his famous "plumed knight" speech nominating James G. Blaine for the presidency.

similar. There were some who resisted the new intellectual currents and rejected any modification of inherited theological formulations. There were others who came to believe that the traditional forms of faith were no longer relevant and must be discarded and replaced with idioms and practices that were forthright expressions of a scientific world-view. A third group occupied an intermediate position between the two extremes, seeking to effect adjustments that would do justice both to the essential elements of the inherited faith and to the newer scientific patterns of thought. The radical tendency never loomed large on the American scene, and the moderate "liberal" tendencies in Roman Catholicism were arrested by papal intervention. But both Reformed Judaism (see chap. XIII) and liberal Protestant evangelicalism were destined to flourish.

Protestant liberalism

The mood of most Protestant churchmen at the close of the Civil War was reflected in the proceedings of the Congregational National Council which met in Boston on July 14, 1865. The assembly listened "with profound attention for two full hours" to an opening sermon on the text: "Ask for old paths" (Jer. 6:16), and then proceeded to adopt a Declaration of Faith to serve as a bulwark "for the defense of the Word of God now assailed by multiform and dangerous errors." This was not an entirely ritualistic performance, for the Council was aware of new and urgent problems. But many of the errors it had in mind were those of an earlier generation which the "old paths" had been designed to skirt, and it soon became obvious that signposts pointing to "old paths" were to have only limited utility in helping Christians avoid the perils and pitfalls of the theologically unmapped terrain of the postwar years.

Henry Ward Beecher (1813–87), pastor of Plymouth Congregational Church in Brooklyn from 1847 to 1887 and easily the most prominent preacher of his time, was one of the earliest to recognize that the mere repetition of ancient doctrines would no longer do. In 1872, as the first Lyman Beecher lecturer at Yale, he warned the students of the Divinity School of the danger they faced of being left behind by "the intelligent part of society."

> There is being now applied among scientists a greater amount of real, searching, discriminating thought . . . than ever has been expended . . . in the whole history of the world put together. . . .

If ministers do not make their theological systems conform to the facts as they are; if they do not recognize what men are studying, the time will not be far distant when the pulpit will be like a voice crying in the wilderness. And it will not be "Prepare the way of the Lord," either. . . .

The providence of God is rolling forward in a spirit of investigation that Christian ministers must meet and join.

The one thing ministers cannot afford, insisted Beecher, is to become "apostles of the dead past" by letting "the development of truth run ahead of them." [4]

THE FUNDAMENTAL ISSUE OF BIBLICAL AUTHORITY. The most heated initial debate centered on the notion of biological evolution, for it was a dramatic issue and, by its apparent contradiction of the Bible, Darwin's theory seemed to strike at the very root of a biblically grounded faith. Charles Hodge, the towering theological oracle of Princeton Theological Seminary, declared in 1874 that "a more absolutely incredible theory was never propounded for acceptance among men," and Mark Hopkins, the equally distinguished president of Williams College, denounced the whole concept as "essentially atheistic." A different verdict, however, had been pronounced three years earlier by Hodge's neighbor James McCosh (1811–94), president of Princeton University. "I am inclined to think," he said, "that the theory contains a large body of important truths." If one distinguished the "major assumptions" of the biblical accounts of creation from their literary form, McCosh saw no reason why creation as described in Genesis should be regarded as inconsistent with developmental theories. Holding fast to the traditional doctrine of design in nature, he interpreted "natural selection" as the product of "supernatural design." [5]

A similar resolution of the problem was proposed by John Fiske (1842–1901). In his *Outline of Cosmic Philosophy* (1874) and subsequent volumes, he transmuted the struggle for survival into a struggle for the lives of others. Infusing the whole process with divine purpose, Fiske coined the sentence—"Evolution is God's way of doing things"—which was later popularized as a slogan by Lyman Abbott (1835–1922). In the meantime, Henry Ward Beecher had given further impetus to this type of

[4] *Yale Lectures on Preaching* (N.Y., 1872–74), I, 87–89. See C. E. Clark, *Henry Ward Beecher: Spokesman for Middle Class America* (Champaign, 1978).
[5] See Charles Hodge, *What Is Darwinism?* (N.Y., 1874), and James McCosh, *Christianity and Positivism* (N.Y., 1871).

adjustment by announcing in the *Christian Union* (Aug. 2, 1883) that he was "a cordial Christian evolutionist." [6] But perhaps the most reassuring evidence to many faithful Christians that evolutionary views could be assimilated without harm to the Christian faith was provided by Henry Drummond (1851–97), the author of *Natural Law in the Spiritual World* (1883). This gifted young Scottish theologian was an intimate friend of Dwight L. Moody, and when Drummond visited the United States in 1887 Moody enlisted his aid both at Northfield and in his revival meetings.

The theory of biological evolution was actually the least serious of the intellectual problems which the churches were being compelled to face. While it could be handled by construing the first chapter of Genesis allegorically or by contending that the Bible was never intended to be a scientific encyclopedia, other problems could not be side-stepped so easily. This was notably true of the issues that were being raised by the "scientific" study of the Bible, for the new biblical studies were making it increasingly evident that any attempt to justify even the "major assumptions" of the Christian faith by an appeal to the authority of Scripture was fraught with difficulty. Biblical scholars were demonstrating that at many points of Christian doctrine conflicting evidence could be adduced from within the biblical text itself.

In 1867 these difficulties were pointed out by Thomas F. Curtis (1816–72) of Bucknell University in *The Human Element in the Inspiration of the Sacred Scriptures,* and the measure of the confusion he evoked is indicated by the reaction to his book of a fellow Baptist, Henry G. Weston (1820–1909), who was soon to become president of Crozer Theological Seminary. "I am all at sea," wrote Weston, "except so far as a dogged belief in inspiration goes, without being able to define what 'inspiration' is or what its metes and bounds are." Small wonder that Weston was determined to hold fast to a belief in inspiration, for this had been the major line of defense of the whole dogmatic structure.[7]

The central issue was the authority of the Bible. Few great religions have been so dependent as Christianity upon a sacred book. Preaching

[6] For Beecher and Abbott, see Beecher's *Evolution and Religion* (N.Y., 1885), and Abbott's *The Theology of an Evolutionist* (N.Y., 1897).

[7] See J. W. Brown, *The Rise of Biblical Criticism in America, 1800–1870* (Middletown, Conn., 1969), and N. H. Maring, "Baptists and Changing Views of the Bible, 1865–1918," *Foundations* (July, 1958), 52–78; (Oct., 1958), 30–61. W. B. Glover, *Evangelical Nonconformity and Higher Criticism* (London, 1955) is suggestive for interpreting the American scene.

elucidated its texts. Prayer claimed its promises. And theology and conduct alike were grounded on its teachings. While both Protestants and Roman Catholics had long regarded the Bible as the inspired and inerrant Word of God, the Roman Catholic Church had found it necessary at the Council of Trent (1545–63) to supplement biblical teaching with that of "tradition," and at the first Vatican Council (1870) to affirm papal infallibility in the interpretation of Scripture and tradition. Protestants, on the other hand, had clung to the sole authority of Scripture, which in the first half of the nineteenth century was almost universally understood in terms of an inspired and infallible text. Since they had no recourse to any supplementary authority, the questioning of biblical inspiration was peculiarly threatening to Protestants. Once this point was surrendered, a thoroughgoing reconsideration of the whole basis of the Christian faith was required. Ultimately Protestants were to work out different ways of understanding biblical authority, but first many of them were to seek in "evangelical liberalism" and in "scientific modernism" other sources of authority.

EVANGELICAL LIBERALISM. The striking feature of the liberal movement in Protestantism which began to take shape during the 1870's was its conservative intent. The leaders of the movement were evangelicals, standing firmly within the church, cherishing their Christian experience, and uncompromising in their loyalty to Christ. They had little in common with the earlier rationalistic liberalism which had become dominant in Unitarianism. The central concern of the evangelical liberals was quite explicitly apologetic. They wished to preserve the truth of the gospel as it spoke to the hearts of men. In the face of what many feared might be fatal assaults on the Christian faith, they sought to restate the essential doctrines of evangelical Christianity in terms that would be both intelligible and convincing and thus to establish them on a more secure foundation.

Henry Ward Beecher was the most conspicuous of the early liberal leaders and it would be easy to overestimate his importance.[8] The influence he exerted was great, but he was no theologian. At most he was a

[8] F. H. Foster made this mistake in *The Modern Movement in American Theology* (N.Y., 1939), devoting a whole chapter to "The School of Henry Ward Beecher," J. W. Buckham also asserted that, next to Horace Bushnell, Beecher was "the greatest liberator of American theological thought." *Progressive Religious Thought in America* (N.Y., 1919), 32.

popularizer—a "weather cock" some called him. The real theological task of adjusting the inherited formulations of the faith to the new "scientific" climate of opinion was the work of other men.

While isolated individuals in various parts of the country helped to fashion what came to be called the "New Theology" and "Progressive Orthodoxy," the most important contribution was made by a notable group of pastors in prominent New England pulpits, all of whom had been deeply influenced by Horace Bushnell. In neighboring churches on the New Haven green, Theodore T. Munger (1830–1910) and Newman Smyth (1843–1925) gave new luster to a tradition of distinguished theological preaching that had been exemplified in these same pulpits by Jonathan Edwards, Jr., and Nathaniel W. Taylor. Munger, at the United (Congregational) Church was the author of *The Freedom of Faith* (1883) which the *New York Times* called the "most forcible and positive expression" of the new theology to appear in this country; [9] while Newman Smyth, at the Center (Congregational) Church, had argued the same case in three pioneering volumes: *The Religious Feeling* (1877), *Old Faiths in New Light* (1878), and *The Orthodox Theology of Today* (1881). In Boston, Phillips Brooks (1835–93) at Trinity (Episcopal) Church and George A. Gordon (1853–1929) at Old South (Congregational) Church were making Copley Square a center of the new theological outlook. Washington Gladden (1836–1918) was less philosophically inclined than Munger, Smyth, and Gordon, but he was equally creative in his own way and was the most effective propagandist of the new point of view. As early as 1873 he had written for the *Independent* (July 3, 1873) an editorial entitled "Immoral Theology," which exhibited the journalistic flair that won such a widespread circulation for his subsequent books dealing with current theological issues: *Burning Questions* (1886), *Who Wrote the Bible?* (1891), *Ruling Ideas of the Present Age* (1895), *Seven Puzzling Bible Books* (1897), and *How Much Is Left of the Old Doctrines?* (1899). By the time these books were published, Gladden had left New England, having resigned his Springfield pulpit in 1882 to accept a call to the First Congregational Church of Columbus, Ohio. All these young men were responding in the immediate post-Civil War years to the practical necessity of relating the Christian faith from week to week to questions that were uppermost in the minds of alert and inquiring congregations.

[9] C. H. Hopkins, *The Rise of the Social Gospel in American Protestantism* (New Haven, 1940), 61.

Meanwhile in theological seminaries a less conspicuous intellectual ferment was taking place, the consequence in part of the stimulus provided by an increasing number of younger members of the faculties who had spent a period of study abroad where they had imbibed the relatively advanced theological thinking of the German universities. The most dramatic shift occurred at Andover Theological Seminary, which had been established in 1808 as a counter to Unitarian tendencies at Harvard and had been shackled with a creed designed to prevent any deviation from orthodoxy. A new type of thinking began to be introduced at Andover in the 1860's, but no open break occurred until 1880 when William J. Tucker (1839–1926) qualified his subscription to the creed.

> The creed which I am about to read and to which I subscribe I fully accept as setting forth the truth against the errors which it was designed to meet. No confession so elaborate and with such intent may assume to be the final expression of the truth or an expression equally fitted in language or tone to all times.[10]

When Edwards A. Park (1808–1900), the last great champion of New England orthodoxy, retired the following year, the liberals were left in complete control. Three years later the faculty began publication of the Andover Review to elucidate their "progressive orthodoxy."

While this developing liberal sentiment was indebted to insights supplied from abroad by Friedrich Schleiermacher (1768–34) and Albrecht Ritschl (1822–89), it was mediated in part through British scholars and scholarship. It also had indigenous rootage in categories and understandings provided by Horace Bushnell who earlier had been influenced by Schleiermacher and Coleridge. Bushnell was perhaps the key figure, for in many ways it was Bushnell who eased the difficult transition for evangelical Christians from the old to the new theology. As early as 1844 Bushnell had provided the basis for an adjustment to evolutionary views when he asserted that "growth and not conquest" was "the true method of Christian progress."[11] Through his analysis of the use and limitations of language, he also offered a way of escape

---

[10] See D. D. Williams, *The Andover Liberals* (N.Y., 1941), 28.

[11] See Buckham, *Progressive Religious Thought*, 11. Bushnell, of course, also had found much that was suggestive in the English theologian Frederick Denison Maurice (1805–72). For some of the points at which he diverged from the German theologians, see Fred Kirshenmann, "Horace Bushnell: Orthodox or Sabellian?" *Church History*, XXXIII (1964), 49–59.

from bondage to the verbal forms in which doctrinal statements had been cast. But the real key to the influence Bushnell exerted upon his younger contemporaries was his success in fashioning a definitely Christocentric theology that was based upon Christian experience rather than upon any external dogmatic authority. Thus the believer was no longer under compulsion to find his security in biblical proof texts. He could accept the conclusions of the biblical scholars with relative equanimity and appropriate the results of other scientific investigations without great difficulty because his faith was validated by the inward testimony of the heart. Bushnell had discovered this path of escape from his "arrant doubts" at the very beginning of his ministry. What shall I do with the doctrine of the Trinity, he asked, when "logic shatters it all to pieces and I am all at the four winds"?

> I am glad that I have a heart as well as a head. My heart wants the Father; my heart wants the Son; my heart wants the Holy Ghost—the one just as much as the other. My heart says the Bible has a Trinity for me, and I mean to hold by my heart.[12]

Secure in the conviction that "the heart has its reasons, which reason does not know," Bushnell found a freedom denied to those who felt compelled to meet a rationalistic assault with a purely rationalistic defense.

In keeping with their apologetic concern, the starting point of all theology for the heirs of Bushnell in pulpit and classroom was to be found in Christ. Christ stood at the heart of the religious experience they were seeking to defend. Christ alone, declared Egbert C. Smyth of Andover Theological Seminary, "fulfills the aspirations and harmonizes the discords in man's religious history."

> The history of religion leads on and up to him, and he possesses all the resources requisite for its greatest possible future growth. He is the Alpha and Omega; the Absolute, revealed; the Infinite, personally disclosed; the eternal Power that makes for righteousness, realized in the Righteous One. . . . A theology which is not Christocentric is like a Ptolomaic astronomy; it is out of true relation to the earth and heavens, to God and the universe.[13]

Thus, while there was much that earlier generations had affirmed that

---

[12] *Life and Letters of Horace Bushnell*, ed. M. B. Cheney (N.Y., 1880), 56; quoted by Mead, *Lively Experiment*, 136.
[13] *Progressive Orthodoxy*, by the Editors of the *Andover Review* (Boston, 1886), 35-36.

could be surrendered as nonessential and much that had to be adjusted and accommodated to new knowledge, the person and work of Christ as the clue to the nature of God, the worth of human personality, and the meaning of life was indispensable. His life and teachings constituted "the final principle" of "interpretation," the standard by which all else must be judged. The goal of the New Theology, as William Adams Brown (1865–1943) was to point out in 1898 in his inaugural address as professor of systematic theology in Union Theological Seminary, was no more than "the old cry, 'Back to Christ.' Let no theology call itself Christian which has not its center and source in him."

Although these evangelical liberals clung tenaciously to the Bible and repaired to it for consolation and inspiration, they viewed it as a document which recorded the historical experience out of which the Christian faith had emerged, a vivid personal record of suffering and travail which culminated in the disclosure in Christ of true and perfect communion with God. It was a record not of a theology but of an experience that was to be reproduced "in our own times and in our own souls." While it told them what they knew of Christ, there was no need to seek "scientific arguments for Christian truth," for their own experience of Christ was self-authenticating. "The foundation of spiritual faith is neither in the church nor in the Bible, but in the spiritual consciousness of man." [14] The doctrines which "form the subject matter of theology," declared Brown in his inaugural address, are not "dogmas to be received on authority"; they are "living convictions, born of experience, and maintaining themselves in spite of all opposition because of the response which they wake in the hearts and consciences of men."

Few of these men exhibited any great metaphysical interest, but those who did found in idealistic philosophy a way of theologizing that did not depend upon complicated processes of biblical criticism. Some, like George A. Gordon, appropriated the "monistic" form of idealism of which Josiah Royce (1855–1916) was the most conspicuous American representative. Others, mostly fellow Methodists, adopted the "personalism" of Borden P. Bowne (1847–1910) of Boston University. The greater number, however, were content to give only passing attention to philosophical issues and to structure their theological thinking within more familiar biblical categories. Typical in this respect was William Newton Clarke (1840–1912), the Baptist theologian at Colgate Theological Semi-

[14] See Lyman Abbott, *Reminiscences* (Boston, 1915), 451, 461-62.

nary, whose *Outline of Christian Theology* (1898) was so widely used that it has been called "virtually the Dogmatik" of evangelical liberalism.[15]

The great advantage of this New Theology of evangelical liberalism was that it enabled its proponents both to maintain what to them was the heart of their inherited faith and at the same time to come to terms with the whole intellectual temper of the modern world. The stress upon self-authenticating religious experience permitted them to bridge the gap between the natural and the supernatural, and enabled them to give due recognition to the claims of science and of the scientific method. The acceptance of the idea of development made it possible to view the Bible in a way that was congenial to both their religious and their cultural orientation, allowed them to share to varying degrees the growing confidence in man and his future, and fostered an openminded attitude toward differing opinions and new modes of thought.

SCIENTIFIC MODERNISM. While evangelical liberalism continued to be the dominant liberal current in American Protestantism, a more radical approach to the issue of the relation of science to religion began to emerge in the first years of the twentieth century. Those who in retrospect have been called "scientific modernists"[16] stood in marked contrast to the conservative intent of the evangelical liberals, for they viewed as a lost cause the endeavor of the evangelical liberals to maintain continuity with the inherited faith by abstracting religion from the realm of scientific verification. These men recognized that the sanctuary of the heart which the evangelical liberals sought to preserve inviolate had been invaded by the scientists. "Science," E. D. Starbuck had proclaimed in 1899, "has conquered one field after another, until now it is entering the most

---

[15] The phrase is that of Sydney E. Ahlstrom, "Theology in America," *The Shaping of American Religion*, ed. Smith and Jamison, 292. G. B. Smith described it as "perhaps the most influential book of its kind in American religious thinking." *Current Christian Thinking* (Chicago, 1928), 83. W. A. Brown's *Christian Theology in Outline* (1906) was largely based upon Clarke's text. Kenneth Cauthen, *The Impact of American Religious Liberalism* (N.Y., 1962), 42–43. Insight into the changing attitude toward the Bible can best be gained from William Newton Clarke's *Sixty Years with the Bible* (N.Y., 1909), a moving autobiographical account of the development of his own views through six decades.

[16] The term was coined by Sidney E. Mead. While exact lines of demarcation between the evangelical liberals and the scientific modernists are difficult to draw, there was a clear difference of intention and emphasis. The liberals were committed first and foremost to the Christian tradition and from that vantage point attempted to effect any necessary adjustments. The scientific modernists took their stand with the presuppositions of science, and then sought to reclaim what they could of the traditional faith. For them the scientific method was accepted as the starting point for all human investigation. Complicating the picture is the fact that evangelical liberals frequently called themselves "modernists."

complex, the most inaccessible, and of all the most sacred domain—that of religion." The scientific modernists were impressed by the way in which psychological and sociological analysis was able to explain not only religious experience, but also doctrinal concepts and ecclesiastical practice, in terms of inner personal drives and conditioning social forces. Thus they were ready to grant "to the data of religious experience the same scientific status as the data of the physical sciences," and then to fashion a religious faith "out of the materials furnished by the several sciences." [17] They did not seek a complete break with the Christian past, as is made clear in Shailer Mathews' classic definition of modernism—"the use of the methods of modern science to find, state, and use the permanent and central values of inherited orthodoxy in meeting the needs of a modern world." [18] The values of orthodoxy were not to be ignored, but "science" was the arbiter in determining what they were and how they were to be stated and used.[19] It is safe to assume, Mathews was to assert, that "scientists know more about nature and man than did the theologians who drew up the Creeds and Confessions." The whole tendency, therefore, was to become less and less concerned with a distinctively Christian witness and more and more interested in general religious affirmations based on a "scientific world-view."

Unlike liberal evangelicalism which initially was the product of the reflections of men who were pastors of churches, scientific modernism was indigenous to the theological seminaries. The great center was in Chicago where William Rainey Harper (1856–1906) and John D. Rockefeller had established their Baptist super-university in 1892, assembling for that purpose a faculty of many of the most noted scholars in America. While many pastors found comfort and reassurance and themes for sermons in the reports that filtered down to them from the psychologists and sociologists that religious beliefs integrated personality, fostered mental health, and served socially useful ends; the theological professors at Chicago, with John Dewey, Albion W. Small, and George Herbert Mead numbered among their university colleagues, were compelled to face the fundamental

[17] E. E. Aubrey, "Religious Bearings of the Modern Scientific Movement," in *Environmental Factors in Christian History*, ed. J. T. McNeill *et al.* (Chicago, 1939), 368.

[18] See the portion of Mathews' *The Faith of Modernism* which is reprinted in Smith, Handy, Loetscher, *American Christianity*, II, 238–45.

[19] A typical monograph was that of George A. Coe, "What Does Modern Psychology Permit Us to Believe in Respect to Regeneration?" *American Journal of Theology*, XII (1908), 353–68.

theological issue that was raised by the empiricism upon which these new disciplines were based.

The Chicago approach to theology (they hesitated to call it more than a theological method) was not fully elaborated until after World War I, but its basic character was clearly evident much earlier. The key figures of the Divinity School faculty, in addition to a distinguished corps of biblical scholars headed by Harper himself, were Shailer Mathews (1863–1941), George Burman Foster (1858–1918), and Gerald Birney Smith (1868–1929); while Edward Scribner Ames (1870–1958)—simultaneously professor of philosophy in the university, pastor of the University Church of the Disciples of Christ, and dean of the Disciples Divinity House—also provided strong leadership in the task of theological reconstruction. The dominant emphasis, exemplified pre-eminently by Mathews, was upon a socio-historical approach to theology which viewed all doctrinal statements as reflections of historic cultural patterns, and consequently were functional and not normative, changeable and not permanent. They were to be tested and applied "in the same way that chemists and historians reach and apply their conclusions," and they must be stated in terms that would make sense to intelligent men and women within the contemporary cultural context. "The God of the scientifically minded will assume the patterns of science." [20]

In spite of the fact that some members of the Chicago group moved to a nontheist position and others found it difficult to find anything either unique or normative in the Christian faith, the influence they exerted in the life of the churches was far from insignificant. This was partly due to the fact that for a period of thirty or forty years a very large proportion of professors in other theological seminaries received their graduate training at Chicago. Scarcely less important was the fact that most of the key figures remained stanch churchmen and played a leading role in ecclesiastical affairs. Shailer Mathews, for example, was president of the Federal Council of Churches from 1912 to 1916 and of the American (Northern) Baptist Convention in 1915. Finally, the men at Chicago exhibited an intensely practical propagandist zeal. William Rainey Harper set the pattern when he became superintendent of the Hyde Park Baptist Sunday School in order to put his theories into practice, and with the stimulus of

[20] *The Faith of Modernism*, as reprinted in Smith, Handy, Loetscher, *American Christianity*, II, 240–41; and Shailer Mathews, *The Growth of the Idea of God* (N.Y., 1931), 184.

Harper's interest the University of Chicago pioneered in the new "scientific" approach to religious education. One of the most effective means of penetration was a scheme of adult education known as the American Institute of Sacred Literature, through which books, pamphlets, and study courses in a steady stream were made available and were widely used in Protestant churches throughout the Middle West.

Protestant conservatism

The mounting accommodation within Protestantism to the new intellectual climate did not go unchallenged. From the beginning resistance was both vocal and widespread, but the opposition seldom grappled profoundly or creatively with the issues involved. The response was mainly limited to strong dogmatic denials grounded in a pietistic indifference to the new "scientific" studies. Charles Hodge, in an earlier debate, had set the tone of the unyielding defensive posture of the conservative elements when he declared: "We can even afford to acknowledge our incompetence to meet them in argument, or to answer their objections; and yet our faith remains unshaken and rational." [21] There was no prominent theologian to play a constructive role comparable to that of a P. T. Forsyth (1848–1921) in Britain or a Martin Kähler (1835–1912) in Germany, unless the attempt of Augustus H. Strong (1836–1921) to find a mediating position qualifies him to be ranked with his European contemporaries. Nevertheless, when the defenders of the inherited formulations of the faith chose to fight the battle on the basis of biblical inerrancy, they were astute enough to recognize that the central issue was the authority of the Scriptures even if they failed to recognize that there may have been a more tenable position than a doctrine of "inspiration" upon which to base their defense.

THE HERESY TRIALS. The Congregationalists and Baptists, with their loose form of organization, offered the freest field for the growth of liberal sentiment.[22] Neither denomination had any ready means of taking

[21] *Princeton Review*, XXIX (1857), 662.

[22] The Disciples offered an equally free field but among them the issue assumed a somewhat different form. The division was between those who placed primary emphasis upon the Disciples' traditional theme of the "restoration" of the primitive church and those who gave major stress to the equally traditional theme of Christian unity. Such men as Peter Ainslee and Charles Clayton Morrison gained their chief distinction as advocates of Christian unity. Herbert L. Willett, of course, made a major contribution to the field of biblical study, and Edward Scribner Ames was one of the most prominent of the "scientific modernists." By 1906 the rigidly biblistic wing of the Disciples—the "Churches of Christ" of the middle South—had gone its separate way.

action to enforce conformity to doctrinal standards. Once installed in a church, a pastor was secure as long as he retained the support of his own congregation, and most of their theological seminaries were independently organized and not subject to denominational control. Although Ezra P. Gould (1841–1900) was dismissed from Newton Theological Seminary in 1882 and Nathaniel Schmidt (1862–1939) from Colgate in 1896, all the northern Baptist seminaries were firmly in the liberal camp by the end of the century. This was also true of the Congregational seminaries, with Andover's status having been clarified in 1892 when the Supreme Court of Massachusetts sustained the trustees and voided the action of the Board of Visitors in dismissing Egbert C. Smyth from the faculty.

The Methodists had the means of closing ranks to prevent doctrinal innovation, but in the North at least they exhibited little inclination to do so. In spite of the fact that such men as Nathan Bangs (1778–1862), Daniel D. Whedon (1808–85), and Miner Raymond (1811–97) had whetted their theological scalpels and used them with great effectiveness in running debates with Calvinists, the Methodists as a result of their continuing emphasis upon the centrality of heart religion had developed no sharply defined theological position. To the extent that they held to any external tests of fellowship, their stress was upon morality rather than dogma. When charges of denying the inerrancy of Scripture were leveled in 1904 against Hinkley G. Mitchell (1846–1920) of the Boston University School of Theology and then against Borden P. Bowne, the General Conference of 1908 put a stop to any further proceedings of this type by relieving the bishops of responsibility for investigating charges of erroneous teaching in Methodist schools. While there were to be subsequent flurries of controversy among northern Methodists, the official policy of the denomination hewed closely to the line represented by John Wesley's oft-repeated dictum: "Is thy heart as my heart? Then give me thy hand." The Protestant Episcopal Church followed a similar policy of comprehension, with the trial of Algernon S. Crapsey (1847–1927) in 1906 being the only conspicuous exception. And even Crapsey probably would not have been summoned to defend his heterodox theological views had he not embarrassed his bishop by combining his doctrinal errors with radical attacks upon the existing economic order.

The Lutherans, in contrast to these other denominations, maintained an almost solidly unbroken orthodox front. The most liberal of the major Lutheran bodies—the General Synod of the Lutheran Church in the United States—tightened its discipline in 1895 and affirmed that its doctrinal basis was "the Word of God as the infallible rule of faith and practice, and the unaltered Augsburg Confession as throughout in perfect consistence with it—nothing more, nothing less." Thus the heresy trials which gained so much attention in the public press were largely confined to the reunited Presbyterian church in the North.

Among northern Presbyterians the issue was raised as early as 1874 when Francis L. Patton (1843–1932) of McCormick Theological Seminary lodged charges of heresy against David Swing (1830–94), pastor of the Fourth Presbyterian Church in Chicago. The local presbytery acquitted him, but when Patton filed notice of his intention to appeal the verdict, Swing resigned his pastorate and established an independent congregation. During the following decade several other men, including William C. McCune of Cincinnati, W. W. McLane of Steubenville, Ohio, and J. W. White of Huntington, Pennsylvania, were dismissed from the ministry on doctrinal grounds. The most celebrated trials, however, were those of Charles A. Briggs (1841–1913) and Henry Preserved Smith (1847–1927).[23]

The Briggs case was precipitated in 1891 by his inaugural address as the first occupant of the newly created chair of biblical theology in Union Theological Seminary (New York), an address in which he vigorously condemned "the dogma of verbal inspiration." [24] There were two immediate consequences. First, the Presbyterian General Assembly withheld its approval of his appointment. Second, charges of heresy were filed with the presbytery of New York. Briggs was acquitted by the presbytery, but the General Assembly set aside the verdict and suspended Briggs from the ministry. The veto of his appointment by the General Assembly was brushed aside by the Seminary as irrelevant. Two decades earlier the Seminary had granted the General Assembly the right to confirm appointments to its faculty. In this instance, however, Briggs had been a member of the faculty since 1874 and the Seminary contended that the authority it had conferred upon the General Assembly did not extend to a transfer

[23] For the context of these trials, see L. A. Loetscher, *The Broadening Church: A Study of Theological Issues in the Presbyterian Church since 1869* (Philadelphia, 1954).

[24] A portion of the address is in Smith, Handy, Loetscher, *American Christianity*, II, 275–79.

within the faculty from one chair to another. In the end, the Seminary revoked its earlier grant of authority, severed this somewhat tenuous official connection with the Presbyterian church, and retained Briggs who solved the problem of his ministerial standing by becoming an Episcopalian.

At the same time the Briggs affair was before the General Assembly, the case of Henry Preserved Smith, a professor in Lane Theological Seminary, was also being adjudicated. Smith had come to the defense of Briggs and was convicted of heresy on similar grounds in 1892 by the presbytery of Cincinnati, a verdict which was sustained by the General Assembly. This meant the end of his relationship to Lane Seminary, but Union Seminary provided him with a haven as librarian and Smith transferred his denominational affiliation to the Congregationalists. A few years later another member of the Union faculty, Arthur Cushman McGiffert (1861–1933) had charges preferred against him, and to avoid another heresy trial he quietly withdrew from the Presbyterian church and became a Congregationalist.

The heresy trials failed to halt the growing theological cleavage even among the Presbyterians. Not only did the trials bring the issues to the fore and publicize them, they awakened popular sympathy for the "persecuted." And this sympathy in turn was exploited and heightened by widely read novels such as Margaret Deland's *John Ward, Preacher*, and Mrs. Humphrey Ward's *Robert Elsmere*. Henry Van Dyke (1852–1933), minister of Brick Presbyterian Church in New York City, spoke for many laymen when he declared: "This great city wants the bread of life. Don't give it the stone of controversy instead." A church that had cast out a warmly devout Professor Briggs was reminded by Van Dyke that it had

> Something to learn and something to forget:
> Hold fast to the good, and seek the better yet:
> Press on, and prove the pilgrim-hope of youth—
> That creeds are milestones on the path to truth.

If orthodoxy was to flourish, Van Dyke insisted, it must breathe the air of freedom. "The best way to defend the Bible is in the open air and in the light of the facts." [25] His admonitions were not without effect, and after the turn of the century at least two of the Presbyterian seminaries—Auburn in

[25] Tertius Van Dyke, *Henry Van Dyke A Biography* (N.Y., 1935), 129.

upstate New York and McCormick in Chicago—were exhibiting definite liberal tendencies.

CENTERS OF CONSERVATIVE STRENGTH. The theological climate of the country varied from section to section. By the time of World War I, New England had long been the great stronghold of Protestant liberalism. New York State, with its Yankee heritage and "New School" tradition, was scarcely less liberal in its dominant theological mood. The Middle West was generally moderate, with radicals of both the "right" and the "left" exerting influence within the churches. The Pacific coast was beginning to manifest its distinctive sense of freedom in a variety of new sects and cults, but otherwise its tone was conservative. The South had witnessed a few attempts to break with orthodoxy. Alexander Winchell (1824–91) at Vanderbilt had contradicted the Genesis account of creation in 1878, thereby provoking a pointed censure by the General Conference of the southern Methodist church of those who bend "all the energies of their most exalted genius to the inculcation of theories which are calculated, if not designed, to destroy the credibility of the Holy Scriptures." [26] When Winchell refused to resign, the university abolished his position. The following year Crawford H. Toy (1836–1919) was forced to resign from the faculty of the Southern Baptist Theological Seminary at Louisville, Kentucky, for teachings which allegedly undercut the absolute authority of Scripture. And in 1886 James Woodrow (1828–1907), uncle of Woodrow Wilson and professor at Columbia Theological Seminary, was condemned and dismissed from his post by the General Assembly of the southern Presbyterian church for suggesting that the theory of evolution could be reconciled with a "not unreasonable interpretation of the Bible." [27] Such incidents were significant only as an occasion for the closing of ranks by the southern churches against any departure from the inherited theological formulations. A placid and undisturbed orthodoxy continued to prevail throughout the South as a whole.

Pennsylvania and New Jersey stood in marked contrast to their neighboring states to the north, for they were dominated by a vigorous, articulate, and strongly intrenched conservatism. This was the Presbyterian citadel, and it was a Presbyterianism that was shaped by the

[26] K. K. Bailey, *Southern White Protestantism in the Twentieth Century* (N.Y., 1964), 10.
[27] *Ibid.*

unyielding orthodoxy of Princeton, Western, and Pittsburgh (United Presbyterian) theological seminaries. Also contributing to the conservative cast of the Middle Atlantic states was the strength of the denominations of German origin in this area. The rallying center of the conservative forces was Princeton Theological Seminary, where the mantle of Charles Hodge had been bequeathed first to his son Archibald Alexander Hodge (1823–86) and then to Benjamin Warfield (1851–1921), both of whom were as convinced as the elder Hodge that the truth of the gospel had been definitively set forth in the Westminster Confession of 1646. In response to the issues raised by biblical criticism, the younger Hodge and Warfield fashioned the "Princeton doctrine of Inspiration" which became a major defense of biblical inerrancy.[28]

Meanwhile, throughout the northern half of the United States, a new movement was arising that was to give added strength to the conservative forces. This was a movement which found its inspiration in the "dispensationalist" and "premillennialist" speculations of J. N. Darby (1800–82) in England. It was spearheaded in America by itinerant evangelists, popularized at "prophetic" Bible conferences which met annually after 1876, and supplied with leadership by newly established "Bible Schools." [29] Displaying little concern for denominational peculiarities, the proponents of this "prophetic" understanding of the Scriptures made inroads in practically all the Protestant denominations. This penetration was greatly facilitated by the popularity of the *Scofield Reference Bible,* an annotated edition of the Bible prepared by C. I. Scofield (1843–1921), which imposed a rigid schematization on the complex biblical materials by relating each part of Scripture to a timetable of "dispensations" which were to culminate in the return of Christ to reign in glory. Among the leaders of the movement were such men as Reuben A. Torrey (1856–1928), J. W. Chapman (1859–1918), A. C. Dixon (1854–1925), and James M. Gray (1851–1935), all of whom were related in one way or another to the Moody Bible Institute in Chicago. Associated with them in New England were A. J. Gordon (1836–95) and A. T. Pierson

28 For their doctrine, of inspiration, see article by Hodge and Warfield reprinted in Smith, Handy, Loetscher, *American Christianity,* II, 324–32.

29 See C. N. Kraus, *Dispensationalism in America* (Richmond, 1958); C. B. Bass, *Backgrounds to Dispensationalism* (Grand Rapids, 1960); and F. E. Gaebelein, *The Story of the Scofield Reference Bible* (N.Y., 1959). The larger context of "dispensationalism" is discussed by E. R. Sandeen, *The Roots of Fundamentalism British and American Millenarianism, 1800–1930* (Chicago, 1970).

(1837–1911), both of whom had also been influenced by the "holiness" emphasis of the Keswick conferences in England.[30] These men tended to interpret every manifestation of theological liberalism as the work of Satan, and they constantly voiced their alarm. This preoccupation with heresy led them to identify specific doctrinal items—the verbal inerrancy of Scripture, the deity and virgin birth of Christ, the substitutionary atonement, the physical resurrection of Christ, and his bodily return to earth—which could be utilized to spot any heretic by a few pointed questions.

Most Protestant conservatives hesitated to identify themselves with the "Bible School" men, for they were not willing to accept the "dispensationalist" doctrine which colored their premillennialist interpretation of the Bible. On occasion, to be sure, the old-line conservatives welcomed "dispensationalist" support when other issues were at stake. And in 1910 the northern Presbyterian General Assembly appropriated the "dispensationalist" technique when it named five "essential and necessary" doctrines which were to be used as tests of orthodoxy. Though not mentioning premillennialism, these "five points" were adopted by many of the Bible School group as a convenient means of detecting heresy.

While party alignments did take place in every denomination during the years which bridged the turn of the century, the centering of attention on the theological debates between conservatives and liberals can be misleading. Few of the rank-and-file members of the churches were caught up in the controversy. To the extent that they were theologically self-conscious, the great body of American Protestants were undoubtedly conservative and traditional in their basic beliefs, but they were not rigidly so. They had no thought of abandoning the faith of their fathers, but, having been subjected to several solvents, their definition of that faith was somewhat vague and imprecise. What was most admired was not the rigid stance of embattled theologians, but the great-heartedness of a Dwight L. Moody who did not stickle at working with those whom he could not regard as doctrinally sound at all points. In the theologically relaxed atmosphere of late nineteenth-century evangelicalism, Daniel Dorchester (1827–1907), the eminent Methodist historian, probably pronounced the

---

[30] The Keswick conferences were held each summer for the purpose of "promoting practical holiness," and had been initiated in 1875 by men who had been influenced by Dwight L. Moody during his British tour of 1873–75. See Ernest R. Sandeen, *The Roots of Fundamentalism: British and American Millenarianism* (Chicago, 1970).

verdict of the majority when he rejoiced that theology had become "less scholastic and repulsive," had been "lubricated and broadened," and was "the better for its siftings." [31]

Variant radical responses

During these same years much more radical attempts to come to terms with the new intellectual climate were taking place outside the established churches. Most of them were not numerically significant, but they are important in illustrating the ferment that had been precipitated. Some were sober attempts at a thoroughgoing reconstruction of religion without a "supernatural" dimension, others were impressed by "discoveries" in the field of comparative religion, but the most successful were those that constructed a new "science" out of evidence supplied by mesmerism and utilized it as the basic datum for a whole new system of religious belief. What bound these diverse groups together was a common revolt against any accepted understanding of the Christian faith.

THE RELIGION OF HUMANITY. On Memorial Day in 1867 the Free Religious Association was formed by a militant group of young Unitarians who had become convinced that organized Christianity, even in its Unitarian form, had become the chief enemy of freedom and progress. They were devotees of science who experienced the influence of the positivist philosophy of Auguste Comte (1798–1857) and were persuaded that with the tools of science man could become the master of his own destiny.[32] But to release the latent energies of men and to awaken the necessary idealism for the fashioning of a new society in which the peoples of the world would be united in a universal brotherhood, they believed that the inspiration of religion was required. The religion they had in mind betrayed many overtones of the transcendentalism of Ralph Waldo Emerson and Theodore Parker, but its major thrust was toward an empirical and scientific naturalism. Conventional theism was abandoned. This was made clear by Octavius Brooks Frothingham (1822–95), president of the Association, when he declared in *The Religion of Humanity:* "Whether there shall be peace or war, rule or misrule, purity or corrup-

---

[31] *The Problem of Religious Progress* (N.Y., 1881), 41.
[32] There were other more explicitly Comtean societies, including the Positivist Society which was formed in New York City in 1871 and two Societies of Humanity, one of which Leon Trotsky attended.

tion, justice or injustice, . . . are questions which men must answer for themselves. There is no higher tribunal before which they can be carried; there is no super-human or extra-human will by which they can be dealt with. If things go well or ill rests with those who are commissioned to make them go." [33]

The fundamental convictions of the "religion of humanity" were summarized in "Fifty Affirmations" which Francis Ellingwood Abbot (1836–1903) published in each issue of the *Index*, the official organ of the Association. The Affirmations begin with the assertion that "religion is the effort of man to perfect himself." This is the oft-times hidden but universal element in all historical religions, and the objective of free religion is the perfecting of man by emancipating him from outward laws and winning him to a voluntary obedience to the inward fundamental law of true humanity. Perhaps the spirit of this free religion was best expressed in the lines of Walt Whitman:

> If I build God a church it shall be a church to men and women.
> If I write hymns they shall be all to men and women.
> If I become a devotee, it shall be to men and women.[34]

Although the Free Religious Association had its origin in Boston, it had representatives elsewhere. Abbot moved to Toledo in 1870, and the Association's most prominent pulpit was in New York City where Frothingham preached each Sunday in the Lyric Hall to a congregation that included notable figures in the arts and letters. The watchwords of the movement were freedom and unity, and because its strong-minded members believed so wholeheartedly in freedom there was often little unity and frequently considerable dissension.[35] By 1890 most of the Free Religionists had been reabsorbed into Unitarianism.

The "religion of humanity" found more permanent institutional expression in the Society for Ethical Culture founded by Felix Adler (1851–1933) in 1876. Adler had been trained for the rabbinate but had revolted against his religious heritage. For a time he was president of both his own society and the Free Religious Association. The Ethical Culture movement was never large. It enjoyed, however, a slow but steady growth

[33] *The Religion of Humanity*, 3rd. ed. (N.Y., 1875), 171.
[34] *Walt Whitman's Workshop* ed. C. J. Furness, (Cambridge, Mass., 1928), 43.
[35] For the inability of the Free Religionists to act on the basis of complete freedom, see Stow Persons, *Free Religion: An American Faith* (New Haven, 1947), 93–94.

287

as long as Adler lived. In 1926 there were six societies in the United States with a membership of more than two thousand and perhaps an equal number of peripheral adherents.

ESOTERIC WISDOM FROM THE EAST. Theosophy was a faith which capitalized, on a more popular level, upon much the same interest which had led to the formation of the Free Religious Association. It also emphasized fundamental truths which lay behind all the great religions, assimilated in a curious way the discoveries of modern science, and stressed the godlike potentialities of men and the universal brotherhood of the human race. The founder of the movement was Madame Helena P. Blavatsky (1831–91) who came to New York in 1872 and three years later established the Theosophical Society.[36] As the wife of a Russian general, she had led a peripatetic existence in the Orient where she had busied herself accumulating occult lore. She claimed that during a visit to Tibet she had been instructed in the esoteric wisdom of the ages by a group of "adepts" or "masters"—gifted seers who stood in direct succession to Moses, Krishna, Lao-tze, Confucius, Buddha, Christ, and other great religious prophets. Her teaching combined many features of Spiritualism with a bowdlerized understanding of Buddhism, and interpreted reincarnation as an extension of the evolutionary process. Indicative of her central emphasis are titles of two of her many books: *Isis Unveiled: A Master Key to the Mysteries of Ancient and Modern Science and Theology* (1877), and *The Secret Doctrine: the Synthesis of Science, Religion, and Philosophy* (1893).

After Madame Blavatsky's death the movement was divided into two camps when Mrs. Annie Besant (1847–1933) [37] began to replace some of the characteristic Buddhist doctrines with concepts derived from Hinduism. Mrs. Besant, with a suave and cultured Hindu brahmin sleeping outside her door to guard her against intrusion, was the leading sensation at the World's Parliament of Religions in 1893. But the conference with the words of Malachi as its motto—"Have we not all one Father? Hath not one God created us?"—provided an opportunity for other representatives of Eastern religions to gain a hearing. The Vedanta Society, a Hindu cult, had its American origin here in the teaching of Swami Vivekananda. A

[36] See C. E. B. Roberts, *Mysterious Madame, Helena Petrovna Blavatsky* (N.Y., 1931), and A. B. Kuhn, *Theosophy* (N.Y., 1930).

[37] See the two-volume biography by A. H. Nethercot, *The First Five Lives of Annie Besant* (Chicago, 1960) and *The Last Four Lives of Annie Besant* (Chicago, 1963).

similar movement was the Yogoda Sat-Sanga or Self-Realization Fellow-ship which taught the Hindu practice of yoga. Baha'i, of Moslem origin, received some notice in 1893 at Chicago, but its real American rootage dates from the arrival of 'Abdu'l-Baha in 1912.[38] It had been founded in Persia in 1853 when Mirza Husayn 'Ali (1817–92) announced that he was the Baha'-u'llah—"the Glory of God." Operating from the premise that God is unknowable except through a "manifestation," he claimed to be the manifestation for this age commissioned by divine command to unify humanity within one faith and one order. When he died in 1892 he left a testament appointing his son 'Abdu'l-Baha—"the Servant of God" —as his authoritative interpreter. In its stress upon human brotherhood and the essential unity of all religion, Baha'i is scarcely distinguishable from Theosophy, except in pressing the necessity for full and unquestion-ing acceptance of Baha'-u'llah as the authoritative manifestation of God.

SCIENCE, RELIGION, HEALTH. An interest in "mental healing" had been developing in America prior to the Civil War. It was based on the experiments with hypnosis by a German physician, Franz Anton Mesmer (1733?–1815), who concluded that a mysterious magnetic fluid was the explanation of the mental power that one person could exercise over another. Phineas Parkhurst Quimby (1802–66) of Portland, Maine, was one of the many who became intrigued by the therapeutic power of mesmerism. Ultimately he became convinced that disease could be cured by cultivating healthy attitudes—positive thoughts instead of negative ones—through suggestion and without the use of hypnotism. Sickness, he insisted, was the consequence of wrong beliefs. The remedy, therefore, was to displace the erroneous ideas of the ill with healing truth.

One of Quimby's patients was Mary Baker Eddy (1821–1910), the founder of Christian Science.[39] As a child she suffered from what appears to have been nervous disorders and perhaps hysteria. Her ill health continued to plague her through three marriages. Although she was helped by Quimby in 1862 and 1864, she and her followers have insisted that she was guided through her own experience to an original discovery of the

[38] See William M. Miller, *Baha'ism; Its Origin, History, and Teachings* (N.Y., 1931).
[39] Robert Peel, *Mary Baker Eddy: The Years of Discovery* (N.Y., 1966). See also E. F. Dakin, *Mrs. Eddy: the Biography of a Virginal Mind* (N.Y., 1929), L. P. Powell, *Mary Baker Eddy* (N.Y., 1930), and E. S. Bates and J. V. Dittemore, *Mary Baker Eddy* (N.Y., 1932).

divine law of life which surpassed in importance Newton's discovery of the law of gravitation when he saw the apple fall. Whether she built upon the foundation provided by Quimby or gained her insight from a unique revelation, Mrs. Eddy was soon embarked upon an independent healing career based upon the conviction that the Eternal Mind is the source of all being, that matter is nonexistent, that disease is caused by erroneous thought (compounded, to be sure, by the Malicious Animal Magnetism projected by one's enemies), and that power is released through Christian Science to overcome all the illusions that have troubled mankind. "The control mind holds over matter," she declared, "becomes no longer a question when with mathematical certainty we gain its proof and can demonstrate the facts assumed." In Christian Science this proof has been reduced to a scientific statement that "furnishes a key to the harmony of man and reveals what destroys sickness, sin, and death." [40]

In 1875 Mrs. Eddy formed a small group of adherents into a society at Lynn, Massachusetts, and published the first edition of the authoritative textbook of Christian Science doctrine, *Science and Health with Key to the Scriptures*. The movement did not prosper, however, until she shifted her base of operation to Boston and established the Massachusetts Metaphysical College to train "practitioners." In 1892 complete control of the movement was vested in the self-perpetuating board of trustees of "the Mother Church" in Boston. Membership multiplied rapidly thereafter. By the time of Mrs. Eddy's death in 1910, the Church of Christ, Scientist, with its various local units, had grown to almost one hundred thousand members.

There were other heirs of Quimby. The most important were his former patients Julius A. Dresser (1838–93) and Warren Felt Evans (1817–89). [41] The latter was a former Methodist minister who had become a Swedenborgian. Evans began to practice "mental medicine" at Claremont, New Hampshire, and set forth the principles of the new science in a series of books: *The Mental Cure* (1869), *Mental Medicine* (1872), *Soul and Body* (1876), and *The Divine Law* (1881). In Boston other disciples of Quimby who had formed the Church of the Divine Unity were joined by Dresser in 1882. The movement spread rapidly under many names—Mental Science, Higher Thought, Higher Life, and Divine Science. The term

[40] *Science and Health* (Boston, 1875), 9.
[41] See J. A. Dresser, *The True History of Mental Science* (N.Y., 1899), H. W. Dresser, *A History of the New Thought Movement* (N.Y., 1919), and C. S. Braden, *Spirits in Rebellion: the Rise and Development of New Thought* (Dallas, 1963).

"New Thought" was coined in 1889 by William Henry Holcombe (1825–93), a homeopathic physician; and in 1894 this was chosen as the title of a little magazine published in Melrose, Massachusetts. The first national convention was held in San Francisco in 1894 under the auspices of the Divine Science Association and five years later the name of the sponsoring body was changed to the New Thought Alliance. The annual conventions failed to develop any centralized organization and the movement continued to be highly individualistic, with considerable variation in doctrine, and with personal preference dictating the choice of name by local groups. One current, represented by M. J. Barnett's *Practical Metaphysics* (1889), interpreted New Thought doctrine within a theosophical context; another current was strongly influenced by Spiritualism. The most prolific of the New Thought writers were Ralph Waldo Trine (1866–1958) and Emmet Fox (1886–1951), whose books were widely read by people who had no connection at all with the movement.

A less amorphous expression of the "mind cure" idea was the Unity School of Practical Christianity founded at Kansas City, Missouri, by Charles and Myrtle Fillmore.[42] They had been attending Christian Science and New Thought lectures in 1886 when "Truth" came to Myrtle Fillmore. It was a discovery of the power of positive thinking— "the establishment of a healing consciousness through the constant repetition of an affirmation, 'I am a child of God and, therefore, I do not inherit sickness.' " With this new power, the Jesus-power, the power to release through divine affirmations the electronic forces sealed in the nerves, the Fillmores began to advertise themselves as "Healers and Teachers." Gradually a small group of adherents was formed which they named the Society of Silent Help. In 1889 a periodical, *Modern Thought*, was launched to publicize their views, and two years later the name "Unity" was seized upon as more adequately expressing their basic principle.

> Unity! . . . Unity! . . . That's the name for our work! The name I've been looking for! . . . It embodies the central principle of what we believe: unity of the soul with God, unity of all life, unity of all religions, unity of the spirit, soul, and body; unity of all men in the heart of truth.[43]

[42] See J. D. Freeman, *The Household of Faith: the Story of Unity* (Lee Summit, Mo., 1951), and C. S. Braden, *These Also Believe* (N.Y., 1949).
[43] Freeman, *Household of Faith*, 44, 61–62. Cf. Marcus Bach, *They Have Found a Faith* (Indianapolis, 1946), 223.

The Fillmores denied that they were starting a new sect; they were only teaching a practical philosophy to supplement the teachings of the existing churches. To make it evident that a break with one's present religious affiliation was neither intended nor required, the name of the Society of Silent Unity was changed in 1903 to the Unity School of Practical Christianity.

Unity, for all its practical down-to-earth emphasis was far from simple. It developed a highly complex metaphysical system which incorporated ideas of reincarnation and spirit-communication borrowed from Theosophy and Spiritualism. It also emphasized the power of positive thinking to guarantee economic prosperity as well as physical health. "God will pay your debts," declared Fillmore.

> Do not say money is scarce; the very statement will drive money away from you. Do not say that times are hard with you; the very words will tighten your purse strings until Omnipotence itself cannot slip a dime into it. Begin now to talk plenty, think plenty, and give thanks for plenty. . . . It actually works.
>
> Every home can be prosperous, and there should be no poverty-stricken homes, for they are caused only by inharmony, fear, negative thinking and speaking.[44]

Basically Unity became a vast publishing enterprise, producing a constant stream of literature that had an astonishingly large circulation among members of conventional churches. While the practice of holding propagandist meetings in hotels and other public halls was an early phenomenon, it was not until the middle of the twentieth century that Unity began to establish churches of its own.

Such were the disparate religious responses to the new intellectual climate. It was a difficult time for the churches, for their whole system of thought had been challenged at many points. But this was not the only problem with which the churches had to grapple. They had to come to terms at the same time with revolutionary changes in the economic and social order which were being made manifest by the rapid pace at which the country was becoming urbanized and industrialized. This challenge demanded changes in practice as well as in thought.

[44] Charles Fillmore, *Prosperity* (Kansas City, Mo., 1938), 103–4, 117.

XII

New Frontiers for the Churches

While the mind of America was being reshaped by the intellectual revolution of the years of midpassage from 1865 to 1914, the outward aspects of American life were undergoing swift and bewildering change as a result of rapid technological advance. "Steam and electricity have tremendously increased the pace of life," reported an observer in 1896.

> Everybody is in a hurry. . . . St. Martha is the patron saint of the women, and St. Vitus of the men. Nervous prostration is our characteristic disease. Leisure is a word for whose meaning we consult the dictionary. In the clatter of the train, in the click of the keys at the telegraph office, the spirit of the age finds speech.[1]

The click and the clatter were symbols of a surging industrial advance sped by a flood of inventions. In contrast to the fewer than 62,000 patents that had been issued prior to 1865, the number granted by the Patent Office in the following thirty-five years was in excess of 637,000. Large-scale steel production was made possible by the introduction of the Bessemer con-

[1] George Hodges, *Faith and Social Service* (N.Y., 1896), 6.

verter. The efficiency of the railroads was multiplied by automatic couplings and Westinghouse air-brakes. Refrigerator cars made feasible the centralized slaughterhouses of the meat-packers. The discovery of oil, coupled with the use of tank cars and pipe lines, gave further impetus to industrial development. The McCormick binder, the typewriter, the transatlantic cable, the telephone, the incandescent lamp, the electric motor, and the gasoline engine, each fostered growing commercial enterprises. Before the end of the century the linotype, the automobile, and the motion picture had made their appearance. Meanwhile, through an increasing utilization of machinery and the adoption of interchangeable parts, the factory system had been established in almost all areas of production. By 1894 the United States had become the leading manufacturing nation of the world, with its production of manufactured goods surpassing the combined output of its two closest rivals—Great Britain and Germany.

Many rubrics have been used to characterize the impact upon society of this massive industrial development. Some have viewed these years as "the gilded age"; others have called it "the tragic era." To some these were "fifty years of progress"; to others they were "years of unrest and corruption." The most obvious label has been "the age of big business," for this was the era of the empire builders—the steel kings, the coal barons, the railroad magnates, the merchant princes, the Napoleons of finance, and the potentates of the stockyards, the oil wells, and the street railways. Another rubric has been "the rise of the city," for these were the years when cities were "springing up and growing great and splendid as it were in a night." A further facet of this adolescent period in the emergence of modern America has been suggested by Harold U. Faulkner's phrase "the quest for social justice." And those who placed the period against a larger canvas have used the term "imperial America" to convey the expansionist spirit of an awakening industrial giant. All these aspects of this new industrial society—the problems and opportunities posed by the city, the economic order, and the outward thrust of imperialism—were to replace the West as urgent new frontiers for the churches.

The challenge of the cities

Urbanization spawned a wide variety of human needs, for in its wake came slums, poverty, vice, and political corruption. Each of these needs was to claim the attention of the churches, but the most pressing problem was the basic task of evangelism. Even before the Civil War extensive sections of rural America had begun to experience a steady and persistent decline in population as people moved from farms and backcountry villages to growing commercial centers and newly established mill towns. After the war the process was vastly accelerated. Previously tilled acres reverted to woodland and whole villages disappeared, leaving only a few foundation stones as monuments to the past. The cities, in contrast, were lusty infants. During the three decades from 1860 to 1890, the population of Detroit and Kansas City grew fourfold, Memphis and San Francisco fivefold, Cleveland sixfold, Chicago tenfold, Los Angeles twentyfold, and Minneapolis and Omaha fiftyfold and more. Even such previously major centers as New York, Philadelphia, and Baltimore more than doubled in population. "There is a city of thirty-five thousand added to Chicago, and one of fifty thousand added to New York, every year," reported Josiah Strong in 1887. With the overwhelming proportion of the churches located in rural areas and with many of them left stranded to dwindle and die as people departed, it became more obvious than ever that the future influence of the churches in the life of the nation was to be decisively conditioned by their success or lack of success in evangelizing the cities.

At the outset most of the urban inhabitants came from the farms and villages of the hinterland where many of them had been regular in church attendance. They may not have been conspicuous for piety and they may not even have been church members, but they had been accustomed to going to church. When they pulled up their roots and moved to the city, this pattern of habit and custom was broken, the emotional ties to a particular church were severed, and the pressure exerted by the expectation of friends and neighbors was removed. In their new environment, the tendency was for these former churchgoers to drift into "indifference." Later the problem of re-evangelization was complicated by the sweeping tide of population arriving from abroad.

Conspicuous as were the effects of urban revival campaigns and Sunday school activity, the greatest successes were won in the smaller commercial and industrial centers where social relationships remained relatively intimate. In these communities, where employer and employee lived in somewhat close proximity, patronized the same stores, sent their children to the same schools, and frequently knew each other by name, the churches were able to bridge the gap between the social classes. In this respect the American experience duplicated that of the English churches. Even the Primitive Methodists of England who were famed for bringing the gospel to people who were "rude, poor, and even brutish" did not bring the gospel to more than a very small portion of the rude and poor, and what success they had was restricted to the smaller industrial settlements.[2]

In larger industrial communities, whether in America, Britain, or France (and presumably in the developing urban concentrations of Belgium, Germany, and northern Italy), the working-classes tended to be impervious to the message and ministry of the churches.[3] It was not that the churches had "lost" these people; they never had most of them. If people generally attended church from habit, most of the laboring group who were born in the city never had the habit. And it was to this habit of nonattendance that newer additions to the urban labor force conformed.

Among other portions of the urban population churchgoing was a normal, mannerly, and even a fashionable activity. Signs of the popularity of the churches abounded. The churches were well attended. Costly and imposing edifices were being built to match the increasing prosperity of their clientele, and congregations vied with one another to possess the tallest steeple as a symbol of wealth and prestige. Pipe organs were installed, paid soloists were employed, and the preachers were polished orators who ranked in status with the most substantial citizens. Some of the preachers—men like Henry Ward Beecher and T. DeWitt Talmage in Brooklyn, Phillips Brooks and George A. Gordon in Boston, David M. Swing and Frank W. Gunsaulus in Chicago, Russell Conwell in Philadelphia, and Washington Gladden in Columbus—were figures of national prominence, but every city boasted eloquent preachers who could hold their congregations spellbound and who were regarded with deference and respect. Furthermore, the most influential leaders of business and society—Jay Gould, J. Pierpont Morgan, John D. Rockefeller, Samuel Colgate, Jay Cooke, Cyrus McCormick, Marshall Field, James J. Hill,

[2] K. S. Inglis, *Churches and the Working Classes in Victorian England* (Toronto, 1963), 10–13, 327.
[3] For France, see H. Desroche, *Archives de Sociologie des Religions*, VI (1958), 197–98; cited by Inglis, *op. cit.*, 327. The Roman Catholic Church in the United States provided the major exception to the prevailing situation, and the strength it developed among working people was closely related to the insecurities of their immigrant status.

William H. Vanderbilt, P. D. Armour, G. A. Swift, A. J. Drexel, John Wanamaker, and many others—were prominent churchmen, active in religious enterprises, and frequently Sunday school teachers.

To many of the immigrants from abroad, the Roman Catholic Church was the one familiar landmark in a strange and alien land, and its role in easing the transition to a new life in America helped it to retain the loyalty of many of the urban workers. With this single major exception, the great evangelistic successes of the city churches were won among the white-collar workers who had come from the rural areas, not to work in a mill, but to "clerk" in a store or an office, and who aspired to win, if not a fortune, at least a comfortable competence in the city. These young men, their wives, and their children, constituted the greater portion of those who were recruited for the churches by the revival campaigns, the Sunday school, and the Y.M.C.A. Beyond this potentially middle-class group was the hard core of nonchurchgoers—the urban masses, they were sometimes called, the poor, the destitute, the day-laborers—who were to constitute a continuing challenge to the churches.

NEW TECHNIQUES FOR CITY CHURCHES.   In 1865, almost before Grant had time to haul the artillery from the Virginia battlefields, James S. Yeatman (1818–1901) of St. Louis—banker, philanthropist, and head of the Western Sanitary Commission during the Civil War—had drafted a *Circular of Inquiry* calling attention to urban religious needs and proposing that the energy devoted to wartime service to combatants be redirected to peacetime service in the cities. He noted the comparative ineffectiveness of the Protestant churches in urban communities and suggested that they were handicapped by four major deficiencies—"want of knowledge" of the true "moral condition" of the cities; "lack of organization of the wealth, piety, and labor which exist there"; need of information concerning the "best agencies" for city work; and "want of trained, tried, permanent laborers in the various spheres of city labor." [4] As a result of his initiative, those who had been active in the United States Christian Commission (the agency of the churches in ministering to soldiers) met in Cleveland in the autumn of 1865 and organized the American Christian Commission to help the churches develop a systematic program of urban missionary endeavor. They viewed the task of the Commission as twofold:

[4] A. I. Abell, *The Urban Impact on American Protestantism, 1865–1900* (Cambridge, Mass., 1943), 11.

(1) to ascertain the actual conditions prevailing in the cities, and (2) to assemble information concerning the "experience already gained" as to the best methods to be employed to gain the ends desired.

Information, based on a personal investigation of thirty-five cities by the two secretaries of the Commission, was presented the following year. "Greatly as these cities differ in most respects," they declared, "certain causes are in operation to a greater or less extent in each that necessitates special missionary effort." Fortunately, while "no mission field is more necessitous," there is "none more easily accessible, none which appeals to so many interests of the Christian patriot and philanthropist as this in our very midst." In addition to authorizing the secretaries to make a survey of the cities, the Commission established a department of foreign correspondence to gather intelligence of European experience, in ministering to the unchurched masses of the cities. The purpose was to secure helpful suggestions for American churches, and the information that was compiled was given wide circulation through the Commission's monthly periodical, *The Christian at Work*.

The investigators had discovered that most American churches did little in any systematic fashion for those "who neglect the house of God." The city mission societies and the Y.M.C.A., to be sure, sponsored street-preaching and tract distribution, and occasionally there were citywide revival campaigns. While these activities were to be encouraged, the Commission believed that the great need was to recover "the simplicity and entire consecration of the early Christians," when "every disciple was a missionary and every church a missionary society," so that the church itself would reach out to people where they live. The most obvious means of doing this was by regular house-to-house visitation of working-class neighborhoods. Many of the poverty-stricken, it was contended, had been alienated "because in their affliction they were not visited," and the only remedy was "personal, living, love-convincing" contact between the churchgoer and the nonchurchgoer. This, of course, demanded lay effort. Pastors of churches in densely populated communities were urged to "seek out and employ all such talent in their congregations as they shall believe to possess qualifications for this important and pressing work." [5]

The volunteer visitation program never worked too successfully. Even when the Evangelical Alliance picked up the idea of a cooperative

[5] *Ibid.*, 12–13, 15, 33.

monthly citywide house-to-house visitation and, as a result of vigorous promotion, had put it into operation by 1889 in forty cities, the actual implementation was sporadic. As an alternative, the utilization of female assistants or women missionaries was strongly advocated. It was recognized that women could be especially effective in going into the homes, and considerable support developed for the establishment of sisterhoods or deaconess orders patterned after the German model. In an eloquent plea for the churches to adopt the German practice, a speaker at the 1868 convention of the Commission asserted that the "theory that woman has no place in the church deprives America of two-thirds of its Christian force." The eloquence of the proponents of the use of women workers, however, was not sufficient to quell popular hostility. In 1857 William A. Muhlenberg had aroused a storm of opposition among his fellow Episcopalians when he established a deaconess order in New York. A Lutheran attempt after the Civil War was equally abortive. The Methodists were somewhat more successful, but official recognition was withheld until 1889. By the end of the century, the Lutherans and the German Reformed were making extensive use of deaconesses, the Episcopalians had established a training school, and even the Congregationalists and Baptists had taken a few tentative steps toward the employment of deaconesses. The Methodists, however, were far in the lead, having nearly as many deaconesses as all other denominations combined. In the next few years the number of deaconesses began to decline. Perhaps their quaint hats and distinctive dress militated against any continuing popularity. But the battle over the employment of women had been won and the churches generally began to make use of women as church visitors and missionaries.

A second problem highlighted by the Commission and underscored in the actual process of house-to-house visitation was the fact that often no churches were located in the neediest neighborhoods. The city mission societies were encouraged to establish mission chapels in these areas. Most of these were conventional in character. Much more dramatic were the "rescue missions" designed to reach and reclaim the dregs of society—vagrants, alcoholics, former convicts, jobless men, and fallen women. While the Water Street Mission in New York was the most famous and the Pacific Garden Mission in Chicago the most successful of these rescue operations, by the 1880's every city boasted one or more missions of this type. The real pioneer of the movement was Jerry MacAuley (1837–84) who founded the Water Street Mission in 1872, and his own early career was typical of those to whom he sought to minister. He had arrived in New York from Ireland at the age of thirteen. Living in the streets, he soon became a petty thief and then graduated to gambling, organized burglary, and drunkenness. At the age of nineteen he was sentenced to a fifteen-year term in prison, and while confined he was converted by an ex-prizefighter. Back on the streets after having been pardoned in 1864, he resumed his criminal career until he was finally redeemed by agents of the Howard Mission. He then established his own mission outpost in his former neighborhood, ministering primarily to the homeless men who congregated there.

Among both the conventional missions and the rescue missions, there was a growing conviction that attention must be given to immediate material necessities before spiritual needs could be fully met. The managers of the North End Mission in Boston put it quite bluntly: "Till the cravings of hunger are satisfied, we cannot develop the moral nature," adding that they believed this to be "the biblical way of reaching the heart." [6] As a result of this conviction the rescue missions began to provide food, lodging, and employment services, while missions of all types launched a wide variety of enterprises which included model tenements for the poor, homes for working mothers, and hospitals for the care of sick children.

Yeatman's initial *Circular of Inquiry* had emphasized the importance of "trained" leadership for the specialized tasks of city work, and a number of institutions were established to meet this need. [7] A further step in this direction was taken when followers of Jerry MacAuley organized the Convention of Christian Workers in 1886. John C. Collins, a Yale graduate and manager of the Union Gospel Mission in New Haven, was the guiding spirit. By means of annual gatherings a type of "in-service" training was provided through the sharing of experience with new methods and techniques. Within little more than a decade it had gained more than

---

[6] *Ibid.*, 36.

[7] Among these schools were Stephen H. Tyng's Home of the Evangelists (1870) in New York, T. DeWitt Talmage's Tabernacle Lay College (1872) in Brooklyn, and Dwight L. Moody's Chicago Evangelization Society (1886) in Chicago. The latter institution was designed "to raise up men and women who will be willing to lay their lives alongside the laboring class and the poor and bring the gospel to bear on their lives." They were to do work that ministers could not do—"get in among the people and identify themselves with the people." W. G. McLoughlin, *Modern Revivalism*, 272–73.

2,500 members, and Graham Taylor (1851–1938), professor of Christian sociology at Chicago Theological Seminary, declared the annual Convention of Christian Workers was "a great exhibit of the work and working forces of modern Christianity" and "as nearly ecumenical a gathering of the church in America as is held on this continent." The *Christian Union,* which had been founded as Henry Ward Beecher's personal journal, was equally enthusiastic, asserting that the stenographic reports of the conventions furnished "the best literature on practical Christian work that can be secured." [8]

Meanwhile a new instrument of urban evangelization had made its appearance. This was the Salvation Army.[9] It had been founded in London in 1878 by William Booth (1829–1912), an ex-Methodist preacher. Booth had come to the conclusion that "we can't get at the masses in the chapels," and consequently he was determined to move out into the streets. Organized on the basis of strict military discipline, the Army was geared for a many-sided attack on the problems of the city. The program was spelled out in Booth's famous volume, *Darkest England and the Way Out* (1890). The familiar brass band and tambourines which were used to gather a crowd for street-preaching was only an incidental feature of a broad range of activities. Booth aimed to supply the poverty-stricken people of England with at least the three things that any dray horse enjoyed—"shelter for the night, food for its stomach, work allotted to it by which it can earn its own corn." In addition to the usual provision made by rescue missions for meals, lodging, and an employment service, the Army moved out into the community with its Slum Brigades, Sewing Battalions, and visiting nurses. Legal aid bureaus were opened, day nurseries for children set up, and rescue homes for prostitutes established. And to give men and women the benefit of a new and wholesome environment, farm colonies were founded. Although the Salvation Army was ultimately to take on the characteristics of a church, its initial intention was to serve only as a recruiting agent of the churches among the most neglected elements of the population.

The Salvation Army was introduced into America in 1880, but its

---

[8] Abell, *Urban Impact on American Protestantism,* 97–98.

[9] The English background is summarized by Inglis, *Churches and the Working Classes in Victorian England,* 175–214; and is given in detail by Robert Sandall, *The History of the Salvation Army,* Vol. I, *1865–1878* (N.Y., 1947). For its American career, see H. A. Wisbey, *Soldiers without Swords: A History of the Salvation Army in the United States* (N.Y., 1955).

major expansion took place after 1886 when Booth's son, Ballington Booth (1859–1940), was sent over to take charge. A schism occurred in 1896 when Ballington Booth refused to obey his father's order that he return to England. Instead he and his wife founded the Volunteers of America, which patterned its activities after the parent organization but was organized on a more democratic basis.

THE INSTITUTIONAL CHURCH. The problem of city churches was complicated by the mobility of the urban population. As commercial establishments encroached upon residential areas and housing grew old and deteriorated, the more prosperous sought newer and more spacious accommodations on the outskirts, leaving room at the center for newer arrivals. Without endowments to sustain them, most churches seemed to face the choice either of following their congregations or of being marooned in poverty and left to eke out a dwindling existence. Rather than subject themselves to a lingering death, many churches elected to follow their congregations and erect new edifices in the areas to which their members had moved. It was this solution to their problem that necessitated the founding of mission chapels in sections formerly occupied by churches. The whole process became deeply disturbing to sensitive Christians as they became aware of what was taking place. Instead of moving the church and then seeking to discharge its responsibility to the people of its former neighborhood by proxy through missions of various types, some proposed that the churches adapt themselves to the changing population of the inner city by adopting and utilizing techniques that were being developed by the missions.

The "institutional church," a strange name, was proposed as a means of enabling churches to survive in central city areas instead of moving. The problem was to entice new arrivals in changing neighborhoods into existing churches. The solution put forward was for churches to provide the newcomers with a variety of "services" or "added attractions." Edward Judson (1884–1914) was the pre-eminent theoretician of an institutional ministry. He defined an institutional church as "an organized body of Christian believers, who, finding themselves in a hard and uncongenial social environment, supplement the ordinary methods of the gospel—such as preaching, prayer meetings, Sunday school, and pastoral visitation—by *a system of organized kindness*, a congeries of institutions, which, by touching people on physical, social, and intellectual sides, will conciliate them and draw them within reach of the gospel."[10] With the slogan "open church doors every day and all the day," institutional churches became hives of activity with gymnasiums, athletic programs, reading rooms, day nurseries, sewing classes, lecture series, choral societies, drama clubs, concerts, and entertainments.

The honor of establishing the first institutional church probably belongs to Thomas K. Beecher (1824–1900), one of the numerous Beecher progeny, who was pastor of the Park Congregational Church in Elmira, New York, from 1854 to 1900. In 1872 he induced his congregation to build a block-long structure equipped for a full range of services. Mark Twain, his brother-in-law, described the building with its gymnasium, lecture rooms, library, and free public baths in his *Curious Dreams and Other Sketches* (1872) and commented that "we have at least one sensible but very curious church in America." Within two decades there were many of these "sensible" churches. By 1900 one observer listed 173 churches with a full-blown institutional program and acknowledged that there were probably others which had escaped his attention. In addition, scores of churches were appropriating parts of the institutional program.[11]

When the Open and Institutional Church League was formed in 1894 to promote "educational, reformatory, and philanthropic" activities by the churches as an evangelistic device, its leaders self-confidently proclaimed that the question "how to reach the masses" had been "practically solved." It was true that institutional churches were experiencing phenomenal growth. By 1900 the Baptist Temple in Philadelphia, in process of fathering what was to become Temple University, had become the largest congregation in America. St. George's Episcopal Church in New York, which had been ready to close its doors when it had only six families left, now numbered five thousand members. Congregationalists reported that their institutional churches had six times as many additions as the average church. But there were problems. For one thing, an institutional church was an incredibly costly enterprise. Not many churches could command the necessary financial support. St. George's was fortunate in having J. Pierpont Morgan as a member of its initial

---

[10] "The Church in Its Social Aspect," *Annals of the American Academy of Political and Social Science*, XXX (Nov. 1908), 436. For an impressionistic appraisal of the institutional church, see G. G. Atkins, *Religion in Our Times* (N.Y., 1932), 69–85.

[11] Many new "suburban" churches also felt they should have a gymnasium with a stage so that they too could adopt the tactic of the "added attractions" by having made adequate provision for athletics and theatricals.

remnant. St. Bartholomew's, whose parish house was erected by Cornelius Vanderbilt and his mother, had an annual budget of over one million dollars.[12] Edward Judson's begging expeditions were successful in tapping the resources of John D. Rockefeller. Furthermore, as Edward Judson noted, the involvements of an institutional program "are so difficult and fascinating that they easily absorb all a minister's time and energy." The tendency is for him to neglect "his study and the care of his flock," to lose "his priestly character," and to become "a mere social functionary."[13] Becoming absorbed in manifold activities which initially were intended to serve as a bridge into church membership, the ideal of mere humanitarian service tended to replace the earlier evangelistic concern. As a result the congregations of institutional churches, as their novelty disappeared, dwindled almost as rapidly as they had increased. In the end, far from being a means of building up a congregation to support a ministry in areas of deterioration, many institutional churches became social agencies which other churches had to find money and leadership to support. Meanwhile, store-front churches began to make an appearance in the surrounding neighborhoods to demonstrate that "added attractions" were not needed to "draw" people "within reach of the gospel." Few noted the irony of this development.

The churches and the economic order

The decade preceding the great railroad strike of 1877 has been described as the "summit" of American economic complacency. This complacency was as evident among churchmen as it was among other Americans. Leaders of the churches may have disagreed about many things, but they displayed remarkable unanimity in their approbation of the existing economic order and of the "principles" or "laws" of political economy which provided its theoretical foundation. Gone was the radical criticism and ferment of the 1830's and 1840's. Henry F. May has observed that "in 1876 Protestantism presented a massive, almost unbroken front in its defense of the social status quo," [14] and this was equally true of Roman Catholicism. Within a dozen years, however, this situation

---

12 Abell, *The Urban Impact on American Protestantism*, 150–51.
13 "The Church in Its Social Aspect," *op. cit.*, 437.
14 *Protestant Churches and Industrial America* (N.Y., 1963), 91. This is an important study based on an analysis of the periodical literature of the major Protestant bodies.

began to change as a result of people being shocked from their complacency by outbreaks of violent social conflict. Roman Catholics remained cautious,[15] but by the 1890's vigorous demands for social reform were being voiced in every major Protestant denomination and a few of the leaders were calling for the complete reorganization of society. By the turn of the century the adherents of two antithetical gospels— "the gospel of wealth" and "the social gospel"—were locked in combat and were struggling for predominance.

THE GOSPEL OF WEALTH. For many Americans the years following the Civil War marked the beginning of a period of unrivaled prosperity. Rapidly as the population increased, the nation's wealth multiplied three times as fast. Those who benefited by this tremendous economic expansion were confident that they were living in the best of all possible worlds. The American economy had been tested and had not been found wanting. This smug self-satisfaction lent an aura of eminent reasonableness and even sanctity to the *laissez-faire* economic doctrines which had been fathered by Adam Smith, popularized in America by Francis Wayland (1796–1865),[16] and given strong reinforcement by the teachings of Herbert Spencer. The most persuasive argument for allowing economic self-interest free play was the seemingly obvious fact that it worked for the economic betterment of men generally. Perhaps it worked, as the *Congregationalist* put it, because there were "thousands upon thousands of acres of magnificent soil" beyond the Mississippi that could be secured "at a merely nominal price" so that "no man who is blessed with health and willingness to work, be his family large or small, need come to the poorhouse." [17] But it worked nonetheless, at least for a time.

The classic statement of "the true gospel concerning wealth," obedience to which will "solve the problem of the rich and the poor," was

[15] Francis J. Lally has pointed out that Roman Catholics gave little evidence of being "socially progressive" prior to the New Deal years. The papal encyclical *Rerum Novarum* (1891) had little immediate impact in America, and the few occasions when Roman Catholics displayed an interest in social reform were "sporadic and mostly short-lived." This was true of the 1919 "Bishops' Program of Social Reconstruction" which did not receive strong support until the 1930's. Participation in the labor movement was the single notable exception to the generally conservative outlook. *The Catholic Church in a Changing America*, 47–48. For an account of developing social consciousness among Roman Catholics, see A. I. Abell, *American Catholicism and Social Action* (N.Y., 1960).

[16] Wayland was president of Brown University and the author of *The Elements of Political Economy* (1837). The most popular textbook on the subject, it went through many printings.

[17] March 17, 1870; quoted by May, *Protestant Churches and Industrial America*, 55.

written by Andrew Carnegie (1835–1919), the steelmaster of Pittsburgh, and was published in the June, 1889, issue of the *North American Review*.[18] Carnegie insisted that "civilization depends" upon the triple law of the "sacredness" of private property, free competition, and free accumulation of wealth. This triple law, which allows free play to economic forces, is indispensable to all progress, and nothing should be permitted to interfere with its operation. Its indispensability is one of the facts of life which cannot be changed. One can only make the "best of it." It is true that a price is exacted, since the law of competition forces the employer "into the strictest economies, among which the rates to be paid to labor figure prominently," and this often creates friction. But even if the operation of the law "may sometimes be hard for individuals," it is "best for the race, because it insures the survival of the fittest in every department" and produces "a wonderful material development" that benefits all. "The laborer has now more comforts than the farmer had a few generations ago," "the farmer has more luxuries than the landlord had," and the landlord has more than "a king could then obtain." This inequality is much better than the "universal squalor" that would otherwise prevail.

The harshness of Carnegie's views was somewhat tempered by his view of the proper use of wealth. In words reminiscent of John Wesley's slogan, "Gain all you can, save all you can, give all you can," he declared that "the man who dies . . . rich, dies disgraced." [19] Instead of leaving vast sums to one's children or even making bequests for public purposes, Carnegie insisted that one's wealth should be distributed in ways that served the common good during one's own lifetime. Indiscriminate charity, of course, could only serve "to encourage the slothful, the drunken, the

[18] Carnegie's brief dissertation on "Wealth" is reprinted, with other essays, in *Democracy and the Gospel of Wealth*, ed. Gail Kennedy, *Problems in American Civilization: Readings Selected by the Department of American Studies, Amherst College* (Boston, 1949), and in *The Gospel of Wealth and Other Essays*, ed. Edward C. Kirkland (Cambridge, Mass., 1962). The former includes Ralph Gabriel's analysis of "The Gospel of Wealth of the Gilded Age," reprinted from *The Course of American Democratic Thought*.

[19] Wesley's concern, of course, was different. "Religion," he said, "must necessarily produce both industry and frugality, and these cannot but produce riches." And "whenever riches have increased," religion "has decreased in the same proportion." "Is there no way to prevent this—this continual declension of pure religion?" What way "can we take that our money may not sink us to the nethermost hell? There is but one way, and . . . no other. . . . If those who 'gain all they can,' and 'save all they can,' will likewise 'give all they can'; then the more they gain, the more they will grow in grace." *The Works of John Wesley*, 4th ed. (London, 1840–42), XIII, 246–47.

unworthy." The race has never been improved by almsgiving, for it rewards vice rather than aids virtue. "Those worthy of assistance, except in rare cases, seldom require assistance." The objective should be to help those who will help themselves. "The best means of benefitting the community is to place within its reach the ladders upon which the aspiring can rise." Parks, museums, libraries, schools are ways of returning surplus wealth to the masses in a form "best calculated to do them lasting good."

Carnegie's gospel of wealth was closely intertwined with the doctrine of stewardship of time, money, and talent that had been staple-fare in Protestant moral teaching. Consequently it was but a small step for current principles of economics to be translated into laws of God's providential ordering of society. Phillips Brooks, Henry Ward Beecher, and a host of lesser luminaries of the Protestant pulpit embraced the gospel of wealth with fervent devotion, but Russell Conwell—with his lecture on *Acres of Diamonds* (they are in one's own backyard) and his exhortation that everyone has a "duty to get rich"—was its most eloquent clerical spokesman.[20]

Roman Catholics, for the most part, represented an older conservatism which enjoined passivity and acceptance of one's lot in society, God permits poverty as "the most efficient means" of fostering "some of the most necessary Christian virtues." Charity should be directed to the relief of suffering and not to its elimination, for "a country where there are no beggars" would be "a veritable branch of hell." It was suggested that "to let well enough alone is a very wise old saw." Liberal Catholics, on the other hand, took a more positive view of the benefits derived from the free play of economic forces. Bishop Spalding assured a graduating class at Notre Dame that "the organs of the social body" had never been so healthy, and Cardinal Gibbons applauded Carnegie's essay on "Wealth." Archbishop Ireland insisted that "respect" for capital "must be supreme," and admonished Roman Catholics to stop considering money as evil and—with "will," "energy," "pluck," "push," and "ambition"—to set about acquiring some. "It is energy and enterprise that wins everywhere," he declared with the briskness of an entrepreneur; "they win in the

[20] For Brooks and Beecher, see H. F. May, *Protestant Churches in Industrial America*, 64–72. For Conwell, see W. S. Hudson, *The Great Tradition of the American Churches*, rev. ed. (N.Y., 1963), 180–86. There is no standard text of Conwell's *Acres of Diamonds*, for it underwent constant revision.

Church, they win in the state, they win in business." In 1890 the *Catholic World* published a minor classic of the gospel-of-wealth literature which pointed out that the three men Christ restored to life were all men of wealth and recommended that, after praying for faith, hope, and charity, Catholics should add the petition: "O Lord! give me good sense. Give me hard, practical, everyday gumption. If I had a little of that, I shouldn't act as foolishly as I generally do; I shouldn't waste my time nor money." The ability to make "frequent and handsome donations" to the church, it was suggested, is a "pretty" sure indication "that a man has the right sort of zeal." [21]

Many wealthy men had this "right sort of zeal," for this was a great age of philanthropy. Even without the incentive of benefit to be derived from income-tax exemption, benefactions were large and numerous. George Peabody, with gifts amounting to eight and one-half million dollars, was only one of many who, in the words of William Gladstone, demonstrated "how a man may be master of his fortune, not its slave." There were, of course, incongruities symbolized by the image of Daniel Drew as both "master fleecer of the lambs" and "founder of a theological seminary." Jay Cooke presented a curious picture as a skilled corrupter of legislatures and president of the Education Society of the Protestant Episcopal Church. Considerations of self-interest may have spurred the Armour brothers to lavish more than a million dollars on a mission in Chicago. But many took their stewardship seriously. John P. Crozer, whose many benefactions included the theological seminary which bears his name, was not exceptional when he confessed his perplexity as to "how I shall use, as I ought, the great and increasing stores of wealth which God has bestowed upon me."

> Excuses are so easily framed, and the heart of man so deceitful, that one can easily reason himself into the belief that, all things considered, he has done pretty well. I find such a process of reasoning in my own mind, but calm reflection tells me that I have not done well. I am a very unprofitable servant to so good a Master.

Troubled lest the good he designed be lost in the mere satisfaction of giving, he asked the Lord to direct him "clearly and decisively" to the "path of duty and usefulness." Commenting on Crozer's careful assessment of his responsibility, Sidney E. Mead observed that "only the sneering

[21] R. D. Cross, *Emergence of Liberal Catholicism in America*, 107–09, 111–12, 163–64.

souls of the mean in mind" could belittle such transparently "honest and consecrated devotion" to sacred duty.[22]

THE RISE OF SOCIAL DISCONTENT. The prosperity of a booming economy was not equally shared by all sections of the population, and the result was smoldering discontent among both farmers and workingmen. The woes of the farmers, apart from the natural hazards of the weather and periodic insect infestations, were due to their growing dependence upon the railroads and a system of mass marketing, both of which were susceptible to manipulation by the "moneyed interests." [23] The earlier subsistence farming had been replaced by the production of money crops—bought, shipped, and processed by others. Selling in a distant market in open world competition, the farmer purchased his machinery, supplies, and personal necessities in a market subsidized by protective tariffs. And his shifting fortunes from year to year frequently made him dependent upon credit to finance his next crop. The great enemy was the triple alliance of railroads, banks, and tariff-protected industry.

Caught in a web woven by railroad monopolists, buccaneering market speculators, tight-fisted money-lenders, and hardheaded industrialists, the farmers rose in sporadic movements of protest and revolt. The Grangers of 1867, the Greenbackers of the 1870's, the Farmers' Alliance of the 1880's, the Populists of 1891, and Bryan's "free silver" campaign of 1896—all were expressions of this agrarian discontent which sought to impose systematic government control over the economic life of the nation to mitigate the plight of the farmers. The *Congregationalist Record* of Boston represented the attitude of most eastern churchmen when it described the leaders of the agrarian protest as "dangerous characters of the inflammable and covetous West." Lyman Abbott of Plymouth Congregational Church in Brooklyn was probably equally representative when he spoke disparagingly of William Jennings Bryan as a western "medicine man" who set up his tent to hawk "one medicine which will cure all the ills to which humanity is subject." [24] The evangelical religion of the rural and village churches of the Midwest and South, however, was implicated in the farm revolt and contributed to its continuing impetus.[25] Unfortunately the relationship of evangelical religion to rural radicalism has received little

[22] *The Lively Experiment,* 149.
[23] See R. B. Nye, *Midwestern Progressive Politics: A Historical Study of Its Origins and Development, 1870–1950* (East Lansing, Mich., 1951).
[24] *Ibid.,* 5.
[25] *Ibid.,* 160. The Grange, for example, was and has continued to be closely related to the churches.

detailed study, partly because the religious press gave little attention to the agrarian problem. The religious press was urban oriented and its attention was absorbed by the much more spectacular labor uprisings.

The plight of the workers was even more serious than that of the farmers. Wages were low, hours were long, and working conditions were almost uniformly bad. Where women and children were employed, they labored from dawn to dusk for a pittance. And the situation steadily worsened, for the mounting national wealth was being concentrated in fewer and fewer hands. As early as 1867 a magazine reported that ten men owned one-tenth of the taxable property in New York City, and it listed their holdings. By 1890 it was estimated that 1 per cent of the families of the country received one-quarter of the national income, and seven years later one-tenth of the American people were said to own nine-tenths of the national wealth. Wages, to be sure, were rising. From 1860 to 1881 they increased 31 per cent, but prices rose 41 per cent and more than offset the gain.[26] The crises came, however, when workers were laid off in large numbers or had their pay cut as the result of recurring financial crashes. The crash of 1873 set off the first crisis. This was followed by the panic of 1884 and then by the disastrous depression of 1893, when Coxey's "army" marched on Washington.

Numerous workingmen's associations were being formed throughout these years, and their efforts to improve the lot of the workers led to large-scale labor warfare. Strikes were frequent and bloody. Four were particularly frightening to the nation as a whole. The first was the railroad strike of 1877 in which pitched battles were fought in many cities, arousing widespread fear of imminent revolution and anarchy. The second was the McCormick Harvester strike of 1886. On May 3 six pickets were killed in a clash with the police. The following day at a protest meeting of the workers in Haymarket Square a bomb was exploded which killed a policeman and injured many others. In the subsequent riot ten more persons died. The third was the Homestead strike of 1892 at the Carnegie Steel Plant in Pennsylvania where ten were killed and sixty wounded in a battle between the workers and three hundred "Pinkerton" men. The fourth, the Pullman strike of 1894 which affected rail transportation in twenty-seven states,

[26] See Charles B. Spahr, *An Essay on the Present Distribution of Wealth in the United States* (N.Y., 1896), 128 ff.; Robert Hunter, *Poverty* (N.Y., 1912), 61 ff.; Washington Gladden, *Applied Christianity* (Boston, 1894) 120; W. E. Garrison, *March of Faith*, 62, 120.

was accompanied by widespread burning, looting, and killing, and was finally brought to an end by President Cleveland's use of federal troops.

The reaction of the churches to the revolt of the workingmen was one first of shock and then of panic. Orthodox economic theory had taught them that labor was a "commodity," subject "like all other commodities" to "the imperishable laws of demand and supply," and that in a free country the sole responsibility of government to both capital and labor was "the simple duty of enforcing contracts" and preserving peace.[27] Thus they were more shocked by the riots of the strikers than by the conditions which caused the strikers to riot. The whole fabric of society seemed in danger of being torn apart, and many of the Protestant periodicals responded with almost incredibly brutal denunciations of the workers. The issue is between "law and anarchy," declared the *Independent* on July 26, 1877. The safety of society demands that no concessions be made to rioters. A week later its mood was near hysteria. "If the club of the policeman, knocking out the brains of the rioter, will answer, then well and good; but if it does not promptly meet the exigency, then bullets and bayonets, canister and grape . . . constitute the one remedy and the one duty of the hour." The *Christian Union* agreed. "There are times when mercy is a mistake," it asserted.[28] But there were others who were deeply troubled. Washington Gladden, for example, in the late 1860's had defended the cause of the strikers in North Adams, Massachusetts; and in 1876 he published his first book on social questions, *Workingmen and Their Employers*. By the 1880's many were to share his concern.

Roman Catholics were often equally intemperate in their denunciation of strikes. James R. Bayley, archbishop of Baltimore, took a dim view of labor unions, insisting that "no Catholic with any idea of the spirit of his religion will encourage them," and a Catholic periodical asserted that the proper solution for economic troubles was for the workers to "Pray, Pray, Pray." [29] The Knights of Labor, the first really effective mass labor union, was condemned in Quebec by papal decree in 1884, and Archbishop Corrigan of New York insisted that membership in the Knights was forbidden in the United States as well. Cardinal Gibbons, on the other

[27] *Watchman and Reflector*, June 4, 1874, quoted by May, *op. cit.*, 55; and the *Independent*, July 26, 1877, quoted by Garrison, *March of Faith*, 64.

[28] May, *Protestant Churches and Industrial America*, 92–93.

[29] *The American Apostolate*, ed. L. R. Ward (Westminster, Md., 1952); Cross, *Emergence of Liberal Catholicism*, 118.

hand, believed that many of the workers' grievances were just, and he was alarmed by the prospect of major defections from the church if the censure was maintained. In 1888, with the help of Ireland and Keane, Gibbons obtained a ruling from Rome which stated that the Knights could be "tolerated." Gibbons then proceeded to warn the Knights against the use of strikes and boycotts. While the liberals sympathized with the plight of the workers, they tended to oppose any proposals that would restrict free economic activity. Even the great labor encyclical, *Rerum Novarum* (1891), provided no clear guidance in America, for the workingmen's associations sanctioned by Leo XIII were to be Catholic societies and were to include employers as well as employees. Joseph Schroeder, the conservative leader at Catholic University, quickly pointed out that these approved associations were a far cry from anything to be found in the United States.[30]

THE SOCIAL GOSPEL.[31]   The developing social concern among American Protestants was stimulated in part by influences from abroad. The writings of Thomas Chalmers (1780–1847), the Scottish theologian and philanthropist, were widely read and exerted the earliest influence in this direction,[32] and immediately after the Civil War interest in the distinctively English "Christian socialism" of Frederick Denison Maurice (1805–72) and Charles Kingsley (1819–75) was aroused by their books and novels.[33] Later the "Christian socialists" of Germany and Switzerland contributed a strong theological emphasis upon the centrality of the doctrine of "the kingdom of God." The chief American precursors were Henry M. Dexter (1821–90), a New England clergyman, who published

[30] *Ibid.*, 118. For Gibbons' defense of the Knights of Labor and for portions of *Rerum Novarum*, see Smith, Handy, Loetscher, *American Christianity*, II, 377–91.

[31] The term "social gospel" did not come into common use until after 1900. Prior to this the term most widely used was "social Christianity." See R. C. White and C. H. Hopkins, *The Social Gospel: Religion and Reform in Changing America* (Phila., 1976); R. T. Handy, ed., *The Social Gospel* (N.Y., 1966); James Dombrowski, *The Early Days of Christian Socialism* (N.Y., 1936).

[32] Chalmers' *The Application of Christianity to the Commercial and Ordinary Affairs of Life* was reprinted at Hartford and at Boston in 1821, at Lexington, Ky., in 1822, and at New York in 1855. His *Christian and Civic Economy of Large Towns*, first published in 1821, was considered to be of such value that an abridgment was published in 1900 by Charles R. Henderson, professor of Christian sociology at the University of Chicago.

[33] English nonconformists, such as Andrew Mearns, A. M. Fairbairn, C. Silvester Horne, John Clifford, and Hugh Price Hughes, may have exerted even greater influence in America because they were not "handicapped by ties with an aristocratic and partly feudal establishment." H. F. May, *Protestant Churches and Industrial America*, 149, 150.

The Moral Influence of Manufacturing Towns in 1848, and Stephen Colwell (1800–1871), a Philadelphia iron merchant, who became preoccupied with social problems in the 1850's.[34]

The indifference and, on occasion, the hostility of the churches to the cause of the worker was due largely to ignorance. Consciences were disturbed and sympathy and support were enlisted when the clergy became personally acquainted with the workingman's plight. Typical in this respect was the sturdy defense of the workers in the great Pullman strike of 1894 by William H. Carwardine. He was no student of the labor question. He had no theory to support his opinions. But he was the minister of a Methodist church in Pullman, Illinois, and he was drawn by his immediate and firsthand experience of conditions there into a firm belief in the justice of the strikers' demands. For Washington Gladden, the conversion was not so sudden and dramatic. He was first exposed to the plight of the workers during his pastorate at North Adams, Massachusetts, and when he was called to Springfield he found the situation there much more acute. But his views did not mature until the Hocking Valley coal strike of 1884 when he was minister of the First Congregational Church of Columbus, Ohio. The officials of the coal company were members of his congregation, and Gladden was aware of the lengths to which they were prepared to go to crush the strike and break the union. This they succeeded in doing at great cost to the men and to themselves, only to have a new strike break out a year later. This time the miners won. A contract was signed, and the manager of the company admitted to Gladden that it was much better to bargain with the union over a table than to attempt to deal with a mob.

The social gospel leaders represented no unified point of view. They shared a common concern and they were agreed that the people in the churches needed to be exposed to the "facts." Most Protestants were isolated from the scenes of industrial conflict and had no personal acquaintance with the lot of the worker. To remedy this situation, socially minded clergymen organized forums and study groups to discuss industrial problems and invited representatives of labor to speak before men's brotherhoods in the churches. In addition they busied themselves with producing a voluminous literature dealing with social issues from a

---

[34] Colwell's books were *New Themes for the Protestant Clergy* (1851), *Politics for American Christians* (1852), and *The Position of Christianity in the United States* (1854). He also wrote the Preface to William Arnot's *The Race for Riches* (1853).

Christian point of view.[35] But beyond this common pattern of activity, there were deep divergences.

Washington Gladden represented a rather mild "progressivism" which recognized the rights of labor, advocated municipal ownership of public utilities, and placed strong emphasis upon the Golden Rule as the royal law of brotherhood. The latter theme was picked up and romanticized by Charles M. Sheldon (1857–1946), minister of the Central Congregational Church of Topeka, Kansas, in a parable-novel that was destined to win a place beside *Uncle Tom's Cabin* and *Ten Nights in a Bar Room* as one of the great American tracts. *In His Steps, or What Would Jesus Do?* (1897) [36] was the story of the revolution which occurred in a small city when members of a single congregation resolved to live for a year in accordance with the teachings of Jesus. At the opposite pole from Sheldon's nonprogramatic sentimentalism was the demand for a radical reconstruction of society voiced by such men as George D. Herron (1862–1925), professor of applied Christianity at Grinnell College, and W. D. P. Bliss (1856–1926), an Episcopal clergyman in Boston and guiding spirit of the Society of Christian Socialists. A "scientific" approach to social problems was represented pre-eminently by a Chicago coterie whose chief luminaries were Shailer Mathews, Graham Taylor, and Charles R. Henderson (1848–1915). Social melioration based upon careful sociological analysis was their forte, and they were strong advocates of the utility of "social settlements" in forwarding the necessary process of social adjustment.

The social settlements were patterned after Toynbee Hall, a pioneer settlement house established in London in 1884. Their purpose was to bring together a company of university-trained social workers who would live together in the slums where they could study conditions at first hand and initiate projects of social betterment. Two of the best known American "settlements" were in Chicago—Hull House, founded by Jane Addams, and Chicago Commons, with Graham Taylor as its guiding light. Others were to be found in most of the major cities, usually being established in connection with either a university or a seminary.

[35] Typical in this respect was Gladden's own literary output which included *Working People and Their Employers* (1876), *The Christian League of Connecticut* (1883), *Applied Christianity* (1886), *Tools and the Man* (1893), *Ruling Ideas of the Present Age* (1895), *Social Facts and Forces* (1899), *Social Salvation* (1902), *Christianity and Socialism* (1905), *The Church and Modern Life* (1908), *The Labor Question* (1911).

[36] Its circulation has been estimated to have exceeded 20 million copies. Conwell's *Acres of Diamonds* occupied much the same place in the gospel-of-wealth literature.

In terms of continuing influence, Walter Rauschenbusch (1861–1918) was the outstanding prophet of the social gospel. His social awakening occurred during ten years spent as pastor of a small Baptist church of German immigrants in New York City. Participation in Henry George's campaign for mayor helped shape his views, as did his experience among the tenements and his association with two other young pastors, Nathaniel Schmidt and Leighton Williams.[37] In 1897 Rauschenbusch was appointed to the faculty of the Rochester Theological Seminary and in 1907, when *Christianity and the Social Crisis* was published, he was thrust into national prominence. Of equal note was his *Prayers of the Social Awakening* (1910), one of the few devotional classics America has produced.

Rauschenbusch is difficult to classify in relation to other social gospel leaders. His fellow Baptists at the University of Chicago dismissed him as "rhetorical" rather than "scientific." [38] He called himself on occasion a "Christian socialist," but he was careful to distinguish his reformist position from any doctrinaire socialism. While he did not wholly escape the sanguine temper of his time, he showed few traces of the sentimental optimism that characterized so much of the social gospel literature. As early as 1892 he had rejected the "comforting" doctrine of "the inherent upward forces of nature," and in 1907 he spoke strong words of caution to those who had imbibed the heady wine of inevitable progress.[39] After a brief flirtation with uninhibited hopefulness which found expression in *Christianizing the Social Order*, he returned to a more sober view of human nature in *A Theology for the Social Gospel*. As the title of the latter volume indicates, his interest was much more theological than most of the others, and his great contribution was to clothe the social gospel with passion and a sense of destiny. He did this by relating the social gospel in dynamic fashion to the concept of the kingdom of God, placing it in juxtaposition to the inherited, massive, and stubbornly resistant structures of the kingdom of evil.[40]

Rauschenbusch's flurry of optimism just prior to World War I was rooted in the growing popular support and official recognition that was

[37] Henry George had an astonishing influence in awakening Christian social concern in England. Schmidt, Williams, and Rauschenbusch linked themselves in a Society of Jesus which was later expanded to become the Brotherhood of the Kingdom.

[38] For Mathews and Rauschenbusch, see W. S. Hudson, "Rauschenbusch and the New Evangelism," *Religion in Life*, XXX (1961), 416–20. See also 429–30.

[39] *Ibid.*, 421–22; and Hudson, *Great Tradition*, rev. ed. (N.Y., 1963), 228–30.

[40] See Smith, Handy, and Loetscher, *American Christianity*, II, 402–07.

being won by advocates of the social gospel. The social concern reshaped the curricula of theological seminaries, induced some of them to move from isolated hamlets to urban centers ("What medical school," asked Graham Taylor, "is thus remote from the centers of suffering men, and deprived of hospital clinics?") and prompted others to provide students with a summer's exposure to urban problems.[41] Most major denominations established commissions to forward social concerns, and in 1908 the Federal Council of Churches (predecessor of the National Council of Churches) was formed to enable churches to deal jointly with the problems of an industrial society. A "Social Creed of the Churches" was adopted,[42] addressed: "To the toilers of America and to those who by organized effort are seeking to lift the crushing burden of the poor, and to reduce the hardships and uphold the dignity of labor," pledging them sympathy and help in "a cause which belongs to all who follow Christ."

Apart from sincere concern to combat injustice, this official "social Christianity" was motivated by a desire to overcome an assumed alienation of the workingman from the churches. Washington Gladden had noted that only one-tenth of his congregation were wage earners, whereas the census reported that almost one-fourth of the population were of the laboring class. It is "all too evident," he declared, "that the proportion of working people who attend church is much smaller than the proportion of churchgoers to the entire population." [43] The assumption was that the gap between the churches and the workingmen would be closed if the churches would only exhibit an interest in their plight and support them in their struggle for justice.

Middle-class Protestantism, however, was mistaken in assuming that there was such an alienation of workingmen. They simply did not belong to middle-class churches. Overlooked had been the existence of "a working-class social Christianity" running parallel to "the more widely known and well-studied social gospel" of middle-class critics of society. A study of labor periodicals has made it clear that Christian rhetoric, imagery, and motivation were characteristic of labor leadership and that the workingmen found religious sanction for their discontent and union activ-

41 Abell, *The Urban Impact upon American Protestantism*, 224–45.
42 Reprinted in Smith, Handy, Loetscher, *American Christianity*, II, 396–97. It had been drafted and adopted by the Methodist Episcopal Church earlier in 1908.
43 From "The Working People and the Churches," *The Independent*, July 23, 1885.

ities in the evangelicalism of traditional American Protestantism.[43a] The tactic of wooing workers into middle-class churches by a show of concern for their plight, however, met with little success. Immediate gains rather than expressions of sympathy interested them. Indeed, the 1896 election witnessed a massive shift in the labor vote from its traditional democratic affiliation to the Republican party of Mark Hanna and William McKinley.[44] Practical issues were decisive, for neither party in its urban strongholds (Republicans in Philadelphia and Chicago, Democrats in Boston and New York) offered programs of thoroughgoing social and economic reform.

THE "PROGRESSIVE" MOVEMENT. Middle-class support of "social Christianity" was related to Theodore Roosevelt's "Square Deal" and "Bull Moose" platforms. Most social gospel leaders were involved in "progressive" politics, and the 1912 Progressive party campaign had a strong religious flavor. The party convention had as its theme song "Onward, Christian Soldiers," a response to his ringing challenge to them before the convention met, "We stand at Armageddon and we battle for the Lord." Ministers campaigned openly from the pulpit for the party, and one justified himself by maintaining that, while "it is not the province of the pulpit to say that any man ought to be elected president," it is "the province of every pulpit to say that the principles of the Progressive party should guide the nation for the next four years." [45]

Progressivism, like the social gospel, was almost exclusively a manifestation of middle-class idealism. Middle-class opinion had been deeply shocked by the muckrakers' exposure of widespread vice and corruption, of the ruthless tactics employed by the trusts, and of the special privileges accorded "vested interests" by city governments, state legislatures, and the national Congress. The progressives had no consistent philosophy and their program was a miscellaneous collection of reforms which included direct primaries, womans' suffrage, the initiative, referendum, and recall, regulation of interstate commerce, revision of banking and currency laws, effective antitrust legislation, municipal ownership of public utilities, the income tax, the eight-hour day, prohibition of child labor,

[43a] Herbert Gutman, "Protestantism and the American Labor Movement: the Christian Spirit in the Gilded Age," *American Historical Review*, LXXII (1966), 74–101.
[44] S. P. Hays, *The Response to Industrialism, 1885–1914* (Chicago, 1957), 46–47. Democrats did not recover their urban strength until the elections of 1928 and 1932.
[45] *Ibid.*, 93.

safeguards against industrial accidents and occupational diseases, and either strict regulation of the liquor traffic or its outright prohibition.

The related issues of conspiracies in restraint of trade and the corrupting of government officials were the great objects of concern. When most of the reforms designed to curb the "vested interests," restore power to the people, and eliminate other abuses, had been adopted, attention was concentrated upon women's suffrage and the abolition of the liquor traffic as the final goals to be achieved. Each was regarded as something of a universal panacea for the ills of society. The women's vote, it was believed, would strengthen at every point the cause of virtue, morality, altruism, and humanitarian endeavor. The crusade for prohibition, which was equally integral to the progressive program, was viewed from a similar universal perspective.

The liquor industry with its increasing monopolistic tendencies was regarded by the progressives as the most dangerous and predatory of all big business. It was lavish in its expenditures both to gain desired legislation and to thwart the enforcement of bothersome regulations adopted as concessions to public opinion. Often arrogant in its control of government, the liquor industry had been exposed again and again by the muckrakers as a principal source of political corruption and a strong ally of political reaction. Its links with vice and crime were more indirect but nonetheless real. As a progressive reform, prohibition drew upon the same moral idealism as the rest of the progressive program. It was popularly believed that the abolition of the liquor traffic would eliminate at a single stroke a primary cause not only of political reaction, corruption, vice, and crime, but also of poverty, disease, economic inefficiency, marital discord, and broken homes. While some of the progressives disliked the reform, believing it to be too extreme, this loss of support was more than compensated by that received from conservative Protestants. But the leadership which pushed the adoption of the Eighteenth Amendment remained with the socially liberal progressives.[46]

The temperance cause had long been gaining ground in the United States, and it had become much more vigorous with the organization of the Woman's Christian Temperance Union in 1874.[47] The emphasis shifted

[46] See J. H. Timberlake, *Prohibition and the Progressive Movement, 1900–1920* (Cambridge, Mass., 1963).

[47] More study could profitably be devoted to the W.C.T.U. Its influence was great, and its literature reveals a wide-ranging social concern. Frances Willard, friend and colleague of Susan B. Anthony, was the key figure in the organization.

from temperance to total abstinence to a full-scale attack upon the saloon. By 1900 five of the forty-five states had adopted statewide prohibition laws which banned the manufacture and sale of intoxicating beverages, and others had made provision for local option. The big thrust, however, was launched with the formation of the Anti-Saloon League in 1895, an agency which was to become an instrument of sophisticated political action. It was manned by socially progressive Protestant churchmen, and also enlisted the support of liberal Catholics.[48] As was true of the progressive movement as a whole, the drive for prohibition found its greatest strength in an alliance between the old-stock middle-class element in the cities and the rural and small-town population, both groups being stanchly Protestant and united in their determination to rid the cities of vice, crime, poverty, and corruption. Unless this was accomplished, it was feared that the growing influence of the cities would subvert the character of American society and thwart all further attempts at progress and reform.

The drive to suppress the liquor traffic had the great advantage of enlisting the support of both liberal and conservative Protestants, and in the end it became a great Protestant crusade. By April, 1917, twenty-six states had gone "dry," and before the end of the year a constitutional amendment to ban the liquor traffic had been passed by Congress and submitted to the states for ratification. With the approval of forty-five of the forty-eight states, the Eighteenth Amendment came into effect on January 16, 1920. Later in the same year the Nineteenth Amendment, which established the right of women to vote, came into operation. Of the major reforms sought by the progressives, the only unfinished business was a federal ban on child labor. The national child labor statute was declared unconstitutional by the Supreme Court in 1918, and subsequent attempts to secure a child labor amendment were to be unsuccessful.

Imperialism and world missions

A third frontier of the new industrial society that was to be of urgent concern to the churches lay beyond the seas. Conscious of its growing industrial power, the United States had begun to assume a more positive and vigorous role in international affairs. Foreign trade had mounted

---

[48] Bishop John J. Keane attended the Anti-Saloon League's founding convention, Archbishop Ireland served as one of the vice-presidents, and Catholic clergymen regularly addressed subsequent conventions.

rapidly and American entrepreneurs were eager to exploit the untapped markets of Latin America and eastern Asia. James G. Blaine, as secretary of state under Presidents Garfield and Benjamin Harrison, championed vigorous action to expand American economic and political influence abroad, and negotiated reciprocal trade agreements and arbitration treaties to further American interests. As early as 1878 a United States naval base was established on the Samoan Islands and the process of reducing the Hawaiian Islands to an American possession had begun. President Cleveland's bold defiance of Great Britain in the Venezuelan crisis of 1895 was symptomatic of the new temper which led to the Spanish-American War of 1898 and to the prompt support of Panama's revolt against Colombia in 1903. As an aftermath of the war with Spain, Puerto Rico, Guam, and the Philippines were claimed as United States possessions, and "protectorates" were established in several Caribbean countries. In the meantime the United States was intervening in China to preserve an "open door" for American commerce.

DOLLAR DIPLOMACY AND RELIGION. American imperial expansion was accompanied by a mounting enthusiasm among the churches for overseas missions. In its more bellicose form this enthusiasm was utilized as an excuse for territorial aggrandizement and what came to be called "dollar diplomacy." This was the note struck by President McKinley when he sought to explain to some Methodist friends how he had come to change his mind with regard to the acquisition of the Philippine Islands.

> I am not ashamed to tell you, gentlemen, that I went down on my knees and prayed Almighty God for light and guidance more than one night. And one night late it came to me this way. . . . There was nothing left for us to do but to take them all and to educate the Filipinos and uplift and civilize and Christianize them, and by God's grace do the very best we could by them, as our fellow men for whom Christ also died.

Senator Albert J. Beveridge was not troubled by such hesitation and uncertainty, and his defense of annexation was positive and to the point.

> We will not renounce our part in the mission of the race, trustee under God of the civilization of the world. . . . He has marked the American people as his chosen nation to finally lead in the regeneration

of the world. This is the divine mission of America. . . . The judgment of the Master is upon us: "Ye have been faithful over a few things; I will make you ruler over many things."

The possibility that Scripture provided a different interpretation of American policy was made clear when Senator George F. Hoar rose to his feet in response to Beveridge and quoted another biblical text: "The Devil taketh him up into an extremely high mountain and showeth him all the kingdoms of the world and the glory of them and saith unto him, 'All these things will be thine if thou wilt fall down and worship me.'[49]

Without the results of public opinion polls there is no way to determine which senator represented majority opinion in the churches. Many shared the militant spirit of Senator Beveridge, but influential churchmen who had supported the conflict with Spain as a war of liberation in keeping with America's anticolonialist tradition were appalled when it became an occasion for launching the United States on an imperial career of overseas expansion.[50] When their efforts to exclude provisions for annexation from the peace treaty were defeated, they mounted a continuing campaign to promote the cause of peace and international justice. Peace societies multiplied. Dollar diplomacy and the "big stick" (the naval construction program) were attacked. The newly organized Federal Council of Churches established a department of peace, and the Student Y.M.C.A. enlisted hundreds of young people for foreign mission work, inspiring them with the ideal of human brotherhood and a warless world. On February 10, 1914, twenty-nine of America's most distinguished religious leaders—Protestant, Roman Catholic, and Jewish—formed the Church Peace Union to coordinate the activities of all religious groups into a single thrust for a peaceful settlement of international disputes. Andrew Carnegie provided an endowment to underwrite the program, and so great was his optimism that he included as a proviso of his gift that "after war is abolished" the income may be used "to relieve the deserving poor . . . , especially those who have struggled long and earnestly against misfortune

[49] Charles S. Olcott, *The Life of William McKinley* (Boston, 1916), II, 110–11; Mark Sullivan, *Our Times, the United States, 1900–1925* (N.Y., 1926–35), I, 47–48. Garrison, *March of Faith*, 174.

[50] W. S. Hudson, "Protestant Clergy Debate the Nation's Vocation, 1898–99," *Church History*, XLII (1973).

and have not themselves to blame for their misfortune." [51] One of the first projects of the new organization was to aid in the establishment of the World Alliance for International Friendship through the Churches. This was accomplished in August, 1914, the month which marked the beginning of World War I.

THE EVANGELIZATION OF THE WORLD. When William R. Williams (1804–85), a scholarly Baptist preacher, wrote in 1846 that "our heavenly Father has made us a national epistle to other lands," [52] he was reiterating a conviction that had long been held by most American Christians. Until late in the nineteenth century, however, Great Britain had taken the lead in the foreign-mission enterprise and the United States had served as the junior partner. At the close of the century this role was reversed.

The expansion of American commercial and political interests abroad riveted the attention of the churches upon the needy people beyond the seas. In 1885 Josiah Strong, in a little book entitled *Our Country*, summoned the churches of America to assume their full responsibility for the Christianization of the world. [53] American ideals, he insisted, rather than its national power should be the focal point of concern in America's relationship to other lands. The Anglo-Saxon race in general and the American people in particular, he contended, are the bearers of two great interrelated ideas—"civil liberty" and "spiritual Christianity." And but for the "salt" provided by the second, the first would "speedily decay." These in turn are the "two great needs" of all mankind.

> Without controversy, these are the forces which, in the past, have contributed most to the elevation of the human race, and they must continue to be, in the future, the most efficient ministers to its progress.

The obvious corollary of this fact was that "the Anglo-Saxon [in the United States all immigrants by the alchemy of the 'melting pot' quickly became Anglo-Saxons [54]], as the great representative of these two ideas,

[51] Charles S. MacFarland, *Pioneers for Peace through Religion: Based on the Records of the Church Peace Union* (N.Y., 1946), 22.
[52] John R. Bodo, *The Protestant Clergy and Public Issues, 1812–1848* (Princeton, 1954), 241.
[53] *Our Country: Its Possible Future and Its Present Crisis*, ed. Jurgen Herbst (Cambridge, Mass., 1963). The quotations that follow are taken from chaps. XIV and XV, pp. 201–3, 205, 210, 212, 215–18, 252, 256.
[54] *Ibid.*, 203.

the depository of these two great blessings, sustains peculiar relations to the world's future" and "is divinely commissioned to be, in a peculiar sense, his brother's keeper."

Strong was more eloquent than exact in his terminology. His words sound "racist," but he states that Anglo-Saxon superiority "is due in large measure to its highly mixed origin," it being "almost universally admitted by ethnologists that the mixed races of mankind are superior to the pure ones." Thus the Anglo-Saxon is not to be defined in terms of a racial strain but as the heir of a dual tradition—"civil liberty" and "spiritual Christianity"—of which he is the custodian. And the influence of these twin concepts served as a corrective to the inevitable temptation to exercise tyrannical domination over other peoples. Nor did Strong explain the energy and vigor of the Anglo-Saxon in terms of "blood" or "genes." It was largely the product of climate and diet.

As Strong reviewed past history, it seemed evident to him that, with "two hands," God had been "preparing in our Anglo-Saxon civilization the die with which to stamp the peoples of the earth" and at the same time, through the revolutionary ferment that contact of Christian with heathen nations was creating, had been "preparing mankind to receive our impress."

> The door of opportunity is open in all the earth; organizations have been completed, languages learned, the Scriptures translated, and now the triumph of the Kingdom awaits only the exercise of the power committed to the church.

Whether the perils which threaten to delay "the coming of the kingdom wherein dwelleth righteousness" will be permitted to retard its advance "is now being swiftly determined" by the men and women of this generation. Living as they do in one of the plastic moments of history, Strong declared, "it is fully in the hands of the Christians of the United States, during the next ten or fifteen years, to hasten or retard the coming of Christ's kingdom in the world by hundreds, and perhaps thousands, of years."

Strong's stirring summons elicited a remarkable response the following summer among the students gathered for a conference at Dwight L. Moody's Mt. Hermon School. The enthusiasm was sparked by Robert P. Wilder (1863–1938) who had just graduated from Princeton, and he was aided and abetted by Luther D. Wishard (1854–1925), secretary of the

Student Y.M.C.A. at Princeton, and John R. Mott (1865–1955), a student at Cornell. Before the conference was over an even one hundred had volunteered for foreign-mission service. The delegates carried their contagious enthusiasm back to their campuses, Wilder made a whirlwind tour of the colleges, and by the end of the succeeding year the number of volunteers had grown to more than two thousand.[55] In 1888 the growing enthusiasm was channeled into a permanent organization, the Student Volunteer Movement, which adopted as its slogan "The evangelization of the world in this generation." For the next three decades this organization was to enlist the very ablest men and women on the college campuses of the nation and to send them to the far corners of the earth.

The motivation which lay behind this surge of foreign-mission interest was varied. A. T. Pierson (1837–1911) and A. J. Gordon (1836–95), both of whom played a part in arousing Wilder's concern, were premillennialists who believed that the gospel had to be preached throughout the world as a prerequisite to the second coming of Christ. Others were distressed at the thought of millions of souls being lost forever. J. Hudson Taylor (1832–1905) at the Student Volunteer convention at Detroit in 1894 declared:

> There is a great Niagara of souls passing into the dark. . . . Every day, every week, every month, they are passing away! A million a month in China . . . are dying without God.[56]

Democratic and humanitarian sentiment, however, seems to have played the strongest role in winning support for missions. Robert E. Speer (1867–1947), who with Wilder and Mott constituted the great triumvirate of the Student Volunteer Movement, emphasized this when he asserted that the great need for the world was "to be saved from want and disease and injustice and inequality and impurity and lust and hopelessness and fear."[57]

The whole foreign mission enterprise was marked by widespread interdenominational cooperation. Not only did the mission boards recruit

[55] R. W. Braisted, *In This Generation: The Story of Robert P. Wilder* (N.Y., 1941).
[56] *The Student Volunteer Enterprise: Addresses and Discussions of the Second International Convention of the Student Volunteer Movement for Foreign Missions* (N.Y., 1894), 48.
[57] *Christianity and the Nations: the Duff Lectures for 1910* (N.Y., 1910), 29.

their personnel through the joint endeavors of the Student Volunteer Movement; they allocated territory on a comity basis in the mission fields and formed interdenominational councils in mission lands for purposes of consultation and sharing of experience. At home the work of the denominational boards was coordinated through the formation of the Foreign Missions Conference of North America in 1893, and later it was also coordinated through the International Missionary Council which grew out of the Edinburgh conference of 1910. In 1902 the Missionary Education Movement was launched to quicken missionary interest in all the major denominations. A continuing problem, of course, was to provide sufficient financial support for the youth who were offering themselves in increasing numbers for missionary service. A Presbyterian layman, John B. Sleman, Jr., sought to meet this need. He had been deeply moved when thousands of college students had gathered in Nashville in 1906 for a Student Volunteer convention. As a result of his prodding the Laymen's Missionary Movement was organized in the autumn of that year to challenge laymen throughout the nation to match the devotion of youth with the dedication of their dollars. Until the outbreak of World War I, the Laymen's Missionary Movement was carried forward with the same surge of enthusiasm that characterized the Student Volunteer Movement.

The years of midpassage following the Civil War had introduced many changes into American life and had presented the churches with multiple problems of adjustment. These problems had been met with varying degrees of success, but never were they tackled with more exuberance than during the first decade and a half of the new century, which Gaius Glenn Atkins described as "the age of crusades." The unusual moral idealism and superabundance of zeal which found expression in the allied enterprises of the missionary movement was channeled into a whole galaxy of causes, only a few of which have been noted in this chapter. World War I brought to an end all these peaceful crusades by diverting the idealism and zeal of the American people into the one great crusade to end war and make the world safe for democracy through military power.

World War I also marked the end of the years of transition. The era of the frontier was brought to an end in 1912 when Arizona and New Mexico were granted statehood, and the great tide of immigration was cut off in 1914 when the German armies smashed through Belgium and into France. The economic effect of the war was to hasten the process of industrial development and to bring to maturity the urban world of modern America. In most parts of the country the agrarian democracy of earlier years was to be little more than a memory as backcountry villages and smaller cities were brought within the orbit of great metropolitan centers.

The changes introduced by World War I were not immediately apparent. By the time the United States entered the war in 1917 the attention of the American people had long been absorbed by the dramatic news of the conflict in Europe. When the United States joined the struggle, President Wilson's "Fourteen Points" made the issues at stake seem clear cut, and the churches responded to the national summons with zeal and unanimity. Few voices of dissent were heard as "preachers presented arms," utilizing their sermons to depict the iniquity of the Central powers and the righteousness of the Allied cause.[58] Prominent clergymen exhibited their enthusiasm for the president's crusade by volunteering to go abroad with the troops as Y.M.C.A. workers. Others served at home as "Minute Men," promoting the sale of Liberty Bonds. Then, with American troops having scarcely arrived on the field, the war ended. So quickly had it rushed to its conclusion that only the most perceptive had had time to contemplate the possibility that the old days were gone and that the world would never be the same again.

[58] See Ray H. Abrams, *Preachers Present Arms* (N.Y., 1933).

PART IV

MODERN AMERICA

1914–

XIII

The Shifting Religious Configuration

By 1914 when the onset of World War I brought to an end the massive influx of new Americans, the religious configuration of the nation had been sharply modified. Mounting Roman Catholic immigration had continued to reduce the numerical predominance of Protestantism, and in the two decades preceding the outbreak of war both Judaism and Eastern Orthodox Christianity made the striking gains which transformed them into numerically significant communities. At the same time, marked Lutheran growth, the emergence of new "disaffected" Protestant groups, and the growing strength of Negro churches had altered the Protestant spectrum.

Judaism

Of all the religious traditions and groups that emerged into relative numerical prominence for the first time at the turn of the century, Judaism had the longest history. As children of Abraham, the ancient Hebrews had known troubled times and prosperous times, times of strife and times of peace. Their epic included escape from bondage in Egypt, only to spend forty years in the wilderness before reaching the Promised Land. Recurring wars ended with exile in Babylon, from whence they returned to rebuild the temple in Jerusalem. Greeks and Romans came as conquerors, followed by an heroic insurrection. Again the temple was destroyed and this time the Jewish people were dispersed into almost all parts of the known world. Here and there, scattered in small communities, from Spain to India and from northern Africa to the Danube and the rivers of Gaul, the Jews survived. Sometimes they prospered; frequently they were harried; and always the dispersion continued. In 1654, fleeing from Portuguese harassment in Brazil, twenty-three Jews arrived in New Amsterdam as initial representatives of what was to become one of America's major faiths and in time the largest Jewish community in the world.

Jewish life found its focus in the giving of the Law to Moses some three thousand years ago and in the consciousness of being a people chosen of God to exhibit both his righteousness and mercy.[1] The Temple in Jerusalem was the center of Jewish worship. The synagogue appeared for the first time during the Babylonian exile and was given definite shape by Ezra after the return to Jerusalem where it occupied a subordinate position to the renewed Temple worship. Among Jews of the Diaspora (those living outside Palestine), except for a rare pilgrimage to Jerusalem, the synagogue provided the sole opportunity for communal worship. While its prayer services were modeled after the Temple service, the central emphasis was upon the instruction of the people rather than upon priestly acts performed in a sacred place. The Torah (the Law contained in the Pentateuch, the five books of Moses) was read and explained and applied to the needs of daily life. When the Temple was again destroyed in A.D. 70 and the Jewish nation dispersed, synagogue worship took on heightened significance as a corporate reminder of the ancient bond symbolized by the Temple and its Ark of the Covenant.

Closely related to the developing life of the synagogue were the rabbis. The rabbis, or teachers, were businessmen or workers who had devoted their leisure to studying the heritage of Israel and, as learned scholars, had been recognized as competent authorities of Jewish law.

---

[1] For an account of Jewish faith and practice, see Milton Steinberg, *Basic Judaism* (N.Y., 1947), and Arthur Hertzberg, *Judaism* (N.Y., 1961). Jacob Neusner, *American Judaism: Adventure in Modernity* (Englewood Cliffs, N.J., 1972), Nathan Glazer, *American Judaism* (Chicago, 1972), and Joseph Blau, *Judaism in America* (Chicago, 1976), are compact accounts of the American Jewish experience.

Although they had no official relationship to the synagogue, the rabbis had always played a prominent role in synagogue life as spokesmen and interpreters of God's claim upon his people. After the shattering events of A.D. 70, the rabbis gradually gained a more central position. Broken and forlorn, the members of the scattered Jewish communities were groping for guidance and comfort. The rabbis gave them both, for in their preaching they reinterpreted the Law to make it applicable to the new situation and at the same time combined this instruction with glowing words of encouragement and hope. Official leadership, to be sure, did not belong to the rabbis. Others conducted the services of worship, reciting the prayers and reading from the Torah. But it was the rabbi who won the full respect and esteem of the community. More than a millennium was to pass, however, before it became customary to provide the rabbi with a salary, and even as late as the fifteenth century this was far from a universal practice.

REFORM JUDAISM. Life in America introduced a significant change in Jewish life. In medieval Europe a pattern of Jewish life developed which tended to be perpetuated in some areas until the twentieth century. These European Jewish communities were tightly knit enclaves set apart from the larger community. An individual Jew had no independent civic status. But within the ghetto there was considerable self-government, with the Jewish leadership being responsible for maintaining order, levying taxes to satisfy the demands of the civil government, and imposing additional assessments to meet their own communal needs. The synagogue was but one of several communal institutions, and it both embraced and was controlled by the total Jewish community.[2] In America these self-contained Jewish enclaves disappeared. The synagogue became the primary institution of Jewish life, with membership a matter of individual choice. Instead of one synagogue there could be several within a given area. And the synagogue was controlled by its own congregation rather than by the whole Jewish community, some of whom might not be members of any synagogue. In a sense the synagogue was the community, for it exercised whatever social control there was.

The first Jews to arrive in America were "Sephardim," Jews of Spanish or Portuguese antecedents who came by way of Brazil beginning in 1654, but they never came in large numbers. Until the last decade of the nineteenth century, most American Jews were "Ashkenazim," German-

[2] See Glazer, *American Judaism*, 18–19.

speaking Jews from central Europe. Both groups were thoroughly orthodox, differing in ritual but not in doctrine. What may be called Jewish
denominationalism dates from 1802 when a group of Philadelphia Jews
who wished to adhere to the practices of the Ashkenazic rite formed a
separate synagogue. This was a time of small beginnings, of course, for in
1825 there were only about a half-dozen active congregations in the United
States and in 1848 there were not more than fifty.

Almost everywhere throughout the world Jews had been forced to
regard themselves as a separate entity, living apart from the general
community and governing themselves, to the extent that they were permitted to do so, by Talmudic law.[3] In the United States the legal
restrictions which fostered this isolated life were absent. Jews could
become full citizens. They could be Americans of Jewish faith rather than
an alien people. In this situation a growing number of Jews came to
regard many of the ancient laws as anachronistic. Particular sources of
embarrassment were some of the ancient folk customs associated with
synagogue worship, and the general lack of decorum and dignity of the
religious services. An initial attempt to simplify synagogue worship and to
make it more comprehensible and appealing was made at Charleston in
1824. While this was abortive, a similar effort in 1836 was more successful. The first congregations that were founded to foster Reform were Har
Sinai of Baltimore in 1842 and Emanu-El of New York in 1845.

American Jews, of course, were few in number. The great impetus for
Reform came from Germany where the Jews had been emancipated by
constitutional changes. At Frankfort-on-the-Main in 1843 the Frankfort
Society of the Friends of Reform was organized and issued the following
declaration:

> First, we recognize the possibility of unlimited development
> in the Mosaic religion. Second, the collection of controversies, dis-
> sertations, and prescriptions commonly designated by the name Talmud
> possesses for us no authority from either the doctrinal or practical
> standpoint. Third, a Messiah who is to lead back the Israelites to the
> land of Palestine is neither expected nor desired by us; we know no
> fatherland except that to which we belong by birth or citizenship.[4]

[3] The Talmud is a distillation of the biblical interpretation and wise counsel of the
ancient rabbis.
[4] David Philipson, *The Reform Movement in Judaism* (N.Y., 1931), 122.

These were to be the classic guiding principles of Reform Judaism. As a result of the storm of protest the declaration aroused among the more conservatively inclined, many German Jews sympathetic to Reform emigrated to the United States where they greatly strengthened the Reform cause.

The great leader of Reform Judaism in America was Isaac M. Wise (1819–1900) who arrived in the United States in 1846. He served as rabbi of a small congregation in Albany until 1854, and then spent the rest of his career in Cincinnati. His great concerns were to effect a national organization to give a degree of unity to the independent Jewish congregations, and to establish a college to train rabbis. Primarily through his efforts the Union of American Hebrew Congregations was formed in 1873, and the Hebrew Union College was founded in 1875. His Reform views were promoted through the pages of the *American Israelite*, a paper which he founded and edited. In the area of doctrine he discarded belief in a personal Messiah and in the resurrection of the dead. He also made a distinction between the Torah of God (the Ten Commandments) and the Torah of Moses(the rest of the Pentateuch), the latter being simply an application of divine truth to specific circumstances and becoming outdated as conditions changed. In terms of practice he insisted upon equal rights for women (family pews, for example, instead of segregation by sex), and introduced into the service the use of both English and instrumental music. The prayer book he compiled was an abbreviation and simplification of the traditional liturgy, with references to the Messiah and the resurrection being modified to conform to his views. Other reformers were much more radical than Wise, making a sharper break with the past, introducing original prayers into the service, and substituting Sunday for Sabbath worship. Wise's adjustment to the problem posed by a Saturday morning Service was to shift it to Friday evening, an innovation which had little support during the nineteenth century but which was to become the general practice of Reform, Conservative, and even some Orthodox synagogues in the middle of the twentieth century.

By 1880 Reform had become the dominant version of American Judaism, although a placid orthodoxy continued to find expression in scattered synagogues. The extent to which Reform leaders were willing to effect accommodation to American life, however, was soon to create a further division. The growing restiveness of a minority who were nominally within the Reform camp was brought to a head in 1883 by the serving of shrimp (a violation of the dietary laws) at a banquet honoring the first graduates of Hebrew Union College. This produced a deep emotional shock among some of the more conservatively inclined. Rallied by Sebato Morais (1823–97), the disaffected groups in 1886 founded the Jewish Theological Seminary in New York City, an institution which was to become the chief center of Conservative Judaism. Occupying a middle position between Reform and Orthodox Judaism, the Conservative synagogues did not prosper greatly until the atrocities of the Nazi era in Germany heightened the sense of Jewish identity and created a growing desire among Jews to re-emphasize the historic continuities of Judaism.

THE GREAT IMMIGRATION. The wave of Jewish immigrants which poured into the United States for three and one-half decades after 1880 introduced a new strain into American Judaism and completely changed the character of the whole Jewish community. It has been estimated that in 1880 there may have been as many as 250,000 Jews in the United States.[5] They were a relatively homogeneous group, largely German in background, and quite widely dispersed throughout the country. Most of them were related to the synagogue, that is to say, to a Reform Temple. By 1914 the Jewish segment of the population numbered not far from three million. This new Jewish population was markedly different in cultural background and represented a quite different type of Judaism. The recent arrivals were refugees from eastern Europe. They were poverty-stricken and heterogeneous. They came from different lands, and their common Yiddish tongue was spoken in varied dialects. A few were distinguished scholars, but some were illiterate and most were without skills. Unlike the older Jewish inhabitants, they crowded into the eastern cities.

The Jewish flight from eastern Europe was a response to harsh anti-Semitic pressures and pogroms. In 1882 the Russian government issued a series of decrees designed to make Jewish life impossible. The objective was stated with cynical frankness by the Tsar's most trusted advisor: "One-third of the Jews will emigrate, one-third will be baptized, and one-third will starve." [6] A similar policy was pursued in other countries of eastern Europe, most notably in Romania and Galicia (Austrian Poland),

[5] Interpretation of Jewish statistics is complicated by the fact that until well into the twentieth century, numbers were computed in terms of "heads of families." Nor are Jewish statistics comparable to those of most other religious bodies, for they usually refer to total Jewish population rather than to synagogue membership.

[6] Bamberger, *The Story of Judaism*, 324.

and the pressure continued with varying intensity until the outbreak of World War I.

Among the Jews of eastern Europe there had been three responses to the tragic condition in which they found themselves. The majority, without hope of securing full status as citizens through political and social assimilation in the lands of their birth, retreated into a rigid orthodoxy, finding inner security in an unquestioning piety and a strict observance of the Torah. Their cultural outlook was almost totally unaffected by cultural movements among the peoples about them. A second major group, those who had had some contact with contemporary thought, reacted in a fashion quite different from that of the Jews of Germany and America. Instead of seeking to create a Reform Judaism that would be consonant with modern culture, they tended to renounce Judaism and identify themselves with radical antireligious movements of social reform. The passion and intensity with which the religious Jews of eastern Europe clung to traditional forms of thought and practice made the prospect of altering these forms seem utterly hopeless, while the political structures were so repressive and class-oriented that only a thoroughgoing social revolution seemed to offer the possibility of emancipation. Emerging from this second group was a third faction, rather insignificant at the outset, which cast its revolutionary fervor into a nationalistic mold. Taking their cue from the liberation movements of the Poles, Czechs, Ukrainians, and other oppressed peoples of eastern Europe, these "Lovers of Zion" emphasized the national rather than the religious character of Judaism and began to think in terms of securing emancipation through the establishment of a Jewish state. Each of these groups was represented in the east European immigration.

Nathan Glazer has reported that the Jewish immigrants who came from eastern Europe were "a frightening apparition" to "the established, middle-class, Americanized German Jews of the 1880's."

> Their poverty was more desperate than German Jewish poverty, their piety more intense than German Jewish piety, their irreligion more violent than German Jewish irreligion, their radicalism more extreme than German Jewish radicalism. It is not surprising that the American Jews viewed this immigration with mixed feelings, and some even suggested the possibility of deflecting or preventing it.

The American Jews did not know which was the most objectionable: the strident orthodoxy of the immigrants (as distasteful to the dignified Orthodox who opposed Reform as it was to the adherents of Reform synagogues), the antireligious views of the social radicals, or the political separatism of the Jewish nationalists. By the end of the century, however, the antipathy had been pushed sufficiently to one side for the leaders of the older Jewish communities to engage in strenuous efforts to "uplift" the immigrants and ease their adjustment to American life. One specific project of considerable future significance was the injection of new life into the Jewish Theological Seminary which had been slowly dying as its original base of tradition-oriented synagogues had dwindled. Under the leadership of Cyrus Adler (1863–1940) the financial support of Reform Jews was enlisted to transform the seminary into an agency for civilizing the east Europeans by providing them with modern English-speaking rabbis. A fund of more than a half million dollars was collected for this purpose, Solomon Schechter (1847–1915) was brought from England to be the new president, and a distinguished faculty was assembled.

RECONSTRUCTIONISM AND ZIONISM. By 1920, 80 per cent or more of the Jewish population in the United States was of east European background, and the adherents of Reform Judaism were far outnumbered by members of Orthodox synagogues. Those unaffiliated with any synagogue, however, exceeded the combined total of all religious Jews, and the proportion of the unaffiliated was growing. The flight from Judaism, which had begun in the old country, was accelerated as a concomitant of the process of Americanization. Repelled by the "foreignness" of the religious observances of their parents, children of Orthodox immigrants drifted into indifference and even hostility to religion. Few exhibited any inclination to transfer their loyalties to more modern synagogues. The results of a 1935 survey in New York City, which revealed that approximately 75 per cent of Jewish young people between the ages of fifteen and twenty-five had attended no religious service during the preceding year, were not regarded as atypical.[7] Social centers, growing out of such social agencies as the settlement houses and the Young Men's and Young Women's Hebrew Associations, were more often the focal points of Jewish life than the synagogues.

A creative response to this situation was the Reconstructionist

[7] Glazer, *American Judaism*, 85.

movement led by Mordecai M. Kaplan (b. 1881) of Jewish Theological Seminary. Kaplan's views evolved out of the synagogue center movement which he initiated in 1918. Others had experimented with making the synagogue more attractive by developing "institutional" temples patterned after the institutional churches of the Protestants, but Kaplan's aim was a new type of Jewish community with its focus not religion but "Jewishness." His approach to religion was sociological and he sought to strengthen Judaism by relating it closely to all aspects of Jewish life—political, cultural, intellectual, and philanthropic. His central contention, fully elaborated in *Judaism as a Civilization* (1934), was that Judaism was not a religion but a religious civilization in which nonreligious as well as religious Jews shared. The synagogue should be the rallying center of Jewish people and Jewish culture even for those who did not feel strongly about Jewish religion. Traditional rituals and ceremonies were viewed as important for their instrumental value as cement which helped to bind the Jewish people together. Conservative Judaism, with its ambivalent stance between Reform and Orthodox Judaism, was best equipped to assimilate Kaplan's Reconstructionist emphasis upon both tradition and modernity. In general the Conservative synagogues adopted Kaplan's policy of fostering a broad, inclusive Jewishness while rejecting some of the more radical features of his philosophy.

Closely allied to Kaplan's view of Judaism as a civilization was the older Zionist view of Judaism as a nation. Zionism had east European roots among the nineteenth-century "Lovers of Zion" but was given its more definitive shape by Theodor Herzl (1860–1914), a Viennese reporter who was present in Paris at the trial of Captain Alfred Dreyfus. In 1894 Dreyfus had been falsely charged with treason and was subsequently convicted, a victim of virulent anti-Semitic feeling in the French army. In a state of high emotional excitement Herzl wrote a pamphlet entitled *The Jewish State* (1896). The only salvation for Jews, he insisted, was national rebirth. This necessitated a homeland, preferably in Palestine. Herzl was hailed by many as a prophet, and in 1897 the first World Zionist Congress was held in Basel, Switzerland.

The Zionist issue became the subject of prolonged debate. While Zionist leaders tended to be nonreligious, many Orthodox Jews embraced Zionism since it could be reconciled with the ancient expectation of the restoration of Israel. Conservative Jews had even fewer reservations and tended to become ardent Zionists. Reform Jews, on the other hand, were generally hostile, viewing Judaism as a religion and advocating a policy of assimilation at other points. After Hitler's persecution of the Jews began in 1933 and thousands of German Jews emigrated to Palestine, the Zionist question became much less theoretical. By 1935 a majority of the Reform rabbis had moved into the Zionist camp, and in that year the Central Conference of American Rabbis abandoned its official policy of opposition to Zionism and adopted in its stead a position of neutrality. The subsequent holocaust, in which six million Jews were murdered by the Nazi state, further strengthened both the Zionist cause and the sense of Jewish solidarity. When the State of Israel was established in 1948, American Jews rallied to ensure its survival by raising astonishingly large sums through the United Jewish Appeal to aid the resettlement of refugees who were streaming into Israel from many parts of the world.[8]

THE JEWISH RELIGIOUS REVIVAL. While the Hitler years heightened Jewish self-consciousness and drew many into participation in Jewish activities, there was no great return to the synagogue. The surge of growth in synagogue membership was to be a phenomenon of the post-World War II period. In 1937 the *American Jewish Year Book* estimated that the Reform congregations had 50,000 member families. The Conservative congregations, having gained recruits from the children and grandchildren of Orthodox immigrants, had passed the Reform group and numbered some 75,000 member families. The Orthodox congregations had the largest constituency, with about 200,000 families. Thus the combined synagogue membership represented between one and one and one-half million Jews, not much more than one-fourth of all the Jews in the country. By 1956 there was a marked change. Synagogue life was flourishing, with most of the gains having been made in the last decade. Member families of Reform temples numbered 255,000, a fivefold increase over 1937. The growth rate of Conservative synagogues was smaller, but their member families had almost tripled in number and stood at 200,000. While Orthodox Judaism represented a declining portion of the total Jewish religious community, it too was exhibiting signs of vigorous life, and its most notable intellectual center, Yeshiva College, had become a flourishing university.

[8] The total amount raised in 1948 was $201,000,000. In subsequent years the amount declined, but in 1955 it still exceeded $100,000,000.

Apart from numbers, there was a marked increase in the practice of piety. The proportion of Jewish population attending religious services at least once a month increased from 18 per cent in 1947 to 31 per cent in 1955. Even among Reform Jews there was a strong tendency to reemphasize traditional values, customs, and ceremonies. The Friday evening family Kiddush with its candle lighting became more common and holidays more widely observed. In the mid-1950's it was said somewhat skeptically that the modern Jew "does more" but "knows less." This verdict was scarcely supported by available evidence. Not only had there been a vast increase in the number of children receiving a Jewish education through weekday classes, the Sunday school, and Jewish day schools, but publishers had discovered that there was a growing market among adults for books dealing with Jewish theology and religious life.

The revival of synagogue life may have been related to a change in the Jewish community. In the 1930's Jews had been predominantly working class in status, but by the 1950's only a small segment could be classified as "blue collar" workers. As a result of a driving zeal for education, second- and third-generation east European Jews had been remarkably successful in imitating earlier Jewish immigrants by moving into business and the professions. Their children and grandchildren also shifted their place of residence from inner city slums to better neighborhoods and then to the suburbs. Having become a relatively homogeneous and prosperous community, mid-twentieth century Jews tended to conform to the churchgoing pattern of other middle-class Americans. They conformed in other ways as well: in their denominationalism, in the lay control and autonomy of congregational life (there was no "chief rabbi" as in Europe), and in their activism and emphasis on Judaism as a "way of life," not doctrine.

Eastern Orthodox Christianity

The Eastern Orthodox churches also have a long history.[9] They look back to the early Christian Fathers, and to Athanasius, the Cappadocians, Pseudo-Dionysius, and "the seven ecumenical councils," as the source of their tradition. Perhaps Orthodox Christianity can best be identified in

[9] See Nicolas Zernov, *Eastern Christendom* (London, 1961); Ernst Benz, *The Eastern Orthodox Church: Its Thought and Life* (Chicago, 1963); and Timothy Ware, *The Orthodox Church* (Baltimore, 1963).

terms of the two separations which gave the Orthodox churches their geographical locus. The first separation was that of the smaller eastern churches—the Nestorians of Syria, Persia, and ultimately China, and the Monophysites (the Jacobite and Coptic churches) of Armenia, Syria, Egypt, and Ethiopia—which took place in the fifth and sixth centuries. The second separation was the product of a growing cleavage between the Greek-speaking and the Latin-speaking areas of the old Roman Empire. Although the ecclesiastical division was beginning to be apparent as early as the end of the sixth century, the final separation is commonly dated from 1054. As a result of these two separations, Eastern Orthodoxy was bounded on both its eastern and western sides, but it was able to expand to the north among the Slavic peoples. As the Greek power of Byzantium dwindled, the newer Orthodox churches of the north increased in importance. After the fall of Constantinople in 1453, Moscow—"the third Rome"—tended to assume Byzantium's role as protector of the Orthodox world.

THE ORTHODOX CHURCHES. Distributed throughout eastern Europe, in Russia, and along the eastern coast of the Mediterannean, Orthodox Christianity is a family of self-governing churches, united by a common faith and order. Apart from areas of more recent expansion, these churches are: the ancient Patriarchates of Constantinople, Alexandria, Antioch, and Jerusalem; the national churches of Russia, Romania, Serbia (Yugoslavia), Greece, Bulgaria, Georgia (U.S.S.R.), Cyprus, Czechoslovakia, Poland, and Albania; and the Holy Monastery of Sinai. While the Patriarch of Constantinople is known as the Ecumenical or Universal Patriarch and enjoys a position of special honor, he has no power to intervene in the affairs of any church other than his own. His position is much like that of the Archbishop of Canterbury in the Anglican communion, which is also composed of self-governing churches spread throughout the world. Because the overwhelming proportion of Orthodox Christians (perhaps as many as 55 million) are behind the "iron curtain," it is difficult to estimate their total number. The four ancient Patriarchates have more than 2,500,000 adherents, and the churches of Greece and Cyprus have a combined total of almost 8 million adherents.

Although the Orthodox have much in common with Roman Catholics, there are significant differences in emphasis, practice, and even doctrine. The whole mood is much more mystical and much less legalistic. The mode of baptism is triple immersion. Communion is in both kinds, the communicant receiving both the bread and the wine. Infants are confirmed and receive communion immediately after being baptized. Statues (rounded images) are not permitted, and in their stead icons (paintings and mosaics) are used. Priests may marry prior to ordination, but bishops must be unmarried. The date of Easter is different (being reckoned by the Julian rather than the Gregorian calendar), and church architecture is distinctive. The doctrines of purgatory and the immaculate conception of Mary are not generally accepted; and instead of extreme unction for the dying, the sick are anointed for the recovery of health. The most crucial difference is the authority Roman Catholicism confers upon the Roman Pontiff as the vicar of Christ and the infallible teacher and ruler of the faithful. Where Roman Catholics insist upon obedience to the Bishop of Rome, Orthodox Christians stress the role of the bishops in the government of the church and the authority of General Councils in the determination of matters of faith.

ORTHODOXY IN AMERICA. Eastern Orthodoxy had its beginnings in North America when missionary monks came to Alaska in the 1790's and were successful in converting large numbers of the natives. A seminary was established at Sitka in 1848 and a diocese was formed in 1867 when Alaska became a territory of the United States. In 1872 the seat of the diocese was transferred to San Francisco, and in 1905 to New York. In addition to the Russians, a few Greek communities had churches prior to 1900, but the major Orthodox influx came after the turn of the century. During the latter years of the great Jewish immigration, Slavic peoples (and Romanians) were also arriving from the countries of eastern Europe. Many of the non-Jewish east Europeans were Roman Catholic, but a large portion of them were Orthodox. And Orthodox strength was augmented by Uniates, Roman Catholics of an Eastern rite, who were reconciled in America to Orthodoxy (see pp. 342–43). Unlike the Jews, these other east Europeans did not crowd into the coastal cities. They had been recruited to labor in the mines and steel mills, and hence they were dispersed throughout Pennsylvania and along the periphery of the Great Lakes. The only significant exception to this pattern of Orthodox settlement was represented by non-Slavic immigrants, principally Greeks and Syrians (including Armenians), who were largely independent entrepreneurs and were widely scattered throughout the country.

From a total membership of not more than one hundred thousand in 1900, the number of Orthodox in the United States had risen to more than two million in 1960,[10] subdivided into at least fifteen national or jurisdictional groups. Before World War I all Orthodox Christians in America were united in a single organization under the jurisdiction of the Russian church, since it was the Russians who first brought Orthodox Christianity to the United States. The subsequent multiplicity of jurisdictions was a consequence of the Russian Revolution of 1917. With the Russian church becoming involved in a difficult and controversial relationship to the new Soviet regime, each of the Orthodox nationality groups formed separate organizations.

The Orthodox churches in America had a confused history in the post-World War I years as a result of the readjustments which then took place. The Greek church has been the largest (1,500,000 members in 1962) and most stable, but it was troubled by such disorders and frictions that it was not until 1930 that its life was fully regularized as the Greek Archdiocese of North and South America. The Russians had less unity. In 1919 a convention of Russian Orthodox, meeting in Pittsburgh, declared the Russian church in America to be "temporarily autonomous." Five years later, at a convention in Detroit, what was to become known as the Russian Orthodox Greek Catholic Church of America was formally constituted. This is the second largest Orthodox church, with a reported membership in 1962 of 755,000. A second Russian church, the Russian Orthodox Church Outside Russia, was formed in 1920 by Russian emigrés in Europe. With 55,000 of its members in America, it shifted its headquarters to the United States in 1950. The sole point of difference between these two groups is that the first group is willing to affirm spiritual loyalty to the patriarch of Moscow if he will recognize its administrative and legislative autonomy, while the second group insists that the Moscow Patriarchate has forfeited its right to be considered a true Orthodox church. A third Russian church, the Russian Orthodox Church in America (Patriarchal Exarchate) maintains an official tie with the Orthodox in the Soviet Union. It is the creature of the Moscow Patriarchate, and is so small as to be insignificant. The fourth Russian group, the American Carpatho–Russian Orthodox Greek Catholic Church with a membership in 1962 of 102,000, is a former Russian Uniate church which returned to Orthodoxy early in the century. The Ukrainians in America not only split

[10] According to the *Year Book of the American Churches* the total in 1960 was 2,680,633. This figure is no more than an approximation, for Orthodoxy, like Judaism, has tended to estimate its adherents in terms of total ethnic or national groups. Membership is generally reported in round numbers.

away from the Russians; they have suffered a threefold division among themselves. The two oldest groups are the Ukrainian Orthodox Church of U.S.A. (87,000 members in 1962) and the Ukrainian Orthodox Church of America (40,250 members in 1962). The latter was formerly a Uniate group in communion with Rome. The Holy Ukrainian Autocephalic Orthodox Church (5,000 members in 1962) was formed by World War II refugees in 1950. The Albanian, Bulgarian, Romanian, Serbian, and Syrian Orthodox were not fragmented, but their churches did not become fully stabilized in organization until around 1930.

Troubled by cultural and administrative divisions, the Orthodox churches in America began to gain full maturity only after World War II. Of the several theological seminaries which were established, those in New York and Boston became distinguished centers of theological scholarship. Paralleling the theological awakening was evidence of growing sentiment for greater unity among the Orthodox. In 1954 the Council of Eastern Orthodox Youth Leaders of America was formed which drew together most of the Orthodox youth organizations, and in 1960 a committee of Orthodox bishops began periodic meetings under the presidency of the Greek archbishop. The Orthodox churches also exhibited vitality in adjusting to the American environment. The use of English in worship, the introduction of mixed choirs and instrumental music, the installation of pews for the seating of the congregation, the development of parish organizations, and the adoption of church dinners as an important aspect of church life, were the kind of adaptation that other immigrant bodies had made prior to becoming fully integrated into American life. There were several attempts, mostly by former Episcopalians, to form an indigenous Orthodox church that would be at the same time both more American and more "catholic" and thus attract converts from other traditions. These met with little success and received little encouragement from Orthodox leaders, although at least four of these bodies were able to maintain a precarious existence with a handful of adherents.

"Disaffected" Protestants

One of the consequences of religious liberty is the opportunity for disaffection to find free and open expression. Many of the groups born of disaffection in the nineteenth century lived on into the twentieth century, some of them growing in strength, others declining. Among those which have been discussed in preceding chapters are Mormonism, Millerism, and Spiritualism; New Thought, Christian Science, and Unity; Theosophy, Baha'i, and the Vedanta Society. But there were other groups which were to have a surge of growth in the post-World War I years. Of these, with the exception of the Fundamentalist movement (see pp. 365–73), the Holiness and Pentecostal churches and Jehovah's Witnesses were perhaps the most significant. These latter groups, on the whole, were more traditional in orientation than those previously considered. One might refer to them as "sects" rather than "cults." [11] They may best be described as disaffected Protestants, for they claimed no new revelation and their intention was to recover past tradition.

THE HOLINESS MOVEMENT. The quest for perfect sanctification or holiness is as old as Christianity. In nineteenth-century America it had received powerful reinforcement from the generally optimistic temper of the time ("Jacksonian perfectionism"), from the hunger for holiness generated by the revivals, and more specifically from the pervasive influence of the strong Wesleyan emphasis upon the doctrine of Christian perfection.[12] Among the non-Methodists who responded to this "perfectionist" climate of opinion, Charles G. Finney and his colleagues at Oberlin were the most prominent. Beginning in 1839 the Oberlin group exhibited a growing interest in "the higher Christian life," and through their influence the concern for sanctification penetrated most of the Protestant denominations during the decades immediately preceding and following the Civil War.[13] The holiness revival, however, found its pre-

[11] As is true of many words, "cult" and "sect" have a variety of meanings. In this context, "cult" is used to denote those groups which are based on a claim to new revelation and/or the authoritative teaching of a new prophet. A cult tends to be forward-looking and is frequently eager to come to terms with what is considered to be "modern" thought. "Sect," on the other hand, is used to denote groups which make no claim to new revelation but instead seek to recover what they regard as an important but neglected aspect of past tradition. Thus they are backward-looking and usually highly resistant to "modern" thought.

[12] Wesleyan perfectionism was defined by nineteenth-century Methodists in terms of a "second blessing"—a work .of grace (sanctification) subsequent to conversion (justification) which imparted perfect love of God and liberation from sin. Wesley never claimed sanctification for himself, and sometimes he seemed to imply that it was the culmination of a growth in grace rather than an instantaneous experience. For Wesley's views, see Harold Lindström, *Wesley and Sanctification*, trans. H. S. Harvey (London, 1946).

[13] For Asa Mahan's statement of the Oberlin views, see selection in Smith, Handy, Loetscher, *American Christianity*, II, 42–48. Wesleyan and Oberlin perfectionism had much in common, but the former tended to stress the instantaneous change wrought by the "second blessing" while the latter emphasized the more gradual change resulting from growth in grace. See Timothy L. Smith, *Revivalism and Social Reform* (N.Y., 1957), 108–12, and J. L. Peters, *Christian Perfectionism and American Methodism* (N.Y., 1956).

eminent expression among the Methodists, where it was sparked by the enthusiasm of a remarkable woman, Phoebe Palmer, and where it gained momentum through her evangelistic tours and through the organized promotional efforts of the National Association for the Promotion of Holiness which had been founded in 1867.

Methodism as a whole continued to be preoccupied with the quest for holiness throughout the latter half of the nineteenth century.[14] In spite of this unanimity, it was nonetheless a potentially disruptive emphasis, for it tended to cultivate an absolutist state of mind which brooked no compromise. This was illustrated by the Wesleyan Methodist defection of 1843 which was rooted in a demand for moral perfection on the slavery issue. After the Civil War the disruptive issue was the growing "worldliness" of the Methodist churches and their members.

Methodists had been a plain people—plain in dress, behavior, and worship. But as Methodism gained in numbers, wealth, and social status, signs of laxity began to appear. As early as 1856 the stringent rules prohibiting the use of specific items of ornamentation in dress were reduced in the *Discipline* to a general admonition, an admonition that was not sufficiently rigorous to deter Bishop Matthew Simpson's wife from appearing in ruffled silk, expensive lace, and fine jewelry. A similar loss of simplicity in worship occurred as costly edifices were built, and choirs, organs, and instrumental music were introduced. A correspondent of the *Christian Advocate* reported in 1868 that in the cities of the western states—in Ohio, Indiana, Michigan, Wisconsin, Illinois, and Iowa—the tendency was to erect "one hundred thousand dollar churches" where "wealth and style and fashion gather, and the poor have not the gospel preached to them." Two years earlier a writer in the same journal had noted with satisfaction that "by virtue of the habits which religion inculcates and cherishes, our church members have as a body risen in the social scale, and thus become socially removed from the great body out of which most of them were originally gathered." While he regarded this development as "natural" and "not undesirable," there were to be some among the less privileged who were to regard it as a betrayal of the

---

[14] The southern bishops constantly emphasized this theme, and the northern bishops were equally firm, as they declared in 1884, that "the mission of Methodism is to promote holiness." See *The History of American Methodism*, ed. E. S. Bucke (N.Y., 1964), II, 614–18.

summons to holiness.[15] By the end of the century the grievances were multiplying, with notice being taken of the "church theatricals" and "fairs" that were being held, and of the increasing number of church members who "dance, play cards, attend theaters, [and] absent themselves from revivals."[16]

A foretaste of what was to be a continuing disaffection was supplied in 1860 with the formation of the Free Methodist Church at Pekin, New York. Taking its stance on the declaration that "those who are sanctified wholly are saved from all inward sin" and "all their thoughts, words, and actions are governed by pure love," the new church proceeded to denounce the proud and aspiring, to voice opposition to all "superficial, false, and fashionable" Christians, and to demand of church members an affirmative response to the question: "Will you forever lay aside all superfluous ornaments and adorn yourself in modest apparel . . . , not with broidered hair or gold or pearls or costly array?" Organs, instrumental music, and pew rentals were also condemned.[17]

The Free Methodist revolt was restricted to three relatively small areas in western New York, Michigan, and Illinois, but in the 1880's evidence of more widespread disaffection found expression in the formation of numerous independent Holiness groups throughout much of rural America. While some of these "come-outer" groups were composed of people from various denominations, the larger portion were formed by dissident Methodists. By the 1890's the local fellowships had begun to coalesce into larger groupings. Most were to remain numerically unimportant,[18] but there were a few that were to exhibit a capacity for sustained growth during the first half of the twentieth century. One of these was the Church of God (Anderson, Indiana), founded in 1881 with a dual stress on holiness and Christian unity. From its initial base in the rural Midwest, it spread gradually into the South and to the Pacific coast.[19] Another

[15] W. C. Barclay, *History of Methodist Missions,* Vol. III (N.Y., 1957), 49. May, *Protestant Churches and Industrial America,* 62.

[16] *History of American Methodism,* ed. E. S. Bucke, II, 624.

[17] *Ibid.,* 346, 352, 356, 357n., 359.

[18] Some of these were the Hephzibah Faith Mission Association formed in Iowa in 1892, the Church of Daniel's Band formed in Michigan in 1893, the Metropolitan Church Association formed in Illinois in 1894, the Church of Christ (Holiness) formed in Alabama in 1894, the Church of God (Apostolic) formed in Kentucky in 1897, the Missionary Bands of the World formed in Indiana in 1898, the Missionary Church Association also formed in Indiana in 1898, and the Pillar of Fire Church formed in Colorado in 1901.

[19] See C. E. Brown, *When the Trumpet Sounded: History of the Church of God* (Anderson, Ind., 1951).

group, the Christian and Missionary Alliance, was founded by a Presbyterian minister, A. B. Simpson, in 1887. But the most successful was the Church of the Nazarene, established by a Methodist district superintendent at Los Angeles in 1895, which numbered 307,629 members by 1960.[20] By this latter date the Holiness groups as a whole, including the Salvation Army, had a total membership of more than 1,500,000.

THE PENTECOSTAL CHURCHES. Growing out of the Holiness movement were the "pentecostal" churches, also having a combined membership in 1960 of approximately 1,500,000. Their distinguishing feature, in addition to faith healing, was an emphasis on baptism in the Holy Spirit, manifested by speaking in unknown tongues.

Modern pentecostalism was first known as the Latter Rain Movement, a name derived from the "former rain" and "latter rain" of Joel 2:23, interpreted as a dual prophecy of the speaking in tongues on the first Pentecost (Acts 2:4) and of the descent of the Spirit immediately prior to Christ's premillennial return. The movement originated in 1901 among students of C. F. Parham's Topeka Bible College, but its greatest momentum came from the 1906 Azusa Street revival in Los Angeles initiated by Parham's student, W. J. Seymour, a fledgling Negro preacher. The Azusa Street Mission became a nursery of pentecostal leadership, with Florence Crawford establishing headquarters in Portland, Oregon, and C. H. Mason and G. B. Cashwell carrying the gospel to the southeastern states. The Church of God in Christ, the largest Negro pentecostal group was shaped and nurtured by Mason, while Cashwell's ardent preaching led to A. J. Tomlinson's Spirit baptism. Tomlinson's activity, supplemented by R. G. Spurling's preaching, led to a bewildering array of Church of God organizations. The largest (170,261 members in 1960) is known as the Church of God (Cleveland, Tennessee). There were at least three offshoots with the same name, two with headquarters in Alabama, one with headquarters in Cleveland. Confusion was somewhat reduced when the latter group adopted the designation Church of God of Prophecy.[21]

Apart from the Church of God groups of the southeast, most other Pentecostal bodies were more Reformed than Wesleyan in background.

[20] See Timothy L. Smith, *Called unto Holiness: The Story of the Nazarenes* (Kansas City, Mo., 1962).
[21] See Vinson Synan, *The Holiness-Pentecostal Movement* (Grand Rapids, 1971) and C. W. Conn, *Like a Mighty Army*, rev. ed. (Cleveland, Tenn., 1977).

The Pentecostal Holiness Church, organized in 1911, belongs to this wing of the movement, but the largest group is the Assemblies of God founded in 1914 at Hot Springs, Arkansas.[22] The terminology of the latter group is somewhat misleading for the local units of the Assemblies of God are frequently called full gospel tabernacles or full gospel churches. The Assemblies of God differ from the Wesleyan wing of the movement in that they regard sanctification as a gradual process rather than an instantaneous work of grace. Consequently, for them, speaking in tongues is an independent experience of the Holy Spirit. Beginning with an initial membership of 6,000, the Assemblies of God numbered over 41,000 adherents in 1926; 318,478 in 1950; and 508,602 in 1960. Furthermore they had launched a bold foreign-mission program and had won notable successes in many parts of the world.

A more streamlined pentecostalism was represented by the Foursquare Gospel of Aimee Semple McPherson (1890–1944). With a magnetic personality, striking beauty, a flair for the dramatic, and an ability to turn the unfavorable publicity generated by her sensational adventures to her own advantage, Mrs. McPherson gathered a large following in Los Angeles where she erected the Angelus Temple. After its dedication on January 1, 1923, the Temple quickly became a major tourist attraction. Emphasizing Christ as Savior, Healer, Baptizer, and Soon-Coming King, Sister Aimee gathered branches of her Four Square Gospel Church in various parts of the country. In 1927 these branches and the mother church were incorporated as the International Church of the Foursquare Gospel. After Mrs. McPherson's death, her son Robert continued her work. But without the vitality and excitement she had contributed, its growth lagged. In 1960 the church had 82,624 members.

MILLENNIALISM. While premillennial views were held by some of the Holiness and Pentecostal groups, there were other disaffected Protestants who seized upon the expectation of Christ's return to judge the quick and the dead as their major theme. This emphasis offered both present and future consolation to those who felt alienated and disinherited by the "fashionable" churches of the privileged classes. Part of the comfort was the satisfaction to be derived from the assurance that the established denominations were clearly apostate, and further consolation was gained

[22] For Assemblies of God, see W. W. Menzies, *Annointed to Serve* (Springfield, 1971).

from the conviction that the tables would soon be turned, with the mighty being put down and the humble exalted, the hungry being filled with good things and the rich sent empty away.

The "dispensationalism" of the Darbyites and the Scofield Bible (see pp. 284–85) had made significant inroads among members of many of the older churches during the latter years of the nineteenth century, and after 1920 it was to produce a growing number of independent Bible churches and gospel tabernacles. It also was to contribute to most of the Fundamentalist defections. An older premillennial tradition in America, stemming from the Millerite excitement of the 1840's, was represented by the Seventh-day Adventists and the smaller Advent Christian group. After maintaining an undramatic and modest witness for more than half a century, the Seventh-day Adventists, who had been chiefly known for their sanitariums and for fathering the breakfast-food empires of the Kelloggs and the Posts, experienced a surge of new life in the twentieth century.[23] From 62,211 members in 1906, they grew to 110,998 in 1926, to 237,168 in 1950, and to 317,852 in 1960. But these statistics tell less than half the story, for twice this number of Seventh-day Adventists were to be found outside the United States as a result of far-flung missionary endeavor during these same years. Quite surprising in view of their firm belief in the imminent end of the world was their heavy investment in publishing houses, hospitals, homes for the aged, and especially educational institutions. Not only did they maintain numerous academies, colleges, graduate schools, and both a theological seminary and a medical and dental school; but they also established a widespread network of elementary schools. Noting their many good works, one observer has commented that seldom, while expecting a kingdom of God from heaven, has a group worked so diligently for one on earth.[24]

Of all the Adventist or millennial groups, Jehovah's Witnesses are in many ways the most conspicuous and vigorous.[25] After the onset of the depression in 1929 the Witnesses often seemed omnipresent, selling the *Watchtower* on busy street corners, and ringing doorbells endlessly in an

[23] See M. E. Olsen, *Origin and Progress of Seventh-day Adventists* (Washington, D.C., 1932), and David Michell, *Seventh-day Adventists in Action* (N.Y., 1958).
[24] Gaustad, *Historical Atlas of Religion in America*, 115.
[25] The best account of the movement by an outsider is H. H. Stroup, *The Jehovah's Witnesses* (N.Y., 1945). See also Marley Cole, *Jehovah's Witnesses: The New World Society* (N.Y., 1955), and J. A. Beckford, *The Trumpet of Prophecy* (N.Y., 1975).

effort to gain an opportunity to present their message of salvation. Then with the end of World War II, Kingdom Halls began to multiply. But it was their encounters with the law that gained the Witnesses most notoriety. Much of their trouble stemmed from their refusal to salute the flag, register for the draft, and permit their children to receive blood transfusions. Not only did these several refusals bring them before the courts, but they served to engender a popular hostility which found expression in attempts to harry the Witnesses by charging them with minor infractions of municipal codes—disturbing the peace, trespassing, violating Sunday "blue laws," and peddling without a permit.

The Witnesses have been known under a variety of names—Millennial Dawnists, International Bible Students, members of the Watchtower Bible and Tract Society, Russellites, and Rutherfordites. The founder was Charles Taze ("Pastor") Russell (1852–1916), a haberdasher and member of a Congregational church in Allegheny, Pennsylvania, who had been troubled by the notion of eternal damnation and by doubts as to the reliability of the Bible. "Stumbling," as he put it, upon an adventist preacher, he found help that was sufficient to re-establish his "wavering faith." By 1872 Russell was meeting with a small group of earnest Christians to examine the teaching of Scripture "relative to the coming of Christ and his kingdom." [26] Soon he had elaborated a millennial scheme of his own. In 1879 he began the publication of a magazine, and the following year he published his first book, *Food for Thinking Christians*. By 1884 he had won enough adherents to justify forming them into the Zion's Watch Tower Society. To disseminate his message, Russell traveled incessantly, trained "preachers," and issued a constant stream of publications, including several million copies of a multivolumed *Studies in the Scriptures*. Attention was focused on 1914 as the year when "the kingdoms of this world" will be brought to an end, and "the full establishment of the Kingdom of God will be accomplished." [27] When the year passed without the expected heavenly intervention, a re-examination of Scripture disclosed that it was Christ's return "in spirit" that had taken place in 1914, and that this was but a prelude to his visible return to lead the righteous into battle against the hosts of evil. This imminent Armageddon would mark the beginning of the millennium.

[26] Stroup, *Jehovah's Witnesses*, 4, 6.
[27] *Jehovah's Witnesses in the Divine Purpose* (Brooklyn, 1959), 55.

When Pastor Russell died in 1916 his following was not large, numbering not many more than 15,000, but positions of leadership in the Society were sufficiently coveted to occasion a severe struggle for power. The victor was Joseph Franklin ("Judge") Rutherford (1869–1942), legal counsel of the Society and Russell's attorney in his divorce proceedings and in his imbroglio over the sale of "miracle wheat." Judge Rutherford injected new life into the Society, substituted his writings for those of Pastor Russell, popularized the slogan "Millions now living will never die," [28] introduced the name "Jehovah's Witnesses" (1931), and equipped the Witnesses with phonographs so that they could utilize transcriptions of his talks in their house-to-house calls. As before it was a personality-centered operation, with Judge Rutherford replacing Pastor Russell as the authoritative teacher and leader. All this was changed when Rutherford died in 1942. This time there was no "palace intrigue," no struggle for control, for a collective leadership took over and the "personality cult" was eliminated.[29] A board of directors assumed control with Nathan H. Knorr (b. 1903) as president. Unsigned pronouncements replaced the writings of Judge Rutherford, and the portable phonographs disappeared. Henceforth the Witnesses were to be trained to do their own talking instead of relying on the transcribed voice of a leader.[30]

With Rutherford's death, Jehovah's Witnesses entered the period of their greatest growth. Activity was stepped up both at home and abroad. During the five years from 1942 to 1947 in the midst of World War II the worldwide membership almost doubled, increasing from 115,240 to 207,552; and the rate of growth was even greater during the next five years, with the total membership reaching 456,265 in 1952. By 1960 the number of Witnesses throughout the world was nearly one million, with the United States accounting for slightly more than one-quarter of the total.[31]

The message, elaborated successively by Pastor Russell, Judge Rutherford, and the directorate headed by Nathan Knorr, was calculated to appeal to the multiple resentments of those who are euphemistically described as the "culturally deprived." The central contention was that Satan's power is wielded through "the religious, commercial, and political

[28] This was the title of one of his early publications (1920).
[29] Marley Cole, *Jehovah's Witnesses*, 107–8.
[30] *Ibid.*, 211–12.
[31] *Ibid.*, 212. For detailed statistics, see pp. 220–28.

combine" which is united in oppressing the righteous.[32] These three elements in society are so intimately linked that each does the bidding of the others. All churches and religious organizations are "tools of Satan" and are utilized by the clergy as a means of securing cash income. The clergy both support and are supported by the proud and arrogant commercial class which dominates, subjugates, and exploits the poor. The wealthy in turn are protected by the governments of the world, all of which are equally wicked since they are ruled by Satan. The righteous, however, are not without hope, for the evils of the world are soon to be rectified at the battle of Armageddon when the forces of Jehovah led by Jesus will defeat the hosts of Satan; and Jesus, with the living Witnesses and the resurrected righteous among the dead, will reign for one thousand years.

While few of the Holiness, Pentecostal, and millenarian groups were as direct or as comprehensive in their appeal to the frustrated and the resentful as Jehovah's Witnesses, they all tended to thrive among those who for one reason or another felt either alienated or disinherited. And since this was a common feeling among many mid-twentieth-century Americans, these diverse expressions of disaffection—including the related Fundamentalist groups—represented a combined membership in 1960 of almost 8,500,000 persons.

The Negro churches

In many ways Negro religious life reflected the patterns and trends that prevailed in the general religious life of the nation. Most of the larger "white" denominations had Negro members. This was true of the American Baptist Churches, the United Methodist Church, the two major Presbyterian churches, the Protestant Episcopal Church, the Roman Catholic Church, and the United Church of Christ. Some of these Negro members belonged to predominantly white congregations, but most were in separate Negro congregations.[33] These "integrated" churches, however,

32 See Stroup, *Jehovah's Witnesses*, 155–61.

33 On the congregational level the separation could be regarded as a natural grouping because of residential patterns, but the Methodists and Presbyterians carried the separation a step further by grouping Negro congregations in separate ecclesiastical units. In 1964, however, the Methodist Church made provision for the gradual liquidation of its segregated "Central Jurisdiction," and in 1967 the last Negro presbytery of the United Presbyterian Church was dismantled.

accounted for only a small fraction of Negro church membership, for the overwhelming proportion of Negroes belonged to Negro denominations. Outwardly these denominations closely resembled the churches of the white majority. Of the eleven million members of Negro denominations in 1960 (up from three million in 1900), slightly more than 70 per cent were Baptists and 22 per cent were Methodists. But this outward resemblance was somewhat deceptive.

As a result of social forces to which Negroes were subjected, a separate Negro world had been created. The Negro's church was partly the product of this segregated society with a distinctive life of its own.[34] The worship featured a variety of liturgical innovations designed to encourage group participation. The theology stressed both the consolations of heaven and the this-worldly promise of a near-approaching Day of Jubilee. Congregational singing was deeply moving. Both the emotional pitch of the services and their eschatological focus found expression in the "spirituals" which have been called the most original and enduring contribution of the Negro church.[35] With most avenues of social expression cut off and with the ministry one of the few professions open to the Negro, the church assumed an importance that has seldom been duplicated among other groups.[36] Since there was little opportunity elsewhere for a Negro to gain recognition and to exercise authority, there often was a scramble for leadership and a tendency for the churches to become personal fiefs of the pastor. This highly competitive situation led to numerous schisms, withdrawals, and reorganizations. Negro Methodists splintered into at least eight different denominational bodies. Baptist strength among the Negroes is explained at least in part by the ease with which an individual pastor could pursue an independent course, but the Baptists suffered a major denominational schism in 1917 when the National Baptist Conven-

[34] See C. G. Woodson, *The History of the Negro Church* (Washington, D.C., 1945), E. F. Frazier, *The Negro Church in America* (N.Y., 1974), B. E. Mays and J. W. Nicholson, *The Negro's Church* (N.Y., 1933), and H. V. Richardson, *Dark Glory* (N.Y., 1947). For the ambivalent relationship to the larger American community, see G. S. Wilmore, *Black Religion and Black Radicalism* (N.Y., 1972) and L. I. Sweet, *Black Images of America* (N.Y., 1976).

[35] See Howard Thurman, *The Negro Spiritual Speaks of Life and Death* (N.Y., 1947), and D. J. Epstein, *Sinful Tunes and Spirituals: Black Folk Music to the Civil War* (Champaign, Ill., 1977).

[36] The importance of the church in the Negro community was reflected in the fact that by the 1930's a larger proportion of Negroes were church members than was true of members of the white population.

tion split into two rival organizations—the National Baptist Convention, Inc. and the National Baptist Convention of America. Other schisms resulted in the short-lived New Era Baptist Convention and in a larger and enduring Progressive National Baptist Convention.

The large-scale movement of Negro population into the major industrial centers of the nation, which began during World War I and continued thereafter at a steadily mounting tempo, introduced marked changes into Negro church life. Many of the urban churches became much more formal and restrained. The emotionalism of earlier days declined, "spirituals" were sung less frequently, the itinerant evangelist was less prominent, and preaching gave less emphasis to otherworldly aspects of the faith. Attention was increasingly devoted to advancing the interests of the Negro through practical action. The Supreme Court decision of 1954, which put an end to the "separate but equal" doctrine in public education, triggered a massive civil rights movement in which the Negro churches played a prominent role. A spectacular illustration of this was the bus boycott in Montgomery, Alabama, in 1955–56, which was led by the local Negro clergy and which made Martin Luther King, Jr., a national figure. Subsequent "freedom rides" to eliminate discrimination in interstate travel, "sit-ins" and "demonstrations" to obtain equal access to public accommodations, and voter registration drives, were usually planned and organized in the Negro churches and often led by their pastors.

The growing decorum and "worldliness" of many of the city churches produced much the same reaction among some of the new Negro urban dwellers as had occurred among segments of the white population. Tiny store-front churches, which reproduced the intimacy and informality of the rural churches, multiplied, and the Holiness and Pentecostal movements found ready recruits among those Negroes who looked back with nostalgia to the uninhibited emotionalism of their childhood religious experience. A whole cluster of new Negro denominations emerged—the Church of God in Christ, Christ's Sanctified Holy Church, Church of the Living God, House of the Lord, Apostolic Over-coming Holy Church of God, Fire-Baptized Holiness Church of God, Triumph the Church and Kingdom of God, Church of Our Lord Jesus Christ of the Apostolic Faith, Bible Way Churches of Our Lord Jesus Christ, Kodesh Church of Immanuel, and Free Christian Zion Church of Christ. Most of these groups were small, some almost miniscule in membership, but taken together they had almost 750,000 adherents in 1960. The Church of God in Christ accounted for half this total. Founded in 1897 with a stress on sanctification and then adding an emphasis on the gift of tongues, the Church of God in Christ experienced rapid growth after 1936, numbering 392,635 members in 1960.

Like urban whites who toyed with the teachings of Psychiana, the Rosicrucians, the "Mighty I Am," and Zen Buddhism, Negroes also developed exotic cults in the urban environment.[37] The House of Prayer for All Nations of Bishop "Sweet Daddy" Grace was a product of the depression years which gained added income from the sale of Daddy Grace coffee, Daddy Grace cold cream, and Daddy Grace toothpaste. Although Daddy had given God a vacation, the faithful were assured they need not despair, for they could still be saved by grace—Daddy Grace. The Peace Mission of Father Divine was equally bizarre for he claimed to be God and his followers were "angels." In 1932 he established "heavens" in Harlem where he fed thousands. Later Philadelphia became a major center. After World War II, the Peace Mission lost much of its momentum. Both Daddy Grace and Father Divine emphasized nonracial brotherhood, but other movements took an opposite tack. The "Black Jews" of W. S. Crowdy, F. S. Cherry, and W. A. Matthew, for example, stressed Negro separateness and superiority. A similar view was represented by Marcus Garvey's "Black Nationalists" who appealed to "the God of Africa," and Drew Ali's "Moorish Americans" who found their inspiration in the Koran. In the 1960's the "Black Muslims" of Elijah Muhammed's Islam, which blended emphases derived from Garvey and Drew Ali, was reported to be the fastest growing movement among Negroes in America.[38] This seemed an overenthusiastic verdict until the brief but charismatic leadership of Malcolm X (1925–65) and the conversion of Cassius Clay (Muhammad Ali) gave major impetus to the Muslims. Overenthusiastic or not, the comment called attention to unusual ferment in the urban Negro community, and Muslim growth pointed to a forthcoming repudiation of "Negro" and adoption of "Black" as the proper term of identification.

[37] See A. H. Fauset, *Black Gods of the Metropolis* (Phila., 1971).
[38] C. E. Lincoln, *The Black Muslims* (Boston, 1961), 4. See also Malcolm Little, *Autobiography of Malcolm X* (N.Y., 1965). Wallace Deen Muhammad, assuming leadership on the death of his father, Elijah Muhammad, in 1975, gave the Nation of Islam both a new direction and in 1980 a new name, American Muslim Mission. By 1980 membership now including whites and other races had doubled, debts had been paid off, and democratic control established.

The mid-twentieth-century religious profile

An accurate assessment of the balance of religious forces in the United States is difficult to make. It is clear that several shifts took place during the first half of the twentieth century, but available statistics are not always comparable. As officially reported, Protestant church membership in 1960 was approximately 64,000,000, the Roman Catholic total was 42,000,000, the number of Jews was 5,500,000, and the Eastern Orthodox total was roughly 2,650,000. But the Roman Catholic figure included baptized infants, while the Protestant statistics generally did not.[39] The Jewish and Eastern Orthodox figures, on the other hand, tended to be estimates of total ethnic or national groups rather than of specific religious affiliation.

Within Protestantism significant shifts in numerical strength took place during the post-World War I period. Methodists increased from 7,600,000 to 13,150,000 between 1916 and 1960, but were displaced as the largest Protestant grouping by the Baptists who had grown from 7,000,000 to 21,000,000. Lutherans surged forward from 2,500,000 to 8,000,000 to become the third largest Protestant group. Presbyterians and Reformed slipped to fourth place with a gain from 2,800,000 to 4,800,000. The growth of the Protestant Episcopal Church from 1,100,000 to 3,300,000 was somewhat deceptive, for the first figure was communicant membership while the second was the total number of baptized. The merger of the Congregational Christian Churches with the Evangelical and Reformed Church put the United Church of Christ in sixth place with 2,200,000 members in 1960. The related Churches of Christ (from 300,000 to 2,100,000) and Disciples of Christ (from 450,000 to

---

[39] Information supplied by the U.S. Census Bureau and the American Institute of Public Opinion indicates that the Protestant–Roman Catholic membership figures give at least a rather accurate picture of proportionate strength. A Census Bureau study in 1958 reported that of 119,330,000 Americans fourteen years of age and older, 66.2 per cent (78,952,000) regarded themselves as Protestant, 25.7 per cent (30,669,000) regarded themselves as Roman Catholic, 3.2 per cent (3,868,000) regarded themselves as Jewish, 1.3 per cent (1,545,000) identified themselves with other faiths, while 3.6 per cent (4,300,000) claimed no religious preference or were not reported. The Protestant predominance was reduced to a rough conformity with official membership figures when active identification, as reflected in church attendance, was taken into account. A survey by the American Institute of Public Opinion in 1958 reported that 44 per cent (34,740,000) of those who considered themselves Protestant had attended church the preceding Sunday, while 74 per cent (22,700,000) of those who considered themselves Roman Catholic had attended.

1,600,000) were followed by a group which had only a tenuous relation-ship to Protestantism, the Latter-day Saints, or Mormons, which had grown in number from 450,000 to 1,600,000 during the years between 1916 and 1960.[40]

While interesting and illuminating in some respects, such a tradi-tional classification of the relative strength of various Protestant groupings serves to obscure one of the most significant shifts that was taking place in twentieth-century Protestantism. This was a shift that divided Protes-tantism into two or three loosely defined camps.

The traditional classification was largely based upon differences in polity and church government which had little relationship to the divisive issues of the twentieth century, for the latter were theologically and sociologically grounded in a way that by-passed the older distinctions. The traditional classification fails to give adequate weight, for example, to the 1,500,000 members of Holiness churches, the 1,500,000 members of Pentecostal bodies, and the 500,000 members of Adventist or Premillen-nialist groups. Moreover some of the smaller Baptist, Methodist, Presbyte-rian, and Reformed groups should more properly be classified as part of the 4,800,000 members of Fundamentalist denominations. And the Funda-mentalist total ought to be even larger to take into account many individual churches, such as the Park Street Congregational Church in Boston and the Tenth Street Presbyterian Church in Philadelphia, which held Fundamentalist views and actively supported Fundamentalist agen-cies.[41] What is needed in place of the traditional grouping of Protestants into denominational families is a classification that takes into account the actual realignment within American Protestantism.

The dominant Protestant group at mid-century was composed of those mildly "liberal" or "progressive" denominations affiliated with the National Council of Churches. Frequently referred to as "cooperative Protestantism," these bodies represented a constituency of some

[40] The long-established smaller religious groups met with varying success in the twentieth century. The Mennonites doubled their membership in the 1916–1960 period (from 80,000 to 160,000), as did the Church of the Brethren (100,000 to 200,000). The rapid growth of Christian Science ended about 1940, after having tripled in number of churches during the preceding three decades. Quakers, Unitarians, and Universalists, on the other hand, had steadily declined during the first forty years of the century, but each of them made small but significant recoveries after World War II—with respective memberships of 125,000; 100,000; and 70,000 in 1960.

[41] Their respective pastors, Harold J. Ockenga (b. 1905) and Donald Grey Barnhouse (1895–1960), were prominent Fundamentalist leaders.

37,000,000 members. Approximately 24,000,000 conservative Protestants were "non-cooperative" in the sense that they were not affiliated with the National Council of Churches.[42] These included such major groups as the Southern Baptists with over 10,000,000 members, and almost 5,000,000 Lutherans belonging to the American Lutheran Church and the Lutheran Church—Missouri Synod. In addition there were 8,500,000 "disaffected Protestants," members of Fundamentalist, Adventist, Holiness, and Pentecostal churches. This classification does not produce neat packages, for it does not take into account the fracturing of Protestantism along racial lines. Nor do the formal figures give any hint that "disaffected Protestantism," having given up hope of gaining control of the major denominations of "cooperative Protestantism," continued to exhibit astonishing vitality during the 1930's and 1940's and was succeeding in penetrating old-line denominations at the grass-roots level.[43] Many individuals and congregations grouped with "cooperative Protestantism" actually were providing major support for the institutions of the "disaffected." Thus one may say that by mid-century there was roughly an even division numerically between liberal and conservative (or "evangelical") Protestants.

The emergence of Judaism and Eastern Orthodox Christianity as prominent components of an American religious scene that was becoming ever more multiform and diverse has been discussed in some detail. Major Protestant and Roman Catholic developments during the period that followed World War I, however, were more complicated and need further attention before the bubbling ferment affecting all religious groups in the 1960's can be assessed.

[42] Some did have their own cooperative organizations, such as the National Association of Evangelicals, the smaller American Council of Churches, and a variety of cooperative missionary, evangelistic, educational, and publishing agencies. See Joel A. Carpenter, "Fundamentalist Institutions and the Rise of Evangelical Protestantism, 1929–1942," *Church History*, XLIX (1980), 62–75.

[43] Ibid., 65–68.

XIV

Protestantism's Years of Drift and Indecision

For American Protestantism, World War I marked the end of an era. Kenneth Scott Latourette observed that "Protestant Christianity had entered the nineteenth century on a rising tide" and noted that it had come to the end of the century "on a rapidly ascending curve." [1] The momentum of almost two hundred years of vigorous advance had not yet been spent, and the first years of the new century found Protestantism at the peak of its apparent strength and influence. Churches were crowded, financial support was generous, programs were proliferating, and a host of good causes elicited eager and ardent devotion. It was a time of unusual moral idealism generated in part by a widespread determination among church members to "win the world for Christ in this generation." By the time Warren G. Harding was installed in the White House, however, much of the contagious enthusiasm exhibited by the churches in the prewar years had begun to be dissipated. By 1925 the usual indices of institutional health—church attendance, Sunday school enrollment, missionary giving—showed a downward trend that was to continue for at least a decade. Although not

[1] *A History of the Expansion of Christianity* (N.Y., 1937–45), IV, 458, VI, 5.

many at the time were aware that the forward thrust had been seriously blunted, it is clear in retrospect that by the middle 1920's an ebb tide had set in.[2]

The transitional years

The blunting of the long Protestant advance was foreshadowed by the fate of the Interchurch World Movement of 1919 and 1920. This was an ambitious enterprise, launched with a flourish of trumpets, that was designed to push to rapid completion the task of Christianizing the world, a Christianizing that was defined in terms of "the complete evangelization of all of life." The major Protestant denominations cooperated to make a detailed survey of urgent needs both at home and abroad, to chart a common strategy for meeting them, to allocate specific responsibilities to the different mission boards, and then, through a concerted campaign patterned after the great wartime drives for funds, to secure the necessary financial resources to carry out the plans.[3] Each denomination had its own financial goal and its own "movement" or campaign for funds, and these coordinated drives were to be supplemented by a general campaign which would tap the supposedly vast potential support of public-spirited citizens who could not be reached through denominational channels. At first a goal of $300 million was suggested, then $500 million, and the final figure was one billion dollars, with $335 million to be raised initially. Although large sums were raised by the participating denominations,[4] the joint cam-

---

[2] See Robert Handy, "The American Religious Depression, 1925–35," *Church History*, XXIX (1960), 2–16. "Depression" may be too strong a word to describe the plight of the churches; "recession" would be better. While church attendance, Sunday school enrollment, and missionary giving declined, the decline was not precipitate. The advance was slowed, then halted, but there was no shattering "crash." Vigorous activity continued, and up to 1930 there was an increase in the amount spent on new church buildings. With few exceptions church members and clergy remained confident and optimistic. Statistical trends, of course, become evident only in retrospect, and the onset of the depression in 1930 may have contributed to a delayed response to the loss of momentum. Consequences of the economic depression were so overwhelming that other debilitating factors were obscured. Curiously gains being made by "fringe" churches were simply ignored.

[3] For the objectives of the Movement, see H. W. Schneider, *Religion in the Twentieth Century*, 95ff. The scope of concern is indicated by a survey to ascertain "all the facts about the religious, social, moral, physical, and economic environments through the world." D. B. Meyer, *The Protestant Search for Political Realism*, 9. The full story is told by Eldon Ernst, *Moment of Truth for Protestant America* (Missoula, Montana, 1974).

[4] The New World Movement of the Northern Baptists was the most successful on the basis of per capita giving, but only half the $100,000,000 goal was raised. The

paign was a costly and dismal failure which left the denominational mission boards saddled with debts incurred in the cooperative phases of the endeavor. But this was only half the story. Confident that the goals would be reached, the mission boards had overextended their commitments. Programs were expanded, new projects undertaken, and additional personnel employed. When the anticipated funds were not forthcoming, drastic and painful retrenchments had to be made.

The failure of the Interchurch World Movement can be attributed in part to the economic recession of 1920–22. Prospects for success may also have been blighted by the report of the Movement's commission of inquiry which surveyed the needs of the steelworkers and their families. The inquiry coincided with the 1919 strike of the steelworkers, which sought the elimination of the twelve-hour day and the seven-day week. The sympathetic tenor of the commission's report was not calculated to win the support of the wealthy public-spirited citizens, which was one of the objectives of the campaign. Furthermore, the report was issued at a time when the Boston police strike had created widespread fear of anarchy and when the anti-Red hysteria associated with the activities of A. Mitchell Palmer, Wilson's Attorney-General, was fostering intense antilabor sentiment. But there were more deep-seated reasons for the failure of the Interchurch World Movement. A marked shift in the mood of the American people was perhaps the most important. Moreover, long smoldering tensions within Protestanism broke out into open conflict at the close of the war, diverting to internecine strife energies which might have been otherwise employed. And finally, Protestanism was beginning to reap the consequences of a long period of acculturation.

THE POSTWAR GENERATION. For two decades Protestants had been engaged in a series of crusades to refashion the face of America and to reshape the life of the world (see Chap. XII). The war itself was but the greatest of these crusades, enlisting as it did the idealism generated by the churches in "a war to end war" and to "make the world safe for democracy." The United States had entered the conflict with banners flying, but it proved to be a dirty unheroic war which few participants remembered with anything but distaste. The peace proved equally disap-

---

Methodists, with five times as many members, raised the largest total amount. The much more modest $40,000,000 goal of the Methodist Centenary Movement had been set before the interdenominational effort had been fully elaborated, and it was far exceeded, with more than $100,000,000 being subscribed. But in the end the Methodists had many unpaid pledges and soured hopes.

pointing. Little idealism was apparent in the treaty negotiations at Versailles, and Woodrow Wilson was pilloried at home as a fool trapped by the wily diplomats of Europe. Harding's call for a "return to normalcy," a summons to put aside idealistic crusades and far-flung responsibilities, mirrored the mood of a tired and disenchanted people. Small wonder, in this climate of opinion, that the new crusade envisioned in the Interchurch World Movement met with so disappointing a response.

The postwar generation, however, was suffering from a more severe malady than mere weariness with crusades. Nor was the disenchantment which stemmed from the machinations of the diplomats at Versailles sufficient to account for the waning of idealism. The latter was more largely the product of a profound revolution in morals. Wars tend to be followed by a breakdown in public and private morality, and World War I was no exception. For many people the war was a liberating experience. Young men were uprooted and introduced for the first time to the amoral standards of army life. Women were drawn from their homes to engage in war work. The movement of population into the cities was accelerated. Each of these represented a break with accustomed patterns of life. But the war also imposed its own restrictive discipline. Those at home were driven to strenuous exertion by the effort to win the war, and those in the army were subjected to the unfamiliar and unpleasant regimentation of military life. From this perspective, it was the end of the war that brought a welcome release from the stern requirements of duty and evoked a heartfelt desire to relax and enjoy the satisfactions of a less disciplined existence. This mood, quite apart from the brutalizing effect of war, was normal for a postwar period. Parallels in other postwar epochs can be found for the scandals of the Harding administration and the heedless preoccupation of the business community with making "a fast buck." But these were symptoms only of a widespread moral laxity, a laxity that was mostly covert and did not represent an open flouting of accepted standards of morality. The more serious malady was quite different in character, venting itself in a candid and undisguised revolt which bluntly attacked the whole system of traditional manners and morals.

The revolution in morals of the 1920's is most frequently depicted in terms of "flaming youth" and the "jazz age," of "speakeasies" and "gang wars," of the gay antics of Jimmy Walker in New York and the crude boasts of Big Bill Thompson in Chicago. But it was much more than this. It was a revolution that affected all classes of society and tore people loose from their old moorings. Its roots are extraordinarily difficult to assess. As William E. Leuchtenburg has pointed out, historians have given the revolution almost no attention,[5] and others have naïvely attributed it almost solely to the breakdown of law enforcement occasioned by prohibition. It can be seen in part as an aftermath of war, but its fundamental rootage was much more remote. Technological advance, of course, had multiplied material satisfactions and weakened religious sanctions, and the booming prosperity of the twenties was a heady experience. The "status revolution" which undercut the authority of those who had traditionally set the moral standards—the "professional" classes (ministers, lawyers, teachers), the "rural gentry," and the "urban patricians"—was also involved. And not least in importance was the erosion of family solidarity and authority, which was one of the consequences of the increasing urbanization of American society and the growing emancipation of women. But it was the popular appropriation of insights derived from the teachings of such men as John Dewey and Sigmund Freud that contributed as much to the new hedonism as anything else. "Self-expression" and "self-fulfilment" became magic words, and anything that smacked of "repression" was regarded as a threat to the "psyche." While these tags of popular understanding distorted carefully devised philosophies, they had the effect of giving a supposedly scientific imprimatur to self-indulgence.

The major prophets of the moral revolt were literary figures—Theodore Dreiser, Sinclair Lewis, H. L. Mencken, George Jean Nathan, F. Scott Fitzgerald, and a host of other luminaries. Their rebellion was full of "sound and fury" and took the form of a frontal attack on what they called America's "puritanism"—an epithet for anything that interfered with the new freedom. Religion was dismissed as antiquated, false, and absurd—a blend of prudery, cant, and sanctimoniousness from which individuals must emancipate themselves if their spirits were not to be suffocated. To Joseph Wood Krutch, "sin" and "love" were empty words, and he insisted that "all the capital letters in the composing-room cannot make the words more than that which they have become—shadows, as essentially unreal as some of the theological dogmas which have been completely forgotten." [6] Concerned with the individual rather than with society, with private rather

[5] *The Perils of Prosperity, 1914–32* (Chicago, 1958), 290.
[6] *The Modern Temper: A Study and a Confession* (N.Y., 1929), 191–92.

than public experience, these writers had no interest in social reform. "Doing good" was either a dull business or, as Mencken insisted, "in bad taste." "The great problems of the world—social, political, economic, and theological—do not concern me in the slightest," wrote George Jean Nathan.

> If all the Armenians were to be killed tomorrow and if half of Russia were to starve to death the day after, it would not matter to me in the least. What concerns me alone is myself, and the interests of a few close friends. For all I care the rest of the world may go to hell at today's sunset.[7]

Not all were as blunt and callous as Nathan, but social nihilism was a fundamental theme of the *avant garde* novelists and poets. Even the care with which most of them avoided adjectives and sought to make do with unadorned nouns and verbs was part of a studied and self-conscious rejection of all idealistic sentiment.

While the cynical and deeply pessimistic hedonism of the novelists and poets and literary critics was not without influence, the revolution in morals found much more temperate and prosaic expression in the population as a whole. Spurred on by handbooks of popular psychology and carried forward in home and classroom, the revolution produced a less sin-ridden and more self-indulgent people. But, unlike the despair of the "intellectuals," the popular mood of "the booming twenties" was optimistic and affirmative, and the new freedom was geared to an increasingly undisciplined pursuit of more tangible forms of personal fulfillment. Whereas the intellectuals had lost faith in progress, the great mass of Americans were content to believe that the promises of the past had become the realities of the present. Here the waning of idealism had complacency, and even smugness, as its hallmark, and it manifested itself in the demise of the progressive movement. The only alarm was that directed against those who seemed to threaten the existing order.

In 1912 progressivism, with its zeal for reform, had been triumphant. In a three-cornered race, Taft had been far outdistanced by both his progressive rivals—Woodrow Wilson and Teddy Roosevelt. Moreover, Eugene Debs, the Socialist candidate, had amassed almost a million votes. Four years later Wilson and Hughes, who were almost equally progressive in outlook, had vied for the White House. But in 1920 progressivism was

[7] Quoted in Leuchtenburg, *The Perils of Prosperity*, 150.

buried under the Harding landslide, and only a remnant could be resurrected by the LaFollette-Wheeler banner in the 1924 campaign.

The churches were not unaffected by this shift in mood of the American people. The demise of progressivism was accompanied by the decline of the social gospel which in prewar years had given American Protestantism much of its verve and contagious enthusiasm. As a typical social gospel project, the Interchurch World Movement had been one of the first casualties of the fading idealism implicit in the new morality. It is true that interest in social Christianity survived in some circles, just as there were still progressives to be found, but it was mostly confined to clerical ranks and had ceased to be important as a powerful ferment in the life of the churches. The clergymen who continued to issue social pronouncements were generals with few troops. They were tolerated by their congregations, but their summons to action sparked little response.[8] Even among the clergy much of the social concern was diverted into a pacifist crusade. Shamed and humiliated by the role of many churchmen in propagating hatred during World War I [9] and revolted by the horrors of trench warfare, a large percentage of the clergy vowed that the church should not bless war again and that they would neither personally support nor participate in any future conflict.

THE FUNDAMENTALIST CONTROVERSY. If the Protestant advance was blunted by the shifting mood of the American people, it also was impeded by an intramural conflict which broke out in 1920 between two hostile and embattled factions within Protestantism. The protagonists were the "Liberals," or "Modernists," who sought to adjust the inherited faith to the new intellectual climate (see pp. 269–78), and the "Fundamentalists," who insisted that the old ways of stating the faith must be preserved unimpaired.[10]

[8] A failure to make this distinction weakens Robert M. Miller's otherwise cogent demonstration of a continuing interest in social Christianity in his *American Protestantism and Social Issues, 1919–1939* (Chapel Hill, N.C., 1958). See also Donald B. Meyer, *The Protestant Search for Political Realism, 1919–1941* (Berkeley, Calif., 1960).

[9] See R. H. Abrams, *Preachers Present Arms* (N.Y., 1933), as qualified by J. F. Piper, "The Social Policy of the Federal Council of the Churches of Christ," Duke University Ph.D. thesis (Durham, 1964).

[10] Stewart G. Cole, *The History of Fundamentalism* (N.Y., 1931) is an early account of the controversy. See also G. M. Marsden, *Fundamentalism and American Culture: The Shaping of Twentieth-Century Evangelicalism, 1870–1925* (N.Y., 1980), E. R. Sandeen, *The Roots of Fundamentalism* (Chicago, 1970), and T. P. Weber, *Living in the Shadow of the Second Coming: America Premillennialism, 1875–1925* (N.Y., 1979).

Theological tension, of course, had been developing over a long period of time, but it had subsided after the heresy trials of the latter years of the nineteenth century. A common enthusiasm for reform made it possible to subordinate theological differences and to gloss over divergent theological positions with pious ambiguities.[11] Almost every prominent professional evangelist regarded himself as being engaged, through his revivals, in a work of social reformation. A few, like B. Fay Mills, went all the way with the social gospel. Others, like Sam Jones, Milan B. Williams, Burke Culpepper, William E. Biederwolf, and Rodney "Gypsy" Smith, limited themselves to "civic reform" and occasionally stressed the "social service" motif. And some, like J. Wilbur Chapman, placed primary stress on personal morality. But whatever their emphasis, they tended to be welcomed as allies in the progressive movement for human betterment and were drawn unwittingly into its orbit.[12] And they, in turn, tended to mute their points of theological dissent.

Not everyone, to be sure, was bemused by this happy state of affairs. For the first time since Finney's day, a significant opposition to mass revivalism was beginning to develop within evangelical Protestantism. Even among conservatives doubts were arising as to the effectiveness of the old techniques. In 1899 George E. Horr (1856–1927), a Baptist editor, pointed out that Dwight L. Moody had acknowledged that the day of great "hippodrome" services was drawing to a close. The following year George F. Pentecost (1843–1920) abandoned his career as an itinerant evangelist, having become convinced that conversions should be obtained by patient pastoral work and not in "after meetings" where "indiscriminate 'workers' with a few texts of Scripture" seek to "railroad inquirers" into hasty and shallow decisions. This growing disenchantment with revivalism was bound to create tension, but it was the more ardent "dispensationalists" (see pp. 284–85) within the revivalist camp who were primarily responsible for introducing discord into the general harmony.

Unlike other professional evangelists, the "dispensationalists" had their own scheme of reform which reflected the general expectancy and enthusiasm of the time, a scheme expressed in terms of their premillennial

[11] See McLoughlin, *Modern Revivalism*, 350, 353–54, 361–63, 386–87, 393, 397, 402, 411.

[12] Biederwolf and Gypsy Smith, for example, were active in the Men and Religion Forward Movement of 1911–14, which had liberal leadership and a strong social service orientation.

views. Furthermore, they were not of a mind to compromise their convictions by glossing over theological differences. In 1905 Amzi C. Dixon (1854–1925), shortly to become minister of the Moody Church in Chicago, published a book in which he announced that there could be no reconciliation between science and religion any more than socialism and free enterprise could be reconciled. The duty of the church, he insisted, was to convert individuals, to keep out of politics, and to remember that there could be no true revival that was not led by "believers in the inspiration and infallible authority of the Word of God." [13] It was, however, in reaction to the intransigence of Reuben A. Torrey (1856–1928), superintendent of the Moody Bible Institute in Chicago, that the issue was fully joined.

On Moody's death, Torrey had laid claim to his mantle and had embarked on a worldwide series of revival campaigns. Late in 1905 Charles S. MacFarland (1866–1956), a Congregational pastor who had spent two summers investigating the impact of Torrey's evangelistic work in the British Isles, reported that representatives of every school of thought in Britain believed that on the whole Torrey's influence had been harmful. They objected particularly to Torrey's intemperate denunciations of those who differed from him theologically, to the artificial "machinery" of his campaigns, and to his excessive commercialism. Within a few months after the publication of MacFarland's report, ministers of various denominations in America were urging churches to dissociate themselves from Torrey's campaigns.

In response to this criticism, Torrey and Dixon launched a vigorous counterattack which culminated in 1910–15 with the publication of 12 small volumes entitled *The Fundamentals*, which sought to reduce the Christian faith to clear essentials. These brief treatises were written by various men but were edited by Dixon and Torrey, and their distribution was financed by two wealthy residents of Los Angeles, Milton and Lyman Stewart. They were sent free of charge "to every pastor, evangelist, missionary, theological student, Sunday school superintendent, Y.M.C.A. and Y.W.C.A. secretary" whose address could be obtained, and eventually three million copies were distributed.[14] It is likely that serious strife would

[13] McLoughlin, *Modern Revivalism*, 348, 352–53.
[14] *Ibid.*, 352, 370. N. F. Furniss, *The Fundamentalist Controversy*, 12. Charges that fright among wealthy laymen aroused by radical social views accounts for Fundamentalist financial support at this time are unfair.

have been provoked then had not the agitation been interrupted by the outbreak of World War I.

The career of Billy Sunday (1862–1935)—the professional baseball player turned evangelist, whose antics in the pulpit did more than anything else to discredit revivalism—bridged the prewar and postwar periods.[15] In many ways he was a transitional figure, whose early popularity was derived in part from the alacrity with which he jumped on the bandwagon of civic reform and moral uplift, and who then rode to fame on the crest of the wave of reaction against the social gospel. Even during the early phase of his career, his denunciations of liberal theology were frequent and coarse. He had no use for the "bastard theory of evolution" or for the "deodorized and disinfected sermons" of "hireling ministers" who gave up the old faith to please their liberal parishioners. Furthermore, he complained of those who try to "make a religion out of social service with Jesus Christ left out," noting that this was why the Men and Religion Forward Movement was "a lamentable failure." He exhibited nonetheless a marked ability to blend his "old-time religion" with the progressive emphasis on reform. He advertised his revivals as "civic clean-ups" which would make any town a better place in which to live. He appropriated many of the indictments leveled by the "muckrakers," and this led many progressives and social gospelers to believe that he was buttressing their cause. Even his vulgarity and "vaudeville stunts" were defended as necessary means of reaching the masses. One contemporary observer was confident that "it is as a reformer that Mr. Sunday has warmed the hearts of all who desire better things." His ideas of reform, however, turned out to be extremely limited and did not extend much beyond the suppression of the liquor traffic.[16]

Sunday was quick to respond to changing climates of opinion. From the beginning he had preached a masculine "muscular" Christianity which equated salvation with decency and manliness ("the man who has real, rich, red blood in his veins instead of pink tea and ice water"). Under the excitement of war this masculine Christianity was transformed into a barnstorming, tub-thumping "100 per cent Americanism" which insisted that "Christianity and patriotism are synomous terms" just as "hell and

---

[15] See W. G. McLoughlin, Jr., *Billy Sunday Was His Real Name* (Chicago, 1955), and *Modern Revivalism*, 400–54.

[16] McLoughlin, *Modern Revivalism*, 399, 410–12, 429, 437.

traitors are synonomous." Soon he was attributing German atrocities to the baneful influence of biblical criticism upon the German people. And when labor unrest developed at the close of hostilities, he was in full cry after all foreign-inspired, godless social radicalism.

In spite of Billy Sunday's diatribes, most prominent Protestant leaders at the end of the war believed that the struggle to win acceptance for new ways of understanding the Christian faith had been won, and they were prepared to resume the humanitarian advance of the prewar years.[17] But Billy Sunday was demonstrating how hostile sentiment could be aroused in the postwar climate. The American people were in no mood for any further tampering with the social order, and it was easy to demonstrate to the satisfaction of many that "modernism" and "communism" were but reverse sides of the same coin.

Perhaps the decisive factor in thrusting the controversy into public attention was the championship of the Fundamentalist cause by William Jennings Bryan, the "peerless leader" of the old populist element in the Democratic party. When Bryan entered the fray in 1920, he was able to claim a national audience and to use his magic voice and moving rhetoric to transform isolated protests into a more or less unified crusade. Soon every denomination was embroiled in conflict, with the initial attack being directed against the Interchurch World Movement and its denominational counterparts. This was followed by strenuous efforts to ferret out evidence of heresy in every area of church life and by insistent demands that remedial action be taken to guarantee doctrinal orthodoxy. Harry Emerson Fosdick (1878–1969), a Baptist preacher filling the pulpit of the First Presbyterian Church of New York City, added fuel to the flames in 1922 when, dismayed by the demoralizing effects of the Fundamentalist attacks which he had observed on a visit to the mission fields of Asia, he seemed to fling down the gauntlet in a sermon entitled, "Shall the Fundamentalists Win?"

The qualifying phrase describing the Fundamentalist movement as a "more or less" unified crusade is important, for it did embrace diverse elements. Thus far the gathering disaffection has been depicted almost wholly in terms of the Bible School "dispensationalists" who sought to detect heresy by a standardized summary of key points of faith (see p. 285),

[17] For the eager enthusiasm of church leaders, see Meyer, *Protestant Search for Political Realism*, 12–13.

with its stress on the verbal inerrancy of Scripture (including the Genesis account of creation) and the premillennial return of Christ, as the standard of orthodoxy. But this was initially a fringe position. The movement derived much of its strength at the outset from men who stood more squarely within the traditional life of the churches.[18]

Curtis Lee Laws (1868–1946), Baptist editor of the *Watchman-Examiner,* who coined the label "Fundamentalist" in 1920 to designate those who were prepared to battle for the "fundamentals" of the faith, was associated with a large body of genuine "conservatives," whose concern was to conserve and defend the integrity and continuity of the Christian faith. The key issue, as these moderate Fundamentalists saw it, was the authority of the Bible, for Protestantism historically claimed the authority of Scripture for the whole structure of its thought. While continuing to revere the Bible as a treasury of religious devotion, there had been a growing tendency in liberal circles to reject it as being in any sense normative. It was a suitable subject for historical study and useful for devotional purposes, but the canons of truth were to be found in religious experience. It was this tendency to forget that the Christian faith had any objective standard of truth which alarmed the conservatives. These men were far from obscurantist in their attitude toward modern knowledge. While they centered attention on the question of biblical authority, few of them wished to make an issue of evolution, biblical inerrancy, or premillennialism. They represented the type of reaction to the more extreme modernist tendencies that had long been present in Protestant seminaries. The views expressed by John A. Faulkner (1857–1931) at Drew Theological Seminary in *Modernism and the Christian Faith* (1921) and by Augustus Hopkins Strong (1836–1921), former president of Rochester Theological Seminary whose *Outlines of Systematic Theology* was widely used as a textbook in the more conservative seminaries, were typical of this broad current of concern.

Strong frankly accepted the doctrine of evolution and the methods of biblical criticism. "Neither evolution nor the higher criticism," he said, "has any terrors to one who regards them as parts of Christ's creating and educating process." The composite authorship of the Pentateuch and the existence of two Isaiahs did not disturb Strong. "Any honest Christian," he

[18] For this distinction, see the chapter by Norman H. Maring, "Conservative but Progressive," in *What God Hath Wrought,* ed. G. L. Guffin (Philadelphia, 1960), 17–28.

affirmed, ". . . has the right to interpret Jonah and Daniel as allegories rather than histories." The Bible, he insisted, is the record of a progressive revelation, "shaped in human molds and adapted to ordinary human intelligence." It is a "human composition," but it is also "God's Word," presenting "divine truth in human forms." The danger of historical criticism of the Bible, he declared, is not in the method itself but springs from the presuppositions of those who use it. "The 'historical method' of Scripture interpretation, as it-is often employed, ends without Christ because it begins without him." It makes the mistake of "treating Scripture as it would treat any unreligious or heathen literature" and ignores the fact that properly to interpret the Bible one must adopt a frankly confessional stance. The point is "not how man made the Scripture for himself, but how God made the Scripture through the imperfect agency of man." To abandon the Bible as the authoritative testimony to Christ and thus in a derivative sense the authoritative ground of faith, Strong contended, would be to cut the "taproot" and imperil the very existence of Protestantism.[19]

The moderate Fundamentalists, however, were quickly upstaged by more radical and noisy elements, whose quarrel seemed to be with almost every facet of modern life. Viewed from this perspective, Fundamentalism can best be understood as a phase of the rural-urban conflict, drawing its strength from the tendency of many who were swept into an urban environment to cling to the securities of their childhood. While this characterization does less than justice to the moderate wing of the movement, it does point up the fact that in many ways Fundamentalism was as much the product of a cultural as a religious concern. It is significant that it arose among rural-oriented people in the cities before it penetrated the small towns and villages of the countryside. Furthermore, the mores which were emphasized as indispensable to the Christian life had, in the words of H. Richard Niebuhr, "at least as little relation to the New Testament and as much connection with social custom" as did those aspects of behavior which were condemned, while the cosmological and biological notions which were stressed as integral to the gospel were equally culturally conditioned.[20] Fundamentalist sentiment also was not unrelated to the sweeping tide of hyperpatriotism which was so conspicu-

[19] *Outlines of Systematic Theology* (Philadelphia, 1903), ix, 55–62. See also Strong's *Tour of Missions* (Philadelphia, 1918), 177, 181, 186–87, 191, 203.
[20] *Christ and Culture* (N.Y., 1951), 102.

ous a feature of the early 1920's. "One hundred per cent Americanism" tended to be regarded as the normal corollary of "old-time religion," and "Back to Christ, the Bible, and the Constitution" was a typical slogan. While Fundamentalism had no direct connection with the resurgent Ku Klux Klan of the 1920's,[21] the more extreme wing of the Fundamentalist movement was in some respects a parallel phenomenon.

The great body of Protestants was never fully committed to either side of the controversy, but when the more belligerent Fundamentalists took charge of the movement and formed themselves into a power bloc intent on seizing control of the various Protestant denominations and placing them in a rigid theological strait jacket, the effect was to push middle-of-the-roaders into a defensive alliance with the liberals. This shift in alignment was most clearly evident at Princeton Theological Seminary which long had been the citadel of Presbyterian orthodoxy and where Fundamentalism had its ablest spokesman in the person of J. Gresham Machen (1881–1937). Nowhere was the Fundamentalist case stated with more clarity and cogency than in Machen's writings,[22] but his ill-advised dogmatism in personal relationships and his determination to dominate the life of the seminary drove even stanchly conservative colleagues to make common cause with the Auburn "Affirmationists." [23] Among the Baptists, the initiative was seized by a radical triumvirate—J. Frank Norris, William B. Riley, and T. T. Shields—who formed the Baptist Bible Union to promote their views and succeeded in placing their stamp on much of the movement within the Baptist ranks. Here too the bitter-spirited intransigence of the extremists caused some of the prominent early leaders of the movement to defect and work out a policy of coexistence with the liberals. By 1925, when a national comedy was acted out in the "monkey trial" at Dayton, Tennessee, with William Jennings Bryan and Clarence Darrow in the starring roles, the obscurantism, violent language, and "smear" tactics of the more vociferous Fundamentalists had so alienated public opinion generally that there was little prospect that the Fundamentalists would gain control of any major Protestant denomina-

[21] John Roach Straton, the most prominent Fundamentalist leader in New York City, publicly castigated the Klan. Others condemned the Klan's tactics, suggesting that its members should take off their masks and make their fight in the open.

[22] See his *Christianity and Liberalism* (N.Y., 1923).

[23] The "Auburn Affirmation" is printed in Armstrong, Loetscher, Anderson, *The Presbyterian Enterprise*, 284–88.

tion. In 1929 Princeton Seminary was reorganized, and Machen departed to found Westminster Theological Seminary and the Orthodox Presbyterian Church.

Most of the denominations continued to be troubled by controversy throughout the 1930's, and among the American (Northern) Baptists peace was not restored until after World War II. The ranks of the latter group were depleted by two additional schisms. The first occurred in 1932 when a group of dissidents withdrew to form the General Association of Regular Baptists, and the second took place fifteen years later with the formation of the Conservative Baptist Association of America. While Fundamentalism was a declining force throughout these years in the major denominations, it maintained itself in many local congregations, and expanded its influence through the formation of independent Bible churches and the capture of some of the smaller denominational bodies. A major source of its continuing strength was its ability to supply, through graduates of Bible schools or institutes strategically located throughout the nation, ministerial leadership to impoverished churches.

PROTESTANT ACCULTURATION. Despite the distractions of controversy and despite the shafts of ridicule directed by the "intellectuals" against those who made profession of religious faith, the mood of the Protestant churches in the 1920's was remarkably complacent. Curiously enough, during the very decades when Protestantism was reaching the peak of its prestige and apparent influence, the nerve which had impelled two centuries of advance was being cut. A long process of theological erosion had opened the way to a rather complete assimilation of Protestantism to the model of the world.[24] With its basic theological insights largely emasculated, Protestantism was robbed of any independently grounded vision of life and became more and more the creature of American culture rather than its creator. In this respect the culturally conditioned character of Fundamentalism was typical of Protestantism as a whole, the tension within Protestantism arising primarily out of the differing cultural orientation of the older agrarian and the newer urban society. "If the theology of the fundamentalists was archaic and anachro-

[24] For elaborations of this point, see W. S. Hudson, *The Great Tradition of the American Churches*, 157–225, and *American Protestantism*, 131–43; S. E. Mead, *The Lively Experiment*, 134–87; H. Richard Niebuhr, *The Kingdom of God in America*, 164–98, and *The Church Against the World* (N.Y., 1935).

nistic," Sidney E. Mead has observed, "that of the liberals was secularized and innocuous." [25]

While there were exceptions to this general characterization, by and large the Protestant churches had become victims of their own success. They had succeeded in creating a culture that in mood and spirit was recognizably Christian, and then during the first two decades of the twentieth century practically all the reforms that had been proposed to remedy the ills of society had been set in operation. Proud of their achievements and pleased that their mission had been so largely accomplished, the churches relaxed and made peace with the world.

From satisfaction with the culture, it was but a small step to the placing of confidence in the culture to nurture and sustain the Christian faith. Even before the end of the nineteenth century, Phillips Brooks had declared: "I do not know how a man can be an American, even if he is not a Christian, and not catch something with regard to God's purpose for this great land." How else could one explain "all the secular, all the studiously irreligious, all the even blasphemous attempts at education and the development of character?" The most impressive feature of American life, to Brooks, was the way in which men "outside the churches" were impelled by the spirit of America to do that which "the churches and Christianity" seek to do, being led to do "Christian work in the spirit of Christ" even when they "studiously" or "vehemently" disown him.[26] By thus investing the culture with intrinsic redemptive power, scant room was left for any special redemptive work of Christ. The distinction between the Church and the world, between the Christian and the non-Christian, was largely obliterated; and little independent wisdom and guidance was available to the Christian believer. The churches, as a result, became increasingly composed of adherents whose religious affiliation was determined more by accident of birth and persistence of custom than by conscious conviction.

The missionary thrust of a religion is one of the most sensitive indices of its vitality. Evidence was accumulating throughout the 1920's of a growing missionary apathy, which indicated how ill-prepared the churches were to withstand the effect of the general American retreat into isolation. Missionary giving steadily declined during this period of boom-

[25] *The Lively Experiment*, 186. For a defense of liberalism, see W. R. Hutchison, *The Modernist Impulse* (Cambridge, Mass., 1976), esp. 274–87.
[26] *National Needs and Remedies: Discussions of the General Conference of the Evangelical Alliance* (N.Y., 1890), 301–11.

ing prosperity, and the Foreign Missions Conference reported in 1929 that, in contrast to the 2,700 students who had volunteered for foreign service in 1920, only 252 had volunteered in 1928.[27] It was this waning interest in missions that led to the Laymen's Foreign Missions Inquiry in 1930, whose report in 1932 reflected the questioning of the mission enterprise as it had been traditionally conceived.

The Laymen's Inquiry was instigated by a group of Baptist businessmen and financed by John D. Rockefeller, Jr. Its purpose was to study existing mission projects, evaluate their effectiveness, and determine what was worthy of continued support. Research specialists were sent abroad to collect factual information, and then, armed with this data, a "Commission of Appraisal" visited the mission fields before issuing their report.[28] The chairman of the commission and editor of the report was William E. Hocking (1873–1966), professor of philosophy at Harvard. While urging that missionary endeavor be continued, the report declared that there is no ground for "a renewed appeal for the support, much less for the enlargement, of these missions as a whole in their present form and on their present basis." A typical "big business" bias, which equated centralization with efficiency, was evident in the critical attitude of the report toward all operations based upon separate denominational entities. "A single administrative unit," free of all church control, it maintained, should be given "administrative direction of missionary effort in all fields." But the report went much farther than this. Not only did it question much of the work that was being done on the mission fields, it brought the whole philosophy of Christian missions under attack. Educational and philanthropic work was commended, but the report insisted that the missionaries should be freed from any responsibility for "conscious and direct evangelization." Far from making any overt presentation of the claims of Christ, the missionary must adopt a stance of openness toward other religions and "regard himself as a co-worker with the forces within each such religious system which are making for righteousness." As Christians, we must "be willing to give largely without any preaching, to co-operate wholeheartedly with non-Christian agencies for social improvement." The basic philosophy,

[27] See Handy, "The American Religious Depression," *Church History*, XXIX (1960), 4–5. The United Stewardship Council reported that per capita gifts for benevolence fell from $5.57 in 1921 to $3.43 in 1929.
[28] *Re-Thinking Missions: A Laymen's Inquiry after One Hundred Years* (N.Y., 1932). The factual material that had been assembled was published in the seven-volume *Laymen's Foreign Missions Inquiry . . . Supplementary Series* (N.Y., 1933).

which was fully explicated two years later by Archibald G. Baker in *Christian Missions and a New World Culture,* was to foster an intercultural penetration which would bring about a synthesis or reconception of all religions into one universal faith.

A similar indecision and hesitancy with regard to any forthright presentation of the Christian faith was evident at home. Home missions underwent the same metamorphosis that was recommended in the Laymen's report, with mission centers being transformed into social agencies. "A decreasing emphasis upon a specific church program and intensification of efforts to help the immigrant worker in the struggle for economic security and social recognition," a study sponsored by the Institute of Social and Religious Research concluded, "suggest themselves as the most constructive items on the future program of mission work." [29] As for the professional evangelists who had sought to maintain the tradition of mass evangelism, their day also was over. Finding it no longer possible to secure the necessary cooperation of the churches for citywide campaigns, most of them settled down, accepting pastorates or founding churches (or tabernacles) of their own. [30]

The churches were under considerable pressure during these years, quite apart from uncertainty as to their own vocation. Less and less reliance could be placed on habit and custom to maintain active participation in church life. In addition to the free and easy atmosphere generated by the revolution in morals which enabled many to ignore the Sabbath and neglect church attendance without compunction, there were other features of American life which made the task of the churches more difficult. The population was increasingly urban and mobile. By 1930 ninety-six metropolitan areas had emerged, twenty-two of them straddling two or more states. And once within the urban orbit, there were many who did not stay put long enough to develop strong ties to a church. Nor could the churches count on the family as an ally to the same extent as formerly, as was made evident by the rising divorce rate and the sharp decline in the practice of family devotions. Automobile production soared at almost a

[29] Theodore Abel, *Protestant Home Missions to Catholic Immigrants* (N.Y., 1933), 107.

[30] McLoughlin, *Modern Revivalism*, 469. C. E. Fuller, M. R. DeHaan, and D. G. Barnhouse captured national audiences by taking to the air-waves with their "Old-Fashioned Revival Hour," "Radio Bible Class," and "Bible Study Hour."

geometric rate, vastly extending the range of an individual's freedom, providing easy access to multiplying golf-courses and setting up the family weekend outing as a counterattraction to the church. Motion pictures and the radio joined the press as rivals of the churches in setting the tone of society.[31] Almost everything—the popular mood, the churches' own sense of uncertainty, urbanization, mobility, competing attractions, the decay of family solidarity—militated against the success of any attempt by the churches to maintain their congregations as a disciplined and fully committed people.

One response to this situation was a frenzied effort by some churches to "merchandise" religion with the huckstering methods of Madison Avenue.[32] "Early to bed and early rise, preach the gospel and advertise," ministers were admonished. "Selling Religion—that is the only business of the Church," proclaimed Lewis S. Mudge, stated clerk of the Presbyterian General Assembly, in supplying the churches with five sure-fire tips on how they might best vend their goods. "The old idea that a minister is above stooping to commercial devices must disappear if the church is to grow," the Methodist *Zion's Herald* informed its readers, for "ministers are salesmen with a wonderfully fine 'line' to sell their congregations." The use of printer's ink and brightly illuminated signs to advertise their services, churches were told, could change the cry of "S.O.S." to "S.R.O."—standing room only Bruce Barton, an advertising executive, made his contribution to the cause by writing a biography of Jesus, *The Man Nobody Knows* (1925), which for two years headed the nonfiction list of best-selling books. Jesus was pictured as a master salesman, psychologist, and forceful young executive, who forged twelve men from the lower ranks into the best management team of all time.

Churches responded to the multiple exhortations·with snappy slogans and promotional stunts. "A friendly church" became a familiar slogan which compared favorably with more flashy punch-lines such as "Be a Sport—Come to Church" or the hard-sell "Worship Increases Your

[31] The press provided much less support for the churches than heretofore. The circulation of religious periodicals dwindled, and there was a marked change in the attitude of the nonreligious press. One study has indicated that, whereas about 78 per cent of published views of religion in 1905 could be classified as favorable, by 1930 the situation was almost reversed with 67 per cent unfavorable. Hornell Hart, "Changing Attitudes and Interests," *Recent Social Trends* (N.Y., 1933), I, 403.

[32] See Miller, *American Protestantism and Social Issues*, 22-26.

Efficiency" and "Business Success and Religion Go Together." Catchy sermon topics—"The Irishmen of the Old Testament," "Two in a Bed," "The Mae West of My Bible"—were used as teasers to draw a crowd. Some of the promotional stunts were equally bizarre.

Churches with a more sedate and prosperous clientele sought to maintain their prestige and popularity by the more dignified expedient of constructing impressive gothic cathedrals, and even the less prosperous invested heavily in more modest gothic structures. In 1921 the total spent on new church buildings was 60 million dollars. Five years later the total had risen to 284 million. John D. Rockefeller, Jr., explained his interest in spending large sums on the construction of a new home for the Park Avenue Baptist Church on Riverside Drive by saying that he did not want the business community to look down on the churches.[33] There were also attempts to make Sunday morning worship more attractive by decorating it with liturgical innovations borrowed from other traditions. Unlike earlier forms of church architecture and liturgical practice which expressed in one way or another the common faith of the congregation, the new eclecticism betrayed little discernible relationship to any fundamental theological convictions.

These same churches also tended to specialize in "progressive" programs of religious education, geared to the immediate interests and capacities of the child. According to George A. Coe's *Social Theory of Religious Education* (1917), the aim of the new educational program was "the growth of the young toward and into mature and efficient devotion to the democracy of God, and happy self-realization therein." The basic assumption was the conviction that religious consciousness is a natural and progressive experience which emerges out of "an experimental pupil-teacher quest for growing values." [34] With this emphasis upon "growth" and a "continuous becoming," there was little point to the old Sunday school "Decision Day." Far from involving any crisis of conversion, church membership was regarded as simply a routine step in the normal unfolding of human life. Since everything revolved around the changing interests and capacities of the child at different age levels, churches were under strong pressure to replace the old "Akron style" Sunday school

[33] *Ibid.*, 25.
[34] See H. Shelton Smith, "Christian Education," in *Protestant Thought in the Twentieth Century*, ed., A. S. Nash, (N.Y., 1951), 241.

378

building, which featured a central assembly room for ungraded "opening exercises," with a more suitable educational "plant." Furthermore, churches were encouraged to employ full-time professional directors of religious education.

Much church life, of course, remained untouched by these newer expedients, for many congregations refused to adopt cheap appeals to attract a crowd and did not have the financial resources to embark upon a building program or to launch a full-blown program of "progressive" education. Moreover, many of them were still old-fashioned enough to believe that a "life-centered" Sunday school curriculum was no adequate substitute for specific instruction in the Bible. But whatever course individual churches pursued, nothing could obscure the fact that the churches were suffering a loss of prestige and authority. Throughout the 1920's overt manifestations of religious interest were being confined more and more to Sunday morning, as midweek and Sunday evening services were dropped in many parts of the country. Nor did religious leaders command the same respect as in former years. This decline was reflected in the relative economic status of ministers and in their participation as members of boards of trustees of universities, colleges, and other philanthropic organizations. In a sample of private institutions, an investigator reported that the number of clergymen who were members of their governing boards decreased from 39 per cent in 1860 to 7 per cent in 1930.[35] It was upon churches thus weakened that the blow of the economic depression of the 1930's fell, and the churches suffered from the crippling effect of the economic disaster along with the rest of the nation. Budgets were slashed, benevolent and missionary enterprises curtailed, and some churches were forced to close their doors.

Variant Protestant "revivals"

Many people expected that the depression into which the nation was cascaded following the crash of the "great bull market" of 1929 would produce a return to religion. A people shorn of their material possessions, it was believed, would turn to God in some spectacular way. By-and-large they did not. Samuel P. Kincheloe of the Chicago Theological Seminary

[35] S. P. Hays, *The Response to Industrialism* (Chicago, 1957), 72.

explained that secularism had become so pervasive that a general revival was impossible.[36] Even churchgoing people looked to Washington instead of to God in their extremit*y*. But there were exceptions. A somewhat *sub rosa* revival did occur among less secularized portions of the population as indicated by the rapidly mounting membership of what Kincheloe dismissed as "minor 'fundamentalist groups,' " the most striking gains being made by Holiness and Pentecostal churches.

At the opposite end of the social spectrum, a quickening religious interest found expression in the "First Century Christian Fellowship" of Frank Buchman (1878–1960).[37] Since 1921 Buchman had been engaged in personal evangelism among students, both in the United States and abroad. Becoming convinced that Park Avenue needed conversion as much as the Bowery, a mission to America was launched in 1930 with headquarters in the Calvary Episcopal Church in New York City. The focus was upon "four absolutes" of perfect honesty, purity, unselfishness, and love, and upon "the five C's" of confidence, confession, conviction, conversion, and continuance, which were the five stages of a "changed" life. The basic "houseparty" technique was supplemented by the activities of a traveling team, and sophisticated use was made of news media and propagandist literature, with such titles as *For Sinners Only* (1932), *I Was a Pagan* (1934), *Life Began Yesterday* (1935), and *How Do I Begin?* (1937). In 1939, after the movement was renamed Moral Re-Armament, 30,000 people filled Hollywood Bowl for its second World Assembly, with an additional 10,000 turned away. Buchman's emphasis was highly individualistic and no great renewal of church life was either intended or effected, but many prominent people professed to have had their lives changed in the "quiet times" of the house parties.

THEOLOGICAL REASSESSMENT. As early as 1928 Episcopal Bishop Charles Fiske (1868–1942) was convinced that there was "evidence of a sad disintegration of American Protestantism," a view shared by Unitarian writer, William L. Sullivan. In an article on "Our Spiritual Destitution," Sullivan noted that religion had become "timorous, unimaginative, quick with comment upon the contemporaneous, but unable in the authen-

36 *Research Memo on Religion in the Depression* (N.Y., 1937), 45 ff., 95.

37 See A. W. Eister, *Drawing-Room Conversion* (Durham, N.C., 1950), and W. H. Clark, *The Oxford Group: Its History and Significance* (N.Y., 1951). For the later Moral Re-Armament phase of the movement, see *Moral Re-Armament: A Study of the Movement Prepared by the Social and Industrial Council of the Church Assembly* (London: Church [of England] Information Board, 1955).

tic manner of its great tradition to judge the contemporaneous by categories that are eternal." [38] Further discontent with Protestantism's theological void and accompanying acculturation was voiced by Edwin Lewis, *Christian Manifesto* (1934), H. Richard Niebuhr, *The Kingdom of God in America* (1937), and Joseph Haroutunian, *Wisdom and Folly in Religion* (1940). Even more stirring was Reinhold Niebuhr's devastating polemics, *Moral Man and Immoral Society* (1932) and *Reflections on the End of an Era* (1934).[39] In spite of the prescience of such men, not more than a handful of ministers were ready to engage in a fundamental theological reconsideration. Harry Emerson Fosdick was a significant exception, having announced in a widely publicized sermon that "The Church Must Go Beyond Modernism."

There were several reasons for the lack of response. In the midst of a depression the working clergy were overwhelmed with the mere task of seeing that bills were paid and church doors kept open. Whatever time was left for reflection tended to be absorbed by efforts to mitigate the plight of their parishioners. Additional energy was siphoned off in an effort to qualify themselves to deal more adequately with the personal problems of anxious and distraught people. It was no coincidence that Charles T. Holman's pioneering book on pastoral counseling, *The Cure of Souls*, was published in 1932. More important was the lingering impact of the Fundamentalist controversy. Attention had been centered on peripheral issues, with both parties driven to more extreme positions than they otherwise would have adopted. Alarmed by the controversy's threat to institutional concerns, denominational officials took charge and, in the interest of harmony, were largely successful in ruling theological discussion out of bounds in church assemblies.

It was otherwise in the seminaries where indications of a theological revival had begun to surface in the 1930's. This revival, however, is difficult to characterize, for it found expression in no single theological system or school of thought.[40] Its most common feature was represented

---

[38] *Confessions of a Puzzled Parson* (N.Y., 1928), 191. *Atlantic Monthly,*   CXXXIII (1929), 378.

[39] Other important books were: Walter Lowrie, *Our Concern with the Theology of Crisis* (1932), George Richards, *Beyond Fundamentalism and Modernism,* and three essays by H. R. Niebuhr, Wilhelm Pauck and Francis P. Miller, *The Church against the World* (1935).

[40] See D. D. Williams, *What Present-Day Theologians are Thinking* (N.Y., 1959, and D. W. Soper, *Major Voices in American Theology* (Phila., 1953).

by Henry Nelson Wieman's announcement in 1932 of his intention hence-forth "to promote a theocentric religion as over against the prevalent anthropocentric one." Influenced by Alfred North Whitehead's process philosophy, Wieman, Douglas C. Macintosh, and also Walter M. Horton moved in a new theological direction which rejected the philosophical idealism of the older liberalism. Destined to be much more influential, however, were views derived from Europe,[41] where the shattered optimism of the post-war years had produced an earlier theological reassessment. Although European-oriented theology in America was generally labeled "neo-orthodox," it was multiform and varied, borrowing insights from such diverse sources as the Jewish thinker Martin Buber, the Russian Orthodox theologian Nicholai Berdyaev, the Spanish existentialist Miguel Unamuno, the French neo-Thomist Jacques Maritain, and the Swedish Lutheran theologians Anders Nygren and Gustaf Aulén. While recognizing this diversity, the European influence can best be summarized as an inter-mingling of neo-Reformation and existentialist emphases, with Karl Barth and Emil Brunner representing primary stress on the Reformation herit-age and Paul Tillich, who came to America in 1933, drawing more heavily on the "existentialism" of Søren Kierkegaard.

Karl Barth (1886–1968) was the towering figure of the theological revival. Although fully accepting the historical criticism of the liberal era, Barth took his stand firmly on the Scriptures as interpreted by the Prot-estant reformers and insisted that it is through Jesus Christ alone that God's Word addresses man. Emil Brunner (1889–1965) was not quite so uncompromising in the rejection of natural theology and was at first more influential in the United States than his Swiss colleague. Americans found Brunner's strong emphasis on one's apprehension of God being derived from a deeply personal "I-thou" encounter less forbidding than Barth's seemingly more harsh statement of much the same position.[42] While both Barth and Brunner had been influenced by "the melancholy Dane," Amer-icans were directly exposed to Kierkegaard's writings through translations

41 See S. E. Ahlstrom, "Continental Influence on American Christian Thought since World War I," *Church History*, XXXVII (1958), 256–73.

42 Douglas Horton introduced Barth to America in 1928 through a translation of Barth's *The Word of God and the Word of Man*, and three years later Wilhelm Pauck presented a sensitive appraisal of his thought in *Karl Barth: Prophet of a New Chris-tianity?* A translation of Brunner's *The Theology of Crisis* appeared in 1929, but *The Divine-Human Encounter*, which was not published in America until 1943, was to be his most influential work.

provided by Walter Lowrie and David Swenson. Paul Tillich (1886–1965) was the chief mediator of the type of existentialist thought represented by Kierkegaard, until the writings of Rudolf Bultmann (b. 1884) and Dietrich Bonhoeffer (1906–45), the German martyr, began to appear in English translations. Preoccupied with the problem of the agonized conscience (the sense of guilt, estrangement, and frustration which once had been so prominently displayed in revival meetings), these men manifested much the same personal concern and introspective analysis that had become fashionable among the *literati*. The self-acceptance they stressed, however, was grounded in the biblical message of justification by faith alone.

Although the tendencies of the theological revival cannot be reduced to a single consistent point of view, major themes can be identified.[43] The first was a reassertion of the sovereignty of God. Even such a neo-naturalist as Wieman thought in terms of a religion of "grace." Second, there was a much less optimistic evaluation of the human situation, and a much more radical stress on the demonic power of sin. Third, there was a renewed appreciation of the centrality of biblical revelation. Fourth, there was a revival of interest in Christology. Fifth, there was a deepening concern to recover a sense of fullness and wholeness in the life of the church. Lastly, there was a tendency among many, while moving to the "right" theologically, to move to the "left" politically. The tone was set by Reinhold Niebuhr's remark in *Reflections on the End of an Era*: "In my opinion, adequate spiritual guidance can come only through more radical political orientation and more conservative religious convictions than are comprehended [at present] in the culture of our era."

For at least three reasons the theological revival proved to be abortive, having little impact beyond the seminaries. First, attention to theological issues was diverted by World War II. Second, attempts at theological reconstruction never got out of the classroom and into the pulpit, to say nothing of making the transition from pulpit to pew.[44] But most important of all, serious theological reflection was overwhelmed by the surging tide of the popular "religious revival" of the post-World War II

[43] Several of these themes are illustrated by selections reprinted in Smith, Handy, and Loetscher, *American Christianity*, II, 438–71.

[44] Presbyterians attempted to make the transition with their *Christian Faith and Life Series* of church school materials, but an ill-equipped laity found it difficult to teach and it was gradually phased out. For the point of view of the series, see Armstrong, Loetscher, Anderson, *Presbyterian Enterprise*, 301–03.

years which peaked in 1957 when Billy Graham had his "finest hour" in New York City.

THE RELIGIOUS REVIVAL OF THE FIFTIES. By the 1950's it was evident that the United States was in the midst of a religious revival. Critical voices became muted, and religion was riding the crest of a wave of popularity. Church attendance soared, contributions mounted, and unprecedented sums were spent on new church buildings.[45] Publishers discovered that religious books were profitable, and the more popular volumes dominated the best-seller lists for extended periods of time. Seldom had religion been held in greater public esteem. The pledge of allegiance was amended to include the phrase "under God," prayer breakfasts were attended by the president and members of his cabinet, a prayer room was installed in the national capitol, and both the American Legion and the National Advertising Council launched "Back to God" and "Go to Church" campaigns. In 1957 the Census Bureau indicated that more than 96 per cent of the American people cited a specific religious affiliation in response to the question: "What is your religion?" Obviously there were many among the 96 per cent whose names did not appear on any church membership roll, but the fact that they so identified themselves is significant.

Unlike earlier religious revivals, the "return to religion" of the 1950's was formless and unstructured, manifesting itself in many different ways and reinforcing all religious faiths quite indiscriminately. It cannot be understood apart from the trauma of World War II and its aftermath. The depression of the 1930's had been a sobering experience, but the "immense and indomitable optimism" of the American people was not really shaken until the bombing of Hiroshima and Nagasaki in 1945 demonstrated the potential destructiveness of the unleashed powers of the atom. The uneasy peace of the "cold war" that followed, with its recurring crises and continuing conflicts, heightened the sense of anxiety and insecurity. Religious overtones also were present in the confrontation with the Communist regimes because of the latter's professed atheism. In this situation,

45 From a base of $26,000,000 in 1945, the amount spent on new churches rose steadily: 1946—76 million; 1948—251 million; 1950—409 million; 1954—593 million; 1956—775 million; 1958—863 million; 1959—935 million; 1960—1,016 million. After 1960 a decline set in. In contrast to attendance figures and in spite of reports to the contrary, church membership was not increasing in proportion to the population. See W. S. Hudson, "Are the Churches Really Booming?" *Christian Century*, LXXII (1955), 1494–96.

it was natural that religion should be viewed as a weapon to be employed in the struggle.

As a result of what Robert Maynard Hutchins, president of the University of Chicago, called "the good news of damnation," the world of the secular intellectuals was prepared to listen to the theologians, most notably to Reinhold Niebuhr and Paul Tillich, in a way and to a degree that had not been true for almost a half century. The comment of *Time* magazine in 1956 that Tillich was an intellectual whom even the intellectuals regarded with awe may have been overly exuberant, but it nonetheless reflected the shift in attitude that had occurred. For the most part, however, the revival flowed through more popular channels.

The heirs of the Fundamentalists gave the revival its most vigorous leadership. The way for their new surge of activity had been prepared by the National Association of Evangelicals, Youth for Christ, and a handful of scholars determined to develop an effective Fundamentalist apologetic. The N.A.E. was formed in 1942 to unite the forces of moderate Fundamentalism,[46] and under the leadership of Harold J. Ockenga it adopted a conciliatory policy designed to capitalize upon the demoralization of the "modernists" and to penetrate the life of major denominations by persuasion from within rather than by leveling criticism from without. In pursuing this goal they successfully appropriated for themselves the name "evangelical" to avoid the Fundamentalist label. Youth for Christ, the second organization spearheading the Fundamentalist recovery, was founded in 1943 to sponsor Saturday night rallies for young people. It quickly became both a recruiting instrument and a training ground for the new "evangelical" leadership. The activity of these two agencies was strengthened by a coterie of young theologians who sought to provide a philosophic defense of the Fundamentalist understanding of the Christian faith and were willing to engage in the give and take of reasoned theological discussion.[47]

The thrust of the new "evangelicalism" was brought into focus by Billy Graham (b. 1918) who had been recruited by Youth for Christ in

[46] See J. D. Murch, *Cooperation without Compromise* (Grand Rapids, 1956). Radical Fundamentalists were drawn together in the American Council of Churches by Carl McInire in 1941 but it had no numerically significant constituency.

[47] The most prominent were Carl Henry, Edward Carnell, and Cornelius Van Til. See A. W. Hearn, "Fundamentalist Renascence," *Christian Century*, LXXV (1958), 528–30.

RELIGION IN AMERICA

1945 to serve as an itinerant evangelist at its rallies. Four years later at a tent meeting in Los Angeles, Graham gained widespread attention through the conversion of three minor celebrities—a local television star, a former Olympic athlete, and an alleged associate of the notorious racketeer Mickey Cohen. The Los Angeles success was followed by an eighteen-day campaign at the Park Street Church in Boston and in 1950 by a citywide revival in Portland, Oregon. Under the tutelage of Ockenga, Graham moderated his sensationalism, expressed a distaste for interdenominational feuds, and deplored "fumbling Fundamentalists" who destroyed their effectiveness by intolerance and sectarianism. He expressed his own willingness to "fellowship with all born-again believers" and announced a decision to refuse any invitation to conduct a revival that was not tendered by a majority of the Protestant clergy of the host city.[48]

Several factors, in addition to his dashing youthful appearance and generally irenic spirit, combined to further Graham's growing prominence and popularity which culminated in his dramatic "invasion" of England in 1954. One was a skillful use of sophisticated organizational techniques and an adroit exploitation of publicity media, including his weekly "Hour of Decision" radio broadcasts, television appearances, and feature-length motion pictures. The second was the care he took to marshall support among all denominations. But the real key to his success, perhaps, was the mounting public anxiety which reached a peak during the Korean conflict and the Red-hunt of the McCarthy era.

The political flavor of Graham's gospel had great appeal to ultraconservative segments of the population. Drawing a contrast with the Garden of Eden where there were "no union dues, no labor leaders, no snakes, no disease," Graham depicted the United States as "falling apart at the seams" as a result of deficit spending, "giveaway" foreign-aid programs, "immorality in high places," the influence of "big labor" and "pinks and lavenders" in Washington, and "the infiltration of the left wing" into schools and churches. The "betrayals" at Yalta and Potsdam, the war in Korea, the bungling United Nations ("they set the policies and we shed the blood and pay the bills") were cited as evidence of the "deadly work" of Communism boring from within and were used to demonstrate that "we

48 See John Pollock, *Billy Graham: Evangelist to the World* (N.Y., 1979); Marshall Frady, *Billy Graham: A Biography of American Righteousness* (Boston, 1979); W. G. McLoughlin, *Billy Graham: Revivalist in a Secular Age* (N.Y., 1960); L. I. Sweet, "The Epic of Billy Graham," *Theology Today*, XXXVII (1980), 85–92.

386

are living in the latter days" with a consequent urgency of repentance. Since Communism was "masterminded by Satan," it was a mistake to think that Satan can be defeated with "flesh and blood and guns and bullets." Only through a great revival, purging America of "the rats and termites that are subversively endeavoring to weaken the defense of this nation from within," could the United States be saved and the battle won, for "the greatest and most effective weapon against Communism today is a born-again Christian." The altar call was simple and direct: "If you would be a true patriot, then become a Christian. If you would be a loyal American, then become a loyal Christian." [49]

The patriotic motif did not represent the full scope of Billy Graham's message. There was much traditional doctrine, and he often spoke to the more personal needs of people. Here the stress was upon the role of religion as a consolation which brings "peace of mind, peace of soul, peace of conscience." This latter emphasis points to another prominent feature of the surge of piety of the 1950's—the "cult of reassurance" of which Norman Vincent Peale (b. 1898), minister of the Marble Collegiate Church in New York City, has been called the "high priest."

New Thought, Christian Science, and the Unity School of Christianity had long exploited the reassurance theme in religion, and in 1937 Henry C. Link, a professional psychologist, in a best-seller entitled *The Return to Religion* had given an aura of scientific authority to an emphasis upon the psychological value of religion in easing social adjustments (bridge-playing and church attendance were equally useful in this respect) and fostering healthy attitudes. But the full-blown cult of reassurance dates from the publication of Joshua L. Liebman's *Peace of Mind* in 1946, which quickly achieved a phenomenal sale. Liebman was a Jewish rabbi, and within a brief period of time preachers of all persuasions, including Monsignor Fulton J. Sheen with his *Peace of Soul* (1949), were capitalizing upon this newly awakened religious interest.

Of all the "peace of mind" evangelists, it was Norman Vincent Peale who most fully captured the public imagination. From his base in New York City he issued a stream of books and other writings, including the fabulously successful *The Power of Positive Thinking* (1952). His was a simple "do-it-yourself" faith, calling for the replacement of "negative thoughts" with "positive thinking," that was strongly reminiscent of the

[49] McLoughlin, *Modern Revivalism,* 505–12.

teachings of Charles and Myrtle Fillmore. You can "make your life what you want it to be through belief in God and in yourself," he informed his readers. You must "think, believe, visualize success"—"think big," "believe big," "pray big," "act big." "When you decide that nothing can defeat you, from that instant *nothing can defeat you.*" How does one "practice faith?" he asked. "First thing every morning before you arise say out loud, 'I believe,' three times." [50]

Peale was referred to by some as "the rich man's Billy Graham," and the two men did hold each other in high esteem. While they differed theologically, they shared common political and economic views. Peale was a sponsor of Graham's New York Crusade and, if the number of decision cards received from the Graham organization was an accurate index, his church reaped the largest harvest. Graham in turn regarded Peale as "a born-again Christian" in spite of his obvious self-help Pelagianism.

While the popular "religious revival" of the 1950's can most easily be depicted by vivid personalities, its substratum was much broader than that suggested by personality cults. Religion-in-general, any religion and all religion, was thoroughly popular, reflecting a simple belief that religion was a "good thing." President Eisenhower stressed the importance of having "faith in faith." Belonging to a church was widely regarded as a badge of respectability. Membership did not always (perhaps seldom) require much commitment, but few doubted that the children of delayed "family formations" (the "baby boom" of the postwar years) would derive great benefit from religious instruction. This was the real revival of the 1950's, expressing itself in increased church attendance, increased church giving, increased church building, and increased public esteem.

Other manifestations of religious vitality

In spite of the pervasive "folk religion" of the time, many of the clergy and coteries of church members continued their attempts to deal realistically, from a Christian perspective, with some of the more urgent problems of national life.

During World War II the churches demonstrated that they had learned a lesson from the uninhibited exuberance with which they had

50 *The Power of Positive Thinking* (N.Y., 1952), 154; *Stay Alive All Your Life* (Englewood Cliffs, N.J., 1957), 22, 104, 211, 263.

blessed World War I. The new conflict was viewed much more soberly. The halting of totalitarian aggression was accepted as a necessity. It was recognized, however, that if the ensuing peace was to be secure, the requirements for the establishment of international order must be clearly defined before the victory was won. To this end a conference was summoned in 1942 to meet at Delaware, Ohio, to draft a report on the prerequisites for a "just and durable peace." [51] Seldom has a report received more serious consideration by the churches. Study guides were prepared and few congregations failed to make use of them. Key political leaders declared that the report was of decisive importance in creating the favorable climate of American opinion that was indispensable to the establishment of the United Nations.

Later in the McCarthy era, the Protestant churches performed yeoman service in calling a halt to the witch-hunt of those years. Methodist Bishop G. Bromley Oxnam and John A. Mackay, moderator of the Presbyterian Church, U.S.A., provided the most signal leadership, but all major denominations repeatedly expressed alarm at the threat to freedom implicit in the practice of character assassination, imputation of guilt by association, use of loyalty oaths as a means of thought control, and curtailment of individual rights on the basis of credence given accusations by undisclosed informers. The boldest action was taken by the Presbyterian General Council in a statement of October 21, 1953, to be read to each congregation, which declared that "detestation of Communism" was becoming a "new form of idolatry" which could be as dangerous as Communism itself, that dissent and treason are not identical, and that true believers in God will not play fast and loose with truth to preserve freedom.[52] The firm strictures of official church bodies played no small part in heartening the defenders of liberty in this difficult time and in encouring the United States Senate to meet the issue without equivocation.

Still later the racial crisis elicited the strong leadership of many churchmen.[53] Two years prior to the 1954 Supreme Court decision outlawing segregation in the public schools, the National Council of Churches adopted an official statement, *The Churches and Segregation*, which de-

[51] The "Statement of Guiding Principles" is reprinted in Smith, Handy, Loetscher, *American Christianity*, II, 522–26.

[52] The statement is reprinted in *ibid.*, II, 549–55.

[53] See Robert Root, *Progress against Prejudice: the Church Confronts the Race Problem* (N.Y., 1957).

clared racial segregation to be "diametrically opposed" to the Christian faith. When the decision of the Court was announced, the National Council quickly issued "Suggestions for Action" to guide the churches in helping speed compliance with the law. Unfortunately, instead of proceeding with "all deliberate speed" to carry out the directive, many southern states adopted a "massive resistance" policy which served to create smoldering discontent in Negro communities. A tragic aspect of the situation was the abdication of responsibility and leadership by southern white churches. After passing a mild resolution commending the Court's decision, the Southern Baptist Convention retreated into silence. The record of other denominations was not notably better, although some local congregations exhibited firm and courageous leadership.

A new phase of the struggle began in 1956 when Negroes of Montgomery, Alabama, put an end to segregated seating in the city's public transportation by a mass bus boycott. The leader of the boycott was a young Negro Baptist minister, Martin Luther King, Jr. (1929–68), who became the principal architect of a drive to attack all forms of segregation through nonviolent action.[54] Other Negro clergymen and particularly Negro college students rallied to his support, as did leaders of northern white churches. Several organizations, including the Southern Christian Leadership Conference of which King became president, were formed to push a program of nonviolent resistance. By 1962 the movement had spread to northern cities, where the focal point of concern was discrimination in housing, employment, and de facto school segregation.

With a succession of "long hot summers" of increasing tension in prospect, the National Council of Churches created a committee on Religion and Race to coordinate the activities of member denominations. Action programs, such as the Episcopal ESCRU (Episcopal Society for Cultural and Racial Unity) and the American Baptist BARB (Baptist Action for Racial Brotherhood), were set in motion. Special funds to aid victims of economic and legal harassment were established. Prominent churchmen joined picket lines, street demonstrations, and "sit-ins," and the top echelon of official leadership was conspicuously present in the massive "March on Washington" on August 28, 1963. In the autumn the nation was shocked by the tragic murder of four Negro Sunday school children in the wanton Sunday morning bombing of a Baptist Church in

[54] See his *Stride toward Freedom: the Montgomery Story* (N.Y., 1958).

390

Birmingham. The following spring, during the lengthy Senate debate on the Civil Rights Bill of 1964, a Daily Protestant Assembly was maintained at the Lutheran Church of the Reformation on Capitol Hill. The prayer services of the Assembly were supplemented by briefings for those who had come to make their views known to their legislative representatives. But it was the careful marshalling of support in local congregations that was of decisive importance in bringing the debate to a successful conclusion.

A further feature of mainline Protestantism at mid-century was a growing trend toward unity. Throughout the nineteenth century Protestants were accustomed to work together in voluntary societies of individuals. Most of them believed "there were sufficient targets to hit without firing at each other." In the twentieth century these voluntary modes of cooperation were replaced by "official" interdenominational agencies to coordinate home mission, foreign mission, and Christian education activities as well as work in other areas of joint concern. The final step in the consolidation of Protestant cooperative activity was taken in 1950 when these several agencies came together to form the National Council of Churches.[55] The national coordinating structure was paralleled by state and local councils of churches, and in rural areas a "grass roots" unity movement developed with the formation of federated and community churches to solve the problem created by a declining rural population. While there were dissident voices, H. Richard Niebuhr was probably correct when he observed that "the increasing unity of American Protestantism" was "more striking than its apparent diversity." [56]

The typical Protestant pattern in America had been to unite in service while preserving diversity in polity and worship, but the vision of organic unity has had recurrent spokesmen. Numerous proposals for broad-scale union were made, but the suggestion which won most serious consideration was made in 1960 by Eugene Carson Blake (b. 1906), stated clerk of the United Presbyterian Church, speaking in the San Francisco Episcopal cathedral at the invitation of Bishop James A. Pike (1913–70). A Consultation on Church Unity (COCU) was convened in 1962 to forward a plan of union that would be "both catholic and re-

[55] *Christian Faith in Action: The Founding of the National Council of Churches* (N.Y., 1951). See also Samuel McCrae Cavert, *Church Cooperation and Unity in America* (N.Y., 1970).
[56] *The Purpose of the Church and Its Ministry* (N.Y., 1956), 16–17.

formed." High hopes were awakened and ultimately nine denominations participated in the continuing consultations.

Denominational "reunions" had more immediate success than more broadly based mergers. Three Methodist bodies came together in 1939 to form the Methodist Church, becoming the United Methodist Church in 1968 with the addition of the Evangelical United Brethren (German Methodist) Church. In 1958 the United Presbyterian Church joined with the Presbyterian Church, U.S.A. to form the United Presbyterian Church in the U.S.A. In 1961 Unitarians and Universalists united in the Unitarian Universalist Association. Meanwhile the 24 Lutheran groups of 1900 were gradually reduced in number until by 1960 almost all Lutherans (96 per cent) belonged to three major bodies—the Lutheran Church in America, the American Lutheran Church, and the Lutheran Church-Missouri Synod. The formation of the United Church of Christ in 1957, bringing together the Congregational Christian Churches and the Evangelical and Reformed Church, was the sole merger which bridged traditional denominational lines of division.

Closely related to movements of Christian unity in America was a growing concern for ecumenical or worldwide unity, which found expression in the formation of the World Council of Churches in 1948. Several currents of interest combined to produce the World Council of Churches. The first stemmed directly from foreign-mission fields where divisions imported from the West seriously impaired the task of evangelism and weakened the small Christian communities that were struggling to maintain themselves in non-Christian societies. Periodic missionary conferences were held to chart common strategies which culminated in the formation of the International Missionary Council at the Edinburgh Conference of 1910. This conference inspired two Americans to pursue alternate paths to unity. Bishop Charles H. Brent, believing that churches should engage in theological discussion to learn from one another and to discover their common faith, was instrumental in organizing the Faith and Order Movement. Charles S. MacFarland took an alternate route. Believing that the way to bring churches together was to have them address themselves jointly to common social tasks, he took the lead in helping initiate the Life and Work Movement. Leaders in all three areas had become accustomed to working together in the World's Christian Student Federation, organized in 1905, and it was natural for them to envision the consolidation of their efforts in an inclusive ecumenical body. Though completion of its formal organization was delayed by World War II until 1948, the World Council immediately achieved a status far exceeding the hopes of those who labored to bring it into being. "Our century has its sad features," Ernest Barker, a distinguished historian of Cambridge University, commented, "but there is one feature in its history which is not sad. That is the gathering tide of Christian reunion." And this gathering tide was reflected in the growing success of the World Council in enlisting non-Protestant churches within its membership. By the late 1950's even the Roman Catholic Church was participating through unofficial observers in some of the conferences and assemblies of the World Council.

The Protestant phase of the "religious revival," during Protestantism's years of drift and indecision, has often been dismissed as an expression of mere religiosity—a booming, surging, culture religion, without depth and with little commitment, which was utilized to lend divine sanction to "the American way of life." While there is much evidence to support this indictment and while there was much that was superficial in Protestantism at mid-century, there were deeper currents which were never wholly submerged. There was also earnest probing and a great hunger for faith. And in the confrontation with McCarthyism and in the struggle for the equal rights of all citizens, it is apparent that not all churchmen had been ready to bow their knees to Baal.

XV

The Maturing
of Roman Catholicism

When Pius X issued the apostolic constitution *Sapienti Consilio* on June 29, 1908, he recognized that the Roman Catholic Church in the United States had come of age by bringing to an end its missionary status. Hitherto the church in the United States had been under the jurisdiction and control of the Congregatio de Propaganda Fide in Rome. Henceforth it was to be administered on a basis of equality with the older branches of the church in Europe. But it was not until after World War I that the Roman Catholic Church in America began to exhibit the full marks of maturity as an indigenous expression of the Roman Catholic faith.

The external marks of maturity

Maturity is an ambiguous word. It may refer to external manifestations of adulthood, or it may connote an inner temper of mind and spirit that is no longer plagued by the insecurities and anxieties of adolescence. Generally in the maturing process, the outward evidence of maturity precedes the inward maturation. The initial concern of this chapter is with the external aspects of a "full-grown" American Catholicism.

THE EFFECT OF WORLD WAR I. The outbreak of war in 1914 cut off the massive influx of immigrants which had contributed so largely to the numerical growth of Roman Catholicism. After the war restrictive legislation put an end to renewed large-scale immigration. This meant that for the first time the Roman Catholic Church had an opportunity to become stabilized in the American environment. Throughout the nineteenth century it had been a church of immigrants—heir of many different national traditions. Parishes were identified by national constituencies—Irish, Polish, German, Portuguese, Italian, French, Slovak, Croatian, Hungarian, and Spanish-speaking. It often was difficult to think of them as constituting a single indigenous church. With the curtailment of immigration, the nationality and language distinctions would normally have tended to disappear over a period of two or three generations, but the process was hastened by the strong Americanizing pressures that were so prominent a feature of World War I and its immediate aftermath. Immigrant languages were abandoned as quickly as possible, and there was a scramble by immigrants to demonstrate that they were 100 per cent Americans. Almost within a single decade thereafter Roman Catholicism ceased to be thought of as an immigrant's church, and by 1955 the "melting pot" had to a great extent eliminated the identification of religion with specific national origins.[1]

A second consequence of the war was a greatly increased organizational unity that was achieved through the formation of the National Catholic Welfare Conference. The last of the plenary councils had been held in 1884, when the triumvirate of Gibbons, Ireland, and Keane was intent on limiting diocesan autonomy in the interest of a unified national policy. Since that time the papal delegate and an annual meeting of the archbishops had been the only channels through which the activities of the church could be coordinated. In practice this meant that the bishop of each diocese set his own policy. Neither the delegate nor the archbishops had the necessary administrative staff for over-all planning; and while the

[1] See Will Herberg, "The Triple Melting Pot," Commentary, XX (1955), 101–08, and 243. Renewed immigration after World War II posed no appreciable problem, but the massive influx of Spanish-speaking Catholics after 1960 from Puerto Rico, Cuba, Mexico, and elsewhere posed the question whether this surging tide could be assimilated in similar fashion within two or three generations. By 1980 a major segment of the Roman Catholic population was Spanish-speaking.

delegate could intervene in a diocese if an emergency situation developed, the authority of the archbishops was limited to the influence they could exert by persuasion and example. The war, however, created a situation in which specific and detailed centralized action was necessary if wartime needs were to be met effectively and with dispatch. For this purpose the National Catholic War Council (N.C.W.C.) was formed in 1917. So "sensible, visible, practical, efficacious" was its work that many bishops became convinced that some permanent form of peacetime organization should be continued as a coordinating agency for Catholic affairs. After some delay occasioned by a few bishops who feared that their independent powers would be jeopardized, the National Catholic Welfare Conference was fully established in 1921 and in the following year was officially approved by the Vatican.

Initially the work of the N.C.W.C. was divided into five departments—Education, Lay Activities, Press, Social Action, and Missions. Later it was reorganized into eight departments, with subsidiary bureaus and committees which embraced almost every area of Catholic interest and concern. The Conference, with its large administrative staff, had no independent authority, being controlled by the entire episcopate, directed by an Administrative Board of ten bishops, and existing solely to advise and assist the bishops. Nonetheless it gained such prestige that it became a highly effective instrument for establishing national policy, for issuing pronouncements in the name of the entire hierarchy, and for fostering a sense of unity and solidarity among American Catholics.

Another mark of growing maturity was the changing roll of American Roman Catholics in the field of foreign missions. For almost a century they had been the recipients of assistance from missionary societies abroad. The war shut off this source of help, and by bringing mass immigration to an end it lessened the need for such aid. The Society for the Propagation of the Faith, with headquarters in Europe, had long been a chief channel through which mission funds had been sent to the United States, but after the war Americans began to supply much of its income. By 1957 about 65 per cent of its total budget was being met by gifts from the United States. In terms of foreign-mission personnel the story was much the same. The Maryknoll Fathers had been founded in 1911, but not until 1918 were the first missionaries sent out. By mid-century, however, Maryknoll Fathers were at work in Asia, Africa, Central and South

America, and the islands of the Pacific. Meanwhile other American orders joined the enterprise, and by 1960 Americans represented about one-ninth of the total Roman Catholic foreign-mission force.

INCREASE IN NUMBERS AND WEALTH. Growing homogeneity, increasing unification, and vanishing dependence upon aid from abroad were not the only signs of maturity. In terms of numbers the Roman Catholic Church was far more than a lusty infant. By 1920 the *Official Catholic Directory* reported a total of 17,885,000 baptized members.

With the flow of recruits through immigration reduced to a trickle, there was hope of strengthening the church through converts. The number of converts did increase, many being the result of mixed marriages. This, of course, was a two-way street, with a Gallup Poll indicating that the movement in both directions was roughly in balance.[2]

Other defections stemmed from the natural tendency of many people to shirk religious obligations, but Roman Catholicism was remarkably successful in holding its own during these years. The officially reported membership was 20,203,702 in 1930; 21,284,455 in 1940; 28,634,878 in 1950; and 42,104,900 in 1960.[3] The latter figure reflects the triple effect of a swelling birthrate, the influx of refugees following World War II, and the "religious revival." In terms of any realistic standards of membership, the church in the United States had become the largest national grouping of Roman Catholics in the world.

In addition to numerical size, the Roman Catholic community in the United States was distinguished by its success in developing the largest private educational system in the world. By 1964 there were 10,902 Catholic elementary schools with more than 4,500,000 pupils; 2,458 high schools with 1,068,424 students; 295 colleges and universities with more than 350,000 students; and 596 seminaries with 48,750 seminarians preparing for the priesthood. All this was accomplished with little or no direct aid from public taxation.

A third indication that American Roman Catholicism had moved far beyond its period of infancy was the fact that it had become the wealthiest

---

[2] Conversion Poll Ends in a Dead Heat," *Christian Century*, LXXII (1955), 411.

[3] Inadequate collection of data resulted in an underreporting of membership at least through 1940. Statistical procedures were gradually improved thereafter. See G. A. Kelly and Thomas Coogan, "What Is Our Real Catholic Population?" *American Ecclesiastical Review*, CX (1944), 377.

national church in the Roman Catholic world. By 1920 it had achieved its financial independence and rapidly became a chief contributor to foreign mission funds. Moreover, as early as 1937 it was estimated that half Rome's current income was supplied by Americans.[4] A decade later Communist takeovers in Poland, Czechoslovakia, Hungary, and Yugoslavia increased the reliance of the Vatican on American support.

Representation in the College of Cardinals is often an index of the importance Rome attaches to a particular segment of the church. Until 1921 there was never more than one prince of the church in the United States, but thereafter the number gradually increased. By 1959 there were six American cardinals, a number approximating Spanish representation and exceeded only by that of France and, of course, Italy. The number of American priests appointed to offices in the Curia and in the Holy See's diplomatic service also reflected the enhanced importance of American Catholicism in the eyes of Rome.

CHANGING STATUS OF CATHOLICS IN AMERICAN LIFE. In the first half of the century attention often was called to the contrast between the number of Catholics and their feeble representation in national leadership positions. The failure to attain prominence in proportion to their numbers was commonly alleged to be the result of a conscious discrimination designed to keep Catholics out of posts of leadership. Few would contend that there were no instances of discrimination, but as an explanation of the lag in status of Catholics in American life, it is much too facile.

First, such an explanation fails to take into account the source of a large portion of Roman Catholic strength. It was derived from recent immigrants, drawn from the underprivileged classes of Europe, who arrived without financial resources. Many were illiterate; of those who were not, many were isolated from the general culture by language barriers. It normally takes at least a generation for children of immigrants to secure education necessary to qualify for professional positions. More often it is not until the third generation that this occurs. Financial resources are only slowly accumulated by unskilled labor, and when there is a desire to provide one's children with an opportunity for higher education, these resources are quickly depleted.

Second, much of the isolation of Roman Catholics was self-imposed. To hold immigrants true to the faith, tightly guarded enclaves were often

4 William Teeling, *Pope Pius XI and World Affairs* (N.Y., 1937), 133, 158 f.

created. Language barriers were perpetuated, and children were separated in parochial schools from other children in the community. The Knights of Columbus, the Catholic Youth Organization, the Newman Clubs, the Catholic War Veterans, and even Catholic "Junior Leagues," served to retard assimilation into the general community and thus made it more difficult for Catholics to gain positions of community leadership.

Third, the Catholic church often projected a negative image. It was most successful in conveying an image of what it was against—birth control, divorce, euthanasia, therapeutic abortion. The Legion of Decency, founded to encourage the production of better motion pictures, became much better known for the films it blacklisted than for those it approved. At several points, including issues relating to public education and American policy toward Franco Spain, Catholic opinion was at variance with that of other citizens. Quite apart from any religious prejudice, Catholic aspirants for public office were sometimes defeated simply because they did not represent majority opinion.

Studies based on information gathered in 1939–40 and in 1948 indicated that Roman Catholics moved up the economic ladder much faster than had generally been assumed.[5] By the latter date differences in class affiliation were rapidly disappearing. No appreciable distinctions in class, occupation, and education were found between Roman Catholics, Baptists, and Lutherans; and the disparity between Roman Catholics and Methodists was not great enough to be statistically significant.

Roman Catholics gained political prominence at an even earlier date. As was to be expected, urban centers where their strength was concentrated provided the arenas where Catholics first gained roles of political leadership. Later they moved in increasing numbers into positions of consequence in state capitals. If Roman Catholics were under-represented in some state governments, it was presumably not because of their religion but because state legislatures were apportioned to give undue predominance to rural rather than urban interests.

The nomination of Alfred E. Smith in 1928 as the Democratic candidate for president was an event which signaled that Roman Catholics had come of age politically on the national scene. Smith faced a hopeless prospect. A candidate of a minority party seeking office in a time of booming prosperity, he had as his opponent a man with a towering repu-

[5] See appendix to Schneider, *Religion in Twentieth Century America*, 225–38.

tation as a great humanitarian who, as secretary of commerce, had guided the nation into such affluence that the slogan, "two chickens in every pot and two cars in every garage," did not seem unrealistic. Moreover, Hoover had the benefit of Republican alliances with big-city machines and organized labor. Later it was said that Smith's religion cost him votes.

Anti-Catholic votes were cast in the election. Methodist Bishop J. M. Cannon (1864–1944) urged Protestants to "vote as you pray," and in the South the traditional Democratic vote was reduced. But prohibition was as decisive as religion in this defection. Elsewhere "the noble experiment" was not yet a sufficiently emotional issue to cause very many to vote against their pocketbooks. Four years later a vote for one's pocketbook coincided with a vote to end prohibition. Smith's Catholicism apparently gained him more votes than he lost. What else would account for his astonishing achievement in lifting the Democratic percentage of the total vote from 34 per cent in 1920 and 28 per cent in 1924 to 40 per cent in 1928?[6] It is likely that a Protestant would have fared much worse. Not only did Smith lift the Democratic total from eight to fifteen million, he did better in proportion to the Democratic vote for Congressmen than any other twentieth-century Democratic candidate prior to Franklin D. Roosevelt. After the election of 1932, Catholic political participation at the national level became commonplace, and John F. Kennedy's election in 1960 finally put to rest the myth that a Catholic could not be elected president of the United States.

Expressions of new vitality

European Roman Catholics have often referred to the "activism" of American Catholicism. With rapidly proliferating parishes to staff, churches to be built and schools to be established, money to be raised and ecclesiastical supervision to be maintained, there was ample cause for energetic busyness. The preoccupation with immediate tasks may explain the absence of any native-born citizen in the ranks of the saints. Mother Cabrini (1850–1917), of course, was elevated to sainthood in 1946, but she was of Italian birth. It is also true that Elizabeth Bayley Seton (1774–1821) was canonized in 1970. But on the whole American Catholics have

[6] R. C. Silva, *Rum, Religion, and Votes, 1928 Re-examined* (University Park, Pa., 1962), 4. Also E. A. Moore, *A Catholic Runs for President* (N.Y., 1956). The nomination of Muskie in 1968 and of Shriver in 1972 for the vice-presidency were interpreted as Democratic efforts to hold the Catholic vote.

been distinguished for virtues other than those calling for veneration by the faithful. It is appropriate, therefore, to begin a consideration of currents of thought and concern that have characterized American Catholicism by centering attention on its "social program."

THE SOCIAL PROGRAM OF THE CHURCH.   For two decades after its founding, the National Catholic Welfare Conference was regarded in public esteem as almost synonymous with its Social Action Department, headed by John A. Ryan (1869–1945), professor of moral theology at Catholic University.[7] In 1919 Ryan wrote a pamphlet, *Social Reconstruction: A General Review of the Problems and Survey of the Remedies*, which became known as the "Bishops' Program of Social Reconstruction." [8] The document pointed to the need for minimum wage legislation, regulation of child labor, protection of the right of labor to organize, public housing, a national employment service, and unemployment, industrial accident, and old-age insurance. With one or two exceptions, the recommendations of the Ryan document became part of the New Deal legislation of the early Roosevelt years.

Meanwhile other Catholics actively forwarded the cause of economic justice. The Catholic League for Social Justice was established in 1932. A year later Dorothy Day (b. 1898) helped found the Catholic Worker movement. In 1937 the Association of Catholic Trade Unionists was formed. Numerous "labor schools" were established to train union members and help them combat both racketeering elements in the unions and Communist infiltration. Moreover, Charles E. Coughlin (b. 1891), the radio priest of the Shrine of the Little Flower in Royal Oak, Michigan, won a large following in the 1930's as a conspicuous spokesman for social justice. When his weekly broadcasts became tinged with anti-Semitic sentiment, however, his ecclesiastical superiors gradually inhibited him from further political activity.

Although the "Bishops' Program of Social Reconstruction" was based on the authoritative teaching of the papal encyclical *Rerum Novarum* (1891), the stance of the church was ambiguous. Some bishops were lukewarm in their support, and many of the laity were recalcitrant. The cooling of social ardor was especially noticeable after World War II when much of the Catholic press became scornful of "do-gooders" and "bleeding hearts." The disposition to give only nominal acceptance to the "social

[7] See F. L. Broderick, *Right Reverend New Dealer: John A. Ryan* (N.Y., 1963).
[8] Reprinted in Smith, Handy, Loetscher, *American Christianity*, II, 407–14.

encyclicals," Bishop William Mulloy declared in 1952, "tended to paralyze the force of the teaching Church in modern American society." [9]

Roman Catholic policy was much more firm during the 1950's in the area of racial justice. Ever since the Civil War work among Negroes had followed a segregated pattern, but in the 1920's a protest movement led to a series of conferences which focused attention on segregation in Catholic institutions. The movement began to bear fruit when the Archbishop of St. Louis in 1947 ended segregation in the schools of his diocese. The following year the Archbishop of Washington followed his example, and in 1953 the Bishop of Raleigh, North Carolina, defied the opposition of Catholics in his diocese and opened the churches, schools, and hospitals under his jurisdiction to people of every race. After the Supreme Court in 1954 declared public school segregation unconstitutional, the unequivocal stands of Archbishops Robert E. Lucey of San Antonio and Joseph F. Rummel of New Orleans were a heartening feature of the situation in the South.

The tenor of Catholic political thought contrasted sharply with the progressive character of other aspects of the church's social program. Tendencies toward accommodation of Catholic tradition to basic assumptions of American democracy had been arrested by Leo XIII's condemnation of "Americanism" in 1899. The alternative, in terms of official teaching, seemed to be to look back to the Middle Ages for normative models, and this alternative appeared to have been commanded by Leo XIII's encyclicals "The Christian Constitution of States" (1885) and "Christian Democracy" (1901) which rejected doctrines of popular sovereignty, government by consent of the governed, and pernicious notions of freedom of religion, freedom of speech, freedom of assembly, and freedom of the press.[10] The encyclicals conceded that, due to circumstances in any given nation, a full Christian political order may not always be possible or practical. Under certain conditions, therefore, the church will not judge it "blameworthy" for "the people to have a share, greater or less, in the government." Indeed, under certain conditions, "such participation . . . may even be of obligation." This concession was the "out" seized upon by American Catholics familiar with papal teaching to effect a practical adjustment to the necessities of American political life. The theory was explicated by John A. Ryan and Moorhouse F. X.

9 Cross, *Emergence of Liberal Catholicism*, 218–19.
10 For the encyclicals, see W. S. Hudson, *Understanding Roman Catholicism*.

402

Millar in the widely used textbook, *The State and the Church* (1922).[11] In the area of political thought, since he was forced to acknowledge that Catholic teaching involved "hard sayings" that smacked of intolerance, Ryan was cast in the role of a reactionary.

Whatever Ryan's intention may have been, the views expounded in his textbook made it possible for many Catholics in the 1950's to defend Senator Joseph McCarthy's activities on the assumption that they were based on "Catholic" teaching. By the late 1940's, however, Catholic theologians began to challenge Ryan's conclusions. Jesuits John Courtney Murray (1904–67) and Gustave Weigel (1906–64) took the lead with a more dynamic view of Catholic political theory, placing it in historical context and demonstrating that political democracy could be firmly grounded on Catholic principles.[12] Within a decade their views were clearly in the ascendency.

INTELLECTUAL LIFE. As early as 1928, in *The Catholic Spirit in America,* George N. Shuster was voicing the complaint that American Catholicism was intellectually asleep and exhibited "a terrible contempt for thought." In 1940 he renewed the charge, stating that the church had "virtually no use for intellectuals." The absence of a strong intellectual tradition may be attributed to several causes. For one thing, American Catholics had been too engrossed in what have been called "brick-and-mortar" enterprises—constructing churches, schools, and other institutions—to allow much energy and imagination to be devoted to intellectual pursuits. Moreover, the average immigrant family lacked both the educational background and the financial resources to foster intellectual interests. Symptomatic of this was the fact that in the late 1940's not a single member of the hierarchy was the son of college-educated parents. Furthermore, throughout the Catholic educational system the tendency had been to emphasize "safeness" at the expense of "excellence" and creative inquiry. But the major reason was the inhibiting effect of the successive condemnation of "Americanism" and "Modernism."

The retreat into "separatism" from American culture which followed Leo XIII's letter of 1899 to Cardinal Gibbons was strongly reinforced by Pius X's comprehensive attack in 1907 on the "modernist" heresies flowing from the historical researches of certain European Catholic scholars.

11 Later revised and republished by Ryan and Francis J. Boland under a new title, *Catholic Principles of Politics* (N.Y., 1940).

12 See Murray's essays, *We Hold These Truths* (N.Y., 1960), and Gustave Weigel, "The Church and the Democratic State," *Thought,* XXVII (1952), 165–75.

Bishops were instructed to exercise minute supervision of both teachers and students. Three years later a decree was issued requiring all Catholics in positions of responsibilty to take a detailed antimodernist oath. Although few in America held the condemned opinions, the effect of the condemnation was to heighten timidity and give full reign to an unquestioning orthodoxy. The spirit inculcated was reflected in the counsel given a young Paulist who was perplexed by intellectual problems. He was advised to "preach the moral law and let dogmas alone." [13]

It was not until after World War II that the situation began to change. The mingling, especially of priests, with non-Catholics in the armed forces ended the isolation which had so largely prevailed. Also the educational level of the Catholic population was rising, thrusting to the fore questions hitherto regarded as "too hot to handle." And an awareness began to seep into academic cloisters of new theological trends in Europe. But the most decisive factor may have been such verdicts as that expressed by an English observer that "the Catholic church in America has counted for astonishingly little in the formation of the American intellectual climate." In 1955 John Tracy Ellis of Catholic University created a minor sensation with an indictment of American Catholics for their intellectual abdication, and three years later Thomas F. O'Dea contributed an even more detailed analysis of the problem.[14]

In the meantime a vigorous controversy had developed between those who were convinced that the general culture was important to Catholics and necessitated their active involvement in it and those who insisted that a strongly guarded defensive posture was indispensable since Catholicism and modern cultural tendencies were diametrically opposed. The first position commanded massive Jesuit support, with John Courtney Murray and Gustave Weigel the outstanding protagonists. Stressing the obligation of the church to the pursuit of truth and drawing heavily upon new biblical and theological studies in Europe, they tended to share the belief, enunciated by Walter Elliott in the 1890's, that one who turned aside from apologetic opportunities involved in friendly contact with non-Catholic scholars was "only a half Catholic." The conservative citadel was

---

13 W. L. Sullivan, *Under Orders* (N.Y., 1944), 111. T. T. McAvoy spoke of the "theological silence" which descended on the church. See *The Great Crisis in American Catholic History*, 344.

14 D. W. Brogan, *U.S.A.: An Outline of the Country, Its People and Institutions* (London, 1941), 65. Ellis, *American Catholics and the Intellectual Life* (Chicago, 1956), originally published in *Thought*, XXX (1955), 351–88. O'Dea, *American Catholic Dilemma: An Inquiry into the Intellectual Life* (N.Y., 1958).

the faculty of theology at Catholic University, where Joseph C. Fenton and Francis J. Connell took the lead in viewing the "openness" of the Jesuits as verging on indifferentism. "Polemics" rather than "irenics" was emphasized as the proper approach to error, for any minimizing of the hard sayings of dogma to avoid offense to outsiders was to trifle with the salvation of the faithful.[15] In the 1960's, partly as the result of the "fresh air" introduced into the church by John XXIII, the conservatives were pushed into a defensive position even within the church. The ranks of the "liberals" had been swelled by recruits from non-Jesuit orders, diocesan seminaries were displaying a new openness, new scholarly journals were being published, and a growing number of Catholic colleges and universities were beginning to be distinguished by the quality of their scholarly contributions and the vigor of their intellectual life.

THE RELIGIOUS REVIVAL. Fulton Sheen (1895–1979) and Thomas Merton (1905–68) were two major symbols of the post-World War II religious revival among Roman Catholics. In public esteem Sheen ranked with Billy Graham and Norman Vincent Peale as the preeminent spokesmen of religion during these years. A teacher of philosophy at Catholic University with a gift of speaking intelligibly and convincingly to a mass audience, Sheen gained fame as a radio and television preacher and then as the author of several widely read books. His role in a number of prominent conversions, both before and after being appointed auxiliary bishop of New York, also made him a focus of attention. These conversions, however, did not prevent him from gaining a wide hearing among Protestants as well as Catholics, since he seldom stressed distinctively Roman Catholic doctrine. Merton was a disillusioned sophisticate who had sought peace in many places, including Greenwich Village, and finally found it in the silence of a Trappist monastery in Kentucky. His autobiography, *The Seven Story Mountain* (1948), was on the list of best sellers for months, and his subsequent writings also aroused widespread interest.

Merton's pilgrimage was part of a striking movement to which his autobiography gave added impetus. Although a Trappist monastery had been established in America early in the nineteenth century, contempla-

[15] See Fenton, "The Direction of Catholic Polemic," *American Ecclesiastical Review*, CXXII (1950), 48–55; "The Church and God's Promises," *ibid.*; CXXIII (1950), 295–308, "The Lesson of *Humani Generis*," *ibid.*, 359–78, and "Catholic Polemic and Doctrinal Accuracy," *ibid.*, CXXXII (1955), 107–17. See also Connell, "If the Trumpet Give an Uncertain Sound," *American Ecclesiastical Review*, CXVIII (1948), 23–30, and "Theological Content of *Humani Generis*," *ibid.*, CXXIII (1950), 321–30.

tive monasticism, with its vows of perpetual silence and rigorous austerity, failed to prosper in the American environment. At the end of World War II, however, a startling change occurred when hundreds of young men began to forsake the world and give themselves fully to a life of prayer and contemplation.

The surge of interest in contemplative life, of course, was restricted to a spiritual elite. A more typical expression of the religious revival was mounting lay participation in the life of the church, much of it associated with the burgeoning parishes of the suburbs. The lay movement was the product of the wedding of traditional American activism with postwar religious enthusiasm and the increased stress of Pius XII on the importance of the lay apostolate. So marked was the development that one clerical observer could speak with confidence of "The Coming Era of the Catholic Layman." [16]

Closely related to the lay movement was a developing liturgical interest which sought to revitalize corporate worship. The religious revival had expressed itself initially among Roman Catholics in the growing popularity of many special nonliturgical devotions—the Forty Hours Adoration of the Blessed Sacrament; novenas to Our Lady of Perpetual Help, Our Lady of Sorrows, Our Lady of Fatima, Our Lady of the Miraculous Medal; and devotions to favorite saints such as St. Ann, St. Jude, St. Anthony, and St. Rita. But attendance at Mass was often little more than fulfillment of solemn obligation. Worshipers frequently had little understanding of the service and sat as mere spectators or performed private devotions by reciting the rosary. This was scarcely an adequate expression of their role as a Christian people or of their lay priesthood, nor did such routine attendance readily relate itself to their apostolate in the world. It was out of concern to renew the life of the church through truly corporate worship that the liturgical movement was born.

The main center of the liturgical revival in America was the Benedictine Abbey at Collegeville, Minnesota, where Virgil Michel (1890–1938) was the outstanding pioneer. Through his initiative the periodical *Orate Fratres* (later known as *Worship*) was founded to promote liturgical renewal. In 1940 annual Liturgical Weeks, conferences for those interested

[16] This was the title of an article by W. R. Fleege in the *Homiletical and Pastoral Review*, LIV (1953), 134–39. For the lay movement, see Leo R. Ward, *The American Apostolate* (Westminster, Md., 1952) and *Catholic Life, U.S.A.: Contemporary Lay Movements* (N.Y., 1959), and L. J. Putz, *The Catholic Church, U.S.A.* (Chicago, 1956).

in liturgical renewal, began to be held. In addition to seeking to instruct the faithful in the meaning of the liturgy, two chief goals of the movement were use of the vernacular instead of Latin and adoption of the dialogue Mass in which the people recite the prayers with the priest. Other aims included restoration of the Holy Week Liturgy, encouragement of daily attendance at Mass, and the use of "people's altars" placed in the midst of the worshiping congregation.[17] By 1960 liturgical renewal was receiving widespread support, many innovations had been introduced, and the movement had deeply influenced the architecture of new church buildings. Three years later the movement received full sanction when Paul VI, on December 4, 1963, promulgated the "Constitution of the Liturgy" which had been approved by the Second Vatican Council.

Interfaith relationships

The middle decades of the twentieth century were marked by increasingly friendly interfaith relationships. The National Conference of Christians and Jews, founded in 1928, was one of the instruments for promoting understanding between adherents of different faiths, utilizing local committees to combat prejudice, ill-feeling, and strained relationships. Broad Protestant and Jewish support was enlisted but Catholic participation was extremely limited. Francis J. Connell voiced the prevailing sentiment when he declared that "the association of Catholics with non-Catholics in such organizations and meetings is a grave menace to the faith of our people." [18] This aloofness from interfaith relationships was in striking contrast to the generally warm, friendly, and even cordial attitudes of Protestants and Jews. Even the Eastern Orthodox churches, while maintaining their doctrinal integrity, felt sufficiently secure to accept membership in both the National and World Councils of Churches. The Catholic problem was complicated by tension at several points of social policy and also by an unresolved difference of opinion as to the proper strategy to be pursued in a religiously pluralistic society.

While feelings were exacerbated by Roman Catholic intransigence on issues of public policy, the greatest problem in reducing tension was

[17] E. B. Koenker, *The Liturgical Renaissance in the Roman Catholic Church* (Chicago, 1954), P. B. Marx, *Virgil Michel and the Liturgical Movement* (Collegeville, Minn., 1957), A. H. Reinhold, *The American Parish and the Roman Liturgy* (N.Y., 1958).
[18] Cross, *Emergence of Liberal Catholicism*, 212.

the self-imposed Roman Catholic policy of isolation. As the ecumenical movement gained momentum in the 1920's and 1930's, it was hoped that Catholics would participate. This hope was dashed in 1928 when Pius XI issued an encyclical on "Fostering True Religious Unity" (*Mortalium Animos*) in which he declared that it was unlawful for Catholics to "take part in these assemblies," and that by giving "such enterprises their encouragement or support," they "would be giving countenance to a false Christianity quite alien to the one Church of Christ." Throughout the 1940's, however, there was growing restiveness at this blanket prohibition.

In retrospect it is clear that a basis for a new attitude was being prepared by a revival of biblical studies which made it possible to distinguish the spiritual from the physical body of Christ. This dual understanding of the church was susceptible of being interpreted to justify regarding Protestants as "separated brethren" and "brethren in Christ." Although European scholars initiated this new type of thinking, a number of American Catholics began to recognize the necessity of breaching the wall of ignorance which separated Catholics and Protestants in the United States. In 1957 John A. Hardon published a book entitled *The Protestant Churches of the United States* in which he noted that Catholics "often have only the vaguest notion of what Protestants believe, how they worship, and what their religion means to them." [19] Nor was Hardon alone in this concern. In 1955 J. J. Kane sought to foster sympathetic understanding with his *Catholic-Protestant Conflicts in America,* as did George H. Tavard in *The Catholic Approach to Protestantism,* and in 1957 Gustave Weigel published *A Catholic Primer on the Ecumenical Movement.*

The elevation of Angelo Giuseppe Roncalli to the chair of Peter as John XXIII late in 1958 inaugurated a new era in the Catholic Church. On January 25, 1959, he announced his intention to summon a General Council of the Roman Catholic Church to bring the church up-to-date (*aggiornamento*) through purification and renewal. By opening a few windows he hoped to make the Church more effective in dealing with the problems of the twentieth century and to provide a basis for furthering Christian unity. When the first session of the Second Vatican Council con-

[19] Two years later Jaroslav Pelikan, a Protestant, made a similar admission in the Introduction to *The Riddle of Roman Catholicism,* stating that many Protestants "know more about the batting averages of the Yankees or the marriages and divorces of Hollywood than they do about the life and workings" of the Roman Catholic Church.

vened on October 11, 1962, seventeen non-Roman Catholic churches had responded to an invitation to send "official observers," and the impact made by their mere presence was felt throughout the whole Roman Catholic Church.

In the United States John XXIII's initiatives led to a dramatic shift in the atmosphere of interfaith relationships. Even in terms of pressing social problems there had been little interfaith cooperation, but within a month of the close of the first session of the Second Vatican Council, Protestants, Roman Catholics, and Jews met at Chicago in a national meeting to chart a common strategy for dealing with the racial crisis. "The bishops were holding back from these meetings out of fear—fear of Rome," one theologian explained. "Now Pope John has given the Church a freedom from fear." [20] The most impressive consequence of the new spirit was the flowering of interfaith discussion in city after city throughout the nation. Reticence gave way to openness and friendliness, and for the first time in more than a half century Catholic clergy with ease of mind could talk freely with representatives of other faiths about points of difference. Equally impressive was the warmth of the response by clergy of other faiths. No surrender of doctrinal positions was intended or expected, but sympathetic understanding was no longer foreclosed by estrangement.

The several tendencies of growing maturity within American Roman Catholicism—a deepened sense of responsibility to society, a heightened emphasis upon intellectual pursuits, a greater stress on the role of the laity, and an intensified concern for liturgical renewal—had been brought into focus and reinforced by John XXIII and the Second Vatican Council. But this remarkable pontiff, who had been expected to serve only a caretaker role made a further contribution. By the openness to the "world" he displayed, American Catholics were enabled to shed the last vestiges of an immigrant mentality and with Americans of other faiths they were learning, in the presence of diversity, to live together in a way that was mutually enriching rather than impoverishing.

Learning this latter lesson was to be especially important for the years ahead, for both churches and nation were about to enter a troubled time which would tax the wisdom, strength, and resources of everyone.

[20] R. B. Kaiser, *Pope, Council, and World* (N.Y., 1963), 254.

XVI

A Time of Disarray and Disaffection

The Eisenhower years (1952–60) were quiet years, years of relative affluence and stability. The Korean War ended. Joseph McCarthy was "put down." And most Americans were content to relax and enjoy themselves. Some tumult was precipitated by the 1954 Supreme Court decision ordering school desegregation "with all deliberate speed." But even on the racial front, in spite of the emphasis on "deliberate" in school desegregation, there was hopefulness, a confidence that through sit-ins, ride-ins, and legal proceedings steady progress was being made in eliminating discrimination in public accommodations. An important source of calm and hope was President Eisenhower himself. To most people he was a reassuring father figure. "We like Ike" was the slogan that expressed the majority feeling. Still there was an undercurrent of disaffection.

The academic community felt displaced after the heady years of the Roosevelt "brain trust." Their subsequent hero, Adlai Stevenson, had twice gone down to defeat, and "Engine Charlie" Wilson was a chief symbol of Eisenhower's "businessmen's government," to which they found it difficult to relate. A more radical disaffection began to surface in 1957 with the "beatniks" who represented a deep sense of alienation from the whole style and quality of life of the Eisenhower years of affluence.[1]

Disaffection also began to surface among Protestant theological professors who were dismayed by the superficiality of the "religious revival." Earlier criticism of culture religion, form without substance, was revived. Analyses of what was disparagingly called "religion-in-general" ("a passionate faith in the Great Whatever" was William Lee Miller's designation) were accompanied by calls for more substantive religious renewal than that represented by middle-class piety.[2]

While the Protestant phase of the revival peaked in 1957 with all indices of growth leveling off thereafter, Roman Catholic momentum was maintained somewhat longer, pent-up disaffection not being fully released until Vatican Council II had relaxed the fetters that inhibited expressions of discontent. The momentum of Judaism continued and was reinforced by a surge of pride in "Jewishness" that followed the unexpectedly quick victory in the "six days' war" in 1967. Of the larger groups, only the Eastern Orthodox and Negro churches departed from a general pattern of incipient disaffection. Eastern Orthodoxy was busy pursuing internal regrouping and consolidation. The Negro churches were to experience a revival of their own with a focus on "blackness"—black religion, black theology, black churches, black power, black liberation.

Protestantism's quest for meaning and vocation

Awareness of Protestant acculturation and accommodation led to a loss of a sense of vocation among the clergy. Not being content with a

---

[1] Jack Kerouac, Ken Kesey, and Allen Ginsberg were among the more important literary figures. For Kerouac's account of "The Origins of the Beat Generation," see Thomas Parkinson, *Case-book on the Beat* (N.Y., 1961). For a poet's biting satire, see "Boom!" by Howard Nemerov, *New and Selected Poems* (Chicago, 1960), 18–19.

[2] See A. R. Eckardt, *The Surge of Piety in America* (N.Y., 1958); M. E. Marty, *The New Shape of American Religion* (N.Y., 1959); Peter Berger, *The Noise of Solemn Assemblies* (Garden City, N.Y., 1961). Will Herberg had indicated how differing religious affiliations were little more than acceptable ways of being an American, *Protestant-Catholic-Jew* (Garden City, N.Y., 1955).

housekeeping role of merely maintaining the institutional life of churches and tutored by historians and theologians of a Barthian cast, clerical leadership at the end of the 1950's embarked briefly once again on the task of theological recovery, seeking to rediscover in the Christian gospel a source of identity and meaning which transcended its cultural expressions.[3] This endeavor was aborted, however, partly because theological energies were diverted to a church union proposal and partly because the 1960's began with a new flare of hope for society.

The story of the quest for church union is briefly told. The first Consultation on Church Union (COCU) met in 1962 with the Presbyterian Church, the Episcopal Church, the Methodist Church, and the United Church of Christ as participants.[4] A decade later the Consultation received a crippling blow by the withdrawal of the United Presbyterian Church. The Presbyterian action was symptomatic of general disquiet. There was conservative resistance in each church. What tipped the scale was a defection of liberal support, a defection grounded in growing distrust of bigness and centralization and growing stress on localism and dispersal of decision making.[5] These advocates of "participatory democracy," taking advantage of a preoccupation with "restructuring," in 1969 also attempted to dismantle the National Council of Churches by reducing it to a loose federation of autonomous "task forces."

NEW CULTURAL ACCOMMODATIONS.   The new flare of hope, which aborted the brief effort of theologians to disengage the churches from cultural accommodation, was awakened by the election of John F. Kennedy in 1960. The striking feature of the Kennedy administration was a change in style. "Intellectuals" once again were recruited from the academic community and brought into inner circles of government. Kennedy had élan, flair, style. He had a romantic aura—youth, a young and beautiful wife, little children. He became a symbol of hope, not only in the United States but—in stark contrast to the old men of

3 One expression of the attempted theological recovery was the *Christian Faith and Life Series* developed for Presbyterian church school classes.
4 George L. Hunt and P. A. Crow, *Where We Are in Church Union* (N.Y., 1965). Ultimately nine denominations participated in the Consultations.
5 In 1980 COCU discussions were revived by a faithful remnant of earlier participants who, refusing to accept defeat, presented a new Plan of Union to be considered by the churches and acted upon in 1986.

Europe, Adenauer, De Gaulle, De Gaspari—throughout the world. This change in mood produced a change in Protestantism's quest for vocation. If theological leadership had spoken disparagingly of culture-bound religion during the Eisenhower era, it was because of disenchantment with existing social and cultural prospects. With a more hopeful prospect in view, seminary and bureaucratic leadership began to turn to the easier task of seeking a vocation for church and clergy within the society and culture to which the churches already had become accommodated. The quest was pursued along several parallel and often converging paths.

In the field of theology, the new optimism found expression among those who styled themselves "radical" or "death of God" theologians.[6] While the word theology was retained, there was a forthright rejection of the past (theological language, theological categories, and "God-talk") as no longer meaningful and acceptance of the present (modern man and secular culture) as normative. With existentialism a strong influence, meaning was sought in the present. One spoke of "doing theology"—an emphasis on "style" (standing beside the neighbor) rather than on "substance" (principles, rules, standards). When one engaged in reflection, it was reflection derived from present action and present experience.

If meaning was to be found in the present rather than the past, the vocation of church and clergy had to be present-oriented. In theological schools this meant for many a shift from theology to sociology. With consciences having been sensitized to the plight of the disadvantaged, the scandal of discrimination, and the growing stratification and consequent isolation of various segments of society in self-contained residential enclaves, many churchmen became fascinated with the central city as the place where cleavages could be transcended and injustices rectified.

[6] See the essays by Thomas Altizer and William Hamilton, *Radical Theology and the Death of God* (Indianapolis, 1966). In differing ways, Paul Van Buren, *The Secular Meaning of the Gospel* (N.Y., 1963), and John A. T. Robinson, *Honest to God* (Phila., 1963) were related to the new cultural or "secular" Christianity. Present-mindedness and rejection of theological "principles" was represented in the field of ethics by Joseph Fletcher, *Situation Ethics: The New Morality* (Phila., 1966). For a critique of this type of thinking, see Kenneth Hamilton, *What's New in Religion: A Critical Study of New Theology, New Morality, and Secular Christianity* (Grand Rapids, 1968).

The preoccupation with the city had a double thrust, both being fully explicated by Gibson Winter in 1961.[7] The first was a romanticizing of the "inner city" as a locus where all kinds of people could be found, a place, therefore, where experimental ministries could foster "congregations" (groups) that would be truly "inclusive." The basic motivation was anti-elitist as a counter to the exclusivism of existing churches. In many instances, however, this anti-elitist thrust was deflected into a paternalistic ghetto type of activity. The second thrust spelled out by Winter was specifically elitist, being preoccupied with social management and utilization of technology to transform the metropolis into the New Jerusalem. The vocation of the clergy was to be "change-agents," social engineers, "evangelizing" the structures of society by infiltrating community organizations, zoning boards, planning commissions, as well as penetrating the corporate structures of business and industry and developing cadres among the professions.

The sociological emphasis led quite naturally to a stress on sociological expertise as a means of "doing theology" and discovering a meaningful clerical vocation. A popular way of describing this sociological vocation was to speak of clergymen as "enablers" who initiated community change by helping lawyers, doctors, engineers, architects, business executives, and others, discover their duty and do it.

An alternate way of finding a meaningful role for church and clergy in a present-oriented culture religion was to seek it in the field of psychology. This therapeutic Christianity was derived from a variety of "cultural ideologies"—from Freud, Jung, Fromm, Erikson. But the most immediately influential figure was Carl Rogers, beginning with his *Casebook of Non-Directive Counseling* (1947) and extending to his *Carl Rogers on Encounter Groups* (1970). Multiform and diverse, the development of therapeutic Christianity is difficult to chart, but its general movement is reasonably clear—from the pastor as individual therapist in a one-to-one relationship to a utilization of group dynamics and group process. Beginning with small groups for personal renewal, the progression was to therapy groups, encounter groups, sensitivity groups, and group marathons. Sometimes a contrived chaos was

---

[7] *The Suburban Captivity of the Churches* (Garden City, N.Y., 1961). The emphases were further elaborated by Winter, *Metropolis as the New Creation* (N.Y., 1963), and by Harvey Cox's best seller, *The Secular City* (N.Y., 1965).

fostered to free individuals from the ordered structures of church life and thus facilitate creativity, innovation, and self-discovery.

PROTESTANT DISARRAY.   Although "faith" had ceased to "abide" (I Corinthians 13:13) for "radical theologians" and their fellow accommodationists, "love" was still available, and a cultural confidence gave ground for "hope." For William Hamilton, two events of January 4, 1965, signaled the final shift from pessimism to optimism—the death of T. S. Eliot, with his wasteland and hollow men, and the inaugural address of Lyndon Johnson, with its depiction of "the great society."[8]

While Hamilton was late in recognizing it, the promise of "the golden sixties" was not to be fulfilled. The 1960's turned out to be a decade when almost everything went wrong. Beginning with the Bay of Pigs fiasco, the Vietnam intervention, the triple assassinations of President Kennedy in 1963 and of Martin Luther King and Robert Kennedy in 1968, the decade witnessed mounting unrest, discontent, burnings, and bombings. The civil rights movement achieved its initial goals, but instead of diminishing the racial crisis was intensified. Urban programs multiplied, but the problems of the cities became intractable, desperate, and unmanageable.

Mainline Protestant churches were thrown into disarray by their misplaced confidence in the culture. With few social achievements to validate them, the "secular" thrusts of theologians and ecclesiastics had little effective impact. In 1957, according to the Gallup Poll, only 14 per cent of Americans believed that religion was losing its influence. A decade later 57 per cent held this opinion, and in 1970 those who believed religion was losing influence increased to 75 per cent. After 1957 church attendance began to level off and then decline. Church membership of several major denominations failed to keep pace with the increase in population. In 1968 ten of the largest Protestant churches had fewer members than in the preceding year. This decline in numbers continued into the 1970's. The United Methodist Church, a denomination that once out-paced all others, leaping forward like a brush fire, in 1972 reported a net loss of 518,000 members in the preceding four years. Financial contributions also fell off, while the decline in church school enrollment began earlier and was more drastic than the decline in church membership. From 1958 to 1971 the foreign

[8] Altizer and Hamilton, *Radical Theology,* 159.

mission personnel of six representative denominations was reduced by one-third.[9]

The new "secular" emphases and programs of the churches were scarcely calculated to stimulate church renewal and augment religious interest. The reductionism of "secular theology" had scant appeal and little compelling power. Its most provocative slogan—"the death of God"—appeared at face value to be an announcement of the irrelevance of religion. Psychological therapy, moreover, was no monopoly of the church and required no return either to church or religion. Therapy groups were everywhere available to those who wished to embark upon a process of self-discovery. The "secular city" (Gibson Winter's "metropolis" as "the new creation") thrust was more preoccupied with action than reflection, more interested in power than in piety, more concerned with effecting political coalitions than communicating Christian insight. Small wonder that these emphases were more productive of apathy than renewal, of dissidence than growth. After an initial "shock" appeal, they even failed to titillate the interest of the non-church public. The religious book market, which had been so profitable in the 1950's, collapsed, and major publishing houses began abandoning their religious book departments.

Most major Protestant bodies experienced widespread dissension centering on social issues that was referred to as a "gap between clergy and laity." One exception was the Lutheran Church—Missouri Synod where the issue was doctrinal. Schism was narrowly averted in 1971, but this only postponed the ousting of professors at Concordia Theological Seminary for unsound views of biblical authority which resulted, in turn, after efforts at reconciliation failed, in a formal split. Theological disputes also continued to trouble Southern Baptists.

Meanwhile Protestant churches were being buffeted by demands of caucuses of blacks and of women—demands that were met in varied ways and to varying degrees. Provision was made for minority representation in executive councils, funds were allocated to meet minority needs, and women achieved a status of greater equality. Baptists, Congregationalists (United Church of Christ), Friends, Methodists, and some other groups had long ordained women and occasionally elected

[9] For statistics, see D. M. Kelley, *Why Conservative Churches Are Growing* (N.Y., 1972), 1–11.

them to high church office, but mostly women were restricted to serve small churches. United Presbyterians and the Lutheran Church in America had begun to ordain women, and Presbyterians had elected a woman moderator of their General Assembly. Episcopalians were more laggard, ordaining women only after a stiff fight which led to a defection by "traditionalists."

One of the sadder aspects of the era of Protestant disarray was the closing of many theological seminaries which had long and distinguished histories. Suffering from confusion of purpose and costly curricular innovations, many theological schools were beset by mounting deficits. Some casualties resulted from merging smaller seminaries to create stronger institutions, such as the Lutheran School of Theology at Chicago and the United Theological Seminary of the Twin Cities in Minnesota. Others, such as Bexley Hall and Crozer Theological Seminary, sought to survive by adding their students and income to the greater resources of Colgate Rochester Divinity School. Berkeley Divinity School also adopted this recourse, uniting with Yale Divinity School in 1971. Some sought strength by sharing resources in "consortiums." And some simply disappeared. Oberlin School of Theology, with a record of notable alumni stretching back to the time of Charles G. Finney but with few resources of its own, was absorbed almost unnoticed by Vanderbilt Divinity School. Hartford, with an equally distinguished history, a magnificent library, and the fourth largest endowment of any theological school, but with few students, announced in 1972 that it was closing its doors as a theological seminary and would use its funds for a dispersed "ministry support" program featuring "action-research," "parish renewal," and "professional development" projects.

Roman Catholic euphoria, vacillation, and dissidence

Roman Catholic growth peaked in 1959. Thereafter a slowly eroding plateau was maintained until 1965 when the erosion accelerated. This halt and decline was apparent only in retrospect, only after sufficient time elapsed for statistical comparisons to be made. Moreover, for the first years the decline was partly obscured and partly arrested by the heady excitement following John XXIII's election to the papal office in 1958, by John F. Kennedy's election to the presidency in 1960, and by the surprising events of the initial session of Vatican II. Of the three, the Vatican Council (1962–65) had the most important consequences. Not since the sixteenth-century Council of Trent was the church subjected to such transformation. Few aspects of church life were left untouched—shape and language of worship, devotional practices, ecclesiastical administration, relationships to other Christians, attitudes of clergy and laity. Ripples set in motion by the Council ran far and wide.[10]

EUPHORIA AND VACILLATION. If Vatican II initiated profound changes in the church, expectation of change often outran the speed and extent of reform. The response of most American bishops was hesitant and cautious. They were slow to move partly out of habit and partly because they had other pressing problems. The heady excitement of reform may have made the problems seem less pressing to others, but with urgent day-to-day problems to meet, the bishops were not permitted this luxury. They knew that the church was in deep trouble.

A dramatic decline in conversions, perhaps a result of the new ecumenical spirit, was paralleled by declines in accessions by birth and immigration. More serious were declines in the number of seminarians and religious vocations among young women, accompanied by increases in the number of priests and members of teaching orders returning to lay life.[11] Parochial schools also demanded attention. Even with enrollment dropping and schools closing, the loss of low-paid personnel precipitated a crisis, for it meant increased dependence on more highly paid lay teachers. The problem was aggravated by a questioning of the value and quality of parochial education, some arguing that the whole system should be phased out.[12] There also was the problem of parishes left stranded by the shift of Catholic families from slums to suburbs. New churches had to be built in the suburbs, while inner-city churches were left with half-empty houses of worship and inadequate means to

---

[10] For an account of this period, see "The Changing Church" in J. T. Ellis, *American Catholicism*, rev. ed. (Chicago, 1969).

[11] Seminarians dropped from 48,046 in 1966 to 22,963 in 1972; nuns from 181,421 to 146,914; lay brothers from 12,255 to 9,740.

[12] Mary P. Ryan, *Are Parochial Schools the Answer?* (N.Y., 1964).

support the decaying parish facilities. Thus the bishops had to make agonizing reappraisals of priorities and reallocations of resources.

Both the Roman Curia and the National Conference of Catholic Bishops were slow in issuing guidelines for reforms approved by the Council, and with few exceptions individual bishops were tardy in instituting reforms once guidelines were provided. The "Constitution on the Sacred Liturgy," for example, was promulgated in 1963, but Cardinal McIntyre of Los Angeles, who believed lay participation distracted attention from "contemplation of the mystery of the Eucharist," kept the liturgical life of Los Angeles unchanged throughout the decade. Most bishops were less laggard, but few kept pace with expectations aroused in important segments of the church. Eager young priests with enthusiastic support of youthful parishioners took things into their own hands and embarked on liturgical experiments which sometimes took the form of "underground" or "house" churches but more often were unauthorized innovations introduced into regular church worship. Approval of change frequently came a year of more after the fact of change. Official changes were dramatic enough—use of English instead of Latin, freestanding "people's altars" with the priest facing the people, congregational responses, singing of hymns—often Protestant hymns. By the time approval was given, reformers had proceeded with further experimentation of their own.

Gradually other reforms were instituted. Discipline was relaxed at many points. The laity were given more active roles. Advisory school boards and parish councils were established. Diocesan priests' councils or senates were instituted, and in 1968 these were linked in a National Federation of Priests' Councils. In 1966 the bishops sought greater cohesion and coordination among themselves by electing a president of the National Conference of Catholic Bishops.

DISSIDENCE. A curious consequence of Vatican II is that it created dissidence on both right and left. Apprehension and dismay were aroused as well as exhilaration and expectation. The so-called "fish on Friday" syndrome is a conventional way to illustrate the disarray that followed the ending of compulsory Friday abstinence. Of little consequence in itself, "Friday's fish" was of great symbolic importance in distinguishing Catholics from other Americans. When such a symbol is changed, much else is called into question. And alterations were introduced in other items of symbolic importance. With the changes in customary practices and disciplines, gnawing identity anxieties were awakened.

The Latin Mass was symbolically the most important feature of traditional church life, and the introduction of a vernacular liturgy was a point at which conservative opposition first coalesced. The Catholic Traditionalist Movement issued its first manifesto in 1965. Other groups, such as Catholics United for the Faith, were organized. Meanwhile the National Federation of Laymen was organizing financial boycotts to withhold funds from parishes which allowed their schools to teach "humanistic" and "Freudian" values. An anomaly of traditionalist dissidence was that it led to open disobedience to church authority and to blunt criticism of the Pope. Of Paul VI, William Marra of Fordham grumbled: "He looks at all the heresy that is rampant in the chanceries, and all that he can do is weep."[13]

Among "progressives," the vacillation of the bishops also precipitated a crisis of authority. The church's teaching began to be questioned on subjects as diverse as the Incarnation, birth control, obligatory celibacy of priests, and papal infallibility. The issue of obedience was publicly dramatized in 1967 at Catholic University when Charles S. Curran failed to have his contract renewed and was denied the promotion recommended by the faculty. To the consternation of the authorities, this led to an almost total boycott of classes by faculty and students, including large numbers of graduate student priests and nuns. The ecclesiastical authorities capitulated and Curran was promoted.[14]

Participation of the priests and nuns in the boycott at Catholic University was symptomatic of widespread disaffection. Caught up in a crisis of change, younger priests were unsure of who they were and what they were to do. Responding to this malaise, the bishops in 1967 appointed a committee to sponsor sociological and psychological studies to ascertain the scope of the problem. The results were illuminating.

[13] "Catholic Right," *New York Times,* March 14, 1971. See also James Hitchcock, *The Decline and Fall of Radical Catholicism* (N.Y., 1971).

[14] The capitulation was eased by J. E. Walsh's redefinition of a Catholic university's role being "the Church *learning*" instead of being part of the "*teaching* function of the Church." *Academic Freedom and the Catholic University,* ed. Edward Manier and J. S. Houck (Notre Dame, 1967), 109.

Customary devotional practices were being abandoned. Of younger priests, 60 per cent did not pray privately each day, 85 per cent did not say the breviary each day, 50 per cent did not say it at all. The church's teaching authority also was questioned. Of those under 35, 87 per cent did not support the official teaching on birth control. An equal percentage of all priests would not refuse absolution to those who would not promise to stop using contraceptives. Sixty per cent of all priests did not think divorce was forbidden by divine law.[15]

The identity-crisis of priests was accentuated by the relaxing of their psychological isolation. The 1964 decree on "Ecumenism" led to an extraordinary fraternizing with other Americans. Some used their new freedom to gain a further sense of liberation by engaging in "dialogue" and "honest discussion" and by experimenting with "sensitivity" training. Others began to think of their "rights"—demanding the right to be heard, advocating the right to elect their own bishops, urging the abolition of obligatory celibacy, organizing associations for collective action.[16] Others sought relevance and meaningful vocation by going into the streets "where the action is." Participating in the civil rights march on Selma, Alabama, was an exciting experience. Open housing marches in Milwaukee led by Father James Groppi, involving angry crowds, stern-faced police, multiple arrests, and appearances in court, were even more dramatic. Opposition to the Vietnam conflict enlisted articulate groups of priests and led to highly publicized acts of civil disobedience and lengthy court trials with accompanying demonstrations. The celebrated folk heroes of the movement were Fathers Daniel and Philip Berrigan.[17]

Members of women's religious orders also were in revolt. At the 1972 Berrigan conspiracy trial, Sister Elizabeth McAlister was a codefendant. An act, equally as provocative as those of the Berrigans, occurred on April 30, 1972, when a dozen nuns disrupted a Mass conducted by Terrence Cardinal Cooke at St. Patrick's Cathedral in

[15] Andrew Greeley, *Priests in the United States* (Garden City, 1972), 55–56, 65–66; and D. P. O'Neill, *The Priest in Crisis: A Study in Role Change* (Dayton, Ohio, 1968).

[16] The Association of Chicago Priests, formed in 1966, was duplicated elsewhere. A principal objective of the National Association for Pastoral Renewal was to gain support for optional rather than obligatory celibacy.

[17] See Daniel Berrigan, *No Bars to Manhood* (Garden City, 1970), and Philip Berrigan, *Prison Journals of a Priest Revolutionary* (N.Y., 1970).

New York City to protest Catholic apathy toward the Vietnam war. The nuns prostrated themselves in the center aisle before the Cardinal until they were dragged from the cathedral by the police and arrested for disorderly conduct.

Emancipation of nuns began in 1954 with the founding of the Sisters Formation Conference. Small progress was made before 1966 when the number of sisters dropped alarmingly. Changes thereafter were rapid and startling. There were changes in garb (street clothes were adopted by some orders) and experiments in living in small groups without a superior. Many wished to be regarded as persons rather than members of a community, freedom to relate more closely to outsiders, and opportunities to be relevant to their own moment in time. On July 20, 1967, the *Saturday Evening Post* featured an article on "The New Nuns," and in December the cover-story of *Newsweek* was "The Nun: Going Modern." By 1972 the National Coalition of American Nuns issued a "Declaration of Independence" demanding full equality in churches, including women priests, and suggested boycotting collection baskets to speed the end of oppression.[18]

Episcopal authority was in obvious disarray when priests no longer hesitated to criticize and rebuke their bishops on issues of policy. Still the general public was surprised in 1971 when the Association of Chicago Priests publicly censured John Cardinal Cody for failing to represent the views of his priests at the National Conference of Catholic Bishops. The focus of their anger was the "silence" of the Cardinal and his auxiliary bishops on the issue of compulsory celibacy when they knew that the survey commissioned by the hierarchy had revealed a majority of priests to be in favor of optional celibacy.

The subject of birth control provoked the greatest crisis of authority. Left dangling by Vatican II, the issue was submitted to a distinguished panel of experts. This Commission agreed that opposition to all forms of artificial birth control should be modified. In 1966 Paul VI postponed a decision and remanded the subject to the Papal Commission for further study. For Charles Davis, England's best known Roman

18 Hans Küng, the German theologian, supported their cause by asserting that there is no biblical or theological reason for an all-male priesthood. *Why Priests?* (Garden City, 1972), 81–82. The women's liberation movement enlisted much of its most vigorous leadership among Roman Catholics, *e.g.*, Sally Cunneen, Mary Daly, Elizabeth Farians, Rosemary Ruether, and Elizabeth Woo.

Catholic theologian, the postponement had "the effect of igniting a spark." The stated reasons for delay seemed so morally insensitive, exhibiting a "lack of concern" both "for truth" and "for persons," that they presented him with a "question of conscience."[19] After much searching of mind and heart, Davis felt morally constrained to leave the church. In 1968, brushing aside the conclusions of his own carefully selected Commission, Paul VI issued *Humanae Vitae*, which rigidly reaffirmed the position of Pius XII.

Most of the laity seemed unaffected by the stress and strain among the clergy. True they had begun behaving like other Americans, taking their religious obligations more casually. The cork was out of the bottle, and the froth had begun to fizz. Unlike their grandparents who docilely accepted the words of their bishops and priests, they were making up their own minds. A 1971 Gallup survey,[20] reported that attendance at Mass was taken less seriously (only 52 per cent attended regularly, and 42 per cent did not regard absence as a sin); confession was neglected (63 per cent had not made confession in eight weeks); 60 per cent neither prayed together as a family nor said the rosary as a private devotion; 78 per cent believed their children could still be saved if they left the church. Oddly, when confused about what to believe, almost as many relied on Billy Graham as looked to the teachings of the Pope. There was no open revolt. The church's teachings were simply quietly ignored by many. This was notably true in matters relating to sex. Seventy-five per cent of those of childbearing age believed good Catholics could use contraceptives. Nearly half favored liberalized abortion laws, and 60 per cent did not believe that a remarried divorced Catholic was living in sin. Almost half thought priests should be permitted to marry.

These statistics, of course, can be reversed. When reversed, they revealed that large numbers of Catholics still believed and behaved along traditional lines.

Religion on the periphery

As the 1960's progressed there was mounting disenchantment. Vietnam was the major albatross, but equally dispiriting was the

19 *A Question of Conscience* (N.Y., 1967), 97.
20 Reported in *Newsweek*, October 4, 1971.

crumbling enthusiasm of youthful idealists in 1965 when they discovered, in the feckless burning of Watts and the mindless violence at Madison, that idealism had its own potential for explosions of pent-up anger and rage. The earlier "beatnik" disaffection was vastly augmented as disenchanted social activitists adopted changing styles of dress and behavior as symbols of dropping out of established society. But even the counterculture bred its own disenchantment when the euphoria of the 1969 Woodstock "rock" festival was quickly followed by the wanton murder of an innocent by-stander at Altamont. Small wonder that many began to look for inward meaning, seeking it on the periphery in a home-brewed medley of occult lore, in mystic teachings of itinerant gurus from the East, or in a new Jesus cult among the street people. Many of the groups of the periphery originated in California where offbeat religions had long flourished.

THE PURSUIT OF PRIVATE HEAVENS. Fascination with the occult—a mélange of astrology, spiritualism, psychic prediction, and a mixed bag of prescriptions for meeting personal needs, intermingled with notions of reincarnation and astral projection (out-of-body travel)—was not new in America. Psychedelic and drug-induced mind-blowing (consciousness expanding) experiments also had been practiced in California by Aldous Huxley and others. Witchcraft, as a nature religion and fertility cult, had ancient rootage. Even the Scientology of L. Ron Hubbard ("the bridge to total freedom and total power") had connections with nineteenth-century mental healing fads. And Oriental religions had intrigued Americans at the 1893 World's Parliament of Religions.

After World War II the practice of the occult arts became big business, but it was primarily addressed to senior citizens. What was new in the late sixties was a surge of interest and a shift in clientele from age to youth, the occult having developed great attraction for the under-25 generation and their folk-heroes.[21] While Jeane Dixon was the most publicized psychic, Wanda Moore, a self-styled "Aquarian Child," was more typical of a glamorous new breed of spiritual counselors. Mascot of a California motorcycle gang, Wanda turned up

[21] For a popular account of the occult scene of the 1970's with attention to historical antecedents, see John Godwin *Occult America* (Garden City, N.Y., 1972). See also J. Needleman, *The New Religions* (Garden City, N.Y., 1970).

in Greenwich Village in 1967 to found a "hard rock" psychedelic club. After six months she retreated to New Jersey to practice Yoga and immerse herself in occult lore, putting together a patchwork quilt of many things and returning a year later as the New Age Wanda, psychic advisor to a throng of under-30 entertainers and musicians. Others of the occult "glamor elite" were practitioners of witchcraft—Louis Huebner, official witch of Los Angeles county, and Sybil Leek, author of the *Diary of a Witch*. Some younger devotees, turned off by the monetary demands of the professionals, practiced the occult arts as a do-it-yourself religion with accoutrements purchased from occult emporiums. Often they formed rural communes, the nature religion emphasis of witchcraft being congenial to their concerns.

Less home-grown than the occult pursuit was the response to gurus from the East who came like carpet-baggers to the West with new methods to pursue the quest for private heavens of personal religious experience.[22] In 1968 attention was riveted upon eastern alternatives to western religions by the happy guru Maharishi, whose picture adorned the covers of popular periodicals as a result of captivating the interest of Mia Farrow, Shirley MacLaine, the Beatles, the Rolling Stones, and 15,000 lesser mortals with his Spiritual Regeneration Movement. His prescription for "cosmic consciousness" was to practice "transcendental meditation" twice daily for thirty minutes. More colorful than Maharishi devotees were saffron-robed adherents of Hare Krishna, shaven-headed boys and sari-clad girls who gyrated on street corners to the tinkling of little cymbals. Zen Buddhism was a less flamboyant method of seeking enlightenment. Those who turned to Indian mysticism often had used psychedelic drugs which produced a penchant for mind expansion and experience beyond normal consciousness,[23] but the path to Zen usually was taken by those who experienced emptiness in ordinary life and yearned for an inner mystical experience that would restore meaning to their existence.

[22] While proselytizing representatives from the Orient have received much attention, little has been known of the indigenous religion of Asian Americans. For Buddhism this has now been remedied by Emma Layman, *Buddhism in America* (Chicago, 1976), and Tetsuden Kashima, *Buddhism in America: The Social Organization of an Ethnic Institution* (Westport, Conn., 1977).

[23] Related to the drug cult was the interest of some American Indians in a renewal of the Peyote cult as a symbol of Indian identity. The Native American Church was an institutional expression of this interest.

THE JESUS CULT. No one knows where or when it began, but by 1967 there were traces of a reviving interest in Jesus among the "street people," "cop-outs," and "trippers" of California. Perhaps it began with "rock music"—a blend of jazz, blues, country and gospel music with a rhythmic beat of its own. The turning of "rock" to "protest" themes led to secularized religious themes to express and convey their message of disaffection and alienation. Gospel themes became more and more prominent. Even the rock musical "Hair" had religious overtones. "Jesus Christ Superstar" and "Godspell" had explicit Christian themes. Then "Amazing Grace" and "O Happy Day" hit the top of the "hit parade."

The new Christians among hippies, flower children, and drug addicts quickly became known as Jesus Freaks or Jesus People. They were a variegated lot, having no common origin and often exhibiting intense hostility among themselves. Although there were spontaneous beginnings elsewhere, the Jesus cult first gained public notice in California. An early group in the Haight-Ashbury district of San Francisco was related to Ted Wise, a sail-maker from Sausalito, who had been deeply involved in drug use. Late in 1967 he established a coffee house known as The Living Room, forerunner of a commune called The House of Acts. Then Lonnie Frisbee founded a similar commune in southern California, The House of Miracles. Members of these groups dispersed to New Knoxville, Ohio; Rye, New York; and Eugene, Oregon, to extend the influence of the Jesus Way.[24]

By 1970 there were Jesus groups everywhere, representing a surprisingly wide range of ideology. The Children of God, bluntly anti-establishment, legalistic, and authoritarian communalists, demanded complete and disciplined separation (including forsaking and "hating" their parents) from the world which was soon to perish.

The appeal of Jesus to youth who had found organized religion apathetic was not unlike the appeal of Oriental religions to some of their friends. With a pervading sense of emptiness and futility, they found in simple gospel texts meaning and direction which released them from drug-oriented escapes. And their new commitment, while not changing the life-style represented by dress and communes, did

[24] See R. M. Enroth, E. E. Ericson, and C. B. Peters, *The Jesus People* (Grand Rapids, 1972).

result in a shift to sober, disciplined living coupled with new excitement and purpose. While diverse, Jesus people shared some common emphases; a non-intellectual insistence on the simple gospel, a belief that they were living in the last times, an espousal by some of pentecostal gifts, a tendency toward communal living, a bias against organized Christianity, a utilization of the music and vocabulary of the youth culture in their evangelism.

It is difficult to assess how many were involved with the Jesus people. There was much coming and going. For some it meant no more than the first step in going back to Kansas, back to a more conventional life. But numbers were not as important as influence. As a result of media attention, Jesus was definitely "in." He even became commercial, and organizations of conversative bent capitalized on the new interest.

THE AUTHORITARIAN STRAIN. The Children of God demonstrated the appeal of intensely rigid authoritarian discipline. When acutely distraught "flower children" discovered that the counterculture of the "street" provided little support, it is not surprising that some should retreat to the security of a group gathered about a dictatorial father-figure.[25] In addition to the Children of God there were two other rigidly authoritarian religions of the periphery which were to gain notoriety in the 1970's, although they were late-blooming products of the 1960's.

The "Moonies" of Rev. Sun Myung Moon's Unification Church were the first to gain public attention. Moon, a Korean, founded his Holy Spirit Association for the Unification of World Christianity in 1954, mingling messianism with anti-Communism, establishing cordial relations with the Korean government, and amassing a private fortune. In 1973 he shifted his primary base to the United States, having been preceded by emissaries who sought converts by warning of the approaching doom of America because of crime, alcoholism, drug abuse, college radicals, and Communists. Later, at a "God Bless America Festival" in Yankee Stadium, Moon said that his purpose was to "restore confidence in the American dream."

More was involved than the American dream. As the self-

[25] The notorious Charles Manson "family" provides a minor but incredibly shocking example of this type of appeal to forlorn drop-outs of the street.

proclaimed Messiah, commissioned by Jesus on a Korean mountainside to finish his task, Moon's teachings were to be accepted unquestioningly as divinely revealed. Aided by a Stanford graduate as Director of Training, Moon won recruits not from the "street" but from psychologically troubled middle-class youth who had yet to make a break with home and family. Enticed by fellow students to conferences where they were surrounded by loving concern, potential recruits were then persuaded to attend grueling, marathon training sessions which left them exhausted and scarcely able to think for themselves. God's plan for America was spelled out, and they were offered one last chance for salvation. Moon was called "Father" and his command was: "What I wish must be your wish." When parents objected to the iron discipline, recruits were taught to regard them as agents of Satan. Ever smiling and neatly dressed, the "Moonies" were conspicuous as they solicited money for vaguely identified humanitarian causes. Parents complained that their sons and daughters had been brain-washed.

A third authoritarian group of the periphery gained worldwide attention in 1978 with a macabre murder-suicide ritual in Jonestown, Guyana. Jim Jones in Indianapolis had gathered poor blacks and white social activists into his People's Temple, moving them in 1965 to rural Redwood Valley in California. A politically liberal Stanford Law School graduate joined the Temple in 1969 and helped facilitate a move to San Francisco. Whereas Rev. Moon won the acclaim of conservative politicians, Jim Jones' activities among the poor were endorsed by equally prominent liberal political leaders. The People's Temple had a different clientele from either the Children of God or the Moonies, garning its followers from those who had been active in civil rights marches, anti-Vietnam demonstrations, and organizing farmworkers. They turned to Jones as a last hope for securing a better, more humane, and just society. The discipline of the Temple was intense. Jones used the Temple to camouflage his growing fascination with Marxism and his developing paranoia. He patterned his style of leadership after Father Divine, becoming as "father" the personification of God. In 1973 a small party was sent to Guyana to locate a site for an agricultural commune, a venture which ended on November 18, 1978 with the mass suicide and slaughter.

While religions of the periphery gained headlines in the daily press and weekly news magazines, the conspicuous feature of the decade from the mid-sixties to the mid-seventies was the disarray of both Roman Catholicism and mainline Protestantism. Countervailing forces, however, were gaining ground during the latter years of the seventies which were to shift the hitherto dominant trends and give a new cast or profile to both Catholicism and Protestantism. Meanwhile Black Christianity and Judaism were charting independent courses of their own.

Black religion, black theology, and black church

Negro theologians became black theologians in the 1960's. They pursued an independent course which, unlike the emphases of Martin Luther King, had few affinities with traditional theology. King had marshalled a mass following under the banner of a theology of reconciliation. But in 1966, with Stokely Carmichael's cry of "Black Power" during James Meredith's march to Jackson, Mississippi, the stress began to shift to blackness—black pride, black religion, black theology, black church, black liberation. In 1964 Joseph R. Washington, Jr. published *Black Religion: The Negro and Christianity in the United States*, a book which played a curious role in precipitating discussion of black theology. He stressed the inadequacies of black religion, a "folk religion" which lacked and had been denied the theological sophistication and insights of classical Christian theology. The sharp rejoinders which the book elicited indicated that a number of young black leaders already held a view which reversed Washington's negative evaluation of black folk religion, and needed only the prod given by Washington to surface and become the focal point of discussion. As a result of the debate, Washington changed his own position, and in 1967 published *The Politics of God: The Future of the Black Churches* which was to become an important transitional book in the development of a theology of black liberation.

THEOLOGY OF LIBERATION. Two major spokesmen for the theology of black liberation were Albert B. Cleage, Jr. and James H.

Cone.[26] Cleage, with a black Christology brought into focus in his Church of the Black Madonna, sought to bring black religion into the service of political action, economic pressure, and black separation. Cone, no less committed to using the resources of the black church to remedy the powerlessness of the black community, was the more knowledgeable theologian. In sophisticated ways, Cone related a theology arising out of black experience to biblical themes—the bondage of the Israelites in Egypt, the oppression of Jews and Christians under Roman rule, and the manifestation of Jesus as the Black Christ. To the liberationist black theology, explicitly or implicitly, was a strategy for freeing the black mind from beliefs and attitudes which frustrated the thrust for liberation. The cause of liberation took priority over any suffering servant claim of the gospel. "Black theology must say: 'If the doctrine is compatible with or enhances the drive for black freedom, then it is the gospel of Jesus Christ. If the doctrine is against or indifferent to the essence of blackness as expressed in Black Power, then it is the work of the Antichrist.' "[27]

THEOLOGY OF HOPE AND RECONCILIATION.   Black liberation theology had great influence, especially in theological schools where interest was reinforced by another "liberation theology" forged in Latin America. Still it was not unchallenged. Others, no less concerned with black awareness, self-esteem, and liberation, held fast to Martin Luther King's vision of a redeemed society of mutual reconciliation.[28] The courage to be black was a major motif and there was no hint of compromise with racism. But blackness needed to be related to a truth that would be liberating to black and white alike—a truth that would lead

26 See Cleage, *The Black Messiah* (N.Y., 1968) and Cone, *Black Theology and Black Power* (N.Y., 1969) and *A Black Theology of Liberation* (Phila., 1970). See also two anthologies—C. Eric Lincoln, *The Black Experience in Religion* (N.Y., 1974) and G. S. Wilmore and J. H. Cone, *Black Theology: A Documentary History* (Maryknoll, N.Y., 1979).

27 Cone, *Black Theology and Black Power*, 121.

28 See Major L. Jones, *Black Awareness: A Theology of Hope* (N.Y., 1971) and J. D. Roberts, *Liberation and Reconciliation: A Black Theology* (Phila., 1971). A sad feature of the years following King's assassination was the dwindling strength of the Southern Christian Leadership Conference. No one was able to assume his charismatic role. One of his ablest young lieutenants, Andrew Young, provided conspicuous political leadership, first as a member of Congress and then as ambassador to the United Nations. Perhaps the closest approach to King's role was played by another of his young men, Jesse Jackson, with his church-based "Operation Breadbasket" in Chicago and then with his "Push for Excellence" campaign in schools throughout the nation.

to authentic freedom for all people. Black theology, they contended, was necessarily a theology of hope rooted in the gospel message of a "new life" in Christ which knows "neither Greek nor Jew, circumcision or uncircumcision, barbarian, Scythian, bond nor free" (Col. 3:11).

The theologians of hope believed that black churches and black theology had other contributions to make to the larger theological community. They spoke "for a people too long voiceless, too long powerless to preach the good news" as they saw it. In addition to the historic role of calling attention to the redemptive possibilities of suffering so prominent in black spirituality, black theology by "raising the issue of a black messiah or God" had the virtue of forcing "the white Christian to ponder whether his own picture of God and Jesus" is "a tribalized projection of his Westernized self-image."[29] The value of such an acknowledgement of idolatry for white Christianity seemed obvious.

Perhaps Harriet Beecher Stowe was right. She depicted Uncle Tom as a Christ-figure (a black messiah) whose unswerving loyalty and sacrificial death brought redemption to Charles Shelby and to the two blacks who were the instruments of the brutal torture which ended his earthly life. But it was her third from last chapter which may have been more prophetic when she foreshadowed Jones' stress upon a "strong sense of messianic mission" of a people "called of God to deliver black America from its bondage and white America from its lethal folly."[30] Who would they be? A people of "African nationality" was the answer in *Uncle Tom's Cabin*. And from whence would they come? Where but from Africa—from Africans that have learned of Christ but have their own peculiarities, peculiarities which, "if not the same with those of the Anglo-Saxon, may prove to be morally of even a higher type." And out of a period of struggle and conflict, a new era may be born. From its vantage point, the present throes that convulse the nations will be seen as "but the birth-pangs of an hour of universal peace and brotherhood."[31]

[29] William Jones, "Toward an Interim Assessment of Black Theology," *Reflection*, Yale Divinity School, LXIX (January, 1972).
[30] Major Jones, *Black Awareness*, 137.
[31] Harriet Beecher Stowe, *Uncle Tom's Cabin; or, Life Among the Lowly* (N.Y., 1876), 300, 302.

Judaism's uncertain course

As the oldest of what were called "the three major faiths," modern Judaism did not escape the problems troubling most American religious groups in the United States. Still Judaism exhibited some tendencies which suggested that its experience, as well as the black experience, might provide clues to renewal both for other religious communities and the nation. The rhyming comment, "how odd of God to choose the Jews," could have new pertinence as the twentieth century moved toward its close.

Jews had a love affair with America. In the United States they had found a country where they lived as full citizens with "all the rights and privileges pertaining thereunto." True, the United States was not a perfect society. Numerous ills needed to be remedied. But, with political rights having been followed by economic advance and growing social acceptance, Jews felt more completely at home than they had in the lands from whence they had come. They accommodated themselves to American society. They learned to live with a variety of religious opinions within their own ranks. Moreover, they took manifestations of "social radicalism" in stride.[32] Consequently they were not unduly disturbed when some of their youth became radicalized in the 1960's. Nor were they initially disturbed when some became disaffected with the synagogue as a symbol of an affluent Jewish style of life. Still the latter development was a symptom of a malaise from which Judaism was suffering.

What occurred is easy to discern in retrospect, as Arthur A. Cohen noted.[33] The American tradition and the American environment "made it possible for the Jew to become an American without ceasing to be a Jew." Not entirely convinced of this great good fortune and eager to avoid any cause for offense, many Jews divested themselves of that which they deemed most provocative—their religion. The usual process of assimilation was reversed. In Europe assimilation was preceded by conversion; in America Jews were assimilated without conversion. "America was tolerant of the Jew," Cohen observed. The Jew was

---

[32] Social disaffection was a concomitant of life in a ghetto, and social radicalism was one manfestation of the struggle against a ghettoized existence.

[33] The Natural and the Supernatural Jew (N.Y., 1962), 193–94, 202.

intolerant of himself. "He did more than the environment demanded; he paid a higher price than he was asked." There was no need for him to sacrifice his Judaism which was regarded by most Americans as his most positive asset.

The drift from Judaism shifted the focus of many rabbis from conservation of the religious tradition to the issue of Jewish survival. Their strategy was to make Judaism acceptable to secular Jews. For most of the twentieth century the stress was on human values, interpreting Judaism as a way of life with little attention given matters of faith and belief. Cultic practices were perpetuated for the sake of group identification and survival, their meaning being quite peripheral. Secularized Judaism, a religion of Jewishness, served well enough as a basis for group life longer than normally would have been expected, for Jewish solidarity was reinforced, first, by the shock of the Hitler "holocaust," then by concern for the new state of Israel, and finally by a vicarious self-esteem derived from Israel's speedy triumph in the "six-day war" of 1967.

HOLOCAUST THEOLOGY. While widespread euphoria was generated in the Jewish community by the six-day war, there were a few, most conspicuously in Brooklyn, who were less than euphoric. They were more concerned with their immediate situation. Crime in the streets had become common in urban America, and the push for integration precipitated many forms of backlash. Both were present in Brooklyn where Jewish neighborhoods were in transition and hazardous places to live, while "affirmative action" policies threatened the security and advancement of Jews long entrenched in the school system. What made Brooklyn distinctive was not that the backlash was more intense than elsewhere. It was the historical dimension given the plight of the Jews by Rabbi Meir Kahane who, not willing to be intimidated, organized the Jewish Defense League in 1968 with the slogan "never again." Too long, he insisted, Jews had responded passively to threats to their existence. This was true of Jews in Nazi Germany. "Never again" must Jews exhibit such passivity.

Kahane's language and tactics embarrassed leaders of the Jewish community and found scant support among the rank and file. Not until the near defeat of Israel in the Yom Kippur war of 1973 did the type of thinking Kahane represented begin to gain much support from respected leaders. Of those who gave support, the most important was Eliezer Berkovits in his book *Faith after the Holocaust* (1973) where he adopted Kahane's slogan "never again," contended that honor required a Jew to die with a gun in his hands, and asserted that "as a Jew, I can believe in the future of man only because I believe in the future of Israel."[34] From this small beginning an elaborate literature developed in which the Holocaust displaced Sinai as the defining point of Judaism.

JEWISH SPIRITUALITY. Meanwhile the spiritual hunger leading other Americans into a quest for personal religious experience was also present in the Jewish community. By 1970 rabbis on campuses reported widespread interest in discussions of Jewish mysticism, spiritual disciplines, and personal faith. Some younger Jews, disenchanted with what seemed to be the spiritual void of conventional Judaism, sought to develop a renewed or parallel Judaism of their own in communes or "covenanted" communities committed to strict religious discipline.[35] While older members of the Jewish community did not seek such drastic solutions, many shared the same longing for meaning that transcended their daily routine.

The establishment of the state of Israel also posed a problem for thoughtful Jews. It pushed to the fore the issue of defining Judaism in more specifically religious terms. Attachment to the land of Israel and hope for eventual return had been one of the bonds of unity among Jews of the Diaspora (dispersion) whether Judaism was religiously or culturally defined. When it became clear that millions of Jews chose to remain where they were when the way to return was open, the need for a rationale for a continuing Diaspora became acute. If a cultural Judaism was unable to satisfy the spiritual hunger of individuals, it was equally unrealistic to expect Jews in America to find a meaningful existence merely by living vicariously in another land. They had to live where they were and no emotional tie to Israel, however strong, could provide the meaning derived from a common religious vocation to which Jews everywhere had a contribution to make.

With astonishing rapidity Jewish scholars began to mine the rich

34 (N.Y., 1973), 163–67. For the shift from religion to ethnicity as the core of Judaism, see Jacob Neusner in *National Review*, XXXI (1979), 975–79.
35 S. S. Schwarzchild, "Radical Imperatives of Judaism," *Judaism* (1972), 9–15.

resources of Jewish mystical piety. Younger Jews were especially drawn to the Hasidic mystical enthusiasm which had its beginnings in eighteenth-century eastern Europe, attracted partly by the countercultural aspects of Hasidic communal life, but more interested in the Hasidic experience of encounter with God than in rituals and customs. Martin Buber had explicated the teachings of the Hasidic masters,[36] but youthful Jews set about exploring the riches of Hasidic texts for themselves. The mystical piety of Abraham Heschel, who had insisted that Jews by attuning their "yearning to the lonely holiness of this world" will "aid humanity more than by any particular service," became more influential than hitherto.[37] The issue of vocation, so important to Jews of the Diaspora, was a central concern for a group of distinguished scholars, including Eugene Borowitz, Norman Lamm, and Seymour Siegel. Known as "Covenant theologians," they defined the Jewish people in terms of relationship with God, insisting that God established a special covenant with the Jews which imposes on them a special vocation which has relevance and meaning for all humanity. If Vatican II opened windows and allowed fresh air to penetrate the closed confines of Roman Catholicism, it is clear that a freshness of thought and a deepening of spirituality was also penetrating Judaism which was in danger of ceasing to be a living religion.

A PLURALISTIC SOCIETY. Since the time of the emperor Theodosius in the fifth century, most Christians assumed that the Christian faith should embrace all of life in a Christian society. This had been true of both Protestants and Catholics. Faced with diversity within their own ranks, English and American Protestants in the seventeenth and eighteenth centuries made a distinction between the realms of nature and grace to permit them to live at peace in the same society (see p. 111), and this distinction provided a basis for the guarantee of religious freedom in the United States. The distinction was not always kept clearly in mind for pluralism in America was mostly a diversity among Christians and many tended to think of America as a Christian nation.

Adherents of Judaism, however, for two thousand years had been

---

[36] *Hasidism and Modern Man* (N.Y., 1958).
[37] For a moving account of his views and lively faith, see *The Earth Is the Lord's* (N.Y., 1950); see also *Man Is Not Alone* (N.Y., 1951).

compelled to live in two worlds—to maintain their faith while meeting demands for coexistence within a non-Jewish culture and society. As was true of early Christians, they were "in the world" but not at every point "of the world." Such dual allegiance was not easy to maintain. It required strenuous efforts in "schule" and family to preserve the religious tradition. It was doubly difficult when the coercion of the ghetto was relaxed. Still it could be and was done, even in America where the temptation to abandon a dual allegiance was greatest.

Perhaps the greatest contribution of Judaism to the United States will be to help other Americans understand how the United States can be a truly pluralistic society in which the pluralism is maintained in a way that is enriching rather than impoverishing, a society in which the integrity of different faiths is preserved while their respective adherents engage in open dialogue to clarify their own self-understanding. A pluralistic society is a society of dual commitments which need not be in conflict but can be complementary. From the long experience of Judaism, it may be possible for other Americans to learn how this may be done with both grace and integrity.

While black Christians and Jews were following their own independent and sometimes uncertain pursuits, a radical shift in direction for Roman Catholicism and a growing segment of Protestantism was taking place at the end of the 1970's and the beginning of the 1980's. Both were marching to the beat of new drummers. Among Roman Catholics official leadership took the initiative in an attempt to restore order and authority in the Church. Among Protestants, grassroots sentiment, responding to a new breed of conservative leadership, was altering the shape, character, and complexion of Protestantism in America.

XVII

The Turn to Conservatism in the 1970's and 1980's

When Nash K. Burger, book review editor of *The New York Times*, commented in 1971 that, as a result of a "creeping secularism" in religion, "religious book sales and the number of titles published have declined," he was reporting past history. It is true that religious books, such as *Honest to God* (1963) and *The Secular City* (1965) which had been best sellers a few years earlier, no longer titillated widespread public interest. As Burger explained, people had become tired of "religious books" that offered little more than "secular answers to secular questions."[1] But other religious books, not issued by the more familiar publishing houses and hence largely unnoticed in the book trade, were gaining a rapidly expanding readership. These books did provide religious answers to religious questions and their sale was symptomatic of the phenomenon Dean M. Kelley of the National Council of Churches sought to analyze in his book, *Why Conservative Churches Are Growing* (1972).

[1] *New York Times Book Review*, May 23, 1971, p. 56.

The search of many college students for inward meaning has been discussed in the preceding chapter. Paralleling this pursuit was the quest of increasing numbers of all ages to recover, in the midst of what seemed to them a spiritual void, old values, certainties, and assurance. By 1972 a neo-pentecostal or charismatic movement had penetrated the congregations of such staid Protestant denominations as the Episcopal, Lutheran, and Presbyterian churches, as well as having become a significant and highly visible presence within Roman Catholicism. By 1973 growing discontent over a wide variety of issues produced lay revolts and "traditionalist" schisms in several of the old line churches. The swing to conservatism was also evident in the election of 1976. The appeal of a "born-again" Democratic candidate was countered by the pilgrimage of Gerald Ford to Dallas to secure the blessing of William A. Criswell, pastor of the 20,000 member First Baptist Church, while his vice-presidential running-mate ended a one-day, five-state campaign swing in Pontiac, Michigan, to permit him to attend a Billy Graham evangelistic rally held in the covered stadium of the Detroit Tigers and Detroit Lions. In 1979 the deeper yearnings of many Americans were most fully and starkly revealed in the overwhelming enthusiasm of the reception accorded Pope John Paul II. Following his whirlwind visit to the United States, the Gallup Poll reported that John Paul II received one of the highest overall favorable ratings for personal popularity of any individual ever tested by their organization.[2] Protestants were particularly enthusiastic. Part of this outpouring of favorable public sentiment may have been no more than a response to an unusually colorful personality, but most interpreters viewed it as an indication that Americans were eager to welcome a figure who represented so dramatically the importance of moral and spiritual values in national life.

Conventional Protestantism

The religious climate changed during the 1970's. Whereas, according to the Gallup Poll, 75 per cent of the American people in 1970 thought that religion was losing influence, only 46 per cent were of the

[2] *The Gallup Opinion Index*, Report 171, October 1979, pp. 3–4. The other two were Dwight Eisenhower and John F. Kennedy at the peak of their political careers.

same opinion in 1980. The same sample indicated that 84 per cent of the people regarded religious beliefs as important. From a low point in the 1960's, confidence in organized religion posted a sharp gain after 1973. Six years later, 68 per cent of Roman Catholics and 70 per cent of Protestants expressed confidence in organized religion.[3]

In spite of this favorable climate of opinion, the more liberal Protestant churches continued to report declines in membership, declines which had begun in the 1960's (see p. 415). These declines constituted a marked reversal after a century and a half of steady growth. According to statistics drawn from the *1970 Year Book of American Churches* and the *1980 Year Book of American and Canadian Churches*, losses during the decade were suffered by the following typical old-line denominations:

Christian Churches (Disciples of Christ) declined 22.6 per cent
Episcopal Church declined 16.9 per cent
Presbyterian Church in the U.S. (southern) declined 10.3 per cent
United Church of Christ declined 13 per cent
United Methodist Church declined 11.4 per cent
United Presbyterian Church in the U.S.A. declined 23 percent

When measured against growth in population, the actual declines were even greater. The relative declines are further accented when an aging make up of the general population is taken into account, for the upper age brackets are more strongly represented on church membership rolls.

The diminishing membership is partly explained by various degrees of unease and disquiet among the laity (the clergy often being at odds with their congregations) which led some members to become "drop-outs" and others to withdraw to form separate churches. Some of those who dropped out were unhappy with liturgical changes, the abandonment of traditional forms of worship.[4] Episcopalians and Presbyterians were disturbed by the ordination of women, a policy adopted years earlier by a wide spectrum of denominations ranging from the

---

[3] *Ibid.*, Report 166, May 1979, pp. 1–2; Report 171, April-May 1980, p. 7.
[4] A Gallup poll reported that 80 per cent of the Episcopal clergy preferred the 1979 revised *Book of Common Prayer* compared to 37 per cent lay approval.

Salvation Army, many pentecostals, American Baptists, Congregationalists, and Unitarians. Other Presbyterians were upset by a 1978 directive that all congregations elect some women as elders (members of the session, the local governing body), and also by an attempt to deny ordination to a man who would not affirm his agreement with the policy of ordaining women. Even more divisive within old line denominations was the issue of ordaining practicing homosexuals to the ministry, such ordinations frequently being advocated by committees and commissions officially appointed to study the issue. In a few instances, without the policy having received official approval, local officials proceeded on their own with such ordinations.

Perhaps the most divisive issue of all was the commitment of official national leadership to an agenda for specific social and political change. Rightly or wrongly, the tactic of James Forman and his allies in interrupting church services to present a "Black Manifesto" demanding multi-million dollars in "reparations" from church funds for past injustices seemed arrogant and outrageous to many, and the abject response of most denominations in setting up special funds and designating percentages of income to be paid into these funds created further resentment. Efforts to effect community organizations within inner-city areas by enlisting, not the resources of the Southern Christian Leadership Conference or other Christian agencies, but the talents of Saul Alinsky whose initial tactic was to "rub raw the sores of social discontent," was also a source of alienation. The most provocative act may have been the decision of the United Presbyterian Church in 1971 to give $10,000 to the Angela Davis Legal Defense Fund. Most rank and file members of the church found it difficult to understand why, among all blacks needing legal aid, a professed member of the Communist Party (allegedly involved in a shootout that left a judge and three witnesses dead, and not without able defense counsel) should be singled out to receive Presbyterian church funds. Church promotion of grape and lettuce boycotts in support of the organization of migrant farm workers in California, appointment of committees on corporate policy to police and alter activities of multinational firms abroad by economic pressure, and financial aid (for food and medical supplies) extended by the World Council of Churches to liberation movements engaged in guerrilla war and terrorist tactics, all bred resentment among some church members. What was questionable in the eyes of many church members was not financial contributions for social rehabilitation, but the arbitrary ways in which funds were utilized by distant and unresponsive officials. Little opposition was expressed to the abandonment of traditional forms of ministry. The absence of such opposition was striking.

Symptomatic of conventional Protestantism's loss of a sense of mission or even of a Christian identity was *A Lay Person's Guide to Conflict Management* prepared for use in local congregations and published, from within the precincts of the National Episcopal Cathedral, by The Alban Institute, Mt. St. Albans, Washington, D.C. This 1979 guide gave no indication that the Christian faith had anything to contribute to the resolution of conflict even within churches. There is no suggestion that appeal be made for divine guidance, no suggestion that sin and pride and the need for repentance may be involved, no summons to humility and mutual forgiveness as a prerequisite to conflict resolution, no role for the pastor as a "facilitator," since he usually is part of the problem. The prescription is to call in a professional "conflict manager" to initiate the psychological process of "conflict management" to help members of the congregation understand that there are no items of belief or conviction at stake that are of importance to their common ministry or existence as a Christian church. Thus, whatever their differences of opinion, there is no obstacle to their continuing to exist as a group on the basis of the simple formula of agreeing to live and let live with mutual respect.

Small wonder, with this type of guidance, that churches should diminish in membership as people decided they could easily spend their time in more interesting ways. Nor is it surprising that some, disturbed by many things, should seek to recapture some sort of identity through the activities of the Good News Movement among Methodists, PEWS ACTION among Episcopalians, and the Presbyterian Layman's Commission. What is surprising is that there were so few formal departures to found new churches to carry on what they believed to be the true tradition of their denomination. A few small churches were organized such as the Anglican Catholic Church, and the Presbyterian Church in America. Some churches simply withdrew to become independent congregations, while others joined earlier defections such as the Southern Methodist Church or became affiliated with a loose grouping such as the independent Christian Churches and Churches of Christ. But most simply dropped out.

The new conservatism

The growing edge of Protestantism in number of adherents and public attention was either outside or on the fringes of the old-line churches. The new vigor and vitality were represented, in part, by two parallel and sometimes over-lapping movements which had taken on new life after having been on the scene since early in the century. These movements usually were referred to as the "new evangelicalism" and the "new pentecostalism."[5]

THE NEW EVANGELICALISM. If the religious landscape looked different by 1980, it was partly the result of the new confidence and thrust of the evangelicals—the emerging into prominence of what the press called "the born-again movement." To some the new evangelicalism seemed little more than a dressed up version of the old fundamentalism. There were continuities including an insistence upon a conversion experience, an undeviating reliance upon the authority and reliability of the Bible, and an acceptance of the birth, miracles, and resurrection of Christ as supernatural events. But there were also differences. The constituency was more broadly based (drawing support from members of almost all denominations) and more respectable (adherents being recruited from representatives of "high" as well as "mass" culture). The leadership was better educated, less contentious and less obsessed with frailties of personal behavior and more prone to identify with middle class America. And there was a strong tendency, with a few notable exceptions, to lend support to conservative and even overtly right-wing politics.

One reason evangelicals were able to win popular support more effectively than conventional Protestants was that they more explicitly

---

[5] The difference in growth rates of conservative bodies is striking. During the same decade for which statistics of the more liberal churches are cited, the staunchly conservative Southern Baptist Convention netted a gain of 16.5 per cent; the Church of God (pentecostal) 61.8 per cent; the Assemblies of God 48.8 per cent; the Christian and Missionary Alliance 32 per cent; Church of the Nazarene 27.2 per cent; Salvation Army 25.6 per cent; Free Methodists 16 per cent. The rapid growth of the Lutheran Church—Missouri Synod was checked by schism, but the rigidly conservative Wisconsin Evangelical Lutheran Church gained 12.4 per cent.

affirmed popular religious beliefs. A survey by the Gallup organization for *Christianity Today*, reported in the December 21, 1979 issue, noted that 94 per cent of all adult Americans believed in the existence of God, that 80 per cent believed that Jesus was divine, that 50 per cent believed that Adam and Eve were created directly by God; and that almost 50 per cent believed that the Bible contained no errors. A related reflection of the public mind was Gallup's report in another poll that 77 per cent of the American people were in favor of a constitutional amendment to permit prayers in public schools.

A growing awareness of evangelical strength led *Newsweek* to label 1976 "the year of the evangelical." This perhaps was a salute to the election of Jimmy Carter as president. But the editors also could have cited such items as Charles Colson's autobiography, *Born Again*, at the top of the best-seller lists and Black Panther leader Eldridge Cleaver's announcement of his conversion to evangelical Christianity. Indeed, it was becoming almost fashionable to be "born again." The ranks of the reborn included rock stars (Bob Dylan), folk singers (Johnny Cash), and a long list of movie stars, professional athletes, and U. S. Senators.

Newsweek's instinct was sound for there was other evidence of the evangelical surge. Evangelical publishers were flourishing and captured a major segment of the commercial book market. Annual sales of one publisher alone exceeded 45 million dollars in 1980. In the 1970's books by evangelical writers began to head the list of best sellers with some regularity.[6] Evangelical magazines also flourished. *Christianity Today* founded (and heavily subsidized for a number of years by J. Howard Pew of the Sun Oil Company) to counter the influence of the *Christian Century* is one illustration. It claimed nearly 200,000 subscribers in 1980 while the circulation of the *Christian Century* dropped to 30,000.

Another conspicuous feature of evangelicalism's activity was the

[6] These were Kenneth Taylor's *The Living Bible* in 1972 and 1973, Marabel Morgan's *The Total Woman* in 1974, Billy Graham's *Angels* in 1975. Colson's *Born Again* was edged out in 1976 by Bernstein's *The Final Days*. The best selling book of them all (but not in any one year) was Hal Lindsey's *The Late Great Planet Earth* which sold more than 12 million copies in six years following its publication in 1970. Sequels, such as *Satan Is Alive and Well on Planet Earth* (1972), *The Liberation of Planet Earth* (1974), and *The Terminal Generation* (1976) added 4 million copies to Lindsey's sales before the end of the decade. *Time* called attention to the phenomenon when it reported that in 1975 there were almost 50 religious titles in print which had crossed the million copy mark in sales, most of them geared to the evangelical market.

response it elicited among students with organizations such as the Intervarsity Christian Fellowship and Campus Crusade. Intervarsity Fellowship, a 1940 British import with more than 600 chapters on American college and university campuses, assembled 12,000 students at the University of Illinois during the 1970 Christmas vacation ("Urbana '70"), a remarkable achievement when conventional campus religious groups were dwindling. The total attending the bi-annual Urbana conventions of the Fellowship increased to 17,000 in 1977 and again in 1979. Equally impressive, although held at a more convenient time and more highly organized and financed, was Campus Crusade's "Explo '72" which brought 75,000 (mostly young people) to Dallas, Texas, in the summer of 1972. Campus Crusade had been founded in 1951 at the University of California, Los Angeles (UCLA) by Bill Bright, and in 1974 Bright drafted plans for the most ambitious evangelistic campaign since the early years of the Student Volunteer Movement at the end of the nineteenth century. The goal of the "Here's Life America!" campaign, chaired by Texas billionaire Nelson Bunker Hunt, and popularized by the ubiquitious "I Found It" bumper stickers, was to raise one billion dollars to proclaim the gospel to every person on the globe by the end of 1982.

During these years a shift of emphasis was taking place among some evangelical scholars who began to urge that evangelicals should be more concerned with helping people understand the message of the Bible than being preoccupied with attempts to prove its inerrancy in matters of history and science.[7] A potential for disruption was created in 1976 when Harold Lindsell launched an attack upon such opinions with *The Battle for the Bible*, a book which sparked heated debates. Its greatest impact was among Southern Baptists and within the faculties of non-denominational evangelical theological schools.

Billy Graham was a moderating influence in the face of Lindsell's emotional defense of an older fundamentalism. He had become a father-figure to evangelicals in the 1970's and continued to give big name identification to the movement with his network television specials, his weekly Hour of Decision radio programs, and his easy relationship with presidents and such perennial favorite personalities as Bob Hope. Year

[7] D. F. Wells and J. D. Woodbridge, eds., *The Evangelicals* (Nashville, 1975), and Richard Quebedeaux, *The Worldly Evangelicals* (San Francisco, 1978).

444

after year various polls rated him among the "ten most respected men" of the nation. He was a Grand Marshall of the Tournament of the Roses Parade and embraced Richard Nixon in 1968 and 1972. But Graham changed with the years. His opposition to segregation became more vigorous and explicit. He spoke more frequently of the nation's responsibility to the poor. In 1978 he took his crusades to the Communist countries of eastern Europe. Graham had always preached that personal morality is the foundation of social morality, and in the 1980's his words, more mellow in tone, clearly struck a responsive chord among non-evangelicals as well as evangelicals.

THE NEW PENTECOSTALISM. An equally striking manifestation of the turn to conservatism was the mushrooming of the "new pentecostalism" within conventional Protestant denominations and within the Roman Catholic Church. For fifty years charismatic gifts of healing, miracles, prophecy, tongues, and the interpretation of tongues (I Cor. 12:1–11) had been the domain of a cluster of pentecostal denominations (see pp. 347–48), most of them experiencing marked growth after 1960. But late in the 1950's "the pentecostal experience" began to penetrate major Protestant churches without producing defections. It was primarily a lay movement, with informal groups being drawn together by mutual unhappiness with a lackluster spiritual life and a common longing for an intimate experience of God's presence.[8]

In terms of national publicity, neo-pentecostalism surfaced among Presbyterians in 1956 when a Presbyterian minister informed his congregation that he had experienced the gift of tongues, but more sensational treatment was accorded the 1960 announcement of Dennis J. Bennett to his 2000 member Van Nuys, California, Episcopal congregation of his "pentecostal experience." Lutheran and Methodist, as well as some Baptist and Dutch Reformed congregations, also were involved in the movement, but Baptists and Nazarenes were much less receptive than Episcopalians, Presbyterians, Methodists, and Lutherans.

The most important institutional bridge between the old and new pentecostalism was the Full Gospel Businessmen's Fellowship, founded in Los Angeles in 1951 by a wealthy California dairyman, Demos

---

[8] See D. E. Harrell, Jr., *All Things Are Possible: The Healing and Charismatic Revival in Modern America* (Bloomington, Ind., 1975), and Richard Quebedeaux, *The New Charismatics* (Garden City, N.Y., 1976).

Shakerian, and by faith healer Oral Roberts. The intent was to provide opportunity for laypersons in the older pentecostal denominations to promote pentecostal renewal as they saw fit, i.e., without the supervision of denominational officials. Although the fellowship eventually included ministers, it remained an exclusively lay-run organization. The meetings of the fellowship were often held in luxury hotels, and the thoroughly independent, non-denominational character of the gatherings was attractive to persons in conventional churches who had had the pentecostal experience but did not wish to sever their old church connections. By 1980 conventional Protestant and Roman Catholic pentecostals constituted a majority of the fellowship's membership.

Various individuals played key roles in transmitting the older pentecostalism to the new charismatic movement—Shakerian, David duPlessis, Jean Stone, Ralph Wilkerson, among others. Oral Roberts (b. 1918), however, was by far the most important. Originally ordained in a small Wesleyan denomination, the Pentecostal Holiness Church, Roberts began a full-time faith healing ministry in 1948. His skill and reputation for financial honesty quickly moved him to the forefront of big-time faith healers. From 1954 to 1967 Roberts' healing services were carried live on network television. But in the mid-1960's Roberts concluded that the day of tent revivals had passed. With the keen sense of timing and bold innovation that marked his subsequent career, Roberts determined to spread the pentecostal message in more up-to-date ways.

A first step was to become a United Methodist. A second step was to found Oral Roberts University in 1967 as the world's first charismatic university.[9] With its spectacular 200 million dollar Tulsa, Oklahoma, campus, Oral Roberts University in 1980 had an enrollment of nearly 4000 students and one of the best basketball teams in the country. The nearly completed City of Faith, a sprawling sixty-story hospital complex adjacent to the university was erected as testimony to Roberts' emphasis upon the health of the "whole person"—spiritual, intellectual, physical, even financial. Support was gained by a nationwide newspaper column, by a monthly magazine, *Abundant Life*, with over

---

[9] The official sequence was reversed. Roberts' formal reception into the United Methodist ministry was not completed until 1968.

a million subscribers, and by a weekly television program and quarterly network specials. The latter, featuring the racially mixed (and conspicuously attractive) World Action Singers as well as Hollywood celebrities, seemed distinctly secularized to many old-fashioned pentecostals. At the end of the 1970's, the *Christian Century* named Oral Roberts as one of the ten most influential religion leaders of the decade. If by the 1980's pentecostalism had moved "uptown," Roberts clearly must be regarded as one of the principle architects of the transition.

The eruption of pentecostalism within Roman Catholicism began in 1967 with a lay faculty prayer group at Duquesne University in Pittsburgh. Two books deeply influenced them: David Wilkerson's *The Cross and the Switchblade*, an account of his Christian witness among teenage gangs and dope addicts in New York City, and John L. Sherrill's *They Speak with Other Tongues*, a persuasive analysis of "the pentecostal experience." At this point they came into contact with an Episcopalian woman who invited them to attend an informal pentecostal prayer group meeting at the home of a Presbyterian woman. Shortly thereafter, early in 1967, four of the inquirers received the baptism in the Spirit and began to witness to their friends what the Lord had done for them. This culminated in the "Duquesne weekend" of mid-February when about thirty students were touched by the Holy Spirit. From Duquesne the excitement spread to Notre Dame, which was to become the great center of Roman Catholic pentecostalism, then to Michigan State, the University of Michigan, Fordham, and other university centers. An incipient national organization was initiated in 1967 at the "Michigan State weekend" when about 45 persons arrived at Notre Dame from East Lansing for a conference. Each year thereafter a "National Conference on Charismatic Renewal in the Catholic Church" was held at Notre Dame, with 1279 present in 1970, 5000 in 1971, 12,000 in 1972, and between 20,000 and 30,000 in each year in the latter part of the decade. While there was much coming and going between the new pentecostals, both Protestant and Catholic, Protestants tended to insist that tongues must accompany baptism in the Holy Spirit as the "initial physical evidence" of the experience, whereas Catholic pentecostals regarded tongues as one of many possible manifestations of the Spirit.

The extent of the growth of pentecostal churches and the penetration of other religious groups by the charismatic movement is indicated by a 1979 Gallup poll which reported that 29 million Americans called themselves either pentecostals or charismatics, and that at least six million said that they had spoken in tongues.

THE ELECTRONIC CHURCH.   Nowhere was evangelical and pentecostal influence more evident than in their successful use of radio and television to reach a mass audience. In the 1980's religious broadcasting had come a long way from the first fifteen minute religious program on Pittsburgh's KDKA in 1921. Twenty per cent of the radio stations in the United States were classified as principally or exclusively religious, although only four per cent of the television stations fell into this category. Seventy per cent of religious radio programming and ninety per cent of religious television programming was produced under evangelical or pentecostal auspices. One observer judged that these programs were heard or watched by 129 million persons each week. Estimates of the amount of revenue produced by the programs varied widely. Producers of the programs said that contributions amounted to 500 million dollars annually. Some industry analysts, however, calculated that the figure was closer to a billion dollars annually. Whatever the sum there were indications that the lion's share was garnered by fewer than a dozen ministries.

The "big league" television programs were individually produced. They were Jerry Falwell's "Old Time Gospel Hour" from Lynchburg, Virginia; Rex Humbard's "Cathedral of Tomorrow" from Akron, Ohio; "Pat" (M. G.) Robertson's "700 Club" from Virginia Beach, Virginia; and, an offshoot from the "700 Club," Jim Bakker's "PTL Club" from Charlotte, North Carolina. Trailing somewhat behind the four but with annual revenues and audiences still in the millions were Jimmy Swaggert in New Orleans, James Robison in Fort Worth, and two stars in California—Gene Scott in Glendale and Robert Schuller in Garden Grove.[10] Schuller was not an evangelical and his "possibility

10 Billy Graham and Oral Roberts might be included in the list but their broadcast efforts began in the 1950's, and both were primarily identified with other types of ministry. The "World Tomorrow" broadcasts of the Armstrongs' Worldwide Church of God, on the air for decades, was not regarded by evangelicals as theologically orthodox, but its income and audience were comparable to the others. The split between the father and son, of course, created problems for the church.

thinking," derived from his mentor Norman Vincent Peale, was sharply criticized by both liberals and conservatives. Still it is clear that his nationally syndicated television program, "The Hour of Power," strongly appealed to theologically unselfconscious evangelicals.

It is difficult to know who derived the largest total income from the telecasts. It may have been Jerry Falwell, "Pat" Robertson, or Jim Bakker with his PTL Club. Initially PTL stood for "Praise the Lord." Later it was announced that it also stood for "People that Love." PTL's daily two-hour program, patterned after the Tonight Show, was carried by 200 commercial stations and 3,000 cable outlets in the United States, and a Spanish version was beamed to a score of Spanish-speaking countries by satellite. Weekly revenues in 1979 were said to approximate a million dollars.

Despite troubles with creditors and what Bakker called harassment by the Federal Communications Commission, Bakker's long range plans remained undiminished. A Total Living Center, estimated cost 100 million dollars, was under construction across the state line in Fort Mill, South Carolina, although financial problems in 1980 caused the projected date for completion to be pushed far into the future. The center, with village clusters (New England, Hawaiian, etc.) designed for different dreams and tastes, was planned to provide every need as a place to live for Christian families including recreational facilities for youth and nursing care for the elderly. Moreover, there were to be areas within the Total Living Center (e.g., a corner for mobile homes) priced to meet the requirements of every pocketbook. Models of the different settings, displayed during appeals for funds, were almost breath-takingly beautiful. Bakker also had plans to have a Christian television network on the air around-the-clock to provide Christian children's shows, a Christian interpretation of the news, and even the Christian equivalent of soap operas and situation comedies.

There were differences within the leadership of the Electronic Church. Some were pentecostal, emphasizing faith healing and speaking in tongues. Others steered clear of charismatic "gifts." A few were non-political, but most did not hesitate to use their programs on occasion to promote conservative or right-wing causes that had no visible connection with religion. The similarities, however, between these electronic superstars were much more striking. All directed their message to the upwardly mobile lower middle class. All were intensely ambitious men and women (PTL was a husband and wife effort), who were deeply involved in other Christian enterprises, usually a mega-church with thousands of members. All, except Schuller, perceived themselves as modern day prophets, fervently ringing a tocsin to warn civilization that it was perilously close to God's final judgment.

"Arm chair religion" was the label some attached to the Electronic Church. Samples indicated that persons who listened to one program tended to listen to them all. Nothing much was demanded beyond mailing in a weekly or monthly check. Still the influence in shaping the mind-set of the listener was tremendous.

Evangelical political concerns and activity

When Hodding Carter III reviewed David Broder's *Changing of the Guard* (1980), which analyzed the shifts in political power and influence in America, he noted one striking omission. Nowhere did Broder mention "the newly politicized religious fundamentalists" as a significant influence in "the coming years."[11] Traditionally fewer "evangelicals," to use a more moderate and inclusive term, were much less inclined to register and vote than the population as a whole. But by 1980 this was no longer true. Evangelicals had been politicized and had had marked impact upon several contests in the 1978 congressional election.[12]

Since the 1950's there had been vocal right-wing, fundamentalist, anti-communist organizations such as Billy James Hargis' "Christian Anti-Communist Crusade" and Carl T. McIntire's American Council of Churches. But not many paid them much attention. What was new

[11] *Washington Post Book World*, August 31, 1980, p. 2.

[12] In statistical analyses of political sentiment no distinction was made between evangelicals and pentecostals both being given the same label "evangelical." The Gallup Poll used three criteria to identify evangelicals: describing themselves as "born-again Christians" or saying they had a "born-again experience," reporting that they had encouraged others to believe in Jesus Christ, and stating that they believe in a literal interpretation of the Bible or accept its absolute authority. Gallup's use of the term in his December 21, 1979 *Christianity Today* poll was based on more detailed yet less restrictive criteria, for in this instance being "born-again" was reduced to identifying only a sub-category of evangelicals. For his political analyses, Gallup concluded that in 1980 evangelicals constituted about 20 per cent of the electorate or 30,000,000 potential voters. Others, using more lax definitions, suggested that evangelicals constituted 30 to 40 percent of the adult population.

in the last two or three years of the 1970's was the development of a number of heavily financed evangelical organizations designed to elect right-wing conservatives to national office.[13] The largest of these was Moral Majority founded in 1979 by Jerry Falwell. By the fall of 1980 it reportedly had nearly half a million members and claimed to have registered 3 million voters and signed up 72,000 clergymen to serve as precinct workers in addition to accumulating a million dollar war chest. On the west coast another organization called Christian Voice was established by Richard Zone in 1978 which soon boasted 200,000 active supporters, a mailing list of 5 million names, and a 3 million dollar treasury. In Texas, where television evangelist James Robison never hesitated to link the gospel to political interests of the New Right, several thousand ministers were brought together from the mid-South in the late summer of 1980 to listen to Ronald Reagan and to encourage the ministers to promote voter registration drives.

Several factors combined as a catalyst to provoke this political counteroffensive. The first was a perceived threat to the Christian home represented by a majority of unmarried adolescents becoming sexually active, by campaigns for "gay rights," by a Supreme Court decision legalizing abortion during the first trimester of pregnancy, and by the proposed Equal Rights Amendment to the Constitution. The intersection of these concerns in relationship to the preservation of the Christian family as basic feature of the social order was exemplified in the person of singer Anita Bryant. Repeatedly designated by *Good Housekeeping* in the late 1970's as the most admired woman in America, she was subjected to much public opprobrium as an outspoken opponent of gay rights, abortion, and ERA. Though suffering the loss of many contracts, she continued to appear on such television programs as the 700 Club, the PTL Club, and the Oral Roberts network specials.

The other major catalyst was what was perceived as state and federal harassment of Christian private education. The Internal Revenue Service, the Department of Health, Education, and Welfare, and state boards of education each seemed determined to disrupt these schools by

---

[13] Not all evangelicals were wedded to right-wing politics. A number of young evangelicals sought to relate "Biblical" faith to the problems of hunger, racism, and sexism through such magazines as *Radix, The Other Side, Sojourners,* and the feminist *Daughters of Sarah.* See also R. J. Sider's *Rich Christians in an Age of Hunger* (1977).

imposing governmental regulation. In state after state the Christian schools appealed to the courts and sometimes to state legislatures where they won remarkably friendly hearings, gaining the right for the most part to order their educational affairs as they saw fit.

A more diffuse factor was a general unhappiness with the pervasive culture of the nation as exhibited in newspapers, periodicals, movies, and television. At this point, their activities represented a new counter-culture movement. At the very least, it was a reassertion of a long-dormant streak of fierce Christian individualism, yet an element of realism was involved. The highly politicized pressure groups fashioned by the most aggressive evangelical leaders unhesitatingly overlooked religious differences and made common cause with likeminded Mormons, Jews, and Catholics to promote what they called pro-God, pro-family, and pro-America issues. The central aim was to preserve traditional family values by blocking the Equal Rights Amendment and by fighting for other amendments that would prohibit abortion and permit prayer in the public schools. Curiously their tests of orthodoxy also included such domestic and foreign policy goals as balancing the federal budget, increasing defense spending, curtailing the powers of regulatory commissions, repealing the Panama Canal Treaty, and reinstating diplomatic recognition of Taiwan.

Evangelical leaders were cultivating grassroots support in ways that the churches, with the exception of black churches, had not done since early in the century and were doing it much more efficiently by making use of computerized technology. Grassroots opinion had been neglected by the politically-active liberal leadership of the conventional churches, a neglect which limited their effectiveness as spokespersons in forwarding causes for which they had marshalled only partial support among people in the pews. It was not clear at the outset whether evangelicals would be more successful in turning their flocks into a solid voting bloc. Polls for the 1980 presidential election indicated how difficult it is to determine why and to what extent a single group will follow its leadership. Aggressive evangelical leadership was overwhelming in its support of Reagan, yet a Gallup Poll published on September 7, 1980 reported that evangelicals chose Carter over Reagan 52 per cent to 38 per cent, and approved the way in which Carter was handling his job 46 per cent to 42 per cent. The problem was one of conflicting loyalties. Gallup's profile of evangelicals revealed that 33 per cent lived in the South, 42 per cent were Baptists, 36 per cent were non-white, 54 per cent were Democrats. At all these points Carter had the advantage, being from the South, a Baptist, a Democrat, and with major black support. Moreover, he had greater visibility as a "born again" Christian than an opponent who had been divorced and remarried and was intimately linked to, what was to evangelicals, the notorious Hollywood movie industry. In the end, however, Reagan gained great support in areas of evangelical strength. Perhaps issues of inflation, defense spending, national pride, the Panama Canal treaty, and the Iranian hostages counted for more, with many, than religious affinities. Equally important was the strenuous and systematic effort by right-wing evangelical leaders to get evangelicals who shared their political views registered and to the voting booths.

Other conservative churches and religious groups

The broad spectrum of evangelicals, including the Southern Baptist Convention, most other Baptists, and smaller Presbyterian and Methodist churches, does not take into account the large number of other conservative religious bodies in the United States. Some are Protestant while others, most notably the Eastern Orthodox Churches, the Latter-day Saints (Mormons), and Jehovah's Witnesses, are not. The churches of Eastern Orthodox Christianity reach back in history to the patristic period. The Mormons emerged in opposition to all existing churches and based their doctrine on a record that ante-dated the Protestant Reformation. Jehovah's Witnesses regard all ecclesiastical institutions as synagogues of Satan. Other groups included within this loose and ambiguous category are firmly Protestant. None of the above, including the Protestants, would be happy to be placed in a single classification with the others, but they do have in common a theological conservatism, whatever its character, and most of them, measured by membership statistics reported in the 1970 and 1980 *Year Books* of the churches, exhibited a marked degree of vitality and growth.

Jehovah's Witnesses led the list with 519,218 adherents, representing a 55.6 per cent gain for the decade. The Church of Jesus Christ of Latter-day Saints (Mormons) with nearly two million members maintained its remarkably rapid growth, posting a gain of 40 per cent.[14] The Seventh-day Adventists were third with a percentage gain of 35.2 per cent and a membership of 535,705.

The growth of some other churches is more difficult to assess. The (Russian) Orthodox Church of America, for example, has simply reported 1,000,000 members since 1969. The estimates for the Greek Orthodox Archdiocese have been increased from 1,875,000 members in 1965 to 1,950,000 in 1977 for a four per cent gain. Bulgarian, Romanian, Serbian, and Ukrainian Orthodox Churches give similar rounded figures, perhaps having no clearly defined criteria of membership. There is little doubt that the Church of God in Christ, a pentecostal group, experienced the greatest growth rate of any black denomination; but it is possible for questions to be raised concerning the full reliability of its claimed membership of 3,000,000 in 1980. A similar problem exists with regard to the Churches of Christ. It is clear that there was rapid growth during the decade, but it is also clear that the 25 per cent gain, from 2,400,000 to 3,000,000 members, cannot be regarded as precisely accurate. With no central ecclesiastical organization or office to receive reports and collect statistics, it is probable that the Churches of Christ can do no more than offer an informed estimate.

The only major extremely conservative religious body to report a decline in membership for the decade was the hitherto rapidly growing Lutheran Church—Missouri Synod, while its smaller erstwhile partner in defending what both regarded as Lutheran orthodoxy, the Wisconsin Evangelical Lutheran Church, registered a 12.5 per cent gain with a report of 402,972 members.[15] The loss of members by the Missouri Synod was the result of an attempt to put the church in an unusually tight theological straight-jacket. The take-over of the denomination by its most extreme wing was followed in 1974 by the dismissal

14 The smaller 185,636 member Reorganized Church of the Latter-day Saints (led by members of Joseph Smith's family) had a gain of 24 per cent.

15 Small religious bodies with membership concentrated in a restricted geographical area had had difficulty surviving since World War II without an extremely vigorous evangelistic outreach. With the population having become highly mobile, members of such churches became widely scattered. Even with extraordinary effort, it was almost impossible for some of these groups to follow their members with a ministry in their new homes. Often members in any one neighborhood were too few in number to establish a church. The hardest hit were the very smallest groups such as the Seventh-day Baptists, but even larger bodies such as the Church of the Brethren and some Mennonite groups experienced the same problem.

of the president and almost all the faculty of its senior theological seminary, Concordia in St. Louis, and the withdrawal of most of the students. A seminary-in-exile, Christ Seminary, was established. Two years later a number of churches withdrew and founded the Association of Evangelical Lutheran Churches with more than 100,000 members. Several other churches also severed the ties of their former affiliation. In addition to losing members, the energies of the Lutheran Church— Missouri Synod were diverted by the infighting, and its public image suffered.

The potential for such intramural strife was present among several of the conservative bodies, including the Southern Baptist Convention. The possibility for such a disruption among Southern Baptists, however, has never been great for the less conservative of them have usually been ready to make adjustments. Perhaps it will be otherwise with the Seventh-day Adventists and the Mormons, for neither group has dealt decisively with simmering issues which have been troublesome and may cause controversy.

The issue of what happened in 1844—whether Christ entered the heavenly sanctuary at that time and began judging the people in preparation for his return or whether he began raising up a people who would recover the spirit of the Reformation as a prerequisite to his return, was brought to the fore by an Australian scholar in October 1979 at the Adventists' Pacific Union College in California. What was formally at stake was the doctrine of "investigative judgment." What was really at issue, insisted the Australian, Desmond Ford, was the doctrine of justification by faith and sustaining the remarkable evangelistic outreach of the church. Everyone knew, however, that at the heart of the discussion was the exact authority of the visions and writings of Ellen Gould White. One theologian phrased the question: "Are we prepared to test Mrs. White by the Scriptures?" A year later the answer was given by the official leadership when Ford's ministerial credentials were withdrawn, and at least a minor schism was precipitated.[16]

The Latter-day Saints (Mormons) had achieved the height of respectability following World War II as a thoroughly American church

[16] See *Christianity Today*, February 8, 1980, 64–67; October 10, 1980, 76f.

with a claimed rootage extending far back into the American past. Although its growth was worldwide, it projected an image of all-American young men and young women—clean-shaven, well-dressed, and devoted to the virtues of diligence, thrift, honesty, sobriety, and obedience—as its members spread across the nation from its Utah heartland. Both the church and its members prospered, the latter achieving high posts in business, industry, and government. The former was able greatly to expand its multimillion dollar investments in its business enterprises and to build a 33 million dollar headquarters building in Salt Lake City. Still, like the Adventists, Mormons were troubled by problems, pointed out by a few scholars, concerning the authority to be attributed to some of their founding documents. The disturbing issue of the place of blacks in the scheme of salvation was partially resolved in the 1970's, but the treatment accorded a Mormon wife and mother who publicly spoke out against what seemed to her to be official marshalling of opposition to the Equal Rights Amendment may have tarnished somewhat the public image of the church.

Changing the guard in Roman Catholicism

The election of a Pole, Karol Wojytla, on October 16, 1978, as the first non-Italian bishop of Rome in more than 400 years inaugurated a dramatic reversal in the Roman Catholic Church. Unlike the grassroots turn to conservatism in Protestantism and Judaism, the return to old ways in Roman Catholicism was imposed from above by the new pope who took the name of his short-lived predecessor, becoming John Paul II.

John Paul II stood in marked contrast to the conventional image of occupants of the papal office. He was much younger. He was bold, colorful, and charismatic in personality. Virile, vigorous, and athletic, he loved to ski. Outgoing in personality, with a quick wit and a keen sense of humor, laughter came readily to his lips. He related easily to ordinary people, did not hesitate to lead them in singing folk-songs, and established instant rapport with great crowds as well as smaller groups. He was also a poet, a sophisticated philosopher, and a highly skilled linguist. But above all, he had learned the techniques and discipline needed for the church to survive in a hostile environment of a land under Communist rule.

The new pontiff turned his attention immediately to the task of reinvigorating his worldwide flock. His technique was to make dramatic and triumphant visits to carefully targeted countries. In January 1979 he swept down on traditionally anti-clerical Mexico and was followed by millions of people as he pursued his strategically charted tour of the nation. In June he overwhelmed Poland, his native land, in an eight-day visit that astonished the world. Everywhere he was greeted by tumultuous crowds as the whole population seemed to turn out to line the streets and overflow the squares and open fields where he was scheduled to speak or celebrate mass. It was as if he were implicitly challenging the government to interfere. At the end of September he made a three-day visit to Ireland on his way to the United States, being welcomed and heard by over half the population of the Irish Republic. This was followed by a seven-day, six-city conquest of popular sentiment in the United States, beginning in Boston and progressing in triumph through New York City, Philadelphia, Des Moines (and nearby farms), Chicago, and Washington, D.C. Little more than six months later, in May 1980, he visited six new nations in central Africa. Two months later he was in Brazil for a whirlwind tour of the vast and diverse country that reportedly has the largest number of Roman Catholics in the world. The enthusiasm he evoked everywhere was partly a tribute to his colorful personality, his common touch, and his sense for dramatic timing, but it was also indicative of a sense that something was lacking, a widespread longing among many for stability, moral values, and spiritual leadership.

It was clear that John Paul II was not marching to any drum but his own. Wherever he went he did not shorten his step nor lengthen his stride to accommodate local opinion, and he used every opportunity to spell out how he intended to restore order to the church. A sympathetic observer commented that he was a man with a big open heart but a closed mind. He faced issues head on and without equivocation. He was sensitive to human need but unwavering on matters of doctrine and discipline. He was mild with the faithful but stern with the clergy.

During his visit to the United States, John Paul II spoke sharply in opposition to abandoning priestly celibacy and ordaining women. To permit priests to marry would violate traditional Catholic teaching. Priestly celibacy is a sign of total consecration to God and a reminder of the loyalty priests owe to their superiors in the hierarchy.[17] Nor is the priesthood a proper calling for women, and John Paul urged nuns who had discarded their habits to put on once again their distinctive garb. With regard to training for the priesthood, and presumably for sisters also, the pope took a tough stand in support of traditional seminary education and in opposition to any experimentation or innovation.

Perhaps as compensation for the subordinate role assigned women in the church,[18] the new pontiff made every effort in his travels to revive, restore, and exalt the cult of the Virgin which had been the center of much of the popular piety in Roman Catholicism for centuries but which had tended to be played down following the Second Vatican Council. In his fervor to uphold and strengthen devotion to Mary, he made it a point to visit the most prominent shrines to the Virgin, as at Guadalupe in Mexico, the shrine of the Black Madonna in Poland (where he led half a million pilgrims in consecrating their country to Mary), and at Knock in Ireland.

It is possible that John Paul II's concern to give renewed prominence to the Marian devotion was also related to Mary's role as a model for women in their day-to-day life as mothers. The strengthening of family life was strongly stressed and the pope made plain his unswerving opposition to artificial birth control, abortion, divorce, extramarital sex, and homosexual relationships.

In Washington and again in Brazil, John Paul II met with leaders of other Christian churches. Earlier in Chicago he had spoken of his desire to pursue the ecumenical vision of Vatican II by working "humbly and resolutely to remove the real divisions that still exist, and thus to restore the full unity in the faith." At the same time he insisted that Catholic doctrine must not be compromised by undue ecumenical

[17] Perhaps related to this total consecration was the withdrawal from re-election bids in 1980 of two priests who were members of Congress. The withdrawals were in response to the wishes of their superiors who in turn were responding to what everyone agreed was a papal initiative. To someone with John Paul II's background, political office for a priest would likely seem to constitute a conflict of loyalties.

[18] At Philadelphia, in a special mass celebrated by the Pope for those with a religious vocation, the nuns were seated in the basement with closed-circuit television while the priests were ushered into the sanctuary above.

zeal, quoting to this effect the words of Paul VI who had said: "Let the work of drawing near to our separated brethren go on, with much understanding, with much patience, with great love, but without deviating from the true Catholic doctrine."

Meanwhile steps were being taken at the Vatican to bring the church's theologians into line with the official teaching of the church that had received papal approval. The reins were not drawn too tightly but by the end of 1979 theologians had been put on notice. Hans Küng, one of the most liberal and by far the most widely known of the theologians, had been notified that he was no longer recognized by the Sacred Congregation of the Faith as an official theological representative of the Roman Catholic Church and was therefore no longer qualified to serve as a member of the Roman Catholic faculty at Tübingen. A month earlier Jacques Pohier, a French theologian, had been officially censured, a fate parried by the distinguished Dutch theologian Edward Schillebeeckx. Elsewhere, in the United States as in other nations, scholar-priests were being reassigned to new and different duties, the reassignments being most noticeable among the Jesuits.

For many Roman Catholics in the United States the pope demanded radical readjustments. His stand on birth control and divorce ran counter to the practice or opinion of most Roman Catholics. His stand on priestly celibacy was opposed by a majority of both priesthood and laity. His views on the role of women were out of step with the views of many. His cautious approach to ecumenism was foreign to the easy relationships that had developed in the United States. His theological traditionalism was not in tune with much of the thinking of scholars in Catholic universities and seminaries. What was surprising was that there was so little public expression of opposition or even dismay. A few nuns stood silently before John Paul II in Washington as a symbolic act as another nun read a statement of their views of their place within the church. A number of theologians joined in publishing a letter in defense of Hans Küng. But beyond a few such ripples all was silent. Most remarkable of all was the absence of any discussion of the issue of collegiality in the government of the church. Certainly there were undercurrents. But publicly the whole movement was in the direction of order and discipline. Perhaps it was a more popular tendency than many supposed.

The new pluralism and the state of the nation

If polls of public opinion are to be believed, few Americans in 1980 quarreled with the contention that a renewal and recovery of vigor and vitality by the churches was highly to be desired. How many were ready to make a contribution to that end is another question. Still, most Americans believed, as had George Washington, Benjamin Franklin, and Thomas Jefferson in an earlier time, that churches of true believers contributed to the *well-being* of the nation. Almost everyone in 1980 agreed that virtue and morality were in short supply in homes and families, in commerce and industry, in business and government, in what was called the work force and among unemployed youth in the streets. Franklin, genial spokesman for the colonies, a taster of the fare in many churches but a believer in none, had confessed that most people had need of "the motives of religion to restrain them from vice, to support their own virtue, and to retain them in the practice of it until it became habitual." Jefferson in his first inaugural address referred with approbation to the importance of religion, even "though professed and practiced in various forms, yet all of them inculcating honesty, truth, temperance, gratitude, and love of men."[19] A further bonus occurs, he might have added, when the churches encouraged a degree of humility among people who acknowledged their sin of pride and self-righteousness and the consequent need of both divine and mutual forgiveness. All these virtues generated by the churches contributed to the *well-being* of the nation.

But there was another religious dimension to American life. In addition to the diverse and multiform religion of the churches, there was a common religion shared by most Americans, a "civic" or "civil" religion, or a national faith, which served as a bond of unity to a diverse people and was essential to the *being* of the nation itself. (See above, pp. 110–115.) Not everyone was necessarily a believer anymore than every member of a church was necessarily a believer. But most must share the common faith if either a church or a nation is to have any substance beyond historical accident—the persistence of habit or cus-

---

19 Jefferson and others frequently added the qualifying word "benign" to religion, apparently recognizing thereby the possibility that some forms of religion could be demonic.

tom. When most members of a church cease to share common convictions, the church is threatened with disintegration. And when most people no longer share common assumptions about the mission and vocation of their common life as Americans, the nation is in trouble. As forces of habit and custom diminish and the bonds of an acknowledged common relationship cease to exist, Americans will find it increasingly difficult to live together in peace and the nation will find it increasingly difficult to survive. Many observers in the 1980's found the process of dissolution already far advanced. Social fragmentation had become a major problem.

Disenchanted with many aspects of American life and having forgotten how they had adjusted to ecclesiastical diversity and then to a growing religious pluralism, Americans in the latter part of the twentieth century were confronted with a pluralism that was more widespread, diverse, and variegated than anything they had encountered heretofore. Complicating the problem was the fact that much of the new pluralism had slipped upon them almost unnoticed.

An influx of Cubans and others from the Caribbean and Latin America, for example, vastly augmented the Spanish-speaking segment of the population along the east coast hitherto chiefly represented by the Puerto Ricans. Similarly in the southwest the Spanish-speaking population was being swelled by an unprecedented infiltration of Mexicans, with some of them continuing their migration to cities of the midwest. While Puerto Ricans and Cubans gave a new cast to Roman Catholicism of the eastern seaboard, Chicanos in the southwest gave a massive infusion of strength to a heretofore little regarded Hispanic Catholicism.

In similar fashion, from the perspective of the nation as a whole, Asian Americans received little attention until Pearl Harbor when Americans of Japanese ancestry, with the exception of those in Hawaii, were illegally uprooted from their homes and detained in internment camps.[20] For the next thirty years, the Asian segment of the population rapidly increased as a mounting tide of Chinese from the mainland and Taiwan, Koreans, Indians from the subcontinent of Asia, Vietnamese

[20] An illustration of the invisibility of Asian Americans is represented by the *Year Book of American and Canadian Churches* which as late as 1980 tipped its hat to the Buddhist presence by a single listing—the Buddhist Churches of America with 60,000 members.

and others from southeast Asia, and a medley of people from the middle east sought a new life in the United States. Further contributing to the racial, ethnic, and religious mosaic were home grown cults and a resurgence of interest among numbers of Native Americans in recovering their religious rootage in ancient tribal faiths and rituals.

What were to be the bonds uniting so diverse a population? With many questioning what had been cherished values and having been disabused of any sense of American mission, how was the United States to recover a sense of nationhood which united rather than divided the American people? It was clear that the old Hebraic themes of the American faith were no longer ample enough to accommodate so heterogeneous a population. New themes had to be identified and elaborated with clarity and persuasiveness, related to the American past, exemplified in the American present, and spelled out in appropriate myths and rituals. Both the recovery of health by the churches and the restoration of a sense of nationhood constituted unfinished business on the agenda of the American people.

Suggestions for Further Reading

General reference volumes—including bibliographies, a biographical dictionary, an atlas, and a theologically informed multivolume work that gives pertinent and detailed information about almost every American religious group and movement—are listed in the Preface (see p. ix).

Accounts of America's "three major faiths" are included in the University of Chicago's History of American Civilization series; J. T. Ellis, *American Catholicism* (1969); Nathan Glazer, *American Judaism* (1972); W. S. Hudson, *American Protestantism* (1961). For these traditions, see also: J. P. Dolan, *The Immigrant Church* (1975); Philip Gleason, ed., *Catholicism in America* (1970); Joseph L. Blau, *Judaism in America* (1976); Jacob Neusner, *American Judaism* (1972); R. T. Handy, *A Christian America*: *Protestant Hopes and Historical Realities* (1971), and M. E. Marty, *Righteous Empire*: *The Protestant Experience in America* (1970).

For other religious traditions, both old and new, see Timothy

Ware, *The Orthodox Church* (1963); Leonard Arrington and Davis Bitton, *The Mormon Experience* (1979); Stephen Gottschalk, *The Emergence of Christian Science in American Religious Life* (1973); J. A. Beckford, *The Trumpet of Prophecy: A Sociological Study of Jehovah's Witnesses* (1975); R. S. Ellwood, *Alternative Altars: Unconventional and Eastern Spirituality in America* (1979), and Jacob Needleman, *The New Religions* (1970).

Broad-ranging thematic interpretations of Protestantism include H. Richard Niebuhr, *The Kingdom of God in America* (1935); Sidney E. Mead, *The Lively Experiment* (1963), and W. A. Clebsch, *From Sacred to Profane America* (1968). The Puritan-Reformed theological tradition has been effectively made the main current of American religious thought by the preponderance of scholarship devoted to it. Perry Miller's "The Marrow of Puritan Divinity" in his *Errand into the Wilderness* (1956) is the most arresting short treatment of Puritan thought, but for more systematic treatment see W. K. B. Stoever, *A Faire and Easie Way to Heaven* (1978). Later New England theology is concisely surveyed in the Introduction to H. Shelton Smith's *Horace Bushnell* (1965). A neo-evangelical view of Protestant-Reformed thought is given by D. G. Bloesch, *The Evangelical Renaissance* (1973), and by John Woodbridge, Mark A. Noll, and Nathan O. Hatch, *The Gospel in America* (1979). Alternative traditions are discussed by Henry F. May, *The Enlightenment in America* (1976), W. R. Hutchinson, *The Modernist Impulse in American Protestantism* (1976), and, for the mid-twentieth century, Langdon Gilkey, *Naming the Whirlwind: The Renewal of God-Language* (1969). The whole theological development is reviewed in Sydney Ahlstrom's Introduction to his *Theology in America* (1967).

The social dimension of religion has been considered in D. B. Rutman, *American Puritanism* (1970); Alden T. Vaughan and Francis Bremer, *Puritan New England: Essays on Society, Religion, and Culture* (1977); Alan E. Heimert, *Religion and the American Mind from the Great Awakening to the Revolution* (1966); Donald G. Mathews, *Religion in the Old South* (1977); Timothy L. Smith, *Revivalism and Social Reform in Mid-Nineteenth Century America* (1957); George F. Marsden, *Fundamentalism and American Culture, 1875–1925* (1980); W. G. McLoughlin, *Revivals, Awakenings, and*

Reform (1978); and Henry F. May, *Protestant Churches and Industrial America* (1963). Perhaps as important as any of these books dealing with social dimensions of religion is Whitney R. Cross' critique of Frederick Jackson Turner's frontier thesis in his book *The Burned-over District: The Social and Intellectual History of Enthusiastic Religion in Western New York, 1800–1850* (1965). Designed as a case-study of the transit of New England culture westward, the findings are applicable to the whole western migration, whether from New England or elsewhere.

Social aspects of black religion are discussed by Albert J. Rabateau, *Slave Religion* (1978); E. Franklin Frazier and C. Eric Lincoln, *The Negro Church in America and the Black Church since Frazier* (1974); and G. S. Wilmore and J. H. Cone, *Black Theology: A Documentary History* (1979).

The role of women has not been studied extensively but there are relevant chapters in Anne F. Scott, *The Southern Lady: From Pedestal to Politics, 1830–1930* (1970); Joan J. Brumberg, *A Mission for Life* (1980); June Fochen, *Movers and Shakers: Women Thinkers and Activists, 1900–1970* (1973); and the Winter 1978 issue of *American Quarterly*.

Perspectives drawn from the social sciences have continued to enrich the examination of American religion. Anthropological and historical approaches are blended in D. D. Bruce, Jr., *And They All Sang Hallelujah: Plain-folk Camp-meeting Religion, 1800–1845* (1974), and Peter Williams, *Popular Religion in America* (1980). Those interested in the behavioral aspects of religious history will find Irving I. Zaretsky and Mark P. Leone, *Religious Movements in Contemporary America* (1974) and R. F. Berkhofer, Jr., *A Behavorial Approach to Historical Analysis* (1969) especially useful.

Collections of essays of unusual merit have been assembled by J. H. Mulder and J. F. Wilson, *Religion in American History: Interpretive Essays* (1978), and in two volumes edited by J. W. Smith and A. L. Jamison, *Religious Perspectives in American Culture* (1961) and *The Shaping of American Religion* (1961) which form part of the four volume *Religion in American Life.* Equally useful are other collections of distinguished essays: C. Eric Lincoln, *The Black Experience in Religion* (1974); Jacob Neusner, *Understanding American Judaism,* 2 vols. (1975); R. E. Richey and D. G. Jones, *American Civil Religion* (1974); R. E. Richey, *Denominationalism* (1977). In addition to these collections, essays which presented fresh interpretations of specific issues have been reprinted as monographs in the open-ended Facet booklet series by the Fortress Press.

Primary source readings, in addition to the two volumes of H. Shelton Smith, R. T. Handy, and L. A. Loetscher, are found in Perry Miller and Thomas Johnson, *The Puritans* (1963); Alan Heimert and Perry Miller, *The Great Awakening* (1967); Sydney Ahlstrom, *Theology in America: The Major Protestant Voices from Puritanism to Neo-Orthodoxy* (1967); W. G. McLoughlin, *The American Evangelicals, 1800–1900* (1968); William R. Hutchinson, *American Protestant Thought: The Liberal Era* (1968); William R. Miller, *Contemporary American Protestant Thought, 1900–1970* (1972); John Tracy Ellis, *Documents of American Catholic History* (1972). Michael McGiffert has united both source materials and interpretive essays in his *Puritanism and the American Experience* (1969), and from another perspective Giles B. Gunn has provided New World Metaphysics: *Readings on the Religious Meanings of the American Experience* (1981).

INDEX

Index

Abbott, Francis E., 287
Abbott, Lyman, 269, 270n., 275n., 309
Adams, John, 91f., 94, 101, 105, 112
Addams, Jane, 314
Adler, Cyrus, 336
Adler, Felix, 287f.
Adventism, 195–97, 348f., 357; Advent Christian Church, 197; Seventh-day Adventist Church, 197, 349, 454, 455
African Methodist Episcopal Church, 225–26
African Methodist Episcopal Zion Church, 225, 226
Ahlstrom, S. E., ix, 164, 170n., 276n.
Alban Institute, 441
Albright, Jacob, 125
Alcott, Bronson, 175, 189
Alcott, Louisa May, 189
Alexander, Archibald, 160
Alexander, James W., 180
Ali, Drew, 355
Ali, Muhammad, 355
Alinski, Saul, 440
Allen, Ethan, 131
Altham, John, 48
Amana Society, 184
America: church membership, 7, 129f., 329, 356ff., 384n., 397, 415, 417, 439, 442n., 453ff.; civic religion, 110–15, 461f.; destiny, 20f., 110–14, 151, 193, 211f., 320–24; influence of evironment, 12–22; part of European society, 3–5; possibility for reform, 16–18; post-Civil War, 209ff., 265ff., 304f., 309ff.; post-World War I, 361–65; post-World War II, 384f.; religious character, 16, 21f.; religious configuration, 7, 329, 356ff.; sense of expectancy, 18–22; two religions, 110–15, 129, 461f.
American Antislavery Society, 152, 201
American Bible Society, 150, 152
American Board of Commissioners for Foreign Missions, 157
American Christian Commission, 297ff.

American Colonization Society, 152
American Council of Churches, 385n.
American Education Society, 152, 166
American Home Missionary Society, 152, 153, 166
American Lutheran Church, 358
American Missionary Association, 222f.
American Peace Society, 152
American Protective Association, 242ff.
American Revolution: attitude of denominations, 95ff.; effect upon churches, 116ff., 123, 126; Anglican pretensions, 87–92; role of clergy, 96ff.; slogan, 101f., 105
American Sunday School Union, 152, 236
American Temperance Society, 152
American Tract Society, 152
American Unitarian Association, 162, 174
Ames, Edward Scribner, 278, 279n.
Anabaptists, 52
Andover Review, 273
Andover Theological Seminary, 120, 155, 157, 161, 163f., 187, 273f., 280
Anglican communion, 340
Anglicans, *see* Church of England and Episcopalians
Anthony, Susan B., 318n.
Anti-Catholic sentiment, 242ff., 400
Anti-mission sentiment, 149, 168
Anti-Saloon League, 319
Antislavery movement, 199, 201ff.
Arminianism, 32, 65, 79, 163, 180
Armour, P. D., 297, 308
Armstrong, Herbert, 448n.
Arrington, L. J., 191n.
Asbury, Francis, 122f.
Asian Americans, 425, 461f.
Aspinwell, William, 29
Assemblies of God, 348, 422n.
Astrology, 424
Atkins, G. C., 303n., 325
Atlanta University, 223
"Auburn Affirmation," 372